Securing the Connected World

Sabu M. Thampi • Tony Thomas •
Preetam Mukherjee
Editors

Securing the Connected World

Exploring Emerging Threats and Innovative Solutions

Springer

Editors
Sabu M. Thampi
School of Computer Science and Engineering
Digital University of Kerala
Trivandrum, Kerala, India

Tony Thomas
School of Computer Science and Engineering
Digital University of Kerala
Trivandrum, Kerala, India

Preetam Mukherjee
School of Computer Science and Engineering
Digital University of Kerala
Trivandrum, Kerala, India

ISBN 978-3-031-82828-7 ISBN 978-3-031-82826-3 (eBook)
https://doi.org/10.1007/978-3-031-82826-3

This Springer imprint is published by the registered company Springer Nature Switzerland AG
The registered company address is: Gewerbestrasse 11, 6330 Cham, Switzerland

Preface

As technology becomes increasingly embedded in our lives, securing connected systems is indispensable. This book brings together the research efforts of the Connected Systems and Intelligence (CSI) Lab at Kerala University of Digital Sciences, Innovation, and Technology, also known as Digital University Kerala. The book addresses key cybersecurity challenges and offers solutions to create a safer digital ecosystem.

The CSI Lab is dedicated to research across critical areas such as Artificial Intelligence (AI), Internet of Things (IoT), the Internet of Drones (IoD), Cognitive Surveillance, Software-Defined Networking (SDN), Digital Twin technology, Quantum Computing, and Smart Systems. The lab also has a strong focus on AgriTech research and FinTech security, developing research solutions to address the unique security needs within these sectors. Through partnerships with industry and academia, the lab aims to deliver practical solutions with a positive societal impact.

This book is divided into two sections. The first section, Foundations and Frontiers of IoT Security, addresses fundamental topics in IoT security, including attack modeling, vulnerability analysis, intrusion detection, fraud detection, secure communication protocols, and SDN-IoT policy management. It concludes with approaches to securing 5G-enabled IoT networks to support the next generation of connectivity.

The second section, Advances in Internet of Drones (IoD) Security, examines the specific security needs of drone networks. This section discusses advancements in authentication, dynamic access control, multi-attack detection, and trust management for robust IoD frameworks. Additionally, it explores physical security concerns and ethical frameworks in IoD-based surveillance.

We hope this book will be a valuable resource for researchers, professionals, and policymakers committed to advancing digital security. Our sincere thanks to Springer for their support and to all contributors and reviewers who made this work possible.

Trivandrum, India

Sabu M. Thampi
Tony Thomas
Preetam Mukherjee

Contents

Part I
Foundations and Frontiers of IoT Security

Introduction to IoT and IoT Security

Anjana Jimmington, Aswin Payyampally, B. Bhagya, Blessy Thomas, Lakshmi R. Nair, and S. Niman

1 Understanding the Internet of Things

The Internet of Things (IoT) is perhaps the revolution in which man interacts with the physical world seamlessly through connectivity as well as intelligent data exchange within common objects and their digital networks. This section presents a comprehensive overview of tracing IoT, where it would be defined and evolved into its core components and operational mechanisms.

1.1 Definition and Evolution of IoT

The Internet of Things is the network of presently interconnected physical devices embedded with sensors, actuators, software, or other technologies, which enables these objects to collect and exchange data over the Internet. This interconnectivity allows for the remote monitoring, control, and automation of different processes, thus enhancing efficiency and the creation of new functionalities [4]. The term Internet of Things was first coined by Kevin Ashton in 1999 and has foreseen that physical objects could talk and even interact autonomously to improve efficiency and convenience [5].

A. Jimmington (✉) · A. Payyampally · B. Bhagya · B. Thomas · L. R. Nair · S. Niman
Connected Systems and Intelligence Lab, School of Computer Science and Engineering, Digital University Kerala, Trivandrum, India
e-mail: anjana.res21@duk.ac.in; aswin.res21@duk.ac.in; bhagya.csres23@duk.ac.in; blessy.res21@duk.ac.in; lakshmi.csres23@duk.ac.in; niman.res21@duk.ac.in
https://duk.ac.in

S. M. Thampi et al. (eds.), *Securing the Connected World*,
https://doi.org/10.1007/978-3-031-82826-3_1

Since its inception, IoT has had exponential growth with tremendous improvement through rapid development in wireless communication, sensor technology, and data analytics. The initial phases of IoT were actually more M2M type, enabling simple data exchange between devices for monitoring and control purposes [10]. Later, with technological advancement, a shift to incorporating Cloud computing was inevitable because this approach furnished necessary scalable storage and processing capabilities in order to process and manage very large amounts of data generated by the IoT devices [22]. AI and edge computing have transformed IoT further in recent years because the real-time processing of data and intelligent decision-making are now implemented at source, reducing latency and increasing the responsiveness of the system [32].

1.2 Core Components of IoT Systems

An IoT system contains several core components, which work in coordination to obtain the required goals. Such key components include.

- Tools and Sensors. These are the physical parts of an IoT system, that have sensing and effecting parts to interact with the real world. Sensors capture data such as temperature, humidity, motion, and other pertinent parameters. Actuators produce actions based upon the processed information given in [27].
- Connectivity: This layer includes the communication technologies and protocols that allow data to be transmitted from the IoT device to the central systems. Among the most popular options for connectivity are Wi-Fi, Bluetooth, Zigbee, LoRaWAN, and cellular networks, each of them offering a different range, data rate, and power consumption profile that is suited for a different application [6].
- Data Processing and Analytics: the collected data is transmitted wirelessly to cloud-based or edge-based systems, which carry out the data processing and analytics. Here, advanced analytics that includes machine learning algorithms are applied to extract meaningful outcomes, recognize patterns, and support clear decision-making processes [38].
- User Interface: This shall be the part through which the user will interact with the IoT system. User interfaces vary from mobile applications to web dashboards and even voice-controlled assistants where one can see system status, control different devices, and visualize data as well [8].
- Security and Privacy Mechanisms: The security and privacy of data are highly important in IoT systems by implementing good encryption, authentication mechanisms, and access control to ensure protection against unauthorized access, data breaches, and other cyber threats [33].

1.3 How IoT Works

The functioning of the Internet of Things (IoT) relies on a layered structure that advances the complete cycle of data acquisition, transfer, handling, and application. Below explains how IoT works with respect to the three basic layers, the Perception Layer, the Network Layer and the Application Layer, as shown in Fig. 1.

- Perception Layer
  The Perception Layer is the base component of the IoT system. It should gather data from the physical world. The perception layer is composed of different types of sensors and devices that measure and monitor the conditions in the environment, for example, temperature, pressure, motion, and others. The key components of the perception layer include sensors and actuators. Sensors sense the actual time data from the physical world. Actuators are devices that interact with the environment based on received instructions (e.g., opening valves, turning on lights, adjusting machinery).
  These sensors and actuators provide the raw data that drive the entire IoT system. The data is then passed to the next layer for transmission.
- Network Layer
  The Network Layer is responsible for communication across the devices of perception layers and the upper layers of the system. In particular, it uses various wireless technologies such as Bluetooth, Wi-Fi, Zigbee, LTE/5G, etc.
  These communication protocols enable seamless data transfers from the IoT devices to servers or edge nodes/ cloud platforms, which further elaborate the data. It is considered an intermediate source that ensures safe and secure data transfer in the presence of very large data volumes, as produced by IoT devices.

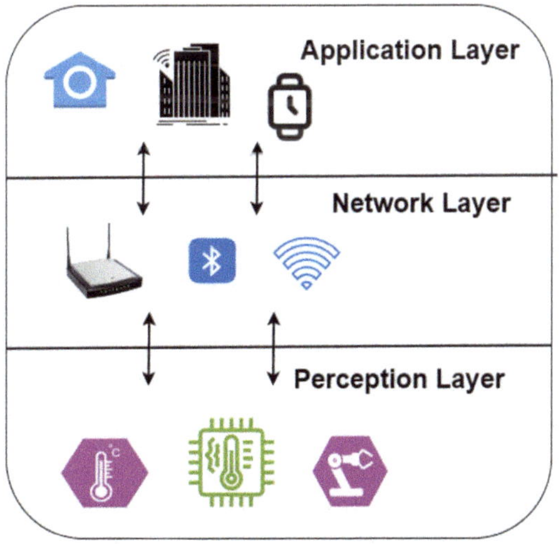

Fig. 1 IoT architecture

– Application Layer
  This is the Application Layer, where all the IoT data gets processed, analyzed, and changed into actionable insights. It provides specific services and functionalities that are different according to the use case. Some of these are smart homes, industrial automation, health care, and urban monitoring, among others.

  Some examples of other industries could include:

- Smart Home Systems: Manage devices like a thermostat, security cameras, lighting systems, etc.
- Industrial IoT: It provides predictions based on machinery and production lines to maintain them better.
- Wearables: Monitoring of health metrics with the aid of smartwatches and fitness trackers.

  This layer further provides processed data to end-users through dashboards, mobile applications, or control systems, and hence, this layer also constitutes the most user-facing part of any IoT system.

Interaction Amongst Layers
The Perception Layer exchanges with the real world. It transfers data to the Network Layer, which forward passes the data towards the Application Layer, processes and analyzes such data to provide real-time feedback and actionable insights. Communication also flows in opposite directions as commands can be fed from the application to devices in the perception layer through the network to suit particular instantiations, for instance, adjusting a thermostat or controlling industrial robots in real-time.

2 The Landscape of IoT Applications

Figure 2 of IoT applications offers a complete overview of the several domains in which the Internet of Things is being employed. It demonstrates different applications in healthcare, smart cities, transportation, agriculture, and industry. Each category is a distinct industry with unique benefits of IoT adoption and use cases. The picture shows the spectrum of IoT applications and how this technology has the potential to revolutionize several sectors. Overall, the image demonstrates the enormous impact that IoT is having on modern society as well as how it may provide new possibilities and improve people's quality of life.

The Internet of Things (IoT) is interconnected nodes of physical items or "things" linked to the Internet and may exchange data and perform different functions. The IoT has several uses across numerous sectors, and those uses are continually growing.

– Smart Homes: IoT gadgets may be utilized in smart homes to automate various tasks, including climate management, lighting, security, and entertainment. It is handy for homeowners to manage their houses since these gadgets can be

Fig. 2 IoT applications

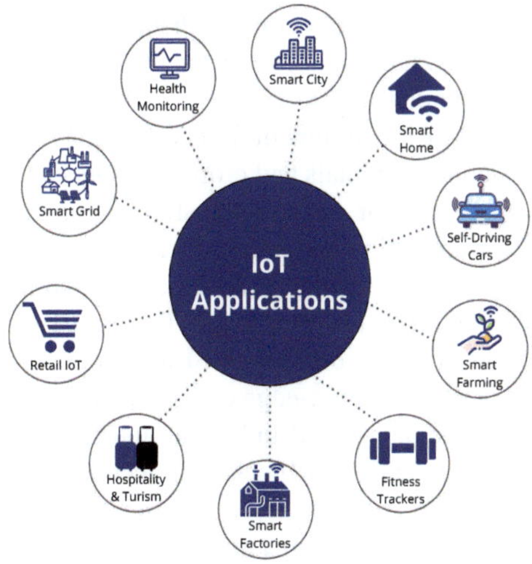

operated remotely using a smartphone or tablet. The authors address the potential advantages of using IoT technology in smart grid and smart home applications [34], despite the limited number of existing examples. The authors reviewed the literature before developing a comprehensive framework for incorporating smart home devices into an IoT-based cloud-centric solution. The framework includes a smart home management model and tasks and practical design issues like data processing and communication protocol interoperability.

– Healthcare: The IoT has several uses in the healthcare sector, from remote patient monitoring to intelligent medical equipment. IoT-enabled gadgets may monitor patient health data and notify medical staff of any adjustments that need to be made. Kim and Kim [15] describe the findings of their study to assess user preferences for an Internet of Things (IoT) healthcare application for managing lifestyle diseases. According to the survey, consumers preferred applications that offered straightforward user interfaces, personalized health recommendations, and wearable device integration. Age, gender, income, and education level were among the other characteristics the survey found to influence user choices. Overall, the report emphasizes the need to consider user preferences when designing and developing IoT healthcare applications.
– Agriculture: The IoT may be utilized in agriculture to manage and monitor animals and crops. Sensors can be installed in fields and barns to gather information on soil moisture, temperature, and humidity. Crop productivity optimization and animal health advancements may be made using this data. Recently a green IoT system in the cloud for healthcare and agriculture was created in [26]. To monitor and regulate environmental factors for optimum plant development and to track patient health-related data, the design incorporates a variety of sensors and IoT devices. The authors note the GAHA system's potential advantages, including increased agricultural yields and lower healthcare costs, as well as its role in encouraging sustainable practices in agriculture and

healthcare. They contend that the GAHA system can significantly influence these fields and enhance the quality of life for people in both communities and as individuals.

- Industrial Automation: The IoT may be utilized in agriculture to manage and monitor animals and crops. Sensors can be installed in fields and barns to gather information on soil moisture, temperature, and humidity. Crop productivity optimization and animal health advancements may be made using this data. In [23] analyses the weaknesses of traditional centralized access control methods and protocols to support future IoT-enabled industrial automation. For this, an effective decentralized access control mechanism is required. The authors examine cutting-edge concepts that leverage 5G-enabled IoT as a foundation for blockchain-based industrial automation in various applications, demonstrating the potential for blockchain technology to transform a wide range of industrial sectors. Additionally, they compare and contrast the current proposals while analyzing the problems and difficulties of 5G-enabled IoT for industrial automation based on blockchain.
- Transportation: The IoT may be applied to the transportation sector to increase efficiency and safety. IoT devices may track traffic patterns and modify traffic signals accordingly. In order to cut down on travel time and fuel usage, they may also be used to track cars and optimize routes. IoT applications in transportation include eco-friendly cruise control for public transit, heat, power management in buildings, and other solutions to increase urban sustainability [19]. While the latter optimizes the speed and acceleration of public vehicles to lower fuel consumption and emissions, the former leverages data from IoT sensors to improve heating, ventilation, air conditioning, and lighting. The report underlines the opportunity for IoT applications to enhance urban sustainability and calls for more study in this field.
- Retail: The IoT may be applied to retail to enhance customer satisfaction and optimize inventory control. IoT-enabled gadgets may be used to track consumer traffic and modify store layouts accordingly. They may also monitor inventory levels and automatically place new orders for goods when supply is short. IoT technology adoption in the retail sector has certain potential advantages. The authors [14] discuss how IoT may enhance customer experience, supply chain optimization, and several other elements of retail operations. In addition, they discuss potential difficulties with IoT implementation in retail, such as privacy and data security issues.
- Energy Management: Utilizing the IoT in energy management may lower energy use and increase sustainability. IoT devices may track energy use in buildings and modify HVAC and lighting systems as necessary. These kinds of IoT technologies can aid in reducing energy waste and bringing down energy costs. Also, [20] propose an intelligent edge-computing framework to manage energy consumption in smart cities. The framework utilizes the Internet of Things (IoT) to collect and analyze energy data and employs edge computing to process the data in real-time. The authors describe the framework's architecture in the article

and present a case study demonstrating its application in a smart building. The results show that the framework can effectively control energy usage and reduce energy costs. Overall, the authors conclude that the intelligent edge computing framework has the potential to play a critical role in the future development of smart cities.

In conclusion, there are several uses for the IoT network in numerous industries, and those applications are continually growing. Energy management, healthcare, and smart homes are areas where the Internet of Things changes how we live and work. We anticipate even more cutting-edge IoT applications as technology develops.

3 Introduction to IoT Security

Security is a technique that safeguards against unauthorized access, physical harm, theft, or loss to an object by maintaining high confidentiality and integrity of information [16, 17]. As a result of the rise in connected devices, IoT networks are growing increasingly and exposed to more cyber attacks. The development and deployment of IoT applications are now critically dependent on the security of the IoT network. IoT network security strives to prevent unauthorized access, and malicious behavior from compromising the confidentiality, integrity, and availability of the data. This demands a thorough security plan encompassing safe device authentication, secure communication protocols, ongoing monitoring and upgrading of security measures.

3.1 Why IoT Security Is Critical

IoT security is essential because connected devices like smart home gadgets, medical devices, and industrial sensors manage sensitive data and control critical operations. If these devices are not properly secured, they can be easy targets for hackers who can steal personal information, take control of devices, or disrupt essential services. Many IoT devices have weak security due to limited computing power and are often shipped with default passwords or outdated software, making them highly vulnerable. As the number of IoT devices grows, the risks of attacks also increase, raising concerns about privacy, data breaches, and the safety of everyday systems like transportation, healthcare, and energy grids [33].

A good example of this happened in 2016 with the Mirai botnet attack [3], where hackers took control of thousands of IoT devices, such as security cameras and routers, to launch a massive cyber attack. These devices were vulnerable because they used default passwords and lacked proper security updates. This incident highlights the urgent need for stronger IoT security, including regular software updates, strong passwords, encryption, and better device authentication. As IoT technology becomes more widespread, securing these devices is critical to preventing attacks that could impact both individuals and large-scale systems [29].

3.2 Common IoT Security Threats

IoT devices are everywhere—smart homes, health monitors, and industrial systems, while they make life easier, they also come with serious security risks. Some of the most common threats to IoT security include [29, 33, 36]:

Weak Passwords and Default Settings: Many IoT devices come with default usernames and passwords, like "admin" or "password," which are easy for hackers to guess. If users don't change these settings, it gives attackers an easy way to break in and take control of the device.

Unpatched Vulnerabilities: IoT devices often have outdated software that isn't regularly updated. These outdated systems might have security flaws that hackers can exploit. If manufacturers don't provide software updates or if users don't install them devices remain vulnerable to attacks.

Physical Attacks Since many IoT devices are deployed in the field or public spaces, they are vulnerable to physical tampering. Attackers can physically access devices to alter their functionality, steal sensitive information, or introduce malware.

Privacy IoT devices often collect personal information without users realizing it. For example, smart home devices can track daily habits, and this data can be misused if not properly protected. This creates privacy risks, especially if the data is shared with third parties without consent.

Eavesdropping and Surveillance IoT devices like smart cameras and voice assistants are prone to eavesdropping if not securely configured. Hackers can take control of these devices and use them to monitor users' activities without their knowledge.

Securing IoT devices requires users to change default passwords, install updates regularly, and use encryption to protect data. As IoT continues to grow, both manufacturers and users need to stay vigilant about these common security threats to ensure their devices remain safe.

3.3 Challenges in IoT Security

The interfering waves can damage wireless signals utilized for communication between sensor nodes. Furthermore, IoT devices frequently function in outdoor settings, and physical assaults against IoT sensors and devices are feasible, allowing attackers to tamper with hardware components. Finally, as the sensors and RFIDs utilized in the physical layer have limited storage, power, and compute capabilities and are regularly relocated throughout the network topology, the system is exposed to threats and assaults [1]. Attacks like Replay Attacks, Timing Attacks, Node Capture Attacks, and Malicious Data Injection can compromise identification information, encryption keys, and data integrity, which in turn puts confidentiality in the network layer in danger [37]. DoS attacks can also be carried out by draining nodes' energy and preventing them from using their energy-saving sleep mode. IoT's network layer is susceptible to passive monitoring, eavesdropping, traffic analysis, and other forms of passive monitoring, as well as DoS attacks and assaults on confidentiality and privacy. In addition, the network layer is highly vulnerable to Man-in-the-Middle attacks, which might compromise secure communication channels if keying information is intercepted [1]. Due to the variety of network components, compatibility is a problem in the IoT, making it challenging to create effective security measures and employ existing network protocols. The objects of the network must also be safeguarded since they need to be able to keep an eye on the network's health and defend themselves from attacks. Effective protocols and software can enable things to react to unusual circumstances and actions that can compromise their security [29]. Security issues in application security have been caused by the absence of global standards for controlling IoT development and interaction. Integration is challenging, as data privacy and identity authentication are unknown due to the different authentication methods used by different apps. Huge volumes of data are produced by connected devices, which can slow down applications and affect the availability of services. Moreover, user engagement, data disclosure, control tools, and knowledge of data consumption must be considered while creating IoT applications [21]. Addressing these challenges requires the implementation of robust security measures such as encryption and access controls to ensure the protection of data, the integrity of the network, and the reliability of services in IoT environments.

4 Security Measures in IoT

4.1 Vulnerability Analysis

Vulnerability of IoT networks refers to security weaknesses or flaws in the IoT network [35]. Attackers can exploit these weaknesses to alter data, steal sensitive information, or even disrupt critical infrastructure. These weaknesses can appear in the hardware, software, or communication protocols of IoT devices.

IoT networks have increasingly become targets for cyberattacks, and this trend is expected to grow rapidly as more vulnerabilities in IoT devices are discovered. This is why conducting a "vulnerability of IoT networks"—which is the process of identifying and prioritizing weaknesses in a network—is crucial. By identifying these potential weak spots, cyber security professionals can take proactive steps to prevent attacks. This allows them to implement security measures that reduce risks and help protect the overall integrity and safety of IoT systems. Network scanning tools identify the vulnerabilities in the network, which in turn helps to take necessary steps to keep the network secure. Common Vulnerabilities and Exposures (CVE) is a publicly available database that lists commonly known cyber security vulnerabilities and exposures [24]. The details about the identified vulnerabilities through network scanning tools can be obtained from the CVE database. The Common Vulnerability Scoring System (CVSS) helps in evaluating the severity of vulnerabilities [9]. In addition to helping prioritize remediation activities, it offers a standardized technique for assessing the risk connected with a vulnerability. With this ongoing vulnerability analysis, organizations can prevent attackers and help in maintaining the security of the system.

4.2 Intrusion Detection

Today's connected world requires network security since data and communication technologies are vital to personal and professional life [25]. As the digital world changes, so do attacks on sensitive data and vulnerabilities. People and organizations use numerous technology and methods to avoid such risks. An intrusion detection system (I.D.S.) is a vigilant digital sentinel, watching network activity and system operations for unusual patterns and behaviors [11]. Its main job is to spot possible computer system or network security breaches or unauthorised access. An I.D.S. uses a wide range of strategies and tools to do this.

- **Signature-Based Detection:** I.D.S. frequently uses signature-based detection as a strategy [30]. The system examines incoming data packets or system activity against a database of recognised threat signatures. When an I.D.S. detects a match, it raises a warning or takes a predetermined action to lessen the hazard. This technique works very well at spotting well-known and well-documented attacks.
- **Anomaly-Based Detection:** Anomaly-based detection, instead of signature-based detection, focuses on locating departures from established baselines of typical behavior. An I.D.S. using this method continually adjusts to the typical network patterns and detects any deviations as potential intrusions [12]. Although this approach is good at identifying new threats, it may also result in false positives if it does not calibrate correctly.
- **Hybrid Approaches:** Several current I.D.S. systems incorporate signature- and anomaly-based approaches to improve accuracy and decrease false alerts. These hybrid strategies use each strategy's advantages, offering a more thorough defence against a constantly changing threat scenario [18].

4.3 IoT Malware Analysis

Malware attacks are one of the crucial security threats in IoT devices. Due to the characteristics of IoT devices and the rapid hike in the number of devices in use, malware writers regularly deploy numerous malware into the web. These malwares utilise various vulnerabilities related to the devices and cause a massive loss of money and crucial data, also becoming hazardous to human life. Various methods are available to detect and analyse malwares. However, due to the distinct specialities of IoT malware [2] with other malwares, malware detection is a critical task that needs the researcher's immediate attention.

The two popular methods to detect malwares are static analysis and dynamic analysis. Static analysis tries to extract malware features without executing them, whereas dynamic analysis extracts the malware features by running them in a controlled environment. Conventionally, the analysis is performed by humans or with the help of specific rules. However, due to the excessive presence of new malware in the IoT domain, utilising machine learning and deep learning for malware analysis [31] became an inevitable part of the malware analysis process. In this book chapter, we included the most advanced static malware detection methods, the description and details about the features utilised for malware analysis and the methods used to extract the features. Advanced static analysis helps to extract features from binary codes, hex codes, opcodes and control flow.

Additionally, the chapter describes the methods to incorporate a machine learning model with a demonstration of a malware detection method. Instead of conventional signature-based detection, machine learning and deep learning models can detect malware with maximum speed and accuracy. No human intervention is needed to detect if new malware approaches the detection system. The generalisation property of machine-learning algorithms can extend its ability to identify malicious behaviour from a group of inputs. Thus, the application of machine learning and deep learning makes the detection system more advanced and helps to become accurate in its actions.

5 Security Enhancements in IoT

5.1 SDN-IoT Policy Management

The flexibility of controlling the network resources is what Software-Defined Networking (SDN) provides, thus as an enabler of modern day's internet of things (IoT) systems; it calls for such agility and flexibility. Policy management in IoT environments which contain several disparate devices, protocols and use cases is important in promoting and enhancing communication, management of security as well as resource management. Thus, SDN through separating control from data forwarding allows centralized policy management where policies are enforced by software applications rather than being baked into network devices. This approach mitigates the challenges of managing IoT network traffic given the dynamic and high scalability demands of such networks due to variation of network loads.

- Policy Enforcement:
  In SDN-IoT, the SDN controller enforces policies for access control, traffic prioritization, and security management. For example, access control restricts communication only to authorized IoT devices, while traffic prioritization ensures that critical applications (e.g., healthcare sensors) receive low-latency data transmission. Security policies can reroute or filter traffic during threats like DDoS attacks, enhancing network resilience [7].
- Adaptive and Dynamic Policy Management:
  SDN enables dynamic policy adaptation, which can translate high-level policies quickly into more granular commands. In smart-city applications, it makes possible for the SDN controller to change communication rules, simultaneously managing traffic congestion in real-time so that the system remains scalable and efficient even in unstable environments [13].
- Scalability and Conflict Resolution in Policy:
  SDN solves policy conflicts, such as security vs. performance, by applying rules of priority in the controller. Centralized control also improves scalability in a sense that administrators will easily manage policies across thousands of IoT devices without manual reconfiguration, streamlining network troubleshooting and monitoring [28].
- Integration with Other IoT Frameworks:
  SDN could complement already existing IoT management systems, more easily in policy specification terms; it can also interface with security frameworks to effect dynamic adjustments in mitigation based on real-time anomaly detection.

5.2 5G-IoT Security

The 3GPP-standardized 5G core network architecture is made to fulfill the demands of diverse applications and services for more throughput, lower latency, and improved reliability. All 5G functionalities are consolidated under a cloud-based, service-oriented architecture (SBA) known as the 5G core. This covers session management, end-to-end device communication, security, and authentication. With a focus on Network Functions Virtualization (NFV) as a fundamental architectural principle, the 5G core makes use of software functions that are virtualized and deployable within the network. There is widespread use of 5G technology in the Internet of Things (IoT) space. Although 5G technology offers enormous speed and scale for Internet of Things activities, it also brings with it a new set of security risks. The 5G core network's security is crucial. To protect 5g, comprehensive mechanisms are required.

6 Security Applications in IoT

6.1 Fraud Detection

Implementing techniques and technologies designed to detect malicious activities in interconnected devices and systems and fraud detection in IoT has remained a crucial topic. Indeed, the rapid growth of IoT-connected devices, now amounting to more than 15 billion globally, creates significant vulnerabilities that cybercriminals may exploit to steal data or disrupt operations. The most important channel for IoT fraud is online financial transaction management. Here, vulnerabilities in the security devices and network infrastructures are prone to manipulation. Advanced machine learning and deep learning techniques are used here to monitor and analyze network traffic to identify anomalies and abnormal behavior that could point toward fraudulent activity. Generally, an accomplishment in fraud detection in an IoT scenario depends more on strong security architectures that ensure the non-interruption of data confidentiality. Confidence against advanced cyber threats toward IoT networks can also be achieved by this preventive measure alone.

7 Conclusion

This chapter offers a clear overview of IoT's architecture, applications, and the evolving security challenges, focusing the importance of proactive measures like vulnerability analysis, intrusion detection systems, and malware detection techniques. To keep IoT networks secure, it's essential to adopt strong security frameworks that include encryption, authentication, and dynamic policy management through Software-Defined Networking (SDN). With the integration of 5G, the IoT ecosystem introduces new risks but also gains opportunities to enhance security through advanced protocols, ensuring safe operations. As IoT adoption grows, collaboration between manufacturers, network operators, and users will be essential to protect these systems from emerging cyber threats. This chapter highlights the importance of continuous monitoring, timely updates, and flexible security solutions to protect data, devices, and networks. In the following chapters, we discuss advanced IoT security strategies, real-world applications, and future trends that influence the IoT landscape in detail.

References

1. Abomhara, M., Køien, G.M.: Security and privacy in the internet of things: Current status and open issues. In: 2014 International Conference on Privacy and Security in Mobile Systems (PRISMS), pp. 1–8. IEEE (2014)

2. Alasmary, H., Khormali, A., Anwar, A., Park, J., Choi, J., Abusnaina, A., Awad, A., Nyang, D., Mohaisen, A.: Analyzing and detecting emerging internet of things malware: A graph-based approach. IEEE Internet Things J. **6**(5), 8977–8988 (2019)
3. Antonakakis, M., April, T., Bailey, M., Bernhard, M., Bursztein, E., Cochran, J., Durumeric, Z., Halderman, J.A., Invernizzi, L., Kallitsis, M., et al.: Understanding the mirai botnet. In: 26th USENIX Security Symposium (USENIX Security 17), pp. 1093–1110 (2017)
4. Ashton, K., et al.: That 'Internet of Things' thing. RFID J. **22**(7), 97–114 (2009)
5. Atzori, L., Iera, A., Morabito, G.: The Internet of Things: A survey. Comput. Netw. **54**(15), 2787–2805 (2010)
6. Bandyopadhyay, D., Sen, J.: Internet of things: Applications and challenges in technology and standardization. Wirel. Pers. Commun. **58**, 49–69 (2011)
7. Ben-Itzhak, Y., Barabash, K., Cohen, R., Levin, A., Raichstein, E.: Enforsdn: Network policies enforcement with SDN. In: 2015 IFIP/IEEE International Symposium on Integrated Network Management (IM), pp. 80–88. IEEE (2015)
8. Botta, A., De Donato, W., Persico, V., Pescapé, A.: Integration of cloud computing and internet of things: a survey. Future Gen. Comput. Syst. **56**, 684–700 (2016)
9. Forum of Incident Response and Security Teams. CVSS. Website, FIRST (2023). Available at https://www.first.org/cvss/
10. Gubbi, J., Buyya, R., Marusic, S., Palaniswami, M.: Internet of things (IoT): A vision, architectural elements, and future directions. Future Gen. Comput. Syst. **29**(7), 1645–1660 (2013)
11. Gupta, N., Jindal, V., Bedi, P.: A survey on intrusion detection and prevention systems. SN Comput. Sci. **4**(5), 439 (2023)
12. Jyothsna, V., Prasad, K.M.: Anomaly-based intrusion detection system. Comput. Netw. Secur. **10**, 35–49 (2019)
13. Karmakar, K.K., Varadharajan, V., Tupakula, U., Hitchens, M.: Towards a dynamic policy enhanced integrated security architecture for SDN infrastructure. In: NOMS 2020-2020 IEEE/IFIP Network Operations and Management Symposium, pp. 1–9. IEEE (2020)
14. Kaur, J., Santhoshkumar, N., Nomani, M.Z.M., Sharma, D.K., Maroor, J.P., Dhiman, V.: Impact of Internet of Things (IoT) in retail sector. Mater. Today Proc. **51**, 26–30 (2022)
15. Kim, S., Kim, S.: User preference for an IoT healthcare application for lifestyle disease management. Telecommun. Pol. **42**(4), 304–314 (2018)
16. Kizza, J.M., Kizza, W., Wheeler: Guide to computer network security, p. 8. Springer (2013)
17. Koien, G.M., Oleshchuk, V.A.: Aspects of Personal Privacy in Communications-Problems, Technology and Solutions. River Publishers (2013)
18. Kwon, H.Y., Kim, T., Lee, M.K.: Advanced intrusion detection combining signature-based and behavior-based detection methods. Electronics **11**(6), 867 (2022)
19. Kyriazis, D., Varvarigou, T., White, D., Rossi, A., Cooper, J.: Sustainable smart city IoT applications: Heat and electricity management & eco-conscious cruise control for public transportation. In: 2013 IEEE 14th International Symposium on "A World of Wireless, Mobile and Multimedia Networks" (WoWMoM), pp. 1–5. IEEE (2013)
20. Liu, Y., Yang, C., Jiang, L., Xie, S., Zhang, Y.: Intelligent edge computing for IoT-based energy management in smart cities. IEEE Netw. **33**(2), 111–117 (2019)
21. Mahmoud, R., Yousuf, T., Aloul, F., Zualkernan, I.: Internet of things (IoT) security: Current status, challenges and prospective measures. In: 2015 10th International Conference for Internet Technology and Secured Transactions (ICITST), pp. 336–341. IEEE (2015)
22. Miorandi, D., Sicari, S., De Pellegrini, F., Chlamtac, I.: Internet of things: Vision, applications and research challenges. Ad Hoc Netw. **10**(7), 1497–1516 (2012)
23. Mistry, I., Tanwar, S., Tyagi, S., Kumar, N.: Blockchain for 5g-enabled IoT for industrial automation: A systematic review, solutions, and challenges. Mech. Syst. Signal Process. **135**, 106382 (2020)
24. MITRE Corporation. CVE. Website, MITRE (2024). Available at https://cve.mitre.org/
25. Nagajayanthi, B.: Decades of internet of things towards twenty-first century: A research-based introspective. Wirel. Pers. Commun. **123**(4), 3661–3697 (2022)

26. Nandyala, C.S., Kim, H.K.: Green IoT agriculture and healthcare application (GAHA). Int. J. Smart Home **10**(4), 289–300 (2016)
27. Perera, C., Zaslavsky, A., Christen, P., Georgakopoulos, D.: Context aware computing for the internet of things: A survey. IEEE Commun. Surv. Tutorials **16**(1), 414–454 (2013)
28. Pisharody, S., Natarajan, J., Chowdhary, A., Alshalan, A., Huang, D.: Brew: A security policy analysis framework for distributed SDN-based cloud environments. IEEE Trans. Depend. Sec. Comput. **16**(6), 1011–1025 (2017)
29. Roman, R., Najera, P., Lopez, J.: Securing the Internet of Things. Computer **44**(9), 51–58 (2011)
30. Shaikh, A., Gupta, P.: Advanced signature-based intrusion detection system. In: Intelligent Communication Technologies and Virtual Mobile Networks: Proceedings of ICICV 2022, pp. 305–321. Springer (2022)
31. Shaukat, K., Luo, S., Varadharajan, V.: A novel deep learning-based approach for malware detection. Eng. Appl. Artif. Intell. **122**, 106030 (2023)
32. Shi, W., Cao, J., Zhang, Q., Li, Y., Xu, L.: Edge computing: Vision and challenges. IEEE Internet Things J. **3**(5), 637–646 (2016)
33. Sicari, S., Rizzardi, A., Grieco, L.A., Coen-Porisini, A.: Security, privacy and trust in internet of things: The road ahead. Comput. Netw. **76**, 146–164 (2015)
34. Stojkoska, B.L.R., Trivodaliev, K.V.: A review of internet of things for smart home: Challenges and solutions. J. Clean. Prod. **140**, 1454–1464 (2017)
35. Waraga, O.A., Bettayeb, M., Nasir, Q., Talib, M.A.: Design and implementation of automated IoT security testbed. Comput. Secur. **88**, 101648 (2020)
36. Weber, R.H.: Internet of things–new security and privacy challenges. Comput. Law Secur. Rev. **26**(1), 23–30 (2010)
37. Wen, Q., Dong, X., Zhang, R.: Application of dynamic variable cipher security certificate in internet of things. In: 2012 IEEE 2nd International Conference on Cloud Computing and Intelligence Systems, vol. 3, pp. 1062–1066. IEEE (2012)
38. Zanella, A., Bui, N., Castellani, A., Vangelista, L., Zorzi, M.: Internet of things for smart cities. IEEE Internet Things J. **1**(1), 22–32 (2014)

An in-Depth Exploration of Attack Modeling and Vulnerability Analysis in IoT Networks

Blessy Thomas, Sabu M. Thampi, and Preetam Mukherjee

1 Introduction

The Internet of Things (IoT) has brought about a new era of interconnection in which devices are implanted with sensors, software, and connections, allowing them to gather and exchange data via the Internet. Due to the efficient features and functionalities of IoT, the network is expanding, and a greater number of devices are linked to the Internet. Many of these devices are designed to be low-power, compact, and easy to deploy, which makes their security vulnerabilities more pronounced. Consequently, the IoT network is susceptible to attacks, and attackers frequently exploit the vulnerability to gain unauthorized access. These attacks can have severe consequences, including the disclosure of private information, the destruction of vital infrastructure, and even physical harm. IoT devices increase the number of attack surfaces that can be used by attackers to compromise the integrity, confidentiality, and accessibility of data as they grow more widespread and interconnected. So it is necessary to identify the vulnerability that exists inside the network to prevent attackers. Organizations can address these weaknesses by recognizing them in advance. Failure to identify this will lead to significant loss. By adopting a proactive and ongoing vulnerability analysis strategy, organizations can strengthen their security posture and lower the likelihood of successful attacks.

Attackers often use the easiest paths to get inside the network. After identifying and prioritizing the vulnerabilities, it is important to model the attacker's pathways in advance to prevent all the possibilities of an attack [39]. Graphs can effectively illustrate vulnerability relations in a network since they are good at depicting

B. Thomas (✉) · S. M. Thampi · P. Mukherjee
Connected Systems and Intelligence Lab, School of Computer Science and Engineering, Digital University Kerala, Trivandrum, India
e-mail: blessy.res21@duk.ac.in; sabu.thampi@duk.ac.in; preetam.mukherjee@duk.ac.in; https://duk.ac.in

S. M. Thampi et al. (eds.), *Securing the Connected World*,
https://doi.org/10.1007/978-3-031-82826-3_2

relationships between elements [9]. The use of graphs in attack modeling has prevailed for the last several decades. Several graphical representations, such as attack graphs [16], attack trees [38], Attack - defense trees [22], are in use. Among these attack models, attack graphs are most widely used in representing vulnerability relations. The attack graph can show the attacker's paths to reach the desired system state [16]. The dynamic and quickly changing nature of IoT networks makes it difficult for traditional attack modeling techniques to keep up. This is where the power of Machine learning (ML) and Deep learning (DL) comes into play. With the help of enormous datasets, machine, and deep learning technologies thrive at finding hidden patterns, spotting abnormalities, and foreseeing future risks with a level of precision and speed that was previously unattainable. Deep learning and machine learning have shown remarkable promise in transforming the cybersecurity environment. Deep learning uses complicated neural networks to simulate the operations of the human brain, while machine learning is characterized by its capacity to learn from data and make informed judgments. Their algorithms can analyze enormous volumes of data, detect subtle patterns, and adjust to new threats making them ideal for providing security in IoT networks. ML and DL methods can assist with the automatic generation of attack graphs based on system parameters and recognized vulnerabilities.

This book chapter focuses on securing IoT networks with vulnerability analysis and attack modeling to enhance security in the rapidly evolving IoT landscape. The chapter starts by reviewing importance of vulnerability analysis in IoT networks. It emphasizes how urgently these networks need to be protected from growing cyber-attacks. We propose a new taxonomy for vulnerability assessment by including all the important elements in the spectrum of vulnerability assessment. It also lists the principal vulnerabilities and attacks, then further discusses different ML and DL based techniques in vulnerability analysis and attack modeling.

2 Importance of Vulnerability Analysis in IoT Networks

When referring to multiple interconnected devices, sensors, and networks constituting the IoT ecosystem, the term "vulnerability of IoT networks" refers to security weaknesses or flaws in the IoT network [50]. These flaws can be used by an attacker to modify data, steal confidential information, or take down vital infrastructure. Vulnerabilities could present in any of the devices' hardware, software, or even communication protocols. IoT networks have been the target of numerous cyberattacks in recent years, and more of these attacks are expected to occur exponentially in the years ahead due to numerous vulnerabilities found in IoT devices. Thus, conducting a "vulnerability analysis"–the process of finding weaknesses in a network–is essential for identifying potential entry points that attackers might exploit. By anticipating cyberattacks before they happen, cybersecurity experts can implement proactive measures to address these identified vulnerabilities. This allows them to put procedures in place to mitigate risks and protect the integrity and security of the IoT ecosystem.

2.1 Types of Vulnerabilities, Notable Vulnerabilities and Exploits

The vulnerabilities can be separated into software, hardware, protocol, network, and web-based vulnerabilities [10, 37, 54, 56, 58]. The Fig. 1 shows this classification.

- Software Vulnerabilities: Software vulnerabilities are flaws or weaknesses in the code or design of software that an attacker could use to get into the system without authorization. Buffer overflow is an example of a software vulnerability. A buffer overflow vulnerability occurs when data written to a buffer exceeds its size, which happens when a program tries to store more data in the buffer than it designed to store. CVE-2021-22908, buffer overflow vulnerability in Windows File Resource Profiles in version 9.X allows a remote authenticated user with privileges to browse SMB shares to execute arbitrary code as the root user.
- Hardware vulnerabilities: Hardware vulnerabilities are weak points or flaws in the physical parts of a device or system that attackers can use to obtain access without authorization, steal data, or interfere with the system's functionality. They may also be more harmful since they may damage every piece of the compromised hardware, even if the software is protected. Spectre Variant 1, also called "Bounds Check Bypass" is a security vulnerability that impacts modern microprocessors. This flaw allows attackers to misuse the speculative execution feature of CPUs, where the processor preemptively executes tasks before confirming their necessity. As a result, attackers may gain the ability to read sensitive data from memory that they are not authorized to access. CVE-2017-5753, allows systems with microprocessors that use speculative execution and branch prediction can potentially expose sensitive information to an attacker who has local user access.
- Protocol Vulnerabilities: Protocol vulnerabilities are weaknesses in communication protocols. These defects may result from implementation issues, design flaws, or deficiencies in the protocols themselves. Attackers can use protocol flaws to intercept or alter data sent between devices, resulting in data theft, unauthorized access, or other malicious behavior. KRACK (Key Reinstallation Attack) is a vulnerability found in the WPA2 protocol, which is used to

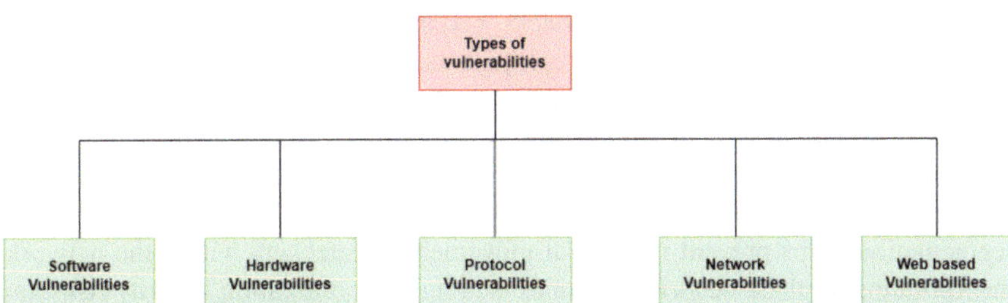

Fig. 1 Types of vulnerabilities

secure Wi-Fi networks. It allows attackers to read and decrypt data transmitted over the network and inject malicious data into the communication stream. With CVE-2017-13077, Wi-Fi Protected Access (WPA and WPA2) permits the reinstallation of the Pairwise Transient Key (PTK) and Temporal Key (TK) during the four-way handshake. This vulnerability allows an attacker within radio range to replay, decrypt, or spoof network frames.

- Network Vulnerabilities: Network vulnerabilities are weaknesses in the architecture of the network that attackers can use to obtain unauthorized access, interfere with network operations, or steal confidential data. They may be brought on by several things, such as improperly configured network devices, out-of-date software or firmware, poor network design and weak passwords. An example of a network vulnerability is a poorly managed firewall. For instance, if the firewall is not properly managed, it may allow data packets to be routed through the network without inspection, enabling attackers to access sensitive information or even take control of the entire network. No specific CVE can be pointed out. However, poor configuration practices can lead to severe security incidents.
- Web vulnerabilities: Web-based vulnerabilities are weak points or faults found in web applications or websites that attackers can use to compromise system security or steal personal information. A common example of a web vulnerability is SQL Injection, where an attacker enters malicious SQL code into the database. This can result in unauthorized access to sensitive data, modification of data, or even data deletion. CVE-2021-28242 is a SQL Injection vulnerability found in b2evolution, a popular open-source content management system (CMS) and blog engine, allows remote attackers to obtain sensitive database information by injecting SQL commands into the "cf_name" parameter when creating a new filter under the "Collections" tab.

2.2 Lessons Learned from Historical Incidents

Over the past few decades, several attacks on IoT devices have exposed serious vulnerabilities and highlighted the need for proper security measures. These attacks provide insights into how attackers exploit these weaknesses, leading to significant security breaches. Table 1 shows a few IoT attacks and the security issues that allowed them to succeed. These attacks revealed the importance of improving security of current and future IoT deployments. The attackers exploited zero-day vulnerabilities, underscoring the need for continuous monitoring and patching of IoT systems to address such vulnerabilities before they can be exploited. Attackers took advantage of default credentials, highlighting the need for strong password policies and enforcing the change of default credentials on all IoT devices. Network segmentation helps prevent the lateral movement of attackers within the network. Incorporating all these security practices is crucial for mitigating security risks and vulnerabilities to prevent from future attacks.

Table 1 Summary of historical IoT attacks

Attack	Description	Reason
Stuxnet (2010) [25]	Cyber weapon that specifically targeted industrial control systems, causing physical damage to centrifuges used by Iran in its uranium enrichment program as part of its nuclear development efforts	Exploited multiple zeroday vulnerabilities in industrial IoT systems.
Target Data Breach (2013) [41]	Attackers gained access to Target's network through a compromised POS system, leading to the theft of 40 million credit card numbers.	Lack of network segmentation allowed attackers to move from the compromised device to gain critical data.
Jeep Cherokee Hack (2015) [36]	Security researchers demonstrated that hackers could remotely control a Jeep Cherokee by exploiting vulnerabilities in the car's entertainment system, which was connected to the mobile data network	Lack of regular security updates left the vehicle vulnerable to attack.
Mirai Botnet (2016) [3]	The attack targeted IoT devices to create botnet, which was then used to launch a massive Distributed Denial of Service (DDoS) attack.	Exploited default credentials that were left unchanged by users and manufacturers, making devices easy targets for attackers.
Persirai (2017) [19]	A botnet that specifically targeted IP cameras, taking control of them by exploiting vulnerabilities for further attack.	Took advantage of unpatched vulnerabilities in IP cameras.
BrickerBot (2017) [5]	A destructive malware that permanently damages IoT devices by corrupting their firmware, rendering them unusable. This attack is known as a Permanent Denial of Service (PDoS) attack.	Exploited devices with weak security configurations, including default credentials
Reaper Botnet (2017) [35]	A botnet that infected and controlled a vast number of unpatched IoT devices by exploiting known vulnerabilities.	Took advantage of unpatched vulnerabilities in IoT devices.
Verkada Camera Hack (2021) [17]	Hackers gained access to security cameras, exposing sensitive video footage and compromising privacy.	Used exposed admin credentials leading to massive breach.

2.3 Overview of Vulnerability Analysis

In cybersecurity, vulnerability analysis helps to have a deeper understanding about the security weaknesses within a system. Vulnerability assessment is the process of identifying, classifying and prioritizing vulnerabilities in the system. The objective of vulnerability analysis is to determine the root causes of the identified vulnerabilities and detailed strategies to mitigate them before they are exploited. Automated tools can be used to detect existing vulnerabilities and misconfigurations. Manual testing and attack modeling techniques are used to identify the reachability of attackers by exploiting the existing weakness in the system. After identifying vulnerabilities, they need to be classified based on their severity (e.g., critical, high, medium, low). The type of each identified vulnerability is also categorized (e.g., software bugs, configuration errors, weak passwords). Once they have been classified, it is necessary to assess the risk posed by each vulnerability, as not all will present the same level of risk. This helps prioritize vulnerabilities, allowing organizations to focus on addressing the most significant threats first. After this step the organizations can move deeper into understanding of root causes of these weakness which further helps in providing appropriate mitigation strategies. Mitigation strategies involve applying patches, reconfiguring systems, or implementing other appropriate security measures. The overall process of vulnerability analysis is not a one-time procedure but rather a continuous activity of assessing the weakness in the network to identify the susceptability of the network to future and attempted attacks. As new vulnerabilities emerge, ongoing monitoring and regular vulnerability analysis are required to maintain a strong security posture [48].

2.4 Integrating Vulnerability Analysis into IoT Security Frameworks

IoT security frameworks offers a secure design and implementation roadmap that gathers, evaluates, and acts on data from multiple devices. A IoT system's design often consists of several layers interacting to gather, process, and transmit data from sensors and devices to other devices, networks, or cloud services. Each layer has its own security issues, highlighting the need to integrate a vulnerability analysis module to build a secure IoT framework

The IoT system is built on the IoT end Nodes (first layer). It includes devices like sensors for gathering environmental data. This layer in IoT faces three main security concerns. First, interfering waves can damage wireless signals utilized for communication between sensor nodes. Furthermore, IoT devices frequently function in outdoor settings, and physical assaults against IoT sensors and devices are feasible, allowing attackers to tamper with hardware components. Finally, as the sensors and RFIDs utilized in this layer have limited storage, power, and compute capabilities and are regularly relocated throughout the network topology, the system is exposed to threats and assaults [1]. Attacks like Replay Attacks, Timing Attacks, Node Capture Attacks, and Malicious Data Injection can compromise identification information, encryption keys, and data integrity, which in turn puts confidentiality in this layer in danger [51]. DoS attacks can also be carried out by draining nodes' energy and preventing them from using their energy-saving sleep mode.

Managing the communication between devices in the IoT system falls within the responsibility of the network layer. IoT's network layer is susceptible to passive monitoring, eavesdropping, traffic analysis, and other forms of passive monitoring, as well as DoS attacks and assaults on confidentiality and privacy. In addition, the network layer is highly vulnerable to Man-in-the-Middle attacks, which might compromise secure communication channels if key information is intercepted [1]. The application layer is responsible for processing the data gathered by IoT end nodes and producing insights that can be used to improve corporate operations or user experiences. Security issues in application security have been caused by the absence of global standards for controlling IoT development and interaction. Integration is challenging, as data privacy and identity authentication are unknown due to the different authentication methods used by different apps. Huge volumes of data are produced by connected devices, which can slow down applications and affect the availability of services. Moreover, user engagement, data disclosure, control tools, and knowledge of data consumption must be considered while creating IoT applications [24].

Mitigation mechanisms such as encryption, authentication, and access control are often incorporated into all layers of IoT frameworks, but they are not sufficient to identify vulnerabilities and prevent attackers from exploiting these weaknesses. Integrating vulnerability analysis at each layer can help build a secure IoT framework by identifying vulnerabilities in advance and preventing them from being exploited.

2.5 Vulnerability Assessment in IoT Networks

Vulnerability assessment involves defining, identifying, classifying and prioritizing the vulnerabilities within the system. This process helps the organizations to identify threats and risk background in their environment. Vulnerability assessment process can discover different types of weaknesses in system or network which needs a variety of tools and scanners. Different types of vulnerabilities assessment scans are discussed below.

- Network-based scans: Helps in identify vulnerability accross both wireless and wired network.
- Host-based scans: This helps to identify the vulnerabilities in servers, work stations or any other network hosts. These scans inspect ports and services

that network-based scans might give but provide more detailed insights into the configuration settings and patch history.
- Application scans: It helps in detecting software vulnerabilities and incorrect configuration in network or web applications.
- Database scans: These scans are used to identify weakness in database systems. They review the database configuration, access permissions, and stored data for weaknesses like improper permissions, injection flaws, or unsafe settings.

Vulnerability assessment helps the organization to know the risk associated with the weaknesses in their environment which is often a part of detailed vulnerability analysis. There exists several standards, tools that helps in identifying and evaluating these weaknesses, which is discussed below.

2.5.1 Common Standards in Vulnerability Assessment

- CVSS- The Common Vulnerability Scoring System (CVSS) [8] is a methodology for evaluating the severity of vulnerabilities in software and hardware systems. In addition to helping prioritize remediation activities, it offers a standardized technique for assessing the risk connected with a vulnerability [26]. The CVSS Score has three components namely,

  1. **Base score:** which evaluates the intrinsic qualities of a vulnerability and the ease with which it can be exploited. It considers aspects including access complexity, access vector, and the effect on confidentiality, integrity, and availability.
  2. **Temporal score:** This element considers elements that could change over time, such as the ease of access to patches, working exploit code, or the amount of support for the impacted system.
  3. **Environmental score:** It evaluates how the vulnerability would affect a particular environment, such as the likelihood of loss in the network of an organization.

- CVE: Common Vulnerabilities and Exposures, or CVE [44]. It is a publicly accessible dictionary of terms commonly used to identify cybersecurity vulnerabilities and exposures. CVE aims to facilitate data sharing so that all parties involved in cybersecurity are aware of the most recent vulnerabilities and can take countermeasures. A CVE is a security hole that has been given a CVE ID number e.g.: CVE-2020-35848, it is a CVE disclosed in 2020 and which is a type of SQL injection vulnerability.
- CWE: A community-developed collection of software and hardware weaknesses called CWE (Common Weakness Enumeration) [45] serves as the foundation for efforts to identify, mitigate, and prevent vulnerabilities. It is maintained by MITRE Corporation, a non-profit organization that runs research and development facilities funded by the US government.

Buffer overflows, injection flaws, and unsafe encryption are only a few of the typical software and hardware issues covered in detail by CWE. It also provides instructions on how to identify and avoid these weaknesses and illustrations of actual vulnerabilities brought on by these flaws.

- CWSS: A method for prioritizing weaknesses in software in a standardized, adaptable, and open way is provided by the Common Weakness Scoring System (CWSS) [46]. It is a community-based collaborative attempt that addresses the requirements of its stakeholders in the public sector, higher education, and business. Base Finding, Attack Surface, and Environmental Metric Groups comprise the CWSS organizational structure. A CWSS score for a weakness is calculated using several metrics from each category, often referred to as factors.
- CPE: A standardized naming method CPE (Common Platform Enumeration) [43] is used to identify software programs and operating systems. It is a structured naming strategy used to determine a product's platform, including the vendor name, product name, and version details. CPE was created to offer a standardized method of identifying the software items and their corresponding versions installed on a system, making it simpler to manage and secure the system.

National Vulnerability Database The National Vulnerability Database is known as NVD [28]. It is a database supported by the U.S. government that acts as a central repository for security flaws and exposures. The National Institute of Standards and Technology (NIST) is in charge of maintaining the database, which includes details on known flaws in hardware, firmware, and software products. Access to vulnerability data from a variety of sources, including vendors, researchers, and the security community, is made possible via the NVD. Each vulnerability is given with the CVE identifier, so that it may be recorded and referred to easily.

2.5.2 Tools and Techniques for Vulnerability Assessment

The specific features of IoT network, with their growing number, has made it challenging to protect these network from attackers. An efficient and systematic vulnerability assessment should be conducted to secure the IoT network from these attackers. In this context, we here discuss techniques and tools for assessing vulnerabilities in the network.

(a) Vulnerability and Network Scanning Tools: The attacker can misuse the information about the vulnerabilities in the network to gain unauthorized access [47]. Providing necessary defense and precautions from attacks requires adequate knowledge of the network. Network scanning tools identify the vulnerabilities in the network, which in turn helps to take necessary steps to keep the network secure. Some the commonly used tools are Nmap [14], Nessus [42], Wireshark [52], OpenVAS [11] and Metasploit [34].

(b) Honeypots: Honeypots are security methods used to identify, deflect, and monitor efforts that threaten the security of the system. They are made to look like trustworthy systems or services so that they can trick attackers into interacting with them, which further helps to identify the attack strategies the attackers could use. In IoT, honeypots often mimic a particular sort of IoT device to examine attack vectors in a certain scenario. Example of such honeypots includes, IoTPot, IoTBoX, HIoTPoT, HostaGe and SIPHON.

(c) Web-based Vulnerability assessment tools: Web applications provide access points to databases containing essential application data and resources [7]. It is vital to identify the web application's weaknesses to provide security to the network assets. Web application scanners aid in lowering the number of vulnerabilities in web applications. It investigates an application by crawling over its web pages. These scanners conduct penetration testing, an active website investigation by simulating attacks on it. AppScan, WebKing, WebInspect, and NTOspider are a few.

(d) Fuzzy Techniques: An automated software testing technique called fuzzing, commonly called fuzz testing, is used to identify weaknesses and vulnerabilities in IoT devices. Security researchers can find security holes in IoT systems and devices using fuzzing techniques, and they can cooperate with manufacturers to remedy such problems before attackers can use them. Fuzzing is simple to scale up to big-scale applications and requires little understanding of the target applications. A few fuzzing techniques include file format fuzzing, kernal fuzzing, and protocol fuzzing [23].

(e) Attack modeling: Attack modeling helps identify the attack paths use by the attacker to traverse the network by exploiting vulnerabilities, thereby aiding in understanding the most critical vulnerabilities. Graph-based attack modeling techniques are prevailing due to their effectiveness in offering a simple and clear approach for showing the relationships between various system components and how they can be exploited. In this chapter, we have included different graph-based attack and defense modeling techniques that will be discussed later.

2.5.3 Vulnerability Assessment Report

A vulnerability assessment report is of utmost significance for ensuring an organization's security environment. It serves as an all-inclusive manual for locating and comprehending security flaws in IT systems and applications. Beyond merely identifying them, it is crucial to prioritize remediation efforts and make sure that the most serious flaws are fixed right away to reduce risks. With the help of this research, decision-makers will be able to reach well-informed decisions on resource allocation, financial planning, and overall cybersecurity policies. The six key elements in a vulnerability assessment report include:

1. Executive Summary The findings and suggestions from the assessment are succinctly but critically summarized in this section. It offers a summary of the objectives, scope, and critical vulnerabilities found in the assessment. Key findings are emphasized, with a focus on vulnerabilities with a high degree of severity or significant potential impact. In terms of potential financial and operational consequences, it provides a risk assessment that describes the possible effects.

2. Scan Results This section thoroughly describes each vulnerability, including its name, severity rating (typically based on the Common Vulnerability Scoring System or CVSS), and a summary of its features and probable consequences.

3. Methodology It provides an accurate understanding of the methodology, resources, and methods employed throughout the evaluation process. This section makes it clear whether a black-box, white-box, or gray-box approach was used to conduct the assessment. Along with the testing methods used, the assessment's objectives and scope are all clearly stated. This thorough overview guarantees the evaluation process's legitimacy and transparency, allowing stakeholders to fully understand its methodology and approach.

4. Findings Here, an in-depth presentation of the discovered security flaws is given. The specific devices impacted by each vulnerability, along with their IP addresses or hostnames for quick identification are provided.

5. Risk Assessment The evaluation of potential hazards connected to the discovered vulnerabilities is the main focus here. Prioritizing vulnerabilities based on their criticality will help organizations deploy resources effectively and handle the biggest threats as soon as they arise. With risk assessment, organizations can develop and implement efficient risk mitigation techniques to lower total risk exposure.

6. Recommendations Recommendations offer practical advice for reducing or eliminating the vulnerabilities that have been found. The actions that should be performed to improve the organization's security posture are detailed in this section. According to the severity and potential impact of the vulnerabilities, recommendations are often prioritized.

The vulnerability assessment report is the primary source of information about the organization's security flaws and vulnerabilities. It offers a thorough list of vulnerabilities along with their explanations, ratings for their severity, and probable effects. Organizations can monitor the application of countermeasures and determine whether they have successfully decreased the risks associated with identified vulnerabilities.

2.6 Challenges in Securing IoT Through Vulnerability Analysis

IoT network is rapidly expanding. The heterogeneity of IoT ecosystem complicates vulnerability analysis process, as different devices may require different tools and methods for identifying and mitigating risks. These devices come from manufacturers with varying security standards, therefore ensuring that all devices are adequately protected is difficult. Due to the growing number of diverse IoT devices have led to the expansion attack surfaces, which is the potential entry points for attackers. Each new device adds another weakness creating a new path for attacker, this makes vulnerability analysis challenging. Unknown vulnerabilities, which is referred to as zero-day vulnerabilities, present security flaws in IoT networks. These vulnerabilities are not yet discovered by security researchers or developers. The existing techniques fails to identify these vulnerabilities leaving IoT devices exposed to attacks. Since these vulnerabilities are unknown they are not accounted for existing mitigation strategies. The dynamic nature of IoT network enables devices to join and leave the network. To conduct a proper vulnerability analysis it is very essential to have an up-to-date inventory of all connected devices. In the case of dynamic IoT network, this information will get outdated, leading vulnerabilities go undetected. As new devices are introduced and older ones are updated or replaced, the nature of potential attacks can change. Attacker tries to exploit the weakness in the newly connected devices. The advanced tactics of attackers to gain access to the network also making it challenging. Therefore new techniques are required to efficiently capture the weakness in the system to keep up with the evolving attack surfaces.

3 Advancements in Vulnerability Analysis Techniques

As attackers develop new methods to exploit vulnerabilities, traditional security measures often fall neccessiting the need of advanced techniques to safeguard critical assests. In parallel standardization of vulnerability analysis is increasingly important. Adopting a common standard ensures consistency and reliability in managing vulnerabilities. This section discusses the need of new advanced vulnerability analysis techniques due to dynamic threat landscape in IoT and the importance of standardization in vulnerability analysis.

3.1 Evolving threat Landscape

The IoT threat landscape has rapidly evolved with the explosion of connected devices, many of which lack adequate security protections. As IoT devices like IP cameras, home routers, and industrial control systems become more common, they have become prime targets for increasingly sophisticated cyberattacks that exploit their vulnerabilities.

A notable example of this is the Mirai botnet. Mirai specifically targeted devices running the Linux operating system, exploiting weak or default credentials to gain control. Once compromised, these devices–often called "zombies"– will be a part of botnet that launched massive Distributed Denial of Service (DDoS) attacks. The speed and scale of Mirai's spread highlighted the destructive nature of IoT-based attacks.

Several key trends characterize the evolving threat landscape [15]:

Increasing Exploitation of Vulnerabilities: Unpatched vulnerabilities in IoT devices remain a critical issue. Attackers are quick to exploit these weaknesses, especially in devices that do not receive regular security updates. Outdated firmware and insecure APIs further expose IoT devices to cybercriminals.

Advancement in Attack Techniques: IoT botnets are not just increasing in number; they are becoming more sophisticated. New botnets like IoT Reaper and Hajime are exploiting various software vulnerabilities, sometimes within weeks of their discovery, showing how attackers are focusing on specific vulnerabilities to create more effective botnets.

Monetization of Compromised Devices: After taking control of IoT devices, attackers typically use them to spread malware, join command-and-control ($CandC$) networks, or launch further attacks. For instance, devices compromised by Mirai and similar botnets have been used to launch large-scale DDoS attacks, disrupting critical online services.

Dynamic Nature of IoT Threats: The IoT threat ecosystem is highly dynamic, with rapidly changing malware infrastructures and evolving attack methods. Botnets quickly adapt and incorporate new vulnerabilities, making them a persistent and growing threat.

Physical vulnerability: Many IoT devices are situated in remote locations and are often left unattended, meaning they aren't regularly monitored or interacted with. This lack of oversight makes many types of IoT devices more susceptible to unauthorized access by malicious actors. For instance, in South Africa, thieves targeted mobile-connected traffic lights, breaking into the connectivity units and stealing SIM cards, which were then used in other devices.

Interconnectedness: IoT devices are connected each other sharing a common infrastructure making vulnerable to security threats. One of the most frequent risks involves man-in-the-middle attacks on user Wi-Fi network, which can lead to financial fraud and other serious consequences.

Diversity of devices: Securing IoT devices is significantly more complex than managing security for a limited range of traditional ICT devices like smartphones, PCs, and IT infrastructure. Enterprises must address the security vulnerabilities of a wide array of devices, spanning from generic IoT deployments to specialized use cases.

Given the emergence of these threats, it is crucial to continuously monitor and adapt security strategies to protect IoT devices. As the number of connected devices continues to rise, so too will the challenges in securing them against an increasingly sophisticated and aggressive threat landscape.

3.1.1 Integration of Artificial Intelligence in Vulnerability Analysis

The term " Artificial intelligence" is used popularly when a computer demonstrates traits like human cognitive processes, such as "learning" and " problem-solving,". The importance of learning for machines has led to the development of the AI area known as machine learning. Machine learning techniques make it possible for computer programs to automatically enhance performance via experience. The capabilities of machines have increased as a result of major advancements made in machine learning techniques over the previous couple of decades. Deep learning, a specialized subset of machine learning methods, is an important endeavor on this path. Deep learning focuses on developing neural networks that can be trained to emulate the complex structure and operation of the human brain. Deep neural networks–also referred to as "neurons", are made up of several layers of interconnected nodes. These networks can automatically recognize patterns, characteristics, and representations in data by analyzing a massive amount of information. They are capable of detecting anomalies and identifying vulnerabilities more effectively. They are also capable of predicting future attacks by analyzing emerging trends, helping to identify vulnerabilities that could be targeted next. ML and DL models can identify zero day vulnerabilities by quickly recognising unusual patterns. Vulnerabilities in dynamic IoT network is often difficult to predict, due to changing connectivity and configurations. Al models helps in identifying vulnerabilities by noticing the changes in the network. Integrating AI in vulnerability analysis can reduce the number of false positive rates by learning from previous patterns. Therefore AI in vulnerability analysis enhances speed and efficiency in identifying and mitigating vulnerabilities.

3.1.2 Standardization Efforts and Best Practices

To ensure vulnerability analysis is efficient, organizations should adopt standardized practices into their processes. CVSS provides a standardized method for assessing the severity of vulnerabilities. It offers a comprehensive scoring system that considers multiple factors, including the ease of exploitation and impact on system integrity. A detailed vulnerability assessment report should be prepared to identify the risk associated. The best practices to be followed in vulnerability analysis is discussed here,

- Regular updates: Ensure that all systems and devices are regularly updated. Updates always include patches and enhancements to existing security features.
- Discover, prioritize, remediate, validate, report: Vulnerability scanning tools helps to identify the vulnerabilities that attackers could exploit. Standard scores like CVSS helps to priortize the identified vulnerabilities. Start with the most critical vulnerability, develop a strategic plan to remove vulnerabilities. Validation process should be conducted to verify that the remediation process have successfully removed vulnerabilities. Finally, for transparency and continous improvement a detailed report have to be prepared.
- Attack modelling: With the identified vulnerabilities, find all the attack paths that attackers could use to reach the network.

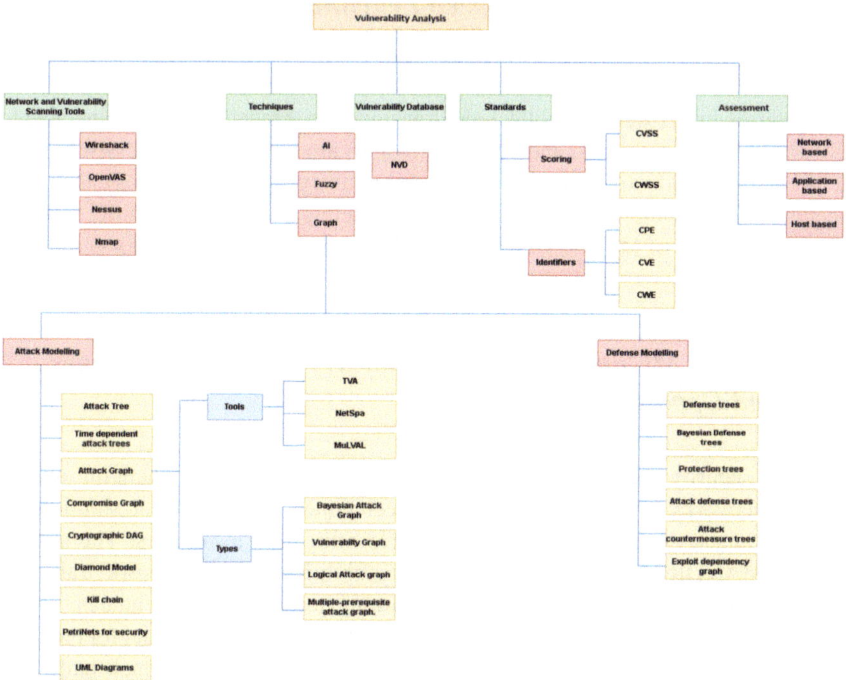

Fig. 2 Proposed taxonomy

- Risk based prioritization: Using attack model, identify critical attack paths and analyze the risk pose by each such paths therefore priority can be given to them while applying security mechanisms.
- Mitigation strategies: After identifying vulnerabilities and assessing attacker reachability, appropriate strategies can be implemented to eliminate vulnerabilities, effectively cutting down potential attack paths.
- Establish a vulnerability management program and put it into use: Organizations should go beyond traditional vulnerability analysis that focus identification and remediation and choose solutions. They must establish a powerful framework to ensure that vulnerability analysis are part of a comprehensive and connected security program.
- Assess vulnerabilities in build time and deployment time: Vulnerability analysis process should addresses vulnerabilities in both build time and deployment time. Conducting thorough vulnerability assessments during the build phase significantly reduces risks when it comes time for deployment.

Figure 2 shows the proposed taxonomy that includes prominent tools, techniques, standards, analysis domains, and a database for vulnerability analysis, providing an understanding of the key elements to consider for effective vulnerability analysis.

4 Machine Learning and Deep Learning in Vulnerability Analysis

The devices in IoT network collect and transmit data, rendering them vulnerable to different security risks. DL and ML technologies are becoming progressively more important for conducting thorough vulnerability analysis in the IoT ecosystem. This section discusses the importance of attack modeling in IoT vulnerability analysis and later the role of ML and DL in the generation and analysis of attack graphs.

4.1 Role of ML and DL in Vulnerability Analysis, Challenges and Opportunities

Existing security measures are ineffective against continuously changing attacks in IoT networks, therefore DL and ML techniques offer potential solutions to improve attack detection and suggest suitable mitigation techniques. The authors in [4], MANDRAKE, aims to detect vulnerabilities in IoT network traffic by analyzing packet traffic using machine learning techniques. This analysis helps identify potential vulnerabilities in traffic encryption, which is essential for ensuring the security of IoT networks. If defenders are aware of all the attack paths that an attacker can create by exploiting vulnerabilities to access the network, they can implement effective strategies to prevent these attacks. Attack models help to understand attack paths and the reachability of attacker into the network. Graph-based attack models are user friendly and intuitive. This aids network administrators in understanding the current state of the networks and helps in maintaining the network secure. The most prominent attack model is attack graph which shows the relationship between vulnerabilities and the possible attack paths that the attacker could use for traversing the network. ML algorithms can assist with the automatic generation of attack graphs based on system parameters and recognized vulnerabilities. Lack of high quality data is one of the core challenges in using ML and DL models for vulnerability analysis and identifying attack paths as they leads to poor predictions. Nowadays attackers are using advanced techniques, models trained on historical data are not sufficient to detect the advanced attack patterns. The lack of explainability in ML and DL models are also a concern. Security administrators should aware of the reason in predicting certain vulnerabilities or attack paths as crucial. Besides these challenges, ML and DL model provides significant opportunities in enhancing the efficiency in predicting and mitigating vulnerabilities in complex systems. They are powerful in automatic detection of vulnerabilities by real time analysing network traffics. Unsupervised learning techniques like clustering and autoencoders are capable of detecting unknown vulnerabilities that traditional methods miss. These advantages of ML and DL models highlights the potential in identifying, predicting and mitigating security risks in IoT network.

4.2 Understanding Attack Graphs and Their Role in Vulnerability Analysis

Network Vulnerability Scanners can detect known vulnerabilities in a target network. However, these vulnerabilities are typically isolated and independent. Since nodes in a network are interconnected, a single vulnerability alone is unlikely to pose a significant threat to the entire network. When multiple exploitable vulnerabilities are combined and interrelated, they form an attack path, enabling an attacker to reach the target resource. One or more of these attack paths make up an attack graph.

Attack graphs are important in cybersecurity for locating and visualizing probable attack paths that an attacker could use to breach a system. Security experts can better understand the security posture of their systems and spot possible vulnerabilities that can be fixed to increase overall security by analyzing attack graphs. By concentrating on the most important vulnerabilities and attack paths, attack graphs can also assist in prioritizing security spending. Attack graphs can be created using several tools, including TVA, MulVA[29], and NetSPA[13]. We need network and vulnerability information to build an attack graph. Nessus [42], Nmap [14], OpenVAS [11], Metasploit [34], and other network analyzer programs can scan the network and produce this information. Vulnerabilities are stored in the NVD (National Vulnerability Database) [28] with a specific CVE (Common Vulnerability Exposure) [44] ID. One can establish both the preconditions necessary for exploiting a vulnerability and the postconditions that can be realized from the detailed information recorded in NVD.

In [40] the authors introduced the idea of attack graphs and suggested an automated process for creating and analyzing them, which is a significant contribution to cybersecurity. The methodology consists of three basic steps: modeling the network, modeling the abilities and goals of the attacker, and creating the attack graph. The authors use formal methods, such as model checking, to verify the correctness of the generated attack graph.

Later in [2] according to the notion of monotonicity proposed by the authors, the precondition of one exploit is never become invalid by the successful use of another attack. With this assumption, even very large networks can be analyzed because the complexity of the analysis issue is reduced from exponential to polynomial. To gain knowledge about why an attack happens, in [30] the authors introduced the idea of a logical attack graph. The node of the graph is a logical statement. This logical statement only encodes a portion of the network's state rather than the complete state. From the logical attack graphs, we can know the reasons why attacks happen. A logical attack graph's ability to explicitly specify the causal relationships between system configuration data and an attacker's possible rights.

The multiple-prerequisite attack graph, which scales almost linearly as the size of a typical network increases, is a novel sort of attack graph that the authors have developed to describe big and complicated networks [12]. It is necessary to incorporate the probability of change in attacks during the lifetime of the system. In

[32] authors propose a Bayesian Attack Graph, which calculates the presence of a non-zero probability corresponding to the scenario where the attacker cannot exploit the vulnerability even though all the preconditions are met, a Local Conditional Probability Distribution(LCPD) is used to depict this probability for each network.

When there are a lot of vulnerabilities in the target network, the state explosion problem causes the computation of attack graphs to degrade. Attack graph processing can be done in parallel to mitigate this issue. The authors in [18] have introduced the concept of distributed attack graph generation. It is a memory-based parallel and distributed method that creates attack graphs based on vulnerabilities on a distributed multi-agent platform. In [9] the authors introduced a vulnerability graph for a vulnerable network. The nodes in the vulnerability graph represent vulnerabilities and the edges represent the relationship. The vulnerability graph gives a visual depiction of the vulnerabilities in IoT edge devices and can help with risk mitigation strategies.

The majority of above methods employed their formulation for the graph's nodes and edges. Attack graphs show possible attack paths and weaknesses in a system or network. Organizations can proactively plan and implement defensive measures to disrupt or prevent these attack vectors by including countermeasures in these graphs, which will lower the likelihood of successful attacks. ML algorithms can assist with the automatic generation of attack graphs based on system parameters and recognized vulnerabilities.

4.2.1 Attack Graph Visualization Technologies

Attack graphs are useful security methods for modeling and examining probable attack scenarios on systems, networks, or applications. Tools generate attack graphs to aid system administrators in visualizing attack pathways and taking appropriate defensive measures. Different attack graph visualization tools are reviewed in this section [55].

1. MulVAL (Multi-host, Multi-stage Vulnerability Analysis Language): MulVAL (Multi-host Multi-stage Vulnerability Analysis) is an open-source project developed at Kansas State University. It takes input files such as a vulnerability configuration file. The MulVAL framework consists of five main components: interaction rules, security policies, a logical execution engine, an analytical database, and unauthorized access and attack path tracing.

   Interaction rules define how different parts of the network interact and affect security. Using the configuration data from the analytical database, reasoning rules simulate an attacker's behavior within the network. Security policies, managed by system administrators, define the network's security attributes, represented as simple Datalog tuples that list the allowed data access rules for users. Based on the analytical database, interaction rules, and security policies, the logical execution engine generates attack graphs. These graphs provide a textual or graphical (PDF) representation of attack paths, highlighting violations and tracing possible attack routes for users.

2. TVA (Topological Vulnerability Analysis): TVA is an attack graph tool developed by George Mason University that uses data from the Nessus vulnerability scanner. It automatically analyzes network vulnerabilities and identifies weaknesses to generate an attack graph. TVA creates state transition diagrams based on attack procedures and conditions, enhancing the scalability of network vulnerability analysis.
3. Cauldron: Cauldron is the commercial version of the TVA network topology vulnerability analysis tool developed by George Mason University. Cauldron operates in three main steps: first, it collects all relevant information from the target network; second, it correlates this information with known vulnerability datasets; and third, it performs 'What-if' analysis and displays attack graphs using its modeling environment. Cauldron can utilize vulnerability scanners, such as Nessus, to support its analysis.
4. Attack Graph Toolkit: The Attack Graph Toolkit, developed by Oleg at Carnegie Mellon University, is an open-source tool designed for Linux platforms with a user-friendly graphical interface. It comprises three main modules: network modeling tools, a scene attack graph builder, and a graphical user interface (GUI). The toolkit takes inputs such as network specifications, host and network configurations, and action libraries. Using the results from the network modeling tools, the scene attack graph builder generates attack graphs, providing a clear visualization of potential attack paths
5. NetSPA (Network Security Planning Architecture): NetSPA was developed by Ingols and Lippmann at MIT's Lincoln Laboratory to visualize network attack graphs. It identifies the most critical attack paths based on the network topology and helps identify potential routes that attackers could exploit to pose long-term threats. NetSPA uses information from individual hosts, running services, and overall network data to create attack graphs that illustrate how hackers can infiltrate the system.
6. FireMon: FireMon is the commercial version of the NetSPA network security management tool. It defines and manages risk scenarios based on identified threats and vulnerabilities related to assets. Once these scenarios are set up, the FireMon Risk Analyzer evaluates and reveals the risks associated with those assets. It also provides a summary report detailing accessible assets and their potential vulnerabilities.

4.2.2 Limitations of Traditional Attack Graph Modeling

Traditional attack graph modeling techniques have certain limitations in dynamic IoT environment with complex connetivities [20]. As the size of the network grows the nodes and edges of the attack graphs grows exponentially leading to dense graphs which are difficult to visualize and analyze. As the size of the network increases, the time required to generate attack paths and assess their security implications grows significantly. The unknown vulnerabilities and advanced attack techniques generate new attack paths, which cannot be generated with existing attack generation techniques. IoT network is dynamic with changes such as the addition or removal of devices and variations in network configurations. Existing attack graph generators lack the capability for real-time monitoring to quickly capture these changes. These limitations necessitate more advanced ML and DL methods that can dynamically update, scale to larger environments, and detect advanced attack tactics.

4.2.3 Automatic Generation and Analysis of Attack Models Using ML and DL, Benefits

IoT ecosystems are incredibly complicated and dynamic since numerous devices are always producing data and interacting with one another. Security professionals can better comprehend the security landscape by using attack graphs that are created using this data to visualize potential attack paths and scenarios. The automatic generation and analysis of attack graphs is now necessary for defending IoT systems. This generation and analysis of attack graphs make use of machine learning and deep learning techniques to find emerging dangers and weaknesses in the IoT ecosystem. Machine learning and deep learning techniques enable real-time monitoring, rapid threat response, and proactive defense, making the automatic generation and analysis of attack graphs indispensable for safeguarding IoT systems against cyberattacks.

The authors in [31] propose a methodology for building attack circuits that uses input/output pairs created by natural language processing (NLP). The weights are also calculated using conventional security score metrics, and attack circuits are assessed using effective optimization methods. The contribution consists of a methodology that analyses possible attack vectors depending on their impact, exploitability, or overall risk.

The authors use Fuzzy Petri Net (FPN) to establish an attack model and improve Q-Learning through FPN in [53]. They define the attack gain from the attacker's perspective to determine the best attack path. The paper introduces a quantitative indicator for analyzing the impact of cyber attacks on the real-time operation of power grids. The contribution is an attack model that enhances a Q-Learning algorithm with the use of FPN's fuzzy reasoning capabilities and further uses the Q-Learning algorithm to identify the network system's vulnerable part.

An autonomous security analysis and penetration testing framework (ASAP) that uses attack graphs to identify security threats and attack paths in a network is introduced in [6]. The framework incorporates a state-of-the-art reinforcement learning algorithm based on Deep-Q Network (DQN) to determine the optimal policy for performing penetration testing. It also includes a domain-specific transition matrix and reward modeling to capture the importance of security vulnerabilities and the difficulty in exploiting them. The ASAP framework generates autonomous attack plans and validates them against real-world networks, making it applicable to complex enterprise networks.

The attack involves injecting a predefined subgraph into a testing graph, causing the GNN classifier to predict an attacker-chosen target label for that graph. The attack is shown to be effective with minimal impact on the GNN's prediction accuracy for clean testing graphs.

4.3 An Example of Real-world Scenario

Smart cities promise an increased quality of life, efficiency, and sustainability through the merging of innovative technologies, data-driven infrastructure, and creative urban planning. Smart cities, however, confront a growing number of security and vulnerability issues as they become increasingly integrated. The complicated security issues that result from this technological integration make them a compelling subject of study. By concentrating on a smart city use case, we seek to investigate and analyze the security concerns and flaws that develop in such environments.

Figure 3 shows an example of a smart city network. The network is integrated with a city transportation system, which functions as a central hub for regulating, monitoring, and alerting traffic situations throughout the city by maintaining connectivity with the city airport management system, city surveillance system, city vehicle management system, and city bus system. The city bus system module concentrates on enhancing public transportation services. It has capabilities includ-

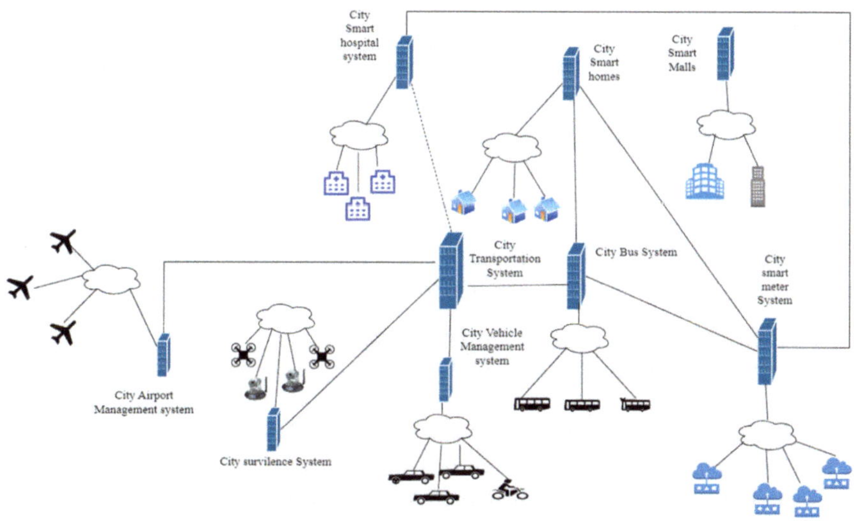

Fig. 3 Example of a smart city network

Table 2 Vulnerability details

Hosts	Vulnerability
LAN user	CVE-2017-11783
Traffic surveillance management server	CVE-2014-2246
Hospital management server	CVE-2017-3167
Drone	CVE-2021-34125
IP camera	CVE-2018-10660
Traffic management server	CVE-2021-3154
Fleet management server	CVE-2022-2199
Hospital surveillance management server	CVE-2017-12708

ing contactless payment options, real-time bus tracking, and smart bus stops. IoT sensors on buses and at stations can provide information for route optimization, cut down on waiting times, and improve the user experience. To assist residents in planning their departures more effectively, a smart bus system is connected with smart homes allowing residents to receive timely updates on bus arrivals. The connection between a smart home system and a smart hospital system enables monitoring of patient's health and well-being, particularly those with chronic diseases or those who require ongoing medical care. The smart malls in the city are connected with smart homes which facilitate shopping and receive real-time notifications on special offers and promotions. A city's smart meter systems are connected to smart homes, malls, hospitals, and smart transportation systems. Residents who use these meters can manage and optimize their energy use from their smart homes by receiving real-time energy consumption data from the meters. Based on data from smart meters, energy efficiency measures implemented at hospitals and smart malls can reduce costs and support a sustainable urban environment. The integration of the same with smart transportation systems guarantees effective electric vehicle charging and route planning.

Assume that the attacker aims to get access to the traffic management server. The entire traffic control system can be affected by an attack on the traffic management server. The attacker can manipulate traffic patterns causing traffic delays, accidents, and a chaotic driving environment.

Table 2 listed different vulnerabilities in the network. The vulnerability information, network details including connectivity, and firewall rules are used to create the attack Graph. Figure 4 shows the attack graph with different possible attack paths and associated CVSS scores towards the traffic management server.

- *There exist two attack paths in the attack graph.*
- *The critical attack path LAN user—Fleet Management Server—Traffic Management Server.*
- *Critical due to high CVSS scores in the vulnerabilities belonging to that path. If they get exploited, there will be severe loss in the network.*
- *Countermeasure: Remove the vulnerability in the LAN user, as it is connected to multiple servers, if not removed other paths will also emerge.*

Fig. 4 Attack graph

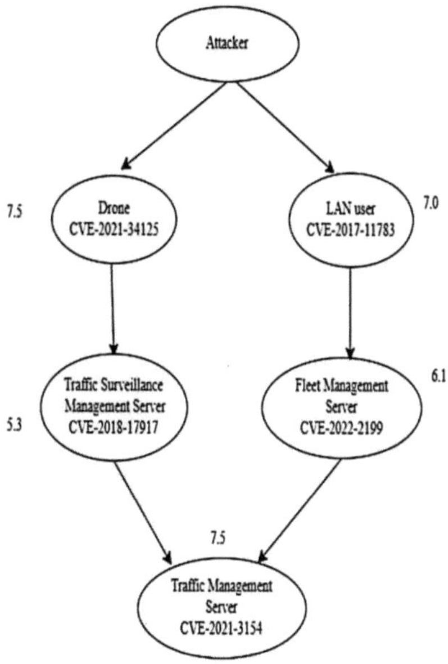

This exploration of security vulnerabilities and their consequences helps to reduce risks and strengthen defenses against potential attacks.

5 Recent Developments in Attack Modeling Techniques

In work [21] authors introduced a method of generating attack Graphs for computer networks using machine learning. The approach uses machine learning to train a model to recognize attack paths in attack graphs. The training data is based on vulnerability databases. The process of generating an attack graph consists of using the trained model to recognize attack graph features in the given network topology.

Authors in [33] proposed a method for anomaly detection and attack modeling in cyber physical power systems using deep learning models. A Graph Convolutional Long Short-Term Memory (GC-LSTM) model is used to predict network traffic patterns accurately. Additionally, the normal traffic data is used to generate the OT network topology using a Traffic Dispersion Graph (TDG), which visually represents the network's communication patterns. In the second step, the trained GC-LSTM model's traffic predictions are used to train a Deep Convolutional Neural Network (CNN) specifically for Time Series Classification (TSC). This process results in a trained CNN model capable of classifying OT network traffic as normal or anomalous. The third step involves real-time monitoring of the OT network traffic. The trained GC-LSTM and Deep CNN models work together to classify each network node as either normal or anomalous based on the observed traffic data.

Finally, the results from the node classification step are combined with the OT graph data generated in the first step to create an attack graph. This visualization helps identify and map potential attack paths within the network, enhancing situational awareness and supporting the identification of active cyber attacks in near real-time. In paper [49], they have extended traditional attack graphs with weights. The nodes and edges are associated with a weight to understand its significance in attack. They have also introduced an algorithm for computing shortest attack trace. A budget constraint strategy to harden the network elements has been proposed to increase the difficulty in short attack trace. In [57] authors introduced "attack function" as a new way to represent attacks within an attack graph. The work shows that the generation of two types of attack graphs–state enumeration graphs and exploit dependency graphs–from the attack functions. This approach allows different forms of attack graphs to be derived from a single representation of the network, improving the ability of analysing. The paper [27] introduces SAGE (IntruSion alert-driven Attack Graph Extractor), a novel framework that automatically generates attack graphs directly from intrusion alerts without relying on prior expert knowledge, vulnerability data, or network topology information. SAGE employs a suffix-based probabilistic deterministic finite automaton (S-PDFA) to model the temporal and probabilistic dependencies between alerts. This model brings infrequent, severe alerts into focus while summarizing the paths leading to them, offering an explainable and interpretable approach to understanding attacker strategies. The framework generates attack graphs on a per-victim, per-objective basis, extracting actionable intelligence about attacker strategies from large volumes of alerts.

6 Conclusion and Future Directions

The surface area for attacks grows as more IoT-based devices are linked to the Internet. Therefore more security solutions need to be developed to secure the user's security and privacy. The change in the dynamics of IoT requires real-time monitoring and implementation of security solutions. AI and machine learning can be used to analyze massive amounts of data from IoT devices and spot anomalies or unusual behavior that can point to an attack. The implementation of machine learning models in identifying the attack paths and critical attack points will help in better security defense. Most of the existing works on attack modeling used simulated networks to analyze the performance. In the future real-time attack modeling of real-world applications including critical path identification and suitable countermeasures is highly in demand.

The existing works focus on threats and attacks in one IoT network. There can be multiple IoT networks that are connected to each other, in such a scenario the vulnerability in one network may indirectly affect the vulnerability in another network, therefore development of models to prevent the transmission of threats from one IoT network to another IoT network is required.

With the development of technologies, more and more solutions are emerging to strengthen security. The defenders are occupied in finding new defensive mechanisms and attackers are often working to crack it. The attackers are already known about the attack paths and defensive strategies. Organizations have to implement security within a given budget, therefore defenders often implement strategies only considering the most prominent attack points. Therefore they often try to find new paths that are not secured. The development of an attack model that is capable of providing the best defensive strategies within the allocated budget by incorporating all possible attack paths can be future work. This chapter has covered an integrated view of security issues and vulnerabilities prevailing in IoT networks. We have also incorporated the importance of attack and defense modeling techniques. Previous studies on attack graphs and prominent works on providing hardening strategies have also been included. Definitely, the literature and the addition of future works provide new insights to further research in the domain of vulnerability and attack modeling in IoT networks.

References

1. Abomhara, M., Køien, G.M.: Security and privacy in the internet of things: Current status and open issues. In: 2014 international conference on privacy and security in mobile systems (PRISMS), pp. 1–8. IEEE (2014)
2. Ammann, P., Wijesekera, D., Kaushik, S.: Scalable, graph-based network vulnerability analysis. In: CCS '02, pp. 217–224. Association for Computing Machinery (2002)
3. Antonakakis, M., April, T., Bailey, M., Bernhard, M., Bursztein, E., Cochran, J., Durumeric, Z., Halderman, J.A., Invernizzi, L., Kallitsis, M., et al.: Understanding the mirai botnet. In: 26th USENIX security symposium (USENIX Security 17), pp. 1093–1110 (2017)
4. Brezolin, U., Vergütz, A., Nogueira, M.: A method for vulnerability detection by iot network traffic analytics. Ad Hoc Netw. **149**, 103247 (2023)
5. Brierley, C., Pont, J., Arief, B., Barnes, D.J., Hernandez-Castro, J.: Paperw8: an iot bricking ransomware proof of concept. In: Proceedings of the 15th International Conference on Availability, Reliability and Security, pp. 1–10 (2020)
6. Chowdhary, A., Huang, D., Mahendran, J.S., Romo, D., Deng, Y., Sabur, A.: Autonomous security analysis and penetration testing. In: 2020 16th International Conference on Mobility, Sensing and Networking (MSN), pp. 508–515 (2020). https://doi.org/10.1109/MSN50589.2020.00086
7. Fong, E., Okun, V.: Web application scanners: definitions and functions. In: 2007 40th Annual Hawaii International Conference on System Sciences (HICSS'07), pp. 280b–280b. IEEE (2007)
8. Forum of Incident Response and Security Teams: Cvss. Website, FIRST (2023). Available at https://www.first.org/cvss/
9. George, G., Thampi, S.M.: Vulnerability-based risk assessment and mitigation strategies for edge devices in the internet of things. Pervasive Mobile Comput. **59**, 101068 (2019)
10. Girma, A.: Analysis of security vulnerability and analytics of internet of things (iot) platform. In: Information Technology-New Generations: 15th International Conference on Information Technology, pp. 101–104. Springer (2018)
11. Greenbone: Openvas. Website, Greenbone Networks (2023). Available at https://openvas.org/
12. Ingols, K., Lippmann, R., Piwowarski, K.: Practical attack graph generation for network defense. In: 2006 22nd Annual Computer Security Applications Conference (ACSAC'06), pp. 121–130. IEEE (2006)

13. Ingols, K., Chu, M., Lippmann, R., Webster, S.E., Boyer, S.W.: Modeling modern network attacks and countermeasures using attack graphs. 2009 Annual Computer Security Applications Conferenc, pp. 117–126 (2009)
14. Insecure.Org: Nmap. Website, Insecure.Org (2023). Available at https://nmap.org/
15. Insights, T.: The evolving iot security threat landscape. Blog, Transforma Insights (2023). Available at https://transformainsights.com/blog/evolving-iot-security-threat-landscape#:~:text=Ten%20key%20aspects%20of%20the%20evolving%20IoT%20security,8%208.%20Diversity%20of%20devices%20...%20More%20items
16. Jha, S., Sheyner, O., Wing, J.M.: Two formal analyses of attack graphs. Proceedings 15th IEEE Computer Security Foundations Workshop. CSFW-1, pp. 49–63 (2002)
17. Kashman, S.: Google dorking or legal hacking: from the cia compromise to your cameras at home, we are not as safe as we think. Wash. JL Tech. Arts **18**, 1 (2023)
18. Kaynar, K., Sivrikaya, F.: Distributed attack graph generation. IEEE Trans. Dependable Secure Comput. **13**(5), 519–532 (2015)
19. Kolias, C., Kambourakis, G., Stavrou, A., Voas, J.: Ddos in the iot: Mirai and other botnets. Computer **50**(7), 80–84 (2017)
20. Konsta, A.M., Lafuente, A.L., Spiga, B., Dragoni, N.: Survey: automatic generation of attack trees and attack graphs. Comput. Secur. **137**, 103602 (2024)
21. Koo, K., Moon, D., Huh, J.H., Jung, S.H., Lee, H.: Attack graph generation with machine learning for network security. Electronics **11**(9), 1332 (2022)
22. Kordy, B., Mauw, S., Radomirović, S., Schweitzer, P.: Attack–defense trees. J. Logic Comput. **24**(1), 55–87 (2014)
23. Li, J., Zhao, B., Zhang, C.: Fuzzing: a survey. Cybersecurity **1**(1), 1–13 (2018)
24. Mahmoud, R., Yousuf, T., Aloul, F., Zualkernan, I.: Internet of things (iot) security: current status, challenges and prospective measures. In: 2015 10th international conference for internet technology and secured transactions (ICITST), pp. 336–341. IEEE (2015)
25. Matrosov, A., Rodionov, E., Harley, D., Malcho, J.: Stuxnet under the microscope. ESET LLC (September 2010) **6** (2010)
26. Mell, P., Scarfone, K., Romanosky, S.: Common vulnerability scoring system. IEEE Secur. Privacy **4**(6), 85–89 (2006)
27. Nadeem, A., Verwer, S., Moskal, S., Yang, S.J.: Alert-driven attack graph generation using s-pdfa. IEEE Trans. Dependable Secure Comput. **19**(2), 731–746 (2021)
28. NIST: Nvd. Website, National Institute of Standards and Technology (NIST) (2023). Available at https://nvd.nist.gov/
29. Ou, X., Govindavajhala, S., Appel, A.W.: Mulval: A logic-based network security analyzer. In: USENIX Security Symposium (2005)
30. Ou, X., Boyer, W., McQueen, M.: A scalable approach to attack graph generation. Proceedings of the 13th ACM Conference On Computer and Communications Security (ACM CCS'06) (2006)
31. Payne, J., Budhraja, K., Kundu, A.: How secure is your iot network? In: 2019 IEEE International Congress on Internet of Things (ICIOT), pp. 181–188. IEEE (2019)
32. Poolsappasit, N., Dewri, R., Ray, I.: Dynamic security risk management using bayesian attack graphs. IEEE Trans. Dependable Secure Comput. **9**(1), 61–74 (2011)
33. Presekal, A., Ştefanov, A., Rajkumar, V.S., Palensky, P.: Attack graph model for cyber-physical power systems using hybrid deep learning. IEEE Trans. Smart Grid **14**(5), 4007–4020 (2023)
34. Rapid7: Metasploit. Website, Rapid7 LLC (2023). Available at https://www.metasploit.com/
35. Research, C.: Iotroop botnet: the full investigation. Website, Checkpoint (2017). Available at https://research.checkpoint.com/2017/iotroop-botnet-full-investigation/
36. Ring, T.: Connected cars–the next targe tfor hackers. Netw. Secur. **2015**(11), 11–16 (2015)
37. Samtani, S., Yu, S., Zhu, H., Patton, M., Chen, H.: Identifying scada vulnerabilities using passive and active vulnerability assessment techniques. In: 2016 IEEE Conference on Intelligence and Security Informatics (ISI), pp. 25–30. IEEE (2016)
38. Schneier, B.: Attack trees. Article, Schneier on Security (1999). Available at https://www.schneier.com/academic/archives/1999/12/attack_trees.html

39. Sheyner, O.M.: Scenario graphs and attack graphs. Carnegie Mellon University (2004)
40. Sheyner, O., Haines, J., Jha, S., Lippmann, R., Wing, J.M.: Automated generation and analysis of attack graphs. In: Proceedings 2002 IEEE Symposium on Security and Privacy, pp. 273–284. IEEE (2002)
41. Shu, X., Tian, K., Ciambrone, A., Yao, D.: Breaking the target: an analysis of target data breach and lessons learned. Preprint (2017). arXiv:1701.04940
42. Tenable: Nessus. Website, Tenable Inc. (2023). Available at https://www.tenable.com/products/nessus
43. The MITRE Corporation: Cpe. Website, MITRE (2024). Available at https://cpe.mitre.org/about/
44. The MITRE Corporation: Cve. Website, MITRE (2024). Available at https://cve.mitre.org/
45. The MITRE Corporation: Cwe. Website, MITRE (2024). Available at https://cwe.mitre.org/
46. The MITRE Corporation: Cwss. Website, MITRE (2024). Available at https://cwe.mitre.org/cwss/cwss_v1.0.1.html
47. Tundis, A., Mazurczyk, W., Mühlhäuser, M.: A review of network vulnerabilities scanning tools: types, capabilities and functioning. In: Proceedings of the 13th International Conference on Availability, Reliability and Security, pp. 1–10 (2018)
48. Tunggal, A.T.: What is a vulnerability assessment? and how to conduct one. Website, UpGuard (2023). Available at https://www.upguard.com/blog/vulnerability-assessment#:~:text=Vulnerability%20analysis%3A%20Decide%20whether%20the%20identified%20vulnerability%20could,first%20based%20on%20their%20wormability%20and%20other%20risks/
49. Wan, Y., Lin, X., Sabur, A., Chang, A., Xu, K., Xue, G.: Iot system vulnerability analysis and network hardening with shortest attack trace in a weighted attack graph. In: Proceedings of the 8th ACM/IEEE Conference on Internet of Things Design and Implementation, pp. 315–326 (2023)
50. Waraga, O.A., Bettayeb, M., Nasir, Q., Talib, M.A.: Design and implementation of automated iot security testbed. Comput. Secur. **88**, 101648 (2020)
51. Wen, Q., Dong, X., Zhang, R.: Application of dynamic variable cipher security certificate in internet of things. In: 2012 IEEE 2nd International Conference on Cloud Computing and Intelligence Systems, vol. 3, pp, 1062–1066. IEEE (2012)
52. Wireshark: Wireshark. Website, Wireshark Foundation (2023). Available at https://www.wireshark.org/
53. Wu, R., Gong, J., Tong, W., Fan, B.: Network attack path selection and evaluation based on q-learning. Appl. Sci. **11**(1) (2021). https://doi.org/10.3390/app11010285. https://www.mdpi.com/2076-3417/11/1/285
54. Xie, W., Jiang, Y., Tang, Y., Ding, N., Gao, Y.: Vulnerability detection in iot firmware: a survey. In: 2017 IEEE 23rd International Conference on Parallel and Distributed Systems (ICPADS), pp. 769–772. IEEE (2017)
55. Yi, S., Peng, Y., Xiong, Q., Wang, T., Dai, Z., Gao, H., Xu, J., Wang, J., Xu, L.: Overview on attack graph generation and visualization technology. In: 2013 International Conference on Anti-Counterfeiting, Security and Identification (ASID), pp. 1–6. IEEE (2013)
56. Yu, M., Zhuge, J., Cao, M., Shi, Z., Jiang, L.: A survey of security vulnerability analysis, discovery, detection, and mitigation on iot devices. Future Internet **12**(2), 27 (2020)
57. Zenitani, K.: From attack graph analysis to attack function analysis. Inf. Sci. **650**, 119703 (2023)
58. Zolanvari, M., Teixeira, M.A., Gupta, L., Khan, K.M., Jain, R.: Machine learning-based network vulnerability analysis of industrial internet of things. IEEE Internet Things J. **6**(4), 6822–6834 (2019)

29. Sheyner, O.M.: Scenario graphs and attack graphs. Carnegie Mellon University (2004)
30. Sheyner, O., Haines, J., Jha, S., Lippmann, R., Wing, J.M.: Automated generation and analysis of attack graphs. In: Proceedings 2002 IEEE Symposium on Security and Privacy, pp. 273–284 (2002)
[illegible]

Advanced Intrusion Detection Techniques and Trends in IoT Networks

Aswin Payyampally, Sabu M. Thampi, and Preetam Mukherjee

1 Introduction to Intrusion Detection System in IoT Network

IoT networks employ intrusion detection systems (I.D.S.) to identify and prevent possible cyberattacks using various data types. These data types comprise system data, which records information on device settings, operating systems, and applications, as well as network traffic data, which offers details on interactions between IoT devices and their servers. I.D.S. also uses behavioral data to analyze patterns of typical and unusual IoT device behavior to identify suspicious activity. Additionally, I.D.S. can improve its detection capacities by using external threat intelligence data, such as well-known malware signatures or dangerous I.P. addresses. Ultimately, the fusion of different data kinds enables I.D.S. to identify and address security issues in IoT networks quickly. An intrusion detection system monitors incoming and outgoing network traffic. It continuously scans network traffic for departures from typical patterns and alerts an administrator whether they find any as shown in Fig. 1. After evaluating these signals, the administrator implements the necessary defenses to mitigate the risk.

IoT networks need intrusion detection systems (I.D.S.) to identify and prevent harmful activity. These systems function by continuously observing network traffic and analyzing it for indications of intrusion or unusual behavior. Data collection, analysis, detection, and response comprise the information flow in an I.D.S. for IoT networks. Figure 2 shows the information flow in an I.D.S.

A. Payyampally (✉) · S. M. Thampi · P. Mukherjee
Connected Systems and Intelligence Lab, School of Computer Science & Engineering, Digital University Kerala, Trivandrum, India
e-mail: aswin.res21@duk.ac.in; sabu.thampi@duk.ac.in; preetam.mukherjee@duk.ac.in; https://duk.ac.in/

S. M. Thampi et al. (eds.), *Securing the Connected World*,
https://doi.org/10.1007/978-3-031-82826-3_3

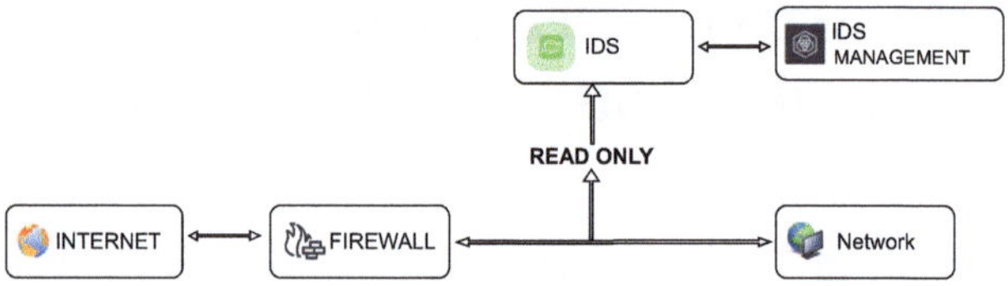

Fig. 1 Intrusion detection system overview

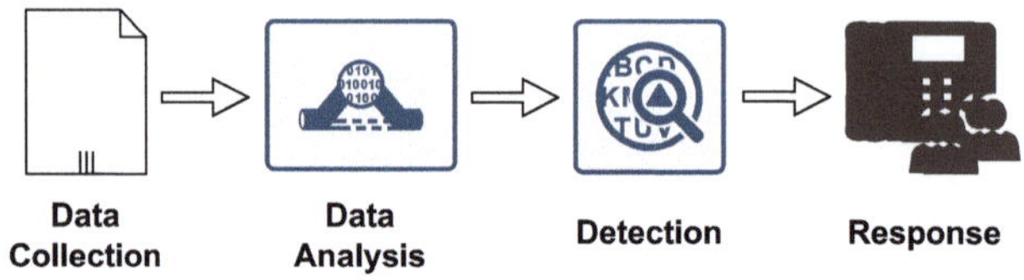

Fig. 2 Information flow of intrusion detection system in IoT network

Data collection is the initial step in the information flow of an I.D.S. Data is gathered from various sources, including network devices, IoT devices, and other pertinent sources. After filtering out noise and unimportant information, only the crucial information is left for analysis.

Once the data is collected, the next stage is data analysis. This stage involves using various techniques such as statistical analysis, machine learning, and rule-based algorithms to analyze the data for signs of intrusion or abnormal behavior. The analysis process may involve comparing the collected data with known attack patterns or identifying deviations from normal network behavior.

In an I.D.S. in IoT networks, detection is the third step in the information flow. In order to assess if an intrusion has occurred or not, the system now employs the data analysis findings. In the case of an intrusion, the I.D.S. will sound alert or take other necessary steps to stop additional harm.

The response is the last phase of the information flow. The I.D.S. responds to the detected intrusion at this point by taking the proper action. If malicious traffic is detected, it may be blocked, the problematic device is isolated, or network administrators are notified.

Data gathering, analysis, detection, and response are all ongoing processes in an I.D.S. for IoT networks. By identifying and stopping harmful activity, this method contributes to the security of IoT networks.

The Fig. 3 depicts a taxonomy of features and terms in Intrusion Detection Systems (I.D.S.), which includes I.D.S. types, I.D.S. analysis strategies, types of intrusions, I.D.S. placement strategies, and several datasets. Overall, this taxonomy provides a comprehensive understanding of the key features and terms in I.D.S., which can aid in selecting the right I.D.S. type, placement, and analysis strategies to secure a network or system. The following sections will discuss about the each in detail.

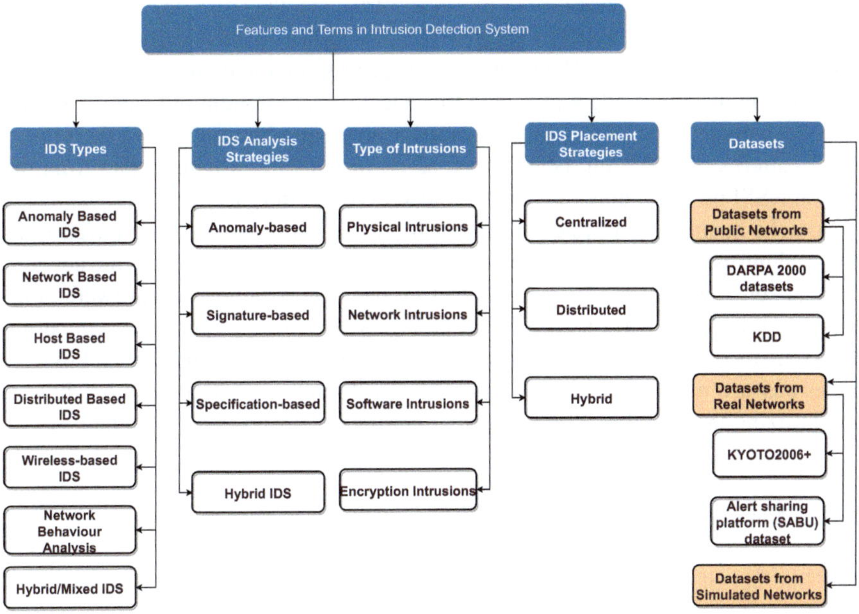

Fig. 3 Taxonomy of some features and terms in intrusion detection system

1.1 Types of Intrusions

Unauthorized access to a computer network, system, or data is called intrusion into a network. Several kinds of network intrusions, such as physical intrusions, occur when an unauthorized individual enters a physical area, such as a server room. On the other side, network intrusions occur when an attacker uses social engineering or vulnerability-based exploits to obtain unauthorized access to a network. Software intrusions happen when an attacker utilizes software flaws, such as viruses or malware, to enter a system. Attackers that want to access sensitive data without authorization try to defeat or go around encryption methods. These network intrusions can be wrong for a company since they can result in data breaches, financial losses, and reputational harm. The different intrusions are discussed in detail in the following sub-sections

1.1.1 Physical Intrusions

In recent years, as more gadgets have been connected to the Internet and can communicate with one another, the Internet of Things (IoT) has grown in popularity. IoT networks comprise several hardware elements that gather, process, and transfer data, including sensors, actuators, and gateways. IoT networks' foundation is built on these hardware elements, which are essential to ensure that they operate correctly.

As a result of their vulnerability to physical intrusions, they also provide a security concern. The authors in [83] explored the possibility of physically breaching a Bluetooth-connected area. The security strategy proposed in their research suggests that one can detect intruders using the Received Signal Strength Indicators (RSSIs) of beacon-based tags. The strategy involves observing and analyzing the typical RSSI patterns of migrating newcomers. Abnormal RSSIs, which deviate from the typical RSSI patterns, may indicate the presence of an intruder.

Attacks against the physical components of an IoT network are referred to as physical intrusions. Attackers could try to obtain unauthorized access to the network or steal sensitive data by gaining control of and manipulating the hardware components. Physical intrusions can entail taking or destroying equipment, tampering with sensors or other hardware, or intercepting data sent between devices. Physical intrusions are more likely as IoT networks proliferate and become more linked, emphasizing the need for robust security measures to thwart these attempts.

1.1.2 Network Intrusions

The Internet of Things (IoT) has increased the number of linked devices, making networks increasingly susceptible to cyberattacks. Network intrusion, which includes unauthorized access to network resources by an external entity, is one of the most frequent assaults against IoT networks. Network intrusions try to interrupt the IoT network's regular operations by interfering with network activity or stealing essential data. The network may suffer serious harm; as a result, leading to downtime, data loss, and financial losses. Access to sensitive data and resources, such as private information, financial data, and intellectual property, can also be gained through network intrusions. Because of this, IoT network administrators need to implement robust security measures, such as firewalls, intrusion detection systems, and encryption, to stop network invasions and safeguard the IoT network and its assets.

Moustafa et al. [62] presented a collaborative network intrusion detection technique to stop destructive behaviors like botnet attacks, particularly against the DNS, HTTP, and MQTT protocols frequently used in Internet of Things networks. The responses consist of many parts.

1. The authors thoroughly examine the TCP/IP model to extract several properties from the MQTT, HTTP, and DNS network traffic protocols. In addition to developing a new extractor module that can provide additional statistical aspects of transactional flows, they employ the BroIDS tool for the fundamental features. Together with Bro-IDS, this module functions.
2. Selecting the essential characteristics using correlation coefficient analysis is crucial in reducing the computing cost of Network Intrusion Detection Systems (NIDS). This feature selection approach aids in removing just the essential characteristics needed for NIDS functioning.

3. In the suggested method [62], network data is distributed using AdaBoost, and decision trees, naive Bayes, and artificial neural networks are used to identify attacks. Computations of the correntropy measure support the employment of these approaches. AdaBoost enhances detection performance using an error function to consider minor feature vector variations. Which learners can correctly classify each occurrence is determined by the function.

1.1.3 Software Intrusions

Software intrusions are unauthorized access to computer networks and systems to compromise confidentiality, integrity, and availability. Most of the time, these intrusions make use of malicious software, such as Trojan horses, viruses, worms, malware, or other types of malware that can change the data stored in system resources and impact the way the system functions. The attacker uses social engineering tactics to acquire unauthorized access to a system and secretly install harmful software. To provide its customers with personalized experiences, IoT devices–especially wearables–collect enormous quantities of personally identifiable information (PII) [44]. Additionally, many IoT gadgets use PII to deliver user-friendly services like voice-activated online purchasing. Cybercriminals, however, may utilize PII to launch attacks and steal sensitive data, including purchase history, user passwords, and personal information.

Viruses are self-replicating programs that connect to and propagate across the system on top of genuine software. Worms, on the other hand, may move quickly over networks and multiply without a host, severely harming system resources. Software applications to carry out evil deeds like stealing confidential data or interfering with a system's regular operation are called malware. Trojan horses are software applications that appear to be trustworthy programs when installed on a system while actually being programmed to carry out harmful operations. If any of these dangerous software programs are not identified or dealt with, they might threaten the security of a system and cause severe damage.

1.1.4 Encryption Intrusions

Sensitive data can be secured using encryption to prevent unauthorized access. Public and private keys are used in the encryption process to encrypt and decode data. Data is encrypted using public keys and decrypted using private keys. Attempts to obstruct this procedure by tampering with the encryption keys are known as encryption intrusions. The security of the data may be threatened by attempts to modify or steal the keys.

Getting unauthorized access to sensitive data is one of the main reasons people attempt encryption attacks. To decode and access sensitive data, attackers may utilize stolen encryption keys. Governments, businesses, and people might all suffer serious harm due to this. Additionally, encryption incursions may be used to alter encrypted data, threatening its integrity. This issue might be hazardous in financial transactions when seemingly insignificant changes could have significant repercussions. Utilizing robust encryption algorithms, secure essential management procedures, and routine audits of encryption processes are some proactive actions that must be taken; as a result to avoid encryption intrusions.

A revolutionary technology called BlindIDS [17] analyses encrypted communication using Deep Packet Inspection (DPI) to look for possible breaches. The optimal intrusion detection mechanism for encrypted traffic is the security architecture underpinning the system. Proper security proofs have validated the key features of the system. Creating a secure market environment depends on systems like BlindIDS, which are the first to achieve a balance between network security and privacy. It enables safe communication between security editors and service providers, delivering value-added security services while preserving the privacy of end-user data.

1.2 I.D.S. and Its Types

The security policy of every organization should include intrusion detection systems (I.D.S.). There are numerous I.D.S. types available, each with particular characteristics and abilities. Anomaly-based I.D.S. uses machine learning techniques to find anomalous behavior patterns that could point to an intrusion. Network-based I.D.S., or NIDS, analyses network traffic for known attack patterns and notifies managers in real time. Host-based I.D.S., or H.I.D.S., can identify unauthorized access or suspicious activities. In order to analyze traffic across many networks, distributed-based I.D.S., or DIDS, uses numerous sensors. Network behavior analysis (N.B.A.) I.D.S. analyses traffic patterns over time and can spot sluggish, continuing assaults that other I.D.S. kinds might miss. Hybrid/mixed I.D.S. combines several I.D.S. types to offer complete security coverage. The organization's infrastructure and unique security requirements will determine which I.D.S. type is best. It is essential to pick an I.D.S. that offers sufficient security, is affordable, and keeps the system up. The Different intrusion detection systems are discussed in detail below.

1.2.1 Anomaly Based I.D.S.

An intrusion detection system (I.D.S.) using an anomaly-based approach is created to spot network and computer misuse by tracking system activity and classifying it as standard or odd. This method establishes a baseline of typical system activity using statistical models and machine learning techniques, then identifies any suspicious behavior that deviates from that baseline.

The I.D.S. goes through a training period when it is first put into use, during which it monitors and records typical system behavior to create a baseline. The I.D.S. will continually monitor system activity after establishing a baseline, comparing it to the baseline to determine if the behavior is typical or atypical. Any action that deviates from the accepted standard is marked as possibly malicious and looked at further. Since anomaly-based I.D.S. does not rely on pre-existing signatures or patterns of known attacks, it can identify previously unknown or unnoticed attacks. This tactic makes it a potent tool for spotting zero-day attacks using a system's previously undiscovered weaknesses. However, anomaly-based I.D.S. can produce many false positives by detecting user behavior that deviates from the predetermined baseline. The I.D.S. must consequently be adjusted to reduce the number of false positives while still providing adequate protection. An effective tool for identifying network and computer breaches and misuse is an intrusion detection system using an anomaly-based methodology. It can spot possible threats that other forms of I.D.S. might overlook by keeping track of system activity and classifying it as typical or atypical. However, careful tuning and maintenance of the I.D.S. are required to reduce false positives and ensure that genuine user behavior is not unduly marked as suspicious.

This study by Maniriho et al. [57] proposes a novel anomaly-based technique for Internet of Things networks that combines the Random Forest algorithm with a hybrid feature selection engine to categorize each communication stream as normal or abnormal. The researchers tested the suggested method using the IoTID20 dataset [90], and it accurately identified attacks, including DoS, MITM, and scanning. The researchers trained and evaluated the Random Forest classifier using a subset of the dataset taken from IoTID20, which produced excellent results regarding TPR, FPR, Precision, Recall, high accuracy, and low error rate.

1.2.2 Network Based I.D.S.

Network-based intrusion detection systems (NIDS) are strategically positioned gadgets that watch network traffic going through the gadgets installed passively. They are made to identify unauthorized access to a computer system or network without actively obstructing network traffic flow. In order to analyze network data and notify users of any malicious activity or potential security breaches, NIDS devices employ a variety of approaches, including signature-based detection, anomaly detection, and behavioral analysis.

NIDS devices are frequently positioned at a network's entrance and departure points and important internal hubs for network traffic. They may detect fraudulent traffic patterns thanks to their passive monitoring capabilities without altering the operation or performance of their installed devices. Identifying security breaches and unauthorized access attempts by analyzing network traffic makes NIDS devices crucial to network security.

The researchers developed a novel Network Intrusion Detection System (NIDS) using Graph Neural Networks (GNNs)[55]. GNNs are a kind of deep neural network that uses structured graph data. The researchers proposed E-GraphSAGE, a GNN method that expresses training and assessment data using flow records in a graph structure, a standard NIDS format. This GNN method captures topological information and graph edge attributes for Internet of Things network intrusion detection. To their knowledge, this is the first verified and practical technique of using GNNs to tackle the flow-based data problem of network intrusion detection for the Internet of Things. Their deep experimental investigation of four NIDS benchmark datasets demonstrated that their technique beat the state-of-the-art in key classification criteria. These findings inspire further investigation and show GNNs' network intrusion detection.

1.2.3 Host Based I.D.S.

Security tools called host intrusion detection systems (H.I.D.S.) are used to identify and stop malicious activity or unauthorized access to a computer or network device. The purpose of H.I.D.S. is to monitor a device's incoming and outgoing packets. They can work as standalone hosts or as linked devices. H.I.D.S. operate by taking a picture of the system files as they are and comparing them to an earlier image, which is a reliable technique to find any unauthorized system changes or alterations.

After being notified by the H.I.D.S. of any fraudulent or malicious behavior, the system administrator may then take the required steps to stop any possible security breaches. The administrator will be notified immediately by the H.I.D.S., for instance, if a file has been deleted or changed without permission. The administrator may then look into the situation and, if required, take remedial action. H.I.D.S.'s ability to identify anomalous network traffic patterns or login behavior may indicate a possible security breach.

H.I.D.S. utilization can be seen in mission-critical computers whose layout is not expected to alter. It is crucial to keep it updated to guarantee that the H.I.D.S. is already identifying novel threats and weaknesses. The organization may ensure that any possible security risks are found and handled promptly and effectively, reducing the impact of any security breaches by implementing H.I.D.S. on mission-critical devices, such as servers or financial systems. H.I.D.S. is a crucial security tool that observes a device's activity, files, and network traffic. It may provide real-time notifications to the administrator, allowing them to take fast action to stop any security breaches.

The usage of smart home products is expanding, and so are the security concerns that follow. The author advises [71] using IoT-IDM, an intrusion detection and mitigation framework, to monitor the network activity of intended smart devices in household contexts and investigate any suspicious or malicious activities. The framework's modular design enables users to modify machine learning techniques for detection depending on known attack patterns. The author uses software-defined networking technology and the enabling communication protocol OpenFlow to realize this framework. A prototype of IoT-IDM is developed and tested on a real IoT device, a smart light bulb, to show the framework's efficiency in providing computer security services for risks associated with smart IoT devices in the home.

1.2.4 Distributed Based I.D.S.

A distributed intrusion detection system (DIDS) is a network security strategy that uses several intrusion detection systems (I.D.S.) dispersed over an extensive network. Connecting all I.D.S. to a single server makes advanced network monitoring possible. In a DIDS, cooperative intelligent agents are placed throughout the network to construct the intrusion detection system in a distributed setting. These agents monitor network traffic and look for suspicious or unusual activities. A DIDS can offer a more thorough and robust defense against network assaults by utilizing numerous I.D.S. working together.

Over a centralized I.D.S., a DIDS's distributed architecture has several benefits. A DIDS, for instance, can employ multiple I.D.S. to offer redundancy, fault tolerance, and easier scaling to handle extensive networks. Furthermore, combining warnings from many I.D.S., a DIDS can lower the possibility of false positives and increase the precision of intrusion detection. A DIDS does, however, also have certain drawbacks, including the requirement for coordination across I.D.S. and the possibility for additional complexity and administration burden.

Recently, researchers have implemented several strategies to enhance IoT security, including utilizing distributed I.D.S.and attack detection techniques. In [88] and [18], the authors proposed two strategies for detecting anomalies, where each node monitors its neighbors and cuts the data link if it detects any anomalous behavior. Butun et al. [16] highlighted the difficulties associated with cloud-centric IoT devices and distributed private datasets. Moreover, to detect cyberattacks in cloud-centric IoT systems works in [3] and [24] developed distributed deep learning algorithms. Rajasegarar et al. [75] presented a clustering algorithm that integrates IoTD measurements before delivering a condensed description of their data to other nodes to reduce communication overhead. In [42], the authors presented an on-chip machine learning method to identify side-channel attacks in IoTD chips, while [41] presented a similar approach.

1.2.5 Wireless-based I.D.S.

A security solution made particularly for wireless networks is the wireless intrusion detection system (W.I.D.S.). It is up to W.I.D.S. to monitor wireless traffic and spot any potential dangers or shady behavior inside the network. They can identify numerous dangers, such as malicious attacks, rogue access points, and unapproved devices.

According to the authors [52], an Intrusion Detection System (IDS) is a system that automatically monitors computer systems or networks and spots possible signs of interference. An IPS not only detects prospective intrusions but also takes steps to lessen the effect of recent and upcoming events[100].

W.I.D.S. functions by recording wireless information and examining it for patterns that could point to a security problem. To find possible threats, they can also use a variety of approaches, including anomaly detection, behavior analysis, and signature-based detection. The W.I.D.S. will record the occurrence and notify security staff to take proper action when a threat is identified. Organizations may defend their wireless networks from security breaches by utilizing a W.I.D.S. to ensure they are safe and secure.

1.2.6 Network Behaviour Analysis

Network behavior analysis (N.B.A.) is a security technique that helps organizations track and assess security issues. N.B.A. systems employ machine learning methods to create a baseline of typical network behavior, which may be used to spot trends and abnormalities in network traffic. N.B.A. can identify any unexpected behavior that can signify a security problem by continuously monitoring network activity and comparing it to the pre-defined baseline.

N.B.A. is an additional security threat detection method for those that employ packet signatures. In order to identify possible risks, packet signature-based techniques use pre-defined patterns or signatures of recognized security concerns. They are unable to recognize recent or zero-day assaults in any case. While signature-based techniques cannot detect previously undiscovered or zero-day threats, N.B.A. is built to spot anomalies from typical network behavior.

The behavior-based detection system employs a technique that analyzes attack patterns and activities in the system's processes, registry, and network to detect intrusions. This technique overcomes the limitations of signature-based analysis. The behavior-based detection method divides into two categories: system-based detection, which analyzes activities within the computer system, and network detection, which analyzes activities within the entire network [60, 61, 68].

Advanced persistent threats (A.P.T.), malware, phishing, and other forms of cyberattacks are just a few of the many cyber threats that the N.B.A. can effectively identify and stop. N.B.A. can assist organizations in enhancing their entire security posture and reducing the risk of cyberattacks by recognizing risks in real-time and notifying security staff to take relevant action.

1.2.7 Hybrid/Mixed I.D.S.

Through the integration of many I.D.S. approaches, intrusion detection system (I.D.S.) technologies can improve network security. A hybrid I.D.S. is produced by combining two or more I.D.S. methodologies, such as behavior analysis, anomaly detection, and signature-based detection. Due to this, the hybrid I.D.S. can detect more security risks than any other I.D.S. technology and give a more complete and accurate view of network activities. The hybrid I.D.S. may provide a full image of the network system by fusing host agent or system data with network information.

In recent wireless networks, intrusion detection systems have become a fundamental processing unit due to increased intruders and lack of security. Similarly, As a heterogeneous network, IoT faces security threats comparable to those of wireless networks. Thus, developing an intrusion detection system is necessary to prevent performance degradation in IoT networks. The proposed research by Smys et al. [81] analyzes various types of attacks in IoT and suggests a hybrid convolutional neural network module incorporating a long short-term memory process.

The hybrid I.D.S. is more successful than other intrusion detection systems since it can use various detection techniques. For instance, another I.D.S. technique may be able to identify a specific threat if one approach cannot do so. By cross-referencing warnings from several detection techniques, the hybrid I.D.S. can also lower the number of false positives and false negatives. Prelude is a hybrid intrusion detection system integrating several detection methods to offer a more complete and potent intrusion detection solution.

1.3 Notable Intrusion Detection Systems in IoT

- **Snort:** An adaptable network intrusion detection system called Snort scans packets and traffic for suspicious behavior. This versatile and strong architecture is helpful for intrusion detection systems, especially those for Internet of Things networks. It can identify many types of attacks by using packet capture and real-time traffic analysis. Raspberry Pi's defense against hypothetical network attacks was evaluated in a recent Snort study[79]. Attacks that cause a denial of service and unwanted access are stopped by Snort. By adopting particular environments for the Raspberry Pi's low-power CPU, Snort showed off its hardware adaptability. IoT gateways were safely and effectively monitored by Snort on Raspberry Pi. Snort's speed and accuracy were improved after a number of network attack scenarios were assessed. Without sacrificing efficiency, this improved gateway security. The IoT security advantages of Snort are emphasized in[79]. Snort defends IoT networks from growing internet threats with its flexibility and detection range.
- **Bro I.D.S.:** Real-time analysis and deep packet inspection make Zeek, formerly Bro IDS, a powerful open-source network monitoring tool. Vern Paxson created Bro IDS, an event-based network management system, for high-bandwidth and high-throughput networks. This is very useful for identifying suspicious behavior fast and doing in-depth traffic analysis. Health monitoring applications like Wireless Body Area Networks need Bro IDS for IoT architecture security. Bro IDS identifies threats early via network data. Monitor and analyze encrypted traffic with Bro IDS to prevent healthcare IoT data breaches and protect patient data. These systems convey crucial health data. A University of Abdelmalek Essaadi research incorporated Bro IDS into an Internet of Things architecture to monitor human health via WBANs [79]. Numerous network-based attacks threatened data confidentiality and integrity. Integration allowed Bro IDS to evaluate every network layer, from the perception layer (direct sensor input) to the network and application layers (data aggregation and user interface).IoT devices are low-

power and computationally restricted, therefore installation required Bro IDS configuration changes. IoT-specific scripts and signatures targeted anomalies such unusual outbound traffic patterns and unwanted access attempts.Bro IDS improved IoT security by detecting threats in real time and giving detailed logs for forensic analysis. Proactive monitoring maintained system integrity and boosted user tech trust. Case studies illustrate how Bro IDS improves network security and protects private data in healthcare IoT architectures. Companies may customize Bro IDS to meet IoT needs to mitigate the risks of growing connected device ecosystems. This solution ensures data integrity and compliance with demanding healthcare and other essential industry data protection regulations.

- **Suricata:**Suricata is a community-driven, open-source, high-performance network IDS and security monitoring engine. It is notable for its scalability, ability to handle millions of packets, and widespread usage. The Open Information Security Foundation (OISF) developed Suricata, a real-time threat detection engine. Suricata's multi-threading and quick data stream processing make it ideal for IoT applications like health monitoring Wireless Body Area Networks. This makes it ideal for high-volume data sets where traditional IDS systems struggle to analyze and execute in real time. The report shows Suricata's IoT healthcare monitoring potential. Through packet inspection and real-time threat analysis, Suricata found health data security issues. In network simulations, Suricata repelled malware, phishing, and DDoS attacks for the company. Suricata protects IoT data circulation. WBAN proves their Internet of Things architecture protects health monitoring data[79]. It shows Suricata's adaptability and IoT complex threat avoidance expertise.
- **OpenWIPS-ng:** The open-source, modular WiFi 802.11 Intrusion Prevention System (IPS) OpenWIPS-ng. It enhances the Intrusion Detection System (IDS) to monitor and protect wireless networks from unwanted access and malicious attacks. OpenWIPS-ng is crucial to wireless security, especially in corporate, hospital, and public WiFi situations[32]. Wireless networks face Evil Twin attacks, rogue access points, and WiFi deauthentication attacks. OpenWIPS-ng addresses these concerns with real-time monitoring and active attack response. In a conventional setup, OpenWIPS-ng requires sensors, a server, and an interface to work. The sensors monitor traffic throughout the network and provide data to a central server for analysis. After detecting a threat, OpenWIPS-ng may warn administrators or neutralize a malicious source. The deployment of OpenWIPS-ng in a wireless network protects wireless data transmission. It protects wireless networks by monitoring, identifying, and addressing threats in real time. A multi-layered security strategy must incorporate physical security, strong encryption, and regular security audits, like any IDS/IPS system. In operationally critical wireless communication environments, OpenWIPS-ng is fundamental to the security architecture.
- **Cisco IoT Threat Defense:** Cisco's IoT Threat Defense provides complete security for IoT setups. Cisco's complete IoT security architecture protects network connections, data integrity, and device authenticity. Due to the variety of IoT deployments, Cisco IoT Threat Defense is essential for security. IoT

devices entering critical industrial and consumer sectors need strong security requirements to avoid unwanted access, data breaches, and sabotage. Cisco IoT Threat Defense combines threat prevention, secure connection, and segmentation to reduce risks and improve reliability. Cisco IoT Threat Defense in a manufacturing facility may combine secure networking hardware with real-time threat assessment software. Improvements in security operations include fewer security breaches and the ability to monitor and update vulnerabilities. This technology protects key industrial activities and follows strict data security and privacy regulations [11]. Compliance and security sustain IoT ecosystem trust.

- **Kismet:** The open-source wireless network detector, sniffer, and intrusion detection system Kismet can accommodate several wireless interfaces. Kismet supports various wireless protocols than 802.11. It can detect network intrusions, wireless traffic, and security threats. In wireless networks with high radio frequency (RF) activity or dense IoT device deployments, Kismet is critical. This program secretly collects wireless network data to find hidden networks and risky gadgets. Kismet identifies dangerous conduct using data and real-time analysis[67]. Kismet secures corporate and airport WiFi networks. These systems benefit from Kismet's security breach detection. Kismet detected a malicious device utilizing anomaly-based detection in an unauthorized corporate network access event. It was necessary to prevent data leaks. So, network administrators and security professionals should constantly carry Kismet. For those accustomed to modern wifi settings. Wireless network security depends on its precise wireless spectrum awareness.

1.4 I.D.S. Analysis Strategies

In order to identify and eliminate security threats, intrusion detection systems (I.D.S.) are a crucial part of the infrastructure for network security. I.D.S. offer real-time monitoring and analysis of network traffic. I.D.S. uses various analytic techniques to identify security risks, such as hybrid detection, anomaly detection, behavior analysis, and signature-based detection. A reliable method for identifying known malware and assaults, signature-based detection depends on pre-defined patterns or signatures of security risks. Contrarily, anomaly detection entails creating a baseline of typical network behavior and keeping an eye out for departures from this baseline in network data. The more sophisticated I.D.S. analysis method, behavior analysis, uses machine learning techniques to find patterns and abnormalities in network data. To give a more thorough picture of network activities and detect a larger spectrum of security risks, hybrid I.D.S. integrates different detection algorithms. Organizations must carefully assess their I.D.S. needs and capabilities to choose the best analysis strategy for their environment, even though hybrid I.D.S. can be more successful than single-method I.D.S.

1.4.1 Anomaly-based

In order to identify network intrusions, anomaly-based intrusion detection systems (I.D.S.), compare the abnormalities to attack patterns. Any deviations or anomalies from a network's normal behavior should be detected. The system examines the behavior of the network as a whole. These abnormalities are compared to well-known attack patterns to assess if there has been a security breach. The main objective of anomaly-based intrusion detection systems is to identify any deviation by understanding the normal behavior [7, 52].

The I.D.S. builds user profiles based on system operations analysis after an abnormality has been found. User profiles are generated to track down the network's various users' and devices' unique behavioral patterns. The system may create a baseline of typical behavior by examining the actions of each person or device. This baseline can then be used as a benchmark to identify future abnormalities.

Any deviation from the user profile while using an anomaly-based I.D.S. is considered an incursion. As a result, the network and the data it holds are protected since the system can recognize and react to any security breaches rapidly. Employing an anomaly-based I.D.S. enables organizations to proactively defend their networks against fresh attacks, enhancing their systems' security and reliability.

1.4.2 Signature-based

Known assaults can be found using signature-based intrusion detection systems (I.D.S.), a cybersecurity defense system. In order to find possible threats, these I.D.S. systems employ a database of attack signatures to compare with network traffic. The I.D.S. system searches for patterns and behaviors in network traffic that correspond to well-known attack signatures. If a match is made, the system will notify the security staff of the possible danger. The attack signature database is continuously updated when new assaults are found, enabling the I.D.S. system to remain abreast of the most recent dangers.The signature-based I.D.S.detects intrusions by comparing monitored behaviors with pre-defined intrusion patterns. This method identifies attacks by searching for specific patterns in the data that match known attack signatures [7, 52].

One advantage of signature-based I.D.S. is its ability to identify known threats accurately. However, they can only partially identify fresh or unidentified assaults that have not yet been submitted to the signature database. Attackers can also try to get around signature-based I.D.S. by employing polymorphic malware, which alters its signature each time it infects a new machine. Because of this, even while signature-based I.D.S. can be a valuable tool in a company's cybersecurity strategy, they should be used in concert with other security measures to offer a complete defense against cyber attacks.

1.4.3 Specification-based

Specifying-based intrusion detection systems (I.D.S.) depend on the ruleset specifying the behavior profile of network elements like nodes, routers, and servers. The routing table and protocol-related data are included in the behavior profile. The specification-based I.D.S. monitors network traffic and provides an alert when there is a departure from the established requirements. This tactic suggests that the functionality of the specification-based I.D.S. is comparable to that of the anomaly-based I.D.S. in that both systems provide warnings if there is any departure from the intended behavior.

The specification-based I.D.S.identifies when adverse nodes break protocol rules and detects topology attacks. Many environments have used this method, including securing sensors and ad hoc network protocols. However, despite attempts to profile the RPL protocol, none have successfully detected RPL topology attacks [49]. Existing RPL profiles either lack verification and implementation or are designed only for conformance testing. Attackers may compromise network performance by using crucial behaviors that these profiles do not reflect, such as not adhering to rank rules, not maintaining consistent ranks, and generating redundant control messages. Therefore, researchers must develop a more compelling profile considering these crucial behaviors.

The specification-based I.D.S. is a powerful security tool since it can immediately identify possible security breaches and notify network managers. As a result of the system's comparison of network activity with a set of predetermined criteria, it has a high degree of accuracy in recognizing known assaults. Furthermore, including specifications makes it possible to identify more subtle and complex assaults that an anomaly-based system could overlook. In order to safeguard network infrastructure from cyber attacks, the system may thus provide organizations with a complete security solution.

1.4.4 Hybrid I.D.S.

An intrusion detection system is a vital security tool for detecting and preventing unauthorized access or malicious activity on a network (I.D.S.). I.D.S. is often divided into three groups: signature-based, anomaly-based, and specification-based. By integrating the advantages of all three I.D.S. types, a hybrid I.D.S., on the other hand, delivers a more resilient and effective security solution. Signature-based I.D.S. compares incoming traffic to a database of known attack signatures, anomaly-based I.D.S. identifies suspicious activity by comparing network traffic to a reference set of acceptable behavior, and specification-based I.D.S. use formal rules and specifications to identify deviations from expected behavior. Compared to other I.D.S. types, a hybrid I.D.S. may identify various assaults and abnormal behaviors with greater classification accuracy and detection rates.

IoT links devices over the internet, offering various services and applications that impact people's lives as the number of gadgets increases every day with varying forms, sizes, and complexity. However, IoT has serious security flaws that open it to several threats. When network security is compromised, intrusion detection systems can spot such attacks. In this article, researchers propose a hybrid convolutional neural network model-based intrusion detection system for Internet of Things (IoT) networks that can identify various assault types. The results show that the proposed hybrid model [81] has superior sensitivity to assaults in the IoT network and is suited for various IoT applications when they validate and compared it with classic machine learning and deep learning models.

1.5 I.D.S. Placement Strategies

I.D.S. placement strategies are essential for network security, and they comprise placing I.D.S. sensors strategically to identify and prevent unauthorized access. The centralized strategy concentrates all I.D.S. sensors in one area, allowing for centralized visibility and administration, but it also introduces a single point of failure. The distributed strategy distributes I.D.S. sensors at numerous locations, resulting in redundancy and greater resilience, but it can be more challenging to manage. The hybrid strategy gives centralized visibility and local monitoring by fusing features of the two approaches. Considering network size, security needs, and financial limits can help choose the best I.D.S. placement approach. To choose the optimal approach for their organization, security experts must carefully weigh the benefits and drawbacks of each strategy.

1.5.1 Centralized

The I.D.S. agents are set up at a router or another central network component in a centralized intrusion detection system (I.D.S.) placement strategy. The primary goal of the I.D.S. is to monitor the network and look for any abnormal behavior or attempted intrusions. With a centralized I.D.S., the central node of the network keeps track of all requests made to other nodes. This strategy may be helpful for large organizations or intricate networks that need a thorough security architecture. Managing and monitoring the network from a single location is one of the benefits of a centralized I.D.S. Analyzing and monitoring network traffic is more straightforward when the I.D.S. agents are positioned at the heart of the network. This tactic makes it possible for security analysts to discover potential risks quickly. In addition, centralized I.D.S. systems can offer a more comprehensive picture of the network, making it simpler to detect and address security events. However, this strategy has certain drawbacks, including scalability and single points of failure, which may need further steps to solve these problems.

In their study, Wallgren et al. [99] propose a centralized strategy that entails installing the Intrusion Detection System (IDS) in the border router. Finding attacks in the physical domain is the aim of their suggested remedy. The authors suggested using a heartbeat protocol rather than watching the traffic that passes through the border router. According to this protocol, the border router must periodically send ICMPv6 echo queries to all LLN nodes and wait for answers to identify attacks or availability problems. The authors showed through experiments that the LLN nodes do not need to allocate more memory to perform the heartbeat algorithm and that the energy overhead is negligible, even though the suggested method increases network traffic.

1.5.2 Distributed

The IoT network is made up of several physical parts that are susceptible to hacker attacks. Intrusion Detection System (I.D.S.) agents are placed on each physical part of the network to guarantee network security. A distributed I.D.S. placement method is used to put these agents, ensuring the network is guarded against numerous threats. This approach guarantees that the network has many points of failure, that any intrusion attempt is rapidly discovered, and that the proper steps may be taken to limit additional harm. The I.D.S. agents must be optimized for very effective intrusion detection since they are deployed on each physical component of the IoT network. This optimization entails creating algorithms capable of spotting even the most complex assaults and categorizing them as either malicious or lawful. Real-time network traffic analysis is another essential skill for efficient I.D.S. agents since it allows them to spot suspicious behavior quickly. The optimization approach also compromises the detection and false-positive rates to prevent incorrectly identifying legal network activity as dangerous. The IoT network must be generally protected against cyberattacks thanks mainly to optimizing I.D.S.agents.

The distributed placement of nodes may include giving them the extra responsibility of keeping an eye on nearby nodes. Sometimes people refer to these nodes as watchdogs because they perform monitoring tasks. In order to identify and prevent possible attacks, Cervantes et al. [18] developed INTI (Intrusion detection of Sinkhole attacks on 6LoWPAN for the Internet of Things) as a solution in 2015.

1.5.3 Hybrid

The distributed and centralized I.D.S. placement techniques are combined to provide the hybrid I.D.S. placement strategy, which offers the advantages of both methods. According to this technique, each network cluster has a central I.D.S. node that controls and coordinates the operations of other cluster nodes. The central I.D.S. node serves as a centralized hub for the cluster and tracks and analyzes the data gathered by the dispersed sensors or nodes. The distributed sensors gather data from diverse sources inside the cluster, and the central I.D.S. node evaluates the data and offers insights into network behavior and potential security concerns. Companies can balance the advantages of distributed and centralized I.D.S. placement strategies by employing a hybrid I.D.S. placement strategy. The cluster is well-covered by distributed sensors, which can identify threats and security issues from various directions. On the other hand, the central I.D.S. node offers a centralized administration and monitoring strategy that enables more effective data processing, faster reaction times, and more significant insights into network behavior. The hybrid I.D.S. placement technique is an efficient method for boosting network security and reducing potential security threats.

Creating clusters inside the network and placing an instance of an Intrusion Detection System (IDS) within each cluster is one method for accomplishing hybrid placement. The other nodes in the cluster are then under the control of this I.D.S.node, even though this definition is in line with the work of Cervantes et al. [18].

1.6 IoT-Specific Intrusion Detection Challenges

In particular, for applications with high stakes, like those in the medical and industrial areas, integrity, confidentiality, and availability are crucial factors to consider in IoT systems. Since these apps are frequently real-time, network latency and delays can significantly influence how well they run. Security issues are a severe problem in applications like e-health systems since attacks like DoS, DDoS, probing, and RPL attacks can seriously impair the usefulness of these programs. Thus, IoT networks must have robust security mechanisms to protect the network and its resources with the least possible adverse effects on system performance and user privacy. Table 1 shows the various detection techniques with their pros and cons.

Additionally, IoT-based smart environments include a variety of gadgets, sensors, and objects from different vendors and IoT platforms. As a result, interoperability issues prevent IoT technology from being widely used [72]. Therefore, it is crucial to address standardization and interoperability issues while developing intrusion detection systems for IoT-based smart environments.

The need for a lightweight intrusion detection system (IDS) with few compute operations arises from the power efficiency difficulties faced by IoT networks. In the case of a Host-based I.D.S.(HIDS), IoT devices must simultaneously execute computational activities for the I.D.S.and IoT services. The design must take power and battery life into account. IDSs for IoT-based smart environments must consider performance parameters like energy consumption, processing time, and performance overhead since IoT devices have limited processing power and memory. Therefore, there is a need for more studies to address these difficulties in the context of HIDS for these contexts.

Ensuring privacy in IoT systems and avoiding intrusive techniques such as deep packet inspection is crucial. Such methods can harm IoT applications, services, and vital and real-time applications in medical and industrial fields. We need to implement a more intelligent system that does not rely on deep packet inspection and guarantees the protection of all operations within the IoT system against

Table 1 Comparison of several intrusion detection methods

Detection techniques	Pros	Cons
Anomaly-based detection	Ability to detect and minimize the number of false alarms from unauthorized intruders.	The volume of observed behavior or features affects how accurately something is detected.
	Ability to detect unexpected and previously discovered weaknesses in security.	Even widely used attack techniques may go undetected throughout the detection procedure if an attack matches a specified profile.
	The system is not heavily dependent on the operating system and can spot instances of privilege abuse.	Over time, an unauthorized person might progressively change their profile.
		It may take time to set up profiles.
Signature-based detection	By comparing suspicious signatures with a database of recognized harmful patterns, the system analyzes to find and highlight future attacks.	Unknown attacks or variants of established attack techniques are challenging to identify and prevent.
	Utilizing the specific signatures of known attacks is an easy and effective way to recognize them.	In order to avoid being identified by well-known attack signatures, malicious actors might alter their attack plans.
Stateful analysis	Includes stateful properties in regular protocol analysis.	Tracking and analyzing protocol state requires significant computing resources.
	Detects command sequences that deviate from the predicted pattern.	The system is limited in its ability to identify attacks that match the protocol's expected behavior.
Rule-based	It is easy to detect known attacks.	The system cannot identify or detect unknown or unfamiliar attacks.
Supervised ML	Can train complex and malicious models	Retrieving and encoding rulesets can be complex and time-consuming.
		It is rarely used in real situations as it requires much-labeled data.
Unsupervised ML	Can work with unlabeled data in expertized domains without requiring specialized knowledge.	The performance of unsupervised machine learning is lower compared to supervised machine learning.

unauthorized access to address this issue. Additionally, we need a new I.D.S.design with high detection accuracy and low FPR to meet the requirements of vital and real-time applications, as more than traditional IDSs may be required.

When using an IDS, a hybrid intrusion detection approach is crucial for identifying different types of attacks across distinct computing contexts. To identify attacks in IoT networks, particularly in Wireless Sensor Networks (WSNs), the I.D.S.must be compatible with the 6LoWPAN protocol. Successful deployment in the IoT context also requires an autonomous I.D.S.that can identify intrusions without the assistance of a person.

The positioning of the I.D.S.is a crucial consideration when developing any intrusion detection system (IDS) for an IoT network. Throughout the design of both Network-based I.D.S.(NIDS) and Host-based I.D.S.(HIDS), one must consider the location of the IDS. The IDS's placement within the IoT network affects how effective it is. One can use either a centralized or distributed approach to perform I.D.S.placement. A centralized approach can make management more straightforward, but it might also cause processing overload, which could lower the quality of service (QoS) for IoT networks. The distributed method can reduce the amount of monitored traffic and increase processing capacity. However, it might be challenging to deploy I.D.S.in various parts of an IoT network due to management problems.

Having both normal and anomaly databases that are constantly updated and easily connected with IoT applications and services is ultimately critical. In order to successfully and meaningfully compare different I.D.S.kinds and approaches in IoT scenarios, these datasets will be helpful (Table 2).

1.7 Existing Intrusion Detection Techniques

Figure 4 shows a taxonomy of methodologies for intrusion detection systems. It divides methods into three broad groups: those based on machine learning, those based on deep learning, and those based on fuzzy computing. This graphic depiction demonstrates the variety of methods for increasing network security and identifying currently available intrusions.

1.7.1 Machine Learning Based Methods for I.D.S.

Computers can now learn from data and make predictions, a subset of artificial intelligence. It uses statistical techniques to find patterns and connections in datasets.In the supervised learning category, trained models on labelled data, and in the unsupervised learning category, discover hidden data structures. Machine learning's subset of deep learning, which employs neural networks with several

Table 2 Contributions and limitations of the previous works

Paper	Year	Methods and tools	Contributions	Limitations
[65]	2016	Sensor-cloud computing	Integrating Green ICTs for IoT Sustainability. Sensor-cloud integration for sustainable application development.	Lack of specific analysis on smart home system vulnerabilities and security threats. Scalability concerns for accommodating numerous smart home devices and users.
[5]	2016	Identity-based encryption, stateful encryption .	Lightweight Encryption Scheme for Smart Homes. Security and Efficiency Analysis	Lacks details about specific vulnerabilities and security threats in smart home systems, thus limiting the overall understanding of the security landscape. Does not address the scalability of the proposed scheme.
[45]	2018	Deep Learning, Parallel computation	Set up a distributed deep learning approach for fog-to-things computing cyber-attack detection. Presents an architectural and methodological re-engineering of intrusion detection mechanisms. The paper acknowledges the unique challenges posed by fog-to-things computing networks	Using just the NSL-KDD dataset may not adequately reflect real-world cyberattacks. Computational and resource requirements for fog-to-things computing environments are not addressed.
[45]	2018	Conjoint analysis, XLSTAT statistical package	Introduces crucial aspects that might greatly affect IoT healthcare service adoption. It underscores the significance of safety and trustworthiness in healthcare services, demonstrating that users prioritize these aspects over additional functionality.	Online survey data may be biased and unrepresentative. Lack of detailed examination of respondent demographics hinders insights into IoT healthcare service preferences.
[62]	2018	Network Intrusion Detection System, correlation coefficient feature selection, AdaBoost ensemble learning algorithm	The paper delves into the problems arising from the lack of interoperability, including vendor lock-in, increased operational costs, and concerns related to product functionality and stability.	Limited coverage for various IoT protocols, focusing primarily on MQTT, DNS, & HTTP. Unverified real-world robustness and adaptability against evolving cyber-attacks, warranting further research.

(continued)

Table 2 (continued)

Paper	Year	Methods and tools	Contributions	Limitations
[72]	2018	Event-driven Service Oriented Architecture, WS-web service, REST web services	Introduces a Network Intrusion Detection System (NIDS) using statistical flow characteristics and an AdaBoost ensemble learning algorithm, which advances intrusion detection. Implementation of feature selection using the correlation coefficient (CC) method within the NIDS, enhancing its performance by retaining relevant features and eliminating unnecessary ones.	IoT plans limit cross-domain interoperability, save oneM2M, UbiROAD, and SEG 3.0. Complexity in interoperability testing, requiring extensive manual testing & hindering small business involvement. scalability lacks in current IoT interoperability solutions, & tailored to specific scenarios.
[41]	2019	Machine learning, Power Analysis Attacks Detection	Introduces compact and power-efficient sensors integrated on-chip for runtime detection of Power Analysis Attacks (PAAs), Shows how the suggested technique might strengthen current Integrated Circuits (ICs) against side-channel attacks, contributing to hardware security.	Centralized IDSs are unfeasible for large-scale IoT systems.
[42]	2019	Mixed-signal circuit, max-voting circuit, Machine Learning	Introduced Independent Double-Gate FinFET (IDG-FinFET) transistors as a novel component for designing machine learning (ML) classifiers. Implementation of a compact and low-power ML classifier architecture using IDG-FinFET transistors, resulting in significant area and power savings over current linear classifiers.	Considering dataset fluctuations and operating settings, the IDG-FinFET classifier's scalability and practicality require more study. Consultation of external sources or further analysis is recommended to gain insights into potential limitations and challenges associated with deploying the IDG-FinFET classifier.

(continued)

[53]	2019	Edge computing, Deep reinforcement learning (DRL) algorithm, Deep Q-learning	Novel way to minimize urban energy usage by using edge computing to effectively manage dense IoT data in smart cities. Integrating IoT technologies, edge computing infrastructure, and deep reinforcement learning algorithms into a strong and efficient energy management system for smart cities' complex urban landscapes is this research's biggest contribution.	It does not evaluate energy management methods or alternatives. The system's scalability and viability in big smart city contexts are still unknown.
[57]	2020	anomaly-based intrusion detection, Random Forest algorithm	New anomaly-based intrusion detection method for IoT networks using a hybrid feature selection engine and Random Forest algorithm. It protects sensitive data from malicious users, improving IoT network security. It shows how it can react to changing IoT threat environments by identifying both current and emerging sophisticated attacks.	Limited generalization to heterogeneous IoT environments may impact model adaptability.
[81]	2020	Hybrid Intrusion Detection System	An innovative IoT intrusion detection solution using a hybrid convolutional neural network model that blends machine learning and deep learning.	The paper omits discussions on scalability, adaptability to diverse IoT applications, and real-world implementation challenges, limiting its practical applicability in IoT environments

(continued)

Table 2 (continued)

Paper	Year	Methods and tools	Contributions	Limitations
[7]	2020	Deep learning-based IDS	Narrowing its scope to provide an in-depth exploration of the role of deep learning within intrusion detection systems. The paper introduces a novel fine-grained taxonomy for deep learning-based IDSs. This research critically evaluates and compares various experimental solutions proposed as deep learning-based IDSs.	
[102]	2022	Hidden Markov multi-step attack detection models	Presents a revolutionary multi-step assault detection model pre-training strategy. This technique improves hidden Markov-based model recognition by using the high semantic similarity of warnings within the same assault phase. Clustering semantically similar warnings and pre-classifying each alert into its attack phase. This pre-classification step improves multi-phase assault detection. Suggests a technique to convert the distance of alert vectors to each attack stage into probabilities.	The assessment uses three datasets, which may not reflect multi-step attack situations. The assumption of high semantic similarity among alerts in the same attack stage may not hold in real-world scenarios, potentially affecting accuracy.
[55]	2022	Graph Neural Network based Network Intrusion Detection	introduces the E-GraphSAGE framework, which leverages GNNs to effectively capture both edge features and topological information in IoT network data. The suggested method is the first successful and thoroughly tested use of GNNs for flow-based network intrusion detection in IoT contexts.	Limited Generalization of E-GraphSAGE due to its reliance on transductive graph embedding. Scalability and computational complexity concerns with the E-GraphSAGE model are not addressed.

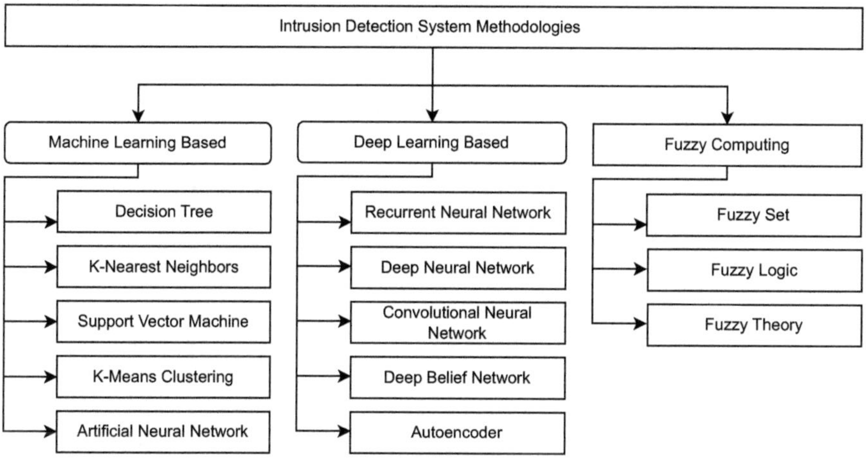

Fig. 4 An overview of I.D.S. several methodologies

layers, is particularly good at complex tasks like image identification and natural language processing. Across a wide range of sectors, machine learning is essential for automating procedures and enhancing decision-making (Fig. 5).

Supervised Learning

1. **Decision Tree:** Decision Trees (D.T.) are foundational algorithms for supervised machine learning capable of performing classification and regression problems for datasets. These algorithms create a model resembling a tree with nodes, branches, and leaves by applying a series of decisions or rules. Each node in the structure represents a characteristic or trait, while the branches and leaves represent judgements or guidelines and alternative outcomes, respectively. One noteworthy aspect of D.T. is its capacity to autonomously choose the best characteristics for tree building, followed by a pruning procedure intended to remove pointless branches, preventing overfitting. Several well-known D.T. models, including CART, C4.5, and ID3 [74], are often used in practice. Additionally, more sophisticated machine learning algorithms, such as Random Forest (R.F.) and XGBoost, use ensembles by merging several decision trees to improve forecast accuracy and resilience in different applications.

   Using a composite architecture of three decision trees, [85] introduces a novel method for improving intrusion detection in IoT-based smart grids. In the domain of IoT-based smart grid intrusion detection, the solution outperforms traditional methods like Support Vector Machine (S.V.M.), K-Nearest Neighbours (K.N.N.), and Decision Tree (D.T.). Tests were conducted rigorously on the effectiveness of the suggested technique using the NSL-KDD dataset, and the findings unmistakably demonstrate that it outperforms other approaches in safeguarding IoT-based smart grids against intrusions.

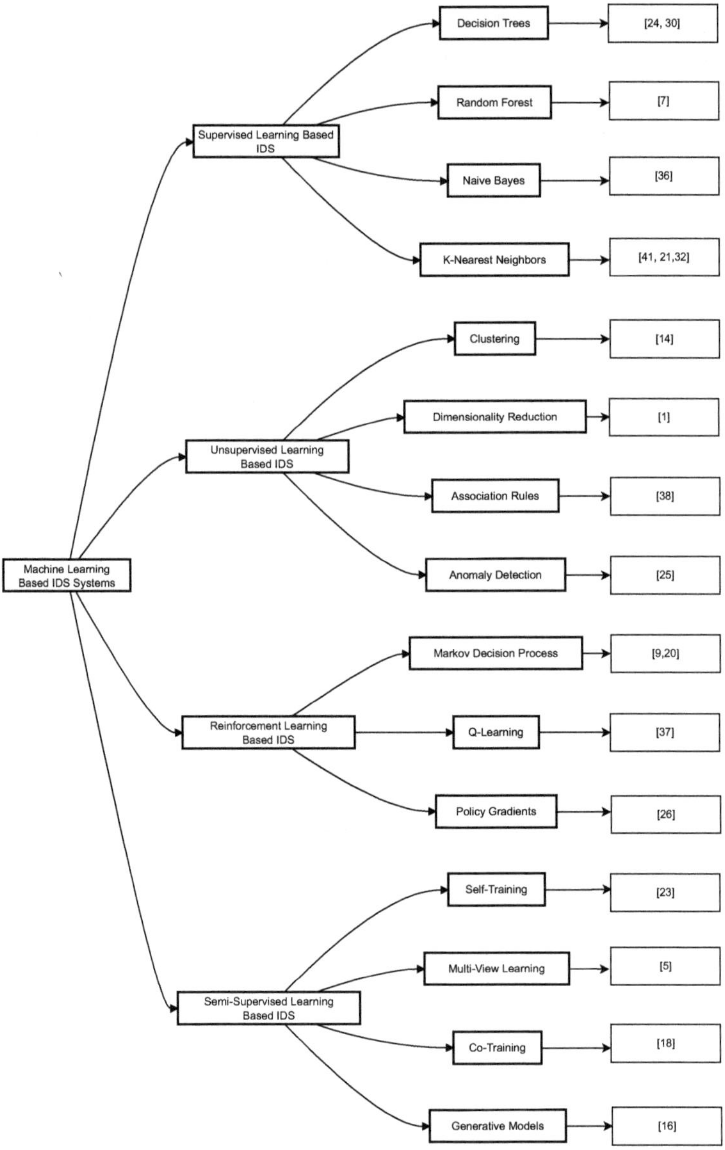

Fig. 5 Machine learning based intrusion detection systems state of art

The Decision Tree (D.T.) generates a test at each node using a top-down approach. Taghavinejad et al. [85] employ the distinct decision tree variation known as the CART method. Unlike other decision tree algorithms, CART divides parent nodes into precisely two groups of children and then recursively branches until it generates additional branches. The Gini index, a crucial param-

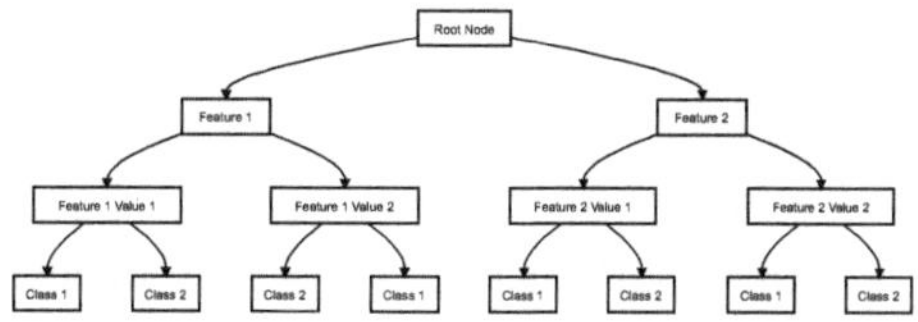

Fig. 6 A decision tree generated using C.A.R.T. algorithm

Algorithm 1 CART Algorithm Basic steps

---

procedure CART(Dataset)
  Step 1: Identify the optimal split point for each input.
  Step 2: Determine the overall "best" split point by considering the results from Step 1.
  Step 3: Split the selected input based on the determined "best" split point.
  Step 4: Iterate through the splitting process until a predefined stopping criterion is met or no further beneficial splits can be achieved.
end procedure

---

eter, is used by the CART decision tree to direct node selection. In particular, it aims to reduce the Gini index as the tree's information density rises. This approach involves an iterative procedure including trial and error to identify the ideal separator point for each characteristic, boosting the tree's efficacy and discriminative ability.The CART method utilizes the Gini Impurity notion to partition the dataset and construct a decision tree. This procedure comprises pursuing optimum homogeneity while guided by the Gini index requirement for the resulting subnodes. CART aims to find the point of split that maximizes homogeneity within each subnode by minimizing the Gini score as shown in Eq. (1) (Fig. 6).

$$Gini = 1 - \sum_{i=1}^{n} (pi)^2 \tag{1}$$

2. **Random Forest:**
   An effective ensemble learning method called Random Forest has found beneficial uses in intrusion detection systems (I.D.S.). It uses the collective intelligence of several decision trees to improve detection accuracy and robustness in the context of I.D.S. To mitigate the risk of overfitting and improve generalization, Random Forest constructs each decision tree by randomly selecting a subset of the training data and features. We then combine the outputs of individual trees from the classification process through voting or averaging to create a more dependable and robust intrusion detection model. Random Forest is ideally suited for the complex and dynamic nature of network security threats because of its capacity to manage high-dimensional data, deal with unbalanced datasets, and provide insights about feature relevance. Its capacity to adapt to incremental learning and real-time intrusion detection scenarios further strengthens its link to I.D.S., making it an effective weapon in the continuous struggle against changing cyber threats. A new Hybrid Network-based Intrusion Detection System (H.N.I.D.S.) that combines the Improved

Random Forest (I.R.F.) technique with the Enhanced Genetic Algorithm and Particle Swarm Optimisation (EGA-PSO) algorithm [12]. This method's primary goal is to improve overall detection accuracy while successfully addressing data imbalance concerns usually encountered in intrusion detection. The test findings conclusively show the effectiveness of the proposed H.N.I.D.S. since it outperforms numerous well-known machine learning techniques, including SVM, R.F., L.R., NB, LDA, and CART, when assessed on the NSL-KDD dataset. Experiments demonstrate the potential of our H.N.I.D.S. as a robust and efficient intrusion detection and network security solution. Equation (2) accurately quantifies the Mean Square Error (M.S.E.) for a Random Forest (R.F.)."

$$MSE = \frac{1}{ND}\sum_{k=0}^{n}\binom{n}{k}(P_i - D_i)b^2 \tag{2}$$

Equation (2), 'ND' represents the number of distinct data points. 'P_i' signifies the output or prediction made by model 'D_i' for each specific data point, with 'i' indicating the particular data point under consideration.

3. **Naive Bayes:** In intrusion detection systems (I.D.S.), the probabilistic classification technique known as Naive Bayes has widespread use. Due to its efficacy in finding harmful activity in network traffic, efficiency at doing so, and simplicity of usage, it plays a crucial role in I.D.S. Naive Bayes essentially uses the Bayesian theorem to determine the likelihood of an event occurring in the presence of specific circumstances or data. These events might represent an attack or a network incursion in the context of intrusion detection. The "naive" part of the algorithm makes the assumption that characteristics are conditionally independent, which makes computations easier but may not necessarily be true in reality. Naive Bayes may be used to implement I.D.S. by simulating the probability distributions of several network parameters, including packet headers, source and destination I.P. addresses, and protocol types, based on legitimate and malicious network traffic. Based on these probability distributions, the algorithm determines if a new network packet or event is likely related to an incursion. A given occurrence is labelled an incursion if its likelihood exceeds a specific limit. Naive Bayes is essential for intrusion detection because it can quickly and efficiently identify network data as benign or malicious with little computational overhead. This technique makes it especially appropriate for high-speed networks where rapid decision-making is necessary. However, because of feature independence and might result in false positives, its simplicity can be a drawback when dealing with sophisticated assault patterns. Naive Bayes nonetheless adds a further line of defence against network attacks when used with other I.D.S. approaches, helping maintain a strong security posture.

   The "Bayes Theorem", an essential element of probability theory and statistics, permits the computation of an event's likelihood while considering the likelihood of an earlier event occurring. The following equation effectively expresses Bayes' Theorem mathematically as in Eq. (3). In this context, A and B represent distinct events. Where $P(B) \neq 0$.

$$P(A|B) = \frac{P(B|A)P(A)}{P(B)} \tag{3}$$

The Bayes theorem may now be applied to our dataset in the manner described below Eq. (4):

$$P(y|X) = \frac{P(B|A)P(A)}{P(B)} \tag{4}$$

In this context, "y" symbolises the class variable, and "X" denotes a dependent feature vector of size "n," describing the analysis's essential variables. $X = (x_1, x_2, x_3, \ldots, x_n)$

Vishwakarma and Kesswani [92] presents a novel strategy that employs an ensemble of recurrent neural networks (R.N.N.) to improve intrusion detection and strengthen the security of Internet of Things (IoT) systems. This approach blends hybrid metaheuristics with deep learning approaches. In particular, Long Short-Term Memory (L.S.T.M.) and Gated Recurrent Unit (G.R.U.) models detect and categorize different attacks inside IoT networks. Add the fractional derivative mutation to the Harris Hawk Optimization technique to enhance accuracy before executing the feature selection procedure.

4. **K-Nearest Neighbors:** It calculates the separations between data points and the samples nearby. The parameter 'k' selection inside the K.N.N. algorithm is crucial to the method's overall performance. A deficient "k" number makes the model vulnerable to overfitting, whereas a high "k" value results in incorrect categorization of data examples [101]. To solve these issues, researchers like Karatas et al. [40] evaluated the performance of various machine learning algorithms using the CSE-CIC-IDS2018 benchmark dataset, a recent benchmark dataset. To address the imbalance in the dataset, the Synthetic-Minority-Oversampling-Technique (S.M.O.T.E.) dramatically boosted the detection rate of minority class attacks.

   Researchers focus on developing an intrusion detection system (I.D.S.) that primarily uses deep learning and machine learning techniques to increase the security of IoT networks [82]. The attack detection model in the research uses the Long Short-Term Memory (L.S.T.M.) and K-Nearest Neighbours (K.N.N.) algorithms, with a comparative evaluation based on important metrics, including detection time, kappa statistic, geometric mean, and sensitivity. By utilizing the Bot-IoT dataset, we meticulously evaluate the effectiveness of this I.D.S., underscoring the imperative for security in IoT networks and accentuating the utilization of machine learning techniques, particularly L.S.T.M. and K.N.N., in crafting a successful I.D.S. Additionally, it emphasizes how crucial it is to assess an I.D.S.'s performance using real-world data, such as the Bot-IoT dataset, to determine its relevance and efficacy in protecting IoT networks.

K-Nearest Neighbours (K.N.N.) is significant in the context of Intrusion Detection Systems (I.D.S.) for Internet of Things (IoT) networks. The primary function of K.N.N. is classifying data points in a feature space according to the dominant class among their k-nearest neighbours. K.N.N. is crucial in intrusion detection since it identifies and categorises network traffic patterns. Comparing current network behaviour to previous data assists in detecting abnormalities and enables the system to identify variations suggestive of possible threats or intrusions. The flexibility of K.N.N. to the dynamic and developing nature of IoT networks, where intrusion patterns can quickly alter, makes it particularly beneficial in the IoT environment. Additionally, K.N.N. enables interpretability and transparency, enabling security staff to understand the background of intrusion warnings and design tailored security actions. As a result, K.N.N. is a reliable and adaptable tool inside the I.D.S. framework, contributing substantially to the security and integrity of IoT networks against new threats.

Algorithm 2 K-Nearest Neighbors (K.N.N.) Algorithm [84]

```
Load the training and test data
Choose the value of K
for each point in the test data do
    Find the Euclidean distance to all the training data points
    Store the Euclidean distances in a list and sort it
    Choose the first K points
    Assign a class to the test point based on the majority of classes present in the chosen points
end for
```

5. **Support Vector Machine:** A supervised solid machine learning technique called the Support Vector Machine (SVM) creates a maximum-margin separation hyper-plane inside an n-dimensional feature space. This method easily handles linear and nonlinear problem areas, serving a dual function. When dealing with nonlinear issues, SVM utilizes kernel functions to transform the initial low-dimensional input vector into a higher-dimensional feature space. Here, achieving an ideal maximum margin hyper-plane that serves as the deciding boundary is the goal using the vital support vectors [76]. SVM appears as a valuable tool in the context of Network Intrusion Detection Systems (NIDS), improving the effectiveness and precision of intrusion detection jobs by expertly differentiating between legitimate and malicious classes, hence strengthening network security [96].
6. **K-Means Clustering:** A key idea in data analysis is clustering, which aims to organize related data points into coherent clusters for easier understanding and analysis. K-Means, an iterative centroid-based clustering technique that works without labelled data, is one of the most extensively used clustering algorithms. In K-Means, the letter 'K' represents the number of centroids that serve as cluster centres. We often use Euclidean distance in the distance calculations to assign data points to clusters. The goal is to produce well-defined, meaningful clusters

that promote efficient data processing and pattern detection by minimizing the total distance between data points and the centroids of each cluster [48].

To address the issues with I.D.S., Yao et al. [97] developed a brand-new multilevel intrusion detection system called Multilevel Semi-Supervised ML (M.S.M.L.). Pure cluster extraction, pattern discovery, fine-grained classification, and model updating are the four distinct components of this comprehensive strategy, which combines clustering techniques with the Random Forest (R.F.) model. The basic concept is to transfer suspicious instances across the modules progressively; if one module cannot identify an attack, it sends the instance to the next for further detection. The authors of [97] used the KDD Cup'99 dataset to thoroughly assess the recommended method's effectiveness.

7. **Artificial Neural Network:** Authors have designed the supervised machine-learning method, the Artificial Neural Network (ANN), after the intricate functions of the human nervous system. Input, hidden, and output layers are only a few of the layers that make up artificial neural networks (ANNs), which employ the backpropagation approach. Its capacity to handle nonlinear modelling, especially when subjected to large datasets, is a crucial benefit. The difficulty, however, comes from the time needed to train an ANN model because of its intrinsic complexity. In addition to slowing down learning, this complexity may provide less-than-ideal results. Thus, it must be applied with caution [13].

   Huang et al. [31] developed the Extreme Learning Machine (E.L.M.) neural network design in response to the limitations of conventional Artificial Neural Networks (ANNs). This innovative technique uses a single hidden layer feed-forward neural network. It utilizes input weights and hidden layer bias in a new way, eliminating the requirement for laboriously fine-tuning and analytic calculation of output weights. Li et al. [50] developed the Fast Learning Network (F.L.N.). This model smoothly combines a multilayer feed-forward neural network with a single-layer feed-forward neural network that operates in parallel. The F.L.N. architecture significantly advances neural network design since it offers outstanding performance and stability while needing fewer hidden nodes and significantly less processing time.

   Ali et al. [8] developed a model called PSO-FLN based on fuzzy logic networks (F.L.N.) and particle swarm optimization (PSO) to handle the Intrusion Detection System (I.D.S.) challenge. In order to compare the effectiveness of F.L.N. with other optimization strategies, they conducted their tests using the KDD Cup'99 dataset. Their research findings supported PSO-FLN's superiority over other F.L.N. models that used various optimization techniques, including Genetic Algorithm, Harmony Search Optimisation, and Ameliorated Teaching Learning-Based Optimisation. Another significant result of their research was that accuracy increased as the number of neurons in the buried layer rose. However, a severe flaw appeared in the lower attack classes' lowered detection rate accuracy.

Unsupervised Learning

1. **Clustering:** In intrusion detection systems (I.D.S.), clustering methods are crucial because they help discover and mitigate security threats in intricate network settings. By dividing network data into discrete groups based on similarity patterns, clustering techniques like k-means or hierarchical clustering can distinguish between legitimate network activity and potentially harmful activity. Because departures from established cluster norms might point to intrusion attempts or abnormalities requiring further study, this segmentation helps with anomaly detection. By concentrating I.D.S. resources on relevant data subsets, clustering also helps to reduce the dimensionality of network data, improving computing performance. Clustering allows I.D.S. to increase threat detection efficiency and accuracy while also making it easier to build baselines for typical network behaviour, which are essential for fast and accurate intrusion detection in dynamic and changing network environments.

   Using multiple-kernel clustering (M.K.C.) methods, in [30] proposes a unique intrusion detection methodology that emphasises ensuring the security of crucial business networks in the dynamic 5G and IoT contexts. By using similarity computations to fill in the gaps left by missing traffic features, this technique successfully handles the common problem of anomaly identification. The method considerably improves clustering accuracy for incompletely sampled data, lowers the sensitivity of the anomaly detection model to the selection of traffic characteristics, and increases its resistance to wrongly gathered traffic data. The primary advancement is the development of many base kernels, each of which captures a unique feature attribute. The researchers then improve the performance of clustering by integrating these basic kernels as shown in Algorithm 3. They rigorously tested the effectiveness of the proposed solution, conclusively establishing its ability to improve clustering accuracy while simultaneously reducing detection sensitivity, thus advancing the state-of-the-art in network security for 5G and IoT contexts.

Algorithm 3 Anomaly Detection Based on MKKC

Require: Properties vector $X = \{x^{(1)}, \ldots, x^{(M)}\}$, each $x^{(i)}$ has L properties; kernel matrix K, number of Clusters N
Ensure: N disjoint clusters $\{C_1, C_2, \ldots, C_N\}$
1: **for** each $x^{(i)} \in X$ **do**
2:     **for** each property p of $x^{(i)}$ **do**
3:         Encode and Normalize p with Eq. (13) and (14);
4:     **end for**
5:     Construct kernel matrix K based vector X;
6:     Fill the incomplete kernel matrix K with algorithm 2;
7:     Perform Multiple Kernel K-Means with algorithm 1;
8: **end for**
9: **return** $\{C_1, C_2, \ldots, C_N\}$

2. **Dimensionality Reduction:** Due to the inherent complexity and high dimensionality of network data in such situations, dimension reduction significantly impacts intrusion detection systems (I.D.S.) used in IoT networks. IoT networks produce enormous amounts of data from multiple sensors and devices, frequently distinguished by various traits or properties. Principal Component Analysis (P.C.A.) and t-distributed Stochastic Neighbour Embedding (t-SNE), two alternative techniques for dimensionality reduction, significantly reduce the number of variables in this dataset while maintaining their core characteristics. I.D.S. may improve computational efficiency, minimise resource needs, and increase the scalability of intrusion detection algorithms by lowering the dimensionality of the data, which is essential in resource-constrained IoT environments. Reduced dimensionality also makes network data visualisation easier, which helps security analysts better understand complicated threat environments. As a result, dimensionality reduction improves the effectiveness of intrusion detection models and equips security professionals to watch over better and defend IoT networks from constantly changing threats.

Algorithm 4 Dimensionality Reduction and IDS Construction [2]

1: Utilize Auto-Encoder (AE) and Principal Component Analysis (PCA) for dimensionality reduction in network intrusion detection systems.
2: Perform dimensionality reduction with Auto-Encoder (AE) by conducting a feedforward pass on training instances, resulting in reduced features from the hidden layer.
3: Employ Principal Component Analysis (PCA) to discover a transformation that reduces data dimensionality while preserving maximum variance.
4: Project the original dataset into a lower-dimensional subspace using PCA while retaining essential data characteristics.
5: Utilize the resultant low-dimensional features obtained from AE and PCA to construct various classifiers for the Intrusion Detection System (IDS).
6: Evaluate the IDS performance based on metrics such as Detection Rate (DR), F-Measure, False Alarm Rate (FAR), and Accuracy.

In order to reduce feature dimensionality in network intrusion detection systems, Abdulhammed et al. [2] used Auto-Encoders (A.E.) and Principal Component Analysis (P.C.A.). For a powerful Intrusion Detection System, the inquiry examines classifiers like Random Forest (R.F.), Bayesian Network, Linear Discriminant Analysis (LDA), and Quadratic Discriminant Analysis (Q.D.A.). A.E. and P.C.A. dimension reduction improves crucial performance measures including D.R., F-Measure, FAR, and Accuracy. The research successfully reduced feature dimensions in the CICIDS2017 dataset while retaining an exceptional accuracy rate of 99.6% in binary and multi-class classification. The paper offers a novel Multi-Class Combined performance measure (Combined Mc) to examine classification systems based on FAR, D.R., Accuracy, and class distribution propertiThe dataset contained a novel uniform distribution-based class imbalance solution. It makes the suggested IDS more robust and user-friendly.

3. **Association Rules:** In IoT network intrusion detection, association rules, a key idea in unsupervised learning, play a significant role. Discovering latent patterns and associations within data constitutes a critical aspect of unsupervised learning, and practitioners often extract association rules without relying on previously labelled data. By exposing patterns of network activity that differ from established standards, association rules play a crucial role in the specific context of IoT network security since they help identify suspicious behaviours and probable intrusion attempts. This analysis method allows for the early discovery of aberrant behaviours and departures from expected network patterns by examining interactions between various network entities, devices, or services. Association rule insights enable security systems to swiftly send alerts and proactively mitigate security risks, enhancing overall IoT network resilience and protecting them from continuously developing attack techniques and vulnerabilities. In order to improve the security posture of IoT networks, association rules in unsupervised learning emerge as a crucial element. They offer a priceless method for proactive intrusion detection and threat mitigation.

   In the CNN-IDS paradigm, convolutional neural networks (CNN) are the cornerstone [95] presented a novel network intrusion detection model was developed in this research to address the inherent shortcomings of traditional intrusion detection techniques. In order to systematically remove redundan t and unnecessary characteristics present in network traffic data, CNN-IDS deliberately uses dimensionality reduction techniques. This technique improves computing performance and the data quality required for effective intrusion detection. The CNN architecture then employs deep learning capabilities to extract critical characteristics from the dimensionality-reduced dataset automatically. Detection effectiveness is further increased by carefully using supervised learning approaches to obtain finely tuned insights necessary for accurate intrusion identification. The original traffic vector format is converted into an image format to enable more streamlined and resource-effective processing to maximise computational resources. ACCORDING TO RIGOROUS EMPIRICAL EVALUATIONS, the CNN-IDS model performs better than conventional algorithms, which is especially clear in the increased accuracy, decreased false alarm rates, and increased real-time detection capabilities.

Algorithm 5 Feature Extraction using Association Rules in IDS

1: Collect and preprocess network data with relevant attributes.
2: Transform the preprocessed data into transactions.
3: Apply association rule mining algorithms (e.g., Apriori or FP-growth) to discover frequent patterns.
4: Evaluate discovered association rules using support, confidence, and lift metrics.
5: Select rules based on predefined support and confidence thresholds.
6: Extract features from the selected association rules to create a feature set for intrusion detection.
7: Optionally, perform feature selection to reduce dimensionality and improve efficiency.

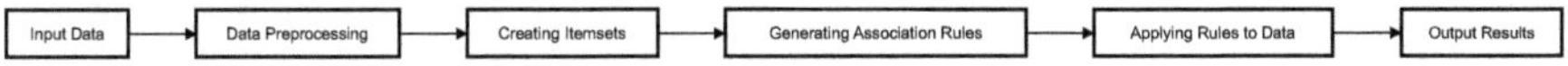

Fig. 7 Association rules usage in feature selection

4. **Anomaly Detection:** Techniques for unsupervised learning anomaly detection play a crucial part in bolstering the security of IoT networks because of their natural capacity to recognise anomalous patterns or behaviours in the absence of labelled data. In intrusion detection systems (I.D.S.) designed for Internet of Things (IoT) networks, these approaches establish a baseline of typical network behaviour and signalling any variations as probable intrusions or abnormalities. Unsupervised learning anomaly detection's importance in IoT-based I.D.S. is due to its proactive propensity to identify emerging risks and undiscovered attack pathways. These approaches recognise intricate and dynamic intrusion attempts by methodically examining network traffic, device interactions, or data trends. As a result, IoT networks are more resilient to a constantly changing threat scenario. Clustering, autoencoders, and isolation forests are just a few examples of unsupervised learning techniques that present a data-centric and adaptable paradigm that blends seamlessly with the fluid and heterogeneous characteristics of IoT environments, making them indispensable tools for preserving the security and integrity of IoT networks. The aim to increase the security of IoT networks by using machine learning methods to detect anomalies in the IoT Network Intrusion Dataset with a high degree of accuracy and effectiveness. The authors in [54] emphasize the inherent difficulties in protecting IoT devices, primarily from their constrained computing capabilities, and advocate using an Intrusion Detection System (I.D.S.) as a cutting-edge security solution. In the report, excellent accuracy rates for anomaly identification range from 99 to 100%, providing persuasive proof for the efficacy of their suggested strategy. This study highlights the crucial part that I.D.S., supported by machine learning algorithms, plays in enhancing the security posture of IoT networks. Given the complexity and weaknesses of IoT device limitations, it is crucial and will eventually help build a more stable and resilient IoT ecosystem (Fig. 7).

Reinforcement Learning

1. **Markov Decision Process:** A Markov Decision Process (M.D.P.) is crucial for improving Intrusion Detection Systems (I.D.S.) in IoT networks. M.D.P.s provide a solid framework for proactive security decision-making in the complex IoT environment, where diverse devices interact and create enormous data streams. Modelling the IoT network as an M.D.P. captures the dynamic and unpredictable character of network traffic, enabling the I.D.S. to make the best decisions at the moment. This character translates into the capacity to adjust and successfully counter emerging threats. In order to increase the network's resilience against cyberattacks, M.D.P.s provide I.D.S.s with the ability to intelligently allocate

resources, such as bandwidth and processing power, for anomaly detection and incident response. Furthermore, M.D.P.s enable the integration of reinforcement learning techniques, enabling I.D.S.s to learn and enhance their intrusion detection procedures over time, essential for avoiding sophisticated and adaptable threats in the IoT ecosystem. A systematic, adaptable, and intelligent approach to threat detection and mitigation is provided by M.D.P.s and I.D.S.s in IoT networks, highlighting their importance in boosting cybersecurity measures.

Benaddi et al. [14] and Kalnoor and Gowrishankar [39] proposes the Reinforcement Learning Intrusion Detection System (RL-IDS), a ground-breaking intrusion detection system designed specifically for Internet of Things (IoT) networks that use Wireless Sensor Networks (W.S.N.). The revolutionary use of computational analysis for thorough network performance evaluation across many security parameters makes it stand out for its capacity to significantly increase detection rates while concurrently minimising false alarms compared to conventional approaches. The RL-IDS uses the extended Markov Decision Process (M.D.P.) algorithm and Q-network, combining reinforcement learning calculations to enable continuous surveillance of digital threats inside IoT and W.S.N. settings, and it promises to improve intrusion detection capabilities significantly. Furthermore, the study conducts a thorough assessment, pitting the RL-IDS against several deep learning (DL) and machine learning (ML) algorithms, such as Convolutional Neural Networks (CNN) and Long Short-Term Memory Networks (L.S.T.M.). The findings are promising, with the R.L. computation showing exceptional accuracy and Area Under the Curve (A.U.C.), especially in challenging multiclass cases, highlighting its promise as a reliable intrusion detection method. Overall, the research presented in this study shows promise for developing more accurate and effective intrusion detection systems in the complex world of IoT contexts.

The letters (S, A, P, R, γ indicate five essential parts of a Markov Decision Process (M.D.P.):

- S represents the collection of potential states for the system.
- A refers to the agent's list of possible actions.
- The Transition Probability Matrix, or P, describes how states change due to actions.
- R stands for the expenses or immediate benefits of an action.
- Factor γ), the discount factor, influences the agent's preference for current benefits over future ones.

The Transition Probability Matrix (P) and Reward (R) might alter depending on the specific M.D.P. activities. This dynamic nature illustrates how various acts can result in state changes and rewards.

Action-specific Transition Probability Matrix;

$$P^{a}_{SS'} = P[S_{t+1} = S' | S_t = s, A_t = a] \tag{5}$$

Action-Dependent Reward Function;

$$R_s^a = E[R_{t+1} | S_t = s, A_t = a] \tag{6}$$

2. **Q-Learning:** Q-learning, a reinforcement learning method, has much potential in the field of Intrusion Detection Systems (I.D.S.) for Internet of Things networks. IoT networks, characterised by a complex web of linked devices, face significant security problems, underscoring the need for solid anomaly detection techniques. Q-learning, which aims to build the best practices in uncertain situations through a trial-and-error methodology, can remarkably adapt to the dynamic nuances prevalent in IoT networks. The algorithm's capacity to systematically investigate and exploit various network situations fosters versatility, enabling the creation of agile and adaptable I.D.S. methods. Q-Learning enables quick detection of abnormalities or intrusions, including unauthorised access attempts and unusual data flow patterns, enabling real-time monitoring. These skills play a crucial role in enhancing the robustness of IoT ecosystems. In addition, Q-Learning's inherent reinforcement mechanism also fosters continuous learning, enabling I.D.S. systems to dynamically adapt to emerging and changing threats, protecting IoT networks from the pervasive and complex security landscape. In conclusion, incorporating Q-Learning into I.D.S. systems designed for IoT networks provides an excellent technique to supplement security measures, successfully tackling the unique issues in the constantly changing and tightly intertwined IoT world.

   Wu et al. [94] introduces a unique two-layer cooperative intrusion detection method called Q TCID. Its goal is to improve intrusion detection accuracy in Internet of Drones (IoD) systems while resolving the troublesome problems of false positives and negatives. An intelligent dynamic voting algorithm that operates at the host level and an intelligent auditing algorithm that operates at the system level are the two key components that make up the mindfully designed Q-TCID algorithm. These elements are carefully infused with Q-learning optimisation algorithms, encouraging the development of intrusion detection methodologies that steadily get closer to perfection. Thorough simulation tests confirm the Q-TCID algorithm's effectiveness in extending the IoD system's mean time to failure (MTTF), which improves overall system dependability in addition to helping to fine-tune defence methods. Notably, the algorithm's handy energy management, which is especially important in contexts with limited resources, considerably strengthens the resiliency and effectiveness of intrusion detection methods inside the complicated structure of IoD networks.
3. **Policy Gradients:** It is impossible to exaggerate the importance of policy gradients in the context of Intrusion Detection Systems (I.D.S.) used in IoT networks since they represent a basic idea in reinforcement learning. In the complex IoT landscape, distinguished by a complex web of interconnected devices exchanging data constantly, I.D.S. plays a critical role in boosting defences against malevolent behaviour and latent threats. Policy gradients present an adaptive mechanism for fine-tuning intrusion detection policies as they develop

Algorithm 6 Collaborative Q-Learning for Intrusion Detection Systems [94]

Require: Set of nodes NODE, State space S_σ, Action space A_σ, Reward table R_σ, Learning rate α_σ, Discount factor γ_σ, Maximum number of iterations.
Ensure: Final Q-value function Q_σ.
Initialize Q-value function: $Q_\sigma(s_\sigma, a_\sigma) = 0$;
Determine the initial state: $s_\sigma \in S_\sigma$;
while Q-value convergence not achieved **do**
    Use an ϵ-greedy strategy to select an action $a_\sigma \in A_\sigma$ based on the current Q-value function and state;
    Execute action $a_\sigma \in A_\sigma$ to obtain the reward $r_\sigma \in R_\sigma$ and transition to a new state s'_σ;
    Update Q-values Q_V and Q_C using specific update rules, e.g., equations (2) and (4);
    Update the current state to s'_σ;
end while

over time. They function as a dynamic reinforcement learning strategy. Policy gradient-based I.D.S. demonstrates an intrinsic ability to autonomously learn and adapt their detection tactics, utilising past network data and iterative feedback mechanisms. Compared to conventional rule-based I.D.S., this method offers a stark improvement. This intrinsic flexibility is significant in IoT networks, where the network environment is noticeably unstable and prone to the ongoing evolution of attack vectors. Policy gradient-based I.D.S. systems attain a higher degree of precision in recognising novel intrusion patterns through the ongoing refining of intrusion detection rules motivated by learning from earlier security events, strengthening the overall security posture of IoT ecosystems. These systems also can reduce false positives, which are a significant worry in IoT networks with scarce computing resources. In conclusion, policy gradients reveal themselves as a beneficial addition to the multitude of intrusion detection approaches already in use in this area, showing promise for addressing the constantly growing security concerns inherent to IoT networks.

An in-depth examination of intrusion detection within the complex framework of a big data environment is the focus of [56]. It presents a brand-new, potent hybrid deep learning model to improve network intrusion detection effectiveness. The advantages of a Weight-Dropped Long Short-Term Memory (W.D.L.S.T.M.) network–which is skilled at collecting and keeping long-term connections among the extracted features–and a Convolutional Neural Network (CNN) for reliable feature extraction–are proficiently combined in this cutting-edge model. The suggested hybrid model regularly shows higher and dependable performance when compared to established approaches using a publically available dataset. This model stands as a formidable solution for network intrusion detection in the extensive data landscape by combining the deep CNN's skill at extracting essential features from the vast expanse of I.D.S. big data, leveraging its inherent speed advantages through weight sharing, and leveraging the W.D.L.S.T.M. network's capability to discern intricate dependencies among these features. A substantial 97.1% accuracy on the demanding UNSW-NB15 big dataset supports its strengths further after extensive experimental validation. This extraordinary accuracy highlights the model's potential to act as a cornerstone for real-time intrusion detection in intricate and substantial datasets, marking a significant development in intrusion detection systems adapted for extensive data environments. The probability distribution of actions based on a specific state is how a policy is appropriately defined.

$$\begin{gathered}\pi(A_t = a | S_t = s) \\ \forall A_t \in A(s),\, S_t \in S\end{gathered} \tag{7}$$

Semi-Supervised Learning

1. **Self Training:** Semi-supervised Learning, especially using the self-training approach, is essential in Intrusion Detection Systems (I.D.S.) functioning within IoT networks. Due to the complex and constantly changing nature of cyber threats, IoT networks frequently need more labelled data. Semi-supervised learning approaches provide a potent remedy for this problem, using the plentiful unlabeled data in real-world network traffic and the readily accessible labelled data. In the self-training paradigm, a specific instance of semi-supervised Learning, we first train a model on the already-existing labelled data. Then, we apply this model to instances not labelled, producing projected labels that we smoothly merge into the labelled dataset. This ongoing loop gradually expands the I.D.S. knowledge base. As a result, the I.D.S. is well-positioned to demonstrate increased proficiency in identifying new and previously unknown threats, which is essential in IoT networks where traditional signature-based detection techniques frequently fail. The combination of semi-supervised Learning and self-training equips I.D.S. with the versatility and resilience required to grow in parallel with the continuously changing threat landscape by utilising the vast reservoir of unlabeled data inherent to IoT networks. This mutually beneficial integration strengthens the security of IoT networks and improves accuracy and resilience.

   Li et al. [51] Using a deep migration learning model that smoothly combines profound learning principles with intrusion detection technologies, the study offers an IoT feature extraction and intrusion detection algorithm optimised for intelligent cities. Numerous tests performed on the KDD CUP 99 dataset demonstrate that the method dramatically improves detection efficiency and decreases detection times compared to previous approaches. The study also delves into the subtleties of data feature extraction and the modelling of the migration learning model, offering insight into the real-world use of migration learning in IoT security. Given the resource constraints that come with the Internet of Things sensor nodes and the vulnerability of IoT networks to possible assaults, the study emphasises the crucial role that intrusion detection systems play in protecting IoT applications. The research also offers a unique self-learning deep migration learning model that broadens the scope of migration learning to include distributed network integration learning, providing a solid framework for distributed migration network learning algorithms. Together, these contributions improve our understanding and use of cutting-edge intrusion detection approaches in the context of secure IoT and intelligent cities.

2. **Multi-View Learning:** Intrusion Detection Systems (I.D.S.) for IoT networks heavily rely on Multi-View Learning in Semi-Supervised Learning. Traditional single-view approaches frequently need to capture the subtleties of security risks inside the intricate and varied data landscape of the Internet of Things. By using data from several data sources or views, multi-view learning overcomes this difficulty and enables a more thorough study of network traffic, sensor data, and system logs. This multi-modal strategy gives I.D.S. the flexibility to respond to emerging threats while improving anomaly detection accuracy. The flexibility of multi-view learning to use labelled and unlabeled data for model training is particularly beneficial in the IoT setting, where data can be very diverse and dynamic. This benefit protects the integrity and dependability of linked systems by allowing IoT I.D.S. to offer robust security solutions suited explicitly to IoT network's unique features.

   The authors in [10] present MV-FLID, a cutting-edge intrusion detection technology built on federated learning and designed exclusively for Internet of Things networks. The unique feature of MV-FLID is its decentralised training on different perspectives of IoT network data, which makes it easier to identify, categorise, and mitigate a wide variety of assaults. In addition to combining federated learning techniques to assure vital privacy preservation and data security, this novel solution uses multi-view ensemble learning to improve its ability to learn different attack classes quickly. In particular, the assessment findings highlighted in the research demonstrate the efficacy of MV-FLID, displaying its better accuracy when compared to conventional centralised non-federated learning systems, thereby significantly underscoring its potential to strengthen IoT network security.

3. **Co-Training:** Co-training is a potent semi-supervised learning approach with great potential for improving intrusion detection systems in Internet of Things (IoT) networks. Co-training presents a novel approach in the context of IoT, where data quantities might be enormous and labelling data for supervised learning is sometimes resource-intensive and impracticable. It functions on the idea that using several perspectives or feature representations of the data can increase classification precision. Co-training may use this multi-modal data in an IoT environment where numerous data sources and sensors create information from distinct viewpoints. Training different classifiers on various data modalities accomplishes this. This method improves anomaly detection capabilities while reducing reliance on labelled data. Co-training can efficiently identify harmful behaviours inside IoT networks by integrating the insights gathered from many data sources, improving security and addressing the issues brought on by IoT data's dynamic and diverse nature. It also fits well with the resource limitations present in IoT devices, making it an appealing method for enhancing intrusion detection.

Jia and Zheng [37] The field of network security has highlighted the critical relevance of network intrusion detection in light of the growing network threats characterized by greater complexity and frequency. The co-training paradigm, which considers static and dynamic aspects, is its foundation. In further detail, we divide network flow attributes into two groups: static attributes containing intrinsic qualities and dynamic attributes capturing interflow correlations. We use a feature extraction technique based on information entropy and probability distribution theory to enhance the model's feature selection process. In addition, by encoding interaction data in a network flow graph, we make it easier to do graph deep learning. This model's excellent performance in effectively recognizing disguised samples proves its usefulness, achieving a remarkable 99.93% recall rate, 99.47% accuracy, and an astonishing 0.997 F1 score on anomalous samples. This model offers a novel viewpoint on network intrusion detection, and the approach put out here has the potential for broader application in various classification problem domains.

4. **Generative Models:** The efficacy of intrusion detection systems (I.D.S.) in IoT networks can be improved using generative models in the semi-supervised learning space. Models like Generative Adversarial Networks (GANs) and Variational Autoencoders (V.A.E.) make creating synthetic data samples that closely resemble network traffic patterns possible. This feature is especially advantageous, given the challenges of acquiring tagged intrusion data in IoT environments, where such data is often scarce and resource-intensive. This innovation gives I.D.S. a deeper understanding of standard and aberrant network behaviour, significantly improving detection accuracy and decreasing false favourable rates. Additionally, generative models are helpful for data augmentation, allowing the development of complex and varied situations for thoroughly assessing the resilience of I.D.S. methods. In addition to strengthening the reliability of intrusion detection systems inside IoT networks, this multidimensional approach also ensures their flexibility to changing threats and dynamic network circumstances, making them a crucial part of the IoT ecosystem's security. Idrissi et al. [34] introduces a novel host intrusion detection system (I.D.S.) based on a Generative Adversarial Network (GAN) that is unsupervised and explicitly designed for Internet of Things (IoT) devices. This system uses unsupervised learning algorithms to analyse independently and cluster unlabeled data, enabling the identification of hidden patterns and data grouping without any human involvement. This I.D.S., known as "EdgeIDS," was carefully created to meet the problems brought on by IoT devices, which frequently function with limited resources and participate in particular data exchanges. Then, the system used the MQTTset dataset to prove its efficacy and found the results encouraging. For example, the system's ROC-AUC metric of up to 0.99 and its ROC-EER metric of just 0.035 are excellent and astonishingly low. By providing a reliable method for identifying cyber anomalies inside this increasingly linked and susceptible environment, this research sets the door for future advancement in IoT cybersecurity.

1.7.2 Deep Learning Based Methods for I.D.S.

Deep learning, a subset of machine learning, has captured the attention of researchers and practitioners due to its potential utility in Intrusion Detection Systems (I.D.S.). It has proved beneficial in discovering sophisticated patterns suggestive of network breaches because of its capacity to extract hierarchical and complex characteristics from raw data automatically. Convolutional and recurrent neural networks, two deep neural networks, have proven remarkably effective in spotting abnormalities and categorising malevolent behaviour. Deep learning is a potential strategy for increasing the security of contemporary networks because of its ability to handle enormous amounts of network traffic data in real-time and its flexibility to change threats. Nevertheless, the requirement for large labelled datasets and tackling false positives-related problems are still complex.

1. **Recurrent Neural Network:** Recurrent Neural Networks (R.N.N.) are a class of deep learning models that have attracted much attention recently in research because of their extraordinary capacity to analyse sequential data, which makes them ideal for tasks like time series forecasting, speech recognition and natural language processing. A defining feature of R.N.N. is recurrent connections, which enable data to persist and undergo updates throughout time steps. R.N.N.s have had difficulties with long-range dependencies and vanishing gradient concerns despite their usefulness, spurring advancements in the area. Developments like Long Short-Term Memory (L.S.T.M.) and Gated Recurrent Unit (G.R.U.) variations have recently improved R.N.N. performance by reducing these problems. Researchers have also looked at novel designs, such as Transformer-based models and attention processes, which have shown excellent outcomes in sequence-to-sequence tasks. Recent studies have demonstrated the importance of attention mechanisms and Transformer architectures, signalling significant advancements in RNN-related research. Examples include works by Vaswani et al. [91], and Devlin et al. [23]. These breakthroughs continue to advance sequential data processing, shaping the landscape of contemporary deep learning (Fig. 8).

   The following Eq. (8) describe the forward pass of an R.N.N. with a single hidden layer:

$$h_t = f(W_x x_t + W_h h_{t-1} + b_h) y_t = W_y h_t + b_y \tag{8}$$

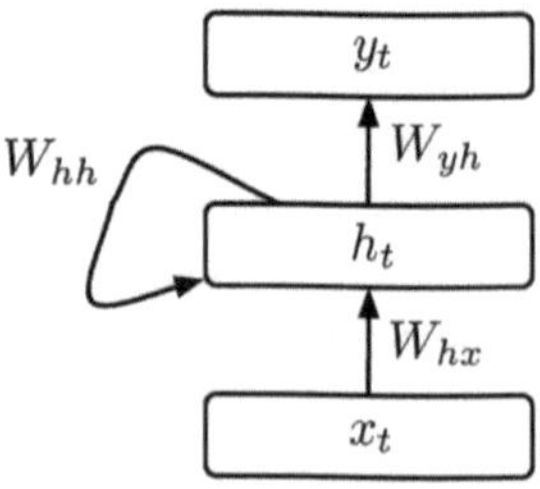

Fig. 8 R.N.N. representation [86]

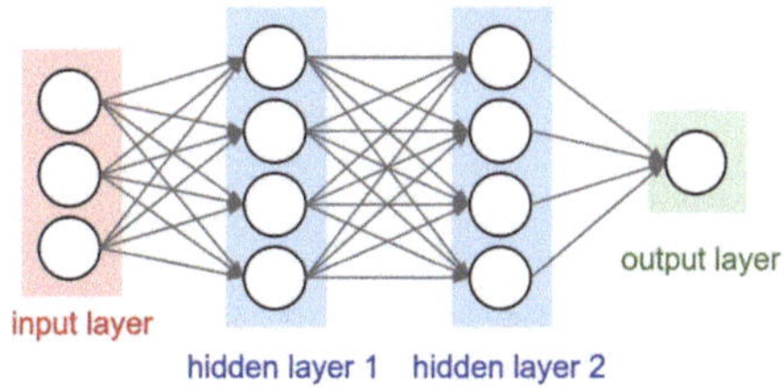

Fig. 9 Deep neural network representation

W_x, W_h, and W_y are weight matrices, while b_h and b_y are bias vectors. h_t is the hidden state at time step t, x_t is the input vector at time step t, and y_t is the output vector at time step t. F is a function that activates something, like the tanh function.

2. **Deep Neural Network:** An essential element of artificial intelligence and machine learning is a Deep Neural Network (D.N.N.), a neural network or deep learning model. Its multi-layered design, which incorporates several hidden levels between the input and output layers, distinguishes it as shown in Fig. 9. A DNN's primary feature is its capacity to automatically learn hierarchical and abstract representations from enormous volumes of data. It makes it particularly good at handling challenging problems in disciplines like computer vision, natural language processing, and speech recognition. A DNN's power rests in its capacity to extract complex characteristics autonomously, gradually deepening its comprehension of the material through more layers. This revolutionary approach, known as feature learning, has driven remarkable advancements in image classification, language translation, and autonomous driving. Deep neural networks are beneficial for jobs with plenty of data. However, it is vital to recognise that training them requires significant computer resources and large datasets, making them potentially tricky for situations with little or unstructured data. Deep neural networks continue to change the face of current technology and fuel advancements in machine perception and decision-making, as they are the engine behind many ground-breaking A.I. applications. Using its capacity to automatically extract sophisticated characteristics from network data for enhanced threat detection and network security, Deep Neural Networks play a crucial role in intrusion detection systems[38].
3. **Convolutional Neural Network:** A crucial deep learning architecture designed specifically for image analysis and recognition applications is the convolutional neural network (CNN). A CNN fundamentally designs itself to automatically and adaptively discover patterns, features, and hierarchical representations from visual input. Convolutional layers of this network design use convolution operations on the input data to efficiently capture local and global information while maintaining spatial links. When used with pooling layers, CNNs are excellent at identifying important characteristics inside pictures, which lower the spatial dimensions and computational complexity. Using fully linked layers enables classification and high-level reasoning based on learned characteristics. As a result of their excellent success in computer vision, object detection, and

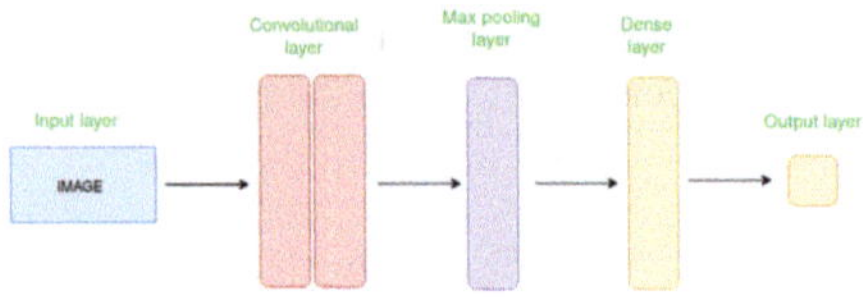

Fig. 10 C.N.N. representation

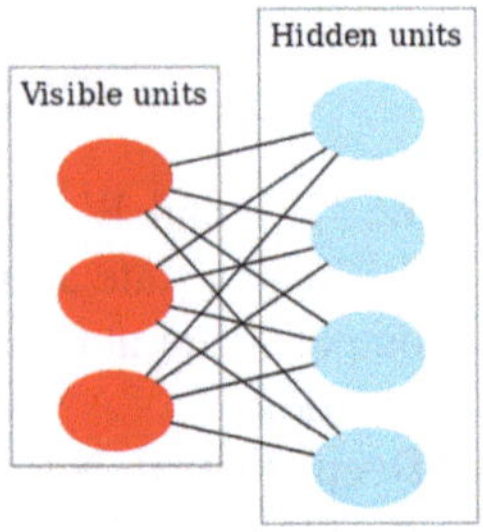

Fig. 11 D.B.N representation [58]

image classification, CNNs have become indispensable in various fields, such as autonomous vehicles, medical imaging, and tasks requiring natural language processing when combined with methods like word embeddings. Xiao et al. [95] proposed an I.D.S. that utilizes CNNs for effective intrusion detection. They employed P.C.A. and A.E. to extract one-dimensional features into a two-dimensional matrix for CNN input. Using the KDD Cup'99 dataset, experiments showed shorter training and testing periods. In contrast to other attack classes, U2R and R2L showed reduced detection rates (Fig. 10).

4. **Deep Belief Network:** A significant development in deep learning and artificial neural networks is the Deep Belief Network (DBN). It consists of several layers of latent, stochastic variables often organised as a stack of restricted Boltzmann machines. DBNs are very good at identifying complex hierarchical representations of data, which makes them adept at identifying complex patterns and characteristics. These networks are used for tasks like dimensionality reduction, feature learning, and pre-training for ensuing supervised learning models because they perform well in unsupervised learning tasks. DBNs' ability to encode high-dimensional input data into a lower-dimensional latent space, which enables data compression and simplicity, is one of its essential properties. Fundamentally, Deep Belief Networks have significantly advanced deep learning, particularly in scenarios involving large, complex datasets where hierarchical feature extraction is essential for achieving superior performance in tasks like image and speech recognition, natural language processing, and more. Marir et al. [58] developed a distributed model for large-scale network intrusion detection using a multilayer ensemble Support Vector Machine (SVM) architecture and Deep Belief Networks (DBN) for feature extraction. The system, based on Apache Spark, demonstrated its effectiveness and applicability for distributed intrusion detection tasks by showing high-performance results in identifying anomalous behaviour across a variety of datasets, including KDD CUP'99, NSL-KDD, UNSW-NB15, and CICIDS2017 (Fig. 11).

5. **Autoencoder:** Researchers use a fundamental type of neural network called autoencoders for dimensionality reduction and unsupervised learning applications. The encoder and decoder in these neural networks cooperate to compress and recreate input data. An autoencoder's primary goal is to provide a compressed representation (encoding) of the input data that preserves important characteristics and patterns. The capacity of autoencoders to extract valuable representations from highly dimensional data proves essential in various domains, including feature learning, anomaly detection, and image denoising. Autoencoders are a valuable tool in the toolbox of deep learning approaches because they may reveal hidden structures and reduce data dimensionality by training on unlabeled data. Yan et al. [96] developed an intrusion detection system (I.D.S.) that used a Stacked Sparse Autoencoder (SSAE) in combination with Support Vector Machines (SVM) in their investigation. SVM was used as the classifier in this innovative strategy, while SSAE was used to extract features. They investigated problems in binary-class and multi-class classification, which allowed them to assess model performance in depth. The NSL-KDD dataset illustrated the model's superior performance compared to several feature selection, machine learning (ML), and deep learning (DL) approaches. Although the model showed great detection rates for U2R and R2L assaults, it had considerable difficulty correctly categorising other attack types in the sample. This finding highlights the difficulties in maintaining balanced intrusion detection across many types.

   The forward propagation of an autoencoder can be represented as follows:

$$z = encoder(x) \tag{9}$$

$$x_hat = decoder(z) \tag{10}$$

   'x' stands for the input data, 'z' stands for the latent representation, and 'x_hat' speaks for the output data that was reconstituted.

1.7.3 Fuzzy Computing Based Methods for I.D.S.

A reliable approach to solving issues with ambiguity or uncertainty is fuzzy computing. Generally, fuzzy set theory and fuzzy logic are the two main elements of this strategy. Fuzzy computing makes it straightforward to get precise and apparent answers from unclear or erroneous settings. A powerful tool for language-based computations, fuzzy set theory, a fundamentally graded notion, allows for partial membership of items inside a set and provides a flexible mechanism to translate linguistic words into fuzzy sets. On the other hand, fuzzy logic's ability to simulate human decision-making while considering ambiguous or approximative data results in exact answers. It may also resolve categorization issues by producing 'IF-THEN' fuzzy rules depending on the information. Fuzzy computing, which includes fuzzy set theory and fuzzy logic, provides valuable answers to challenging issues when faced with ambiguity.

1. **Fuzzy Set:** A "fuzzy set," a fundamental concept in fuzzy logic, may convey ambiguity and uncertainty in data or information. In contrast to the prominent binary membership that is the focus of classical set theory (an item is either related to a set or not), fuzzy sets add the concept of partial membership. As a result, entries in a fuzzy set may have variable degrees of membership, represented as membership values between 0 and 1. These membership values represent how much an element belongs to or how much it possesses the traits listed in the fuzzy collection. In domains like artificial intelligence, decision-making systems, and control theory, where exact binary distinctions may not accurately represent real-world complexity, fuzzy sets are essential for modelling and processing imprecise or ambiguous data.
2. **Fuzzy Logic:** An essential part of fuzzy computing, fuzzy Logic is a mathematical framework that excels at dealing with uncertainties and ambiguous data. This approach, developed by Professor Lofti A. Zadeh, mimics how people make decisions by considering shaky or approximate information and producing exact results. Fuzzy Logic has the benefit of simulating the complexity of actual decision-making, which makes it especially suitable for applications ranging from control systems to artificial intelligence. It significantly resolves categorization issues by generating 'IF-THEN' fuzzy rules based on the given data. Fuzzy Logic's adaptability covers many applications, providing workable answers where standard binary Logic fails owing to uncertainty and imprecision.
3. **Fuzzy Theory:** A key element of fuzzy computing is fuzzy theory, which incorporates a flexible and understandable method for dealing with complicated issues characterised by ambiguity or uncertainty. It supports the fundamental ideas of fuzzy set theory and fuzzy logic, making it easier to extract exact answers from ambiguous or inaccurate situations. The gradational aspect of fuzzy set theory, which accepts partial memberships inside sets, makes it possible to easily translate verbal statements into fuzzy sets, enhancing language-based calculations. Fuzzy logic mimics human decision-making processes and produces exact results while considering ambiguous or rough data inputs. Fuzzy logic also works well for resolving classification issues by producing 'IF-THEN' fuzzy rules based on the existing dataset. In conclusion, fuzzy theory, as it relates to fuzzy computing, is a strong and flexible instrument for tackling complex issues characterised by ambiguity and uncertainty.

Using fuzzy computing in intrusion detection systems (I.D.S.) greatly aids in improving network security and threat detection [36]. I.D.S. can successfully deal with the inherent ambiguity and uncertainty associated with network traffic patterns and intrusion behaviours by utilising fuzzy logic and fuzzy set theory. I.D.S. can model and analyse complex, dynamic network environments thanks to fuzzy computing, which enables the system to react quickly to new threats. It simplifies the development of linguistic variables and fuzzy rules, enabling I.D.S. to assess the degree to which network events belong to established intrusion categories, enabling more sophisticated and context-aware threat detection.

1.8 Datasets Used for I.D.S. in IoT Nework

IoT network security relies on datasets with information about known threats and abnormalities used by intrusion detection systems (I.D.S.). Public network datasets, real network datasets, and simulated network datasets are the three primary datasets utilized in I.D.S. Real network datasets contain details on the behavior and patterns of the network. In contrast, public network datasets are open and offer the most recent threat intelligence. Simulated IoT network environments provide simulated datasets to evaluate I.D.S. under-regulated settings. These datasets are used to test the efficiency of I.D.S. in identifying and reducing possible risks as well as to train machine learning algorithms. Regular updates and expansion of these datasets are essential for the I.D.S. to effectively identify new and developing threats and defend IoT networks from security flaws (Table 3).

1.8.1 Datasets from Public Networks

I.D.S. systems rely on datasets with details on known threats and abnormalities. Public network datasets are one form of the dataset used in I.D.S. for IoT network security. These databases, available to the general public, provide details about recognized security flaws and attacks. In I.D.S., they are frequently used to train machine learning algorithms to find risks and abnormalities. Several advantages come from using public network information in I.D.S., including increased I.D.S. performance, access to the most recent threat intelligence, and the capacity to identify new and emerging threats. These databases are often updated with the most recent threat information, which makes them an essential tool for organizations trying to strengthen their I.D.S. capabilities. Organizations may keep ahead of the curve in IoT network security and prevent possible risks before they might harm the network by using public network datasets in I.D.S.

- DARPA 2000 datasets: well-known dataset frequently used to assess alert correlation studies is the DARPA-2000 dataset. This dataset, which the Lincoln Lab produced at the Massachusetts Institute of Technology (M.I.T.) in the United States, comprises the multi-stage scenarios LLDDOS 1.0 and LLDDOS 2.0.2. A set of attack events intended to start distributed denial of service (DDoS) attacks is included in both attack scenarios. This dataset has been used in some related works to evaluate alert correlation models. The LLDOS 1.0 attack sequence involves five main steps[102]. The attacker performs an IP scan to find active hosts in the first step. The second phase, the adversarial probe, verifies whether the sadmind service is active on the host. In the third stage, called breakins, the attacker gains root access to the host by exploiting a flaw in the sadmind program running on Solaris. The fourth phase, installation, and initialization, involves installing and initializing the trojan mstream DDoS software. Finally, in the fifth and final phase, the attacker launches a DDOS attack on the targeted IP.

Table 3 A few datasets used for I.D.S. in IoT network

Dataset	Description
NSL-KDD	The dataset is a benchmark for evaluating intrusion detection methods and resolving KDD'99 issues. The dataset comprises nearly 4.9 million individual connection vectors, each having 41 attributes and labeled as either a specific attack type or normal. The dataset contains four different forms of attacks: DoS, R2L, U2R, and probing.
Kyoto 2006+	A team produced this dataset by collecting real network traffic data over 3 years. The researchers classified the dataset into three categories: normal, known attacks, and unknown attacks. The dataset includes ten new features and the 14 numerical features from KDD Cup'99.
CSIC 2010 HTTP	This dataset contains many web requests, including normal (36,000) and unusual (25,000) ones. The labeling of the dataset follows the attack type, which includes information collection, buffer overflow, CRLF injection, server-side, XSS, parameter manipulation, file disclosure, and parameter tampering. The requests were automatically created and offered valuable data for researching and identifying potential security issues.
IoTID20	This dataset, one of the newest ones used to simulate network attacks from two smart devices, is designed for Intrusion Detection Systems (IDS). It has 83 network features and three extra features, and it contains five threat types: DoS, Mirai, scan, MITM, and routine threats. The dataset, which has 625,783 records, is an essential tool for network security researchers and practitioners.
DS2OS	This IoT middleware includes data and smart space services. It includes an extensive dataset with 477,426 entries and 14 different attributes per entry. Five attack classes–normal, DDoS, MITM, scan incorrect setup, and data type probing–are used to group the entries.
UNSW's Bot-IoT	This dataset provides a unique combination of botnet and regular traffic, facilitating the study and comparison of the two. CSV, original pcap, and produced argus file formats are all accessible for the source files. A vital resource for cybersecurity research, the dataset comprises a variety of threats, including keylogging, service and OS scanning, DoS, DDoS, and data exfiltration.
KDD-Cup 1999	Researchers utilize the dataset, which consists of almost 5 million records with 41 features categorized into four types of attacks (DoS, R2L, U2R, and Probe), for intrusion simulations and data audits..
UNSW-NB15	The UNSW-NB15 dataset provides nine types of attacks for NIDS research and testing.
ISOT	This dataset, which combines malicious and non-malicious datasets, contains various network trace data, including emails, streaming media, and backup media. The collection includes the Waledac and Zeus botnets. The attacks included in the dataset provide a detailed illustration of network security risks.
ADFA-LD	The dataset contains records for the Linux operating system and data on several types of attacks, including Adduser, meterpreter, Webshell, hydra-SHH, Java-interpreter, and hydra-FTP.This dataset intends to enable researchers to analyze and develop more efficient cybersecurity solutions, particularly in evaluating machine learning- and data-based intrusion detection systems in the cybersecurity industry.

Table 3 (continued)

NN-BaIoT	This dataset includes the botnets Bashlite and Mirai, information on DDoS assaults, and two different forms of botnets.
Alert Sharing Platform (SABU) dataset	The Alert Sharing Platform (SABU) dataset comprises about 10 million alerts and events collected from various security tools like network sensors and honeypots. It contains data about malware infections, network intrusion attempts, and suspicious activities detected by security systems. The dataset also holds contextual information like timestamps, source IP addresses, destination IP addresses, and attack types, which can aid further research and analysis.

- KDD: The KDD 99 Dataset collects network traffic data created based on the information gathered during the DARPA'98 I.D.S.evaluation program. The dataset contains 41 features and is used to evaluate research in Alerts Correlation. The network traffic is labeled as either regular activity or an attack activity. The attacks are classified into four categories, namely, user-to-root attack (U2R), denial of service attack (DoS), remote-to-local attack (R2L), and probing attack. This dataset is widely used in machine learning and data mining research for intrusion detection systems and security applications. Researchers suggested the NSL-KDD dataset as a solution to the KDD-99 cup dataset's drawbacks. Researchers selected a subset of the original KDD records to create the NSL-KDD dataset to address the limitations of the KDD-99 dataset. Researchers explicitly chose this dataset to eliminate the issues present in the KDD-99 dataset and improve its quality. Tavallaee et al. [87] created NSL-KDD to improve KDD-99's limitations and fix its problems. The authors point out several difficulties and potential limits using NSL-KDD, however. For instance, the statistics might not indicate low-footprint attacks [59].

1.8.2 Datasets from Real Networks

Unauthorized access, exploitation, and attacks on computer systems and networks are all things intrusion detection systems (I.D.S.) are made to find and stop. Datasets, including examples of typical and abnormal network traffic, are used by researchers as well as practitioners to train and evaluate I.D.S. algorithms. These datasets may be gathered from real networks or artificially created networks. However, datasets from real networks offer a better representation of real network behavior and attacks. Therefore, real network datasets in I.D.S. creation and assessment can produce more precise and trustworthy findings.

- KYOTO2006+: The Kyoto 2006+ datasets are an essential tool for assessing alert correlation studies. These datasets were produced automatically from total network traffic gathered between November 2006 and August 2009 at the University of Kyoto in Japan. Twenty-four statistical features are included in the datasets, including 14 traditional characteristics taken from the KDD99 datasets and ten novel features[78]. These characteristics help analyze network behavior and security concerns because they offer insightful information about the events and activities that take place there. Researchers researching network security and intrusion detection should use the Kyoto 2006+ datasets as a valuable resource.

- Alert Sharing Platform (SABU) dataset: which compiles intrusion alerts from several intrusion detection systems in diverse organizations, is the first of its kind[33]. Nearly 12 million alerts total is included in the dataset, which was collected from 34 I.D.S., honeypots, and other data sources across three separate organizations. The alerts are categorized using the eCSIRT.net taxonomy and presented using the (IDEA) format. A descriptive data model is utilized with the IDEA format, a contemporary JSON structure. Several research projects have tested the alert prediction and correlation models using this dataset.

1.8.3 Datasets from Simulated Networks

An integral part of intrusion detection systems is datasets from simulated networks. These datasets serve as simulations of real-world scenarios and aid in assessing how well intrusion detection systems work [46]. Web browsing, email correspondence, and file transfers are just a few examples of the different network traffic kinds that customized simulations may replicate. Denial-of-service attacks, port scans, and malware infections are just a few of the attack types that may be included in the created datasets. These datasets allow for the testing and development of intrusion detection algorithms that efficiently identify and reduce cyber risks. These datasets are also essential for creating machine-learning models to identify network breaches precisely.

2 Metrics for Assessing Intrusion Detection in IoT

Based on current research and works, the following metrics have been found and categorized for evaluating intrusion detection systems (I.D.S.) in Internet of Things environments. These metrics are essential for assessing I.D.S.'s timeliness, efficacy, and efficiency in Internet of Things networks.

2.1 Detection Accuracy Metrics

These metrics assess an intrusion detection system's accuracy and dependability in distinguishing malicious and legitimate activity.

- **Accuracy:** As a crucial measure, the system correctly distinguishes between positive and negative events from all recorded occurrences. Researchers often use this metric to evaluate the overall effectiveness of Internet of Things intrusion detection systems.[89]

- **Precision and Recall:** Precision quantifies the percentage of true positives among all identified positives, whereas recall (sensitivity) assesses the system's capacity to identify every true positive. These metrics are essential for assessing detection techniques, which must balance missing and false positive detections.[89]
- **False Positive Rate (FPR):** In IoT networks, a high F.P.R. can result in unwanted interventions and waste of energy in devices with limited resources.[89]
- **Area Under the ROC Curve (AUC-ROC):** This metric provides the tradeoffs between the true and false positive rates at different levels.[73]

2.2 Resource Consumption Metrics

With limited computing power, memory, and energy available in IoT systems, these metrics evaluate how efficient I.D.S. is with these resources.

- **CPU Utilization and Memory Usage:** IoT devices often have limited resources. Thus, it is crucial to monitor their CPU load and memory utilization. A recent study emphasizes the significance of efficient, lightweight models running on Internet of Things (IoT) hardware, such as Raspberry Pi.[19]
- **Energy Consumption:** The use of energy is a significant issue since a large number of IoT devices rely on batteries. In particular, for large-scale IoT installations, energy consumption metrics aid in assessing an I.D.S.'s long-term viability.[26]

2.3 Timeliness Metrics

Critical for real-time applications in IoT networks, these metrics centre on the I.D.S.'s responsiveness and quickness.

- **Detection Time:** The Detection Time metric tracks how long an intrusion detection system (I.D.S.) takes to notice an attack after it has happened. This statistic becomes even more critical when we need to respond quickly to reduce possible harm.[1]
- **Response Time:** This metric evaluates response and decision-making for every I.D.S.'s incoming input. Reducing the reaction time is essential for a time-sensitive and successful intrusion prevention system in IoT applications.[9]

2.4 Other Metrics

- **Scalability:** How well an intrusion detection system (I.D.S.) handles changes in network size and data volume is a measure of its scalability. Internet of Things (IoT) settings must be scalable to accommodate substantial future growth.[25]
- **Resilience:** The resilience of an I.D.S. is the ability to handle environmental changes and various attacks. High resilience is the operation in various network environments.[93]

3 Case Studies and Applications

Intrusion Detection Systems are systems used for surveillance of network traffic and device activity aimed at spotting threatening behaviours and anomalies likely to compromise the system's security. Because devices running in the Internet of Things systems generally have limited resources and operate in highly dynamic, geographically dispersed contexts, intrusion detection systems (I.D.S.) are an essential layer of security in these systems. I.D.S. is vital in IoT since it helps to detect illegal access, data breaches, and cyber-attacks, thereby maintaining the integrity and availability of IoT systems. Intrusion Detection Systems (I.D.S.) improve security but can create problems like resource consumption, false positives, and the complexity of maintaining many Internet of Things devices. Section 3 shows Some cases were Intrusion Detection Systems are being significantly required.

3.1 Case Study I: Fancy Bear IoT Attacks (2024)

The Fancy Bear IoT attacks of 2024 were an attempt at surveillance and disruption by state-sponsored hackers that targeted critical infrastructure and military IoT devices. These Internet of Things devices were prone to complex attacks that attempted to steal data and disrupt services, because they often lacked adequate security measures. The intrusion detection system played a crucial role in these instances by spotting suspicious activity inside the network, such as unusual traffic patterns or illegal access, early on, reducing the impact of the the attack [77].

Russian hackers were behind the Fancy Bear IoT attack, an integrated cyber operation that targeted military and highly susceptible IoT devices. Using the insufficient security mechanisms of the Internet of Things device, the attackers created a massive botnet to allow surveillance and perform Distributed Denial of Service (DDoS) operations. By compromising these machines, the hackers gained access to private data and stopped important operations. By isolating devices impacted by identifying unusual abnormalities in network traffic and patterns of communications, deploying intrusion detection systems across many infrastructues permitted It must to have deactivated the compromised nodes and implemented improved encryption and access restrictions if we are to stop the assault from happening any further.

IoT environments require effective IDS, as the Fancy Bear attack shown. The capacity of IDS to identify and resist the attack prior to its complete penetration of critical infrastructure systems was a significant advantage. Redirecting traffic and upgrading security rules were two of the quick actions made possible by this early notice, which reduced the long-term impact. On the other hand, the attack brought to light a number of drawbacks of IDS in IoT networks, most notably the large amount of false positives caused by the unpredictable behaviors of IoT devices. In addition, IDS has difficulties due to the resource-constrained nature of many IoT devices because real-time monitoring and analysis need a lot of processing power. Considering these challenges, the intrusion detection systems were very crucial in minimizing losses to important assets during the attack.

3.2 Case Study II: Plundervolt (2023)

Plundervolt (2023) is a hardware-based attack that takes advantage of the voltage-regulating capability of Intel CPUs, primarily aimed against Intel Secure Guard Extensions (S.G.X.). In this situation, adversaries alter the voltage provided to the CPU, which causes errors within the secure areas that conduct significant computations. Computers and other electronic equipment are vulnerable to hardware tampering because of their complex behaviour and the limited resources available in their environments. I.D.S. have the capability to do a huge number of tasks, the most essential of that being its capacity to maintain the integrity of computer processes, recognize abnormalities, and minimize the probability that vulnerabilities will be attacked.

The Plundervolt attack made benefits from Intel CPU abilities to scale voltage. Intruders created vulnerabilities that compromised the integrity of the information being processed by making tiny alterations to voltage levels throughout important computations within Intel S.G.X. regions. Considerable breach of privacy or improper use of confidential information may result from this tampering. In order to tackle the matter, Intel introduced microcode modifications that paused CPUs particularly those with SGX technology from undervolting under particular conditions. The approach needed to set up firmware modifications for an enormous amount of IoT devices with insecure Intel CPUs. In order to tackle the matter, Intel introduced microcode modifications that paused CPUs particularly those with S.G.X. technology from undervolting under particular conditions. The approach needed to set up firmware modifications for an enormous amount of IoT devices with insecure Intel CPUs.

Furthermore, hardware attacks such as Plundervolt [63] need very specific detection algorithms that typical I.D.S. systems may not consistently incorporate. Although these challenges, the function of I.D.S. in mitigating hardware

Table 4 Some cases were intrusion detection systems are being significant

Attack	Year	Target	Impact
Stuxnet	2010	ICS, notably Iranian nuclear plants.	The first IoT/ICS malware. It damaged centrifuges and PLCs.
Mirai Botnet	2016	A router, IP camera, and DVR like IoT devices.	The Mirai botnet controlled hundreds of thousands of IoT devices, DDoSing Twitter, Netflix, and Reddit.
BrickerBot	2017	Devices in IoT environment	This spyware corrupted storage on over 10 million devices, leaving them useless. A "permanent denial-of-service" strike.
Prowli Malware	2018	Modems, routers, and NAS are like devices.	Prowli mined bitcoin and implanted malware on over 40,000 devices, demonstrating the financial motivations behind IoT attacks.
Silex Malware	2019	Smart thermostats, cameras, and Routers.	Silex corrupted firmware, deleted data, and rendered IoT devices inoperable like BrickerBot.
Ripple20	2020	Many IoT devices employing Treck's TCP/IP stack.	Ripple20 affected millions of devices in healthcare and critical infrastructure with 19 vulnerabilities. It gave attackers remote device control.
Cicada	2021	military, healthcareand other industries.	A Chinese state-sponsored effort targeting IoT devices to steal high-value target data over time.
Plundervolt	2023	Intel chips in several IoT devices.	Plundervolt caused Intel SGX errors in secure enclaves, possibly leaking data and compromising devices.

vulnerabilities such as Plundervolt is essential for defending critical IoT devices. In the Plundervolt attack, I.D.S. discovered IoT device voltage patterns and behaviors. This instance depicted how I.D.S. may track hardware activities for environmental risks and illegal modifications. Although they could potentially recognize such initiatives, I.D.S. have several drawbacks. False positives from I.D.S. might cause needless IoT interventions, particularly with limited resources (Table 4).

3.3 Case Study III: BlueBorne (2017)

BlueBorne serves a significant risk that influence Bluetooth-enabled IoT devices, such as cell phones, smart televisions, smartwatches, and several connected devices as well. The Bluetooth protocol encountered a breach in security, letting intruders to obtain access to devices without requiring any involvement of individuals. The attack came to light in 2017 and obtained focus for the ability it had to distribute malware by wireless via Bluetooth, providing it particularly unsafe in environments where IoT devices are closely connected and in continuous contact. IDS in IoT perform an essential part in controlling network traffic and communication between devices. They identify anomalies and alert administrators to potential attacks, such as BlueBorne, before significant damage can take place.BlueBorne took advantage of multiple vulnerabilities within the Bluetooth protocol on a range of platforms, such as Android, iOS, Windows, and Linux.

Exploiting these vulnerabilities gave attackers full control over susceptible machines, sensitive information, and remote malware executions. The vulnerability compromised thousands of IoT devices internationally. Systems promptly improve safety by minimizing risk. IDSs must be efficient to stop attacks of this kind. IDS recognized Bluetooth abnormalities, illegal access attempts to harm them, and network attacks. This early detection tactics quarantined attacked endpoints and limited communications, limiting attack severity.IoT intrusion detection remedies are of extreme importance due to security vulnerabilities like BlueBorne. IDS discovered the threat instantly enabling administrators contain it. The complexity of handling intrusion detection systems throughout various connected device environments may make real-time detection challenging, and numerous IoT devices possess constraints on resources that may diminish the effectiveness for specific intrusion detection approaches. Although these challenges, IDS plays an essential role in defending IoT networks against sophisticated attacks like BlueBorne.

3.4 Applications of Intrusion Detection Systems in IoT Network

Monitoring and detecting suspicious activity in IoT environments need Intrusion Detection Systems (I.D.S.). IoT I.D.S. detects unauthorized access and unusual traffic patterns to protect data integrity, confidentiality, and availability. I.D.S. protects significantly distributed devices with different processing capabilities in IoT networks. The following applications are notable contributions that intrusion detection systems can give to protect the IoT network.

- **IoT-based Critical Infrastructure Protection:** IoT device security from cyberattacks is an essential function of intrusion detection systems (IDS) in critical infrastructures [66], including water supply networks, smart grids, and transportation systems. IDS employs lightweight methods for detecting anomalies to enable low latency monitoring, which is essential given that many IoT devices have limited resources. By identifying unusual device behaviors, intrusion detection systems (IDS) secure critical infrastructure system dependability by preventing man-in-the-middle (MitM) and command injection attacks.
- **Advanced DDoS Mitigation in Enterprise Networks:** Large industrial networks need IDS solutions to prevent DDoS attacks. IDS analyze network traffic for anomalous patterns that might indicate a DDoS attack pattern, including traffic flooding targeted activities. In order to assist network administrators in identifying malicious activity and ensuring network availability, the IDS employs machine learning to detect anomalous traffic rises. The IDS automatically eliminates abnormal traffic in conjunction with firewalls and load balancers.

- **Intrusion Detection in Smart Cities and Urban Networks:** Smart cities use IoT devices for trash management, public safety, and traffic control, making IDS important to their cybersecurity architecture [35]. IDS uses artificial intelligence and graph-based learning models in these networks to detect sophisticated multi-vector threats that threaten smart city subsystem integration. Integrating IDS with real-time monitoring may help smart cities avoid major network outages or data breaches that might harm critical infrastructure.
- **Securing Healthcare IoT Systems and Medical Devices:** IDS protects patient data and device reliability in healthcare IoT networks including pacemakers, insulin pumps, and hospital systems. IDS systems with deep packet inspection and anomaly detection can identify unauthorized access, data tampering, and malware infections in healthcare networks [6]. HIPAA-compliant IDS guarantees patient data from external attacks.
- **Industrial Control System (ICS) and SCADA Network Security:** ICS and SCADA networks need IDS to detect cyber-physical threats [21]. Attackers attack these networks to disrupt operations or injure people. Intrusion detection systems (IDS) use behavioral anomaly detection for zero-day attacks and signature-based detection for known vulnerabilities. Intrusion detection systems (IDS) prevent cyberattacks that damage equipment, operational failures, or safety by monitoring important assets like HMIs and PLCs.
- **Cloud and Virtual Environment Security:** IDS systems are becoming more important in identifying and preventing cloud-specific attacks as cloud computing and virtualization rise. A virtualized IDS appliance may monitor cloud container-VM communication for data exfiltration, privilege escalation, and unauthorized VM access. Modern cloud IDS systems link with SDN for dynamic threat monitoring throughout the cloud architecture[80].
- **Securing 5G Networks and Telecom Infrastructure:** IDS defends 5G telecom infrastructure from advanced attacks that threaten network slicing, VNFs, and mobile edge computing. In 5G networks, intrusion detection systems (IDS) utilize distributed detection and AI-driven analytics to identify new threats including signaling storms, SIM-jacking, and attacks that exploit SDN flaws. Since IDS detects threats in real time, 5G services are safe and trustworthy.

4 Emerging Trends and Technologies in I.D.S.

With the expansion of connected devices within the Internet of Things (IoT) ecosystem and the complexity of cyber threats, Intrusion Detection Systems (I.D.S.) have been advancing fast. According to recent breakthroughs, anomaly detection methods, real-time analytics, and machine learning algorithms are the primary concerns that impact the future generation of intrusion detection systems. Improving detection accuracy is only the beginning. These advances are taking on essential problems like scalability, energy efficiency, and reaction speed, which are vital for implementing I.D.S. in contexts with limited resources. Researchers and professionals generally keep a close eye on I.D.S.'s capacity to adapt to dynamic threats, minimize false positives, and optimize resource usage as IoT networks keep growing.

4.1 Blockchain for Intrusion Detection

Blockchain technology is essential in developing and advancing intrusion detection systems for IoT networks; this technology can reduce most security vulnerabilities. The dispersed and resource-constrained networks like Internet of Things (IoT) networks can be protected using the decentralized, irreversible, and transparent properties of Blockchain. Regarding the cons of blockchain technology in intrusion detection systems, traditional systems typically have a single point of failure. The decentralized method removes the problem and makes the I.D.S. more resistant to attacks.

Even though blockchain technology offers intelligent contracts, the intrusion detection system runs automatically to make the detection and response activities [64]. Automatic actions like isolation of devices and alert generation for specific security incidents are made possible by intelligent contracts. The consistency and timeliness of response to various security incidents are kept automated, and the need for human intervention is entirely removed by using this method. Blockchain requires resources like energy and electricity, which remain the primary constraints; the low-powered IoT device may be affected because of this issue. Integrating blockchain with edge computing can help reduce latency resource consumption and employ lightweight consensus methods; it is a discipline of ongoing research focused on solving problems.

4.2 AI and Machine Learning Advancements

More effective intrusion detection systems are required; hence, the number of IoT devices and networks is increasing daily. The sudden increase in IoT devices in the previous decade has caused many risks in terms of security and provides the most effective and versatile intrusion detection system. Studies have found that models made by AI can effectively sort over terabytes of data, detect anomalies, and predict potential safety violations. Due to these enhancements, I.D.S. is now more suitable for setting up IoT scenarios with limited resources, as it concurrently enhances detection effectiveness and minimises resource utilisation. Maintaining reliable safety measures throughout different and dynamic IoT networks is becoming increasingly dependent on applying A.I. and ML into I.D.S. as the number of connected devices and networks increases.

- Explainable A.I. (X.A.I.): The explainable decision-making processes used in artificial intelligence to develop models are called explainable A.I. (X.A.I.), which makes the A.I. model's decisions by providing transparency and accountability. Several rules and boundaries allied with traditional black-box models make it tedious to understand the problems. The X.A.I. achieves the performance of the I.D.S. for IoT by advancing decision-making and strengthening security, allowing network administrators and security analysts to identify risks and understand the logic behind these detections. The X.A.I. is a more crucial and valuable technology in I.D.S. frameworks since the X.A.I. can explain all the reasons and increase the transparency of network traffic and network data.

  Explainable A.I. improves the interpretability of A.I. models without compromising their accuracy [47], and they stand more transparently available for the human understandable mode. In I.D.S., the detection is made more transparent and clear for decision-making. In some critical systems where the decision should be accurate, this transparent model could make the detection and prevention mechanism more possible. The X.A.I. base I.D.S. equally holds the merits and demerits, which are better in transparency, but the model slightly lags regarding complexity. But it still has substantial accuracy.
- Transfer Learning: Transfer Learning (T.L.)'s basic idea is that the starting point for a model on a second task is used as the first task's model or other models developed. Regarding the applicability in intrusion detection systems for IoT networks, cases like limited datasets and the cost to get datasets in specific environments, T.L. used to adapt models on large-scale data. Advanced labelled data needs are replaced by introducing the T.L., which can advance the performance of several targeted areas from information similar to related works [98]. Similarly, it holds a disadvantage in that the information gathered from the related works should only sometimes be compatible with the targeted areas, which reduces the accuracy and performance of the complete system.
- Federated Learning: The federated learning approach keeps data local while training the models across several nodes or devices. This decentralized method simplifies the machine learning methodology[28]. When traditional centralized processes fail or are not viable, problems with privacy and bandwidth emerge, and the same becomes essential. Protecting and maintaining user privacy and network load is the goal of F.L., which the Internet of Things can do while also understanding infiltration tendencies. The F.L. significantly improves the detection system by providing the ability to adapt to different conditions.
- Neuro symbolic A.I.: The symbolic A.I.'s reasoning capability and the neural networks's pattern recognition capability converge to come forward with the trending neuro-symbolic A.I. (N.S.A.I.). Regarding intrusion detection systems, N.S.A.I. provides efficient solutions by utilizing rule-based and data-driven approaches to identify known and unknown threats. Also, the N.S.A.I. enables the I.D.S. to differentiate between emerging and complex threats by being heterogeneous and dynamic in nature. The neural networks and symbolic reasoning can provide many advantages, offering a better I.D.S. system for IoT Networks.

In resource-constrained IoT devices, N.S.A.I. is not practical but is interpretable and has sound reasoning skills.

- Context-aware A.I.: A system that adapts to its current environment is termed Context-aware AI. The intrusion detection systems use the understanding capability of the device or the network's context awareness feature. These technologies are continuously evolving and heterogeneous, more adaptive and responsive to defence techniques. Context-aware A.I. systems deal with all context comparison and data processing, which is more complex in processing and vast in data since it may need more computing power and resources[69].

4.3 Quantum Computing/ML for I.D.S.

Integrating quantum computing and machine learning (ML) into intrusion detection systems makes one of the innovative method of protecting IoT networks. Quantum computing has improved the speed and precision with which machine learning models can analyze data. Quantum machine learning significantly improves the detection of complex and previously unknown attacks in I.D.S. for IoT by doing computations that traditional computers cannot. I.D.S. relies on quantum ML for more robust protection against dynamic cyber attacks in IoT networks due to its ability to handle large data sets swiftly and precisely. Quantum computing is to be stepping into the world of technology; the main cons are that it is not yet accessible to the public and may take a while to make it available. How quantum machine learning can be used and how they can improve the performance of the detection mechanism is discussed in [20]. As per their findings, quantum machine learning can significantly optimize I.D.S. performance.

4.4 Cognitive Computing and IDS

Cognitive Computing mainly incorporates A.I., machine learning, and natural language processing, and it is crucial for enhancing intrusion detection systems (I.D.S.) in IoT networks [43]. Cognitive Computing assists I.D.S. by replicating human cognitive functions, permitting the system to gain insight from historical information, recognize patterns, and make contextually reliable real-time decisions. Cognitive computing enables Intrusion Detection Systems to adaptively respond to emerging threats in IoT networks, defined by devices producing diverse data. Cognitive Computing plays a crucial part in I.D.S. by rapidly processing vast amounts of complex data, reliably detecting abnormalities, and delivering predicting answers. Cognitive Computing has advantages in customization and decision-making; at present, it bears major processing costs, affecting its use in resource-limited IoT devices.

4.5 Zero-Trust Framework

The Zero-Trust Framework is a security paradigm that proposes defaulting to not trusting any entity within or outside a network.This approach dramatically enhances IDS in the IoT network by continuously verifying the identity and behaviour of all network nodes and apps. The zero-trust security mechanism of makes sure that not even a hacked device may access important system components without going through extensive security checks [70]. When it comes to protecting constantly changing IoT environments, where static perimeter defenses don't cut it, zero trust is key. Regardless of its strong security characteristics, zero trust could lead to performance overheads because of the continual need for verification and monitoring.

4.6 Security by Design Strategies in IDS for IoT

The objective of Security by Design is to eliminate vulnerabilities from existing in the first place, by including security measures into technology design and development from the very beginning. With the goal of offering robust, proactive protection, Security by Design in Intrusion Detection Systems (I.D.S.) for the Internet of Things (IoT) focuses on integrating security elements into the design of IoT devices and networks. Due to the variety of devices and data flows, conventional security concepts fail in IoT contexts, making our approach all the more crucial [19]. By lowering the attack surface and guaranteeing continuous security monitoring, which is able to decrease risks, this is why it is significant in IoT I.D.S. Higher overall development expenses as well as complexity due to the need for thorough security integration from the start are probable drawbacks of using these kind of solutions.

4.7 Collaborative Intrusion Detection in IoT

Collaborative Intrusion Detection in the IoT involves utilizing distributed network nodes working together to exchange data and alert details to recognise intrusions. As an outcome of the distributed structure and limited resources of many devices in IoT networks, a collaborative strategy which employs the insights collected by numerous gadgets to develop a comprehensive threat detection improves detection accuracy. The wide IoT environment can be managed by the collaborative framework.

5 Open Research Issues

1. **Detection of persistent attacks:** A.P.T. attacks are frequently highly targeted and customised, making them one of the biggest obstacles to detection. It is tough to create universal detection techniques because of this property. Additionally, A.P.T. attackers frequently employ advanced strategies to avoid detection, including traffic encryption and zero-day flaws.
2. **Detection of Encrypted Traffic Attacks:** Developing intrusion detection systems capable of detecting attacks on encrypted traffic presents a significant challenge due to the content obfuscation inherent to encryption, making identifying malicious patterns difficult.
3. **Intrusion Detection for Low-Power IoT Devices:** Creating intrusion detection systems that can effectively identify attacks on low-power IoT devices is problematic, given these devices' resource limitations, which hinder the deployment of traditional intrusion detection solutions.
4. **Detection of Attacks on A.I. and ML-Based IoT Devices:** Intrusion detection for IoT devices utilizing artificial intelligence and machine learning proves challenging due to these device's inherent complexity and intricacy, which require specialized analysis for effective threat detection.
5. **Deployment on Fog and Edge Computing Devices:** Developing intrusion detection systems deployable on fog and edge computing devices is crucial for achieving real-time intrusion detection and response, particularly in remote and resource-constrained environments with limited connectivity.
6. **Integration with Blockchain Technology:** Exploring the integration of intrusion detection systems with blockchain technology poses an opportunity to enhance the security and transparency of IoT intrusion detection, potentially mitigating issues related to trust and data integrity within these systems.

6 Conclusions and Future Directions

Over the past few decades, intrusion detection systems (I.D.S.) has tremendously advanced. Previously, I.D.S. technology relied on tools like database servers, virtual networks, and NIDS. While these technologies are still in use, I.D.S. has also integrated more recent ones like deep learning, big data, and machine learning. Looking toward the future, the advancement of I.D.S. technology will depend significantly on the quality of training data and machine learning algorithms. Sharing pertinent security data amongst reputable organizations can develop more efficient I.D.S. systems by enhancing the training data for DNNs and machine learning algorithms.

Another benefit of the I.D.S. logging feature is that it can more effectively detect and stop intrusion detections, especially those related to attacks on network systems. In today's global environment, sharing large amounts of data has made data protection critical in organizational settings. Combining multiple intrusion detection strategies, such as those in I.D.S., into a single security solution can significantly reduce management costs. It is, therefore, essential to develop a comprehensive security strategy that can proactively prepare for any potential attack.

The growth of IoT security research and technology continues to face the challenge of increasing the effectiveness of deep learning detection. Achieving 100% detection with 0% false positives while considering IoT resource limitations is a constant struggle. Research often focuses on identifying typical behaviors of the system and relies on typical behavior training techniques while ignoring deviant behaviors. Therefore, more accurate and reliable techniques are needed to deal with harsh real-world conditions. Well-designed techniques are required to extract meaningful knowledge and information from complex data such as unexpected noise, redundancy, and imbalanced datasets. However, working with complex data requires much work and can be exhausting for a lightweight system. In this situation, one can utilize cloud computing to achieve real-time productivity.

Recent research has mainly focused on anomaly detection, with minimal attention paid to anomaly prediction and prevention. New strategies must develop and implement to stop attacks before they occur. Another new concept should be the identification of anomalies in multivariable time series. One should also consider using deep learning for intruder detection systems in smart cars like other smart equipment. There is an urgent need for updated normal and abnormal data sets related to IoT applications and services. These data sets are beneficial for testing different types and methods of Intrusion Detection Systems (I.D.S.) in IoT scenarios. These datasets are essential for making accurate and insightful Intrusion detection systems comparisons.

References

1. Abbas, S.A.A., Ibrahim, A.A.: Fortifying iot infrastructure using machine learning for ddos attack within distributed computing-based routing in networks. Qubahan Acad. J. **4**(2), 569–581 (2024)
2. Abdulhammed, R., Musafer, H., Alessa, A., Faezipour, M., Abuzneid, A.: Features dimensionality reduction approaches for machine learning based network intrusion detection. Electronics **8**(3), 322 (2019)
3. Abeshu, A., Chilamkurti, N.: Deep learning: The frontier for distributed attack detection in fog-to-things computing. IEEE Commun. Mag. **56**(2), 169–175 (2018)
4. Al-Omary, A., Othman, A., AlSabbagh, H.M., Al-Rizzo, H.: Survey of hardware-based security support for iot/cps systems. KnE Eng. 52–70 (2018)
5. Al Salami, S., Baek, J., Salah, K., Damiani, E., Lightweight encryption for smart home. In: 2016 11th International Conference on Availability, Reliability and Security (ARES), pp. 382–388. IEEE (2016)
6. Albalawi, T.S.: Smart-coord: enhancing healthcare iot-based security by blockchain coordinate systems. Int. J. Comput. Sci. Netw. Secur. **24**(8), 32–42 (2024)
7. Aldweesh, A., Derhab, A., Emam, A.Z.: Deep learning approaches for anomaly-based intrusion detection systems: a survey, taxonomy, and open issues. Knowl.-Based Syst. **189**, 105124 (2020)

8. Ali, M.H., Mohammed, B.A.D.A., Ismail, A., Zolkipli, M.F.: A new intrusion detection system based on fast learning network and particle swarm optimization. IEEE Access **6**, 20255–20261 (2018)
9. Alshaeaa, H.Y., Ghadhban, Z.M.: Developing a hybrid feature selection method to detect botnet attacks in iot devices. Kuwait J. Sci. **51**(3), 100222 (2024)
10. Attota, D.C., Mothukuri, V., Parizi, R.M., Pouriyeh, S.: An ensemble multi-view federated learning intrusion detection for iot. IEEE Access **9**, 117734–117745 (2021)
11. Bakhshi, Z., Balador, A., Mustafa, J.: Industrial iot security threats and concerns by considering cisco and microsoft iot reference models. In: 2018 IEEE Wireless Communications and Networking Conference Workshops (WCNCW), pp. 173–178. IEEE (2018)
12. Balyan, A.K., Ahuja, S., Lilhore, U.K., Sharma, S.K., Manoharan, P., Algarni, A.D., Elmannai, H., Raahemifar, K.: A hybrid intrusion detection model using ega-pso and improved random forest method. Sensors **22**(16), 5986 (2022)
13. Bangyal, W.H., Ahmad, J., Rauf, H.T., Shakir, R.: Evolving artificial neural networks using opposition based particle swarm optimization neural network for data classification. In: 2018 International Conference on Innovation and Intelligence for Informatics, Computing, and Technologies (3ICT), pp. 1–6. IEEE (2018)
14. Benaddi, H., Ibrahimi, K., Benslimane, A., Qadir, J.: A deep reinforcement learning based intrusion detection system (drl-ids) for securing wireless sensor networks and internet of things. In: Wireless Internet: 12th EAI International Conference, WiCON 2019, TaiChung, Taiwan, November 26–27, 2019, Proceedings 12, pp. 73–87. Springer (2020)
15. Bizzarri, A., Jalaian, B., Riguzzi, F., Bastian, N.D.: A neuro-symbolic artificial intelligence network intrusion detection system. In: 2024 33rd International Conference on Computer Communications and Networks (ICCCN), pp. 1–9. IEEE (2024)
16. Butun, I., Kantarci, B., Erol-Kantarci, M.: Anomaly detection and privacy preservation in cloud-centric internet of things. In: 2015 IEEE International Conference on Communication Workshop (ICCW), pp. 2610–2615. IEEE (2015)
17. Canard, S., Diop, A., Kheir, N., Paindavoine, M., Sabt, M.: Blindids: market-compliant and privacy-friendly intrusion detection system over encrypted traffic. In: Proceedings of the 2017 ACM on Asia Conference on Computer and Communications Security, pp. 561–574 (2017)
18. Cervantes, C., Poplade, D., Nogueira, M., Santos, A.: Detection of sinkhole attacks for supporting secure routing on 6lowpan for internet of things. In: 2015 IFIP/IEEE International Symposium on Integrated Network Management (IM), pp. 606–611. IEEE (2015)
19. Chaabouni, N., Mosbah, M., Zemmari, A., Sauvignac, C., Faruki, P.: Network intrusion detection for iot security based on learning techniques. IEEE Commun. Surv. Tutor. **21**(3), 2671–2701 (2019)
20. Davis, P.J., Coffey, S., Beshaj, L., Bastian, N.D.: Quantum machine learning for feature selection in internet of things network intrusion detection. In: Quantum Information Science, Sensing, and Computation XVI, vol. 13028, pp. 78–92. SPIE (2024)
21. Deng, P., Huang, Y.: Edge-featured multi-hop attention graph neural network for intrusion detection system. Comput. Secur. p. 104132 (2024)
22. Denning, D.E.: An intrusion-detection model. IEEE Trans. Softw. Eng. **2**(2), 222–232 (1987)
23. Devlin, J., Chang, M.-W., Lee, K., Toutanova, K.: Bert: pre-training of deep bidirectional transformers for language understanding. Preprint (2018). arXiv:1810.04805
24. Diro, A.A., Chilamkurti, N.: Distributed attack detection scheme using deep learning approach for internet of things. Future Gener. Comput. Syst. **82**, 761–768 (2018)
25. El-Sayed, A., Said, W., Tolba, A., Alginahi, Y., Toony, A.A.: Mp-guard: a novel multi-pronged intrusion detection and mitigation framework for scalable sd-iot networks using cooperative monitoring, ensemble learning, and new p4-extracted feature set. Comput. Electr. Eng. **118**, 109484 (2024)
26. Essa, E.I., et al.: Enhanced internet of things intrusion detection model using three-way selected random forest (3-wsrf). Nanotechnology Perceptions 515–536 (2024)
27. Garcia, S., Grill, M., Stiborek, J., Zunino, A.: An empirical comparison of botnet detection methods. Comput. Secur. **45**, 100–123 (2014)

28. Gelenbe, E., Can Gül, B., Nakıp, M.: Disfida: Distributed self-supervised federated intrusion detection algorithm with online learning for health internet of things and internet of vehicles. Internet Things 101340 (2024)
29. He, M., Huang, Y., Wang, X., Wei, P., Wang, X.: A lightweight and efficient iot intrusion detection method based on feature grouping. IEEE Internet Things J. (2023)
30. Hu, N., Tian, Z., Lu, H., Du, X., Guizani, M.: A multiple-kernel clustering based intrusion detection scheme for 5g and iot networks. Int. J. Mach. Learn. Cybern. 1–16 (2021)
31. Huang, G.-B., Zhu, Q.-Y., Siew, C.-K.: Extreme learning machine: theory and applications. Neurocomputing **70**(1–3), 489–501 (2006)
32. Husain, M.S.: Nature inspired approach for intrusion detection systems. Design Anal. Secur. Protocol Commun. 171–182 (2020)
33. Husák, M., Zádník, M., Bartos, V., Sokol, P.: Dataset of intrusion detection alerts from a sharing platform. Data Brief **33** (2020)
34. Idrissi, I., Azizi, M., Moussaoui, O.: An unsupervised generative adversarial network based-host intrusion detection system for internet of things devices. Indones. J. Electr. Eng. Comput. Sci **25**(2), 1140–1150 (2022)
35. Indra, G., Nirmala, E., Nirmala, G., Senthilvel, P.G.: An ensemble learning approach for intrusion detection in iot-based smart cities. Peer-to-Peer Netw. Appl. 1–17 (2024)
36. Jemili, F.: Intelligent intrusion detection based on fuzzy big data classification. Cluster Comput. 1–18 (2022)
37. Jia, D., Zheng, X.: A network intrusion detection model based on static property training and dynamic property correction. In: International Conference on Computing, Control and Industrial Engineering, pp. 757–763. Springer (2023)
38. Jia, Y., Wang, M., Wang, Y.: Network intrusion detection algorithm based on deep neural network. IET Inf. Secur. **13**(1), 48–53 (2019)
39. Kalnoor, G., Gowrishankar, S.: Markov decision process based model for performance analysis an intrusion detection system in iot networks. J. Telecommun. Inf. Technol. **3**(3), 42–49 (2021)
40. Karatas, G., Demir, O., Sahingoz, O.K.: Increasing the performance of machine learning-based idss on an imbalanced and up-to-date dataset. IEEE Access **8**, 32150–32162 (2020)
41. Kenarangi, F., Partin-Vaisband, I.: Exploiting machine learning against on-chip power analysis attacks: tradeoffs and design considerations. IEEE Trans. Circuits Syst. I Regular Papers **66**(2), 769–781 (2018)
42. Kenarangi, F., Partin-Vaisband, I.: Leveraging independent double-gate finfet devices for machine learning classification. IEEE Trans. Circuits Syst. I Regular Papers **66**(11), 4356–4367 (2019)
43. Khan, I.U., Ouaissa, M., Ouaissa, M., Fayaz, M., Ullah, R.: Artificial Intelligence for Intelligent Systems: Fundamentals, Challenges, and Applications. CRC Press (2024)
44. Khraisat, A., Alazab, A.: A critical review of intrusion detection systems in the internet of things: techniques, deployment strategy, validation strategy, attacks, public datasets and challenges. Cybersecurity **4**, 1–27 (2021)
45. Kim, S., Kim, S.: User preference for an iot healthcare application for lifestyle disease management. Telecommun. Policy **42**(4), 304–314 (2018)
46. Koroniotis, N., Moustafa, N., Sitnikova, E., Turnbull, B.: Towards the development of realistic botnet dataset in the internet of things for network forensic analytics: Bot-iot dataset. Future Gener. Comput. Syst. **100**, 779–796 (2019)
47. Kumar, R., Javeed, D., Aljuhani, A., Jolfaei, A., Kumar, P., Islam, A.K.M.N.: Blockchain-based authentication and explainable ai for securing consumer iot applications. IEEE Trans. Consumer Electron. **70**(1), 1145–1154 (2024)
48. Kumari, R., Singh, M.K., Jha, R., Singh, N.K., et al.: Anomaly detection in network traffic using k-mean clustering. In: 2016 3rd International Conference on Recent Advances in Information Technology (RAIT), pp. 387–393. IEEE (2016)
49. Le, A., Loo, J., Chai, K.K., Aiash, M.: A specification-based ids for detecting attacks on rpl-based network topology. Information **7**(2), 25 (2016)

50. Li, G., Niu, P., Duan, X., Zhang, X.: Fast learning network: a novel artificial neural network with a fast learning speed. Neural Comput. Appl. **24**, 1683–1695 (2014)
51. Li, D., Deng, L., Lee, M., Wang, H.: Iot data feature extraction and intrusion detection system for smart cities based on deep migration learning. Int. J. Inf. Manag. **49**, 533–545 (2019)
52. Liao, H.-J., Richard Lin, C.-H., Lin, Y.-C., Tung, K.-Y.: Intrusion detection system: a comprehensive review. J. Netw. Comput. Appl. **36**(1), 16–24 (2013)
53. Liu, Y., Yang, C., Jiang, L., Xie, S., Zhang, Y.: Intelligent edge computing for iot-based energy management in smart cities. IEEE Netw. **33**(2), 111–117 (2019)
54. Liu, Z., Thapa, N., Shaver, A., Roy, K., Yuan, X., Khorsandroo, S.: Anomaly detection on iot network intrusion using machine learning. In: 2020 International Conference on Artificial Intelligence, Big Data, Computing and Data Communication Systems (icABCD), pp. 1–5. IEEE (2020)
55. Lo, W.W., Layeghy, S., Sarhan, M., Gallagher, M., Portmann, M.: E-graphsage: a graph neural network based intrusion detection system for iot. In: NOMS 2022-2022 IEEE/IFIP Network Operations and Management Symposium, pp. 1–9 (2022)
56. Lopez-Martin, M., Carro, B., Sanchez-Esguevillas, A.: Application of deep reinforcement learning to intrusion detection for supervised problems. Expert Syst. Appl. **141**, 112963 (2020)
57. Maniriho, P., Niyigaba, E., Bizimana, Z., Twiringiyimana, V., Mahoro, L.J., Ahmad, T.: Anomaly-based intrusion detection approach for iot networks using machine learning. In: 2020 International Conference on Computer Engineering, Network, and Intelligent Multimedia (CENIM), pp. 303–308. IEEE (2020)
58. Marir, N., Wang, H., Feng, G., Li, B., Jia, M.: Distributed abnormal behavior detection approach based on deep belief network and ensemble svm using spark. IEEE Access **6**, 59657–59671 (2018)
59. McHugh, J.: Testing intrusion detection systems: a critique of the 1998 and 1999 darpa intrusion detection system evaluations as performed by lincoln laboratory. ACM Trans. Inf. Syst. Secur. **3**(4), 262–294 (2000)
60. Modi, C.N., Patel, D.R., Borisaniya, B., Patel, H., Patel, A., Rajarajan, M.: A survey of intrusion detection techniques in cloud. J. Netw. Comput. Appl. **36**, 42–57 (2013)
61. Moon, D., Im, H., Kim, I., Park, J.H.: Dtb-ids: an intrusion detection system based on decision tree using behavior analysis for preventing apt attacks. J. Supercomput. **73**, 2881–2895 (2017)
62. Moustafa, N., Turnbull, B., Raymond Choo, K.-K.: An ensemble intrusion detection technique based on proposed statistical flow features for protecting network traffic of internet of things. IEEE Internet Things J. **6**(3), 4815–4830 (2018)
63. Murdock, K.: Finding and exploiting faults in hardware and software. Ph.D. Thesis, University of Birmingham, 2023
64. Naik, P.K., Mannanuddin, K., Sundaresan, K., Sah, S., Patil, H., Firos, A.: Enhancing iot security with self-adaptive blockchain-based intrusion detection system. 2023 Intelligent Computing and Control for Engineering and Business Systems (ICCEBS), pp. 1 5 (2023)
65. Nandyala, C.S., Kim, H.-K.: Green iot agriculture and healthcare application (gaha). Int. J. Smart Home **10**(4), 289–300 (2016)
66. Negm, N., Alamro, H., Allafi, R., Khalid, M., Nouri, A.M., Marzouk, R., Othman, A.Y., Ahmed, N.A.: Tasmanian devil optimization with deep autoencoder for intrusion detection in iot assisted unmanned aerial vehicle networks. Ain Shams Eng. J. 102943 (2024)
67. Nespoli, P., Díaz-López, D., Mármol, F.G.: Cyberprotection in iot environments: A dynamic rule-based solution to defend smart devices. J. Inf. Secur. Appl. **60**, 102878 (2021)
68. Nissim, N., Moskovitch, R., Rokach, L., Elovici, Y.: Novel active learning methods for enhanced pc malware detection in windows os. Expert Syst. Appl. **41**(13), 5843–5857 (2014). Funding Information: This research was partly supported by the National Cyber Bureau of the Israeli Ministry of Science, Technology and space. We would like to thank Clint Feher, who assisted in the data-set creation and Yuval Fledel for meaningful discussions and comments in the efficient implementation aspects

69. Nitish, A., Hanumanthappa, J., Shiva, Prakash, S.P., Krinkin, K.: Lightweight network context change detection for online defense against heterogeneous iot attacks. In: 2023 International Conference on Computational Intelligence, Networks and Security (ICCINS), pp. 1–6. IEEE (2023)
70. Nkoro, E.C., Njoku, J.N., Nwakanma, C.I., Lee, J.-M., Kim, D.-S.: Zero-trust marine cyberdefense for iot-based communications: an explainable approach. Electronics **13**(2), 276 (2024)
71. Nobakht, M., Sivaraman, V., Boreli, R.: A host-based intrusion detection and mitigation framework for smart home iot using openflow. In: 2016 11th International Conference on Availability, Reliability and Security (ARES), pp. 147–156. IEEE (2016)
72. Noura, M., Atiquzzaman, M., Gaedke, M.: Interoperability in internet of things: taxonomies and open challenges. Mobile Netw. Appl. **24**, 796–809 (2018)
73. Olanrewaju-George, B., Pranggono, B.: Federated learning-based intrusion detection system for the internet of things using unsupervised and supervised deep learning models. Cyber Secur. Appl. 100068 (2024)
74. Rai, K., Devi, M.S., Guleria, A.: Decision tree based algorithm for intrusion detection. Int. J. Adv. Netw. Appl. **7**(4), 2828 (2016)
75. Rajasegarar, S., Leckie, C., Palaniswami, M.: Hyperspherical cluster based distributed anomaly detection in wireless sensor networks. J. Parallel Distrib. Comput. **74**(1), 1833–1847 (2014)
76. Roopa Devi, E.M., Suganthe, R.C.: Enhanced transductive support vector machine classification with grey wolf optimizer cuckoo search optimization for intrusion detection system. Concurren. Comput. Practice Exp. **32**(4), e4999 (2020)
77. Sam, J.: A research report on advanced persistent threat fancy bear (apt28) threat actor https://www.researchgate.net/publication/383606556_Figure_1_A_Research_Report_on_Advanced_Persistent_Threat_Fancy_Bear_APT28_Threat_Actor
78. Sato, M., Yamaki, H., Takakura, H.: Unknown attacks detection using feature extraction from anomaly-based ids alerts. 2012 IEEE/IPSJ 12th International Symposium on Applications and the Internet, pp. 273–277 (2012)
79. Simadiputra, V., Surantha, N.: Rasefiberry: Secure and efficient raspberry-pi based gateway for smarthome iot architecture. Bull. Electr. Eng. Inf. **10** (2021)
80. Singh, O., Vinoth, R., Singh, A., Singh, N.: Navigating security threats and solutions using ai in wireless sensor networks. Int. J. Commun. Netw. Inf. Secur. **16**(4), 411–427 (2024)
81. Smys, S., Basar, A., Wang, H., et al.: Hybrid intrusion detection system for internet of things (iot). J. ISMAC **2**(04), 190–199 (2020)
82. Sugi, S.S.S., Ratna, S.R.: Investigation of machine learning techniques in intrusion detection system for iot network. In: 2020 3rd International Conference on Intelligent Sustainable Systems (ICISS), pp. 1164–1167. IEEE (2020)
83. Sung, Y.: Intelligent security it system for detecting intruders based on received signal strength indicators. Entropy **18**(10), 366 (2016)
84. Syamsuddin, I., Barukab, O.M.: Sukry: suricata ids with enhanced knn algorithm on raspberry pi for classifying iot botnet attacks. Electronics **11**(5), 737 (2022)
85. Taghavinejad, S.M., Taghavinejad, M., Shahmiri, L., Zavvar, M., Zavvar, M.H.: Intrusion detection in iot-based smart grid using hybrid decision tree. In: 2020 6th International Conference on Web Research (ICWR), pp. 152–156 (2020)
86. Talathi, S.S., Vartak, A.: Improving performance of recurrent neural network with relu nonlinearity. Preprint (2015) arXiv:1511.03771
87. Tavallaee, M., Bagheri, E., Lu, W., Ghorbani, A.A.: A detailed analysis of the kdd cup 99 data set. In: 2009 IEEE Symposium on Computational Intelligence for Security and Defense Applications, pp. 1–6 (2009)
88. Thanigaivelan, N.K., Nigussie, E., Kanth, R.K., Virtanen, S., Isoaho, J.: Distributed internal anomaly detection system for internet-of-things. In: 2016 13th IEEE Annual Consumer Communications & Networking Conference (CCNC), pp. 319–320. IEEE (2016)

89. Udurume, M., Shakhov, V., Koo, I.: Comparative analysis of deep convolutional neural network–bidirectional long short-term memory and machine learning methods in intrusion detection systems. Appl. Sci. **14**(16), 6967 (2024)
90. Ullah, I., Mahmoud, Q.H.: A scheme for generating a dataset for anomalous activity detection in iot networks. In: Advances in Artificial Intelligence: 33rd Canadian Conference on Artificial Intelligence, Canadian AI 2020, Ottawa, ON, Canada, May 13–15, 2020, Proceedings 33, pp. 508–520. Springer (2020)
91. Vaswani, A., Shazeer, N., Parmar, N., Uszkoreit, J., Jones, L., Gomez, A.N., Kaiser, Ł., Polosukhin, I.: Attention is all you need. Adv. Neural Inf. Process. Syst. **30** (2017)
92. Vishwakarma, M., Kesswani, N.: A new two-phase intrusion detection system with naïve bayes machine learning for data classification and elliptic envelop method for anomaly detection. Decision Anal. J. **7**, 100233 (2023)
93. Wolf, M., Tritscher, J., Landes, D., Hotho, A., Schlör, D.: Benchmarking of synthetic network data: Reviewing challenges and approaches. Comput. Secur. 103993 (2024)
94. Wu, M., Zhu, Z., Xia, Y., Yan, Z., Zhu, X., Ye, N.: A q-learning-based two-layer cooperative intrusion detection for internet of drones system. Drones **7**(8), 502 (2023)
95. Xiao, Y., Xing, C., Zhang, T., Zhao, Z.: An intrusion detection model based on feature reduction and convolutional neural networks. IEEE Access **7**, 42210–42219 (2019)
96. Yan, B., Han, G.: Effective feature extraction via stacked sparse autoencoder to improve intrusion detection system. IEEE Access **6**, 41238–41248 (2018)
97. Yao, H., Fu, D., Zhang, P., Li, M., Liu, Y.: Msml: a novel multilevel semi-supervised machine learning framework for intrusion detection system. IEEE Internet Things J. **6**(2), 1949–1959 (2018)
98. Yu, X., Lu, Y., Jiang, F., Hu, Q., Du, J., Gong, D.: A cross-domain intrusion detection method based on nonlinear augmented explicit features. IEEE Trans. Netw. Service Manag. 1–1 (2024)
99. Zarpelão, B.B., Miani, R.S., Kawakani, C.T., de Alvarenga, S.C.: A survey of intrusion detection in internet of things. J. Netw. Comput. Appl. **84**, 25–37 (2017)
100. Zhang, X., Li, C., Zheng, W.: Intrusion prevention system design. The Fourth International Conference onComputer and Information Technology, 2004. CIT '04, pp. 386–390 (2004)
101. Zhang, Y., Cao, G., Wang, B., Li, X.: A novel ensemble method for k-nearest neighbor. Pattern Recogn. **85**, 13–25 (2019)
102. Zhang, X., Wu, T., Zheng, Q., Zhai, L., Hu, H., Yin, W., Zeng, Y., Cheng, C.: Multi-step attack detection based on pre-trained hidden markov models. Sensors **22**(8) (2022)

Malware in the Connected World: Advanced Detection Techniques Using System Calls and Graph Analysis

Roopak Surendran and Tony Thomas

1 Introduction

The term computer virus was initially coined by Fred Cohen in his Ph.D thesis [1]. Cohen defined computer viruses as "programs that can infect other programs by modifying them to include a possibly evolved version of itself". Cohen demonstrated a sample virus program which installs itself and modify other programs. In 1986, the first trojan virus called PC-write was developed [2]. It was able to delete the files stored in the computer. This encouraged hackers to create malicious programs for getting unauthorized access to the computing systems. In earlier days, malware apps targeted personal computers for performing various kinds of activities such as stealing the files, key logging, deleting the files, stealing credit card information and so on. Later, people started using smartphones instead of Personal Computers (PC) because of the low cost and portability. Smart phones are devices which can perform functions similar to those found in both PCs and cellular phones. Apart from these functions, smartphones have several resources such as camera, Global Positioning System (GPS), microphone and so on. Marcos Valesco initially developed a proof of concept mobile malware called lasco [3]. It was a Bluetooth worm. If this worm enters a mobile device under symbian Operating System (OS), it prompts the user to install the malware. Timofonica originated in Spain is a first known mobile malware and was detected by anti-malware labs in Russia and Finland in June 2000 [3]. It used to sent Short Messaging Service (SMS) messages to Global System for Mobile Communication (GSM) mobile phones without the knowledge and consent of the user. This prompted the rapid rise of mobile malware applications in cyber world.

R. Surendran (✉) · T. Thomas
School of Computer Science and Engineering, Kerala University of Digital Sciences, Innovation and Technology, Thiruvananthapuram, India
e-mail: roopak.s@duk.ac.in; tony.thomas@duk.ac.in; https://www.duk.ac.in

S. M. Thampi et al. (eds.), *Securing the Connected World*,
https://doi.org/10.1007/978-3-031-82826-3_4

Android smartphones play a critical role in controlling Internet of Things (IoT) devices through various installed applications. However, some of these applications may be malicious repackaged versions of legitimate apps. These kinds of malicious apps can perform privileged operations such as sending SMS to premium rate numbers, making the phone call and so on [4]. Hence, it is essential to protect Android smartphones from the malware apps.

Numerous anti-malware solutions are available on the market, yet many still depend on static and signature-based analysis methods [5]. Static analysis involves inspecting the binary code of an application to identify malicious behaviors, while signature-based analysis checks an application's hash value against a database of known malware hashes to determine if it is malicious. However, these methods can be circumvented by code transformation attacks, making it challenging for traditional anti-malware software to detect modified malware effectively [5]. Therefore, innovative approaches are essential to better characterize and detect malware on Android devices.

The primary goal of malware is to disrupt device functionality or gain unauthorized access. Once installed, malicious software often seizes control of key system resources, which can lead to an increase in CPU and memory usage, reflecting the malware's activities [6]. Although malware initially targeted personal computers, servers, and other networks, smartphones have recently become a major focus due to the growing popularity of third-party apps.

Over the years, several Android-specific malware detection methods have emerged, primarily categorized into static and dynamic analysis. Many of these approaches utilize machine learning models due to their effectiveness in predicting malicious activity in new, unseen data. In this chapter, we present solutions to address the limitations in existing static and dynamic machine learning-based malware detection techniques.

Static analysis methods detect malicious behavior by examining features extracted from an app's source code, such as API calls, permissions, and intents [7]. While these techniques can identify harmful components in the source code, some malware applications exploit runtime vulnerabilities by loading native code through APIs like System.loadLibrary(). Such runtime exploits are not detectable by static analysis alone. Conversely, dynamic analysis captures runtime information, such as system calls, system metrics, runtime APIs, and network packets generated during an app's execution, making it more effective at identifying runtime-based vulnerabilities [8].

Most existing system call-based malware detection mechanisms rely on machine learning algorithms due to their high accuracy in predicting unseen data. However, the performance of these classifiers heavily depends on optimal feature representation, where the goal is to select the most accurate and minimal feature subset from a larger set [9]. Training data often contains noisy features that can degrade classification accuracy and increase both training and testing times. By using only the optimal features that are highly correlated to the class label, detection accuracy can be enhanced, and computational costs can be significantly reduced.

One major limitation of current feature representations for system call-based malware detection is their high dimensionality, which lacks the ability to capture dependency relations between system calls. This results in a "curse of dimensionality," where the excessive number of feature components creates high data sparsity, increasing storage and processing demands for the classifier. High dimensionality also means these systems need to be trained on a larger feature set, further complicating and slowing the detection process.

Moreover, these mechanisms often struggle to detect obfuscated and adversarial malware. Attackers may modify system calls or reorder and inject benign-looking calls to evade detection, making it challenging for models that lack robustness against such adversarial manipulations. Since these traditional approaches do not account for adversarial behaviors in system call sequences, they are vulnerable to evasion techniques, where malicious samples are carefully crafted to bypass detection. Adversarial malware detection requires a more resilient feature extraction approach, capable of recognizing obfuscated patterns and dependencies that are resistant to intentional manipulation, ensuring reliable and efficient malware detection even in the face of sophisticated evasion tactics.

To address these limitations, this chapter discusses recent novel machine learning-based mechanisms for analyzing system call sequences. A graph-based approach is introduced to effectively reduce high dimensionality and enhance malware detection accuracy. By leveraging graph signals to reduce dimensionality and employing graph centralities to select diverse, informative system call features, this approach creates a more compact and meaningful feature space. System call pattern-based binary feature analysis further optimizes this space, improving data efficiency and classifier performance. Additionally, the identification of malicious subgraph segments using eigen-based Graph Convolutional Networks (GCNs) gives resilience against adversarial malware by enabling the detection of subtle, obfuscated patterns.

The rest of the chapter is organized as follows. In Sect. 2, we discuss about Android Operating System and Android malware. The malware analysis mechanisms are given in Sect. 3. Section 4 presents recent advances in system call sequence analysis for malware detection, showcasing innovative mechanisms that integrate binary system call subsequence analysis with graph feature analysis. These approaches improve detection accuracy and efficiency by capturing distinctive behavioral indicators of malicious activity, addressing limitations in traditional detection methods. In Sect. 5, conclusion and future directions for malware research are given.

2 Android Operating System and Android Malware

In this section, we explain the preliminary materials required for a reader to understand the mechanisms proposed in this chapter. In Sect. 2.1, we discuss about the architecture of Android OS in detail. Creation of Android application is given in Sect. 2.2. In Sect. 2.3, we discuss about Google Playstore. In Sects. 2.4, 2.5, 2.6, 2.7, 2.8, and 2.9, we discuss about the decompilation of Android application, Android permissions, Inter Component Communication (ICC), intent filters and device compatibility, ICC vulnerabilities in Android applications and malicious functionalities in Android applications respectively. In Sect. 2.10, a detailed discussion on the types of Android malware and families are given. In Sect. 2.11, we discuss about various malware research datasets. In Sect. 2.12, we discuss about the anti-malware products.

2.1 Architecture of Android Operating System

Android [10] is a Linux-based OS developed by Google. The architecture is shown in Fig. 1.

The components of the Android OS are:

- Applications;
- Application Framework;
- Libraries and Android Runtime (ART);
- Linux Kernel.

2.1.1 Applications

Android applications are software developed to run on devices that use the Android operating system. These applications are typically written in the Java programming language. The core components of an Android application are outlined below:

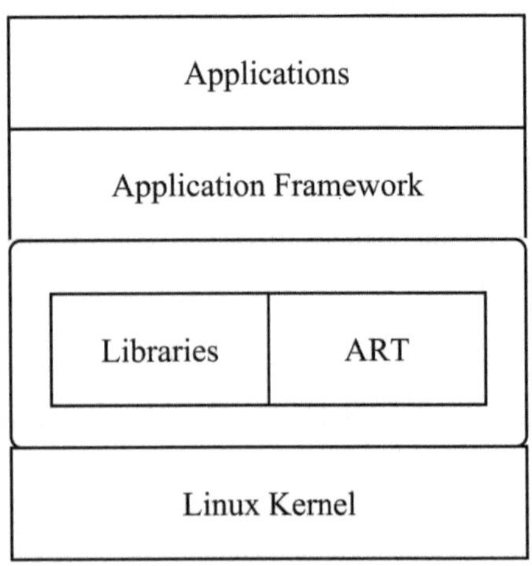

Fig. 1 Architecture of Android OS

- **Activity:** This component serves as the graphical interface through which users directly engage with the application.
- **Services:** Responsible for managing tasks in the background, such as data uploading or downloading, without user visibility.
- **Broadcast Receiver:** This component handles external events like receiving SMS messages or device restarts.
- **Content Provider:** Supplies a standardized interface to facilitate data sharing and access between different applications.

2.1.2 Application Framework

The application framework provides a suite of services in the form of Java APIs, forming the operational environment in which Android applications execute. Applications interact directly with this layer to obtain essential services. Key services within the application framework include:

- **Activity Manager:** Oversees all activities within the application.
- **Resource Manager:** Manages application resources such as layouts, colors, and other assets.
- **Notification Manager:** Allows applications to display alerts or notifications to inform the user.
- **View System:** Offers a range of views for designing and presenting the application's user interface.

2.1.3 Libraries and Android Runtime (ART)

The foundational libraries in Android include SQLite, Secure Socket Layer (SSL), and Media Framework, among others, which support the functionality of the Android OS. SQLite is utilized for data sharing among different applications on the device, while SSL ensures secure communication over the Internet. The Media Framework enables audio and video playback and recording capabilities. FreeType handles the rendering of fonts.

Android Runtime (ART) plays a critical role within the Android OS, as it executes applications in .dex (Dalvik Executable) format. Java bytecode is converted to Dalvik bytecode (in .dex format) using the dx tool to facilitate this process.

2.1.4 Linux Kernel

The Linux kernel functions as the core interface between user-level software and device hardware. It manages system resources and contains essential device drivers, such as those for the camera, Bluetooth, keypad, and display.

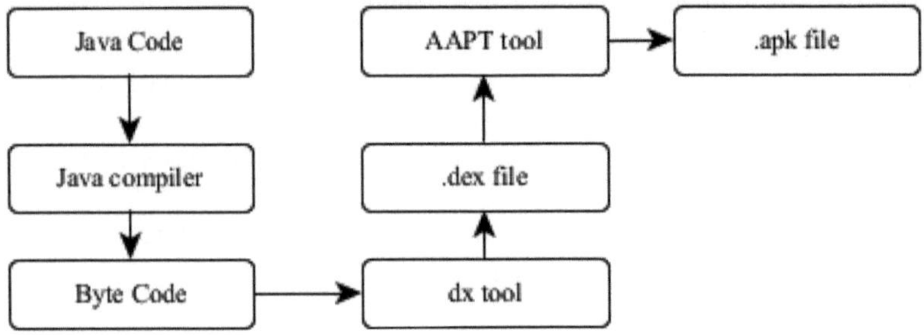

Fig. 2 Stages in android application development

2.2 Creation of an Android Application

Android applications are developed using the Java programming language. The Java code includes the necessary components (such as activities, services, broadcast receivers, and content providers) and API calls required for each function. Initially, the Java source code is compiled into bytecode (.class files) using the Java compiler. This bytecode is then transformed into Dalvik Executable (.dex) files through the dx tool. The final conversion into an Android application (.apk file) is completed using the aapt tool. Figure 2 illustrates the stages in Android app development.

2.3 Google Play Store

The Google Play Store serves as the official marketplace for Android applications. Developers can submit apps to the Play Store for public release. Each application undergoes security verification through an internal system known as Bouncer [11]. While the exact workings of Bouncer are proprietary, it operates by executing the app in a virtual environment to detect malicious behavior. An application is published only if no harmful activity is identified by Bouncer. Once available on the Play Store, users can directly download and install the application on their devices. Android apps on the Play Store span various categories, including:

- Gaming;
- Sports;
- Social networking;
- Banking;
- Education;
- Communication;
- Photography;
- News and magazines;
- Weather;
- Parenting, and more.

2.4 Decompilation of Android Applications

Decompilation is the process of retrieving the source code and associated files of an Android application. Figure 3 shows the steps involved in Android app decompilation. The initial step involves decompressing the Android application, which yields multiple files and folders from the .apk file, including:

- AndroidManifest.xml file: This file stores essential metadata, such as the package name, required permissions, definitions for components like Activities, Services, Broadcast Receivers, or Content Providers, supported versions, linked libraries, etc.;
- Res folder: This folder holds resources such as icons, images, constants, menus, animations, etc., which are compiled into binary codes;
- Assets folder: It contains uncompiled resources such as audio files and images;
- Classes.dex file: This file contains Dalvik bytecode to be executed on the ART;
- Meta-Inf: This directory stores the app developer's certificate signature, used to verify the developer's identity.

In the next step, a reverse engineering tool is used to extract Java source code or Smali code from the classes.dex file. Smali code is the equivalent of assembly language for Android. Some common reverse engineering tools include:

1. Dex2jar: Dex2jar [12] converts Dalvik bytecode (dex) into Java bytecode (jar), and Java code is then extracted using a Java decompiler[13];
2. Apktool: Apktool[14] enables decompiling and recompiling Android apps, providing the source code as Smali code;
3. Dare: Dare[15] assists in analyzing Android applications by converting bytecode into .class files, which are then decompiled to obtain Java source code;
4. Dedexer: Dedexer[16] converts .dex files into Jasmin format;
5. JEB: Jeb[17] is a GUI-based tool for analyzing .apk files and produces Java source code as output;
6. AndroGuard: Androguard [18], written in Python, extracts Java code from bytecode and is also used to detect malware and pirated apps;
7. AndroWarn: Androwarn[19] is a Python-based tool for identifying malware by analyzing Smali bytecode.

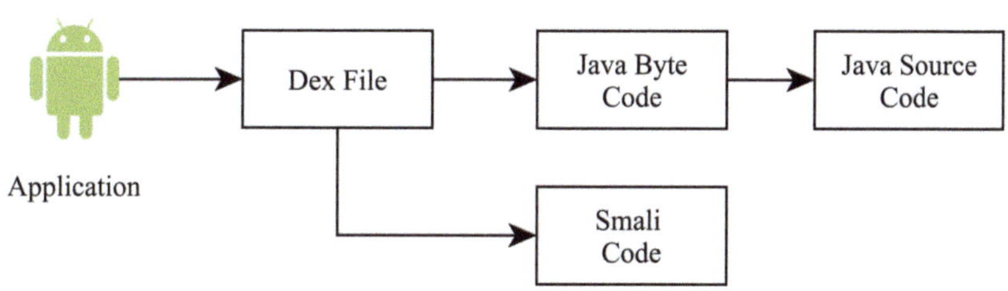

Fig. 3 Android application decompilation process

2.5 Android Permissions

Android's permission-based security model restricts apps from accessing sensitive device functionalities like telephony, network, contacts, storage, and location. Permissions are classified into four levels: normal, dangerous, signature, and signatureOrSystem. Normal permissions are granted by default at installation. Dangerous permissions, considered high-risk, allow access to private data and essential device sensors like the camera. Signature permissions are granted automatically at installation when an app is signed with the same developer certificate, while SignatureOrSystem permissions require the app to be signed with the system's certificate.

2.6 Inter-Component Communication (ICC)

An application component can use intents to initiate components (activities, services, broadcast receivers) within the same or other applications on the device. For instance, an app's activity component can launch the activity component of a browser to display a webpage. Table 1 lists key API calls for intent communication. Android supports two types of intents: implicit and explicit.

- Implicit Intent: An implicit intent does not specify the name of the component to be invoked. For example, an app component can display a webpage in a browser without naming the specific component. A sample code for implicit intent is shown below.

```
URL url=new URL("http://www.example.com")
Intent i=new Intent()
i.setAction(Intent.ACTION_VIEW)
i.setData(url)
startActivity(i)
```

- Explicit Intent: An explicit intent directly names the component to be invoked. For example, an app can switch from one activity (first.class) to another activity (second.class) by specifying the target activity. A sample code for explicit intent is shown below.

```
Intent i=new Intent(first.class,second.class)
startActivity(i)
```

Table 1 API calls for inter-component communication

SI.No	Component	API calls	Description
1	Activity	startActivity(Intent)	Launches an activity
2	Service	startService(Intent)	Starts a background service
3	Broadcast receiver	sendBroadcast(Intent)	Sends a broadcast across the device

2.7 Intent Filters and Device Compatibility

Intent filters allow an application to permit other applications access to its components (activity, service, broadcast receiver). Intent filter elements include:

- Action: Defines the type of action performed by the invoking component, e.g., ACTION_VIEW for content display;
- Data: Specifies the type of data accepted by the intent;
- Category: Indicates where the component will be launched.

In the manifest file, developers can declare required hardware and software resources, such as a camera, and specify minimum and maximum SDK levels for compatibility.

2.8 ICC Vulnerabilities in Android Applications

Applications can exploit ICC vulnerabilities in other applications for various security attacks [20]. Common ICC vulnerabilities include:

- Intent Spoofing: Attackers can invoke vulnerable components of legitimate applications to perform unauthorized actions, such as using the activity component of a payment app to transfer funds;
- Component Hijacking: Attackers can substitute a legitimate component with a malicious one by intercepting intents, such as replacing a login activity with a phishing page to steal credentials.

2.9 Malicious Functionalities in Android Applications

Malware applications may exploit sensitive API calls to perform malicious activities or take advantage of device vulnerabilities for privileged operations. Malware capabilities include [21]:

- Extracting private information like credit card numbers, credentials, and IMEI codes;
- Sending premium-rate SMS in the background;
- Conducting surveillance by secretly taking photos or recording video;
- Recording phone calls secretly;
- Encrypting files and demanding ransom for decryption;
- Locking the device and demanding ransom for unlocking;
- Displaying pop-up ads for revenue generation.

2.10 Types of Android Malware and Families

Malware is classified by functionality, and malware families refer to groups of similar malicious applications [22]. Types and examples include:

- Trojan Spy: Monitors device activity covertly, often keylogging or recording calls. Examples include:
  - Triout: Detected in 2018, capable of recording calls and sending them to a remote server;
  - Bouncing golf: Detected in 2019, it gathers information such as SMS, contacts, and installed apps, sending them to a remote server.
- Trojan SMS: Sends premium SMS messages covertly. Examples include:
  - Boxer: Discovered in 2011, it sends premium SMS messages in the background;
  - Opfake: Discovered in 2012, it operates similarly to Boxer.
- Backdoor: Allows remote control of a device. Example:
  - AndroRAT: Found in 2013, AndroRAT initiates calls, retrieves contacts, and performs other functions.
- Ransomware: Blocks access until ransom is paid. Example:
  - Simplocker: Detected in 2014, it encrypts files and demands ransom.
- Exploits: Leverages device kernel vulnerabilities. Example:
  - Gingermaster: Discovered in 2011, it exploits Gingerbread OS vulnerabilities.
- Botnet: A network of compromised devices, often used in DDoS attacks. Example:
  - Zazdi botnet: Detected in 2019, uses Firebase Cloud Messaging (FCM) for device communication.

2.11 Android Malware Datasets

Popular datasets for Android malware research include:

- MalGenome Dataset: MalGenome dataset contains 1200 malware samples belonging to the period 2010–2011 [23];
- Drebin Dataset: Drebin dataset contains 5560 malware samples from 179 malware families belonging to the period 2010–2012 [24];
- PRAGuard Dataset: Praguard dataset contains 10,479 malware apps. These malware samples were obtained by employing seven different obfuscation

techniques on malware samples in MalGenome and contagio minidump dataset [25];
- AMD Dataset: AMD dataset contains 24,553 malware samples from 71 malware families belonging to the period 2010–2016[22];
- VirusShare Dataset: VirusShare is a growing repository of malware samples. It consists of malware samples belonging to the period 2010–2022 [26];
- AndroZoo Dataset: AndroZoo dataset contains malware/goodware samples from 2010 to 2024. AndroZoo is a growing repository of Android application (both malware and benign) which includes benign applications from Google playstore, ANZHI, AppChina etc. and malware applications from Malgenome Project, VirusShare etc. [27].

2.12 *Anti-Malware Products*

The conventional anti-malware products for desktop and laptop rely on static or signature based analysis to detect the malicious behavior. There are several anti-malware software such as Mcafee, Norton and Kaspersky available for protecting desktop and laptop from malware attacks. These anti-malware software statically scan all the files stored in the system and search for the malicious signatures in it. If a malicious signature is found, it will delete the file immediately. Also, it statically scans the Internet traffic and email messages for finding the malicious content. These kind of signature based anti-malware products are also available in smartphones. Some of the available smart phone anti-malware products are listed below:

- Malware bytes anti-malware;
- AVG Antivirus for Android;
- Avast Antivirus;
  Safe Security;
- Eset mobile Security;
- Avira Antvirus;
- Security Master;
- Kaspersky Mobile;
- Mobile Security.

All these anti-malware products can quickly detect and remove the exact variant of a malware family before installation by analyzing its hash based signatures. The signature of an application will change even with slight changes in its source code. The main advantage of anti-malware products is the very low false positives in detection. These mechanisms can be defeated by employing simple code obfuscation such as identifier renaming, code reordering and dynamic code loading [5]. In dynamic analysis, the application is executed in a VM controlled environment (emulator) and runtime features are collected. These runtime features are analyzed for finding the malicious behavior. The runtime features of an application cannot be changed or hidden with obfuscation techniques. However, the resource consumption and detection time are very high. Hence, anti-malware products are not currently using dynamic malware detection mechanisms. All these anti-malware products have different malware signature databases. That means, the signatures of all malware applications may not occur in the signature databases of all anti-malware products. Hence, it is better to install and use multiple anti-malware products in the device for better malware detection. Furthermore, researchers found that bouncer security mechanism in Google play can be evaded by update attack [28]. Hence, it is essential to develop innovative mechanisms for detecting Android malware applications.

3 Machine Learning Based Static and Dynamic Malware Analysis

Current Android malware detection methods typically rely on either static features, such as API calls and permissions, or dynamic features, such as system calls and network traffic data (or a combination of both [29]) for analysis.

In static analysis, features tied to an application's source code are analyzed to detect malicious behavior. For instance, [30] employed probabilistic machine learning models trained with API call features for identifying malware, while in [31], permissions served as input features for machine learning classifiers to detect harmful applications. Similarly, [32] utilized data flow features for uncovering malicious patterns, and [33] applied intent-based features in a machine learning classifier to identify malware. Across these approaches, API calls, permissions, data flows, and intents are common features for detecting malicious actions. Additionally, [34] examined n-gram opcode frequencies as input to machine learning classifiers, while [35][36] used opcode sequences in CNN-based classifiers for malware identification. Further, [37] used opcode graphs in machine learning models, and [38] trained a deep neural network (DNN) with opcode graph features for malware detection.

However, static analysis approaches can be bypassed through dynamic code loading attacks [5], which unfold in three stages. First, a developer creates an application containing both legitimate and malicious bytecode. Next, they encrypt the malicious bytecode. Finally, a decryption routine embedded in the legitimate bytecode is used to decrypt the malicious code during runtime, effectively concealing it from static analysis methods. This approach allows the malicious code to execute without detection, as it becomes active only at runtime.

In dynamic analysis, applications are executed within an emulator or on a physical device, and features like system calls and network packets are gathered using external utilities. For example, [39] employed runtime API call sequences to detect malware that accesses sensitive device resources. Although effective for identifying malicious applications attempting unauthorized access, this method may sometimes result in false positives, as legitimate applications may also generate sensitive API calls for privileged actions. In [40], CPU and memory usage metrics were used for malware detection, though [41] noted that some malware consume minimal system resources, leading to cases where malicious apps might be misclassified as benign. Network packets were used as features in [42], although certain malware types that do not require an internet connection (e.g., those sending premium SMS messages) evade detection by this approach.

According to Forrest et al. [43], analyzing system call sequences can reveal an application's malicious behavior. Unlike benign applications, which require user triggers for invoking sensitive APIs (such as sendTextMessage() [44]), malware often calls these APIs autonomously [44, 45]. In legitimate applications, user-driven events are passed through the intent system, avoiding inter-process communication (IPC) channels for sensitive data [46]. However, if sensitive APIs are called without user involvement, it will be evident in the system call sequence, indicating possible malicious intent [45]. Consequently, system call traces may offer more relevant insight into malicious actions compared to standalone API calls.

Dynamic analysis techniques leveraging system call data often rely on machine learning (ML) models for detecting malware. These methods typically use either system call frequencies [47], co-occurrence matrices [48], or Markov chain transition probabilities [49] as features for classification. In Crowdroid [50], for example, system calls are collected from devices and sent to a cloud server, where k-means clustering is used to classify applications as malicious or benign. Dimjašević et al. [51] combined system call frequencies and dependencies for detection. Deep4Maldroid [52] used system call graph features in a deep learning classifier, while [53] introduced a model-checking-based approach for system call analysis. Huffman-encoded features for system calls were applied in [54], and Algorithmic Logarithmic Branching Factor (ALBF) from system call graphs was explored in [55] for malware detection. Feature selection methods for finding relevant system calls and TF-IDF (Term Frequency-Inverse Document Frequency) algorithm for feature extraction were proposed in [56] to improve malware detection accuracy.

Existing approaches in Android malware detection face several limitations. High dimensionality in feature vectors, as highlighted in previous studies [57], often leads to the curse of dimensionality, where increased feature numbers result in sparse data. This sparsity unnecessarily inflates storage needs and extends classifier processing time. Additionally, more features require a larger training dataset, which adds to storage demands and computational overhead. Despite these numerous features, the feature vectors frequently lack relevant information, reducing their effectiveness for accurate malware classification. The combination of high dimensionality and extensive datasets further complicates training and testing processes, adding significant complexity. Finally, many current approaches are ill-equipped to detect unknown or adversarial malware due to limited adaptability, making them vulnerable to sophisticated evasion techniques used by modern malware.

To overcome these limitations, a graph-based approach can offer substantial improvements in feature dimensionality, informativeness, and robustness against adversarial malware. By extracting graph signals, we can reduce dimensionality, effectively addressing data sparsity and computational overhead. Utilizing graph centrality measures helps identify diverse and informative system call features, enhancing the feature vector's relevance and reducing the need for excessive data. Additionally, binary feature analysis based on system call patterns enables a more compact and discriminative representation, further streamlining the feature space. For adversarial malware detection, identifying malicious subgraph segments with eigen-based Graph Convolutional Networks (GCNs) can help locate subtle, obfuscated patterns, providing a more adaptive and resilient detection mechanism. This graph-driven approach not only mitigates dimensionality challenges but also improves detection accuracy in the face of unknown and adversarial malware.

4 Advanced Detections Using System Calls and Graph Features

Recent advances in malware detection have increasingly focused on utilizing system call sequences, graph-based features, and machine learning classifiers to effectively identify malicious Android applications. System call graph signal-based detection relies on capturing system call sequences during application execution in an emulator, which are then refined and represented as control flow graphs. These graphs are analyzed to extract informative signal-based feature vectors, which encapsulate both frequency and dependency relationships inherent in the system calls. These features are subsequently used to train machine learning classifiers, such as Random Forest, enabling the detection of potentially malicious behavior in Android applications.

Further enhancement in detection capabilities comes from system call graph centrality analysis, where centrality metrics, including eigenvalues, betweenness, and closeness centrality, are extracted from system call graphs. These centrality measures help reveal the importance and relationships of various system calls within the application, which can be indicative of obfuscated malware behaviors. By removing highly correlated features and selecting the most relevant ones, classifiers can be trained to accurately detect obfuscated malware samples, which often use techniques to evade detection.

Another significant contribution in malware detection is the analysis of binary system call subsequences. This method models system call sequences as first-order Markov chains, leveraging the Asymptotic Equipartition Property (AEP) to capture the statistical properties of malware-specific patterns. These patterns are then used as binary features for machine learning classifiers, allowing for the detection of previously unseen or unknown malware types. This method addresses the challenge of detecting novel malware variants by relying on the inherent structure of system call sequences that are difficult for traditional detection methods to capture.

To further improve detection in adversarial settings, a combination of system call pattern recognition, graph signal analysis, and centrality-based features has been extended using Graph Convolutional Networks (GCNs). GCNs allow for the spectral clustering of system call graphs, partitioning them into subgraphs that highlight potentially malicious behavior. This combined approach integrates the strengths of multiple techniques, such as capturing system call patterns, centrality features, and the power of deep learning with GCNs, to create a robust solution for identifying various malware variants, including common, obfuscated, and adversarial mimicry malware. By enhancing traditional methods with these novel techniques, this approach offers a more comprehensive solution to the evolving challenges in malware detection.

4.1 System Call Graph Signal-Based Malware Detection

In this section, we discuss system call graph signal analysis to identify the most prominent system call based features and use them for malware detection [58] . During classifier training, Android applications are installed in an emulator to capture system call sequences. These sequences are then refined and modeled as control flow graphs, from which informative, signal-based feature vectors are extracted using a graph shift method. These graph signals serve as inputs for training a Random Forest classifier. Here, the classifier training time is only 1.4 seconds.

In the testing phase, graph signals are again extracted and fed into the classifier. As these lightweight signals contain both frequency and dependency information, 98% of malware samples were detected with zero false positive rate using only two system calls. Notably, the signal values from key system calls—especially those related to Inter-Process Communication are highly indicative of malicious behavior.

4.2 System Call Graph Centrality for Malware Detection

This section covers system call graph centrality analysis for obfuscated malware detection [59]. During the training phase, system call sequences are gathered by emulating Android applications, then refined and modeled as control flow graphs. Centrality metrics, such as eigen, betweeness and closeness values are extracted from these graphs. Then, the highly correlated features having Variable Inflation Factor (VIF) value greater than 10 are removed and created feature vectors, which are used to train a Random Forest classifier. Here, the classifier training time is only 5.6 seconds.

In the testing phase, centrality metrics are extracted and classified. These metrics provide diverse and informative features, enabling the detection of over 98% of obfuscated malware samples with a false positive rate of only 2%. Here, All the samples are detected within less than a second.

4.3 System Call Pattern Analysis for Malware Detection

This section explores a method for detecting malware by identifying binary system call subsequences as key features. Here, system call sequences specific to different malware types (e.g., trojans, adware, ransomware) are represented as first-order Markov chains. Using the Asymptotic Equipartition Property (AEP) as outlined by Surendran et al. [60], this approach extracts core malicious patterns indicative of malware activity. These patterns are then converted into binary feature vectors that serve as inputs for machine learning classifiers, allowing for effective detection of both known and unknown malware samples.

With just 50% of the training data, this mechanism achieves a 98% malware detection rate with zero false positives. In this approach, both the training and testing time is only less than 0.5 seconds

4.4 Adversarial Malware Detection

This section presents an approach for detecting adversarial malware by integrating key principles from prior methods, including the identification of malicious system call patterns, extraction of informative graph signals, and use of centrality-based features, in combination with Graph Convolutional Networks (GCNs)[61]. Building upon these principles, the approach first identifies specific malicious system call subsequences that are indicative of malicious behavior. These subsequences are then incorporated into the system call graph, along with centrality features, such as eigenvalues, that capture the importance and relationships of nodes within the graph.

Using the spectral clustering capabilities of EigenGCN, the system call graph is partitioned into two subgraphs, with any malicious behavior residing within one of the subgraphs. The graph Fourier transform-based pooling technique within EigenGCN is then employed to extract informative graph signals from these subgraphs. These graph signals, which incorporate both frequency and dependency information, act as distinctive signatures for detecting malware.

This combined mechanism, which adapts and extends previous principles, achieves high accuracy across various malware types: 98.7% for common malware, 97.3% for obfuscated malware, 97.8% for repackaged malware, and 90% for adversarial mimicry malware. This method can effectively detects not only common malware, but also obfuscated, repackaged, and adversarial mimicry variants in Android applications.

5 Conclusion

Recent works in Android malware detection have demonstrated the effectiveness of system call-based techniques across diverse detection paradigms. System call graph signal analysis has shown promise in identifying critical system call features that enhance detection accuracy with minimal computational overhead, achieving impressive results with limited features. For example, some methods have achieved detection rates as high as 98% with zero false positives by leveraging just two system calls.

Centrality-based approaches, which analyze malware behavior through graph centrality metrics, effectively handle complex obfuscation techniques. By incorporating eigen, betweenness, and closeness centrality metrics, these methods achieve high detection rates with minimal false positives, detecting over 98% of obfuscated malware samples in seconds. Additionally, binary system call pattern analysis, using first-order Markov chains and asymptotic equipartition properties, has demonstrated high accuracy in identifying malware types such as trojans, adware, and ransomware, reaching 98% detection with zero false positives.

Furthermore, adversarial detection methods utilizing Graph Convolutional Networks (GCNs) have addressed the detection of sophisticated attacks, including mimicry and adversarial malware. Techniques like EigenGCN spectral clustering, combined with graph Fourier transform pooling, have achieved high accuracy across varied malware types, effectively detecting common, obfuscated, repackaged, and adversarially crafted malware samples.

These approaches collectively contribute to a comprehensive framework for Android IoT malware detection, offering adaptable and efficient solutions that address various threat types, setting a foundation for continued innovation in IoT security.

Future research in system call-based Android malware detection can harness the strengths of graph-based approaches while focusing on broader applicability and adaptability to dynamic threat landscapes. One key area is addressing concept drift [62], where malware continuously evolves to bypass detection. To counteract this, optimizing training datasets becomes essential. Periodic dataset updates, combined with techniques for removing duplicates and redundant features, can streamline the feature space, reducing both storage and computational load. Active learning approaches can further refine the dataset by prioritizing newly collected, high-impact samples and incorporating real-time feedback from analysts. This targeted dataset optimization can maintain detection relevance without overwhelming the model with unnecessary data.

Another promising avenue is transfer learning [63], particularly in detecting malware targeting lightweight IoT devices. IoT malware often mirrors Android-based attack patterns, making system call classifiers trained on Android malware transferable to these devices. By reusing Android classifiers as a foundation, we can reduce the amount of training data needed for IoT-specific detection, enabling efficient, rapid model deployment for IoT environments where resources are limited.

Expanding the generalization of these detection techniques across Linux-based platforms aligns well with system call-based methods. Since Linux-based IoT devices often share underlying structures with Android, applying graph-based detection models across Linux-based IoT systems could increase the scope and adaptability of malware detection efforts, offering comprehensive protection across diverse IoT applications.

Lastly, improving unknown malware detection beyond Android, particularly in lightweight IoT devices, is vital as malware diversifies across connected devices. Graph-based analysis, which identifies malicious subgraph segments and patterns, can support a more resilient approach to detecting subtle or obfuscated threats across platforms. An adaptive, graph-driven system could generalize malware detection across IoT devices, enhancing resilience against unknown threats and expanding detection capabilities beyond the Android ecosystem.

References

1. Cohen, F.: Computer viruses: theory and experiments. Comput. Secur. **6**(1), 22–35 (1987)
2. Hughes, L.A., DeLone, G.J.: Viruses, worms, and trojan horses: serious crimes, nuisance, or both? Soc. Sci. Comput. Rev. **25**(1), 78–98 (2007)
3. Leavitt, N.: Mobile phones: the next frontier for hackers? Computer **38**(4), 20–23 (2005)
4. Thomas, T., Surendran, R., John, T.S., Alazab, M.: Intelligent mobile malware detection. CRC Press, Boca Raton (2022)
5. Rastogi, V., Chen, Y., Jiang, X.: Catch me if you can: evaluating android anti-malware against transformation attacks. IEEE Trans. Inf. Forensics Secur. **9**(1), 99–108 (2014)
6. Poornachandran, P., Praveen, S., Ashok, A., Krishnan, M.R., Soman, K.P.: Drive-by-download malware detection in hosts by analyzing system resource utilization using one class support vector machines. In: Proceedings of the 5th International Conference on Frontiers in Intelligent Computing: Theory and Applications, pp. 129–137. Springer, Berlin (2017)
7. Aafer, Y., Du, W., Yin, H.: Droidapiminer: Mining api-level features for robust malware detection in android. In: Security and Privacy in Communication Networks, pp. 86–103. Springer, Berlin (2013)
8. Or-Meir, O., Nissim, N., Elovici, Y., Rokach, L.: Dynamic malware analysis in the modern era—A state of the art survey. ACM Comput. Surv. **52**(5), 1–48 (2019)
9. Koller, D., Sahami, M.: Toward optimal feature selection. Technical Report, Stanford InfoLab, 1996
10. Brahler, S.: Analysis of the android architecture. Karlsruhe Inst. Technol. **7**(8) (2010)
11. blog.trendmicro.com: A look at google bouncer [Online]. Available: http://blog.trendmicro.com/trendlabs-security-intelligence/a-look-at-google-bouncer/. Accessed Mar 25, 2016
12. sourceforge.net: dex2jar [Online]. Available: http://sourceforge.net/projects/dex2jar/. Accessed Mar 25, 2016
13. jd.benow.ca: Java decompiler [Online] Available: http://jd.benow.ca/. Accessed Mar 25, 2016
14. ibotpeaches.github.io: Apktool [Online] Available: http://ibotpeaches.github.io/Apktool/. Accessed Mar 25, 2016
15. cse.psu.edu: Dare [Online]. Available: http://siis.cse.psu.edu/dare/. Accessed Mar 25, 2016
16. sourceforge.net: Dedexer [Online]. Available: http://dedexer.sourceforge.net
17. pnfsoftware.com: Jeb [Online]. Available: https://www.pnfsoftware.com/. Accessed Mar 25, 2016
18. code.google.com: Androguard [Online]. Available: http://code.google.com/p/androguard/. Accessed Mar 25, 2016
19. github.com: Androwarn [Online]. Available: https://github.com/maaaaz/androwarn. Accessed Mar 25, 2016
20. Tan, D.J., Chua, T.-W., Thing, V.L.: Securing android: a survey, taxonomy, and challenges. ACM Comput. Surv. (CSUR) **47**(4), 1–45 (2015)

21. Faruki, P., Bharmal, A., Laxmi, V., Ganmoor, V., Gaur, M.S., Conti, M., Rajarajan, M.: Android security: a survey of issues, malware penetration, and defenses. IEEE Commun. Surv. Tutor. **17**(2), 998–1022 (2014)
22. Wei, F., Li, Y., Roy, S., Ou, X., Zhou, W.: Deep ground truth analysis of current android malware. In: International Conference on Detection of Intrusions and Malware, and Vulnerability Assessment, pp. 252–276. Springer, Berlin (2017)
23. Jiang, X., Zhou, Y.: Dissecting android malware: characterization and evolution. In: 2012 IEEE Symposium on Security and Privacy, pp. 95–109. IEEE (2012)
24. Arp, D., Spreitzenbarth, M., Hubner, M., Gascon, H., Rieck, K., Siemens, C.: Drebin: effective and explainable detection of android malware in your pocket. In: Ndss, vol. 14, pp. 23–26 (2014)
25. Maiorca, D., Ariu, D., Corona, I., Aresu, M., Giacinto, G.: Stealth attacks: an extended insight into the obfuscation effects on android malware. Comput. Secur. **51**, 16–31 (2015)
26. virusshare.com: Virusshare [Online]. Available: http://www.virusshare.com/. Accessed Jan 14, 2020
27. Allix, K., Bissyandé, T. F., Klein, J., Le Traon, Y.: Androzoo: collecting millions of android apps for the research community. In: 2016 IEEE/ACM 13th Working Conference on Mining Software Repositories (MSR), pp. 468–471. IEEE (2016)
28. Oberheide, J., Miller, C.: Dissecting the Android Bouncer, vol. 95, p. 110. SummerCon2012, New York (2012)
29. Surendran, R., Thomas, T., Emmanuel, S.: A tan based hybrid model for android malware detection. J. Inf. Secur. Appl. **54**, 102483 (2020)
30. Cen, L., Gates, C.S., Si, L., Li, N.: A probabilistic discriminative model for android malware detection with decompiled source code. IEEE Trans. Dependable Secure Comput. **12**(4), 400–412 (2014)
31. Rovelli, P., Vigfússon, Ý.: Pmds: permission-based malware detection system. In: International Conference on Information Systems Security, pp. 338–357. Springer (2014)
32. Arzt, S., Rasthofer, S., Fritz, C., Bodden, E., Bartel, A., Klein, J., Le Traon, Y., Octeau, D., McDaniel, P.: Flowdroid: precise context, flow, field, object-sensitive and lifecycle-aware taint analysis for android apps. Acm Sigplan Not. **49**(6), 259–269 (2014)
33. Xu, K., Li, Y., Deng, R.H.: Iccdetector: Icc-based malware detection on android. IEEE Trans. Inf. Foren. Secur. **11**(6), 1252–1264 (2016)
34. Canfora, G., De Lorenzo, A., Medvet, E., Mercaldo, F., Visaggio, C.A.: Effectiveness of opcode ngrams for detection of multi family android malware. In: 2015 10th International Conference on Availability, Reliability and Security, pp. 333–340. IEEE (2015)
35. McLaughlin, N., Martinez del Rincon, J., Kang, B., Yerima, S., Miller, P., Sezer, S., Safaei, Y., Trickel, E., Zhao, Z., Doupé, A., et al.: Deep android malware detection. In: Proceedings of the Seventh ACM on Conference on Data and Application Security and Privacy, pp. 301–308 (2017)
36. Li, D., Zhao, L., Cheng, Q., Lu, N., Shi, W.: Opcode sequence analysis of android malware by a convolutional neural network. Concurr. Comput. Pract. Exp. **32**(18), e5308 (2020)
37. Zhang, J., Qin, Z., Zhang, K., Yin, H., Zou, J.: Dalvik opcode graph based android malware variants detection using global topology features. IEEE Access **6**, 51964–51974 (2018)
38. Pektaş, A., Acarman, T.: Learning to detect android malware via opcode sequences. Neurocomputing **396**, 599–608 (2020)
39. Kim, T., Kang, B., Im, E.G.: Runtime detection framework for android malware. Mobile Inf. Syst. **2018** (2018)
40. Milosevic, J., Malek, M., Ferrante, A.: A friend or a foe? detecting malware using memory and cpu features. In: SECRYPT, pp. 73–84 (2016)
41. Gheorghe, L., Marin, B., Gibson, G., Mogosanu, L., Deaconescu, R., Voiculescu, V.-G., Carabas, M.: Smart malware detection on android. Secur. Commun. Netw. **8**(18), 4254–4272 (2015)
42. Zaman, M., Siddiqui, T., Amin, M.R., Hossain, M.S.: Malware detection in android by network traffic analysis. In: 2015 International Conference on Networking Systems and Security (NSysS), pp. 1–5. IEEE (2015)

43. Forrest, S., Hofmeyr, S.A., Somayaji, A., Longstaff, T.A.: A sense of self for unix processes. In: Proceedings 1996 IEEE Symposium on Security and Privacy, pp. 120–128. IEEE (1996)
44. Elish, K.O., Shu, X., Yao, D.D., Ryder, B.G., Jiang, X.: Profiling user-trigger dependence for android malware detection. Comput. Secur. **49**, 255–273 (2015)
45. Xie, L., Zhang, X., Seifert, J.-P., Zhu, S.: pbmds: a behavior-based malware detection system for cellphone devices. In: Proceedings of the Third ACM Conference on Wireless Network Security, pp. 37–48. ACM (2010)
46. Tam, K., Khan, S.J., Fattori, A., Cavallaro, L.: Copperdroid: automatic reconstruction of android malware behaviors. In: NDSS (2015)
47. Amamra, A., Robert, J.-M., Abraham, A., Talhi, C.: Generative versus discriminative classifiers for android anomaly-based detection system using system calls filtering and abstraction process. Secur. Commun. Netw. **9**(16), 3483–3495 (2016)
48. Xiao, X., Xiao, X., Jiang, Y., Liu, X., Ye, R.: Identifying android malware with system call co-occurrence matrices. Trans. Emerg. Telecommun. Technol. **27**(5), 675–684 (2016)
49. Xiao, X., Wang, Z., Li, Q., Xia, S., Jiang, Y.: Back-propagation neural network on markov chains from system call sequences: a new approach for detecting android malware with system call sequences. IET Inf. Secur. **11**(1), 8–15 (2016)
50. Burguera, I., Zurutuza, U., Nadjm-Tehrani, S.: Crowdroid: behavior-based malware detection system for android. In: Proceedings of the 1st ACM Workshop on Security and Privacy in Smartphones and Mobile Devices, pp. 15–26. ACM (2011)
51. Dimjašević, M., Atzeni, S., Ugrina, I., Rakamaric, Z.: Evaluation of android malware detection based on system calls. In: Proceedings of the 2016 ACM on International Workshop on Security and Privacy Analytics, pp. 1–8 (2016)
52. Hou, S., Saas, A., Chen, L., Ye, Y.: Deep4maldroid: a deep learning framework for android malware detection based on linux kernel system call graphs. In: 2016 IEEE/WIC/ACM International Conference on Web Intelligence Workshops (WIW), pp. 104–111. IEEE (2016)
53. Bernardi, M.L., Cimitile, M., Distante, D., Martinelli, F., Mercaldo, F.: Dynamic malware detection and phylogeny analysis using process mining. Int. J. Inf. Secur. **18**(3), 257–284 (2019)
54. Manzil, H.H.R., Manohar Naik, S.: Android malware category detection using a novel feature vector-based machine learning model. Cybersecurity **6**(1), 6 (2023)
55. Bhandari, S., Panihar, R., Naval, S., Laxmi, V., Zemmari, A., Gaur, M.S.: Sword: semantic aware android malware detector. J. Inf. Secur. Appl. **42**, 46–56 (2018)
56. Vinod, P., Zemmari, A., Conti, M.: A machine learning based approach to detect malicious android apps using discriminant system calls. Future Gener. Comput. Syst. **94**, 333–350 (2019)
57. Friedman, J.H.: On bias, variance, 0/1–loss, and the curse-of-dimensionality. Data Min. Knowl. Discov. **1**(1), 55–77 (1997)
58. Surendran, R., Thomas, T., Emmanuel, S.: Gsdroid: graph signal based compact feature representation for Android malware detection. Expert Syst. Appl. **159**, 113581 (2020)
59. Surendran, R., Thomas, T.: Detection of malware applications from centrality measures of syscall graph. Concurr. Comput. Pract. Exp. **34**(10), e6835 (2022)
60. Surendran, R., Thomas, T., Emmanuel, S.: On existence of common malicious system call codes in android malware families. IEEE Trans. Reliab. **70**(1), 248–260 (2020)
61. John, T.S., Thomas, T., Emmanuel, S.: Detection of evasive android malware using eigengcn. J. Inf. Secur. Appl. **86**, 103880 (2024)
62. Bayram, F., Ahmed, B.S., Kassler, A.: From concept drift to model degradation: An overview on performance-aware drift detectors. Knowl.-Based Syst. **245**, 108632 (2022)
63. Li, W., Huang, R., Li, J., Liao, Y., Chen, Z., He, G., Yan, R., Gryllias, K.: A perspective survey on deep transfer learning for fault diagnosis in industrial scenarios: theories, applications and challenges. Mech. Syst. Signal Process. **167**, 108487 (2022)

Fraud Detection in IoT Networks

B. Bhagya, Sabu M. Thampi, and Preetam Mukherjee

1 Introduction

1.1 The Rise of IoT and Its Vulnerability to Fraud

IoT technology is widespread, greatly improving aspects like convenience, efficiency, security, and sustainability. Despite these benefits, the security of IoT devices connected to networks can be inconsistent. Vulnerabilities in less secure devices may provide openings for malicious actors to breach the IoT network. Such vulnerabilities allow unauthorized access to private networks, where fraudsters can alter data and engineer scenarios that benefit them.IoT devices may be susceptible to fraudulent activities due to various factors:

- Numerous IoT devices are equipped with factory-set usernames and passwords, typically identical across several units. Users commonly neglect to modify these default credentials, providing an easy pathway for fraudsters to access the devices.
- Following the launch of IoT devices, emerging security vulnerabilities may lead manufacturers to issue routine patches or updates. Neglecting these updates can compromise device performance and stability. Additionally, updates often introduce new functionalities. However, users indifferent to security concerns or those with limited technical know-how might turn off automatic updates to prevent disruptions. Furthermore, manufacturers typically do not offer updates indefinitely, leaving older devices without the latest security patches.

B. Bhagya (✉) · S. M. Thampi · P. Mukherjee
Connected Systems and Intelligence Lab, School of Computer Science & Engineering, Digital University Kerala, Trivandrum, India
e-mail: bhagya.csres23@duk.ac.in; sabu.thampi@duk.ac.in; preetam.mukherjee@duk.ac.in

S. M. Thampi et al. (eds.), *Securing the Connected World*,
https://doi.org/10.1007/978-3-031-82826-3_5

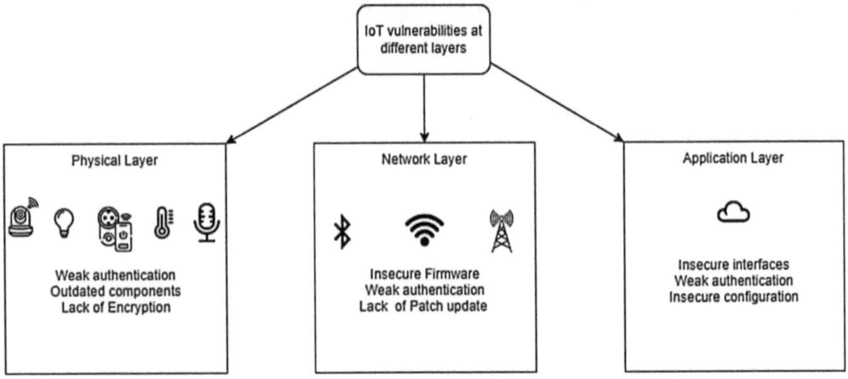

Fig. 1 IoT vulnerability in different layers

- Numerous IoT devices send data without encryption, simplifying the process for fraudsters to intercept and manipulate these devices.
- Sensors or cameras that are exposed to public access are at risk due to their physical accessibility. Fraudsters can circumvent security protocols by directly interfering with these devices.

  Figure 1 shows most common vulnerability in IoT netwroks [6]. The physical layer includes devices like cameras and sensors, susceptible to attacks due to weak passwords and outdated firmware. The network layer, facilitating device communication, often lacks proper encryption and robust authentication, exposing it to unauthorized access and data breaches. The application layer faces threats from insecure interfaces and protocols, compromising data integrity and confidentiality. Effective management of these vulnerabilities requires an understanding of the unique security needs at each layer to implement targeted protection strategies.

  These vulnerabilities represent just a small portion of the growing list of security concerns. To counteract these risks, both users and manufacturers need to implement standard safeguards. Manufacturers should comply with protocols that address potential future vulnerabilities prior to launching new products, while users should adhere to established security best practices for their devices.

1.2 Defining IoT Fraud and Its Scope

IoT fraud involves unauthorized or deceitful actions executed through IoT devices or networks to secure illegal advantages. In an IoT setting, characterized by numerous connected devices, these vulnerabilities may be manipulated, transforming any device into a potential threat. This situation can escalate rapidly, resulting in severe and unforeseen repercussions, similar to a chain reaction. IoT fraud can affect multiple industries such as smart homes, energy systems, healthcare, transportation, utilities, and manufacturing. Each of these sectors is vulnerable to the dangers associated with IoT fraud, underscoring the importance of implementing strong security protocols to protect against these threats.

- **Smart Home [27, 28]**-In smart homes, interconnected IoT devices like Smart Thermostats, Smart Lighting, Smart Plugs, Smart Locks, and devices used for surveillance, such as Smart Security Cameras, improve convenience and enhance security. These devices may act as a substitute for malicious actors to participate in fraudulent actions with serious implications. For example, if a malicious actor gains unauthorized control over a Smart Thermostat, they could suddenly increase energy usage, which increases energy consumption, and the electricity bill will rise abruptly. Beyond the financial impact, such tampering could also serve as a precursor to more severe malicious activities. Another dangerous instance may arise due to unauthorized access to the thermostat. Gaining control over Smart Thermostat allows an attacker to alter the heating or cooling systems, potentially putting them in a cross beyond the safe limits. This could cause the system to overheat and lead to a short circuit. Without timely detection and intervention, such a short circuit could shoot up electrical fires or other critical hazards, significantly endangering the lives of home occupants. Enhancing security is vital to prevent such situations; remote control of IoT devices leads to minor to significant risks, underscoring the urgency of security protocols for a safe, smart home.
- **Health care**-Historically, the physical presence of healthcare professionals has been essential in medical practice, mainly for those patients who require intensive care. Unlike other professionals, medical practitioners need to work 24/7. The monitoring of patients can be done only on-site; they can make quick decisions regarding the treatment. As a person, healthcare professionals also have personal commitments and finite time.

  The rise of IoT technology addresses these challenges. Health monitoring devices such as ECG Monitors, Blood Glucose Monitors, and Blood Pressure Monitors empower doctors to work remotely, allowing off-site supervision and possible timely intervention. This innovation helps doctors balance their workload while ensuring responsible medical care is provided to patients when needed. These technological advancements also introduce considerable risks. Healthcare monitoring devices and connected medical devices are vulnerable to fraud. For instance, an IoT device- an insulin pump could become a target for fraudsters. A fraudster can manipulate the settings of an insulin pump and change the dosage delivered to a patient. Unauthorised access to these medical devices by fraudsters is so harmful, resulting in life-threatening situations. This scenario underscores the importance of unavoidable security in IoT healthcare applications. IoT devices add several advantages in healthcare, such as remote consultation of patients and remote monitoring; they also bring new challenges or risks to the connected world. Securing IoT devices in healthcare is essential to safeguard patients from potential risks and fully utilize this technology's advantages.

- **Transportation**-Contemporarily, most transportation technologies depend more on IoT, especially in the case of intelligent traffic management and automatic toll collection. Despite the increased efficiency, it has become more convenient for users. Again, it opens up new vulnerabilities that fraudsters can exploit to fulfill their malicious intents.

  Intelligent traffic management systems have been designed to optimize traffic flow, minimize the occurrence of congestion, and maximize road safety. However, it has vulnerabilities that allow malicious people or group entities to target one person, a group, or even the government. When these systems are compromised, attackers can deliberately cause traffic congestion or reroute traffic, which creates disorganization in the regular establishment of operations for various malicious reasons. For example, the criminals would initiate road blockades to separate certain cars and commit multiple crimes of robbery, kidnapping, or selective hits. More generally speaking, such disruptions could seriously degrade the necessary emergency services, delay some transportation routes, and spread confusion across a city. This could be part of a larger agenda intended to create public doubts about the government or to provoke the declaration of a state of emergency, with the general welfare and security of the public being impacted. This manipulation will not only result in immediate discomfort and possible risks but also give rise to more critical economic losses and impair essential functionality by necessary transportation infrastructure.

  Another main application of IoT in transportation is to automate toll collection. This allows the streamlining of the tolling process, reduces manual handling, and hastens traffic movement. However, such a system is vulnerable to fraudulent schemes. The data exchanged by the toll collection devices and central systems can be intercepted and modified by individuals having ill intentions. In tampering with such data, such persons can siphon the tolls accrued to legitimate authorities into their accounts. This could expose toll authorities to a huge financial loss and may go undetected for a long time without appropriate monitoring systems in place.

  More importantly, a determined hacker may manipulate the toll collection system to permit specific vehicles to pass through the toll gates free of charge. Such tampering can be conceived for personal benefit or in the fashion of a large-scale con to swindle the tolling mechanism.
- **Utility management**-IoT technology has today become imperative to the modern utility management process, optimizing activities across water services, gas services, electricity services, and waste services. In particular, smart electricity meters represent a significant technological leap. Such devices automatically collect usage data and transmit it to remove the human intervention in meter reading, thus maximizing efficiency and accuracy. However, with smart meters, there are also additional vulnerabilities, such as fraud. Malicious persons can access the meters without an authorization call. Besides, the data reported can easily be changed by the fraudsters. It may add or reduce the recorded energy usage based on the malice behind the act. For example, a fraudster may tamper with the meter so that less electricity than actually was is used, which then leads

to reduced utility bills for the homeowner. This can also arm the fraudulent individual with the influence to require a "commission" or kickback from the homeowner to allow him to continue tampering with the readings. Or, the fraudulent individual might inflate the usage recorded for a property and then blackmail the homeowner out of money to rectify the false readings to avoid high bills. Such activities have serious effects on utility providers and governments. Altering smart meter readings can impact the financial bottom line by allowing the prevention of accurate electricity billing. This leads to a loss of revenue and a diminished perception of the utility management system with potential financial and operational impacts.

- **Manufacturing Industry**-In IoT, different sensors are critical and are used to sense varied conditions, in particular the manufacturing sector, during pre-production and post-production. Unless some proper security measure is taken, all of these IoTs will be compromised by hackers. Intruders would attack such weak systems, manipulate data sensed from sensors, or might even halt an operation by taking advantage of such vulnerabilities. Such security failures can become grave, resulting in defective products, downtime, or even safety issues. In this sense, it is vital to make such comprehensive security analyses and ensure the installation of robust security controls in manufacturing networks. Without these, a company will be left vulnerable to financial loss, its reputation harmed, and the production quality reduced. The risk here can be identified as the necessity of protecting IoT in manufacturing.

2 Navigating the Multifaceted World of IoT Fraud

2.1 Varieties of IoT Fraud

- **Command Hijacking of voice activated IoT [12]**
  In this type of IoT fraud, the primary goal of the fraudsters is to deliberately cause IoT-connected devices to malfunction by manipulating the execution of voice commands. Rather than executing the intended command, the device is tricked into performing actions that align with the fraudster's malicious intentions. This is typically achieved by deploying commands designed to sound similar to legitimate ones, thereby confusing the IoT device into misinterpreting the user's instructions. Such harmful commands are intended to be pronounced to sound more like the actual voice command—in pronunciation or word—which can make such a device confuse the two. At the issuance of such a command, the device might perform an inappropriate action, such as turning off the security system instead of turning it on, and vice versa, or opening a door instead of locking one. Such intentional confusion will harm the normal running of the IoT devices and cause severe security breaches and unauthorized access. The attackers exploit some of the intrinsic weaknesses in voice recognition systems.

The different wording will result in more or less varied consequences. With this malicious wording or design, attackers can overwrite or hijack the legitimate command intended to be used, and thus take over the device to act in their favor, most probably at the user's cost.

- **Data Breach**
  A data breach [21, 23, 33] means unauthorized access and retrieval of confidential information about a person or organization. This can lead to loss in various ways, such as financial loss, reputation loss, and crimes associated with unethical or illegal behavior patterns. Data misuse due to hacks can ultimately be used for committing thefts, fake transactions involving finance, and other forms of malicious use, which may simply devastate the lives of both individuals and organizations alike. Such violations can cause serious damage because they may relate to access to personal information, financial records, trade secrets, or confidential information.

  The prevalence of data breaches is mostly attributed to security vulnerabilities and human errors. More commonly, the mistakes span from misused or stolen credentials. In more detail, weak passwords and unencrypted data make system entry easy for attackers. Furthermore, ransomware can lock out individuals who use their systems, and they will only access it if a ransom is paid. Among them are phishing schemes, where attackers pose under pretenses to trick people into revealing sensitive information. Lastly, exploiting trust relationships within complex interconnected systems, especially in IoT environments, enables attackers to penetrate the network by exploiting one weak link. Each has contributed to the rise in the frequency and severity of data breaches, hence the calls for robust security practices and vigilant monitoring.

- **Fake IoT devices**
  The existence of rogue or fake devices in the system is an overwhelming threat for the IoT environment, as it can do whatever a legitimate device could and carries malicious activities behind it. This would cause an untimely interruption of normal functioning within an IoT ecosystem due to such a counterfeit device, which reaches unauthorized access to sensitive information. The integrity of the network is undermined because they often manipulate and forge data as outputs, misleading decisions, thus weakening decision-making skills. Unrestricted access to critical information poses an instant security threat while allowing for vulnerabilities, eventually leading to sequential assaults on the system. Although it's merely data manipulation, this degrades an IoT system's overall efficiency and reliability due to these fake IoT devices. False information infused into the network makes it prone to skewed analytics, degraded system performance, and misleading automatic processes, eventually decreasing the trust factor of the IoT infrastructure. This has led to significant operational challenges, such as debugging incidents that have become impossible to solve because the fake devices hide their nature. The propagation of such vulnerabilities within the system may then compromise the security of the IoT ecosystem and its accuracy and efficiency, which underscores the critical demand for security measures that can identify and mitigate the potential risks that such threats present.

- **IoT Ransomwares [8]**
  Ransomware is malicious software intended to attack a targeted device and lock up selected services and data hosted on an IoT device. It operates on the system in secret until it sends out a ransom demand. Generally, this malware operates secretly; unauthorized actions run in the background, compromising users' privacy and the system's integrity. When ransomware gains access to secret assets or important documents, it demands the victim's money to restore the system to its original state. The ransom depends on the value of the information stolen. Generally, ransomware is a threat to an individual or an organization.

  Regarding IoT, ransomware could sit quietly for months, even years, silently exploiting vulnerabilities and updating or changing existing firmware. The attack is not discovered until the malware finally reveals itself by demanding a ransom, often after accessing sensitive information or critical system functions. The insidious character of ransomware is that it penetrates and changes the system way in advance without immediately being picked up by the user but only that it exists can be known once it is too late. Thereby, most victims only have the option of frequent ransom demands to regain control of their compromised systems after receiving ransom advice. For this reason, it is strongly advisable to have strong cybersecurity measures.
- **False Data injection attacks in IoT [4]**
  False data injection attacks involve the deliberate insertion of incorrect or misleading information into various nodes within an IoT network. In an IoT environment, where automation of tasks ranging from simple to highly complex is the primary objective, these attacks pose a significant threat. The functioning of IoT systems relies heavily on the accurate exchange of data between interconnected sensors and actuators. Sensors gather data from the environment, which is then processed to trigger appropriate responses from actuators. The integrity of this data flow is crucial for the reliability and efficiency of the entire IoT ecosystem.

  When false data is introduced into the system, it compromises the credibility of the IoT network. This can lead to incorrect actions being taken by the actuators, as the decisions made by the IoT system are based on faulty data. The impact of such attacks can be far-reaching, undermining the decision-making processes and potentially leading to catastrophic outcomes, especially in critical applications such as healthcare, industrial automation, or smart infrastructure. Ensuring the authenticity and accuracy of data within IoT networks is therefore essential to maintaining the trustworthiness and effectiveness of these systems. Robust security measures must be implemented to detect and prevent false data injection, safeguarding the IoT environment from such malicious threats.

3 Proactive Defense: Implementing Effective Measures to Prevent IoT Fraud

Proactive defense in the context of IoT fraud is crucial due to its widespread application across a range of minor to major tasks. Implementing robust security measures is essential for maintaining the integrity of critical infrastructures that support the IoT ecosystem. As the adage goes, prevention is better than cure, and this is especially true for IoT devices, which present more complex challenges in securing compared to traditional PCs. Proactive defense begins with a comprehensive understanding of the potential vulnerabilities and threats to IoT systems. Addressing each risk individually and managing them collectively through the integration of network nodes is key to effective prevention. Despite the many advantages IoT offers in a connected world, it faces significant limitations in security, primarily due to its limited processing power, lack of standardized protocols, and constrained memory capacity. One of the fundamental steps towards establishing a proactive defense for IoT is the deployment of strong authentication and encryption techniques. We can avoid unauthorized access by implementing biometric authentication. The proper encryption mechanisms are only used in some IoT devices. Securing the data in the receiving and transmitting stages is also vital to maintaining authenticity and confidentiality. So, at both ends of transmission, the encryption should be done. Additionally, regular updates and security audits are critical in preventing malicious actors from exploiting vulnerabilities. These audits typically include reviewing system configurations, firmware updates, and patch management processes. Incorporating behavioral analytics and machine learning into the audit process further enhances the reliability of IoT systems. To address risks associated with specific devices, network segmentation and tailored access privileges can mitigate threats effectively without disrupting other nodes within the IoT network.

3.1 Robust Security Architecture [3]

Figure 2 shows the general architecture of an IoT environment incorporating an SDN controller. Integrating Software Defined Networking (SDN) into IoT networks presents a robust strategy to enhance security within increasingly complex and vulnerable IoT environments. We can increase the transparency and visibility of the IoT networks through an SDN controller. The protocol used in SDN is open flow protocol, which decouples the two planes as the control plane and data plane. Open flow protocol operates on a match action paradigm that specifies network traffic handling.SDN controller functions as a central controller, allowing us to program and define rules by which network devices behave. We can deploy dynamic security policies explaining how the network responds if there are any threats. Deploying machine learning models within the SDN controller can proactively find and resolve potential threats by analyzing historical and real-time data to identify unusual network behaviors. This technique boosts the network defenses against threats and ensures the consistency of the IoT network while maintaining its scalability. Combining SDN network management with predictive analytics offers a framework for securing IoT networks, providing a high level of protection where traditional security mechanisms often fail.

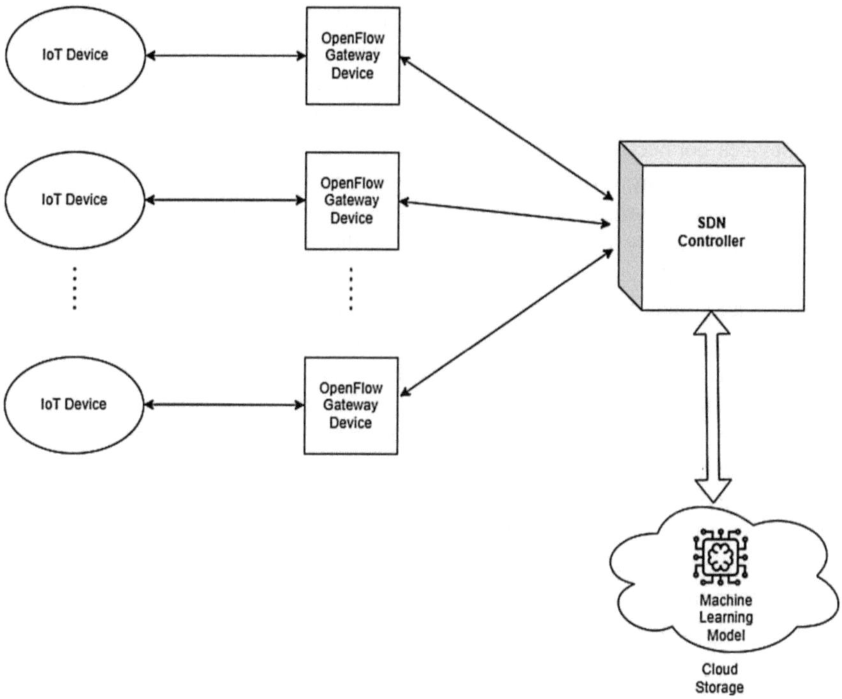

Fig. 2 Robust security architecture

3.2 *Continuous Network Monitoring and Threat Detection*

One way to detect IoT fraud is to monitor network traffic. Monitoring both incoming and outgoing traffic on the IoT network can be achieved through various techniques. Continuous real-time monitoring of network traffic can mitigate the risks posed by compromised devices and vulnerabilities, minimizing the impact of potential damage. However, real-time monitoring presents several challenges due to the heterogeneous nature of traffic types in IoT networks. Monitoring IoT traffic can be classified into several categories:

- **Passive Monitoring:** Passive monitoring captures network traffic without affecting the data flow. This can be achieved by placing passive devices, such as network taps or port mirroring setups, at strategically important points in the network. The captured packets are then analyzed to detect deviations from normal behavior.
- **Active Monitoring:** Active monitoring involves the continuous proactive monitoring of network traffic to and from the IoT network. Unlike passive monitoring, which only observes traffic, active monitoring works in tandem with the network, watching the real-time response of each device. Real-time traffic analysis in

active monitoring can be done mainly through two methods: packet injection and active probing. In packet injection, test packets are injected into the network, and the responses from each device are analyzed. Unexpected behavior may be discovered, revealing fraudulent nodes. In active probing, regular queries are sent to devices connected to the network to evaluate their status. This method also includes emulating various attack scenarios to evaluate how the devices respond.

- **Device-Level Monitoring:** Device-level monitoring provides decentralized or individual security to nodes connected to the network. Fraudulent activities can be detected by closely monitoring each device's communications, resource usage, and data transfer rates, and analyzing their behavior patterns. This ensures the security of even small or isolated components connected to the network. A behavioral baseline can be established for individual devices. Device fingerprinting is another method used to ensure the security of individual devices by profiling their identity based on hardware configurations, firmware, and communication protocols, helping prevent unauthorized attempts to mimic legitimate devices.
- **Network Flow Monitoring:** Network flow monitoring [17] involves analyzing the sequence of packets passing through the network, which provides insights into separating normal and suspicious activities. Protocols like NetFlow, IPFIX (IP Flow Information Export) [19], and sFlow are widely used to collect network flow data from connected devices. These protocols summarize packet flows between different sources and destinations, providing details such as the volume of transferred data, duration of communication, and port numbers. To ensure comprehensive security coverage, flow collectors can be strategically distributed across various points in the IoT network.
- **Cloud-Based Monitoring:** Cloud-based monitoring of IoT network traffic enables centralized management and advanced analytics. Cloud services are used to collect, analyze, and make decisions regarding network vulnerabilities. Data from individual nodes are securely transmitted to the cloud via gateways or local agents. Centralized management allows for the detection of coordinated attacks or fraud across geographically dispersed nodes. The elastic scalability of cloud services ensures that adding more devices to the network does not strain security management.
- **Edge Monitoring:** Edge monitoring involves analyzing and securing data close to the IoT device, avoiding the need to transfer traffic to a centralized location for analysis. This enables immediate detection of vulnerabilities within the local node, reducing latency. Edge monitoring is crucial for applications where data confidentiality is paramount and must not be transmitted outside the local environment. It is also preferred in scenarios requiring immediate response, where latency is intolerable. However, the resources available for processing traffic are limited to those within the local node.

3.3 Data Integrity and Anomaly Detection Techniques

Data integrity refers to the accuracy and consistency of data [12, 14]. The increasing nodes in the IoT environment makes it difficult to keep data integrity. Anomaly detection relies on the assumption that the data being analyzed is trustworthy. If data is compromised, anomaly detection may lead to wrong results. Correct results from anomaly detection techniques can take only the correct decision towards the fraud detection contexts. The incorrect results from anomaly detection may lead to false positives or mask the actual issues. So the data integrity and anomaly detection are interrelated with each other.

Anomaly Detection as a Tool to Safeguard Data Integrity [22]
When an IoT device begins transmitting data that is deviated from the normal behavior, anomaly detection technique can be detected as a fraud or threat occurred in the system or we can say that the data integrity was compromised. Digital sensors connected to IoT network took part in maintaining data integrity. Readings from digital sensors may fail due to various reasons. Data failures in digital sensors can be categorized into 3 types: format failures, timing failures and value failures. Incorrect data in the form of its format is causing format failures of digital sensors. When the data is delayed to receive, then we interpret the source sensor may malfunction due to timing failure. Value failures occur due to the presence of outliers or the values of some attributes extend beyond its ranges. Unless the proper handling of these failures the functioning of IoT may be broken. We can use heuristic rules like nonoverflow, inertia, and inequality rules to keep an eye on sensor data. These rules are used for spotting anomalies by setting limits on what's considered normal data behavior. Additionally, we can use a dual variable-length data monitoring window (VLDMW) [22] to tweak the monitoring process on the fly. A double window mechanism is followed to monitor data integrity: the first window for recovering timing as well as format failures, and the second window for recovering value failures. This way, the system can handle different types of data failures effectively without sacrificing real-time performance or computational efficiency. In more complex situations where simple rules just don't cut it, we can turn to deep learning techniques to model and detect data failures. These models, which are trained on historical data, can spot patterns that might indicate anomalies. However, deep learning models can be pretty demanding in terms of computation and need a lot of data for training, so they might not be the best fit for every IoT application.

Anomaly Detection Techniques

- **Federated Learning for Anomaly Detection** [11] Federated Learning (FL) is a decentralized way for IoT devices to work together to train machine learning models without having to share their raw data. This approach is great for keeping privacy intact while boosting the accuracy of anomaly detection across a network of IoT devices. By combining updates from multiple devices, FL can spot anomalies that traditional, centralized models might miss.

- **Blockchain Integration** [30] Combining blockchain technology with anomaly detection frameworks boosts security by adding an extra layer of protection. Blockchain's unchangeable ledger means that once data is recorded, it can't be tampered with without being noticed. This is crucial in settings where maintaining data integrity is essential. When paired with Federated Learning (FL), blockchain can increase the reliability of the data used to train anomaly detection models.
- **Edge and Cloud-Based Anomaly Detection** [9] In IoT systems, using both edge and cloud computing for anomaly detection is quite common. Edge computing handles real-time analysis right where the data is generated, which is essential for applications that need quick responses. Meanwhile, cloud computing offers the heavy-duty processing power required for more complex analyses and can spot broader anomaly patterns across various devices and locations. By combining these methods, you get a well-rounded solution that benefits from both immediate responsiveness and sophisticated analytics.
- **Machine Learning Techniques** [16] In IoT networks, different machine learning techniques are used to spot anomalies. Supervised learning needs labeled data to learn from known examples of normal and abnormal behavior. Unsupervised learning doesn't need labeled data and is great for finding new types of anomalies. Semi-supervised learning, which uses both labeled and unlabeled data, is especially useful when there's not much labeled data available.

3.4 Secure Device Management and Firmware Updates [13, 18, 24, 32]

Device management and firmware updates are critical in ensuring the security, functionality, and longevity of IoT devices. As these devices are integrated into various aspects of modern infrastructure, including smart homes, cities, and industries, managing them securely while providing continuous firmware updates is paramount to protect against vulnerabilities and cyberattacks.

Importance of Secure Firmware Updates [20]
Firmware updates address vulnerabilities, introduce new features, and patch bugs in IoT devices. However, they also present security challenges, as improperly handled updates can lead to attacks such as firmware tampering, unauthorized access, or malware introduction. Effective firmware management must ensure that updates are authenticated, verified, and securely transmitted.

Over-the-Air (OTA) Firmware Updates
OTA firmware updates are commonly used for remotely updating security patches, new features, bug fixes, or performance improvement. Manual intervention or physical connectivity is not required to provide such updates. OTA updates are provided using two methods: pull and push. In the push method, updates are directly

broadcasted from the server to all clients without explicitly requesting it. In the pull method, whenever the client requests the server, it checks for the updates, and if any update is available, it sends a response.

Threats to Secure Firmware Updates [7]
Firmware updates are exposed to various threats such as rollback attacks, where an attacker reverts a device to a vulnerable firmware version, and mismatch attacks, where firmware intended for another device is installed. Attackers may also exploit unsecured update mechanisms to introduce malicious firmware into IoT ecosystems. Therefore, securing every step of the update process starting from the firmware generation, through to its transmission and installation is crucial.

Blockchain and Cryptography in Secure Updates [15]
Recent advancements in secure device management have integrated technologies such as blockchain and cryptography to enhance firmware update security. For example, blockchain can ensure the integrity and authenticity of firmware updates by maintaining an immutable ledger of update transactions. Cryptographic techniques such as Elliptic Curve Digital Signature Algorithm (ECDSA) and AES encryption are also employed to ensure that updates are securely transmitted and only valid updates are installed.

Root of Trust (RoT) and Secure Boot
A key component in secure firmware updates is the establishment of a Root of Trust (RoT). This hardware-validated boot process ensures that a device can only start using trusted firmware. By employing cryptographic keys embedded in secure hardware components, such as Trusted Platform Modules (TPM), devices can verify the authenticity of the firmware during boot, thus preventing tampering. Secure boot mechanisms further protect devices by ensuring only authenticated firmware is loaded.

Interoperability and Standardization Challenges
The lack of standardization across IoT ecosystems presents a significant challenge in managing secure firmware updates. Devices from different manufacturers use various update protocols and security mechanisms, leading to fragmentation. Industry bodies such as the IETF and Open Mobile Alliance(OMA) have proposed frameworks like SUIT (Software Updates for Internet of Things) and LwM2M (Lightweight Light weight Machine to Machine) to standardize secure update processes across heterogeneous devices [32].

Best Practices for Secure Firmware Management
To ensure secure device management and firmware updates, the following best practices are recommended:

- **End-to-End Encryption**: Ensure that firmware updates are encrypted from the source to the device to prevent interception and tampering during transmission.
- **Authentication and Authorization**: Use cryptographic signatures to authenticate firmware and verify that it comes from a trusted source before installation.

– **Scalability and Device Management**: Implement robust device management systems that can track and manage firmware versions across millions of IoT devices efficiently.

4 From Detection to Resolution: Mitigating IoT Fraud

The travel from detection to resolution for managing IoT fraud is complicated because of its diverse nature and broad deployment. To address IoT fraud, the attack surfaces should be clearly spotted, vulnerabilities need to be identified and corrected, impacts of these attacks should be reverted, and finally, the consistency of the network should be maintained throughout the process. The vulnerable devices often suffer from poor security configurations, outdated firmware, and inadequate patch management, exposing them to potential attacks such as data breaches, device hijacking, and impersonation. The paper "Advances in IoT Security: Vulnerabilities, Enabled Criminal Services, Attacks, and Countermeasures"[29] emphasizes that the detection phase must involve continuous monitoring of network traffic, analyzing behavior patterns using machine learning models, and implementing anomaly detection systems. Machine learning-based detection models help identify unusual patterns, such as abnormal data transfer rates or unauthorized access attempts. Once fraudulent activities are detected, rapid incident response becomes critical. This involves immediate actions like isolating compromised devices from the network, blocking malicious communication channels, and deploying automated countermeasures. The contribution of threat intelligence systems must be perceiving up-to-date data about attack vectors, defining mitigation strategies, and implementing proactive preventive measures. Moreover, AI-powered incident response systems enable automated remediation by learning from past fraud incidents, reducing human intervention and response time.

The resolution phase involves countering the threat and ensuring the system is ready to fight against future attacks. For this, updating device firmware, strengthening authentication mechanisms, and employing robust encryption protocols are required on time. Criminal infrastructures exploiting IoT vulnerabilities, such as Impersonation-as-a-Service (IMPaaS) [29], continuously evolve, requiring dynamic and adaptive countermeasures. Effective fraud mitigation must also account for the growing complexity of these attacks, which often utilize botnets, proxies, and sophisticated malware to carry out large-scale fraud. By incorporating machine learning and deep learning in the detection and resolution phase, reactive to proactive fraud management can be accomplished to enhance the security and flexibility of IoT ecosystems.

4.1 Threat Intelligence and Incident Response Planning

In the context of IoT networks, Threat Intelligence (TI) plays a crucial role in identifying, analyzing, and responding to emerging cyber threats. TI involves the aggregation and interpretation of data related to potential attacks, malicious actors, and vulnerabilities within IoT systems. As outlined in the paper Deep Learning-Enabled Threat Intelligence Scheme in the Internet of Things Networks [2], the integration of AI and deep learning with TI can enhance its capability to predict and mitigate IoT-specific threats. By analyzing large volumes of IoT traffic data, these models are able to detect anomalies, correlate attack patterns, and forecast potential breaches.

One of the primary challenges in IoT security lies in the sheer scale and diversity of devices connected to the network. Many IoT devices have limited computational resources, making them susceptible to attacks that traditional security systems cannot easily mitigate. This is where AI-driven TI systems become invaluable. These systems use deep learning techniques to extract hidden patterns from network traffic and detect cyber threats in real-time. This approach is particularly effective for identifying novel or sophisticated attacks that do not follow previously known patterns. Incident Response (IR) in IoT networks is also crucial due to the real-time nature of these systems. The paper Cyber Resilience and Incident Response in Smart Cities [1] highlights the need for robust IR frameworks that can operate across diverse IoT ecosystems. The stages of IR typically involve preparation, detection, analysis, containment, eradication, and recovery. However, the growing complexity of IoT networks calls for a more dynamic and automated approach to IR. AI and machine learning-based models can help automate the detection and response phases, significantly reducing the time it takes to neutralize threats.

Effective incident response also relies heavily on collaborative threat intelligence. The sharing of real-time TI data across various sectors, such as smart cities and critical infrastructure, enables more coordinated defense mechanisms and faster threat mitigation. Combining TI with automated IR systems can improve the overall resilience of IoT networks by proactively identifying vulnerabilities and initiating countermeasures before attacks can cause significant damage.

4.2 Leveraging AI and Machine Learning for Predictive Fraud Detection

Machine learning and deep learning are revolutionizing fraud detection in IoT networks by using advanced algorithms to analyze and interpret the wide range of fraudulent activities. Supervised learning models, such as Random Forests and Gradient Boosting Machines (GBMs), excel at distinguishing legitimate transactions from potential fraud by modeling the complex, non-linear relationships in data. Unsupervised learning methods, including various clustering techniques, are particularly effective at detecting subtle anomalies within unlabeled data sets, which is essential for spotting new fraudulent patterns. Additionally, deep learning technologies like Long Short-Term Memory (LSTM) networks and Convolutional Neural Networks (CNNs) are adept at processing time-series and image data from IoT devices to identify unusual activities indicative of fraud. These techniques are further enhanced by advanced feature engineering, including feature selection algorithms [5] and Principal Component Analysis (PCA) [5], which optimize the inputs for models and improve their predictive accuracy. In the realm of real-time fraud detection, edge computing is crucial as it processes data directly on IoT devices. This significantly cuts down on latency and network congestion, speeding up response times while also enhancing data privacy by reducing the volume of sensitive information transmitted across networks. However, implementing these technologies in IoT systems presents challenges, such as ensuring data security during model training and achieving scalability across diverse devices and network environments. Looking ahead, the adoption of federated learning offers a more secure and decentralized method for training models, reducing the risks associated with data centralization and boosting privacy. Moreover, integrating reinforcement learning could continually refine fraud detection strategies to effectively respond to evolving security threats, thereby creating a robust detection framework that adapts to the dynamic challenges in IoT environments.

5 Case Studies and Real-world Examples

5.1 Analyzing High-Profile IoT Fraud Incidents

- **Verkada Cyber Attack** Verkada is a cloud-based security platform that provides security by integrating hardware and software for enterprises to monitor, manage, and securely protect physical environments. It primarily offers security solutions through video surveillance, access control, intercoms, alarms, and air quality monitoring. In 2021, the Verkada platform was attacked, compromising customers' valuable and confidential information. The compromised data included video footage from surveillance cameras, Wi-Fi credentials, data from access control products, sales reports, and more. The entry point for the attackers was a misconfigured customer support server that was exposed to the internet. First, the attackers accessed an administrator's credentials from the customer support server. Then, they logged into the customer support web interface using those credentials and gained access to customer devices through the web interface. This was a major breach in Verkada's history. It took 2 hours before the company became aware of the attack. Verkada addressed the security issue through forensic investigation and promptly informed customers about the breach.
- **The Mirai Botnet** The Mirai botnet is mainly focused on IoT devices. These malware convert those devices to bots for propagating distributed denial of

service (DDoS) [25]attacks. It was discovered in 2016, but it was noticed only after releasing the code of Mirai by Anna-senpai publicly. The malware exploits the common vulnerabilities in IoT devices, such as default passwords and open network ports commonly found in unsecured devices. The compromised devices as a whole became a large botnet and acted as a source of disruptive DDoS attacks.

Mirai finds the bots by continuously scanning networks for weak IoT devices with default credentials or open access points, infecting them, and linking them to a centralized command and control server. So that botnet attackers can coordinate attacks by operating thousands of bots simultaneously. To defend against such threats, users of IoT devices need to change default login credentials, restrict unnecessary remote access, and maintain up-to-date firewalls. Also, manufacturers of IoT devices keep reviewing the firmware they release.Manufacturers have also started offering tailored security solutions to mitigate these risks, but vigilance remains crucial to prevent devices from being co-opted into the Mirai botnet.

- **Cold in Finland Cyber attack** In November 2016, a chilling cyberattack hit the city of Lappeenranta, Finland, as cybercriminals managed to cut off the heating in two residential buildings. The attack came at a time when the temperature in Finland was well below freezing, making it a particularly dangerous situation for the residents. The method used was a Distributed Denial of Service (DDoS) attack, which overloaded the heating controllers and caused them to repeatedly reboot. Each time the system tried to restart, the heating would shut down again, leaving the buildings in the cold without proper warmth for an extended period. What made this attack possible was the exploitation of vulnerabilities in the IoT infrastructure. Specifically, the attackers targeted the building's automation system, which was responsible for controlling both central heating and hot water distribution. These systems, connected to the internet, lacked the necessary security measures to protect them from external threats. Without strong safeguards in place, the attackers were able to gain access and flood the system with massive amounts of traffic. This resulted in a cascade of reboots, rendering the heating system inoperative. The attackers capitalized on common weaknesses found in IoT devices, such as the use of default credentials or unprotected open ports. These security gaps are often overlooked but can leave critical systems vulnerable to remote intrusions. In this case, the failure to properly secure the building's heating controllers allowed the cyber criminals to seize control, turning a technical vulnerability into a serious physical threat to the occupants. The incident highlighted the growing risks associated with IoT systems, especially when they are left unsecured, as they can be exploited to cause real-world harm in unexpected ways. This attack served as a wake-up call, showcasing how cyber vulnerabilities can escalate into life-threatening situations, particularly in regions where extreme weather conditions demand fully operational and secure infrastructure.
- **Stuxnet** Stuxnet is one of the most infamous cyberattacks, and it highlights the serious vulnerabilities in the Internet of Things (IoT) within industrial

environments. The attack targeted Iran's Natanz uranium enrichment facility by compromising the Siemens Step7 software, which controlled programmable logic controllers (PLCs) responsible for running the plant's centrifuges. These PLCs, a crucial part of the facility's IoT infrastructure, were connected to Windows systems that Stuxnet exploited. By infiltrating these systems, the attackers were able to manipulate the centrifuges undetected. The breach came to light in 2010 when International Atomic Energy Agency (IAEA) inspectors noticed a high rate of centrifuge failures, leading to the discovery of the malicious Stuxnet worm.

Stuxnet caused significant damage, reportedly disabling 984 centrifuges and reducing uranium enrichment efficiency by 30%. This disruption delayed Iran's nuclear program by years. The attack exposed the vulnerabilities inherent in IoT systems, especially those used in critical infrastructure. It showed how interconnected devices, if not properly secured, can be exploited to cause real-world harm. Stuxnet set a precedent for how cyberattacks can manipulate physical systems, underscoring the importance of securing IoT devices in industrial and sensitive environments.

5.2 *Effective Strategies to Counter IoT Fraud*

Effective strategies to counter IoT fraud are essential due to the increasing prevalence of attacks on IoT devices. One of the most fundamental methods is strengthening device authentication mechanisms. Techniques such as the use of physically unclonable functions (PUF) can significantly boost the security of IoT devices, preventing unauthorized access and mitigating risks like man-in-the-middle attacks or device tampering [31]. PUF-based systems authenticate devices based on their unique physical characteristics, making it nearly impossible to clone or tamper with them. Coupling this with mutual authentication protocols, where devices are authenticated in real-time based on cryptographic methods, offers a robust layer of defense. Additionally, encrypted communication channels are paramount in ensuring that sensitive data exchanged between devices is secure from eavesdropping or interception. For network security, the EPIC (Efficient and Privacy-preserving Traffic Obfuscation) framework is proposed, which obfuscates traffic and prevents attacks that target data traffic patterns. Moreover, IDS (Intrusion Detection Systems) designed specifically for IoT networks are effective in detecting anomalies and protecting the network from wormholes, Sybil attacks, and other malicious activities.

Another critical strategy is securing the software aspect of IoT systems. Lightweight encryption algorithms can provide dynamic, fast communication between IoT devices without compromising on security, especially in power-constrained devices. This addresses the challenge of implementing resource-heavy encryption in environments with limited computational capacity. Additionally, firmware updates play a crucial role in closing security vulnerabilities that arise as IoT devices evolve. Regularly updating devices with the latest patches prevents exploits targeting outdated software. In conjunction with this, behavioral analysis techniques, such as static and dynamic malware detection systems, can be used to detect and neutralize software-based threats. Tools like DroidRanger and DroidAPIMiner, which analyze behavior and permission levels of applications, help prevent unauthorized data access. Finally, integrating blockchain technology for secure data transactions further enhances data integrity and privacy. By decentralizing trust and using attribute-based encryption, only validated users with proper access credentials can decrypt sensitive data, effectively securing IoT networks against data breaches and unauthorized access.

6 Securing Tomorrow: Navigating Future Challenges in Fraud Detection

6.1 Regulatory Landscape Evolution and Compliance Updates

The evolution of the regulatory landscape for cybersecurity in the IoT has gained significant momentum, particularly within the European Union (EU) [10]. The EU Cybersecurity Act, introduced in 2019, represents a major development by establishing a unified framework for cybersecurity certification of ICT products and services. This act strengthens the role of the EU Agency for Cybersecurity (ENISA), granting it more authority to provide expertise and oversight across the Union's digital ecosystem. The regulation sets a clear path for the creation of cybersecurity certification schemes at different assurance levels (basic, substantial, high) based on risk. These schemes help build trust in the digital market by ensuring that IoT products meet established security standards. However, while the certification remains voluntary, there is room for mandatory cybersecurity requirements through Union or national laws, ensuring that IoT products achieve the required security thresholds before they are allowed on the market.

In addition to the Cybersecurity Act, the regulatory framework has expanded to include sector-specific legislation, such as the Radio Equipment Directive (RED), which mandates cybersecurity features in wireless communication devices. This directive ensures that IoT devices like those with Wi-Fi or Bluetooth capabilities are safeguarded against unauthorized access and network exploitation. The Network and Information Systems Directive (NIS2), which is undergoing revision, also broadens the scope of cybersecurity to cover IoT manufacturing, vulnerability disclosure, and supply chain security. The proposed NIS2 extends beyond critical infrastructure to include key IoT sectors, addressing concerns about the lack of security in products entering the EU market. These developments, combined with coordinated efforts across the EU, aim to provide a robust regulatory foundation for securing IoT ecosystems and addressing challenges such as the complexity of interconnected systems and the risk of data breaches.

6.2 Balancing Security with Usability and Privacy Concerns

Balancing security with usability and privacy concerns in the IoT as well as Mobile-Internet of Things (M-IoT) [26] is a significant challenge due to the complex and dynamic nature of the network. The trade-off between securing M-IoT devices and maintaining usability is particularly difficult because increased security measures can often introduce latency, complexity, or resource overhead. Lightweight encryption mechanisms, such as symmetric key encryption, help in ensuring that security protocols do not overly burden resource-constrained devices like sensors and actuators. However, the demand for secure and fast encryption techniques to protect data without hampering device performance remains critical. Additionally, homomorphic encryption allows for performing operations on encrypted data, which helps ensure data confidentiality while maintaining usability in environments where computation on data is required without exposing sensitive information. While these encryption techniques balance security and performance, the trade-off with user privacy is often heightened, especially in cases where complex identity management and access control mechanisms could compromise user experience by requiring frequent authentication procedures or added layers of interaction complexity.

To address privacy concerns, anonymization techniques and attribute-based encryption help maintain user anonymity while ensuring that only authorized entities can access specific IoT data. This approach strengthens privacy but adds complexity to user management. The challenge arises when trying to keep this process seamless and unobtrusive for the user. Furthermore, behavioral analysis and trust management systems can be deployed to detect unusual activities or potential breaches without requiring the user's direct intervention. However, this adds another layer of concern regarding the collection of behavioral data, which may itself raise privacy issues. Balancing the privacy of collected data, ensuring it is not exploited or mishandled, while also maintaining robust security practices, is vital to gaining user trust. Ensuring usability without invasive data collection techniques, all while securing devices from potential vulnerabilities, represents the core challenge in striking the right balance between security, usability, and privacy in IoT environments.

7 Conclusion

As technology continues to advance, bringing new gadgets into our daily lives, it's crucial to address the security concerns associated with IoT. These devices, which make our lives easier and more efficient, also pose risks if not properly secured. For IoT devices, ensuring privacy and security from the outset is non-negotiable. Strict regulations should be in place to only allow devices with robust security measures onto the market. Additionally, manufacturers must commit to providing ongoing updates to combat new security threats, maintaining protection throughout the device's lifetime. Devices must be designed to detect and prevent fraudulent activities automatically. This could involve advanced algorithms that monitor for unusual activity patterns indicative of fraud. By incorporating these preventative measures, we can secure not only individual devices but also the entire interconnected system they form part of. This comprehensive approach to security and fraud prevention is key to maintaining trust and safety in our connected world.

References

1. Ahmadi-Assalemi, G., Al-Khateeb, H., Epiphaniou, G., Maple, C.: Cyber resilience and incident response in smart cities: a systematic literature review. Smart Cities **3**(3), 894–927 (2020)
2. Al-Hawawreh, M., Moustafa, N., Garg, S., Hossain, M.S.: Deep learning-enabled threat intelligence scheme in the internet of things networks. IEEE Trans. Netw. Sci. Eng. **8**(4), 2968–2981 (2020)
3. Al Hayajneh, A., Bhuiyan, M.Z.A., McAndrew, I.: Improving internet of things (iot) security with software-defined networking (sdn). Computers **9**(1), 8 (2020)
4. Ali, K., Rana, Z., Haseeb, R., Niaz, A., Zahid, M., Liang, D.: Detection of false data injection attacks in smart grids via nonlinear interval observer: a review. In: 2024 7th International Conference on Energy Conservation and Efficiency (ICECE), pp. 1–5. IEEE (2024)
5. Alsharif, N.: Ensembling pca-based feature selection with random tree classifier for intrusion detection on iot network. In: 2021 8th International Conference on Electrical Engineering, Computer Science and Informatics (EECSI), pp. 317–321. IEEE (2021)
6. Baho, S.A., Abawajy, J.: Analysis of consumer iot device vulnerability quantification frameworks. Electronics **12**(5), 1176 (2023)
7. Bettayeb, M., Nasir, Q., Talib, M.A.: Firmware update attacks and security for iot devices: survey. In: Proceedings of the ArabWIC 6th Annual International Conference Research Track, pp. 1–6 (2019)
8. Brierley, C., Pont, J., Arief, B., Barnes, D.J., Hernandez-Castro, J.: Paperw8: an iot bricking ransomware proof of concept. In: Proceedings of the 15th International Conference on Availability, Reliability and Security, pp. 1–10 (2020)
9. Chatterjee, A., Ahmed, B.S.: Iot anomaly detection methods and applications: a survey. Internet Things **19**, 100568 (2022)
10. Chiara, P.G.: The iot and the new eu cybersecurity regulatory landscape. Int. Rev. Law Comput. Technol. **36**(2), 118–137 (2022)
11. Cui, L., Qu, Y., Xie, G., Zeng, D., Li, R., Shen, S., Yu, S.: Security and privacy-enhanced federated learning for anomaly detection in iot infrastructures. IEEE Trans. Ind. Inform. **18**(5), 3492–3500 (2021)
12. Ding, W., Liao, S., Cheng, L., Mi, X., Zhao, Z., Hu, H.: Command hijacking on voice-controlled iot in amazon alexa platform. In: Proceedings of the 19th ACM Asia Conference on Computer and Communications Security, pp. 654–666 (2024)
13. El Jaouhari, S., Bouvet, E.: Secure firmware over-the-air updates for iot: survey, challenges, and discussions. Internet Things **18**, 100508 (2022)
14. Friedberg, I., Skopik, F., Settanni, G., Fiedler, R.: Combating advanced persistent threats: From network event correlation to incident detection. Comput. Security **48**, 35–57 (2015)
15. Gong, S., Tcydenova, E., Jo, J., Lee, Y., Park, J.H.: Blockchain-based secure device management framework for an internet of things network in a smart city. Sustainability **11**(14), 3889 (2019)

16. Haji, S.H., Ameen, S.Y.: Attack and anomaly detection in iot networks using machine learning techniques: a review. Asian J. Res. Comput. Sci **9**(2), 30–46 (2021)
17. Hammoudeh, M., Pimlott, J., Belguith, S., Epiphaniou, G., Baker, T., Kayes, A., Adebisi, B., Bounceur, A.: Network traffic analysis for threat detection in the internet of things. IEEE Internet Things Mag. **3**(4), 40–45 (2020)
18. Hernández-Ramos, J.L., Baldini, G., Matheu, S.N., Skarmeta, A.: Updating iot devices: challenges and potential approaches. In: 2020 Global Internet of Things Summit (GIoTS), pp. 1–5. IEEE (2020)
19. Hofstede, R., Čeleda, P., Trammell, B., Drago, I., Sadre, R., Sperotto, A., Pras, A.: Flow monitoring explained: from packet capture to data analysis with netflow and ipfix. IEEE Commun. Surv. Tutor. **16**(4), 2037–2064 (2014)
20. Kolehmainen, A.: Secure firmware updates for iot: a survey. In: 2018 IEEE International Conference on Internet of Things (iThings) and IEEE Green Computing and Communications (GreenCom) and IEEE Cyber, Physical and Social Computing (CPSCom) and IEEE Smart Data (SmartData), pp. 112–117. IEEE (2018)
21. Kolevski, D., Michael, K.: Edge computing and iot data breaches: security, privacy, trust, and regulation. IEEE Technol. Soc. Mag. **43**(1), 22–32 (2024)
22. Liu, G.X., Shi, L.F., Xin, D.J.: Data integrity monitoring method of digital sensors for internet-of-things applications. IEEE Internet Things J. **7**(5), 4575–4584 (2020)
23. Makkar, A., Kim, T.W., Singh, A.K., Kang, J., Park, J.H.: Secureiiot environment: federated learning empowered approach for securing iiot from data breach. IEEE Trans. Ind. Inform. **18**(9), 6406–6414 (2022)
24. Mugarza, I., Flores, J.L., Montero, J.L.: Security issues and software updates management in the industrial internet of things (iiot) era. Sensors **20**(24), 7160 (2020)
25. Salim, M.M., Rathore, S., Park, J.H.: Distributed denial of service attacks and its defenses in iot: a survey. J. Supercomput. **76**, 5320–5363 (2020)
26. Sharma, V., You, I., Andersson, K., Palmieri, F., Rehmani, M.H., Lim, J.: Security, privacy and trust for smart mobile-internet of things (m-iot): a survey. IEEE Access **8**, 167123–167163 (2020)
27. Shouran, Z., Ashari, A., Priyambodo, T.: Internet of things (iot) of smart home: privacy and security. Int. J. Comput. Appl. **182**(39), 3–8 (2019)
28. Sivaraman, V., Gharakheili, H.H., Fernandes, C., Clark, N., Karliychuk, T.: Smart iot devices in the home: security and privacy implications. IEEE Technol. Soc. Mag. **37**(2), 71–79 (2018)
29. Siwakoti, Y.R., Bhurtel, M., Rawat, D.B., Oest, A., Johnson, R.: Advances in iot security: vulnerabilities, enabled criminal services, attacks, and countermeasures. IEEE Internet Things J. **10**(13), 11224–11239 (2023)
30. Varela-Vaca, Á.J., Gasca, R.M., Iglesias, D., Gónzalez-Gutiérrez, J.: Automated trusted collaborative processes through blockchain & iot integration: the fraud detection case. Internet Things **25**, 101106 (2024)
31. Yadav, C.S., Singh, J., Yadav, A., Pattanayak, H.S., Kumar, R., Khan, A.A., Haq, M.A., Alhussen, A., Alharby, S.: Malware analysis in iot & android systems with defensive mechanism. Electronics **11**(15), 2354 (2022)
32. Zandberg, K., Schleiser, K., Acosta, F., Tschofenig, H., Baccelli, E.: Secure firmware updates for constrained iot devices using open standards: a reality check. IEEE Access **7**, 71907–71920 (2019)
33. Zhang, X., Yadollahi, M.M., Dadkhah, S., Isah, H., Le, D.P., Ghorbani, A.A.: Data breach: analysis, countermeasures and challenges. Int. J. Inf. Comput. Secur. **19**(3-4), 402–442 (2022)

Secure Communication Protocols: Safeguarding Information in The Digital Age

I. N. Shahanas and Sabu M. Thampi

1 Fundamentals of Secure Communication

In today's highly globalized world, secure communication is essential for protecting sensitive information and ensuring reliable data exchange. Whether it involves personal interactions, online financial transactions, or confidential corporate data transmitted across networks, the need for secure communication is paramount. It includes a set of principles designed to prevent unauthorized access, tampering, and disruptions, thereby safeguarding the integrity, confidentiality, and availability of information. These principles are critical in fostering trust, preserving privacy, and mitigating cyber threats, which could lead to severe financial or operational consequences. Adopting these foundational principles of secure communication is crucial for individuals, businesses, and governments seeking safety and reliability in an increasingly digital landscape. Secure communication plays a vital role in maintaining the confidentiality, integrity, and availability of data shared across networks, and these principles form the foundation of practices that protect sensitive information from unauthorized access, modification, and disruption.

Figure 1 presents the core principles essential for ensuring secure and reliable communication. It outlines seven key components: Confidentiality, Integrity, Availability, Authentication, Non-Repudiation, Authorization, and Auditing and Monitoring.

I. N. Shahanas (✉) · S. M. Thampi
Connected Systems and Intelligence Lab, School of Computer Science & Engineering, Digital University Kerala, Trivandrum, India
e-mail: shahanas.in@iiitmk.ac.in; sabu.thampi@duk.ac.in

S. M. Thampi et al. (eds.), *Securing the Connected World*,
https://doi.org/10.1007/978-3-031-82826-3_6

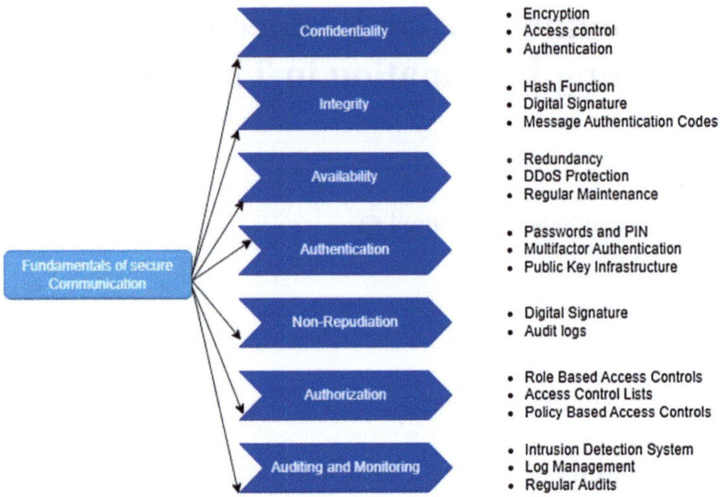

Fig. 1 Fundamentals of secure communication

1.1 Confidentiality

Confidentiality is a core principle of secure communication that safeguards sensitive information from unauthorized access and disclosure, ensuring that only authorized individuals or systems can access specific data. It is crucial for safeguarding sensitive information in various domains such as personal communication, finance, healthcare, and corporate data. Breaches can result in severe repercussions, including financial losses, damage to reputation, legal consequences, and identity theft. Several mechanisms and strategies are employed to effectively maintain confidentiality. Encryption is one of the most crucial methods, involving converting readable data (plaintext) into an unreadable format (ciphertext) using cryptographic algorithms and keys. This means that even if data is intercepted during transmission or accessed without authorization, it remains incomprehensible without the appropriate decryption key. Encryption methods can be categorized into two types: symmetric encryption, which uses the same key for both encryption and decryption (e.g., the Advanced Encryption Standard, or AES), and asymmetric encryption, which uses a pair of keys, a public key for encryption and a private key for decryption (e.g., RSA). Access control is another important aspect of ensuring confidentiality, which involves defining and enforcing policies that dictate who can access specific data and under what conditions.

Access control mechanisms include user authentication methods such as passwords, biometrics, and multifactor authentication to verify the identity of users before granting access to sensitive information. Furthermore, role-based access control (RBAC) assigns permissions based on user roles within an organization, ensuring that only those with the necessary authority can access particular data.

This minimizes the risk of unauthorized access and helps maintain confidentiality. Data masking is another technique to protect confidentiality, especially when real data is unnecessary. This involves obscuring specific data within a database, allowing it to be used for testing or analytical purposes without revealing sensitive information. For instance, when sharing data with developers for software testing, actual customer details can be masked or replaced with fictitious data to protect privacy. Data masking is another technique to protect confidentiality, especially when real data is unnecessary. This involves masking specific data within a database, allowing it to be used for testing or analytical purposes without revealing sensitive information. For instance, when sharing data with developers for software testing, actual customer details can be masked or replaced with fictitious data to protect privacy. The use of secure communication protocols also plays a significant role in maintaining confidentiality. These protocols authenticate the parties involved in the communication and establish an encrypted channel, making it challenging for eavesdroppers to intercept or decipher the data.

1.2 Integrity

Integrity is a fundamental principle of secure communication that ensures the accuracy, consistency, and trustworthiness of data throughout its lifecycle. It guarantees that information remains unchanged and unaltered during storage, transmission, and processing unless modified by authorized individuals. This principle is crucial in various contexts, including financial transactions, healthcare records, and legal documents, where even minor alterations can lead to significant repercussions, such as financial loss, legal liabilities, or compromised safety. To uphold integrity, several techniques and practices are employed. Hashing is one of the most common methods used to verify data integrity. A hash function converts data into a fixed-size string of characters, which serves as a unique digital fingerprint for that data. If the data is altered in any way, the hash value will change, signaling potential tampering. Hash functions are widely used in digital signatures and data verification processes to ensure that the original data has not been modified. Another technique for maintaining integrity is the use of checksums and message authentication codes (MACs). A checksum is a simple method that calculates a value based on the data's contents, which can be checked later to verify that the data remains unchanged. MACs, on the other hand, are cryptographic checksums that use a secret key along with the data to generate a hash. This ensures that only authorized parties can verify the integrity of the data, as the secret key is not shared with unauthorized users. Digital signatures also play a significant role in ensuring data integrity. A digital signature is a cryptographic method that allows the sender to sign a document or message digitally. This signature not only authenticates the sender's identity but also assures that the message has not been altered during transit. If any changes are made to the signed data, the signature will no longer be valid, indicating potential tampering. In addition to these techniques, organizations often implement robust audit trails and logging mechanisms to track changes to sensitive data. By maintaining detailed records of who accessed or modified data and when these actions occurred, organizations can quickly identify unauthorized alterations and take corrective measures.

1.3 Availability

Availability is a fundamental principle of secure communication that ensures that information and resources are accessible and usable by authorized users when needed. This principle is critical across various contexts, including business operations, emergency services, healthcare systems, and online services, where disruptions can lead to significant consequences such as financial losses, compromised safety, and degraded service quality. Maintaining availability is essential not only for operational efficiency but also for maintaining user trust and satisfaction in the services provided. To ensure availability, several strategies and mechanisms are employed. One of the primary methods is redundancy, where multiple systems or components are implemented to take over in case of a failure. Load balancing is another effective strategy for ensuring availability. This technique administers incoming network traffic across multiple servers to prevent any single server from becoming flooded. Regular maintenance and updates are crucial for maintaining availability. Keeping systems up to date and performing routine maintenance helps prevent unexpected failures caused by outdated software or hardware. DDoS protection is increasingly important in ensuring availability, particularly in the face of cyber threats. Distributed Denial of Service (DDoS) attacks overwhelm a system with excessive traffic, rendering it inaccessible to legitimate users. Continuous monitoring and alerting also play a significant role in maintaining availability.

1.4 Authentication

Authentication is a fundamental principle of secure communication that establishes the identity of users, devices, or systems before allowing access to sensitive data or resources. This process is critical in ensuring that only authorized individuals or entities can interact with a system, thereby safeguarding against unauthorized access and potential security breaches. In various contexts, including online banking, e-commerce, and corporate networks, effective authentication mechanisms help maintain the integrity and confidentiality of information. The authentication process typically involves three key factors: something you know, something you have, and something you are. One of the most effective methods of authentication is multi-factor authentication (MFA), which combines two or more of the aforementioned factors. By requiring multiple forms of verification, MFA adds a layer of security, making it much harder for attackers to gain unauthorized access. As the landscape of cybersecurity continues to evolve, maintaining robust authentication practices will be essential for safeguarding data and ensuring secure communication in a risingly interconnected world.

1.5 Non Repudiation

Non-repudiation is a fundamental principle of secure communication that ensures that a party involved in a transaction or communication cannot deny the authenticity of their signature, message, or data transmission. This principle is crucial in establishing accountability and trust in digital interactions, especially in contexts such as online banking, e-commerce, legal agreements, and secure communications within organizations. By providing irrefutable proof of the origin and integrity of messages, non-repudiation helps prevent disputes and enhances the credibility of electronic transactions. The concept of non-repudiation is typically achieved through two main components: authentication and digital signatures. Authentication ensures that the identities of the parties involved in a communication are verified, while digital signatures provide a means to confirm the integrity and origin of a message. Digital signatures use cryptographic techniques to create a unique identifier for a message or document. When a sender signs a message with their private key, a corresponding digital signature is generated. This signature can then be verified by anyone who has access to the sender's public key, allowing recipients to confirm that the message indeed originated from the claimed sender and has not been altered in transit. If the signature matches the message, the recipient can be assured of the message's authenticity and integrity, thus supporting the principle of non-repudiation. As the digital landscape evolves, upholding non-repudiation will be essential for ensuring secure communication and preventing disputes in various applications and industries.

1.6 Authorization

Authorization is an essential principle of secure communication that determines the permissions and access levels granted to users, devices, or systems within a network or application. It is the process of establishing what actions an authenticated user or entity is allowed to perform, ensuring that only authorized parties can access specific resources or perform certain functions. By implementing effective authorization mechanisms, organizations can protect sensitive information and resources from unauthorized access and potential misuse. The authorization process typically follows successful authentication, where a user's identity is verified. Once a user is authenticated, the system evaluates their access rights based on predefined policies, roles, or attributes. This process often involves role-based access control (RBAC), attribute-based access control (ABAC), or discretionary access control (DAC), each offering different approaches to managing user permissions. In RBAC, permissions are assigned to roles rather than individual users. Users are then assigned to specific roles based on their job functions or responsibilities. ABAC evaluates user permissions based on attributes, such as user identity, time of access, location, and the resource being accessed. DAC allows resource owners to make decisions about who can access their resources. In this model, users can grant or revoke access to their data or resources at their discretion. Effective authorization is crucial for maintaining the principle of least privilege, which dictates that users should only be granted the minimum level of access necessary to perform their job functions. By limiting access rights, organizations reduce the risk of unauthorized actions and potential data breaches.

1.7 Auditing and Monitoring

Auditing and monitoring are crucial principles of secure communication that play a vital role in maintaining the integrity, confidentiality, and availability of data and systems. These practices involve the systematic collection, analysis, and evaluation of data related to security events and communications within a network. By applying effective auditing and monitoring mechanisms, organizations can identify potential security threats, ensure compliance with regulations, and enhance their overall security posture. Auditing refers to the process of reviewing and examining records, logs, and activities within a system to ensure compliance with established policies and standards. This process typically involves the following key components Log Management, Regular Reviews, Compliance Checks, and Incident Response. Monitoring, on the other hand, involves the continuous observation of systems and networks to detect suspicious activities or security breaches in real time. Effective monitoring encompasses several practices such as Real-Time Alerts, Behavioral Analysis, Network Traffic Analysis, and User Activity Monitoring. The combination of auditing and monitoring provides a comprehensive approach to security. While auditing focuses on reviewing historical data to ensure compliance and identify past issues, monitoring allows for real-time detection and response to ongoing threats. Together, these practices help to sustain a robust security posture and effectively manage risk.

2 Importance of Secure Communication in Internet of Things

Secure communication in the Internet of Things (IoT) has become increasingly crucial as IoT technology infiltrates various sectors, including healthcare, smart homes, industrial systems, and transportation. These devices continuously generate and transmit immense amounts of sensitive information, ranging from personal and financial data to operational metrics. As their integration into daily life and industrial processes deepens, the importance of ensuring secure communication escalates dramatically. Without effective security measures, the data exchanged between IoT devices becomes vulnerable to interception, modification, or theft, leading to privacy breaches and unauthorized access. Such risks can result in severe repercussions, including financial losses, compromised safety, and operational failures. Given the substantial volume of data involved, prioritizing secure communication is essential. Additionally, many IoT devices store data locally or in the cloud, underscoring the need for robust security protocols to guard against unauthorized access and tampering. The decentralized and resource-limited nature of these devices further heightens their susceptibility to cyberattacks. In critical fields like healthcare, where the integrity of patient data is vital, and in industrial settings, where operational data is crucial for safety and efficiency, any breach of data security can have significant consequences. Thus, implementing secure communication practices is essential for safeguarding data integrity, preserving user trust, ensuring compliance with regulations, and securing the long-term sustainability of IoT technologies.

Because IoT systems are heavily integrated with human environments, the great potential for misuse exists, and many impacts such as physical destruction, financial loss, violations of privacy, and crime can easily come forth from one vulnerability [6]. If ignored, these could be the cause of preventing the full advancement of IoT. Most of the security threats and privacy issues arise from two major causes. First, IoT devices are resource-constrained in terms of energy consumption, memory capacities, and also their computational powers. These resource constraints make it impossible to directly apply traditional Internet techniques such as AES in an IoT-related application. Other techniques, such as TLS or IPsec, for delivering secure communication in resource-rich devices, such as laptops, tablets, and phones, cannot be directly applied to resource-limited IoT devices, hence resulting like security and privacy attacks. Such attacks involve a form of eavesdropping, network side-channel attacks, and even tracking; thus, it is of utmost importance that these techniques are adapted to the paradigm of the IoT in defense against such attacks with its delivery of the requirements of the IoT. Lack of well-investigated security and privacy guidelines, and their proper implementation, are other issues. Such guidelines and techniques will go a long way in helping IoT stakeholders, including developers and manufacturers, build secure IoT systems from the start, which will enhance security and privacy through design. Without such guidelines and countermeasures at the development lifecycle of the IoT system, many attacks and threats can materialize. For example, a policy recommendation can be using a permanent hardware secure booting process that would not allow the launching of malicious code of an IoT system. If an adversary replaces existing executable files of a manufactured process with their malicious version, the lack of following such an advisory could easily lead to compromised devices.

2.1 *Security Attacks In IoT*

The Fig. 2 represents a layered architecture of the Internet of Things (IoT), illustrating various components and technologies across three main layers namely Perception Layer, Network Layer, and Application Layer. The layers are shown with their respective components and associated technologies. The Perception Layer involves devices like wearable watches, temperature sensors, CCTV systems, and control and monitoring tools, using communication technologies like NFC, ZigBee, Wi-Fi, Bluetooth, LoRaWAN, etc. The Network Layer handles data transmission using protocols such as 6LoWPAN, GTSCH, RPL, CoAP, and CDMA over wired/wireless networks. The Application Layer represents IoT services like Smart Healthcare, Smart Agriculture, and Smart Homes, using communication protocols like AMQP, MQTT, CoAP, XMPP, and DDS.

While this layered architecture highlights the essential components and technologies involved in IoT, each layer is susceptible to various security attacks. These attacks differ based on the vulnerabilities and the protocols used at each layer [4, 7].

2.1.1 Perception Layer Attacks

- **Hardware tampering**—An attack that inflicts physical damage on compromised nodes while simultaneously providing access to sensitive information.
- **Fake node injection**—A new counterfeit node is introduced with the purpose of altering the original data and disseminating inaccurate information.
- **Sleep deprivation**—The attacker aims to consume more power than the node will be made to shut down.
- **Node jamming**—Signal interference in wireless communication can occur through the use of a jammer, which disrupts the communication flow for users. Such interference may result in a Denial-of-Service (DoS) attack.

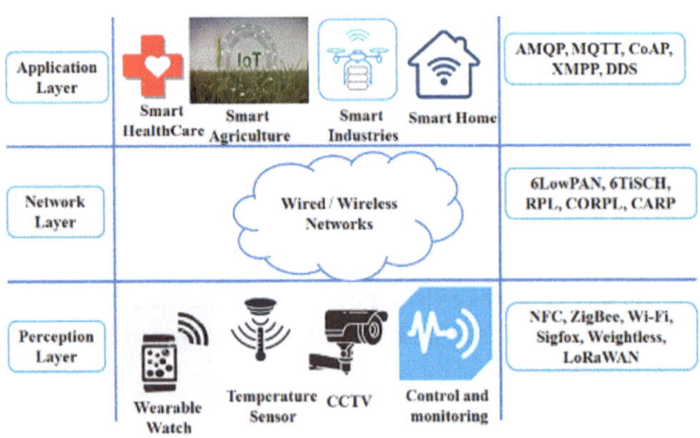

Fig. 2 IoT layered architecture

- **RF interference**—In the context of IoT applications utilizing RFID technology, an attacker may attempt to inject noise signals into the carrier frequency, thereby disrupting communication.

2.1.2 Network Layer Attacks

- **Man in the middle attack**—An attacker secretly intercepts communication between two parties, with the intent to either gain unauthorized access to private information or alter the transmitted data.
- **Traffic analysis attack**—The adversary is likely to target the network by leveraging an analysis and forecast of network information.
- **Spoofing attack**—A node may impersonate another by falsifying data to gain unauthorized access to information. For example, an attacker may modify the header to conceal their true identity, potentially leading to Man-in-the-Middle or Denial-of-Service attacks.
- **Sinkhole attack**—Attacker advertising the fake routing information which intent to attack the network traffic. It will cause other attacks like drops or alter the routing information, and selective forwarding.
- **Sybil attack**—A node may engage in impersonation by falsifying data to gain unauthorized access to information. For instance, an attacker might alter the header to obscure their true identity, which can facilitate Man-in-the-Middle or Denial-of-Service attacks.

2.1.3 Application Layer Attacks

- **Phishing attack**—It aims to access sensitive information like credit card numbers and authentication login credentials in a banking application by masquerading as trusted parties in Electronic communication.
- **Malicious script**—The attacker creates malicious code that compromises the system, rendering it vulnerable to data theft, security breaches, and file corruption.
- **Denial-of-Service (DoS) attack**—This happens when a node inundates the bandwidth or system resources with excessive requests within a defined time frame.

2.2 CISCO's Reference Model For IoT

Having acknowledged these challenges, Cisco rolled out its IoT Reference Model in 2014 [1]. This is an all-encompassing framework (Fig. 3) that takes the best to explain and drive successful IoT solutions, from architecture to security and data management, among others. The Cisco IoT Reference Model facilitates designing

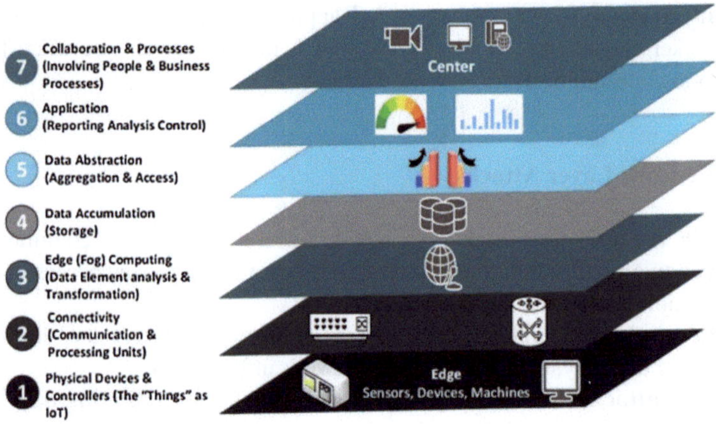

Fig. 3 CISCO's reference model for IoT

scalable, secure, and interoperable IoT systems for covering a wide range of industries and use cases. Cisco's model then breaks down into finer and structured IoT components and how they relate to missing physical devices, connectivity, edge computing, data concentration, and application layers. This approach ensures that every aspect of an IoT implementation is taken into account, mitigating inherent security risks and operational challenges toward the development of robust IoT ecosystems capable of delivering reliable and secure services. The model is composed of seven key layers, each addressing different aspects of IoT system design and implementation.

The first layer, **Physical Devices and Controllers**, involves the foundational components like sensors, actuators, and devices that interact with the physical world, collecting data and performing actions. The second layer, **Connectivity**, focuses on establishing reliable and secure communication channels between devices, leveraging protocols and networking technologies that ensure data can be transmitted efficiently and securely. **Edge Computing**, the third layer, deals with local data processing to reduce latency and bandwidth usage, enabling real-time decision-making close to the data source. This is particularly important in scenarios where immediate response is critical, such as in industrial automation or autonomous vehicles. The fourth layer, **Data Accumulation**, involves the storage and aggregation of data from various sources, ensuring that data is organized and accessible for further analysis. The fifth layer, **Data Abstraction**, is concerned with organizing and filtering data to make it usable for applications and analytics. This layer ensures that raw data is transformed into meaningful information that can be utilized effectively. The sixth layer, **Application**, focuses on deploying data-driven applications and services that provide value to end-users, such as predictive maintenance systems, smart home applications, or healthcare monitoring solutions. Finally, the seventh layer, **Collaboration and Processes**, integrates IoT data with business processes and workflows, driving efficiency and innovation. This layer ensures that IoT systems are not just isolated entities but are seamlessly integrated into the broader organizational context, supporting decision-making and operational improvements. By breaking down the IoT ecosystem into these layers, the Cisco IoT Reference Model provides a clear and structured roadmap for developing IoT solutions. It highlights the importance of security, scalability, and interoperability at each layer, ensuring that IoT systems can be effectively and securely deployed. This comprehensive approach helps organizations navigate the complexities of IoT implementation, fostering the development of robust, secure, and scalable IoT ecosystems capable of delivering significant value across various industries.

Integrating security with Cisco's Reference Model for IoT involves addressing the specific security needs at each layer of the model, ensuring comprehensive protection from physical devices to business processes. At the first layer, Physical Devices and Controllers, security integration includes device authentication, tamper resistance, and firmware security. Device authentication ensures that only authenticated devices can connect to the network, using methods like digital certificates and secure boot processes. Tamper resistance involves implementing physical security measures to prevent tampering, such as secure hardware designs and tamper-evident packaging. Regular firmware updates are crucial to patch vulnerabilities and prevent exploits.

In the Connectivity layer, secure communication protocols like TLS (Transport Layer Security) and IPsec (Internet Protocol Security) encrypt data in transit, ensuring that it cannot be intercepted or altered. Network segmentation isolates IoT devices on separate network segments, reducing the risk of lateral movement by attackers. Implementing strict access controls regulates which devices and users can communicate over the network, providing an additional layer of security. For Edge Computing, local data encryption is essential to protect data processed and stored at the edge from unauthorized access. Ensuring edge device security involves secure configurations, regular updates, and anomaly monitoring. Trusted execution environments (TEEs) are used to run sensitive applications securely on edge devices, protecting against various attacks.

In the Data Accumulation layer, ensuring data integrity through cryptographic hash functions helps detect any alterations to the accumulated data. Secure storage using encryption both at rest and in transit protects against unauthorized access. Implementing role-based access controls (RBAC) ensures that only authorized personnel can access or modify the accumulated data, maintaining data integrity and security. Data Abstraction involves sanitizing and filtering data to remove any malicious input that could exploit applications or services. Keeping data encrypted during abstraction processes maintains confidentiality. Strict access management policies control who can abstract and interact with the data, ensuring that only authorized individuals can access sensitive information. At the Application layer, developing applications with secure coding practices prevents vulnerabilities such as SQL injection, buffer overflows, and cross-site scripting (XSS). Robust authentication and authorization mechanisms ensure that only legitimate users can access application functionalities. Regular security audits and penetration testing identify and mitigate potential vulnerabilities, maintaining application security.

In the Collaboration and Processes layer, integrating security into business processes ensures that workflows involving IoT data are designed with security in mind. Compliance with relevant regulations and standards, such as GDPR and HIPAA, is crucial to maintaining legal and industry-specific security requirements. Developing and implementing an incident response plan allows organizations to quickly address and mitigate security breaches or attacks. Across all layers, continuous monitoring detects and responds to security incidents in real-time, maintaining overall security. Establishing comprehensive security policies and conducting regular training for employees and stakeholders promotes best security practices. Regular risk assessments identify potential threats and vulnerabilities, allowing organizations to apply appropriate mitigation strategies. By integrating security measures at each layer of Cisco's IoT Reference Model, organizations can build a robust and secure IoT infrastructure. This layered approach ensures comprehensive security, protecting against a wide range of threats and vulnerabilities and covering all aspects of the IoT ecosystem.

3 Commonly Used Communication Protocols in IoT And Their Limitations

3.1 Wireless Communication Protocols

In the realm of the Internet of Things (IoT), various wireless communication protocols play a crucial role in enabling connectivity and interaction among devices. Each protocol is designed to meet specific needs based on factors such as range, power consumption, and data requirements [25, 34].

Being a widely used protocol, **Wi-Fi** makes fast internet access possible to a variety of devices. Besides that, it is very effective for applications requiring large data transfer, like video streaming or file sharing. However, Wi-Fi tends to use more power and could be considered a limitation in the operation time of battery-based devices. Another very widely used protocol is **Bluetooth**, which is perhaps most well-known for having very low power usage and being very suitable for short-distance communication. It's widely used in personal devices such as wearables, smart home gadgets, and so on. This is great because it allows easy, seamless connectivity between various devices without quickly draining their batteries, suitable for applications wherein data exchanges between different devices are frequent but over limited distances. **Zigbee** is one among the low-power and low-data-rate applications. It is an ideal application for home automation and industrial control systems because it can support reliable mesh networking. In this type of network configuration, devices extend their coverage area by passing the data to other nodes where the relay continues for a long distance. Hence, in smart lighting, security systems, and temperature monitoring applications where multiple devices have to function together, Zigbee proves effective (Fig. 4).

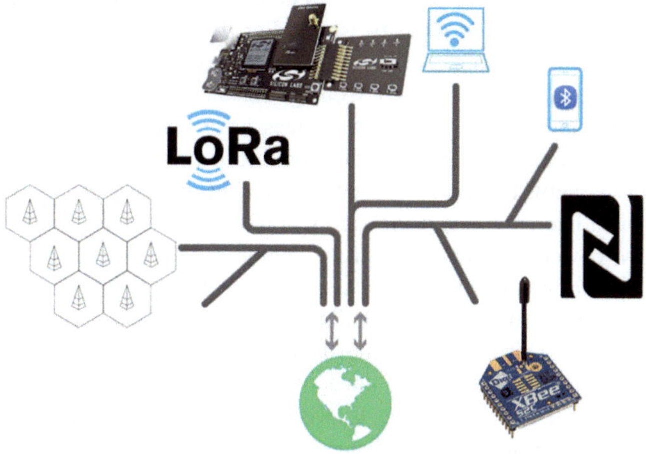

Fig. 4 Types of wireless communication protocols in IoT

LoRaWAN Long Range Wide Area Network is built to accommodate remote transmissions with low power consumption. It makes it excellent for applications in sensing and monitoring, such as agriculture or environmental monitoring [45, 46]. LoRaWAN can reach several kilometers over which is very much required in scenarios where devices are deployed in hard-to-reach areas. Narrowband IoT NB-IoT is cellular technology for low-bandwidth applications. It covers a wide range and penetration, which makes its wide deployment in harsh urban environments where the visual barriers could affect the signal strength. **NB-IoT** supports a large number of devices under the same network, suitable for smart city applications like smart parking management and utility monitoring. **Z-Wave** is primarily focused on low-power home automation and focuses on mesh networking robustness. This protocol allows numerous smart devices, including locks, lights, and thermostats, to operate in a seamless interplay. So, it is a favorite among consumers who want to create holistic smart home environments. The choice of a specific wireless communication protocol depends on an application's need for a certain range, power consumption, and data rates for IoT applications. Therefore, the real understanding of the strengths and limitations of each protocol shall be of prime importance for developing effective IoT solutions against the numerous requirements of modern connected devices.

3.2 Limitations of The Commonly Used Methods

Each of the various wireless communication protocols utilized in IoT has particular limitations. In many ways, such limitations give rise to security issues that pose threats to devices and networks [42, 45]. It is important to be conversant with such concerns in developing secure IoT systems. Wi-Fi, though of extremely fast connectivity, has significant security issues. For decades, this particular protocol has been vulnerable to attacks, including eavesdropping, unauthorized access, and denial-of-service attacks. Although security standards such as WPA3 are more recent and thus much stronger, many devices have not taken advantage of this. Therefore, when a device has been compromised it often becomes an entry point to a much larger network for those attackers. In addition, the scope of Wi-Fi signals can be easier to intercept data if they are within the scope of reception. Bluetooth, with its low power consumption, differs with different security issues. While Bluetooth does offer encryption mechanisms that have authentication, it is still susceptible to a range of attacks—including Bluejacking, Bluesnarfing, and Man-in-the-Middle attacks. This means personal data may be accessed without authorization or that other devices might become unnecessarily interconnected. While Bluetooth is relatively secure at close range, crowded areas can increase vulnerability to being attacked by hackers using advanced technology to take advantage of such weaknesses.

The AES-128 encryption makes Zigbee often thought of as a secure technology. However, vulnerabilities include being susceptible to replay attacks: when an attacker intercepts the retransmission of messages intended to control or disrupt the communications between devices. Moreover, because most networks operated using Zigbee are mesh, compromising one device can be enough for an attacker to gain access to the whole network. Such vulnerabilities can be further accentuated by relying upon the use of weak passwords and poor key management practices, and therefore, the need for developers to use strong security programs is all the more important. Although LoRaWAN has been designed for long-range communication, it suffers from security issues. Although the encryption techniques involve AES, a flaw in the protocol's architecture can prove to be vulnerable to various types of attacks. The authenticating mechanisms provided for devices are limited so that several unauthorized devices might join the network; it is indeed a major threat. LoRaWAN signals possess the properties of long-range communication that make them susceptible to eavesdropping and data interception, especially in less secure environments.

The security features of the cellular network favor the Narrowband IoT but also have some vulnerabilities in store. Since the dependency is on the infrastructure of the cellular networks, once the network itself gets compromised, all the devices connected to it get threatened. Furthermore, even though NB-IoT supports encryption and authentication, its complexity sometimes leads to security misconfigurations that keep bringing risks to devices. Moreover, the operational scalability of NB-IoT networks is questionable while enforcing a standardized security policy over numerous devices. Z-Wave is robust for home automation but poses security issues when encryption is combined with the mesh network design. If one device is compromised, then an attacker may use it as a point of entry to manipulate or gain control over other devices inside the network. On the other hand, Z-Wave also bases its security on device pairing, but this leaves the devices open to unauthorized access if not done securely. It is very nonchalant about firmware updates; thus, devices are often left vulnerable to known exploits. Both of these communication protocols come riddled with meaningful security limitations when used for IoT applications. All these attack vectors expose networks to unauthorized access, data interception, and device manipulation [28]. Hence, developers and users need to implement strong security approaches, including firmware updates, strong authentication methods, and continuous monitoring of suspicious activities [17].

3.3 IoT Messaging Protocols

IoT messaging protocols form the backbone of the Internet of Things (IoT) ecosystem, enabling efficient communication between diverse devices. These protocols facilitate data exchange between sensors, embedded systems, and other devices across a network. Given the diverse nature of IoT devices, which range from low-power sensors to more complex systems, traditional internet communication protocols are not adequate for handling IoT-specific requirements. IoT messaging protocols are designed to be lightweight, efficient, and secure, addressing the unique challenges posed by IoT environments, such as limited bandwidth, power constraints, and varying computational capabilities. Unlike traditional Internet communication protocols, IoT messaging protocols are optimized for transmitting data across distributed and often resource-constrained networks. IoT devices constantly generate and exchange large amounts of sensitive information, including personal, financial, and operational data. These protocols allow devices to communicate while minimizing the consumption of bandwidth and power, ensuring efficient data transfer. As IoT technology pervades many domains, including healthcare, industrial systems, and transportation, the selection of an appropriate protocol becomes critical for ensuring reliable and secure communication.

The architecture of IoT messaging protocols varies significantly to meet the demands of different IoT applications. Some protocols are designed to be extremely lightweight, and suitable for small devices with limited computational resources, while others are built to handle more complex tasks, such as guaranteeing message delivery and maintaining message integrity. In scenarios where devices are expected to communicate intermittently or across unreliable networks, protocols that prioritize minimal overhead and efficient data transmission are crucial. Moreover, the characteristics of IoT messaging protocols often reflect the specific needs of the application domain. For instance, in industrial automation or healthcare settings, where data integrity and security are paramount, more complex protocols with robust security and reliability features may be required. These protocols must ensure that data is transmitted without loss, corruption, or unauthorized access, particularly when sensitive or critical data is involved. On the other hand, in less demanding environments, simpler protocols that prioritize low power consumption and fast communication may be more suitable. As IoT continues to evolve, the importance of selecting appropriate messaging protocols becomes more evident. The variety of IoT applications has led to the development of numerous protocols, each tailored to specific needs such as scalability, reliability, and communication models. The ability of these protocols to handle the unique demands of IoT networks—such as efficient real-time communication, security, and power constraints—is essential for the continued growth of the IoT ecosystem. Given the growing reliance on IoT devices in critical sectors such as healthcare, industry, and smart infrastructure, the selection and use of appropriate messaging protocols play a significant role in determining the success and security of IoT systems. These protocols must balance efficiency, scalability, and security to support the expanding and diversifying IoT landscape. Understanding the nuances of each protocol, including its strengths and limitations, is vital for building secure, scalable, and efficient IoT networks.

3.3.1 Hypertext Transfer Protocol (HTTP)

The **Hypertext Transfer Protocol (HTTP)** is one of the most used protocols over the internet for transferring data between clients and servers. Further to that, in the Internet of Things, HTTP is used to allow communication between devices and applications, or between devices and servers. HTTP, however, was originally developed for web-based applications rather than resource-constrained environments like IoT. Nonetheless, HTTP remains important in some IoT applications: specifically in those applications in which devices need to interact with web services or where IoT platforms are built on top of existing web infrastructure.

- **Use of HTTP in IoT Communication** :
  HTTP operates over **TCP/IP**, the dominant protocol suite on the internet, which ensures reliable and ordered data transmission between devices. Many IoT devices and applications that require connectivity with cloud services use HTTP because of its compatibility with existing web infrastructure, making it a natural choice for IoT systems that need to access cloud-based APIs or exchange data with web servers.In practice, HTTP is often used in IoT for:
  - **Device Configuration and Management**: IoT devices often provide web-based interfaces for administrators or users to configure, update, or monitor device status via HTTP or HTTPS.
  - **Cloud Integration**: Many IoT systems rely on cloud-based platforms for data storage, processing, or analytics. These systems often use RESTful APIs over HTTP to send or receive data.
  - **Web-Based Dashboards and Control Interfaces**: IoT systems, especially in consumer or industrial applications, may provide web dashboards to monitor and control connected devices, with HTTP facilitating this interaction.
  - **Data Reporting**: Devices may periodically send data to web servers using HTTP requests, enabling data aggregation and analysis in centralized systems.
- **Security of HTTP in IoT** :
  To enhance the security of HTTP communication in IoT environments, HTTPS (HTTP Secure), which incorporates TLS (Transport Layer Security), is widely

used. HTTPS encrypts the communication between the IoT device and the server, protecting sensitive data from being intercepted by attackers. The use of HTTPS ensures:

- **Confidentiality**: Data transferred between IoT devices and servers is encrypted, preventing eavesdropping and data leakage.
- **Integrity**: HTTPS protects the integrity of data by ensuring that it is not tampered with during transmission. If any alteration is detected, the connection is dropped.
- **Authentication**: By using digital certificates, HTTPS can authenticate the identity of the server, ensuring that devices are communicating with trusted services.

However, while HTTPS improves security, it can introduce significant challenges in IoT contexts due to the computational and power requirements for encryption, certificate management, and secure key exchanges. Many IoT devices, especially low-power sensors, may struggle with these overheads.

– **Limitations and Challenges of HTTP in IoT** :
Although HTTP can be used in IoT communication, some several limitations and challenges make it less suitable for many IoT applications:

- **High Overhead and Resource Intensity**: HTTP was not designed with resource-constrained devices in mind. It introduces significant overhead because every HTTP request includes headers, status codes, and other metadata, which consume valuable bandwidth and processing power. For small, battery-powered IoT devices like sensors or actuators, these additional data costs can be prohibitive.
- **Stateless Nature**: HTTP is a stateless protocol, meaning that each request from a client to a server is independent, with no memory of previous interactions. This model can create inefficiencies in IoT applications that require continuous, real-time data exchange, as devices must re-establish connections for each communication, adding latency and power consumption.
- **Lack of Native Support for Asynchronous Communication**: Many IoT applications require asynchronous communication, where devices continuously push or receive data in real-time, such as in monitoring systems or industrial automation. HTTP, being primarily a request-response protocol, does not natively support push notifications or bidirectional communication. While workarounds like HTTP long polling or WebSockets exist, these are not always ideal for low-power or highly-constrained IoT devices.
- **Increased Power Consumption**: Maintaining an open HTTP connection, especially over HTTPS, can be power-intensive for IoT devices. The encryption and decryption processes in HTTPS consume additional CPU cycles, draining battery life more quickly, which is a critical limitation in battery-powered IoT devices like smart sensors or wearable devices.
- **Scalability Issues**: HTTP's reliance on point-to-point communication (client-server) makes it difficult to scale in large IoT networks with thousands or

millions of devices. Unlike lightweight protocols like MQTT or CoAP, which are designed for massive scalability and can efficiently handle high volumes of data from distributed devices, HTTP struggles to efficiently support such architectures.

- **Network Congestion**: IoT devices often operate in constrained or unreliable networks (such as low-power wide-area networks or wireless sensor networks). HTTP's reliance on TCP can exacerbate network congestion, as TCP requires multiple packet exchanges to establish a connection (the TCP handshake) and ensure reliable delivery through acknowledgments. This makes HTTP less suitable for networks with high latency or frequent packet loss, which are common in IoT scenarios.

– **Alternatives to HTTP in IoT** :
Due to these limitations, many IoT applications prefer using protocols that are more suited to the unique requirements of IoT environments:

- **MQTT**: As a lightweight, publish-subscribe protocol, MQTT is well-suited for low-bandwidth and resource-constrained devices, allowing efficient and scalable communication with minimal overhead.
- **CoAP**: Designed for constrained environments, CoAP uses a RESTful model similar to HTTP but is optimized for lower power consumption and operates over UDP to reduce transmission costs.
- **AMQP**: Used in more robust systems, AMQP offers reliable message delivery with better support for complex messaging patterns and transactions in IoT environments that require guaranteed delivery.
- **WebSockets**: Provides full-duplex communication over a single TCP connection, which is useful for real-time communication in IoT but still introduces higher overhead compared to MQTT or CoAP.

3.3.2 MQTT And Secure MQTT

The **MQTT (Message Queuing Telemetry Transport)** is a lightweight messaging protocol designed primarily for low-bandwidth, high-latency, or unreliable networks. It uses a publish-subscribe architecture, where clients communicate through a central broker rather than directly with each other. This decoupling allows for efficient communication in systems with numerous interconnected devices, making MQTT a popular choice for various Internet of Things (IoT) applications, such as smart home automation, industrial monitoring, and telemetry data collection [14, 15, 27, 44].

– **Key Features of MQTT**

- **Lightweight Design**: MQTT messages have a small overhead, making it suitable for resource-constrained devices and environments with limited bandwidth.

- **Publish-Subscribe Model**: Devices can publish messages to specific topics on the broker, and other devices can subscribe to those topics to receive messages, enabling scalable and flexible communication.
- **Quality of Service (QoS)**: MQTT provides three levels of QoS, allowing developers to choose the right level of message delivery assurance based on the application requirements:

  * **QoS 0**: At most once delivery (fire and forget).
  * **QoS 1**: At least once delivery (guaranteed delivery but may receive duplicates).
  * **QoS 2**: Exactly once delivery (ensures no message is lost and no duplicates).

- **Retained Messages**: A retained message feature allows the broker to hold the last message published to a topic, providing new subscribers with the latest state immediately upon subscribing.
- **Last Will and Testament (LWT)**: MQTT allows clients to set a "last will" message that the broker will send to a specified topic if the client unexpectedly disconnects, helping in monitoring device status.

– **Secure MQTT**

Secure MQTT refers to the implementation of security measures on the standard MQTT protocol to ensure the confidentiality, integrity, and authenticity of messages exchanged between clients and the broker [26, 32]. While standard MQTT lacks built-in security features, it can be secured through various methods:

- **Transport Layer Security (TLS)**: The most common method for securing MQTT communications is by using TLS (or its predecessor, SSL). TLS encrypts the data transmitted between clients and brokers, preventing eavesdropping and man-in-the-middle attacks.
- **Authentication Mechanisms**: Secure MQTT can implement various authentication methods, such as:

  * **Username and Password**: Simple credential-based authentication.
  * **Client Certificates**: Utilizing public key infrastructure (PKI) for mutual authentication, where both the client and server authenticate each other using digital certificates.
  * **OAuth and Token-based Authentication**: More sophisticated authentication mechanisms that can be employed, especially in environments where third-party services are involved.

- **Access Control Lists (ACLs)**: Brokers can implement ACLs to restrict which clients can publish or subscribe to specific topics, enhancing security by ensuring only authorized devices can communicate over certain channels.
- **Message Integrity**: To ensure that messages have not been altered during transmission, message signing and hashing can be applied. This ensures that the recipient can verify the authenticity and integrity of the messages received.

- **Security of MQTT and Secure MQTT**
  The security of MQTT and Secure MQTT hinges on several critical aspects:
  - **Confidentiality**: By implementing TLS, the data exchanged between MQTT clients and brokers is encrypted, ensuring that even if data packets are intercepted, they cannot be read without the corresponding encryption keys.
  - **Integrity**: Secure MQTT ensures that messages are not tampered with during transmission. If any alteration is detected, the message can be rejected, maintaining data integrity.
  - **Authentication**: Authentication mechanisms prevent unauthorized devices from accessing the MQTT broker, ensuring that only legitimate clients can publish or subscribe to topics.
  - **Authorization**: Using ACLs, brokers can control which authenticated clients have permission to publish or subscribe to specific topics, adding a layer of security to the MQTT framework.
- **Limitations and Challenges of MQTT and Secure MQTT**
  Despite its advantages, MQTT and Secure MQTT come with certain limitations and challenges:
  - **Resource Consumption**: While MQTT is designed to be lightweight, the implementation of TLS encryption adds computational overhead, which can be challenging for very low-power or resource-constrained devices (e.g., microcontrollers). Encryption and decryption processes consume additional CPU cycles and memory.
  - **Latency**: The added security measures, particularly TLS, can introduce latency in message delivery, which may be undesirable in real-time applications requiring immediate responses.
  - **Broker Bottleneck**: The central broker architecture can create a single point of failure in large deployments. If the broker becomes unavailable, all devices relying on it for communication may be affected, necessitating redundancy and failover mechanisms.
  - **Scalability Issues**: Although MQTT can handle numerous devices, the performance of the broker can degrade when managing large-scale deployments with thousands or millions of connected devices. This can lead to increased message latency or even broker crashes if not appropriately scaled.
  - **Complexity of Security Implementation**: Implementing security features such as TLS, client certificates, and token-based authentication can add complexity to the deployment and maintenance of MQTT systems. Developers need to ensure proper management of certificates and keys, which may require additional resources and expertise.
  - **Limited Built-in Security Features**: Standard MQTT lacks built-in security mechanisms, necessitating additional configuration and security best practices. If developers neglect to implement necessary security measures, MQTT systems can become vulnerable to attacks.

- **Message Size Limitations**: MQTT has a default message size limit (usually around 256 MB), which may be restrictive for applications requiring the transmission of large payloads, such as multimedia data.
- **Overhead of QoS**: While the QoS feature enhances message delivery guarantees, higher QoS levels introduce additional overhead, impacting overall network performance and resource usage, particularly in low-power devices.

3.3.3 Advanced Message Queuing Protocol (AMQP)

The **AMQP (Advanced Message Queuing Protocol)** is an open standard application layer protocol that enables message-oriented middleware for message-oriented applications. It was designed to facilitate communication between applications reliably and efficiently, particularly in distributed systems. In the context of the Internet of Things (IoT), AMQP is increasingly utilized due to its robust features that support message queuing, publish-subscribe, and point-to-point messaging patterns, making it suitable for various IoT applications, such as industrial automation, smart grids, and real-time data processing. AMQP is characterized by a few core components:

- **Broker**: The central message broker is responsible for receiving messages from producers, routing them to appropriate consumers, and ensuring reliable delivery. This centralized architecture supports complex routing capabilities.
- **Producers**: These are the clients that send messages to the broker, representing IoT devices or applications that generate data.
- **Consumers**: These are the clients that receive messages from the broker, typically representing applications or services that need to process the data sent by producers.
- **Queues**: Messages are stored in queues until they can be consumed, enabling reliable message delivery even when the consumers are not available at the time of message production.
- **Bindings and Exchanges**: AMQP uses bindings and exchanges to route messages to queues based on routing keys and binding rules, allowing for flexible and dynamic message routing.

- **Key Features of AMQP for IoT**

  - **Reliability**: AMQP ensures reliable message delivery through mechanisms such as message acknowledgments, durable queues, and transactional support, making it suitable for mission-critical IoT applications.
  - **Flexible Routing**: AMQP provides advanced routing capabilities, allowing messages to be directed to one or multiple queues based on specified criteria. This enables complex communication patterns and decouples message producers from consumers.

- **Support for Multiple Messaging Patterns**: AMQP supports various messaging patterns, including point-to-point, publish-subscribe, and request-reply, making it versatile for different IoT application requirements.
- **Message Queuing**: Messages can be queued when consumers are unavailable, ensuring that no data is lost and allowing for asynchronous communication, which is beneficial in scenarios with intermittent connectivity.
- **Interoperability**: Being an open standard, AMQP facilitates interoperability between different systems, applications, and devices, allowing for seamless integration in heterogeneous IoT environments.

– **Security of AMQP in IoT**
The security of AMQP is crucial in IoT applications, as they often deal with sensitive data and require secure communication between devices. AMQP incorporates several security features and best practices:

- **Transport Layer Security (TLS)**: AMQP supports TLS for encrypting data in transit, ensuring confidentiality and protecting against eavesdropping or man-in-the-middle attacks.
- **Authentication**: AMQP allows for various authentication methods, including:
  * Username and Password: Simple credential-based authentication for clients connecting to the broker.
  * Client Certificates: For mutual authentication, where both the client and broker validate each other's identities using digital certificates.
- **Authorization**: AMQP brokers can implement access control policies to restrict which clients can publish or subscribe to specific queues or exchanges, enhancing security by ensuring that only authorized entities can interact with the messaging infrastructure.
- **Message Integrity**: Mechanisms can be employed to verify the integrity of messages, ensuring that they have not been tampered with during transmission. This can include digital signatures or hash functions.
- **Replay Protection**: Some AMQP implementations include replay protection mechanisms to guard against replay attacks, where an attacker could resend valid messages to manipulate systems.

– **Limitations and Challenges of AMQP in IoT**
Although AMQP offers numerous benefits, it also faces certain limitations and challenges when implemented in IoT environments. Its complex protocol design can result in higher resource consumption, which may not be ideal for IoT devices with limited power and processing capabilities. Additionally, the overhead involved in ensuring reliable message delivery can lead to increased latency, making it less suitable for time-sensitive IoT applications.

- **Complexity**: AMQP's feature-rich design and complex architecture can make it challenging to implement and maintain, especially for teams without extensive messaging system experience. This complexity can also lead to higher development and operational costs.

- **Resource Consumption**: Compared to lightweight protocols like MQTT, AMQP may consume more system resources due to its richer feature set and reliance on a broker-based architecture. This can be an issue for low-power or resource-constrained IoT devices that require efficient use of CPU and memory.
- **Latency**: The additional overhead introduced by the AMQP protocol and its broker-based architecture can lead to increased latency in message delivery, which may not be acceptable for real-time applications that require immediate data processing.
- **Broker Dependency**: The reliance on a centralized broker means that if the broker becomes unavailable, communication between producers and consumers is disrupted. This single point of failure requires careful consideration of broker redundancy and failover strategies in critical applications.
- **Scalability Challenges**: While AMQP is designed to support a large number of clients and messages, its performance can degrade under high loads if the broker is not appropriately scaled. Scaling out brokers to handle increased load can complicate architecture and management.
- **Limited Support for Low-Bandwidth Networks**: AMQP is typically designed for more reliable network conditions and may not perform optimally in environments with high latency or frequent disconnections. This can be a concern in some IoT applications that operate in remote or rural areas with unreliable connectivity.
- **Protocol Overhead**: The extensive features and capabilities of AMQP introduce protocol overhead, which may not be suitable for applications that prioritize minimizing data transmission size and processing requirements. This can lead to inefficient use of bandwidth in IoT networks.
- **Implementation Variability**: Different brokers may implement the AMQP specification with variations, leading to potential interoperability issues. Developers must ensure compatibility between the clients and brokers being used in their IoT systems.

3.3.4 Constrained Application Protocol (CoAP)

The **CoAP (Constrained Application Protocol)** is a specialized web transfer protocol designed specifically for use in constrained environments, such as those typically found in the Internet of Things (IoT). Developed by the IETF (Internet Engineering Task Force), CoAP is built to enable simple, low-overhead communication between devices, particularly those with limited processing capabilities, memory, and battery power. CoAP is especially well-suited for applications that require efficient use of bandwidth and low power consumption, such as smart homes, industrial automation, and environmental monitoring [43]. CoAP operates over UDP (User Datagram

Protocol), which provides a lightweight alternative to the more heavyweight TCP (Transmission Control Protocol) used by traditional web protocols like HTTP. The choice of UDP allows CoAP to handle the unique constraints of IoT devices and networks, providing features such as low latency, reduced overhead, and the ability to easily manage multicast communications.

- **Key Features of CoAP**

  - **Lightweight Protocol**: CoAP has a minimal overhead, making it efficient for constrained devices and low-bandwidth networks. The small message size allows for faster transmission, reducing energy consumption.
  - **RESTful Architecture**: CoAP is designed to operate similarly to HTTP, supporting RESTful interactions. It allows clients to interact with resources on a server using standard HTTP methods like GET, POST, PUT, and DELETE, facilitating integration with existing web technologies.
  - **Asynchronous Communication**: CoAP supports asynchronous messaging, enabling clients and servers to send messages without waiting for a response. This feature is particularly useful in IoT applications where devices may need to report data at irregular intervals.
  - **Observation and Notifications**: CoAP allows clients to observe resources on the server. When the resource changes, the server can notify the clients, reducing the need for continuous polling and saving bandwidth.
  - **Multicast Support**: CoAP supports multicast messaging, allowing a single message to be sent to multiple devices simultaneously. This feature is beneficial for scenarios such as broadcasting sensor data to multiple clients.
  - **Built-in Reliability**: CoAP provides a simple reliability mechanism, allowing clients to acknowledge received messages and request retransmissions for lost packets, addressing the limitations of UDP.

- **Security of CoAP in IoT**
  The security of CoAP is crucial, especially in IoT applications that handle sensitive data and require secure communication. To ensure secure operations, CoAP leverages several security mechanisms:

  - **DTLS(Datagram Transport Layer Security)**: CoAP uses DTLS, which provides security over UDP. DTLS protects against eavesdropping, tampering, and forgery by encrypting the data exchanged between CoAP clients and servers.
  - **Authentication**: DTLS supports various authentication methods, allowing devices to authenticate each other using digital certificates or pre-shared keys (PSKs). This ensures that only authorized devices can communicate within the network.
  - **Integrity and Confidentiality**: CoAP messages can be encrypted and signed to ensure their confidentiality and integrity. This means that even if a message is intercepted, it cannot be altered without detection.

- **Access Control**: Implementing access control policies can restrict which clients can access specific resources on a CoAP server, providing an additional layer of security.
- **Message Integrity Codes (MIC)**: CoAP includes a mechanism to verify message integrity, ensuring that messages have not been tampered with during transit. This is achieved through the use of cryptographic hashes.

– **Limitations and Challenges of CoAP in IoT**

While CoAP offers several advantages for IoT applications, it also presents certain limitations and challenges:

- **UDP Limitations**: The reliance on UDP can lead to potential issues with packet loss and message ordering, particularly in lossy networks. CoAP includes mechanisms to handle these issues, but they may not be as robust as the reliability offered by TCP.
- **Complex Security Implementation**: While DTLS provides necessary security features, implementing it can be complex, especially in resource-constrained environments. Managing cryptographic keys, certificates, and secure connections can require significant overhead for low-power devices.
- **Limited Message Size**: CoAP has a default message size limit of 64 KB, which may be restrictive for applications that require the transmission of larger data payloads. This limitation can hinder the protocol's applicability in scenarios that involve multimedia data.
- **Interoperability Issues**: Although CoAP is designed to be interoperable with existing web technologies, variations in implementation among different CoAP libraries and devices can lead to compatibility issues. Developers need to ensure adherence to specifications to avoid these problems.
- **Observation Overhead**: While the observation feature can reduce polling overhead, managing subscriptions and notifications can introduce additional complexity and resource requirements for both clients and servers.
- **Resource Consumption**: Despite being lightweight, CoAP's security mechanisms, especially DTLS, can consume additional resources. This can be a concern for very constrained devices that may struggle to support encryption and decryption operations.
- **Latency Issues**: While CoAP aims to minimize latency through its lightweight design, the added complexity of handling security, acknowledgments, and retransmissions can introduce delays in message delivery, which may not be suitable for real-time applications.
- **Limited Routing Capabilities**: CoAP's design does not inherently support complex routing and message broker functionalities. While it can be used with intermediaries, its architecture is not as flexible as other messaging protocols like AMQP or MQTT when it comes to complex routing scenarios [39].

3.3.5 XMPP

The **XMPP (Extensible Messaging and Presence Protocol)** is a communication protocol based on XML (Extensible Markup Language) that enables near-real-time messaging and presence information. Originally designed for instant messaging, XMPP has evolved to support a wide range of applications, including Internet of Things (IoT) systems. Its flexibility, extensibility, and open nature make it well-suited for connecting heterogeneous devices and applications within the IoT ecosystem. XMPP operates over the TCP (Transmission Control Protocol), which ensures reliable message delivery and ordered message transmission. This makes XMPP suitable for applications requiring consistent and reliable communication, such as smart home systems, healthcare monitoring, and industrial automation.

- **Key Features of XMPP for IoT**
  - **Extensibility**: One of XMPP's primary strengths is its extensibility. It allows developers to define custom XML-based protocols (known as XMPP extensions) to meet specific application requirements. This adaptability enables seamless integration with various IoT devices and services.
  - **Presence Information**: XMPP includes built-in presence functionality, enabling devices to communicate their status (online, offline, busy, etc.) in real time. This is particularly useful for applications requiring awareness of device availability, such as remote monitoring and control systems.
  - **Decentralized Architecture**: XMPP supports a decentralized architecture, allowing multiple servers (XMPP servers) to communicate with each other. This decentralization reduces single points of failure and enhances system robustness and scalability.
  - **Multi-User Chat**: XMPP supports multi-user chat (MUC), enabling multiple devices to communicate in a group chat format. This feature can facilitate collaborative applications in smart environments.
  - **Support for Various Messaging Patterns**: XMPP supports a range of messaging patterns, including point-to-point, publish-subscribe, and presence notifications, allowing for flexible communication scenarios in IoT applications.
  - **Interoperability**: XMPP's standardized nature and open-source implementations promote interoperability among various platforms, devices, and applications, simplifying integration in diverse IoT ecosystems.
- **Security of XMPP in IoT**
  Given the sensitivity of data exchanged in IoT applications, securing XMPP communications is vital. XMPP incorporates several security mechanisms to protect against various threats.
  - **TLS (Transport Layer Security)**: XMPP supports TLS to encrypt data in transit. By using TLS, XMPP ensures the confidentiality and integrity of messages exchanged between clients and servers, protecting against eavesdropping and tampering.

- **SASL (Simple Authentication and Security Layer)**: XMPP supports various authentication mechanisms through SASL, allowing for secure user authentication. Common methods include:
  - ∗ Plain Authentication: Username and password authentication.
  - ∗ Digest-MD5: A more secure method that avoids sending passwords in plaintext.
  - ∗ OAuth: A modern approach for token-based authentication, suitable for web and mobile applications.
- **Access Control**: XMPP can implement access control policies at the server level, restricting which users (devices) can connect and interact with specific resources. This helps prevent unauthorized access to sensitive information.
- **Data Integrity**: XMPP includes mechanisms to ensure message integrity, such as message signing, allowing recipients to verify that messages have not been altered during transmission.
- **End-to-End Encryption**: While XMPP provides security primarily for transport, end-to-end encryption can be implemented using extensions like OMEMO (a modern, encrypted messaging extension) or OpenPGP, ensuring that only the intended recipient can read the messages.

– **Limitations and Challenges of XMPP in IoT**
Despite its advantages, XMPP presents several limitations and challenges when applied to IoT:

- **Resource Consumption**: XMPP is more resource-intensive compared to lightweight protocols like MQTT and CoAP. The use of XML for message formatting and the reliance on TCP can increase memory and bandwidth usage, which may not be suitable for resource-constrained IoT devices.
- **Complexity**: The protocol's extensibility and flexibility can also lead to complexity in implementation. Developers must be familiar with various extensions and configurations, which can increase development time and effort.
- **Latency**: The overhead introduced by TCP and XML parsing can lead to increased latency in message delivery. In applications requiring real-time communication, this latency may be undesirable.
- **Scalability Issues**: Although XMPP supports a decentralized architecture, managing a large number of connections and messages can pose scalability challenges. The performance of XMPP servers may degrade under heavy loads, requiring careful management and infrastructure planning.
- **Firewall Traversal**: XMPP communications may face challenges when traversing firewalls and NAT (Network Address Translation) devices due to its reliance on persistent TCP connections. This can complicate deployments in network-restricted environments.
- **Interoperability Challenges**: While XMPP aims for interoperability, variations in server implementations and support for specific extensions may lead

to compatibility issues. Ensuring seamless communication between different systems can require additional testing and configuration.

- **Limited Built-in QoS**: XMPP does not have built-in Quality of Service (QoS) mechanisms like those found in MQTT. This means that message delivery guarantees are less strict, which may not be acceptable in applications requiring high reliability.

4 Role of Cryptography and Encryption for Secure Communication in IoT

In discussing the widely used wireless protocols in IoT, like Wi-Fi, Zigbee, and LoRa, it is paramount to discuss the security challenges that these protocols face. While most of these data transmissions are passing over public networks not protected, most of them can pose vulnerabilities to all sorts of cyber threats, such as eavesdropping, data interception, and unauthorized access. Key exchange and data authentication protocols will be the paradigm for reducing these risks. These are not only what secure the exchange of data among devices and, therefore, the enhancement of the security of wireless communication but also permit devices to share sensitive information confidentially, between the inherently insecure channels of the Internet. Secure wireless protocols combined with strong cryptographic mechanisms form a base for the creation of secure IoT ecosystems [36].

The cryptography and hence the encryption importance exists specifically in the protection of IoT devices as integrated increasingly into our interconnected environment. The latter includes appliances within the smart home, and industrial sensors that collect and transmit sensitive data. If this sensitive data falls into the wrong hands or is compromised somehow, then critical security breaches might occur. It converts it into an unreadable format allowing decryption only with the decryption key, thus keeping this information highly impossible to have unauthorized access or alteration of data. Encryption is very significant in IoT since devices are open to possible cyber threats. A smart thermostat, or a sensor on the floor of a factory, can be attacked by hackers looking to take down operations or steal proprietary information. Encrypting the data streamed by these devices makes such attacks much more difficult [18]. While the encryption algorithms in the context of IoT security involve not only symmetric key algorithms where one single key is applied for encryption as well as decryption tasks but also asymmetric key algorithms characterized by a pair of keys-one for encryption purposes and the other for decryption so that with the increasing number of IoT devices, grows in its wake the security problem that it brings. Important needs in this area include confidentiality, integrity of the data, authentication, and authorization of incoming information, which protect the devices and the data treated. Cryptography and encryption give thus some of the basic technologies to realize the above security needs, usable and robust mechanisms to protect the data from unauthorized access,

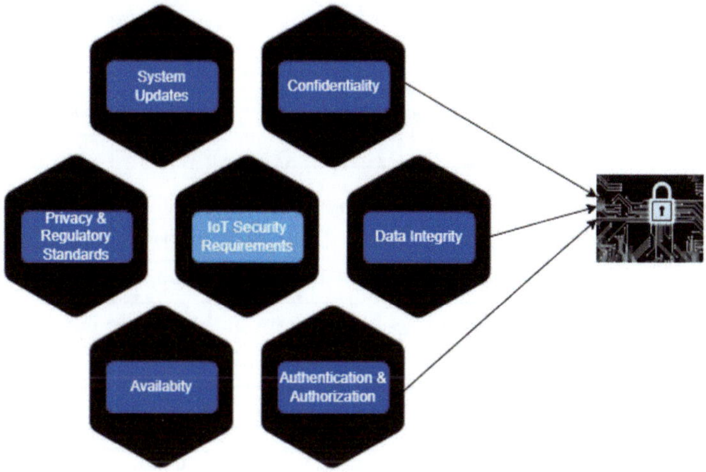

Fig. 5 IoT security requirements

and authenticating communications with a possibility for trusting relations. The following sections detail each one of these security points and how cryptographic techniques can help to bridge the vulnerabilities inherent in IoT systems (Fig. 5).

Given the sizeable amounts of sensitive data being gathered, transmitted, and processed by IoT devices, these devices must be secure. The basic security requirements—confidentiality, integrity, authentication, and authorization—form the bedrock for ensuring the integrity of both the devices and the information processed. Cryptography and encryption are the foundational technologies serving these purposes: ensuring no unauthorized access to data, verifying the authenticity of data received, and maintaining trust in every communication. Probably the most prevalent way of achieving confidentiality in IoT devices is by utilizing encryption and cryptographic methods, such as making sure sensitive information is kept confidential and inaccessible to unauthorized parties. Sometimes while IoT devices are transmitting data to other systems, there is always a threat of intercepting malicious actors. Therefore, the encryption algorithms turn the plaintext data into ciphertext—a format that is jumbled and unreadable. Only the person holding the right decryption can reverse the text back into its original form. This process also means that even though data may get intercepted during its passage, it cannot be accessed or misused by non-legitimate persons. In the context of IoT, confidentiality is critical since most of the devices deal with personal financial, or operational information that can be misused if made public. This means a smart home security system sends video feeds and access logs that, if intercepted, may compromise the safety of the household or its privacy. In this regard, encryption of this data ensures that it can only be accessed and viewed by authorized users, such as the house occupants or security officials. This also protects the privacy of the users plus shields them from security breaches that may result due to unauthorized access. In addition,

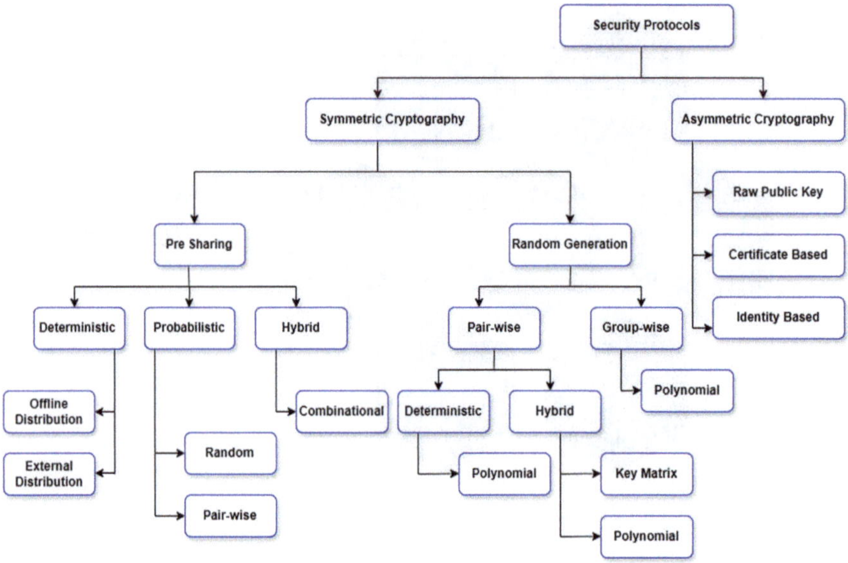

Fig. 6 Types of cryptographic methods used in security protocols

most IoT devices operate in environments that expose them to several cyber threats. Encryption reduces such risks by having a strong layer of security through which data is protected both at rest and in transit. For instance, a medical IoT device that monitors the patient's vital signs and sends the data to healthcare providers must ensure that the sensitive health information is confidential. Using strong encryption algorithms, the device ensures full security of data from the collection point to the destination, thus ensuring patient data privacy and maintaining regulatory requirements in the protection of the data. Secure key management practices are also applied in the encryption used in IoT devices. The process requires generating, distributing, and storing these encryption keys securely to avoid unauthorized access. IoT devices usually tend to balance security with performance using a mix of symmetric and asymmetric encryption. It is faster for resource-constrained devices, like those of IoT, though it needs the same key for encryption as well as decryption. The benefit of more robust security for key exchange and authentication purposes is achieved through asymmetric encryption, which requires two kinds of public and private encryption and decryption respectively. These cryptography techniques become instrumental in including high-level confidentiality in IoT devices and ensuring protection for sensitive data through the lifecycle (Fig. 6).

Data integrity is the foundation of security for IoT devices, otherwise known as Internet of Things devices, where the information transmitted from one device to another remains correct and intact throughout the life cycle. Therefore, in a scenario where IoT devices incessantly send and exchange crucial data, it is imperative to maintain integrity since unauthorized changes may lead to potentially disastrous results. For instance, a faulty temperature sensor on a thermostat may cause an intelligent home to sometimes overheat or cool. In industrial settings, tampered sensor data could compromise a safety protocol or simply make an organization less efficient. Integrity in data is established through the application of two indispensable cryptographic elements: hash functions and digital signatures. A cryptographic hash function is a one-way mapping of any input into a fixed-size string of characters called a hash value or message digest to uniquely identify information. The function is specifically designed so that even a minute change in the input yields a completely different hash value, and this characteristic makes it very useful for data verification. This involves the computation, at the source device's end, of a hash of data when it is ready to send the data to the destination, whether that may be another device or a central server. The receiving party can then, following its transmission, actually compute its hash of the data received and compare it with the hash transmitted over. If they match, then the data integrity has been preserved during transit.

Besides hash functions, digital signatures offer another form of validating integrity and authenticity: they make validating the integrity and authenticity of data relatively powerful. A digital signature is formed by hashing the data and then encrypting that hash value with the sender's private key. This two-layer approach not only proves that the data was not altered but also authenticates who it came from. The recipient uses the sender's public key to decrypt the digital signature, which contains the hash value. By calculating the hash of received data and checking that it matches the decrypted hash, the recipient can thus determine both the integrity of the data and the authenticity of the sender. For additional assurance of data integrity, message authentication codes, and MACs, can be used. With a secret key, the combination of the data produces a unique output—this can then be verified using the output to certify that only the parties in possession of the secret key can authenticate the data. The technique also adds an added layer of security in preventing potential threats to threats altering and manipulating the data and hash or signatures associated with it. The consequences of data integrity compromise in IoT systems are very deep. For example, in healthcare, if the patient's information is erroneously sent out from a medical device due to interference, it could cause inappropriate diagnosis or treatment. In industrial environments, changes in sensor readings of machinery could initiate safety failures or even production downtimes with significant financial and safety implications. Thus, the implementation of cryptographic techniques for data integrity cannot be considered a technical safeguard, but it is a requirement per se in achieving reliability and safety for individuals and also for larger systems.

5 Secure Communication Protocols and Methods

5.1 Key Exchange and Data Authentication Protocols

The relentless growth in IoT calls for secure communication because devices keep on exchanging sensitive information over public and private networks. In this scenario, with every connected device-from smart home appliances to machinery in industrial settings and even healthcare systems-there is a growing risk of cyberattacks, data breaches, and unauthorized access. Two important types of security infrastructure for IoT must be included-they are, namely, key management and data authentication protocols [10, 11].

Key management protocols provide the critical process of creating, sharing, and distributing cryptographic keys to devices in a network. Such keys make use of encryption to preserve data confidentiality. If key management is not properly set up, kinds of attacks such as man-in-the-middle attacks where the creation and manipulation of a key exchange could be intercepted by an attacker for access to encrypted data fall well within a cyber attacker's capabilities. In addition, strong key management is highly required in IoT since devices are often dispersed and are usually resource-constrained in terms of processing and energy. A good key management system needs to ensure all devices can communicate privately with each other but does not bring in heavy overhead to ensure a balance between security and performance.

Data authentication protocols complement key management by ensuring the integrity and authenticity of the data exchange. These protocols ensure that data retrieved by a device is not altered while it is being transmitted and is from the authentic source. Where such compromised data can have disastrous implications in critical sectors such as healthcare, whose accuracy of data is key, authentication assumes even more importance. In this sense, without authentication, malicious actors would gain access to legitimate devices and fake a whole network; they will send bogus commands or altered data. Through mechanisms such as Message Authentication Codes (MACs), digital signatures, and authenticated encryption, IoT systems can, by these means, prove both who the sender is and that the message hasn't been tampered with, thus preventing a wide array of attacks: spoofing and replay [22, 24].

5.1.1 Diffie-Hellman (DH) Key Exchange

The Diffie-Hellman (DH) Key Exchange is one of the foundational cryptographic protocols used to establish secure communication between devices, making it highly relevant for IoT environments. In IoT systems, where devices often communicate over insecure public networks, the DH key exchange allows two devices to generate a shared secret key without exposing it to potential attackers. This shared key can then be used for encrypting data during transmission, ensuring confidentiality and protection against eavesdropping. At its core, the DH key exchange works by leveraging the difficulty of solving the discrete logarithm problem in modular arithmetic. It allows two parties, typically referred to as Alice and Bob, to agree on a secret key even if their communication is monitored by a third party. The process begins with both parties agreeing on a large prime number **p** and a base **g**, known as the generator, which is publicly shared. Each party then selects a private key—randomly chosen integers that remain confidential. They compute their respective public keys by raising the base **g** to the power of their private key, modulo **p**. These public keys are exchanged between Alice and Bob. Upon receiving the other party's public key, each computes the shared secret by raising the received public key to the power of their private key, again modulo **p**. Both parties arrive at the same shared secret key, but a potential eavesdropper, even if aware of the public parameters, cannot easily derive the secret key due to the mathematical difficulty of solving the discrete logarithm problem.

DH key exchange is extremely valuable in the context of IoT since it will let such nodes get into the secure establishment of encryption keys when these nodes have never seen each other or shared common credentials. This is important in many applications of IoT when there is a setting of huge numbers of devices, which may dynamically form networks without human intervention. In the IoT, however, conventional Diffie-Hellman has some important weaknesses. Traditional Diffie-Hellman key exchange requires high computational power and memory usage. In a situation where devices could potentially have resource-constrained hardware, this would make the traditional DH key exchange unsuitable for most low-power or small devices. Instead, the elliptic curve variant commonly replaces it in IoT systems known as ECDH. The basis of ECDH lies in elliptic curve cryptography. Thus, it provides the same security as traditional DH but with significantly smaller key sizes and far less computational load. For example, whereas a traditional DH key exchange might need 3072-bit keys to reach a certain level of security, ECDH can achieve the same security with a 256-bit key. This efficiency is critical for IoT devices, which usually compromise security with limited processing power, memory, and battery life.

5.1.2 Elliptic Curve Diffie-Hellman (ECDH)

ECDH is an advanced version of Diffie-Hellman and very much forms a part of the key exchange protocol while considering the security of the IoT network because it allows the devices to develop a shared secret over a channel of insecure communication. ECDH is an enhanced variant of the classic Diffie-Hellman (DH) key exchange, developed from the mathematical concepts of elliptic curve cryptography (ECC) [37]. It offers the same strength as DH but significantly reduces the sizes of keys and computational requirements. Thus, ECDH is particularly well-suited for IoT environments where the devices generally are resource-constrained regarding processing power, memory, and also battery life. On a high level, ECDH allows two devices, commonly referred to as Alice and Bob, to efficiently and securely agree on a shared secret key without ever transmitting the actual key over the network. The protocol begins with both devices separately picking an elliptic curve mathematical structure defined over a finite field, along with a base point on the curve. Then, each device generates a private key, and based on that, generates a public key obtained by multiplying the base point, which the device itself holds on the elliptic curve. The devices exchange public keys; the private keys remain secret. Both devices will be able to compute the same shared secret, which is a point on the elliptic curve, using its peer's public key and its private key. That shared secret can then be used to derive a symmetric encryption key; all subsequent communications between the devices are thus encrypted and secure.

The main benefit of employing ECDH in IoT systems is connected with its efficiency. A traditional Diffie-Hellman needs very large key sizes for strong security quite long keys, e.g., on the order of 2048–3072 bits in length. ECDH can provide the same security with much shorter keys-for example, a 256-bit ECDH key is as secure as a 3072-bit traditional DH key. This reduction in key size brings down the computation and memory overhead significantly in terms of execution that is required in the performance of the key exchange. For IoT devices, resource constraints are issues that make it essential to reduce the key size. Using reduced key sizes will accelerate not only the key exchange process but also the energy consumption of the devices, thus providing a way to extend the battery life of IoT sensors and nodes. The strength in the mathematics of ECDH comes from the problem of the discrete logarithms of elliptic curves, which are considered harder and more expensive to solve than those involving traditional DH through discrete logarithms. This makes ECDH not just efficient but also secure, requiring an adversary to pose a task that is currently computationally infeasible. Even in case an attacker had sniffed the public keys exchanged between the devices, they could not determine the shared secret even with the private keys because of the elliptic curve discrete logarithm problem.

ECDH In an IoT ecosystem where security often compromised because of primitive capabilities on which devices are built, ECDH stands as a critical balance between security and performance. This is so because it allows safe communication between devices with low power and processing capabilities in line with smart sensors, wearable devices, and embedded systems. ECDH becomes particularly attractive when IoT devices are deployed in large distributed networks such as smart cities, industrial automation, or healthcare scenarios, for which secure communication among the devices is extremely important to safeguard sensitive data and prevent attacks such as eavesdropping or man-in-the-middle attacks. Another reason why ECDH has good scalability is a critical factor in this context. In the large-scale deployments of IoT, where there is a huge requirement to communicate millions of devices with each other, small key sizes in ECDH help save the overall bandwidth required for this secure communication. This, in turn, saves network resources and allows faster, real-time communications critical to applications like autonomous systems or real-time monitoring in smart grids.

5.1.3 Pre-Shared Key (PSK)

Pre-shared key (PSK) is a widely used security mechanism in IoT systems, primarily due to its simplicity and low computational requirements. PSK is a form of symmetric cryptography, where a secret key is pre-distributed to devices before communication begins. This key is shared between all authorized devices and is used to both encrypt and decrypt data, ensuring secure communication across the network. In IoT environments, where devices often have limited resources, PSK offers an efficient way to establish secure connections without requiring complex cryptographic computations. However, despite its advantages in terms of simplicity and resource efficiency, PSK also presents certain challenges, particularly in terms of scalability, security management, and key distribution. In a typical PSK setup for IoT, the shared key is manually or automatically distributed to devices during the initial configuration phase. Once the key is shared, each device uses it to encrypt its outgoing data and decrypt any incoming data from other devices in the network. The key must remain secret; if it is exposed, the security of all devices using that key is compromised. This method works well for small-scale IoT deployments where devices are tightly controlled, such as within a single smart home, where the number of devices is manageable, and the network is relatively isolated.

One of the primary advantages of PSK in IoT is its efficiency. Since PSK relies on symmetric cryptography, the encryption and decryption processes are computationally lightweight, making it suitable for resource-constrained IoT devices with limited processing power and memory. Many IoT devices, such as sensors, wearables, and low-power embedded systems, cannot support the more complex and resource-intensive public-key cryptography used in other key exchange protocols like Diffie-Hellman or Elliptic Curve Diffie-Hellman (ECDH). PSK offers a straightforward solution that enables these devices to establish secure communication with minimal computational overhead. However, PSK is not without its limitations, especially in larger and more complex IoT networks. One of the biggest challenges is key distribution. For PSK to work, the shared key must be securely distributed to all devices before communication can occur. In small networks, this can be done manually, but in large IoT deployments with hundreds or thousands of devices, distributing the key becomes impractical. Additionally, the process of securely updating or rotating keys across such a large network can be cumbersome. If the key is compromised, all devices sharing that key are at risk, and replacing the key across a wide network of devices can be difficult and time-consuming.

Scalability is another concern with PSK. In networks with many devices, maintaining a single pre-shared key for all devices becomes increasingly risky. The more devices that share the same key, the greater the likelihood that the key could be exposed or compromised, either through a vulnerability in one of the devices or through interception during distribution. In such cases, if a single device is compromised, an attacker could potentially gain access to the entire network, since all devices are using the same shared key. To mitigate this, administrators may choose to assign different pre-shared keys to different groups of devices, but this adds complexity to the key management process, especially when the network grows in size. Another significant challenge with PSK in IoT is key management and updating keys. Over time, encryption keys should be rotated or changed to maintain security, particularly in networks with long-lived devices, as old keys can become vulnerable to attacks if used indefinitely. However, updating pre-shared keys across a large and distributed IoT network is not a trivial task. If the key update process is not automated, it requires manual intervention, which can be both time-consuming and error-prone. Moreover, securely distributing new keys to all devices without exposing them to potential attackers is a major security concern. In contrast, other key management protocols, such as Diffie-Hellman or public-key infrastructure (PKI), offer dynamic key exchange mechanisms, which mitigate the need for manual key distribution and management.

From a security perspective, PSK also lacks the flexibility and robustness of more advanced cryptographic techniques. Because it relies on a single shared secret, it does not provide some of the security benefits of asymmetric cryptography, such as non-repudiation (the ability to prove that a specific device sent a message) or forward secrecy (the assurance that even if the current key is compromised, past communications remain secure). Without these protections, PSK-based systems can be more vulnerable to certain types of attacks, such as replay attacks, where an attacker captures and replays previous communications to manipulate the system. Despite these challenges, PSK remains a practical and widely used solution in many IoT applications where simplicity, efficiency, and low computational overhead are prioritized over scalability and advanced security features. For example, in smart home environments, where the number of devices is relatively small and controlled by a single user, PSK offers an effective way to secure communication between devices like smart locks, cameras, and thermostats. Similarly, in industrial IoT systems with fixed devices, PSK may be sufficient for securing communication between sensors and control systems, especially if the network is isolated from external threats.

5.1.4 Message Authentication Code (MAC)

Message Authentication Codes (MACs) play a vital role in securing IoT communication by ensuring the integrity and authenticity of messages exchanged between devices. As IoT systems often operate in environments where devices are exposed to a variety of security threats, MACs provide a way to detect tampering, verify the legitimacy of the sender, and prevent unauthorized access. In resource-constrained IoT networks, where devices frequently communicate over insecure or open channels, MACs offer a lightweight and efficient means of protecting data, making them an essential tool for maintaining trust and security across the network. At its core, a Message Authentication Code is a small block of data generated from a message and a secret key shared between communicating devices. This block is appended to the message itself and sent to the recipient. The recipient, having the same secret key, can generate a MAC independently using the received message and compare it to the one sent by the sender. If both MACs match, the recipient can confidently verify that the message has not been altered during transmission and that it originated from a trusted source. If the MACs do not match, it indicates either tampering or that the message did not come from a legitimate sender. This simple mechanism makes MACs extremely effective in IoT environments, where ensuring data integrity and authenticity is critical.

One of the key strengths of MACs in IoT is their efficiency. Since many IoT devices are resource-constrained, with limited processing power, memory, and energy, security protocols mustn't place an excessive burden on the devices. Unlike public-key cryptography, which can be computationally expensive, MACs rely on symmetric-key cryptography, which is much more lightweight. This makes MACs well-suited for IoT devices such as sensors, embedded systems, and low-power actuators, which may not have the capability to run more demanding security algorithms. By using simple hash functions or block ciphers in combination with secret keys, MACs provide robust protection with minimal resource consumption, enabling even the most constrained devices to verify message authenticity. Several commonly used types of MACs are particularly effective in IoT systems:

- **HMAC (Hash-based Message Authentication Code)**:
  One of the most widely used forms of MACs, HMAC uses cryptographic hash functions (such as SHA-256) in conjunction with a secret key to generate the authentication code. HMAC is widely favored in IoT applications because of its efficiency, simplicity, and flexibility. It can be implemented with various hash functions, allowing developers to choose the most appropriate level of security for their specific IoT use cases. HMAC's reliance on hash functions makes it computationally efficient, which is essential for resource-limited IoT devices, while still providing strong protection against attacks such as data modification or replay attacks.
- **CMAC (Cipher-based Message Authentication Code)**:
  Unlike HMAC, which relies on hash functions, CMAC is based on block ciphers like AES (Advanced Encryption Standard). In IoT systems, CMAC is particularly useful when both encryption and message authentication need to be performed. Since many IoT devices already use AES for encryption, CMAC can be implemented alongside it to provide message authentication without adding significant computational overhead. This dual functionality is especially useful in energy-constrained IoT devices, as it allows encryption and authentication to be handled using the same block cipher, reducing the need for multiple cryptographic operations.
- **Poly1305**:
  This is another form of MAC that is specifically designed for high performance in constrained environments. Poly1305 is often paired with modern encryption algorithms such as ChaCha20 to provide both encryption and authentication in lightweight, high-speed cryptographic protocols. In IoT systems, Poly1305 is advantageous because it offers very fast performance, making it suitable for devices that require high throughput and low latency in communication while still maintaining strong security guarantees.

In an IoT context, MACs protect against a variety of attacks, including message tampering, impersonation, and replay attacks. Since IoT devices often communicate over insecure networks, such as the internet or low-power wireless protocols (e.g., Zigbee, LoRaWAN), they are exposed to attackers who may try to alter messages in transit or impersonate legitimate devices. By generating and verifying MACs, IoT devices can immediately detect if a message has been modified or if it originated from an untrusted source, thereby preventing unauthorized actions or data corruption within the network. Additionally, MACs help to ensure data integrity in IoT systems where even small alterations in data could lead to significant consequences. For example, in industrial IoT applications, sensor readings are critical for monitoring equipment and making real-time decisions. If an attacker were able to tamper with these readings, it could result in incorrect decisions or actions that compromise safety or efficiency. By using MACs, IoT systems can validate that the data they are receiving is accurate and untampered with, ensuring the reliability of the overall system.

While MACs are highly effective, they do have certain limitations, particularly when it comes to key management. Since MACs rely on symmetric keys, the secret key used to generate and verify the MAC must be securely shared and maintained between the communicating devices. In large-scale IoT networks, distributing and managing these keys can be challenging, especially as the number of devices increases. If the secret key is compromised, an attacker could potentially generate valid MACs for malicious messages, bypassing authentication checks. To address this, IoT systems often employ additional key management protocols to securely distribute and rotate keys, ensuring that MAC-based authentication remains robust.

5.1.5 Digital Signatures

Digital signatures are a crucial mechanism for securing communication in IoT (Internet of Things) networks, providing a method to verify the authenticity, integrity, and non-repudiation of messages exchanged between devices. In the context of IoT, where devices often operate autonomously and communicate across public or untrusted networks, digital signatures help ensure that data is both trustworthy and uncompromised, making them a vital part of IoT security. At its core, a digital signature is a cryptographic technique that uses asymmetric encryption (public-key cryptography) to provide strong guarantees that a message was sent by a legitimate sender and has not been altered in transit. The process begins with the sender creating a cryptographic hash of the message, which acts as a unique fingerprint for that specific message. This hash is then encrypted using the sender's private key, creating the digital signature. The signature is sent along with the original message to the recipient. Upon receiving the message, the recipient uses the sender's public key to decrypt the signature, revealing the original hash. The recipient then computes a new hash from the received message and compares it with the decrypted hash. If the two hashes match, the message is considered authentic and unaltered, and the sender's identity is verified. The use of digital signatures in IoT has several key advantages for securing communication.

- **Authentication**: Digital signatures provide strong authentication by verifying the identity of the sender. In IoT networks, where devices communicate with each other without human intervention, it is critical to ensure that the device sending the data is legitimate. For example, in a smart home system, digital signatures can confirm that a message to unlock a door was sent by the homeowner's authorized device and not a malicious actor impersonating the device. By using the sender's public key to verify the signature, IoT devices can authenticate the origin of the message, ensuring that only trusted devices are communicating with one another.

- **Data Integrity**: One of the primary functions of a digital signature is to ensure data integrity the guarantee that the message has not been altered during transmission. In IoT systems, data integrity is essential for ensuring that critical information is reliable and accurate. For instance, in an industrial IoT setting, sensor readings used to control machinery must remain intact from the point of collection to the central control system. Any tampering with this data could result in serious consequences, such as equipment malfunctions or safety hazards. By using digital signatures, IoT systems can detect even the slightest changes to a message, preventing attackers from altering the data without detection.
- **Non-Repudiation**: Another important benefit of digital signatures is non-repudiation. Non-repudiation ensures that the sender cannot deny having sent a message. This is particularly important in IoT systems where critical decisions or actions are automated based on data received from devices. For example, in healthcare IoT applications, medical devices may transmit vital signs to healthcare providers. By signing these data transmissions with digital signatures, the system ensures that the device that generated the data cannot later deny responsibility for sending it. This level of accountability is crucial in applications where trust is paramount, such as in legal or regulatory environments where audit trails are needed.
- **Security in Distributed Environments**: IoT networks are typically highly distributed, with devices communicating across wide geographic areas, often through unsecured public networks such as the Internet. In such environments, the risk of attacks like man-in-the-middle (MITM) attacks or message interception is high. Digital signatures mitigate this risk by ensuring that even if an attacker intercepts the communication, they cannot alter or forge valid messages. Since digital signatures are tied to the sender's private key, only the device with access to that key can generate a valid signature. Even if an attacker gains access to the message, they cannot create a valid signature without the private key, ensuring that any tampering will be detected.
- **Use Cases in IoT**
  Digital signatures are particularly useful in several key IoT use cases:
  - Smart Homes: Devices like smart locks, security cameras, and thermostats rely on secure communication to function properly. Digital signatures ensure that only authorized commands are executed, preventing malicious actors from hijacking devices.
  - Healthcare IoT: Medical devices such as wearable health monitors transmit sensitive health data that must be both accurate and authentic. Digital signatures help ensure that this data can be trusted, preventing tampering or impersonation.
  - Industrial IoT: In manufacturing and automation, digital signatures can secure machine-to-machine communication, ensuring that commands are legitimate

and sensor data is accurate. This is particularly important for ensuring the safety and efficiency of automated systems.
- Connected Vehicles: In autonomous or connected vehicle networks, digital signatures ensure that communications between vehicles, traffic signals, and other infrastructure are authentic, preventing attackers from sending false data that could cause accidents.

– **Challenges of Digital Signatures in IoT**
  Digital signatures offer considerable security advantages but do raise some issues in the IoT context, particularly concerning resource-constrained systems. Creating and checking digital signatures involves computational energy and memory resources that could be limited in a device like a sensor or an embedded system. The public-key cryptography, which is the foundation of digital signatures, is computationally more expensive than its symmetric key-based alternative in terms of MACs (Message Authentication Codes). To solve this problem, key agreement using IoT systems relies mostly on ECC, which provides a security level equivalent to the traditional public-key algorithms, such as RSA, but of much smaller size keys and less computational requirements, which is appropriate for constrained IoT devices. Digital signatures also rely on key management, based on a pair of public-private keys, which require secure storage and distribution. Key management in large IoT networks is quite complex with thousands or even millions of devices. Many rely on PKI with digital signatures for managing keys and certificates, and this can be challenging to deploy and maintain PKI across the IoT environment. To reduce computation overhead by digital signatures in the Internet of Things, researchers and developers are finding lightweight options. These alternatives offer optimized cryptographic algorithms with reduced resource consumption and provide benefits similar to digital signatures, including security advantages. For instance, the Elliptic Curve Digital Signature Algorithm is one such scheme, wherein it derives all its cryptography from elliptic curves and generates signatures that are computationally faster to generate and verify while still offering the same security level. The system is very well-suited to the restricted computational resources of IoT devices.

Key management and data authentication protocols are crucial to maintaining the confidentiality, integrity, and authenticity of data in IoT systems. They ensure that only authorized devices can participate in communication, that data remains encrypted and safe from unauthorized access, and that the data itself remains accurate and trustworthy. Without these security protocols, IoT networks would be significantly more vulnerable to attacks, jeopardizing the reliability and safety of the connected systems they support. These protocols form the backbone of secure IoT communication, enabling trust and resilience across increasingly complex and interconnected environments.

5.2 Light Weight Cryptographic Protocols

Lightweight cryptographic protocols are highly essential for the security of IoT-constrained devices, which generally face resource scarcity with such constraints as low power for computation, memory, and communication capabilities as well as energy resources [16, 20]. These tailored cryptographic solutions are supposed to be designed in such a way that they align security necessities with the inherent resource constraints of such an environment. As the Internet of Things continues to grow, it bridges the digital and physical worlds while making it possible for networks of devices to engage with the real world. However, this growth presents significant security issues, mainly due to the diversity of the devices used. IoT-based systems are inherently asymmetric, consisting of heterogeneously diverse devices, from very low-resource endpoints like sensors and microcontrollers to high-performance platforms that use cloud, fog, and edge computing. Traditional cryptographic protocols cannot be applied to low-resource devices as they are too complex and resource-hungry. Light cryptographic protocols are constructed to satisfy the security requirements of a constrained device with minimum resource utilization without compromising the performance or power efficiency of the device [5, 33]. These protocols have been categorized and studied in detail considering their efficiency, vulnerability, and proper application.

Although these protocols are suitable for constrained devices, an uncautious application of lightweight cryptographic protocols even to relatively more resource-rich nodes used in cloud or fog computing will provide vulnerabilities. Such environments may allow for more computationally intensive cryptographic algorithms to be deployed, thereby opening security vulnerabilities under lightweight protocols. "Elastic Cryptographic Protocols" identifies a problem similar to that in this paper. The notion of such protocols is to operate adaptively concerning the resources that are available at each node within the system so that one can maintain security at every level of the system-from the weakest edge device to the most powerful cloud computing platform. IoT architecture is a multilayered complex with the presence of various devices in different levels such as edge, fog, and cloud. All these interactions increase the complexity of end-to-end security. Against this background, several cryptographic solutions to IoT layers have been proposed keeping in view the specific constraints and capabilities of the layers. The emphasis here is on finding a proper balance between security and performance, where even the weaker devices are secured without consuming all their power or loading up their processing capabilities. There is a need for more adaptive and scalable security mechanisms, such mechanisms that are capable of scaling and adapting the varying profiles of resource availability from IoT devices. Such mechanisms must translate into robust protection even as they can scale and adapt based on the varying resource profiles of IoT devices. Crucial for maintaining security across the system will be the ability of IoT networks to ensure that cryptographic protocols are adaptable to the unique characteristics of the end points, whether constrained or resource-rich.

6 Emerging Technologies and Approaches

6.1 Blockchain and Its Application for Securing IoT Communication

Blockchain technology offers a robust solution for enhancing the security of Internet of Things (IoT) systems. By leveraging its decentralized, immutable, and transparent nature, blockchain addresses many of the security challenges inherent in IoT networks [8, 9, 12, 35].

- **Decentralized Network**
  The traditional IoT-based system, as it relies on a centralized server, is one point of failure and becomes the great target for hackers. Bitcoin's blockchain runs on a decentralized network where all IoT devices are nodes. The scattering of data across multiple points due to this decentralization makes it much tougher for an attacker to compromise the system. The lack of a central authority also decreases the potential for interference with data manipulations and unauthorized access.
- **Public-Key Cryptography**
  Blockchain uses public-key cryptography to secure the communication between IoT devices. According to this technique, each device is assigned a unique pair of public and private keys [29, 31]. To send data to another device, a device encrypts the message by utilizing the other party's public key. Only the recipient can decode the message with the private key, making communication both secret and confidential. It doesn't need middlemen and has other security benefits.
- **Immutable Ledger**
  The most fundamental characteristic of blockchain technology is its immutable ledger. If data recorded in the blockchain is changed, deleted, or modified in any manner, the information's history will not allow such changes. It is because of this immutability that data exchanged from devices in an IoT system cannot be tampered with, thereby proving it tamper-proof and trustworthy. If, for example, data is being changed, it will no longer match the previously existing records on the blockchain. This feature is indispensable for maintaining the integrity of data in an IoT application, and accuracy in the measurement of data becomes a key concern where this feature matters most.
- **Smart Contracts**
  A smart contract is self-executing; this is to say that the terms of the agreement are directly written into code. For instance, in IoT, it is possible to have processes automated and rules enforced without the use of intermediaries. For instance, a good example is that a smart contract can set off actions based on sensor data itself; for example, a smart home would adjust its temperature based on whether the sensor has received information that it has reached a threshold. This automation not only improves efficiency but also ensures that rules are applied with uniformity, thus minimizing the possibilities of human error and fraud.

- **Data Integrity and Transparency**
  A blockchain thereby ensures data integrity by creating a transparent and verifiable record of all transactions. Each transaction receives a time stamp and is connected to the previous one, hence forming a chain of blocks. Such transparency enables verification of the authenticity of data by all participants within an IoT network, reducing tampering and fraud risks. The traceability of data transactions and audits created trust between IoT devices and users.
- **Operational Resilience**
  Its distributed ledger functionality will enable the system to continue operating, even in the event of failure of some nodes in the network. Such critical applications for IoT as healthcare and industrial automation require continuous operations for robustness. Distributed nature also makes it possible for a network to rapidly recover from failures and with little to no disruption to the delivery of IoT services.
- **Secure Data Exchange**
  IoT devices frequently require the exchange of data to operate. Blockchain enables safe data exchange since encryption keys are stored in the blockchain. The sender of an IoT device will create an encrypted message, using the destination device's public key. The decryption of the message becomes possible only through the private key of the destination device, and thus it results in the secure and secretive nature of the communication. This method does not only protect data during transfer but also limits access to only a few authorized devices.

By integrating blockchain with IoT, we can create a secure and reliable environment for IoT communications [13, 19, 21]. This combination addresses many of the security challenges that IoT systems face, such as data tampering, unauthorized access, and privacy concerns, ultimately enhancing the overall reliability and trustworthiness of IoT systems.

6.2 *Quantum Era, Its Affects and Solutions*

Quantum computing introduces a transformative paradigm in computational power, offering unprecedented opportunities but also posing significant risks to IoT security [2, 3]. Leveraging the principles of quantum mechanics, quantum computers can perform calculations at speeds far beyond the capabilities of classical computers. While this holds immense potential for solving complex problems across various fields, it also threatens to compromise the current cryptographic systems that form the backbone of IoT security, potentially rendering them obsolete.

- **Threat to Classical Encryption**
  One of the primary concerns regarding quantum computing is its potential to compromise widely adopted cryptographic algorithms. Currently, IoT security relies extensively on classical encryption techniques, notably RSA (Rivest-

Shamir-Adleman) and ECC (Elliptic Curve Cryptography). RSA is grounded in the computational difficulty of factoring large integers, while ECC is based on the efficient resolution of discrete logarithms. However, quantum algorithms such as Shor's algorithm can effectively break these cryptographic systems, rendering RSA and ECC ineffective. The advent of powerful quantum computers could therefore enable the decryption of IoT communications, the compromise of stored data, and the invalidation of digital signatures, leading to unauthorized access and the exposure of sensitive information.

- **Impact on Authentication and Key Exchange**
  The implications of quantum computing extend to authentication protocols and key exchange mechanisms, which are essential for maintaining robust security in IoT systems. Most IoT devices depend on asymmetric encryption to ensure that only authorized entities can access or control them. However, the vulnerability of asymmetric encryption to quantum attacks compromises these authentication processes, making them susceptible to unauthorized access and manipulation. Similarly, key exchange protocols that rely on the security of discrete logarithms, such as Diffie-Hellman, would become insecure in a quantum computing environment. This would significantly weaken the ability to establish secure communication channels, a fundamental requirement for the safe operation of IoT systems.
- **Data Integrity and Privacy Risks**
  Besides cryptography and authentication weaknesses, quantum computing directly compromises the integrity and privacy of the data sensed and transmitted by IoT devices. It can break cryptographic hash functions: "cracking" of such hash functions may compromise data integrity through the dangers of losing authenticity. Hash functions are employed to authenticate data as authentic and demonstrate the immutability of this data; therefore, should a malicious party win a hash function, there is the possibility to modify data with no chance of being traced. This makes the applications in health, finance, and infrastructure critical to the well-being of modern society all the more worrisome since data integrity is the main issue at hand.
- **Mitigating Quantum Threats**
  The emergence of these new threats has given rise to the field of post-quantum cryptography, which focuses on developing cryptographic algorithms capable of withstanding quantum attacks. Quantum-resistant algorithms are expected to replace existing encryption standards, ensuring security even in the presence of quantum computers. However, implementing these new algorithms in IoT devices will necessitate updates to both software and hardware, given the limited computational and power resources typical of many IoT systems. Additionally, a hybrid approach is essential during the transition to quantum-resistant cryptography. This approach would integrate classical cryptography with quantum-resistant techniques, ensuring comprehensive protection against both classical and quantum threats during the transition period. In this way, IoT devices and communications will remain secure against emerging threats from both traditional and quantum-based attacks.

- **Upgrading IoT Infrastructure**
  Upgrading the existing infrastructure of the IoT will also have to be part of implementing quantum-resistant cryptography. Many IoT devices, especially those with low processing capabilities, would find it hard to support the more computationally intensive quantum-resistant algorithms, so firmware and software updates would need to be incorporated to introduce the new standards for cryptography. Enhancing hardware capabilities would be necessary to ensure other devices could support the newer algorithms in handling the increased computational load.
- **Regulatory and Compliance Considerations**
  Some of the regulatory bodies and standards organizations will have to improve the existing security standards to include quantum-resistant cryptographic requirements. It is essential that all IoT systems remain secure in the postquantum world; therefore, this would require full cooperation within industries as well as from governments to be aligned. This would be possible through shared research, development efforts, and best practices, which would help to accelerate the adoption of quantum-resistant technologies and reinforce a strong defense against quantum-enabled cyber threats.
- **Long-Term Strategies and Research**
  In the long term, future innovative solutions such as Quantum Key Distribution (QKD) might present secure approaches for exchanging keys, based on the fundamental principle of quantum mechanics applied in the detection of eavesdropping. These current advanced technologies are still limited to fiber-optic communications, but new research may lead to applications of QKD in IoT networks. Most importantly, cryptographic algorithms and quantum-resistant technologies should be continually researched and developed to ensure that best practices stay ahead of the latest developments of the quantum computer.

The emergence of quantum computing presents profound challenges to IoT security by threatening the foundational cryptographic techniques currently in use. To mitigate these risks, IoT companies and cybersecurity professionals must adopt quantum-resistant cryptographic algorithms, upgrade IoT infrastructure, and engage in continuous research and development. Preparing for the quantum future is crucial to ensure the continued security and reliability of IoT systems in an increasingly connected world.

6.3 Post Quantum Cryptography for Securing IoT

Post-quantum cryptography, simply PQC refers to a set of new cryptographic algorithms designed to secure communication against the potential threats of quantum computers. Unlike classical computers, which use bits to perform calculations, quantum computers leverage qubits and quantum phenomena, such as superposition and entanglement, to process information at many orders of magnitude greater than classical computational power. While quantum computers promise great challenges to complex problems, they also pose a serious threat to modern cryptographic protocols. The most widely used schemes today include RSA, Elliptic Curve Cryptography (ECC), and Diffie-Hellman key exchange, relying on the hardness of factorization of large numbers or solving discrete logarithms problems that quantum computers can solve through algorithms such as Shor's algorithm very efficiently. In other words, it means much of today's public-key cryptography may go down the tubes when quantum computers can reach sufficient strength, thereby making it liable to unauthorized decryption.

The main target of post-quantum cryptography is to provide algorithms that prove to be resistant to both classical and quantum attacks. The algorithms begin with mathematical problems hard to solve using a quantum computer; some examples include lattice-based cryptography, code-based cryptography, multivariate polynomial cryptography, and hash-based signatures. It does not rely on quantum mechanics' physical properties, as does quantum cryptography, but rather applies classical computing principles to develop cryptographic algorithms resistant to quantum attacks. The central goal of PQC is that it should provide or contribute to replacing the currently vulnerable public-key cryptography methods with quantum-resistant alternatives so that data will remain long-term secure over durations still to be protected decades into the future.

6.3.1 Use of Post-Quantum Cryptography in IoT

While the world is moving towards a quantum era, the unencrypted communication of IoT tends to be a really hard challenge now. IoT technologies are broadly deployed in smart homes and industrial systems, healthcare, transportation, and critical infrastructure facilities. Devices often rely on public-key cryptography for authentication purposes, key exchange, and then establishing secure communication channels. However, the advent of quantum computers threatens classical cryptographical methods. Now, IoT systems are being threatened by future quantum attacks. PQC promises a solution that can overcome the vulnerabilities associated with the use of classical cryptographic schemes in IoT. Here's how PQC can be fitted into IoT systems to ensure long-term security:

- **Securing Key Exchange in IoT**
  The quantum computing attack on IoT security currently targets the key exchange process. Most of the existing IoT systems depend on key exchange algorithms such as Elliptic Curve Diffie-Hellman (ECDH) or RSA in establishing security over an insecure channel a shared key. Quantum computers will be able to break these key exchange algorithms when operational, enabling the attacker to intercept and decrypt IoT communications. Integration of PQC-based key-exchange protocols would enable IoT devices to maintain secure channels in communication even when a quantum threat exists; in fact, these devices have evolved with the development of some promising candidates toward post-

quantum secure key exchange. Such key-exchange schemes rely on the hardness of solving interesting problems in lattices, which could not be efficiently solved on a quantum computer. The two encryption schemes, Kyber or NewHope, are PQC algorithms when deployed in IoT. That would mean that a key exchange technique works quantum resistant-will be protecting the communication between devices, no matter whether the attacker has a quantum computer.

- **Authentication in IoT Networks**
  Authentication is another critical feature of IoT security. It just refers to the procedure a device has to undertake to confirm its identity to the devices or network that it wants to send or receive information from before it's given access to do so. Classical cryptographic algorithms such as RSA and ECC that are utilized for digital signatures in IoT can be broken by quantum computers. The attacker with access to a quantum computer would forge digital signatures such that he would impersonate legitimate devices and inject malware commands in the IoT system. The post-quantum digital signature algorithms are the alternative quantum-resistant methods for the authentication of IoTs. Hash-based signatures like SPHINCS+, lattice-based signatures like Dilithium, and multivariate polynomial-based signatures are strong post-quantum security mechanisms for digital authentication. These protocols ensure to allow the IoT devices a safe authentication even after a post-quantum world. The main reason is that such IoTs are often used in critical places medical devices up to industrial control systems or smart cities, where time reliability and quantum resistance in authentication are highly required to avoid unwanted access or attacks.
- **Data Integrity and Message Authentication**
  Data integrity is an essential aspect of IoT communications as devices often exchange sensor data, control commands, and status updates. Hence, it is essential to maintain data integrity against possible tampering or malicious changes. Classical Mechanisms: The two primary classical mechanisms for proving message authenticity and integrity are HMAC and digital signatures based on RSA. Here again, the problem is that the same are vulnerable to quantum attacks. Post-quantum cryptography may be used to design quantum-safe message authentication codes and signatures for the integrity of data in IoT. For instance, lattice-based signatures FALCON or CRYSTALS-Dilithium could be applied for signing the messages exchanged via IoT communication for that respective quantum-resilience verification of message integrity. This ensures that even if the attacker possesses a quantum computer, he cannot forge messages or alter data in an unnoticed manner, hence the reliability and security of IoT systems will not be compromised.
- **Lightweight Cryptography for IoT Devices**
  Some of the major difficulties in the implementation of Post-Quantum Cryptography in IoT devices are limited resources of the devices of the IoT. Many devices of IoT have very limited processing, memory, and energy capacity, and the implementation of computationally intensive cryptographic protocols is quite challenging in such devices. For example, it has been said that the application of classical public-key algorithms like RSA to IoT devices is already

computationally expensive while many post-quantum algorithms require even larger key sizes and more intensive computations. Researchers are working on lightweight post-quantum cryptography that is best suited for IoT devices. For example, cryptographic schemes based on lattices optimize the computational requirements and memory usage for the scheme to run in resource-constrained environments of IoT devices. In addition, hash-based cryptographic schemes can be quite efficient in terms of computation, so that it becomes capable of operating for applications like digital signatures and authentication for IoT devices. Thus, lightweight post-quantum algorithms can now be adopted for the realization of quantum-resistant security in IoT devices without overloading the limited resources. It would thus become possible to deploy PQC on a broad scale of IoT devices, from low-power sensors to embedded controllers.

- **Future-Proofing IoT Security**
  The most obvious reason for the implementation of Post-Quantum Cryptography in IoT devices is that there's an urgent need for future-proof security. Although the current level of power of quantum computers doesn't reach the strength at which they can break the classical crypto schemes, it is only a matter of time before they become powerful enough to break them. Most of the IoT devices are built to live for years or even decades. For example, the smart meters in utilities or sensors in an industrial environment might continue working for years as long as the threat from quantum computers is going to become very real.

Post-Quantum Cryptography (PQC) offers a robust framework for securing IoT communication against the emerging threat posed by quantum computing. By replacing vulnerable classical cryptographic algorithms with quantum-resistant alternatives, such as lattice-based and hash-based schemes, PQC ensures secure key exchange, device authentication, and data integrity within IoT systems in the post-quantum era. While challenges related to resource constraints and practical implementation remain, ongoing advancements in lightweight post-quantum algorithms make the deployment of PQC in IoT networks increasingly feasible. The adoption of PQC has the potential to future-proof IoT systems, ensuring the long-term security and reliability of connected devices and networks against quantum threats.

6.4 *Quantum Key Encryption for IoT*

Quantum Key Distribution is an emerging technology. Promising to change and revolutionize secure communication by using quantum mechanics principles, QKD stands out from classical encryption methods where mathematical complexity forms the basis of secured communication. Quantum key distribution mainly relies on the laws of quantum physics to create cryptographic keys that are theoretically unbreakable by a quantum computer. QKD can serve as a means that provides the unprecedented security needed for IoT communications, with the assurance that even if quantum computers do break most of the classical schemes, the communications in IoT would be safe [40, 41]. The concept of QKD is based on the principle that any measurement or eavesdropping over a quantum system disturbs that very system in a detectable manner. It is known as the Heisenberg Uncertainty Principle and forms the cornerstone of quantum mechanics; it provides the base for any secure way of the cryptographic keys distribution. QKD is the communication process in which two parties, typically referred to as Alice and Bob, aim to establish a secure key or a cryptographic key. They exchange the quantum bits encoded in the quantum states of particles such as photons. An attempt by the eavesdropper, Eve, to intercept the qubits will disturb the quantum states, and Alice and Bob may know that there is an intruder. Then the key exchange can be aborted and the attempt at eavesdropping defeated. Maybe the best-known QKD protocols are those associated with the BB84 protocol proposed by Charles Bennett and Gilles Brassard in 1984. This protocol allows for two parties to share a cryptographic key securely. Later on, they may encode or decode an arbitrary message using this key in combination with classical encryption methods, like the One-Time Pad.

6.4.1 Quantum Key Distribution in IoT

QKD installed within IoT systems is one promising method of securing communication so the keys used for encryption are safe from both classical and quantum computational attacks. In fact, with IoT approaching the horizon, devices will be more interconnected than ever, and communication will be done over unsecured networks such as the internet or LPWANs increasingly often. This leaves the direction of IoT very open, especially since many of them rely on public-key cryptosystems to implement secure communication schemes. However the advent of quantum computers threatens the security of such classical schemes, therefore necessitating new approaches such as QKD for long-term protection.

- **Securing IoT Key Exchange with Quantum Key Distribution**
  Key exchange is another very important aspect of securing IoT communications. In a traditional IoT network, devices rely on the use of algorithms such as Diffie-Hellman or Elliptic Curve Cryptography (ECC) to share symmetric keys over insecure channels. These algorithms are not secure and will be susceptible to attacks by a quantum computer; therefore, when such computers become available, they may break those protocols of key exchanges. This can provide equal security of key exchange against quantum attackers while using Quantum Key Distribution in IoT networks. In QKD, there is the sharing of a secret key to be utilized for encryption purposes via a quantum channel. After the secure sharing of the key with the devices, the IoT devices can use it as a means of symmetric encryption of their communications [30]. Since QKD-based security is not founded on the mathematical hardness of some problems but on the physical properties of quantum particles, it is therefore safe from attacks by quantum computers. For example, in a smart city's infrastructure, traffic sensors,

smart meters, and streetlight devices may be using QKD for securely exchanging cryptographic keys with each other. Even if it has access to a quantum computer, nothing would be compromised because of this; it simply cannot breach the QKD process, meaning that the keys used in securing communication between such appliances are perfectly safe.

- **Enhancing IoT Device Authentication**
  QKD authentication in the IoT is also a key area in which it can be quite useful since it can serve directly as a source for trusted management data for legitimate architectures of the IoT. Conventional IoT has largely relied on public-key infrastructure as the means of authentication. PKI's two required components are digital certificates and classical cryptographic algorithms, both of which quantum computers could break. Once those certificates were compromised, attackers were able to impersonate legitimate IoT devices injecting malicious commands into the network or stealing sensitive data. This problem can be solved using QKD with quantum-resistant authentication algorithms. In the case of QKD, the IoT devices would receive a secure key that may then be used to sign and verify an authentication message, and the key exchange process will be protected via quantum mechanics to stay safe against quantum attacks. Another advantage that quantum-secured authentication offers is that legitimate devices within the IoT network can only communicate, thus removing impersonation attacks and ensuring the protection of the system. For instance, in the healthcare application of IoT, as medical devices communicate sensitive patient data, the use of QKD to effect key exchange will ensure that only specific authorized devices, such as a wearable health monitor, can self-authenticate and send data to the network. It can even reduce the risk of unauthorized access or malicious activities to a great extent.
- **Securing Critical Infrastructure and High-Value IoT Deployments**
  What's quite promising in QKD use cases for IoT is critical infrastructure and high-value IoT deployment, especially for industrial control systems, energy grids, or defense applications. This is what is most vulnerable to advanced cyberattacks. It's exactly these systems whose security is paramount because a successful attack could have serious consequences from power outage to environmental damage or compromise of national security. The security offered by QKD in high-stakes environments surpasses that which can be achieved by classical cryptography. In fact, by using QKD, operators of critical infrastructure can successfully achieve secure communication between control systems, sensors, and actuators against quantum attacks. For example, smart grids, which monitor and control the flow of energy could use QKD to secure the communication between the substations and the control centers to ensure that even if an attacker has access to quantum computing of the advanced type, they would not be able to intercept, change or even read the communication. More so, using QKD, it will be possible for service providers to exchange encrypted keys for sensitive data in real-time which would practically be almost impossible for an attacker to seize control of the system.

- **Overcoming IoT Resource Constraints with Hybrid Approaches**
  One of the great challenges in using QKD in IoT is that IoT devices are often resource-constrained, having low processing power, memory, and energy. Quantum communication systems normally depend on specially fitted hardware like photon detectors and quantum random number generators which cannot be easily supported in small, low-cost IoT devices. Hybrid solutions that combine QKD with classical cryptography and post-quantum cryptography (PQC) may be the way forward to address this challenge. In a hybrid model, where communications are encrypted between more powerful nodes in a network (like gateways, routers, or edge devices), QKD may be used, while communication to resource-constrained devices can then resort to lightweight PQC algorithms. This hybrid approach will let the IoT network benefit from QKD security without having to put some kind of quantum hardware on every single device. For example, an edge device in a smart city might be a streetlight controller or environmental sensor; it doesn't have the capabilities for direct QKD. However, it will certainly be able to communicate with a gateway or central server that performs the key exchange over a quantum line. Once established via QKD, these edge devices may use this key for symmetric encryption to make communication quantum-secured without requiring the placement of expensive or complex quantum hardware at every node.
- **Future of Quantum IoT Networks**
  In the near future, quantum IoT networks are likely to incorporate quantum communication and quantum computing as core components of the IoT ecosystem. Quantum Key Distribution (QKD) could become the standard method for securing communication within these networks, while quantum sensors and processors may offer enhanced performance and security capabilities for IoT applications. Furthermore, the integration of QKD with both classical and post-quantum cryptography presents a forward-thinking strategy to ensure the long-term security of IoT systems. This hybrid approach would safeguard IoT networks against evolving security threats in both the classical and quantum domains.

QKD could promise a great deal in the future for securing IoT communications because it is a quantum-resistant method of exchanging cryptographic keys. QKD bases this approach on the quantum principles to ensure that any attempt during the transmission process to intercept or tamper with the key exchange is detectable and thus resists attacks both from the classical and quantum realms. Although hardware requirements and resource constraints for IoT devices would still pose the challenge, it's a hybrid approach toward combining QKD with post-quantum cryptography and classical methods that offers much greater practice in this respect. As quantum technology advances, so will the importance of QKD for the future of the security of IoT, where IoT networks will continue to be impregnable against the most advanced cyber threats.

7 Regulatory Compliance and Standards for Ensuring Secure Communication in IoT

As the Internet of Things (IoT) continues to expand, connecting billions of devices globally, the need for regulatory compliance and robust security standards has become increasingly critical. These frameworks are vital for safeguarding user data, preserving privacy, and ensuring the secure operation of IoT devices. Regulatory compliance entails adhering to laws and regulations that govern data protection and privacy, which vary across regions and industries but share the common goal of protecting personal information and holding organizations accountable for their data practices. Compliance is essential for maintaining user trust and avoiding legal consequences. In contrast, security standards focus on the technical and procedural measures necessary to protect IoT systems from cyber threats. These standards outline best practices, including encryption, access controls, vulnerability management, and incident response. By implementing these measures, organizations can effectively mitigate risks and strengthen the security of their IoT ecosystems.

Several key regulations and standards have been established to address these concerns. For example, the General Data Protection Regulation (GDPR) in the European Union sets strict guidelines for data handling and privacy. In the United States, the Health Insurance Portability and Accountability Act (HIPAA) protects sensitive patient information in the healthcare sector. The IoT Cybersecurity Improvement Act sets security standards for IoT devices used by the federal government, while the California Consumer Privacy Act (CCPA) enhances privacy rights for California residents. Additionally, the EU Cybersecurity Act provides a framework for the cybersecurity certification of products and services. These regulations and standards are designed to create a secure and trustworthy environment for IoT devices. By adhering to these frameworks, organizations can ensure that their IoT deployments are safe, secure, and compliant with legal requirements. This not only protects users but also fosters innovation and growth in the IoT industry.

7.1 General Data Protection Regulation (GDPR)

The General Data Protection Regulation is the framework that the European Union has put in place as a comprehensive approach to collecting, storing, and processing personal data from residents of the EU. It was a direct response to growing privacy concerns in the digital age and ultimately offers individuals more control over their information [23]. The rights of the data subjects include access, correction, right to erasure or right to restriction, right to data portability, and objection to various processing activities. An organization has to process the personal data of the organization lawfully, fairly, and in a transparent manner, thereby informing the individuals correctly about the processing carried out on their data. Data shall be collected for specified, explicit, and legitimate purposes and only to the extent and in such a manner as is necessary for the fulfillment of those purposes. The organizations must display awareness of the said compliance with GDPR principles through records that outline processing activities, carrying out DPIAs when relevant, and appointment of DPO when necessary. Appropriate to that purpose and to the nature of the data and categories of data and persons involved, the technical and organizational measures shall ensure the security and confidentiality of the person's data. Failure to comply with the GDPR will result in fines running into millions of Euros, which may be up to €20 million or 4% of the global annual turnover, whichever is higher. Such stringent provisions make compliance with the GDPR very important for any business processing personal data related to EU residents, including those in the IoT sector.

The intersection of IoT and GDPR throws up unique challenges and considerations. IoT devices are prolific in their ability to collect, transmit, and process data, thus raising huge privacy and compliance issues under GDPR. Handling these challenges is crucial for firms so they ensure the protection of the users' data as well as other forms of compliance with the norms and mandates under GDPR.

- **Data Controllers and Data Processors**: Determination of data controllers and data processors is one of the significant matters under GDPR, as such distinctions help draw the difference between the roles of a controller: determining the purposes and means of processing personal data, and the role of a processor: acting only on behalf of and on instructions from the controller. Hence, in the IoT ecosystem, many parties are involved; these include the device manufacturers, service providers, and the owner and operator of cloud platforms. IoT companies shall forthwith make clear their functions, and then formalize them with some appropriate data processing agreements.
- **Personal Data and Data Collection**: One of the core principles of GDPR is the lawful processing of personal data, which includes any information that can be related to an identifiable individual. Through this aspect, IoT companies need to ensure that data collectibles, like health metrics from a fitness tracker, must be collected based on one of the valid legal bases encompassed in the terms of explicit user consent, contract fulfillment, or legitimate interest to meet the requirements set by GDPR.
- **Consent Management**: Alternative, clear privacy notices for obvious and explicit, informed, and revocable consent; such mechanisms must also be in place to make it easy for people to withdraw consent as demanded by GDPR record the same and update the consent requests periodically.
- **Data Minimization and Purpose Limitation**: IoT devices often collect excessive data beyond their core functions, breaching GDPR's data minimization principle. To comply, IoT developers must ensure data collection aligns with intended purposes and not repurpose data without explicit user consent, adhering to the principle of purpose limitation.
- **Data Subject Rights in IoT Ecosystems**: Access, rectification, erasure, and the portability of personal data are granted rights, which make them quite challenging to the IoT ecosystems where the data is diffused across many

different platforms and devices. IoT companies should build mechanisms for efficient management and fulfillment in case of any request for data access. This would mean it should be possible for users, despite the complexity of multi-device environments, to exercise their rights easily.
- **Data Security and Breach Notification**: IoT devices are vulnerable to cyber-attacks due to limited security features, making robust measures like encryption essential to comply with GDPR's mandate to protect personal data. IoT companies must adopt a privacy-by-design approach and develop clear incident response plans, ensuring breaches are reported within 72 hours, despite the complexities of multiple devices and platforms.

By addressing these considerations, IoT companies can better navigate the complex landscape of GDPR compliance, ensuring that they protect user data and uphold the privacy rights of individuals in a rapidly evolving technological environment. While GDPR compliance is mandatory for organizations processing the personal data of EU residents, IoT companies face several unique challenges in meeting these requirements. Below are some of the primary obstacles to compliance:

- **Complex Ecosystems and Data Flows**
  IoT ecosystems comprise multiple devices, networks, platforms, and stakeholders. The data produced by the devices tends to flow across several parties—device manufacturers, cloud service providers, and also third-party developers. In this kind of distributed system, compliance is accordingly considered with a deep understanding of data flows and the roles each party plays. This further complicates the issue by the fact that data is collected continuously in real time, which means there will always be too much information to be processed, stored, and secured. The volume and complexity of the data collected by IoTs are too great for traditional data protection frameworks to comply with.
- **Device Limitations**
  Consumer-grade IoT devices suffer from poor processing and low memory. As such, most of IoT gadgets lack high-level processing capabilities to execute heavy computations that can be required in security features in the form of encryption, multi-factor authentication, or secure firmware updates. Data breaches, therefore, are easily viable possibilities that lead to higher risks. It makes the already difficult requirement of meeting GDPR security even harder to achieve. For instance, it may be extremely difficult to ensure the confidentiality and integrity of information gathered and communicated by these devices when they cannot host strong security in themselves.
- **Cross-Border Data Transfers**
  IoT devices are often spread across different countries, and therefore data is crossing borders. The transfer of personal data from the EU to other jurisdictions is, for example, restricted under the provision of the GDPR which requires there to be adequate safeguards in place to ensure data protection standards are complied with. Interoperability concerns on cross-border data flows for companies involved in IoT while remaining compliant with GDPR is a very significant challenge where cloud services can be used to potentially store data

in different jurisdictions. This requires analyzing data transfer mechanisms and integrating appropriate legal measures, such as SCCs or BCRs.

- **Lack of User Awareness**
  Such personal data is being collected and processed at a scope that users of IoT devices may not be very aware of. This unawareness is a significant hurdle in obtaining meaningful consent because the users may not understand the privacy implications of using such IoT devices. Moreover, with a lack of notification on the types of data collected and availability for access, it is difficult for users to exercise rights as data subjects. Their rights include access, rectification, or erasure of data. This again raises concerns for IoT companies to invest in clear communication strategies and user-friendly interfaces to notify them about data collection practices and rights set under GDPR.

While GDPR compliance is a legal necessity, the unique characteristics of IoT devices and ecosystems present distinct challenges. Addressing these challenges demands a multifaceted approach that involves understanding complex data flows, overcoming device limitations, managing cross-border data transfers, and enhancing user awareness. By effectively tackling these obstacles, IoT companies can align more closely with GDPR requirements and ensure the protection of personal data in an increasingly complex technological landscape.

Different challenges that IoT firms need to address to ensure compliance with GDPR and best practices can be followed in attempting to navigate through these complexities. One of the foundations of GDPR is privacy by design and by default, asking for the embedding of privacy considerations into the development of IoT devices. Firms shall collect only as much data as necessary for their functions, and they shall set the most restrictive privacy settings by default. Furthermore, there are clear and transparent privacy policies. The policies should be easily accessible to users and should be articulate in their language to avoid misunderstandings. Such policies are required to be updated regularly in light of the data processing practices as it showcase transparency and allows gaining trust over time. Good handling of data also plays a very crucial role as far as ensuring the satisfaction of GDP data security standards is concerned. This entails encrypting data in motion as well as at rest, authenticating with secure mechanisms, and regularly updating the firmware to address vulnerabilities. Another great role that compliance plays is in the domain of user control and consent management, such that companies have user-friendly interfaces for use by users that will allow easy management of their data as well as consent preferences. Following these best practices will ensure the protection of user data, and as such, the very building blocks of their loyalties with users.

7.2 *Health Insurance Portability and Accountability Act (HIPAA)*

HIPAA compliance is generally construed as applying to standards and regulations dictated by the Health Insurance Portability and Accountability Act of 1996. This act forms a guideline towards protected health information (PHI) in respect of privacy and security [38]. Compliance involves putting measures in place to ensure the confidentiality, integrity, and availability of PHI in whatever electronic storage, transmission, or processing may be involved. To this end, the covered healthcare providers, health plans, and their business associates must meet some requirements to ensure that PHI is protected. They need to comply with a rule called the Privacy Rule, which specifies what should be done about the protection of an individual's medical records and other personal health information, and the Security Rule, which specifies those administrative, physical, and technical safeguards needed to protect electronic PHI. Covered entities are also mandated to provide notice of a breach of unsecured PHI to affected individuals, HHS, and, if appropriate, the media. The HIPAA rules are enforced by the Office for Civil Rights within HHS, through investigations and imposition of penalties should there be a violation. HIPAA compliance is therefore meant to ensure the security of patients' health information and at the same time maintain the trust between the patients and the healthcare providers.

HIPAA would comprise several major rules and regulations that would guarantee the confidentiality and integrity of health information. The Privacy Rule creates national standards for the protection of protected health information (PHI). It puts limits on the use and disclosure of health records and gives patients rights over their health information, including the right to examine and obtain a copy of their health records and request corrections. The Security Rule describes the safeguards that covered entities and their business associates must put in place to ensure the confidentiality, integrity, and availability of electronic protected health information. The three types of safeguards outlined are categorized under administrative, physical, and technical. Furthermore, the act requires policies and procedures to ensure compliance. Physical safeguards include controls applied at the design level for the protection of electronic systems and related buildings and equipment, as well as from natural and environmental hazards, against unauthorized intrusion. Technical safeguards comprise technology and related policies and procedures that protect ePHI and control access to it. The Breach Notification Rule requires covered entities to notify affected persons, the Secretary of Health and Human Services, and in certain cases, the media, of a breach of unsecured PHI. Business associates should notify covered entities in the event of a breach at or by the business associate. Finally, the Enforcement Rule outlines compliance and investigation provisions, imposition of civil money penalties for violation, and procedures for hearings. This rule ensures entities comply with HIPAA requirements and are dealt with in case they do not, thus pushing them to ensure health information is protected.

The effectiveness of HIPAA on IoT in healthcare is multifaceted, addressing various aspects of data security, privacy protection, compliance challenges, interoperability, breach notification, and ongoing monitoring.

- **Data Security**
  IoT devices in healthcare, such as wearable fitness trackers and remote patient monitoring systems, collect and share various levels of health information. The

Health Insurance Portability and Accountability Act (HIPAA) requires strong security measures to protect this electronic protected health information (ePHI). Encryption is essential both during data transmission and when stored, to prevent unauthorized access. Additionally, access controls must be implemented to ensure that only authorized individuals can view ePHI. Regular security assessments are also crucial to identify vulnerabilities in IoT devices and address them, ensuring the devices remain secure over time.

- **Privacy Protection**
  The HIPAA Privacy Rule ensures that the protected health information collected by IoT devices is kept confidential. It strictly formulates guidance on the use and disclosure of PHI, which means that patient data can be shared only by the regulations that pertain to HIPAA. Rights of Patients There are several rights patients enjoy to their health information: the right to have access to the data and ask for corrections. IoT systems need to be designed to respect and enable these rights; without this, the process of managing healthcare information by the patients is not easy.
- **Compliance Challenges**
  One of the main reasons why HIPAA compliance for IoT devices cannot be guaranteed is within their limited processing power and storage capacity. Within such capacities, it is not possible to offer intricate security features that involve sophisticated encryption and tough authentication processes. Health organizations have to craft their security measures in a manner that is well within the technical capacity of IoT devices but must be suitable enough to satisfy the stringent conditions set by HIPAA. This is often a challenge involving reconciling security requirements with the physically practical capabilities of devices.
- **Interoperability and Data Sharing**
  Through IoT applications in healthcare, data may at times have to be shared between different systems and stakeholders within the healthcare ecosystem. The Security and Privacy Rules of HIPAA ensure that data sharing is done with a keen watch on patient privacy and security. Achieving interoperability without breaching HIPAA is only possible through careful planning, as well as the implementation of secure data exchange protocols. This may include conducting data transfers between devices and systems securely and ensuring that all parties involved in the data sharing are keeping HIPAA regulations alive.
- **Breach Notification**
  Consequently, more and more IoT devices expand the surface area through which breaches may occur. HIPAA's Breach Notification Rule is important for IoT: it requires that notice be given of breaches involving any amount of PHI in a timely fashion. IoT systems need to be designed to quickly notify parties affected by a breach, including patients, the Secretary of Health and Human Services, and, in some cases, the media. The success of this is then followed by lessening harm from a data breach as soon as possible, and patients are then informed of the safety of health information.

- **Ongoing Monitoring and Risk Management**
  Under HIPAA, there is a demand for constant monitoring and risk management, which capability is more complicated under an IoT dynamic environment. There is a regular necessity for healthcare organizations to update their risk assessments to monitor newly created threats and vulnerabilities that emerge with the use of IoT devices. This pertains to implementing ongoing monitoring procedures that ensure lasting security compliance of IoT devices. Updates or patches need to be applied about security threats that tend to appear in order to maintain safe and secured information systems in the realm of IoT devices for patients.

Thus, HIPAA responds to these aspects; the technology supports improvement in patient care and ensures health information is safe and private by use of IoT devices in healthcare. With this, health organizations can see an advantage of the benefits of IoT, as they can use it without compromising compliance and patient trust.

7.3 IoT Cybersecurity Improvement Act

The IoT Cybersecurity Improvement Act is a significant legislation meant to enhance the security of Internet of Things (IoT) devices in use by the federal government and its contractors. It became a law in December 2020, when growing concerns are focused on the vulnerabilities associated with IoT devices, which may oftentimes become entry points for cyber-attacks. The general thrust of the legislation is to ensure security baselines that help mitigate risks and guard sensitive data relative to these devices. Among the significant elements of the IoT Cybersecurity Improvement Act is the determination of minimum security requirements of IoT devices purchased by federal agencies. This act directs the National Institute of Standards and Technology to develop guidelines outlining the minimum required security standards. The requirements include building assured-in-production software, effective authentication mechanisms, and secure out-of-the-box device configurations. In totality, these measures become standards to be met with the act.

The law requires setting standards for security as well as directing federal agencies to conduct risk assessments for their IoT devices. Among others, the requirements include the determination of potential vulnerabilities and assessment of impact these vulnerabilities would create in federal systems. Further, an agency is required to have a strategy for managing risks associated with IoT devices. This also includes periodic monitoring of the security posture of the devices and the update thereof. This proactive approach will allow agencies to get ahead of emerging threats and be ready to respond in a security incident. The IoT Cybersecurity Improvement Act also focuses on information sharing between federal agencies and the public and private sectors. It makes possible the collaboration that enhances the overall cybersecurity posture of IoT devices. The risks that can be mitigated with IoT technology can best be understood if organizations share threat intelligence and best practices. Since this landscape is ever-changing, threats can form very rapidly, and it does call for cooperation.

The act also provides for accountability in the security of IoT devices. It states that the federal agencies are obligated to ensure that any such IoT devices acquired shall comply with established security standards. Accountability is further extended to contractors and other third-party vendors that supply IoT devices to the government. The act holds everyone responsible who is involved in the development and deployment of IoT technologies in a culture of security awareness and responsibility. In a nutshell, it will be a comprehensive effort on the part of federal agencies to improve the security of IoT devices they make use of. This will protect federal systems from the unique vulnerabilities IoT technology has in its use through minimum security requirements, risk assessments, encouraging sharing of information, and accountability. With the onset of IoT devices beginning to crop up in both governmental and private premises, this is an inevitable step toward data safety and national security.

7.4 California Consumer Privacy Act (CCPA)

The CCPA is landmark legislation enacted in California, effective since January 2020. It aims at enhancing the privacy rights and consumer protection of the residents of that state-it, arguably, constitutes one of the most comprehensive data privacy laws in the United States-a piece of legislation that grants Californians increased control over their personal information business organizations may collect from them. Under the CCPA, people have the right to know what personal data is being gathered about themselves, the right to access that data, the right to seek deletion of their data, and the right to opt out of the sale of their personal information. On the other hand, businesses have the obligation of providing clear and transparent privacy notices so that consumers will know how their data is being used. Impact of CCPA on IoT Security: CCPA is significant because the devices under IoT constantly collect sensitive personal data in large volumes. These devices, such as smart home appliances, wearables, and connected vehicles, gather user data continuously and therefore act both as a valuable and vulnerable target for data breaches. This makes the CCPA lay down more stringent demands on companies manufacturing and deploying IoT devices, making them adopt stronger data protection practices. Organizations should ensure data security measures to protect the collection and circulation of personal information carried out through their IoT devices, such as encryption, secure data transmission protocols, and regular security audits.

Another aspect that may impact IoT firms is the focus of CCPA on consumer rights; it will be pretty deciding concerning how the companies should actually deal with data privacy issues. For instance, to ensure that its device offers consumers an easy management of their options, a company may be forced to come up with interfaces that are easier to use for people accessing, deleting, or opting out of data sharing practices. In fact, failure to comply with CCPA brings severe monetary fines that place the manufacturers of IoT on the right path towards proper data protection and consumers' privacy. The organizations are therefore dragged to ensure that their IoT products have aspects of privacy by design, all this from design, ensuring data protection at every step of product life cycles. The CCPA also brings out a new concept of "reasonable security procedures and practices" placed upon businesses in protection of personal information. This would mean that for IoT devices, their manufacturers and service providers have a responsibility to identify vulnerabilities for their products before they develop those products, hence mitigating the risk associated with them. Since many IoT devices also normally possess limited processing power and security capacities, Companies will face difficulties ensuring all their devices fulfill CCPA security requirements. There might arise a need to offer patches and updates after deployment and continued support for security measures.

The provisions of CCPA set a ripple effect throughout the entire IoT ecosystem. As companies strive to comply with the requirements of CCPA, it will prove to be imperative to reassess the manner in which data is shared and collaborated with third-party vendors. It leads towards ensuring that such third parties dealing with processing or storage of personal data maintain similar standards of privacy as well as security, thus incrementally strengthening the protection of data up and down the supply chain. This scrutiny brings a sense of responsibility to the IoT sector, making all stakeholders wary of their actions as much as security and consumer privacy are concerned. Conclusion The CCPA ripples with effects on IoT security since it forces organizations to employ robust data protection means while observing greater respect for consumer rights to privacy. Although data breaches are less concerning in this line of proliferation, compliance with CCPA instills the trust and confidence of consumers into such technologies. Therefore, by embracing the principles under which CCPA stands, manufacturers of IoTs are better placed to navigate the maze of data privacy and security, thereby creating a more secure space for consumers in the digital world.

7.5 Cybersecurity Act, EU

Adopted in the form of Regulation (EU) 2019/881 by the European Union, the Cybersecurity Act aims to improve cybersecurity within its member states. Adopted in June 2019, this regulation outlines a framework for the process of certifying cybersecurity products and services in an effort to boost the general level of cybersecurity within the EU. One of the core objectives of the Cybersecurity Act is the establishment of a unified approach on cybersecurity across the EU, which should be aimed at addressing the challenges and threats in the digital landscape and making possible the proper facilitation for citizens and businesses to trust digital services and products and Internet of Things (IoT) devices.

This great part of the Cybersecurity Act lies in the establishment of an EU-wide cybersecurity certification framework, which is meant to provide assurance on the security and the privacy of IT products, services, and processes. In view of the proliferation of the IoT as a pervasive factor in different sectors such as healthcare, transportation, and manufacturing, this is very important. Under this framework, the European Union Agency for Cybersecurity or ENISA would support the development of cybersecurity certification schemes that can help improve the security of IoT devices and systems. The Cybersecurity Act is meant to put in place standardized certification processes where IoT manufacturers meet specific security requirements that can boost consumer confidence in these products. The Cybersecurity Act underlines adopting a risk-based approach toward cybersecurity, especially through Internet of Things devices. Therefore, it throws a challenge to manufacturers and providers of services to study the particular risks posed by their products to their security and accordingly design and implement countermeasures for that. This may adopt security by design whereby, instead of being an afterthought, the securing elements are developed at the time of designing such gadgets like IoT devices. For example, producers may be required to provide secure code with frequent updates and rigorous encryption regarding data integrity and confidentiality.

The Cybersecurity Act promotes collaboration among various stakeholders in the Internet of Things (IoT) ecosystem, including producers, service providers, consumers, and regulatory authorities. By fostering cooperation and facilitating the exchange of information regarding threats and vulnerabilities, the Act enhances organizations' understanding of their cybersecurity challenges, thereby strengthening the security posture of individual entities and the overall resilience of the European Union's digital landscape. Information sharing is crucial, as it aggregates best practices and industry standards, enabling continuous monitoring and improvement of security measures for IoT devices. Given the rapid evolution of cyber threats, organizations are encouraged to adopt proactive security strategies, such as conducting regular security reviews, penetration tests, and developing incident response plans to effectively address breaches.

The Act also emphasizes the importance of user awareness in securing connected devices. It mandates that manufacturers provide essential information to consumers about the security of their devices and safe usage practices. By empowering consumers with knowledge, the Cybersecurity Act fosters a security-conscious user base that is better equipped to recognize and mitigate risks associated with IoT technologies. Overall, the EU Cybersecurity Act establishes a comprehensive framework aimed at enhancing the cybersecurity of IT products, particularly within the IoT sector. Through standardized certification processes, risk-based approaches, collaboration among stakeholders, continuous monitoring, and user education, the Act enhances the security posture of the IoT ecosystem in Europe, ultimately protecting both consumers and enterprises while bolstering confidence in the digital economy and enabling the safe adoption of innovative technologies.

8 Conclusion

The critical importance of secure communication in the Internet of Things cannot be overstated. As IoT continues to permeate various aspects of daily life and industrial operations, the need for robust security measures becomes ever more paramount. This chapter has explored the intricate landscape of secure communication within IoT, detailing the challenges and proposing viable solutions through advanced cryptographic techniques, innovative technologies, and stringent regulatory compliance. To fully appreciate and harness the potential of IoT, it is essential for researchers, developers, and policymakers to delve deeper into the topics discussed. The integration of blockchain technology and quantum-resistant cryptography, for instance, presents promising avenues for future research and development. Moreover, understanding and implementing comprehensive security protocols tailored to the unique constraints of IoT devices will be crucial in mitigating risks and ensuring the reliability of these systems.

The exploration of blockchain technology offers decentralized communication solutions, enhancing security and trust within IoT networks by eliminating single points of failure and enabling tamper-proof data exchange. Similarly, quantum-resistant cryptography represents a forward-thinking approach to countering future threats posed by quantum computing, ensuring the longevity and robustness of IoT security measures. Comprehensive security protocols, such as lightweight cryptographic algorithms designed specifically for IoT's resource-constrained environments, play a pivotal role in safeguarding data integrity, confidentiality, and authenticity. These protocols must be continually updated and adapted to address emerging threats and vulnerabilities, ensuring that IoT devices can operate securely without compromising performance. Regulatory compliance and adherence to standards like GDPR and HIPAA are vital in establishing a framework for data protection and legal accountability in IoT systems. These regulations not only protect user privacy but also provide a structured approach to managing and securing sensitive information across diverse IoT applications.

To stay ahead of the evolving threat landscape, continuous education and awareness are imperative for all stakeholders involved in the development and deployment of IoT technologies. Engaging with the latest advancements and participating in collaborative efforts to address security challenges will significantly contribute to the creation of secure and resilient IoT ecosystems. The future of IoT depends on our collective ability to address its security challenges through innovative technologies, robust cryptographic solutions, and stringent regulatory frameworks. By fostering a culture of continuous learning and proactive engagement, we can ensure that IoT technologies fulfill their potential in transforming industries and enhancing our everyday lives, while maintaining the highest standards of security and privacy.

Acknowledgments The successful completion of this chapter would not have been possible without the support and contributions of C3iHub Project. I would like to extend my deepest gratitude to C3iHub for their invaluable support and resources throughout the research and writing process.

References

1. Abdul-Ghani, H.A., Konstantas, D.: A comprehensive study of security and privacy guidelines, threats, and countermeasures: an iot perspective.
2. Alhakami, H.: Enhancing iot security: quantum-level resilience against threats. Comput. Mater. Continua **78**(1) (2024)
3. Arya, V., Almomani, A., Han, C.: Analysis of quantum computing-based security of internet of things (iot) environment. Cyber Secur. Insights Mag. Insights2Techinfo **4**, 7–14 (2022)
4. Babun, L., Denney, K., Celik, Z.B., McDaniel, P., Uluagac, A.S.: A survey on iot platforms: communication, security, and privacy perspectives. Comput. Netw. **192**, 108040 (2021)
5. Bhardwaj, I., Kumar, A., Bansal, M.: A review on lightweight cryptography algorithms for data security and authentication in iots. In: 2017 4th International Conference on Signal Processing, Computing and Control (ISPCC), pp. 504–509. IEEE (2017)
6. Hassija, V., Chamola, V., Agrawal, A., Goyal, A., Luong, N.C., Niyato, D., Yu, F.R., Guizani, M.: Fast, reliable, and secure drone communication: a comprehensive survey. IEEE Commun. Surv. Tutor. **23**(4), 2802–2832 (2021)
7. Chanal, P.M., Kakkasageri, M.S.: Security and privacy in iot: a survey. Wirel. Personal Commun. **115**(2), 1667–1693 (2020)
8. Chen, C.-M., Deng, X., Gan, W., Chen, J., Hafizul Islam, S.K.: A secure blockchain-based group key agreement protocol for iot. J. Supercomput. **77**, 9046–9068 (2021)
9. Cherbal, S., Zier, A., Hebal, S., Louail, L., Annane, B.: Security in internet of things: a review on approaches based on blockchain, machine learning, cryptography, and quantum computing. J. Supercomput. **80**(3), 3738–3816 (2024)
10. Cynthia, J., Sultana, H.P., Saroja, M.N., Senthil, J.: Security protocols for iot. Ubiquitous Comput. Comput. Sec. IoT 1–28 (2019)
11. Das, A.K., Zeadally, S., He, D.: Taxonomy and analysis of security protocols for internet of things. Future Gener. Comput. Syst. **89**, 110–125 (2018)
12. Desai, B., Patil, K., Mehta, I., Patil, A.: A secure communication framework for smart city infrastructure leveraging encryption, intrusion detection, and blockchain technology. Adv. Comput. Sci. **7**(1) (2024)
13. Dorri, A., Kanhere, S.S., Jurdak, R., Gauravaram, P.: Lsb: a lightweight scalable blockchain for iot security and anonymity. J. Parallel Distrib. Comput. **134**, 180–197 (2019)
14. Hamad, M., Finkenzeller, A., Liu, H., Lauinger, J., Prevelakis, V., Steinhorst, S.: Seemqtt: secure end-to-end mqtt-based communication for mobile iot systems using secret sharing and trust delegation. IEEE Internet Things J. **10**(4), 3384–3406 (2022)
15. Hintaw, A.J., Manickam, S., Karuppayah, S., Aladaileh, M.A., Aboalmaaly, M.F., Laghari, S.U.A.: A robust security scheme based on enhanced symmetric algorithm for mqtt in the internet of things. IEEE Access **11**, 43019–43040 (2023)
16. Jan, M.A., Khan, F., Mastorakis, S., Adil, M., Akbar, A., Stergiou, N.: Lightiot: lightweight and secure communication for energy-efficient iot in health informatics. IEEE Trans. Green Commun. Netw. **5**(3), 1202–1211 (2021)
17. Javeed, D., Gao, T., Khan, M.T., Ahmad, I.: A hybrid deep learning-driven sdn enabled mechanism for secure communication in internet of things (iot). Sensors **21**(14), 4884 (2021)
18. Kannan, B.M., Solainayagi, P., Azath, H., Murugan, S., Srinivasan, C.: Secure communication in iot-enabled embedded systems for military applications using encryption. In: 2023 2nd International Conference on Edge Computing and Applications (ICECAA), pp. 1385–1389. IEEE (2023)
19. Khan, M.A., Salah, K.: Iot security: review, blockchain solutions, and open challenges. Future Gener. Comput. Syst. **82**, 395–411 (2018)
20. Khan, M.N., Rao, A., Camtepe, S.: Lightweight cryptographic protocols for iot-constrained devices: A survey. IEEE Internet Things J. **8**(6), 4132–4156 (2020)
21. Khan, A.A., Laghari, A.A., Shaikh, Z.A., Dacko-Pikiewicz, Z., Kot, S.: Internet of things (iot) security with blockchain technology: a state-of-the-art review. IEEE Access **10**, 122679–122695 (2022)

22. Kondoro, A., Dhaou, I.B., Tenhunen, H., Mvungi, N.: Real time performance analysis of secure iot protocols for microgrid communication. Future Gener. Comput. Syst. **116**, 1–12 (2021)
23. Kounoudes, A.D., Kapitsaki, G.M.: A mapping of iot user-centric privacy preserving approaches to the gdpr. Internet Things **11**, 100179 (2020)
24. Kumar, A., Farooq, S.A., Gowda, D., Prabhu, S., Reddy, A.M., Tanguturi, R.: Improved secure communication mechanism for iot platform devices. In: 2022 International Conference on Smart Generation Computing, Communication and Networking (SMART GENCON), pp. 1–6. IEEE (2022)
25. Li, F., Xiong, P.: Practical secure communication for integrating wireless sensor networks into the internet of things. IEEE Sensors J. **13**(10), 3677–3684 (2013)
26. Liu, Z., Liang, T., Lyu, J., Lang, D.: A security-enhanced scheme for mqtt protocol based on domestic cryptographic algorithm. Comput. Commun. **221**, 1–9 (2024)
27. Mahajan, R.A., Mahajan, R.G., Tatiya, M., Mandekar, U.H., Shahakar, M., Patil, Y.: Enhancing mqtt security in the internet of things with an enhanced symmetric algorithm. J. Electr. Syst. **20**(1s), 126–137 (2024)
28. Nebbione, G., Calzarossa, M.C.: Security of iot application layer protocols: challenges and findings. Future Internet **12**(3), 55 (2020)
29. Panarello, A., Tapas, N., Merlino, G., Longo, F., Puliafito, A.: Blockchain and iot integration: a systematic survey. Sensors **18**(8), 2575 (2018)
30. Portmann, C., Renner, R.: Security in quantum cryptography. Rev. Mod. Phys. **94**(2), 025008 (2022)
31. Radanliev, P.: Cyber diplomacy: defining the opportunities for cybersecurity and risks from artificial intelligence, iot, blockchains, and quantum computing. J. Cyber Secur. Technol. 1–51 (2024)
32. Rahman, A., Roy, S., Kaiser, M.S., Islam, M.S.: A lightweight multi-tier s-mqtt framework to secure communication between low-end iot nodes. In: 2018 5th International Conference on Networking, Systems and Security (NSysS), pp. 1–6. IEEE (2018)
33. Rana, M., Mamun, Q., Islam, R.: Lightweight cryptography in iot networks: a survey. Future Gener. Comput. Syst. **129**, 77–89 (2022)
34. Rani, D., Gill, N.S.: Review of various iot standards and communication protocols. Int. J. Eng. Res. Technol. **12**(5), 647–657 (2019)
35. Rathee, G., Balasaraswathi, M., Chandran, K.P., Gupta, S.D., Boopathi, C.S.: A secure iot sensors communication in industry 4.0 using blockchain technology. J. Ambient Intell. Humaniz. Comput. **12**(1), 533–545 (2021)
36. Rhee, M.Y.: Internet Security: Cryptographic Principles, Algorithms and Protocols. John Wiley & Sons, Hoboken (2003)
37. Rostampour, S., Safkhani, M., Bendavid, Y., Bagheri, N.: Eccbap: a secure ecc-based authentication protocol for iot edge devices. Pervasive Mob. Comput. **67**, 101194 (2020)
38. Said, A., Yahyaoui, A., Abdellatif, T.: Hipaa and gdpr compliance in iot healthcare systems. In International Conference on Model and Data Engineering, pp. 198–209. Springer (2023)
39. Seoane, V., Garcia-Rubio, C., Almenares, F., Campo, C.: Performance evaluation of coap and mqtt with security support for iot environments. Comput. Netw. **197**, 108338 (2021)
40. Shannon, K., Towe, E., Tonguz, O.K.: On the use of quantum entanglement in secure communications: a survey. Preprint (2020). arXiv:2003.07907
41. Sheng, Y.-B., Zhou, L., Long, G.-L.: One-step quantum secure direct communication. Sci. Bull. **67**(4), 367–374 (2022)
42. Sidna, J., Amine, B., Abdallah, N., Alami, H.E.: Analysis and evaluation of communication protocols for iot applications. In: Proceedings of the 13th International Conference on Intelligent Systems: Theories and Applications, pp. 1–6 (2020)
43. Silva, D., Carvalho, L.I., Soares, J., Sofia, R.C.: A performance analysis of internet of things networking protocols: evaluating mqtt, coap, opc ua. Appl. Sci. **11**(11), 4879 (2021)
44. Singh, M., Rajan, M.A., Shivraj, V.L., Balamuralidhar, P.: Secure mqtt for internet of things (iot). In: 2015 Fifth International Conference on Communication Systems and Network Technologies, pp. 746–751. IEEE (2015)

45. Tightiz, L., Yang, H.: A comprehensive review on iot protocols' features in smart grid communication. Energies **13**(11), 2762 (2020)
46. Tournier, J., Lesueur, F., Mouël, F.L., Guyon, L., Ben-Hassine, H.: A survey of iot protocols and their security issues through the lens of a generic iot stack. Internet Things **16**, 100264 (2021)

Advancing Connectivity and Security in SDN-IoT Networks Through Policy Management

Anjana Jimmington, Sabu M. Thampi, and Preetam Mukherjee

1 Introduction

In the fast-paced world we live in, dependence on technology is intertwined with seamless connectivity. Beginning with simple computer networks, we've evolved into a realm where smart devices abound. The complex nature of this advanced network demands efficient management to ensure smooth operations. Imagine not just your phone or computer being connected but also your fridge, thermostat, and even your coffee maker. This is the "Internet of Things (IoT)". It's like a big web of devices sharing information.

1.1 IoT and Its Network Management Challenges

The Internet has changed a lot over time. It started as a place for information, and now it's becoming a personalized space called the Web of Individualized Things. This change is possible because of advancements in technology that allow different things to connect and communicate without any limits of space or time. This transformation is turning the Internet into a HyperNetwork, like a big web connecting not just people but also objects and information. We call this the "Internet of Things (IoT)," where billions of people and objects are connected. It's a powerful tool humans have created to easily create, change, and share information [55].

A. Jimmington (✉), S. M. Thampi, and P. Mukherjee
Connected Systems and Intelligence Lab, School of Computer Science & Engineering, Digital University Kerala, Trivandrum, India
e-mail: anjana.res21@duk.ac.in; sabu.thampi@duk.ac.in; preetam.mukherjee@duk.ac.in

S. M. Thampi et al. (eds.), *Securing the Connected World*,
https://doi.org/10.1007/978-3-031-82826-3_7

Fig. 1 Internet of Things landscape

The term "Internet of Things" (IoT) was first coined by Kevin Ashton in 1999 during his work at Auto-ID Labs [5]. He used this phrase to describe a system where objects in the physical world are connected to the internet, enabling them to collect and share data. This leads to the definition of the Internet of Things as "The network of interconnected devices or things embedded with sensors, software, and other technologies, allowing them to communicate and exchange data with other devices and systems over the Internet". In essence, IoT extends the capabilities of the internet beyond traditional computing devices to include a wide range of everyday objects, from household appliances and wearable devices to industrial machinery and smart city infrastructure.

Today, there are more connected objects to the Internet than humans. This exponential growth in IoT devices, ranging from smart home gadgets to industrial sensors, shows the integration of technology into every facet of our daily lives, shaping a future where the connectivity of devices surpasses the global human population. Figure 1 shows the landscape of IoT.

The latest IoT Analytics "State of IoT-Spring 2023" report shows that the number of global IoT connections grew by 18% in 2022 to 14.3 billion active IoT endpoints. In 2023, the global number of connected IoT devices grew another 16%, to 16.7 billion active endpoints. IoT device connections are expected to continue to grow for many years to come [66]. The graph in Fig. 2 clearly shows the growth of IoT connectivity over the years.

With great power comes great responsibility, and the rapid adoption of IoT also raises concerns about privacy, security, and ethical considerations [46]. One of the fundamental issues arises from the enormous volume of data generated by IoT devices. These devices, ranging from smart home appliances to industrial sensors, continuously collect and transmit data. The sheer scale of this data presents challenges in terms of storage, processing, and analysis. Furthermore, the network architecture supporting the expanding network of connected devices is becoming increasingly intricate, necessitating more sophisticated management solutions.

The conventional techniques of network management, which revolve around the manual setup of separate devices, do not suffice in the case of the Internet of Things. First, because the manual configuration of individual devices is both ineffective, and

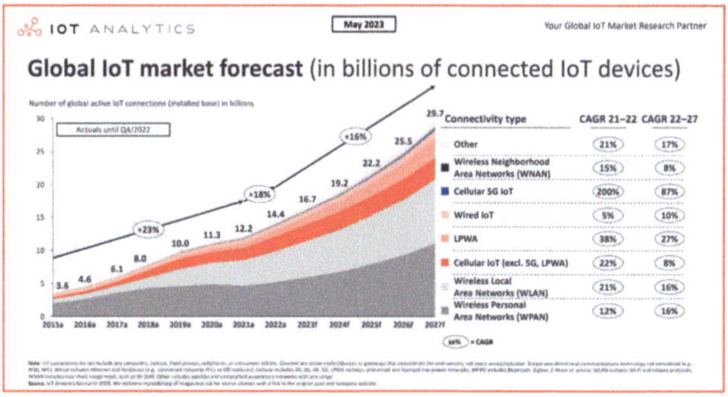

Fig. 2 Global IoT market forecast [66]

takes time to manage, especially with the traffic levels experienced in IoT. Sensors are expected to be responsive in real time which is why the need for such analysis and even decisions is so glaring.

Because of the multidisciplinary nature of the challenges, the necessity of responsible solution making is clear. The massive amounts of personal and sensitive information that IoT components deal with arouses fears in people and therefore requires appropriate measures such as data-breach, and users' privacy protections. Vulnerabilities with regard to security range from access to systems that are not supposed to be available, to system attacks, hence the need for comprehensive cyber security policies and measures. It is likely that the internet of things will be [more] embedded into our daily lives which creates the ethical issues. The ethical use of data, potential misuse of IoT capabilities, and the ramifications for individual rights and social values must all be carefully considered. Maintaining a balance between innovation and risk mitigation becomes critical.

These are some of the aspects that need to be addressed as we progress with the explorations of the Internet of Things. Researchers, policy makers, and industry practitioners need to come together and formulate solutions that will work. Besides that, to ensure that a peaceful coexistence of innovation and privacy or the social well-being of people as a whole, ethical aspects must be factored while designing and implementing such technologies. In this way, the Internet of Things can be embraced in a way that will help promote a well-connected and efficient society.

1.2 Transforming IoT Network Management with SDN

In conventional networks, there is a poor support for flexible flow management and introduction of new network services because both the control plane and data plane are embedded in a single integrated and proprietary device. This centralized architecture makes it very difficult to create new network applications and services that are expected to be programmable and agile. In this regard, SDN aims at

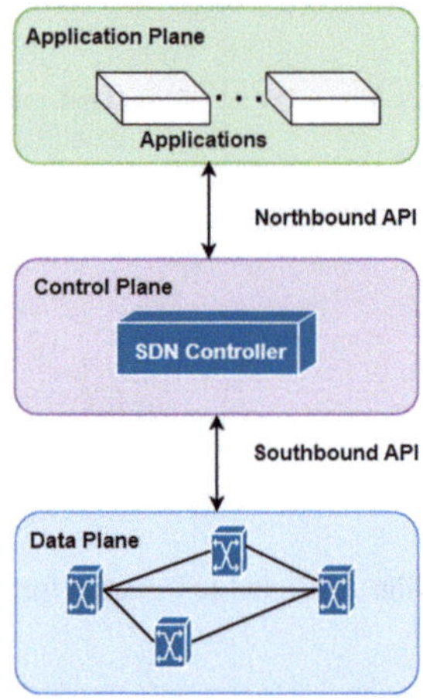

Fig. 3 SDN architecture

addressing the need to fix the conventional architecture, which has been very rigid by looking at the possibilities of separating the control and data planes and providing room for a central programmable network management. This dissociation creates room for innovative network services and allows operators to meet the growing demands of the services with flexibility and speed. This decoupling of the data plane from the control plane is one of the critical and defining features of SDN which paves the way for a more dynamic, malleable and smart network infrastructure [30].

The network's intelligence is represented by the SDN Controller, a software element that serves as the control plane and decides how to handle network traffic. The data plane, represented by the network devices, is in charge of routing traffic according to a predetermined set of rules [30]. The SDN Controller, who has complete knowledge of the network architecture and direct control over the data plane components using a southbound protocol like OpenFlow, formulates and oversees these rules [16].

Figure 3 shows the three layers of an SDN architecture and the APIs facilitating communication between them. The three layers are the Data Plane, the Control Plane, and the Application Plane. Support for communication between the application layer and the control plane layer is provided via the SDN Northbound API. Additionally, it offers assistance for SDN Applications like traffic engineering, routing, firewalls, quality of service, and others. For communication between SDN Controllers and switches, the Southbound API is in charge.

Studying the architecture from bottom to top:

- Data Plane:
  In the SDN architecture, the data plane (DP) is the layer that deals with the actual implementation of the data flow. It comprises switches that receive flow rules from upper levels as instructions to be carried out in the switches flow table. In some circumstances, the switch is in charge of sending the packet to the controller for a decision if it doesn't match any entry in the flow table when it is received.

- Control Plane:
  The control plane (CP) in the middle layer is in charge of implementing the legacy network's control path. This is the most important layer in an SDN architecture since it handles responsibilities related to network administration, traffic engineering, and traffic shaping. Many SDN controllers are available in the market such as NOX [45], OpenDaylight, Ryu [34].
- Application Plane:
  The packet forwarding, policy administration, user management, and Quality of Service (QoS) customization are all handled at the application layer, the top layer, with the aid of a controller. All network operations and monitoring tools in SDN architecture typically fall under the application layer.
- Southbound API:
  The Southbound Interface is a communication mechanism in software-defined networking that uses a Southbound API instruction set to connect the Control plane and the Forwarding Device in the data plane. The controller can be helped by a clearly defined Southbound API interface while programming the forwarding hardware and establishing uniform guidelines for CP and DP communication. OpenFlow, ForCES, and Protocol-Oblivious Forwarding (POF) are a few well-known examples of SI protocols.
- Northbound API:
  Provides the interface for interacting with the application AP and control plane. These Northbound APIs enable the Network Operating System (NOS) to aid in communication among application developers. A northbound API frequently abstracts the implementation of forwarding devices and low-level instruction sets. Northbound APIs have not yet been thoroughly investigated. As a general rule, applications and the control plane are connected by RESTFull APIs.

1.3 Advantages of Integrating SDN and IoT

Integrating Software-Defined Networking (SDN) with Internet of Things (IoT) networks is of great importance, offering a wide range of benefits that address the complexities and challenges inherent in managing and securing IoT ecosystems. SDN's centralized control and programmability are key features that significantly simplify the intricate task of administering IoT networks, particularly for devices located in remote and diverse environments.

When it comes to the management of IoT networks, the control of a SDN remains crucial especially in situations where the networks may contain devices that are too remote to managed manually. This ensures that operations are simplified and quite in control as it allows the administrator to manage thousands of IoT devices through one control plane while ensuring that the network is working at its best. The scope of SDN includes another important characteristic—programmability. Also, administrators can define, and then enforce, specific security controls for interfacing with the Internet of Things, given that such a system needs tight controls around access. This adaptation is important in protecting IoT devices from dynamic threats that evolve over time. The capacity to formulate and enforce differentiated security policies for specific IoT devices and diversity of applications enhances the overall security of the network.

Despite the exponentially increasing number of attached devices, the inherent large-scale growth capability of the SDN architecture ensures that the network infrastructure expansion meets the demand incrementally. And SDN allows management of such networks in a way that different policies can be applied to different devices, use cases, and working scenarios, making it especially useful in the broad category of the IoT. Also, a significant cost-effective factor is the fact of the integration of SDN with IoT networks due to operational efficiency. This has the effect of reducing the overhead costs of management in case of large scale implementation of IoT networks since control is decentralized and routine tasks are automated. This operational efficiency results in cost benefits and allows the IT resources to be channeled into more value adding activities resulting in increased productivity and creativity within the IoT environment.

The addition of SDN integration enhances the overall security in the IoT ecosystem even further. SDN features such as monitoring and controlling the network for suspicious behavior, isolating, quarantining some devices which may prove harmful, and self-healing, help to foster a strong defense against threats incurred from hostile entities. This redundant framework not only helps in malice protection but also ensures the data remains private.

1.3.1 An Example to See

In a smart security surveillance situation, the application of Software-Defined Networking and Internet of Things devices serves as a cornerstone to an effective security system. Given SDN's centralized control, the administrators can tailor the enforcement of the security policy down to each IoT device. SDN has the ability to respond to threats rapidly in which the threat level is assessed at any given time. Once any threat occurs, monitoring is able to take place and action is taken straight away to address the menace. The new devices, which are added to the system, do not automatically imply reduced security thanks to the systems attribute of scalability. Through network segmentation and isolation, it helps in containing the attacks during security breaches, thus increasing the overall system resilience and regular maintenance via SDN reduces the external threats as all the devices will be updated automatically to ensure that the devices are using the current security measures. This enhancement contributes positively in the protection of the surveillance network and the associated benefits of centralized control, dynamic threat response, scalability, isolation for resilience, and security maintenance are properly displayed in an effective security ecosystem.

An example of SD-IoT network can be seen in Fig. 4. Here, we can see how the IoT integrates with the SDN.

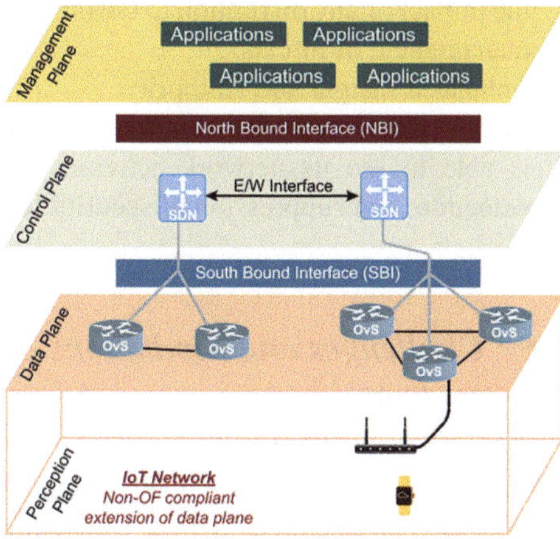

Fig. 4 SDN-IoT: A generic architecture [2]

1.4 Importance of Policy Management

The above-depicted concepts are not only applicable and important in any form of networks, but also they play a crucial role in the context of any policies laid down for the use of the Internet. Most of all, policy management contributes to overall security, risk mitigation, and normal operations in the network. This subsection describes why and how policy management is significant in the aforementioned network developments.

- Improved Security:
  Securing network resources from unauthorized access, misuse, or attack requires effective management of security policy through the design, development, and implementation of preventive measures. An organization employs such means because it expects that there would be threats in the future and seeks to enhance access protection.
- Consistency and Compliance:
  It is equally necessary to ensure that security rules are applied with regard to the entire system. Irrespective of the legal risk posed by the policies, the institution will ensure compliance with them so that policies are not conflicting and no legal provisions are breached. This eliminates legal and financial exposure.
- Enhanced Efficiency:
  Network policies can now be implemented and enforced in a more effective way as a result of the integration of automation. This reduction enhances collective productivity as it eliminates repetitive duties that would have confined IT staff to non-interactive activities and instead allows those staff to be involved in more strategic functions.
- Risk Management:
  Policy management also describes in detail the risks that security policies may create and the tools that are in place to mitigate such risks. This strategy lessens

the impact of any disruption to business caused by a security threat and facilitates management of threats.

- Enhanced Insight and Authority:
  The management of policies from one point proves beneficial in that the company is able to see its network activities clearly. This enables better monitoring, detection, and suppression of security breaches.

1.5 Challenges and Limitations of Current Policy Management Systems

Current implemented policy management systems within IoT networks are highly problematic and limited in their application, especially with regard to security, flexibility, and scalability. One such problem is the management of a variety of different devices with their own capabilities at different levels of IoT systems. Conventional policy systems tend to be even more ineffective in the way they manage the ever-changing and diverse range of devices in the IoT. This, in turn, creates problems with the enforcement of uniform security and access policies throughout the system.

With the increasing expansion of IoT networks, the necessity for real-time decision-making, as well as automated policy enforcement, grows in importance. In this context, conventional access control models, such as Role-Based Access Control (RBAC) or even more adaptable models, like Attribute-Based Access Control (ABAC), experience difficulties in scaling to support millions of devices that are interconnected. This loss of scalability is, however, a huge concern for IoT as the devices may range from high-end sensors to low-powered devices. To mitigate the scaling challenges of IoT, Gusmeroli et al. [18] study capability-based security models. Unfortunately, such models can be very resource-intensive, which is a challenge for IoT resource-constrained devices. Another challenge is the need for more dynamic and context-aware policies that can evolve in response to changing network conditions. Existing systems are largely static, making them inadequate for the highly dynamic nature of IoT networks. Recent efforts, such as decentralized and blockchain-based models like those proposed by Zhu et al. [78], aim to remove central bottlenecks and provide more flexibility in policy management. However, these systems introduce their own set of limitations, particularly in terms of computational overhead and latency.

Additionally, security remains a pervasive issue. Traditional centralized policy management systems are vulnerable to attacks, and the distributed nature of IoT networks exacerbates this problem. Security mechanisms in traditional IT networks often struggle to adapt to IoT environments, where lightweight, decentralized models are necessary. For instance, studies by Kalam et al. [25], El Bouanani et al. [14], etc., have highlighted the need for more resilient and adaptive security models.

2 Policy Considerations in SDN-IoT Networks

2.1 Understanding Policies

Stone et al. [68] offers a comprehensive definition of a policy within the context of network management. According to the definition, a policy is characterized as a collection of rules, with each rule comprising conditions and associated actions. The conditions specified in a policy rule delineate the circumstances under which the rule becomes relevant. Upon activation of a policy rule, one or more actions embedded within that rule may be executed, influencing the behavior of the network or its components. Cuppens et al. extend the understanding of policies, specifically in the realm of security, by presenting a high-level security policy model. This model is abstract in nature and deliberately devoid of any underlying network data. The abstraction at this level allows for a conceptual representation of security policies without getting entangled in the intricacies of the network's underlying structure [13]. The following can be seen as an example of a policy:

> *"Allow external access to the web server while restricting access to the database server".*

However, to operationalize these high-level security policies within a network, Meng et al. [38] emphasize the need for a transformation process. This transformation involves converting abstract, high-level security policies into their corresponding lower-level rules, which encompass the specific and detailed network information necessary for implementation. The lower-level policy rules act as the operational directives that can be executed within the network infrastructure to enforce the intended security policies.

2.2 Policy Languages and Representation

Policy languages in Software-Defined Networking are used to express and enforce network policies. These languages provide a means for administrators to define the desired behavior of the network, specify how traffic should be routed, and manage various network resources. Below we discuss some common policy languages used in the context of SDN:

- Flow-based Management Language (FML): Flow-based Management Language is the first SDN programming language. FML offers a high-level declarative policy language grounded in logic programming. An FML program comprises inference rules defining a function that assigns a set of flow constraints to each packet rewrite, providing a structured approach to packet-level policy enforcement and modification [21].
  A policy to allow flows from TCP port 88 and source host (H_s) with IP 10.0.1.1 is written as:

$$\text{allow}(Flow) \Leftarrow (\text{port} = 88) \wedge \text{Hs} = 10.0.1.1$$

- Nettle: The second programming language to measure the definition of software defined networks (SDN), belongs to the concept of Functional Reactive Programming (FRP). Nettle, therefore, deals with both discrete events, such as manipulating a network switch, and continuous over time changes. This facilitates the introduction of changing policies regarding the modification of network traffic and networks management [72].
  The following code is a simple Nettle example to flood all network packets.

```
floodPackets1 = proc evt -> do
packetInEvt <- packetIns 'precede' evt
returnA 'precede' sendRcvdPacket flood packetInEvt
```

- Frenetic: Frenetic is a domain specific language (DSL) for SDN programming. It helps to represent network policies easily by providing a high-level abstraction. Network operators can express policies in fewer words using Frenetic, and the language takes care of compiling those policies to the low-level OpenFlow commands. This level of abstraction enables one to efficiently manage and control SDN switches [15].
  In Frenetic, a policy to forward all web traffic (destination IP 192.168.1.100, port 80) to port 2 of the switch looks as follows:

```
def forward_web_traffic(switch):
match(switch, dstIP="192.168.1.100",
dstPort="80") >> forward(2)
```

  Pyretic: An advanced programming language for the Software Defined Network (SDN) is known as Pyretic. It simplifies the processes of devising and implementing network policies by using a Python-based syntax. Working with Pyretic, network managers are able to express the policies easily and the Pyretic system transforms these policies into OpenFlow rules for SDN switches [54].
  A policy that blocks traffic from specified IP addresses looks like:

```
def firewall(net):
  #Block traffic from blacklisted IP addresses
  blacklisted_ips = ["192.168.1.50", "10.0.0.20"]
  for ip in blacklisted_ips:
    net.block_traffic(ip)
```

- NetCore: NetCore is a language specifically designed for expressing network policies. It allows the definition of packet-handling rules and network behaviors in a concise and human-readable format. NetCore is often used with the Nettle runtime system for SDN [59].
  The below policy ensures connectivity between two specific nodes.

```
fact: node("h1")
```

```
fact: node("h2")
rule: path("h1", "h2") -> allow
```

- Merlin: Merlin is a language that lets you express high-level network policies like "prioritize web traffic" or "block malicious sites" in a human-readable way. It translates those policies into instructions for your network devices, automating configuration and ensuring consistent enforcement [67].
  In Merlin, a policy to ensure confidential financial data transfers happen only during off-peak network hours, and prioritize security over speed, looks like this:

```
policy secure_financial_transfers = {
predicate: packet(file_type="financial", dstIP="company_
  bank_server"),
time_window: "02:00-06:00",
action: maximize_security,
constraint: bandwidth(5Mbps) }
```

- Procera: Procera is a network control framework with a high-level language, allowing operators to express policies without extensive programming. It is designed to be reactive, responding to dynamic network changes, and supports event-based policy expressions. Procera is both expressive and extensible, enabling users to easily extend the language with new constructs [73].
  For example, a policy that allow only http traffic to IP addresses in subnet 128.36.5.0/24:

```
proc world -> do
    returnA -<
        \req -> if destIP req 'inSubnet'
         ipAddr 128 36 5 0 // 24
            then allow else deny
```

- PonderFlow: PonderFlow is designed for specifying management and security policies in distributed systems. PonderFlow introduces OpenFlow flow rule capabilities to support flow abstraction [8]. It focuses on access control, implementing authorization and obligation abstractions. Authorization policies in PonderFlow define the actions allowed or restricted for group members in target objects, particularly emphasizing the level of access users have in managing OpenFlow switches networks.
  Creating a positive authorization policy allowing all network administrators to add/remove flows and to enable/disable all switches in the network can be written in PonderFlow as:

```
inst auth + switchPolicyOps {
   subject < User > /NetworkAdmin;
   target < OFSwitch > /switches;
   action addFlow(), removeFlow(), enable(), disable();
}
```

– Kinetic: Kinetic is a network policy language leveraging finite state machines (FSMs) for concise control dynamics in response to events [29]. It uses Pyretic's runtime features and composition operators to express FSMs, where states represent distinct forwarding behaviors. Kinetic's event handler listens to events, triggering transitions in the policy, ultimately updating the Data Plane.

2.3 Role of Policies in Dynamic Network Environments

Policies are essential for setting standards, rules, and controls in a dynamic network environment so that the network can operate as efficiently, securely, and optimally as possible. These policies support dynamic network landscape adaptation by managing access, allocating resources, prioritizing data, and enforcing security measures.

Imagine a modern smart home equipped with various IoT devices such as smart thermostats, security cameras, smart door locks, and connected appliances. The goal is to create an intelligent and interconnected living space for convenience, energy efficiency, and security. However, this evolution comes with its set of challenges that necessitate careful consideration and strategic management.

2.3.1 Key Challenges in Building a Smart Home Ecosystem:

– Device Interoperability
  - Seamless Communication: The diverse variety IoT devices often comes with varying communication standards and protocols, creating challenges in achieving seamless interoperability.
  - Manufacturer Diversity: Different manufacturers may have proprietary communication methods, posing obstacles to creating a unified and interconnected ecosystem.

– Security and Privacy
  - Privacy Concerns:
    The integration of IoT devices introduces potential privacy concerns, as these devices often collect and process sensitive information about residents.
  - Security Vulnerabilities:
    The interconnected nature of smart homes raises the risk of security vulnerabilities, including unauthorized access to devices, data breaches, or malicious exploitation.

– Resource Optimization
  - Network Congestion:

With an array of devices constantly communicating over the network, resource contention and congestion can occur, impacting the responsiveness and reliability of smart home functionalities.

- Energy Efficiency:
  Balancing the diverse communication needs of IoT devices while optimizing energy usage becomes crucial to ensuring the sustainable operation of the smart home ecosystem.

To tackle the said issues, there is a need for strategic and systemic thinking. Building a smart home and embedding several IoT-connected devices that work well together while ensuring security, privacy, and efficient resource usage is only possible with succinct and effective policies. These policies serve as a basis for all the developed strategies and carefully orchestrated operations aimed at addressing such challenges as the interoperability of devices, protection of personal data, enhancement of security, and economizing on resources. Above all, policies establish a proven means of preventing the complications of integrating various devices in the smart home system which are so advanced in technology yet need to be secure, private, and efficient in terms of resources used.

2.4 Security and Privacy Concerns in Policy Management

Policy management systems in IoT networks face several security and privacy challenges due to the inherent complexity and interconnectedness of devices. As IoT expands into diverse sectors such as healthcare, smart cities, and industrial systems, ensuring secure and private policy management becomes increasingly crucial.

- Policy Enforcement and Centralized Vulnerabilities:
  One of the core issues with IoT policy management is the centralized nature of traditional enforcement mechanisms. Centralized systems can become single points of failure, making them prime attack targets. In these systems, a compromised central controller can result in widespread network vulnerability. Chen et al. [12] address this problem by proposing a decentralized policy management model for IoT environments, distributing decision-making across multiple nodes to enhance resilience against attacks. It also highlights the need for distributed policy enforcement in dynamic IoT environments, where centralization is infeasible due to the volume and heterogeneity of devices.
- Privacy-Aware Policy Models:
  IoT networks often handle sensitive data, requiring policy management systems to ensure that user privacy is preserved. Many existing models struggle to provide robust privacy guarantees. Loukil et al. [37] emphasize the importance of privacy-aware policies in IoT, proposing the integration of homomorphic encryption to protect data without compromising functionality. Another approach, discussed

by Husnoo et al. [22], leverages differential privacy techniques in policy enforcement to mitigate data leakage risks during policy rule execution.

- Context-Aware and Adaptive Security:
  The dynamic nature of IoT networks makes it difficult to apply static policies. Devices frequently join or leave the network, and network conditions can vary in real time. Alkhresheh et al. [4] propose an adaptive, context-aware policy management system that can adjust security policies based on real-time environmental data, ensuring that security rules evolve as the network changes. This enables IoT systems to maintain robust security even as they scale or change dynamically.
- Policy Interoperability and Heterogeneous Environments:
  Due to the presence of diverse devices, each with its own set of features and security needs, it is nearly impossible to apply a consistent policy in IoT networks. Most importantly, Shaik et al. [62] emphasize that policy management framework should not only exist, but also be flexible and accommodating to the different restrictions imposed by the individual devices. Resembling this, Tiburski et al. [69] see in the future the creation of simple policy protocols, allowing for implementation barriers for a policy universally characterized to all the devices in an IoT.
- Data Integrity and Policy Auditing:
  The other challenging requirement of IoT policy management is data integrity needs to be maintained when policies are imposed across distributed devices. Blockchain-based policy management systems, as identified by Xu et al. [74] hold promising solutions in the form of smart contracts enforcing access control policies in a transparent and auditable manner. Blockchain supports decentralized enforcement of security policies so that no single entity can modify policies without it being detectable.
- Lightweight and Resource-Efficient Security:
  Many IoT devices are resource-constrained, meaning traditional security mechanisms can be too computationally expensive. Policy management systems must employ lightweight protocols to enforce security without overwhelming device resources. Lahlou et al. [32], Pal S et al. [47], etc. discuss the importance of lightweight cryptography in policy management, ensuring that devices can enforce policies without compromising performance.

2.5 Scalability and Efficiency in Policy Management

The swift proliferation of connected gadgets in the internet of things networks come with different security, access, and control requirements, making the scalability and effectiveness of policy management in these networks an important concern. According to [65], the authors have presented a discussion regarding the intricate issues pertaining to the policy management on the constrained resource IoT devices. Their study stressed on the need for large-scale policy management systems that allow for the diversity of the devices, providing a flexible policy deployment system suitable for different devices' features.

Similarly, Shaik et al. [62] handled the issue of policy enforcement for large-scale IoT deployments. Their work developed an idea of making use of edge computing for offloading policy processing from the central server, thereby enhancing the overall efficiency of policy enforcement with low latency. They proved that edge devices are important for low-latency enforcement such that the number of connected devices does not affect the scaling of the management system.

Karimibiuki et al. [27] and Alkhresheh et al. [4], created dynamic policy management model that is capable of being altered in real time with changing network conditions and device states. The model ensures that policy changes take place as smoothly as possible without any additional concerns, when IoT systems grow or experience the deterioration in their network performance, allowing for management solutions that are more aggressive and easily scalable. Their findings stress the necessity of adaptive and context-aware policies in situations characterized by a lot of dynamics.

In another approach Ahmed et al. [1], developed an aggregation based approach to manage resources efficiently in a large scale IoT system by limiting the number of policies to be implemented. By grouping like policies in their approach, which greatly lessens the load on devices, they enhance the overall effectiveness of systems without compromising the security controls of the systems.

2.6 *Policy Conflict Resolution*

Policy conflicts occur when overlapping rules lead to contradictory actions or behaviors in IoT networks. Shah et al. [61] explored a comprehensive conflict detection system in their study, which used a rule-based approach to scan for contradictions in access control and resource allocation policies. This automated method significantly reduces the need for manual intervention, providing a scalable solution to policy conflicts in large-scale networks.

Building on this, Mitropoulos et al. [40], Perumal et al. [50] introduced a priority-based conflict resolution model. In their work, devices are ranked according to their criticality, ensuring that essential devices retain their policies, while lower-priority devices are adapted to resolve conflicts. This automated system ensures consistent network operation without compromising security or resource allocation.

Brew [51], a framework built on the OpenDaylight SDN controller, addresses these issues by detecting and resolving conflicts across flow rules in distributed SDN-based clouds. It extends traditional firewall conflict detection to SDN layers, introducing global rule prioritization and automated or administrator-assisted resolution techniques. Through a visualization scheme for conflict resolution, Brew ensures a consistent, conflict-free implementation of security policies and enhances network reliability without information leakage.

In response to the growing complexity of networks, Varadharajan et al. [71] proposes a policy-driven security architecture for securing end-to-end services in multi-domain SDNs. It introduces a language-based approach for designing fine-grained security policies that control information flow across SDN domains based on attributes like user parameters, devices, and contextual data. The architecture supports dynamic, path-based security enforcement, offering protection from attacks. Its ability to handle intra- and inter-domain communications, coupled with security capabilities distributed as a service layer, is a key contribution in enhancing SDN network security.

Together with the above-discussed works, [52, 60] etc. have contributed to the resolution of policy conflicts in SDN and IoT networks.

3 AI-Driven Policy Management

The inherent complexity and dynamism of Software-Defined Networking (SDN) for the Internet of Things (IoT) environments necessitate a paradigm shift in policy management. Traditional, manual approaches struggle to keep pace with the evolving landscape of threats, device capabilities, and network conditions. Artificial Intelligence (AI) and Machine Learning (ML) techniques offer a promising avenue to address these challenges, promising to transform policy management into a proactive, adaptive, and intelligent process.

The following subsections will delve deeper into the various facets of AI-driven policy management, exploring how these techniques can revolutionize how policies are created, enforced, and adapted in SDN-IoT networks.

3.1 The Role of AI and Machine Learning in Policy Management

Artificial Intelligence (AI) and Machine Learning (ML) have become instrumental in transforming policy management systems, particularly in dynamic and complex environments like IoT networks. The key roles played by AI and ML in policy management include:

- Automating Policy Enforcement: With the developments of AI and Machine Learning techniques, security and network policies may be continuously enforced automatically in real-time without human intervention, reacting to dynamic changes and irregularities in the networks. This is extremely beneficial for scenarios like large-scale networks since it may not be possible to have such a human supervised. For example, by modeling network traffic or user behavior, such systems would be capable of autonomously enforcing any policy or adapting it in an attempt to improve security.

Example: With the help of advanced artificial intelligence systems, it is possible to track the volume of network traffic and, when abnormal situations are observed, turn on certain security mechanisms aiming to avert data loss or breach in the system. Such automated measures are important for the real-time management of such systems where there are many devices and users [6, 11, 48, 75].

- Adaptive Policy Decision-Making: AI and ML provide the possibility of making policy management adaptive by using the previous data as well as based on changing network environments. Such policies can be enhanced or optimized with the help of already available data for better complexity and protection. This is very important for the IoT networks, as devices and threats are added on a very regular basis.
  Example: Studies conducted by Zahid et al. [76] and Rajput et al., [53] reveal that such systems are capable of monitoring internal traffic and other security intelligence in real time in order to modulate the security posture of the institution, indicating an adaptive security management process.
- Predictive Policies: When it comes to predictive policies, AI promotes the development of models which can foresee such unacceptable behavior by the personnel. This ability to foresee enables doing something like making some changes in the security measures in advance, for example, tightening these rules and even restricting some peoples' access before the threats become real.
  Example: Blower et al. [10] validate an approach that utilizes predictive models while designing the authorizing mechanism for edge devices within the IoT networks. To prevent and even deal with these limitations [77], models which are capable of predicting deficiencies by studying and analyzing past addressed attacks are also suggested.
- Conflict Detection and Resolution:
  Policy conflict is one of the arising issues in heterogeneous situations and those encompassing multiple administrative domains and machine learning research is being applied to address it. Especially the types of conflict detection apt algorithms leverage data to discern the presence of conflicting policies and self-resolve such conflicts.
  Example: Conflict management and Resolution in Policy Networks through reinforcement learning and active learning. Apart from most of the Policy conflicts solutions which don't address the soft -conflicts within the system, machine learning approaches including case based and standard conflict resolution are deployed [70].
- Security and Compliance Auditing:
  Policy audit and enforcement assist in regulation compliance through the use of AI-based systems. These systems are capable of monitoring and enforcing organizational policies effectively in line with best practices while also providing alerts on any detected breaches, thus enhancing the overall audit function.
- Explainability and Transparency:
  One of the main problems posed in policy management systems relying on AI is the ability to justify the reasons for a change. The concept of Explainable AI

(XAI) has begun to be applied in the design of policy and enforcement systems, in order to provide audit capabilities for the outputs of systems that make use of artificial intelligence [58].

3.2 Automating Policy Creation

Manual, traditional policy creation and implementation in the SDN-IoT environment involves following tedious and error-prone processes. It requires significant expertise from the network administrators since there are many devices and applications demanding comprehensive configuration and management of policies. The further development and complexity in scale of these networks make this manual process unviable, resulting in imperfection, security gaps, and delayed responses to changes in the network conditions. Toward this end, the field is now looking toward the transformative potential of AI-powered automation, hoping that a good portion of the process of creating policies can be smoothed while still being able to create correct and efficient policies that are also adaptive and personalized toward the dynamic nature of SDN-IoT ecosystems. Figure 5 is a flowchart for automating policy creation.

3.2.1 The Need for Automation

The sheer number and diversity of IoT devices, coupled with the dynamic nature of network traffic and security threats, make manual policy creation an unsustainable approach. Network administrators are often overwhelmed by configuring and managing policies for each device and application, leading to potential gaps in security and network performance. Automation, driven by AI and ML, offers a way

Fig. 5 Automating policy creation

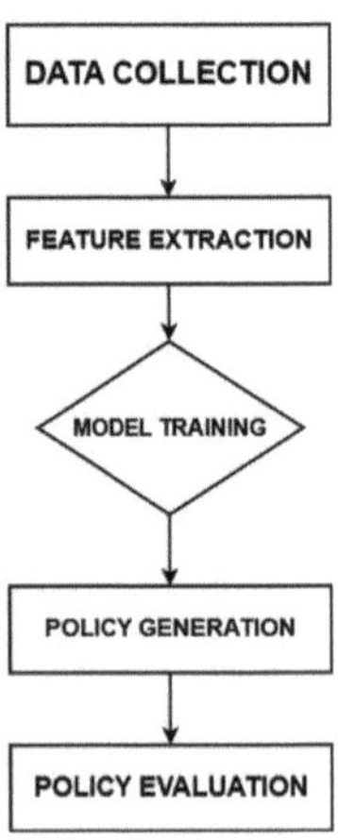

to address these challenges by streamlining the policy creation process and enabling the generation of policies that can adapt to changing conditions in real-time.

3.2.2 Data-Driven Policy Generation

The process of creating policies in an automated manner largely depends on the efficiency of machine learning algorithms in data mining network behavior. This means, detecting and measuring important attributes and trends that can be utilized in predicting network behavior in the near future as well as security threats [49].

This data-driven approach involves several key steps:

- Data Collection:
  Investigating and gathering necessary information from interested parties, for example; network traffic logs, device telemetry, behavior of users, alarms, and so on.
- Feature Extraction:
  Analyzing the focused data and recognizing the particular aspects that will help train the ML models. It can also include some processes such as feature selection and dimensionality reduction, which help in easing the complexity of the data and enhancing the model's accuracy.
- Model Training:
  The resulting features are used to train ML models such as decision trees, random forests, neural networks, or reinforcement learning models.
- Policy Generation:
  Applying the trained models to new, unseen data to generate policies that optimize network performance, security, and resource utilization. This may involve translating model predictions into specific policy rules or configurations that the SDN controller can enforce.
- Policy Evaluation:
  Implementation of feedback and new information to assess the success of the created policies and adjustments to the models.

3.2.3 Reactive and Proactive Policy Generation

The ability to create policies with the help of AI can be understood in two main ways:

1. Reactive Policy Generation Method:
   In this type of method, policies are developed if a predetermined event or trigger occurs. For example, if there is a sudden increase in network traffic from a specific IoT device, it may require the development of a policy which restricts the bandwidth of the device or even bars it from the network entirely. Furthermore, Machine Learning models can also be used for training purposes where the model

learns a pattern of some specific trigger values such as a security breach or a congestion in the network, and an appropriate policy is generated [20].

2. Proactive Policy Generation:
Here, issues are foreseen and policy guidelines developed ahead of time in order to avoid threats. This is made possible with the aid of predictive analytics as well as machine learning, which involves Artificial Intelligence creating an AI model that is able to predict rates of growth on a network and rate of security threats. For example, in a situation where an artificial intelligent model determines that a specific network link will likely be congested during rush hour, it will need to automatically create a policy that will 'rearrange' how that link operates or provide supplementary reinforcement to that particular link [39].

3.3 Automated Policy Enforcement Mechanisms

Few authors have done generous work enforcing network security policies in SDN-enabled IoT networks. Sahay, Ayyoob, Kallol, etc., have shown the different ways of deploying these policies through their work. This section briefly reviews their work.

In [57], the authors introduce a framework to safeguard a ship's communication infrastructure from cyberattacks through SDN. Their goal is to dynamically and automatically mitigate attack traffic within the ship's communication network. They have developed a user-friendly Controlled Natural Language (CNL) for creating security policies, allowing ship crew members with little or no SDN or networking knowledge to participate. The framework connects two crucial components of the ship's infrastructure, the Integrated Bridge Controller (IBC) and the Autonomous Engine Monitoring Controller (AEMC), using SDN-enabled switches to enhance security and functionality. The framework also offers a translation mechanism to convert high-level policies into low-level OpenFlow rules, employs multi-path routing to bolster resilience against cyber threats like DDoS attacks, and allows different controllers to collaborate efficiently. However, some limitations include the simplicity of the implementation topology, potential latency concerns in more extensive networks, and the need to address policy conflicts arising from multiple controllers.

The authors [71] introduced PbSA, a policy-based security framework aiming to secure the end services across multiple domains in an SDN environment. The authors outline a policy language to specify network and security rules crucial for safeguarding SDN services and communications. The framework takes into account a variety of factors related to people, devices, and context information, including location, routing details, services used, and security attributes related to switches and controllers in multiple domains, when defining policies. This framework's ability to describe path- and flow-based security controls, crucial for safeguarding end-to-end services in SDN, is a key component. They implemented an access policy rule that checks the validity of MAC addresses and the original IP addresses of end devices, such as switches, before they are used. When address spoofing is found, this rule is intended to throw packets away. The main emphasis of their work revolved around addressing man-in-the-middle and spoofing attacks. With many components involved, this framework is complex and time-consuming.

Hamza et al. [19] attempts to translate Manufacturer Usage Description (MUD) policies into flow rules that can be enforced using SDN. The proposed system reactively inserts the converted flow rules based on DNS run-time bindings and proactive programming into network switches. The approach's effectiveness was assessed regarding switch flow-table size and the percentage of exception traffic requiring software inspection using traces of 28 consumer IoT devices collected over many months. ARP spoofing, port scanning, TCP/UDP/ICMP flooding, and TCP/SSDP/SNMP reflection are examples of volumetric attacks that the system can detect by sending only a small fraction of exception packets to commercially available IDS. The authors also tried to identify the limitations of flow rules derived from MUD in protecting IoT devices from internal and external network attacks.

Molina Zarca et al. [41] presents a policy-driven, comprehensive cyber-security management architecture that strengthens IoT security through the use of SDN and NFV. The framework may orchestrate security in the IoT dynamically by detecting cyber-security problems and responding appropriately by dynamically enforcing security regulations.

The papers studied can be summarised and seen visually in Table 1.

3.4 Adaptive Policy Management Using Machine Learning

As the Internet of Things continues to grow, managing access and security policies becomes increasingly complex. Traditional methods often struggle to keep pace with the dynamic nature of IoT environments. Adaptive policy management using machine learning offers a solution by allowing systems to automatically adjust policies based on real-time data and contextual changes. This section explores various approaches that harness machine learning, including reinforcement learning, to enhance policy generation, conflict resolution, and overall security in IoT applications.

The desire for better access control mechanisms is escalating as computing environment systems become more complex. Access based on attributes and authorization policies, thus, gave rise to Attribute-Based Access Control (ABAC) systems which present an effective in the resolution of the issue. At the same time, the very flexibility that characterizes most ABAC systems presents difficulties in their enforcement and management especially for federated systems. To that end, Karimi et al. [26] introduce a model which is an instance of an adaptive policy learning approach to ABAC systems whereby the problem is casted in the form of reinforcement learning, thus reducing the manual intervention and effort in the management of authorization control.

With the exponential growth of IoT systems and devices, the problem of adaptive access control policy issues has emerged as a necessity. Unchecked hacked IoT

Table 1 Summarization of the papers studied

		Technology used	Automated	
Paper	Contribution	SDN	NFV	
[63]	Security monitoring framework for cloud environments	Y		Y
[73]	Language for high-level network security policies	Y		Y
[64]	Security framework for OpenFlow security services	Y		Y
[33]	Policy management framework	Y		Y
[6]	Policy management framework	Y		Y
[36]	QoS-based policy automation	Y	Y	Y
[57]	Framework for communication infrastructure in ships Policy Language	Y		Y
[17]	Computer network defense policy deployment framework	Y		Y
[71]	Policy-based security architecture for IoT	Y		Y
[56]	Policy management system Policy Language	Y		Y
[9]	Mechanism to integrate network appliances to SDN	Y		Y
[35]	SDN policy-based architecture	Y	Y	Y
[19]	Framework for MUD policy management	Y		Y
[41]	Security Management Architecture for IoT	Y	Y	Y

devices can cause a lot of problems in particular environments. Answering these challenges, has been formulated new adaptive access control framework which improves in the structure of access policies within the system according to the access behavior between devices. Specific supervised machine learning algorithms will be used in this framework to build models of access behaviors and using a door lock system as an example of the target application of the developed approach shows that the system can achieve a better level of security at the same time being more flexible [3].

The rapid growth of IoT has introduced significant cybersecurity challenges, particularly at the network edge where devices operate under dynamic conditions. Traditional static security policies are often inadequate for the heterogeneous and resource-constrained nature of IoT ecosystems. To address these challenges, Murad et al. [43] proposed a novel adaptive edge security framework to dynamically generate and adjust security policies for IoT edge devices. By integrating conflict detection and resolution mechanisms alongside AI-driven adaptability, this framework produces tailored security measures that respond effectively to changing threat landscapes and compliance requirements.

Together, these studies underscore the importance of adaptive frameworks in managing security and resource allocation within complex IoT environments. By leveraging machine learning, reinforcement learning, and innovative policy frameworks, these approaches address the dynamic nature of IoT networks [44]. As security challenges evolve, the integration of adaptive mechanisms becomes crucial for ensuring the integrity and availability of IoT services while minimizing risks and optimizing performance across diverse applications.

3.5 Challenges and Considerations for AI Integration

Despite the numerous advantages, integrating AI into policy management systems presents several challenges. They are listed below.

- Explainability of AI-Driven Decisions:
  AI-driven policy management systems often face difficulties in providing clear, explainable decisions. Network administrators may struggle to interpret the outcomes from AI models, leading to trust issues. Jagatheesaperumal Xu et al. [23] emphasize the importance of developing Explainable AI (XAI) models to provide transparency and ensure that AI decisions can be audited by human operators. This aids in enhancing the trust and reliability of AI in policy management.
- Computational Costs in IoT Environments:
  AI models generally require significant computational resources, which can be challenging for resource-constrained IoT devices. Jan et al. [24] address this issue by proposing lightweight AI algorithms. These models can be efficiently deployed on edge devices, helping to reduce computational overhead while still ensuring robust policy enforcement in IoT networks.
- Scalability and Data Volume:
  The high volume of data generated by IoT devices presents a challenge for AI-based policy management systems. Real-time processing and decision-making need scalable AI solutions to handle large-scale IoT networks without performance degradation.
- Interoperability Across Heterogeneous Devices: Integrating AI models across diverse IoT devices with varying computational capabilities can be complex. AI systems need to ensure seamless operation across devices with different protocols and architectures.
- Ethical Considerations and Bias:
  AI models are susceptible to bias, which can impact policy enforcement decisions, especially in security contexts. Addressing these biases and ensuring fairness in AI-driven policy management systems is critical for their widespread adoption.
- Security Risks with AI:
  AI models themselves can become targets for adversarial attacks, where malicious actors manipulate AI systems to enforce incorrect policies. Ensuring the security of AI systems and their integration into IoT policy management is an ongoing research challenge.

4 Policy Frameworks and Approaches

Policy frameworks in the context of SDN-IoT networks are essential for ensuring that the communication between devices and controllers adheres to a set of defined rules, which guarantee both performance and security. As IoT deployments grow in complexity, managing policies that dictate network behavior becomes increasingly challenging. SDN offers a solution by allowing for the centralization of policy control, but this introduces new considerations in policy enforcement, verification, and validation. This section examines key policy enforcement aspects, design, verification, and analysis, providing a clear overview of challenges and potential solutions.

4.1 Policy Enforcement in SDN-IoT Networks

The term policy enforcement takes the practical meaning of the actions taken by the network in order to ensure that the devices follow the set operational principles. In an SDN-IoT network, this means ensuring the proper functioning of the IoT devices, the data streams, and their network elements within the functional and security policies in place.

The SDN controllers allow for the centralized application of policies which lessens the variations that are usually seen in a dispensed IoT system. Policies could include access control, traffic shaping, quality-of-service (Qos) constraints, among others. For example, it could be a policy from the controller that only permits selected IoT devices to communicate at specific times of the day or in the case of a smart hospital, precedence is given to traffic from networked medical devices over regular internet traffic.

Key Components of Policy Enforcement:

- SDN-Centralized Control:
  SDN provides a centralized mechanism for the enforcement of policies in IoT networks. This responsibility of the SDN controller is crucial as it translates the high-level policies of the users into detailed flow rules which are transmitted to the IoT and the core networks. Such concentration of control mitigates the issues of policy enforcement harmonization normally experienced with its traditional and federation-based setups.

  In smart homes, for example, the policies relating to communication among the IoT devices such as when a device is allowed to send data or the devices one is allowed to communicate with are controlled from an SDN controller. This makes it less cumbersome to handle the configurations of each device since the SDN controller shields the devices from the users and manages their communication as a whole.

- Dynamic Policy Enforcement:
  In an IoT network, the scope of enforcement of policies is quite dynamic in all aspects. There may be changes in the number of devices on the network, and in the patterns of behaviour of the users on how the devices use the network. Dynamic policy enforcement implies that the policies will be flexible and accept the reality of changing circumstances within the network.
  For example, during a congestion period on a particular network, the controller device can be configured to implement QoS policies in the case where the health-care applications are classified as primary and the entertainment applications are secondary [7].
- Scalability and Complexity:
  The issue of the scale is by far and large, one of the major concerns in the policy enforcement in SDN-IoT networks. The Internet of Things is composed of many applications whose deployment could be on a home, which has very few devices connected to the internet, or on a huge factory, city or country with thousands or even millions of connected devices. It means that the SDN controller will have to also manage the policies within these divergent systems [58].
- Security and Access Control:
  Security is a primary concern in IoT environments, where unauthorized access to devices can lead to privacy breaches, data theft, or even physical harm. SDN can enforce security policies by controlling which devices can communicate with each other and by applying access control lists (ACLs) to prevent unauthorized access to sensitive resources. For instance, an SDN controller in an industrial IoT setting can enforce strict access control policies that ensure only authorized devices or users can interact with machinery or sensitive data [42].

4.2 Policy Framework Design

To achieve scalable, secure, and flexible management of SDN-IoT networks, the formulation of a comprehensive policy framework is a necessity. Many researchers have attempted to review various aspects of policy framework formulation and have examined both the problems and prospects in that area.

One key aspect is how flexible the structure will lend itself to be built. A modular policy framework has the advantage of being scalable since it permits the kinetic of policies being injected into the system while it is running. Their research suggests a layered architecture that uses edge computing to transfer some of the responsibilities involved in policy execution to local agents, which is very useful for IoT systems with a large number of devices. This is in line with the modular approach in our design which also focuses on how policies are spread in heterogeneous networks with respect to IoT.

When it comes to the aspect of dynamic policy adaptation, Krishnan et al. [31] present a multi-level policy framework that allows the capture of policies that can easily be transformed into action enabling a practical configuration of the network in use. This simplifies the policy used in the management of the network in the modern IoT where there are many joining and leaving of devices in the presence of a network. Also, our PDMS tends to have a dynamic policy translation layer that puts out flow rules to SDN devices within no time as laid out in the abstract policies.

Security is one of the foremost concerns in the policy-making aspect. As noted by Sahay et al. [57], when designing the systems, it is imperative to employ several layers of security, especially with respect to the enforcement of the relevant encryption, authentication, and access control policies throughout the entire network. Our framework is also designed the same way by adopting security measures at the centralized policy management level which is the SDN controller, thus the security policies applied here cover all the IoT appliance's devices.

Another important aspect in the design is real-time adaptability. An implementation of a policy framework that incorporates artificial intelligence design in policy formulation to improve given network state policies. The dynamic nature of policies allows the framework to be able to react to any changes in traffic or any security threats. While our framework does not integrate AI, it makes use of feedback loops so as to monitor the network performance and also spot any irregularities before changes are made to the policies, giving it a more real time approach.

Karmakar et al. [28] propose a policy-centric security model for SDN-enabled IoT networks, which underlines the implementation of security policies to control communication between SDN regions. Such approach is of great importance from the perspective of achieving a seamless security coverage in IoT systems.

Key Components of the Framework:

- Policy definition layer:
  High-level policies are derived from the administrator's intent and transformed into implementable prohibitions that are clear and in line with the network objectives.
- Policy translation layer:
  Helps large-scale networks implement modularity and flexibility by turning high-level policies into low-level specific actions.
- Policy enforcement layer:
  Achieves the comprehensive implementation of protective measures through multi-tier applicability of the determined policies.
- Monitoring and feedback layer:
  Stabilizes and keeps the policies in use current and efficient, by using dynamic loops to alter them to suit the changing environments of the network.

4.3 Ethical and Privacy Considerations in Policy Management

As AI-powered policy management systems continue to advance, concerns around ethics and privacy have become crucial. These challenges go beyond technical complexities, touching on broader societal values. A balance must be found between functionality and maintaining user trust.

- Data Protection and User Confidence:
  The Internet of Things pours vast amounts of sensitive information, especially on people's health and their normal or abnormal behavior. Policy frameworks are required for such systems so that they consider the data without risking its safety and its effectiveness. Data protection issues can be exacerbated by the fact that systems using AI often involve an organization collecting large amounts of data about identifiable individuals.
  Take the example of a smart house in which an AI system detects unusual movements, thus allowing the system to heighten the security levels. This improves security but creates concerns over privacy as it means watching everyone's movements, which people may perceive as interference. To this effect, concepts such as federated learning and edge computing are employed and enable local computations on the data so that there is less or no information sent outside devices through the usual servers. In spite of that, the consistence on putting these privacy strategies into practice can be quite difficult.
- Bias and Fairness:
  Policies implemented by using Artificial Intelligence systems can be unfair due to bias embedded in the data. For instance, security systems can be more biased towards certain groups because the training data contains more samples of those groups. Some people may be targeted, while others who may need to be included, may not be included. This creates discrimination and raises probability of ethical implications concerning justice.
  For instance, in network security, Artificial Intelligence may flag some areas or activities as more at risk of attacks based on previous patterns of attacks. Attacking these groups will, however, lead to innocent users being treated differently simply because they fit the description of particular methods of operation. Such bias is mitigated with good practice such as testing and retraining of AIs in use to bring about fairness in implementation of the policies.
- Transparency and Explainability:
  One of the predominant ethical challenges presented by AI faced in the management of policies is the 'black box' aspects of most AI systems. Very often, it is not obvious to the administrator or even a user how the AI has arrived at this or the other decision thus contributing to lack of transparency and accountability.
  Solving that problem, XAI models, or Explainable AI models, are being put together. Such models have the intention of making AI decisions much easier for people to understand them. Thanks to the explanations for the reason why certain policies were enforced, XAI fosters confidence and allows administrators to check and review the decisions made by the system to make sure that the whole process is just and accountable.
- Consent and Autonomy:
  In line with the increasing penetration of IoT, there are challenges associated with seeking clarified consent from users to capture as well as use their data.

Most users may not appreciate how their data is utilized and the bearing of those activities on policy formulation on their freedoms. For example, an intelligent system may adjust security policies without any user intervention, thus altering controls that the users neither authorized nor were aware of.
The necessity of having a straightforward and user friendly consent structure is particularly imperative if there are policies on policy management. This means that users should have power over their own information and how it is likely to be used. This can be achieved by ensuring that there are easy to use interfaces which depict usage of data and policies fairly and in a respectful manner to the users even when driven by AI technologies.

5 Case Studies and Applications

5.1 Industry Use Cases of Policy Management in SDN-IoT Networks

5.1.1 System Overview

The proposed policy mapping framework operates as an application on any SDN controller, as illustrated in Fig. 6. This application is implemented using the

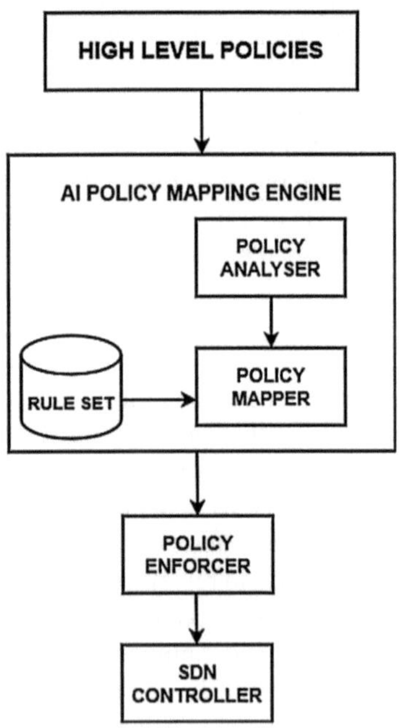

Fig. 6 Policy to rule framework

NorthBound Application Programming Interfaces (APIs) of the controller. The key components of our framework include the policy engine, policy enforcer, and AI integration.

Initially, the framework analyzes high-level policies through the policy analyzer module within the policy engine. This module leverages AI to enhance its understanding of the policy's context and objectives, identifying specific requirements. Once the analysis is complete, the policy is sent to the policy mapper.

The policy mapper, empowered by AI algorithms, assesses the requirements alongside the rule set to determine the most suitable methods and techniques for implementation. By learning from past policy implementations, the AI optimizes the mapping process, ensuring more efficient policy enforcement. After identifying the appropriate rule, the policy mapper passes it to the policy enforcer, which implements the rules on the SDN controller.

In our framework, we view policy and rules as distinct sets. Each policy represents a unique set of security objectives and requirements—for instance, policies related to data protection or access control. Conversely, each rule specifies a set of conditions that, when satisfied, trigger specific actions within the network. The mapping of policies to rules establishes a clear relationship between these two sets, ensuring that the rules are aligned with the objectives outlined in the policies. Thus, the mapping between policy and rules serves as a bridge that connects high-level intentions with low-level implementations.

Policy Engine

This module consists of the policy analyzer, rule set, and policy mapper. The policy analyzer, enhanced with AI capabilities, interprets high-level policies, comprehending their intent and identifying the specific requirements needed for implementation. This information is then forwarded to the policy mapper module. The policy mapper utilizes AI-driven insights to efficiently map these requirements to the corresponding rule set.

Rule Set

In our proposed framework, we define a rule set as a collection of various methods and techniques, each paired with the corresponding rules necessary for policy enforcement. The methods and techniques serve as defense mechanisms linked to the requirements specified in the policy. Depending on the policy's needs, one or more methods can be selected from the rule set. Each method is associated with specific flow rules, ensuring that when a user selects a method from the set, the corresponding rule is also activated. This connection facilitates the implementation of methods within the network to enforce the desired policy effectively.

Table 2 presents a sample rule set we've created, outlining the methods, their associated match fields, and the required actions for rule implementation.

While we acknowledge that the current rule set of methods and techniques is not exhaustive, it is sufficiently robust to support a variety of network policies across different environments and demonstrates the capabilities of our proposed framework.

Table 2 Rule set

Methods/Techniques	Match field	Action
VLAN segmentation	VLAN ID	Drop
Subnetting	IP address	Drop
Web filtering	IP protocol	
	TCP destination port	
	IPv4 destination address: blocked website IP	Drop
IP-MAC binding	IP address	Forward
	MAC address	
Time-based segmentation	IPv4 destination address	Drop
Application firewall	TCP destination port	Forward

5.2 *Policy Management in Smart Cities*

In a smart city, a network of IoT devices continuously interacts to monitor and control various urban aspects, such as traffic management, parking availability, and energy consumption. To maintain secure, efficient, and optimized operations, the city must implement policies governing access to the network, protecting against security threats, and enhancing overall performance. By leveraging SDN, high-level policies can be effectively translated into low-level rules for the IoT network. Below are illustrative examples of how specific IoT devices facilitate the implementation of these policies within a smart city context.

Scenario 1: Controlling Access to Restricted Areas for Authorized Personnel Only
In this scenario, the city aims to restrict access to certain areas, such as government buildings or secure zones, allowing only authorized personnel entry.

A smart access control panel detects when a personnel badge is presented. When a smart lock, as shown in Fig. 7, receives a signal from the access control panel, it verifies the credentials of the person attempting to enter. The smart lock communicates with the AI-enhanced policy analyzer module within the SDN framework. The analyzer assesses the current access policy, utilizing historical data to optimize the decision-making process. If unauthorized access attempts are detected, the analyzer may suggest adjustments to the policy to tighten restrictions. The verified credentials are sent to the AI-powered policy mapper, which evaluates the policy requirements against the existing rule set. The mapper dynamically selects the most effective methods for enforcing this policy, such as applying VLAN segmentation or implementing IP-MAC binding. The determined rules are forwarded to the policy enforcer, which configures the SDN controller to implement the new access rules. This action updates the network devices, ensuring that only authorized personnel can enter restricted areas.

Table 3 shows the policy, methods/techniques, and corresponding rules for Scenario 1:

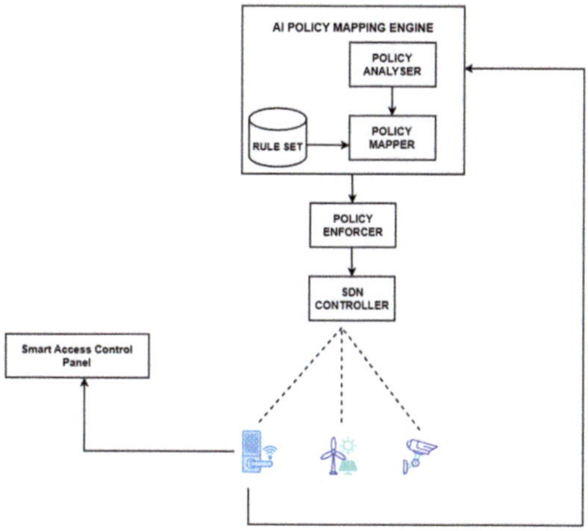

Fig. 7 Scenario 1

Table 3 Scenario 1

Policy	Methods/Techniques	Match field	Action
Restricts access to certain areas of the city to authorized personnel only	VLAN Segmentation	VLAN ID	Drop/Allow
	IP-MAC binding	IP address	
		MAC address	Allow

In this scenario, the interaction between the smart access control panel and the smart lock ensures that only authorized personnel gain entry, enhancing security and maintaining operational efficiency.

Scenario 2: Blocking External Traffic to the City's Internal IoT Network
In this scenario, the city aims to block all traffic from the internet to its internal IoT network to protect sensitive data and prevent potential cyber attacks.

A network firewall continuously monitors incoming traffic from external sources. When a router detects a connection attempt from the internet, it assesses the request against pre-defined security policies. The router communicates with the AI-enhanced policy analyzer. The analyzer evaluates historical threat data and current network load, helping determine the most efficient approach for blocking unwanted traffic while ensuring legitimate internal communications remain unaffected. The data from the AI analyzer is then sent to the AI-powered policy mapper, which selects the best methods for implementing the blocking policy. Techniques such as Network Traffic Filtering (NTF) and VLAN Segmentation are chosen to effectively isolate the internal IoT network from external threats. The policy rules are transmitted to the policy enforcer, which implements the necessary configurations on the SDN controller. This setup ensures that any unauthorized external traffic is blocked, allowing only legitimate internal communications to pass.

Table 4 Scenario 2

Policy	Methods/Techniques	Match field	Action
Block all traffic from the internet to the city's internal IoT network	VLAN segmentation	VLAN ID	Drop/Allow
	NTF	IP address	Drop

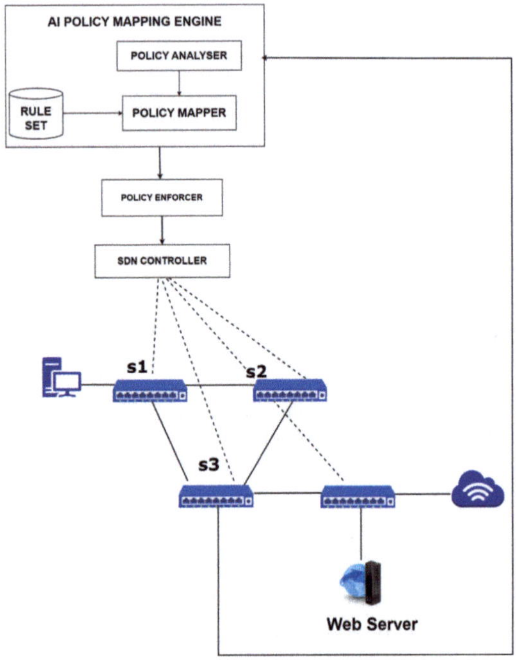

Fig. 8 Scenario 2

Table 4 shows the policy, methods/techniques, and corresponding rules for Scenario 2:

In this scenario, the collaboration between the network firewall and the router ensures that external traffic is effectively blocked, protecting the city's internal IoT network from potential threats. Figure 8 shows this scenario.

Through these interactions, the AI-powered framework enables the smart city to maintain secure and efficient operations while allowing for dynamic adjustments to its policies based on real-time communications among IoT devices. This adaptability is crucial for addressing the evolving needs of the urban environment.

6 Open Challenges and Future Directions

In the rapidly evolving landscape of network technologies, numerous challenges arise as systems become more integrated, complex, and interdependent. This section explores the key open challenges in networking and policy management, focusing on the integration of AI and machine learning, achieving interoperability across heterogeneous networks, and outlining future research directions in policy management.

6.1 Integration with AI and Machine Learning

Artificial intelligence (AI) and machine learning (ML) are transforming how we manage and secure networks. However, significant challenges exist regarding the seamless integration of AI/ML into existing network infrastructures. Current AI techniques often operate in silos, and they struggle with generalization, particularly when faced with novel, previously unseen network behaviors or security threats.

Key Challenges:

- Scalability: As networks grow in size and complexity, AI algorithms must scale accordingly. Traditional AI models often suffer from performance degradation when applied to large-scale networks.
- Real-Time Processing: AI and ML models need to process massive volumes of data in real-time to make network decisions swiftly. Latency and computational requirements can be a bottleneck in time-critical applications such as autonomous network management or real-time security threat detection.
- Generalization: Many AI models are trained on specific datasets, which makes it difficult for them to adapt to dynamic network environments. Research is ongoing to develop models that can generalize across various network conditions and attack types.

Incorporating advanced reinforcement learning (RL) and neurosymbolic AI approaches (combining deep learning with symbolic reasoning) could mitigate some of these challenges. Research efforts like neural-symbolic systems and explainable AI (XAI) offer promising future directions, enabling AI-driven network management systems to be more adaptable and transparent.

6.2 Interoperability Across Heterogeneous Networks

The interconnectedness of the modern world demands a high degree of reliability in all types of communications interconnections that have ever been before. In addition, the emergence of IOT, 5G, and software-defined networking (SDN) systems made the preservation of interoperability even more difficult. One of the most appropriate examples is the communication protocol diversity. Different, and often incompatible, communication protocols (ranging from those used ages ago, such as TCP/IP, to more recent ones like QUIC) create deployment and operation challenges for the everyday management of computer networks. For example, in most instances, older networks are unable to integrate effectively with the modern SDN or IoT based systems, thus compelling the network service providers to implement several gateways for bridging translation.

Security also poses a significant impediment. Conformity and alleviation of threats across numerous networks with varying levels of security are rather impractical, particularly if those networks are required to inter-operate. Consistent security policy application in such an environment is a hot area of concern. On the other hand, new concepts such as Network Function Virtualization (NFV) or SDN are intended to overcome these issues by removing the need for specific network functions and facilitating their management in one location. Wireless Network Function Virtualisation is designed to support a faster and adaptable network with many varied network structures. The approach to networking with increased software solutions is the future for interoperability, where networks will not be static and fixed but will change to improve performance as necessary.

6.3 Future Research Directions in Policy Management

Networking policies have become a key focus of research and development today. The evolution of networking policies is bolstered by the influence of various factors such as automation, intent-based networking, and artificial intelligence, among others. It is worth noting that there are still many areas that require research, particularly in the implementation and management of proper policies in the present day that are both centralized and distributed systems. Some of the Key challenges are:

- The adaptation of policies in real time and systems design compensate changes in real time: Real-time adaptation to changes in policy, threats, users and network requirements is impossible using current policy management frameworks. Accordingly, future work should emphasize the integration of AI and policy management in developing advanced techniques for real time policy management.
- Intent-Based Networking (IBN): It is believed that IBN will change the landscape of network management where it will be possible for nil levels of technical intents to command the network operations. However, there is still more which needs to be known on how these intents are converted to actual policies in specific network environments.
- Privacy-Aware Policy Management: Due to increasing data privacy legislation, networks must guarantee that a given policy organization can offer protection at all levels of policy implementation including data transmission, processing, and storage. Research into privacy-centric solutions such as homomorphic encryption or differential privacy will be critical in this avenue.

Consideration of these research challenges cannot be done without an interdisciplinary integration of AI, policy automation and cybersecurity domains. Activities such as intent-based security policy enforcement give an indication of the future when network policies will be created and implemented in intelligent systems.

7 Conclusion

This chapter ends by emphasizing the complexity of policy management in such SDN-IoT networks and the crucial role played by machine learning and artificial intelligence in overcoming those challenges. Indeed, AI-driven solutions provide scalability, flexibility, and security due to their ability to make use of adaptive frameworks and real-time enforcement mechanisms in cases of dynamic and resource-constrained environments. This shall integrate these technologies together with SDN-IoT, making it more intelligent with more automated decision-making capabilities, changing its policies based on current real-time data, which might give better control over network traffic and access. Such frameworks adopted in SDN-IoT networks can scale up more effectively with connectivity demands while minimizing the risks involved in security through ensuring safe enforcement of policy with consistency and responsiveness. This chapter will be a resource to advance research and industry at the cutting edge of network policy management, revealing the possibilities and challenges in bringing more intelligent and adaptable systems for IoT and SDN integration.

References

1. Ahmed, A., Abdullah, S., Bukhsh, M., Ahmad, I., Mushtaq, Z.: An energy-efficient data aggregation mechanism for IoT secured by blockchain. IEEE Access **10**, 11404–11419 (2022)
2. Alam, I., Sharif, K., Li, F., Latif, Z., Karim, M.M., Biswas, S., Nour, B., Wang, Y.: A survey of network virtualization techniques for internet of things using SDN and NFV. ACM Comput. Surv. (CSUR) **53**(2), 1–40 (2020)
3. Alkhresheh, A., Elgazzar, K., Hassanein, H.S.: Adaptive access control policies for IoT deployments. In: 2020 International Wireless Communications and Mobile Computing (IWCMC), pp. 377–383. IEEE (2020)
4. Alkhresheh, A., Elgazzar, K., Hassanein, H.S.: Daciot: Dynamic access control framework for IoT deployments. IEEE Internet Things J. **7**(12), 11401–11419 (2020)
5. Ashton, K., et al.: That 'internet of things' thing. RFID J. **22**(7), 97–114 (2009)
6. Bari, M.F., Chowdhury, S.R., Ahmed, R., Boutaba, R.: Policycop: An autonomic qos policy enforcement framework for software defined networks. In: 2013 IEEE SDN for Future Networks and Services (SDN4FNS), pp. 1–7. IEEE (2013)
7. Barrera, D., Molloy, I., Huang, H.: Standardizing IoT network security policy enforcement. In: Workshop on Decentralized IoT Security and Standards (DISS), vol. 2018, p. 6 (2018)
8. Batista, B.L.A., Fernandez, M.P.: Ponderflow: A policy specification language for openflow networks. In: Proc. ICN, vol. 215 (2014)
9. Ben-Itzhak, Y., Barabash, K., Cohen, R., Levin, A., Raichstein, E.: EnforSDN: Network policies enforcement with SDN. In: 2015 IFIP/IEEE International Symposium on Integrated Network Management (IM), pp. 80–88. IEEE (2015)

10. Blower, A., Kotonya, G.: A predictive authorization approach for IoT environments. In: Proceedings of the 11th International Conference on the Internet of Things, pp. 80–87 (2021)
11. Cabuk, S., Dalton, C.I., Eriksson, K., Kuhlmann, D., Ramasamy, H.V., Ramunno, G., Sadeghi, A.R., Schunter, M., Stüble, C.: Towards automated security policy enforcement in multi-tenant virtual data centers. J. Comput. Secur. **18**(1), 89–121 (2010)
12. Chen, E., Zhu, Y., Zhou, Z., Lee, S.Y., Wong, W.E., Chu, W.C.C.: Policychain: A decentralized authorization service with script-driven policy on blockchain for internet of things. IEEE Internet Things J. **9**(7), 5391–5409 (2021)
13. Cuppens, F., Cuppens-Boulahia, N., Sans, T., Miège, A.: A formal approach to specify and deploy a network security policy. In: IFIP World Computer Congress, TC 1, pp. 203–218. Springer (2004)
14. El Bouanani, S., El Kiram, M.A., Achbarou, O., Outchakoucht, A.: Pervasive-based access control model for IoT environments. IEEE Access **7**, 54575–54585 (2019)
15. Foster, N., Harrison, R., Freedman, M.J., Monsanto, C., Rexford, J., Story, A., Walker, D.: Frenetic: A network programming language. ACM Sigplan Not. **46**(9), 279–291 (2011)
16. Foundation, O.N.: OpenFlow Switch Specification Version 1.5.1 (Protocol version 0x06). Open Networking Foundation (2015). https://opennetworking.org/wp-content/uploads/2014/10/openflow-switch-v1.5.1.pdf
17. Gao, J., Xia, C., Wang, S., Zhang, H.: A SDN-based deployment framework for computer network defense policy. In: 2015 4th International Conference on Computer Science and Network Technology (ICCSNT), vol. 1, pp. 1253–1258. IEEE (2015)
18. Gusmeroli, S., Piccione, S., Rotondi, D.: A capability-based security approach to manage access control in the internet of things. Math. Comput. Model. **58**(5–6), 1189–1205 (2013)
19. Hamza, A., Gharakheili, H.H., Sivaraman, V.: Combining mud policies with SDN for IoT intrusion detection. In: Proceedings of the 2018 Workshop on IoT Security and Privacy, pp. 1–7. IoT S&P '18, Association for Computing Machinery, New York, NY, USA (2018). https://doi.org/10.1145/3229565.3229571, https://doi.org/10.1145/3229565.3229571
20. Heinl, C.H.: Artificial (intelligent) agents and active cyber defence: Policy implications. In: 2014 6th International Conference on Cyber Conflict (CyCon 2014), pp. 53–66. IEEE (2014)
21. Hinrichs, T.L., Gude, N.S., Casado, M., Mitchell, J.C., Shenker, S.: Practical declarative network management. In: Proceedings of the 1st ACM Workshop on Research on Enterprise Networking, pp. 1–10 (2009)
22. Husnoo, M.A., Anwar, A., Chakrabortty, R.K., Doss, R., Ryan, M.J.: Differential privacy for IoT-enabled critical infrastructure: A comprehensive survey. IEEE Access **9**, 153276–153304 (2021)
23. Jagatheesaperumal, S.K., Pham, Q.V., Ruby, R., Yang, Z., Xu, C., Zhang, Z.: Explainable AI over the Internet of Things (IoT): Overview, state-of-the-art and future directions. IEEE Open J. Commun. Soc. **3**, 2106–2136 (2022)
24. Jan, M.A., Zakarya, M., Khan, M., Mastorakis, S., Menon, V.G., Balasubramanian, V., Rehman, A.U.: An AI-enabled lightweight data fusion and load optimization approach for Internet of Things. Future Gener. Comput. Syst. **122**, 40–51 (2021)
25. Kalam, A.A.E., Baida, R.E., Balbiani, P., Benferhat, S., Cuppens, F., Deswarte, Y., Miege, A., Saurel, C., Trouessin, G.: Organization based access control. In: Proceedings POLICY 2003. IEEE 4th International Workshop on Policies for Distributed Systems and Networks, pp. 120–131. IEEE (2003)
26. Karimi, L., Abdelhakim, M., Joshi, J.: Adaptive abac policy learning: A reinforcement learning approach. Preprint. arXiv:2105.08587 (2021)
27. Karimibiuki, M., Aggarwal, E., Pattabiraman, K., Ivanov, A.: Dynpolac: Dynamic policy-based access control for IoT systems. In: 2018 IEEE 23rd Pacific Rim International Symposium on Dependable Computing (PRDC), pp. 161–170. IEEE (2018)
28. Karmakar, K.K., Varadharajan, V., Nepal, S., Tupakula, U.: SDN-enabled secure IoT architecture. IEEE Internet Things J. **8**(8), 6549–6564 (2020)

29. Kim, H., Reich, J., Gupta, A., Shahbaz, M., Feamster, N., Clark, R.: Kinetic: Verifiable dynamic network control. In: 12th USENIX Symposium on Networked Systems Design and Implementation (NSDI 15), pp. 59–72 (2015)
30. Kreutz, D., Ramos, F.M.V., Verissimo, P.E., Rothenberg, C.E., Azodolmolky, S., Uhlig, S.: Software-defined networking: A comprehensive survey. Proc. IEEE **103**(1), 14–76 (2015). https://doi.org/10.1109/JPROC.2014.2371999, https://www.scopus.com/inward/record.uri?eid=2-s2.0-84919935425&doi=10.1109%2fJPROC.2014.2371999&partnerID=40&md5=26b571f8a284cc9c0f48c3fc0e39a059, cited by: 3226; All Open Access, Green Open Access
31. Krishnan, P., Najeem, J.S., Achuthan, K.: SDN framework for securing IoT networks. In: Ubiquitous Communications and Network Computing: First International Conference, UBICNET 2017, Bangalore, India, August 3–5, 2017, Proceedings 1, pp. 116–129. Springer (2018)
32. Lahlou, S., Moukafih, Y., Sebbar, A., Zkik, K., Boulmalf, M., Ghogho, M.: TD-RA policy-enforcement framework for an SDN-based IoT architecture. J. Netw. Comput. Appl. **204**, 103390 (2022). https://doi.org/10.1016/j.jnca.2022.103390, https://www.sciencedirect.com/science/article/pii/S1084804522000510
33. Lara, A., Ramamurthy, B.: Opensec: Policy-based security using software-defined networking. IEEE Trans. Netw. Serv. Manag. **13**(1), 30–42 (2016)
34. Lara, A., Kolasani, A., Ramamurthy, B.: Network innovation using openflow: A survey. IEEE Commun. Surv. Tutorials **16**(1), 493–512 (2014)
35. Lee, W., Kim, N.: Security policy scheme for an efficient security architecture in software-defined networking. Information **8**(2), 65 (2017)
36. Lekhala, U., Haque, I.: Piqos: A programmable and intelligent QoS framework. In: IEEE INFOCOM 2019 - IEEE Conference on Computer Communications Workshops (INFOCOM WKSHPS), pp. 234–239 (2019). https://doi.org/10.1109/INFCOMW.2019.8845158
37. Loukil, F., Ghedira-Guegan, C., Benharkat, A.N., Boukadi, K., Maamar, Z.: Privacy-aware in the IoT applications: a systematic literature review. In: On the Move to Meaningful Internet Systems. OTM 2017 Conferences: Confederated International Conferences: CoopIS, C&TC, and ODBASE 2017, Rhodes, Greece, October 23-27, 2017, Proceedings, Part I, pp. 552–569. Springer (2017)
38. Meng, Y., Huang, Z., Shen, G., Ke, C.: A security policy model transformation and verification approach for software defined networking. Comput. Secur. **100**, 102089 (2021)
39. Mestres, A., Rodriguez-Natal, A., Carner, J., Barlet-Ros, P., Alarcón, E., Solé, M., Muntés-Mulero, V., Meyer, D., Barkai, S., Hibbett, M.J., et al.: Knowledge-defined networking. ACM SIGCOMM Comput. Commun. Rev. **47**(3), 2–10 (2017)
40. Mitropoulos, S.: Conflict resolution in management policies: case study in cloud computing and internet of things. Int. J. Inf. Priv. Secur. Integrity **5**(2), 93–110 (2021)
41. Molina Zarca, A., Bernabe, J.B., Trapero, R., Rivera, D., Villalobos, J., Skarmeta, A., Bianchi, S., Zafeiropoulos, A., Gouvas, P.: Security management architecture for NFV/SDN-aware IoT systems. IEEE Internet Things J. **6**(5), 8005–8020 (2019). https://doi.org/10.1109/JIOT.2019.2904123
42. Molina Zarca, A., Bagaa, M., Bernal Bernabe, J., Taleb, T., Skarmeta, A.F.: Semantic-aware security orchestration in SDN/NFV-enabled IoT systems. Sensors **20**(13), 3622 (2020)
43. Murad, A., Kraemer, F.A., Bach, K., Taylor, G.: Information-driven adaptive sensing based on deep reinforcement learning. In: Proceedings of the 10th International Conference on the Internet of Things. IoT '20, Association for Computing Machinery, New York, NY, USA (2020). https://doi.org/10.1145/3410992.3411001, https://doi.org/10.1145/3410992.3411001
44. Nassar, A., Yilmaz, Y.: Reinforcement learning for adaptive resource allocation in fog RAN for IoT with heterogeneous latency requirements. IEEE Access **7**, 128014–128025 (2019). https://doi.org/10.1109/ACCESS.2019.2939735
45. Nunes, B.A.A., Mendonca, M., Nguyen, X., Obraczka, K., Turletti, T.: A survey of software-defined networking: Past, present, and future of programmable networks. IEEE Commun. Surv. Tutorials **16**(3), 1617–1634 (2014)

46. Pacheco, J., Ibarra, D., Vijay, A., Hariri, S.: IoT security framework for smart water system. In: 2017 IEEE/ACS 14th International Conference on Computer Systems and Applications (AICCSA), pp. 1285–1292. IEEE (2017)
47. Pal, S., Hitchens, M., Varadharajan, V., Rabehaja, T.: Policy-based access control for constrained healthcare resources. In: 2018 IEEE 19th International Symposium on "A World of Wireless, Mobile and Multimedia Networks" (WoWMoM), pp. 588–599. IEEE (2018)
48. Papanikolaou, N., Pearson, S., Mont, M.C., Ko, R.K.: A toolkit for automating compliance in cloud computing services. Int. J. Cloud Comput. 2 **3**(1), 45–68 (2014)
49. Parker, A., Simari, G.I., Sliva, A., Subrahmanian, V.: Data-driven Generation of Policies. Springer (2014)
50. Perumal, T., Sulaiman, M.N., Datta, S.K., Ramachandran, T., Leong, C.Y.: Rule-based conflict resolution framework for internet of things device management in smart home environment. In: GCC£, pp. 1–2 (2016)
51. Pisharody, S., Natarajan, J., Chowdhary, A., Alshalan, A., Huang, D.: Brew: A security policy analysis framework for distributed SDN-based cloud environments. IEEE Trans. Dependable Sec. Comput. **16**(6), 1011–1025 (2017)
52. Qiu, J., Tian, Z., Du, C., Zuo, Q., Su, S., Fang, B.: A survey on access control in the age of Internet of Things. IEEE Internet Things J. **7**(6), 4682–4696 (2020)
53. Rajput, R.S., Dhoni, P.S., Patel, R., Karangara, R., Shende, A., Kathiriya, S.: AI-Driven Innovations. Cari Journals USA LLC (2024)
54. Reich, J., Monsanto, C., Foster, N., Rexford, J., Walker, D.: Modular SDN programming with pyretic. Technical Report of USENIX **30** (2013)
55. Roxin, I., Bouchereau, A.: The ecosystem of the internet of things. In: Bouhaï, N., Saleh, I. (eds.) Internet of Things: Evolutions and Innovations. ISTE/John Wiley & Sons, London/New York (2017)
56. Sahay, R., Blanc, G., Zhang, Z., Toumi, K., Debar, H.: Adaptive policy-driven attack mitigation in SDN. In: Proceedings of the 1st International Workshop on Security and Dependability of Multi-Domain Infrastructures, pp. 1–6 (2017)
57. Sahay, R., Meng, W., Estay, D.S., Jensen, C.D., Barfod, M.B.: Cybership-IoT: A dynamic and adaptive SDN-based security policy enforcement framework for ships. Future Gen. Comput. Syst. **100**, 736–750 (2019). https://www.sciencedirect.com/science/article/pii/S0167739X1930367X
58. Sarica, A.K., Angin, P.: Explainable security in SDN-based IoT networks. Sensors **20**(24), 7326 (2020)
59. Schlesinger, C., Greenberg, M., Walker, D.: Concurrent netcore: From policies to pipelines. In: Proceedings of the 19th ACM SIGPLAN International Conference on Functional Programming, pp. 11–24 (2014)
60. Sha, K., Yang, T.A., Wei, W., Davari, S.: A survey of edge computing-based designs for IoT security. Digit. Commun. Netw. **6**(2), 195–202 (2020)
61. Shah, T., Venkatesan, S., Ngo, T., Neelamegam, K., et al.: Conflict detection in rule based IoT systems. In: 2019 IEEE 10th Annual Information Technology, Electronics and Mobile Communication Conference (IEMCON), pp. 0276–0284. IEEE (2019)
62. Shaik, M., Venkataramanan, S., Sadhu, A.K.R., Gudala, L.: Envisioning secure and scalable network access control: A framework for mitigating device heterogeneity and network complexity in large-scale internet-of-things (IoT) deployments. Distrib. Learn. Broad Appl. Sci. Res. **3**, 1–24 (2017)
63. Shin, S., Gu, G.: Cloudwatcher: Network security monitoring using openflow in dynamic cloud networks. In: 2012 20th IEEE International Conference on Network Protocols (ICNP), pp. 1–6 (2012). https://doi.org/10.1109/ICNP.2012.6459946
64. Shin, S.W., Porras, P., Yegneswara, V., Fong, M., Gu, G., Tyson, M.: Fresco: Modular composable security services for software-defined networks. In: 20th Annual Network & Distributed System Security Symposium. Ndss (2013)
65. Sicari, S., Rizzardi, A., Miorandi, D., Coen-Porisini, A.: Dynamic policies in internet of things: enforcement and synchronization. IEEE Internet Things J. **4**(6), 2228–2238 (2017)

66. Sinha, S.: 'state of IoT 2023'. IoT Analytics. https://iot-analytics.com/number-connected-iot-devices/
67. Soulé, R., Basu, S., Marandi, P.J., Pedone, F., Kleinberg, R., Sirer, E.G., Foster, N.: Merlin: A language for managing network resources. IEEE/ACM Trans. Netw. **26**(5), 2188–2201 (2018)
68. Stone, G.N., Lundy, B., Xie, G.G.: Network policy languages: a survey and a new approach. IEEE Netw. **15**(1), 10–21 (2001)
69. Tiburski, R.T., Amaral, L.A., De Matos, E., De Azevedo, D.F., Hessel, F.: The role of lightweight approaches towards the standardization of a security architecture for IoT middleware systems. IEEE Commun. Mag. **54**(12), 56–62 (2016)
70. Tripathy, P.K., Shabaz, M., Zaidi, A., Keshta, I., Sharma, U., Soni, M., Agrawal, A.V., Maaliw III, R.R., Sharma, D.: Policy conflict detection approach for decision-making in intelligent industrial internet of things. Comput. Electr. Eng. **108**, 108671 (2023)
71. Varadharajan, V., Karmakar, K., Tupakula, U., Hitchens, M.: A policy-based security architecture for software-defined networks. IEEE Trans. Inf. Forens. Secur. **14**(4), 897–912 (2018)
72. Voellmy, A., Agarwal, A., Hudak, P.: Nettle: Functional reactive programming for openflow networks. rapp. tech. Tech. rep., YALEU/DCS/RR-1431. Yale University, juill. 2010 (cf. p. 31)
73. Voellmy, A., Kim, H., Feamster, N.: Procera: A language for high-level reactive network control. In: Proceedings of the First Workshop on Hot Topics in Software Defined Networks, pp. 43–48. HotSDN '12 Association for Computing Machinery, New York (2012). https://doi.org/10.1145/2342441.2342451
74. Xu, R., Chen, Y., Blasch, E.: Decentralized access control for IoT based on blockchain and smart contract. In: Modeling and Design of Secure Internet of Things, pp. 505–528 (2020)
75. Yu, P., Sendor, J., Serme, G., de Oliveira, A.S.: Automating privacy enforcement in cloud platforms. In: International Workshop on Data Privacy Management, pp. 160–173. Springer (2012)
76. Zahid, N., Sodhro, A.H., Kamboh, U.R., Alkhayyat, A., Wang, L.: AI-driven adaptive reliable and sustainable approach for internet of things enabled healthcare system. Math. Biosci. Eng. **19**(4), 3953–3971 (2022)
77. Zero, E., Sallak, M., Sacile, R.: Predictive maintenance in IoT-monitored systems for fault prevention. J. Sensor Actuator Netw. **13**(5), 57 (2024)
78. Zhu, Y., Qin, Y., Gan, G., Shuai, Y., Chu, W.C.C.: TBAC: Transaction-based access control on blockchain for resource sharing with cryptographically decentralized authorization. In: 2018 IEEE 42nd Annual Computer Software and Applications Conference (COMPSAC), vol. 1, pp. 535–544. IEEE (2018)

Securing Tomorrow's Connectivity: Developing Defenses for 5G-Enhanced IoT Technologies

Lakshmi R. Nair, Preetam Mukherjee, and Subhajit Chatterjee

1 Introduction

The fifth generation of telecommunications systems, or 5G networks, are an international wireless standard. Compared to previous generations, it offers significantly higher data capacities and faster transmission speeds. With its universal ultra-high bandwidth and low latency, 5G guarantees incredibly quick and dependable connectivity for linked devices as well as individual users. Any cellular network architecture's main goals are to meet the demands for higher capacity, faster data rates, lower latency, and higher service quality.

The 5G architecture is entirely built upon the specifications provided by 3GPP. The 3rd Generation Partnership Project (3GPP) is composed of seven standard development organizations called as Organizational Partners. These organizational partners are the Association of Radio Industries and Businesses (ARIB), the Alliance for Telecommunications Industry Solutions (ATIS), the China Communications Standards Association (CCSA), the European Telecommunications Standards Institute (ETSI), the Telecommunications Standards Development Society, India (TSDSI), the Telecommunications Technology Association (TTA), and the Telecommunication Technology Committee (TTC). This collaboration provides a framework for these groups to develop Reports and Specifications that define 3GPP technologies.

L. R. Nair (✉) · P. Mukherjee
Digital University Kerala, Thiruvananthapuram, India
e-mail: lakshmi.csres23@duk.ac.in; preetam.mukherjee@duk.ac.in

S. Chatterjee
Centre for Development of Telematics (C-DOT), Government of India, New Delhi, India
e-mail: subhajit.chatterjee@cdot.in

S. M. Thampi et al. (eds.), *Securing the Connected World*,
https://doi.org/10.1007/978-3-031-82826-3_8

The 3GPP specifications address various aspects of cellular telecommunications, including radio access, core network, and service capabilities, offering a detailed system overview for mobile communications.3GPP started working in 1998 on the third generation of mobile technology, which proposed techniques that all regions could adopt. This global convergence towards 3GPP specifications has enabled remarkable market growth and provided an increasing assurance that broadband cellular, and now the internet of everything, can depend on a stable and forward-looking standardization platform.

5G improves on 4G services in several areas:

- Enhanced Mobile Broadband (eMBB): Higher data rates are specified, offering up to 50 Mbps for outdoor and 1 Gbps for indoor (5GLAN) downlink, with half these rates available for uplink. Case studies include aviation, where eMBB helps deliver a bitrate of 1.2 Gbps to an airborne flight.
- Critical Communications (CC) and Ultra Reliable and Low Latency Communications (URLLC): In some contexts, extremely high reliability is expected. For example, in remote process automation control, a reliability of 99.99% is required, with a user-experienced data rate up to 100 Mbps and an end-to-end latency of 50 ms, supported by Edge Computing.
- Massive Internet of Things (mIoT): 5G must support very high traffic densities of devices, addressing the operational needs of a wide range of IoT devices and services anticipated in the 5G era.
- Flexible network operations: 5G offers features like network slicing, network capability exposure, scalability, diverse mobility, security, efficient content delivery, and migration and interworking.

In 5G networks, Software-Defined Networking (SDN) and Network Functions Virtualization (NFV) are essential for delivering the flexibility, scalability, and efficiency required to support a wide range of applications and services.SDN centralizes control, simplifying network management and allowing real-time adjustments to configurations and policies. It also supports dynamic resource allocation and network slicing, enabling customized virtual networks for specific needs. Both SDN and NFV enhance scalability, support multi-access edge computing (MEC) by positioning functions closer to users, and improve security through centralized policy enforcement.

Integrating 5G and IoT transforms industries by enabling faster, more reliable connections for various devices. With 5G's enhanced speed and capacity, IoT systems can scale up efficiently, supporting more devices and applications than ever.The enhanced security features of 5G, including stronger encryption, mutual authentication, and network slicing, safeguard IoT devices against potential cyber threats, ensuring data integrity and protecting critical infrastructures from unauthorized access.

This chapter provides a comprehensive overview of key topics related to 5G technology and its security landscape. It commences with a detailed examination of the fundamental principles of 5G, establishing a robust framework for understanding its inherent complexities. Subsequently, the chapter analyzes the diverse security challenges faced by 5G networks, emphasizing the unique vulnerabilities that emerge from their advanced architectural features. A thorough review of existing research on 5G security highlights key findings and approaches in the field. The chapter also discusses strategies for protecting the 5G core, emphasizing effective practices and emerging security frameworks. It explores how 5G technology interacts with the Internet of Things (IoT), shedding light on the security challenges that arise in this interconnected environment. Finally, the chapter offers an overview of simulation tools available for 5G, which can enhance our understanding of network dynamics and security testing.

2 5G Basics

This section covers 5G design principles, core architecture, network slicing, and other related topics.

2.1 5G Design Principles

The primary concepts introduced in 5G include Control User Plane Separation (CUPS), Network Slicing, Cloud-Native and Microservices architectures, and Service-Based Architecture (SBA).

Control User Plane Separation (CUPS)
Control User Plane Separation (CUPS) separates the network's control functions from the user data flow. This separation makes the network easier to manage and allows for smoother integration of new applications and services. CUPS improves network components like the Evolved Packet Core, making them better equipped to handle the growing data traffic from smartphones and streaming. By moving the User Plane closer to users in the network, CUPS helps reduce delays and improve service quality.

As smartphones and streaming video apps increase, data traffic is also rapidly growing. For a better user experience, the user plane can be placed at the edge cloud, closer to users. The mobile edge computing concept in 5G allows the user plane to scale and upgrade independently. The communication between the Control Plane and User Plane, will be efficiently managed by the Packet Forwarding Control Plane (PFCP) protocol.

Network Slicing
Network slicing involves providing multiple virtual networks that operate over the same physical network by allocating shared resources. Each slice serves a different purpose with its own functionalities, protocols, and security settings. Through NFV and SDN, the physical layer of the network is separated from the logical structure, enabling the provision of purpose-oriented, independent operational networks.

Cloud-Native and Microservices
There is the possibility to build a service-based architecture using microservices with a cloud-oriented approach for service providers. This technique evolves from virtualized networks with well-defined VMs for capacity provisioning. For 5G, it enhances efficiency for providers by allocating resources based on average, rather than peak, resource consumption. This cloud-native approach to deploying network functions optimizes agility and speed, reducing the risk of vendor lock-in and allowing selection based on the best price and functionality.

Service-Based Architecture (SBA)
The Service-Based Architecture (SBA) for core 5G networks is defined in 3GPP Technical Specification (TS) 23.501, titled 'System Architecture for the 5G System'. SBA uses service-based interfaces for communication between control-plane components, while user-plane components are connected through point-to-point connections.

2.2 5G Core Network Architecture

5G is designed as a single architecture that includes both a point-to-point and a service-based approach. The point-to-point architecture is similar to older systems, with separate interfaces and different protocols connecting each node. This method has drawbacks because it is closed off and not easily programmable. With 5G, service providers want more flexibility and the ability to program in cloud environments, especially because of the wide range of new use cases. At first, most 5G deployments will likely use the point-to-point model because there is some hesitation about switching to the new service-based model.

The Reference Point architecture (Fig. 1) is composed of a series of Network Elements (NEs) interconnected through point-to-point interfaces. Each interface has

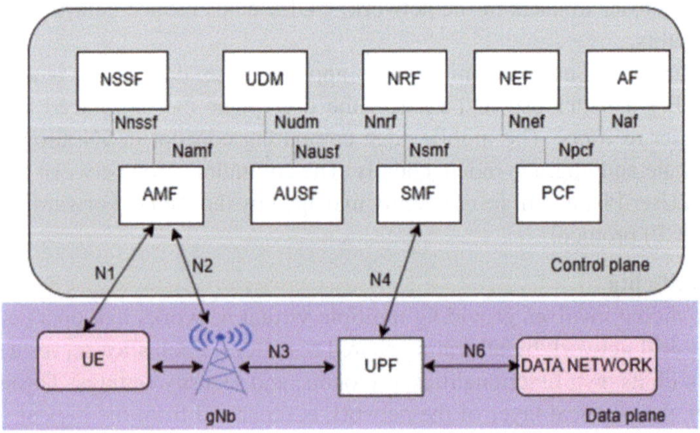

Fig. 1 5G service-based architecture

its own specified signaling procedures. In the Service-Based architecture, Network Elements are transformed into a group of Network Functions (NFs). Each NF offers services to other NFs. The point-to-point interfaces are replaced with a shared communication bus that links all the Network Functions.

The 5G core network is composed of several critical functions, each performing unique and essential roles. The Access and Mobility Management Function (AMF) is responsible for managing user equipment (UE) registration, connection, mobility, and authentication. It is central to handling access and mobility requests, managing the authentication of UEs, and selecting the appropriate network slicing, thereby determining the network services available to users based on their profiles.

The Session Management Function (SMF) is responsible for establishing, modifying, and releasing PDU sessions, as well as managing data plane connectivity according to the functional needs of users and applications. The User Plane Function (UPF) plays a crucial role in data transmission by directing user data packets to and from user equipment and facilitating connections to external data networks. It also implements various spatial data transmission policies related to policy control, Quality of Service (QoS) optimization, and traffic management.

Unified Data Management (UDM) serves as the central hub for storing user subscription data and generating authentication credentials. It plays a crucial role in facilitating interactions between users and the network, ensuring smooth connectivity and user experience. The Policy Control Function (PCF) handles the management of policies, enforcing rules for data flow and Quality of Service (QoS). It manages the allocation of network resources and ensures that users' subscription plans and preferences are properly followed.

The Network Slice Selection Function (NSSF) assigns appropriate network slices to meet specific service needs, contributing to the efficient use of resources and differentiation of services based on user requirements. The Network Exposure Function (NEF) provides network capabilities and functions to third-party developers and service providers through secure, standardized interfaces, enabling a wide range of services and applications within the 5G ecosystem. Together, these functions create a comprehensive, flexible, and efficient framework that supports the diverse services and applications characteristic of 5G networks.

2.3 The 3rd Generation Partnership Project (3GPP)

The 3rd Generation Partnership Project (3GPP) is a initiative which sets standards for mobile networks, with a focus on 5G development and advancement. This particular collaboration unites organizations around the world to establish a consistent set of guidelines for technologies which include GSM, UMTS, LTE, and the latest 5G innovations.

3GPP documents are divided into three types, each serves a specific role in the standardization process. The **Technical Specifications (TS)** which serves as detailed blueprints that outlinine the protocols, interfaces, and operational requirements which are necessary for the development and deployment of network components. These specifications are used by vendors and service providers to ensure optimal performance and compatibility within their systems. The **Technical Reports (TR)** are documents which explore possible alterations or improvements to existing standards, by assessing the integration of emerging technologies within the current framework. The **Change Requests (CR)** are formal proposals which suggests modifications to the existing Technical Specifications and Reports, which contains the justification for changes, the proposed revisions, and the expected impact of these changes.

The organization of these documents is methodical, with a numbering system that reflects their focus areas. For example, the **20 Series** pertains to system architecture and capabilities, elaborating on the interactions between different network elements. The **30 Series** addresses the radio access network (RAN), delineating protocols and procedures essential for communication between mobile devices and base stations. The **40 Series** covers core network and terminal aspects, defining the protocols and operations required for device connectivity and data transmission. Finally, the **50 Series** outlines the procedures for testing and validation, which are crucial to ensure that products and services comply with established standards.

A significant attribute of the 3GPP process is the accessibility and ongoing updates to its documents. This dynamic process, which involves collaboration among various stakeholders, ensuring that the standards remain relevant and effective, focusing on the fast-paced domain of 5G technology development.

Within the context of 5G, network security is critical. 3GPP documents provide guidelines that aims at ensuring security across the network infrastructure. These guidelines considers critical aspects such as authentication protocols, data encryption methods, and secure access controls, which is keyfactor in ensuring a robust defense against potential threats and vulnerabilities.

Overall, 3GPP documents are the documents that contribute to the advancement of 5G technology. They provide detailed guidelines and specifications ensuring interoperability and compliance with performance standards. For more detailed information, the 3GPP official website[1] is a valuable resource, offering access to 3GPP specifications an reports.

2.4 *Advanced Topics*

2.4.1 Network Slicing

5G network slicing is a crucial concept that allows for efficient and flexible network management by creating multiple virtual networks on a single physical

[1] https://www.3gpp.org/.

infrastructure. As outlined in 3GPP specifications, network slicing enables the separation of network resources and services to meet the diverse needs of different applications and user groups.

A network slice is a discrete logical network intended to serve specific needs, functioning autonomously from other networks. Resources like storage, processing power, and bandwidth are allotted to each slice separately. It can also be adjusted with different security policies, QoS settings, and network functionalities. This methodology optimizes the use of resources and raises the general efficiency of the network.

Network slicing in the 5G core network, as described by 3GPP, generates separate and tailored network environments to satisfy different service requirements. To provide high-speed data and huge capacity, one slice could be tailored for enhanced mobile broadband, or eMBB. For ultra-reliable low-latency communications (URLLC), which reduces latency and guarantees high dependability for crucial applications, another slice might be created. Furthermore, a third slice might be able to handle a lot of linked devices at lower data rates by supporting massive machine-type communications (mMTC).

The Single Network Slice Selection Assistance Information (S-NSSAI) is a pivotal concept in the 5G network architecture as defined by 3GPP standards. It serves as a fundamental identifier for network slices, facilitating the selection and management of these slices within the 5G network.

The S-NSSAI consists of two key components (Table 1): the Slice/Service Type (SST) and the Slice Differentiator (SD). The SST represents a broad classification of the slice, which indicates the type of service the slice is designed to support, such as enhanced Mobile Broadband (eMBB), Ultra-Reliable Low Latency Communications (URLLC), or massive Machine-Type Communications (mMTC)., the SD allows the differentiation of slices that share the same SST but belongs to different slices with distinct configurations or characteristics. This combination of SST and

Table 1 Slice/service type (SST) and slice differentiator (SD) in 5G network slicing

Component	Details
Slice/Service type (SST)	SST specifics the overall service behavior and characteristics, such as latency, throughput, and reliability. Common SST values include: – **eMBB**: SST = 1 – **URLLC**: SST = 2 – **mMTC**: SST = 3
Slice differentiator (SD)	SD is a 24-bit value (represented in hexadecimal) that differentiates slices sharing the same SST. It enables finer distinction based on service-specific requirements.
S-NSSAI (SST + SD)	S-NSSAI = {SST, SD} allows for both broad classification and precise customization of network slices, ensuring flexibility in managing service needs and network resources.

SD in the S-NSSAI helps in precise identification and customization of network slices to meet specific service requirements.

The role of S-NSSAI is critical in the operation of 5G networks. When a User Equipment (UE) initiates a connection, it can request for its preferred slices by transmitting one or more S-NSSAIs in the registration request. Thus, the appropriate selection of network slices is facilitated with the help of S-NSSAI. Furthermore, the S-NSSAI facilitates the concurrent use of multiple slices by a single UE. This feature highlights how adaptable the 5G architecture is in providing customized services with unique operational and performance aspects. The S-NSSAI is a key component of the 5G network slicing paradigm, as specified in 3GPP standards like TS 23.501 and TS 24.501. It allows for a new degree of service differentiation and quality assurance in contemporary telecommunications.

3 5G Security Challenges

The introduction of 5G technology brings significant improvements to mobile networks, but it also introduces new security challenges. According to 3GPP specifications and recent research, securing 5G networks requires focused attention on several critical areas.

One of the biggest problems is the bigger attack surface in 5G, shaped by many connected services and devices. The inclusion of the ever-growing Internet of Things (IoT) devices besides mobile brings up possibilities of entry and risks much more within the scope of attackers. Each device creates a risk; thus, stronger security must be taken at every point of the network.

That comes with some real challenges associated with the structure of the network. Network slicing is an important feature of 5G. To ensure that issues in one slice do not bleed into others, there needs to be a set of security rules and protections for each virtual network or slice, automatically bringing layers of complexity in managing network security.

Cloud-based systems and software-defined networking (SDN) underpin 5G. These have associated security issues with it. Threats such as data breaches or misconfigurations against cloud environments, which host network functions, must be countered. Similarly, although SDN brings flexible management of network resources, it also brings risks that must be carefully managed with robust security measures.

The security challenges have been compounded by the flexibility of 5G, including the rapid deployability and flexibility to change network slices and services. Some traditional security solutions may not be strong enough for such an evolving space. Advanced encryption capabilities with layers of security are required to address the challenges that arise.

3.1 5G Core Network Security

The 5G core, the critical component of next-generation mobile systems, and the central element in its operation and efficiency. However, it introduces a range of security challenges unique to its core functions, each of which is vital to the network's performance as a whole.

This includes the authentication, registration, and mobility management of a user by the AMF. Being the main network function , the AMF should be highly secured against denying access and manipulation to users' credentials and session information. Some robust security mechanisms related to the AMF include securing authentication protocols, encryption of communication channels, and constant monitoring systems that are set up to spot and track suspicious activities.

The session management function manages setting, modifying, and closing a data session. Security weaknesses in the SMF easily form through session hijacking or disruption of the session. Such potential threats are highly damaging to a network's stability and user experience, so the encryption provided by the mechanisms set for the data of the session must be very robust, with very tight controls on access and routine security audits in case of vulnerabilities surfacing.

UPF manages and forwards user data. Being the road to the flow of the traffic of the data, it is susceptible to the critical forms of attacks that pass through it in the form of data breaches, unauthorized changes, and denial-of-service attacks. It therefore needs strong encryption protocols when data are on the move, secure path management of data, and highly sophisticated traffic monitoring responses in case of abnormalities.

This would expose the network capabilities through the Network Exposure Function to other applications external to the created network. This would bring forth a new set of security issues in the API management and data access aspects. NEF propagates securing the same by practicing hard-won practices on API security, exercising tight control on accesses, and surveillance over unauthorized accesses to network functions and data.

The network function virtualization infrastructure(NFVI) provides the base for the deployment and running of VNFs. NFVs can pose threats due to the vulnerabilities in the virtual layers, such as weaknesses in hypervisors and isolation of resources. Isolation protocols are strong, with patches updated and updation along with interfaces used for management to secure NFV.

As such, VNF is responsible for orchestration and network resource management. Risks here include unauthorized access to management interfaces, possible misconfigurations, manipulation of network resources, etc. To effectively secure the VNF, robust authentication and authorization protocols, security assessments, and best practices in configuration management, among others, must be followed.

There is no doubt that such inherent security challenges of the 5G core network call for an approach that is extremely thorough and based on core functions. Such advanced security measures, including encryption, access controls, and even continuous monitoring, may safeguard the integrity and reliability of the 5G core network in securing the operation of next-generation mobile services.

We can also use the MITRE FiGHT^{TM} (5G Hierarchy of Threats)[2] framework for a detailed study on attacks and detection techniques possible in the 5G core. The MITRE FIGHT^{TM}(5G Hierarchy of Threats) framework represents a pivotal advancement in the landscape of cybersecurity, especially for new security challenges brought forth by the deployment and operation of 5G networks. Constructed by MITRE with contributions by the U.S. Department of Defense (DoD), the FiGHT framework is designed to systematically catalog and analyze adversarial tactics, techniques, and procedures (TTPs) that could be leveraged against 5G infrastructures.

FiGHT leverages in-depth research and methodologies developed under the leading repository of cyber adversary behaviors: the MITRE ATT&CK framework. However, it is very unique in focused attention to the 5G ecosystem, given the complex interaction among the network architecture, applications, and the diverse nature of connected devices. This focus becomes very important, as the service-oriented and highly distributed architecture of 5G presents increased attack surfaces that might become points of interest for adversaries.

3.2 Network Slice Security

Network slicing of 5G networks makes provision of multiple virtual networks within a common physical infrastructure. The technique would be useful for diverse use cases and demands, allowing the services provided by the network to be appropriately customized. However, network slices do present some security issues. Security of each slice is essential, as well as preventing unauthorized access to any particular slice while keeping the integrity and confidentiality of data and services within that slice intact.

As such, the 3GPP specifications, hence, have isolation between the slices of a network, therefore preventing unauthorized access and secure operations on each slice. Such kind of isolation is hereby through logical and physical mechanisms, which are crucial to protecting integrity and confidentiality in each of the resulting slices.

The NSSF is important in managing network slices by guaranteeing protection on the security level. The NSSF chooses the right slice based on the needs of the users and services. It ensures that only the selected users and services can access a particular slice and enforces access control policies that prevent unauthorized access. For example, the NSSF correctly identifies the slices and, therefore, enjoys the process of authorizing network slices to maintain security for slice-specific resources and services.

---

[2] https://fight.mitre.org/.

Access and mobility management function is another relevant aspect that can be secured through a network slice. AMF manages user authentication, registration, and mobility. It interacts with NSSF to determine which network slice is correctly assigned to users or which users' proper access is carried out. Therefore, AMF must adopt appropriate authentication mechanisms and authenticate communication protocols to safeguard their credentials and session information against threats.

Another added consideration is data security in the slices of the network. The standards of 3GPP indicate that control and user plane data should be encrypted against unauthorized access and theft of data. With this in mind, every slice ought to employ state-of-the-art encryption technologies, as the resultant data is protected while it transits through the network.

Virtualization is very critical in network slicing, and hence, the NFV architecture has to manage VNFs in each slice in a secure way. The VNFM and NFVO would share responsibilities for the management of VNF instances through the deployment mechanisms. Thus, virtualization infrastructure has to be protected and isolated between two different VNFs from any attacks.

It requires ongoing monitoring and management to perpetuate the security of the network slices. It employs SOCs and other network monitoring tools to help them detect anomalies and respond to Security incidents, conforming to any security policy. It requires regular security assessment needed for updates on the ever-emerging threats and for ensuring the further security aspects of network slices.

4 Related Works on 5G Security

The transition to 5G technology introduces a range of enhancements in terms of data rates, latency, and network capacity. However, the increased complexity and novel architectural features of 5G networks bring forth significant security challenges. This literature survey consolidates critical research contributions addressing various aspects of 5G security, including access control mechanisms, network slicing, software-defined networking (SDN), and risk assessment frameworks. The following sections detail key studies, their findings, and identified gaps.

Akon et al. [3] present a formal analysis of access control mechanisms in the 5G core network using the 5GCVerif framework. The study reveals five new classes of privilege escalation vulnerabilities within the 5G core network. These vulnerabilities occur when a registered consumer Network Function (NF) is compromised by a malicious actor, allowing it to pursue unauthorized access to resources and services offered by benign producer NFs. The compromised NF can transmit arbitrary requests, such as *NFUpdateRequest*, *NFDiscoveryRequest*, *accessTokenRequest*, and *NFServiceRequest*, to other NFs within the 5G Core (5GC). However, 5GCVerif does not detect vulnerabilities arising from misconfigurations or implementation-level flaws since it focuses solely on modeling and analyzing specifications. This limitation highlights the need for tools that can address both specification-level and implementation-level vulnerabilities.

Olimid and Nencioni [14] provide a comprehensive overview of security concerns in 5G network slicing. They explore potential attack points and examine security requirements and recommendations from three perspectives: the lifecycle of a network slice, intra-slice security, and inter-slice security. Despite the thorough theoretical analysis, the study notes that large-scale experimental validation of network slice security is needed to confirm these findings. Before such validation, testing must be conducted to bridge the gap between theoretical insights and practical applications.

Abood and Abdul-Majeed [2] classify network slicing threats based on slicing enablers such as SDN, NFV, and cloud computing. The study discusses network slicing, the concept of isolation, and the enablers of slicing while addressing related attacks, risks, and concerns for each enabler. Previous surveys are reviewed, and taxonomies are mapped to illustrate each survey's contribution in presenting threats and attacks against network slicing. However, the paper notes that more research is needed to identify additional threats specific to 5G core networks.

Ghaffar et al. [7] explore the integration of SDN into 5G mobile core architectures. The survey categorizes existing works into four key factors: technology adoption, control plane implementation, evaluation techniques, and overall architecture. The objective is to guide researchers and practitioners in the ongoing development of SDN-based mobile core architectures tailored to 5G networks. However, the study identifies a gap in focusing on data plane implementation, which is critical for securing communication within these networks.

A white paper by Adaptive Mobile Security discusses 5G core network slicing, covering topics such as the 5G architecture, core network slicing, and existing security features related to slicing. It also addresses authorization within the Service-Based Architecture (SBA) using the Network Repository Function (NRF) and Service Communication Proxy (SCP), as well as security from a terminal and user perspective. However, the paper suggests that the security of network slicing could be covered in more depth, particularly concerning specific slicing security challenges.

Wehbe et al. [19] assess the security features introduced in 5G's Service-Based Architecture (SBA) with a focus on the security implications of using HTTP/2 as the signaling protocol. The study highlights that while HTTP/2 introduces several security enhancements, it would benefit from testing other protocols within the same security framework to ensure comprehensive protection. The gap identified here involves the need to test different protocols to evaluate their security implications fully.

Chlosta and Rupprecht [5] examine the vulnerabilities associated with SUCI-Catchers in 5G networks. These tools have traditionally been used to identify and track users by requesting all users' permanent identities within range. While 5G enhances security by encrypting the permanent identifier (now referred to as SUPI) and transmitting it as SUCI, the encryption does not entirely prevent tracking and linking. If an attacker knows a user's identity, they can still probe for it, creating a security loophole. The study points out that while SUCI-Catchers are identified, specific mitigation techniques to counteract them are not provided, leaving a critical gap.

Borsatti et al. [4] discuss the use of 5G and network slicing for mission-critical communications, particularly for Public Protection and Disaster Relief (PPDR) forces. The paper examines the feasibility and effectiveness of running a PPDR communication service as a network slice. While the implementation framework is clearly specified, the study does not discuss the security aspects associated with this use case, highlighting a significant gap that requires further research.

Wijethilaka and Liyanage [21] introduce a security orchestrator for managing security services in 5G network slicing. The proposed orchestrator offers services such as attack detection, proactive and reactive security deployment, and security service lifecycle management. The study specifies the location of a centralized security orchestrator within the traditional network slice architecture. However, it suggests that deploying different orchestrators for different network slices could be beneficial, a concept that remains unexplored.

Gomez et al. [8] investigate the application of security policies within the 5G Policy Control Function (PCF) framework, focusing on Quality of Service (QoS) policies. The paper details how QoS policies are applied to security, specifically in managing user plane detection and policy control. Although the study is comprehensive, it suggests that security policies specific to network functions should be added to enhance the security of 5G networks.

Hoq et al. [9] introduce 5GSPE, a novel approach for evaluating the security posture of 5G networks by combining state auditing and event monitoring. The study uses a Bayesian network model to integrate these inputs and assess the security posture of a 5G network through Bayesian inference. While 5GSPE effectively evaluates the current security posture, it does not predict future security risks, indicating a gap that future research could address.

Kabir et al. [10] propose a security architecture designed to secure 5G networks, particularly at customer edge nodes. This architecture, implemented using SDN and NFV technologies, has been demonstrated to mitigate unauthorized access and prevent denial-of-service attacks effectively. However, the study identifies the need for a comprehensive framework to manage security policies within network slices, particularly in ultra-reliable 5G networks.

Varadharajan et al. [17] explore techniques for securing 5G network services from attacks, focusing on the dynamic establishment of secure and trusted end-to-end services. They advocate for the development of mechanisms to proactively detect and mitigate security attacks in virtualized network infrastructures. The paper notes that ensuring security in the dynamic environment of 5G services over multiple domain networked virtualized infrastructures remains a critical challenge.

Kuo et al. [12] propose RAIN, a risk assessment framework based on an interdependent input propagation network for 5G networks. The framework aims to guide mobile network operators in implementing effective protective measures. However, the study points out that existing risk assessments lack numerical results for cost-efficient decision-making and cannot automatically update with changes in security policies. This limitation highlights the need for a unified assessment framework.

Kholidy et al. [11] address the challenges of securing 5G core networks through a vulnerability assessment approach (VAA). Their study focuses on the deployment of a cloud-based security testbed to evaluate vulnerabilities across various 5G scenarios. Although this approach is valuable, the study emphasizes that the testbed needs further deployment to achieve its full potential.

Mamushiane et al. [13] explore the performance of the User Plane Function (UPF) node within a 5G standalone testbed through stress testing. The research focuses on evaluating the UPF's CPU utilization under different levels of network traffic, highlighting the critical role of UPF in determining network performance. The study notes that additional parameters specific to UPF attacks need to be identified, which represents a gap in the current research.

Wijethilaka and Liyanage [20] conduct a survey on the realization of network slicing for the Internet of Things (IoT) in 5G networks. The study highlights the importance of SDN, NFV, and cloud computing in enabling the creation of virtual networks tailored to specific IoT applications. However, the lack of large-scale implementations and the evolving specifications related to network slicing present challenges that need further exploration. Certainly! Here is the detailed review, incorporating aspects related to procedures and systems, message flow, PDU sessions, and 5G architecture.

3GPP TS 23.501 [1] provides a detailed framework for the 5G System (5GS) architecture that introduces a modular design that separates the control plane from the user plane. This separation will enhance network flexibility and scalability. Essential core network functions defined in this specification are the Access and Mobility Management Function (AMF), which manages user registration and mobility; the Session Management Function (SMF), responsible for session establishment and modification sessions; and the User Plane Function (UPF), which handles user data traffic. The architecture also supports network slicing, which allows multiple isolated virtual networks to operate on a shared infrastructure based on diverse service requirements and application needs.

Regarding procedures and systems in the 5G network, 3GPP TS 23.502 discusses the operational procedures within the 5G system. The processes such as session management, mobility management, and network slicing are detailed in this document. The document specifies the message flows and signaling procedures involved in establishing, modifying, and releasing PDU sessions and managing user mobility across different network regions.

3GPP TS 23.503 introduces network function virtualization (NFV) and its integration with Network Slicing. This document specifies the principles for implementing and operating virtualized network functions within the 5G framework. It then shows how dynamic resource allocation and scaling can be done according to service conditions. The deployment of NFVs across network slices, facilitated by 3GPP TS 23.503, supports efficient resource utilization and the delivery of customized network services.

3GPP TS 23.504 describes the signaling protocols and message flows within the 5G core network. It details how core network functions such as AMF, SMF, and UPF interact to manage user sessions, mobility, and resource allocation. The document includes procedures for session establishment, modification, and release, as well as managing user data traffic and maintaining session continuity. In order to ensure that data flows are efficiently handled and users experience minimal disruption during network interactions, these protocols can be used.

Network management and orchestration in the 5G environment are covered in 3GPP TS 23.505. The document addresses the lifecycle management of network slices, including their creation, modification, and operation. It suggests a framework for integrating network management with service delivery, ensuring that network slices are efficiently operated and optimized according to various service levels and performance criteria.

3GPP TS 23.510 introduces the service-based architecture (SBA) for the 5G core network. It details how network functions interact through service-based interfaces. The SBA framework plays a major role in achieving the required flexibility and scalability for 5G networks.

The procedures for creating, managing, and operating network slices are further detailed in 3GPP TS 23.518. This document provides insights into how slices can be customized to meet specific service requirements and performance criteria. It outlines mechanisms for slice creation, modification, and operation, supporting the segmentation of the network into virtual networks and optimizing resource use.

3GPP TS 38.413 specifies access and mobility management procedures for New Radio (NR), including user equipment (UE) registration, handover procedures, and session management. The document outlines the protocols for managing network access and ensuring seamless mobility, essential for maintaining high-quality service and efficient network operation.

Procedures related to user plane data in NR are detailed in 3GPP TS 38.414. This document covers data transfer, quality of service (QoS) management, and data integrity, supporting efficient data handling and reliable transmission across the 5G radio network while adhering to performance requirements.

For security, 3GPP TS 33.501 describes the overall security architecture and procedures for 5G networks, focusing on encryption, authentication, and integrity protection. It establishes a framework to secure core network elements, user equipment, and radio interfaces from various threats, crucial for maintaining network security and integrity.

3GPP TS 33.502 specifies security assurance requirements, emphasizing the robustness of security mechanisms through extensive testing and validation. It provides guidelines for evaluating the effectiveness of security measures and ensuring they meet necessary standards, which is vital for maintaining a secure network environment.

3GPP TS 33.503 details security procedures specific to the 5G core network, including key management, mutual authentication, and secure signaling. The document addresses potential security threats associated with network slicing and virtualization, ensuring comprehensive protection against various types of attacks and vulnerabilities.

3GPP TS 33.510 outlines advanced security procedures for the 5G system, addressing evolving security challenges and providing enhanced protection measures for network elements and interfaces. This document is key to adapting security protocols to emerging threats and ensuring robust defense mechanisms within the 5G network.

3GPP TS 33.511 focuses on security measures for the User Plane Function (UPF), detailing procedures for protecting user data traffic. The document specifies encryption and integrity protection mechanisms for data transferred between the UPF and other network functions, ensuring the confidentiality and integrity of user data.

3GPP TS 33.512 addresses security for the Access and Mobility Management Function (AMF) and Session Management Function (SMF), providing detailed security protocols for these core functions. The document outlines authentication, integrity protection, and secure communication procedures, which are critical for safeguarding management and signaling processes within the 5G core network.

3GPP TS 33.521 provides guidelines for network security assurance in 5G, emphasizing the need for regular security assessments and compliance checks. It includes procedures for evaluating network security measures, ensuring that they are effective and adhere to established security standards.

4.1 Open Issues

A detailed review of the literature has identified several critical security gaps within the 5G core network (5GC) functions. This review, grounded in the analysis of 3GPP specifications and recent studies, highlights vulnerabilities that arise from the complex and dynamic nature of the 5G architecture. These gaps, which affect various core network functions, underscore the need for comprehensive security measures to address the evolving threats in 5G environments. The following section discusses these identified vulnerabilities in detail, providing insights based on the literature review and relevant 3GPP standards.

As shown in Fig. 2, the primary entry points for attackers into the 5G core network are through the Access and Mobility Management Function (AMF) and the User Plane Function (UPF), as these core functions communicate with external entities. There are several options for attackers to exploit these Network Function Virtualizations (NFVs) to gain unauthorized access to the 5G core network. Another potential attack vector, as depicted in the Fig. 2, involves intercepting the Radio Resource Control (RRC) and Non-Access Stratum (NAS) messages exchanged between the User Equipment (UE), the Radio Access Network (RAN), and the AMF. To ensure the security of the 5G core network, it is essential to address these vulnerabilities and consider the attack vectors highlighted in the Fig. 2.

The other NFVs in the 5G core do not interact directly with external entities. However, if an NFV like the AMF or UPF is compromised, it can transmit fake messages or data to these other NFVs, potentially leading to their compromise. This underscores the importance of securing all NFVs, especially those with external interfaces, to prevent cascading security issues within the network.

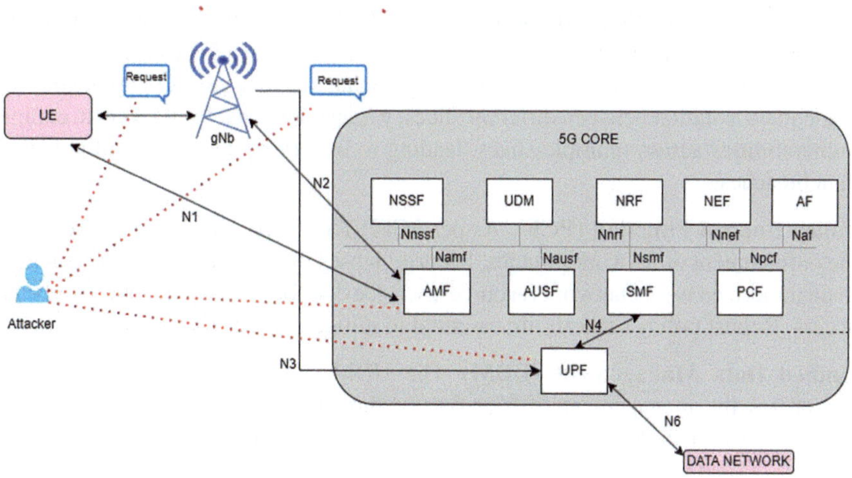

Fig. 2 Possible entry points for an attacker in 5G core

Access and Mobility Management Function (AMF) The AMF is critical in managing the registration, connection, and mobility of user equipment (UE). As per 3GPP TS 23.501, a significant concern is the AMF's requirement to interact with various network entities, including legacy systems. This interaction may necessitate the use of older protocols, which are vulnerable to known security issues. Additionally, the AMF's role in tracking user mobility can be exploited, leading to potential signaling storms or session hijacking, thereby impacting user privacy and network integrity.

User Plane Function (UPF) As per 3GPP TS 23.501, the UPF is essential for data forwarding within the network. A primary security challenge is the isolation of user data. Inadequate isolation can lead to vulnerabilities such as man-in-the-middle attacks and unauthorized data interception, compromising the integrity and confidentiality of user data.

Session Management Function (SMF) The SMF oversees the lifecycle of data sessions, including their establishment, modification, and termination. According to 3GPP TS 23.502, vulnerabilities in the SMF can arise from weak authentication processes, potentially allowing unauthorized entities to initiate or modify sessions. Robust policy enforcement is crucial to prevent unauthorized access and ensure proper session management.

Authentication Server Function (AUSF) The AUSF manages the authentication processes as outlined in 3GPP TS 33.501. Weaknesses in the authentication protocols can expose the network to replay attacks, where attackers intercept and reuse legitimate authentication messages. Ensuring robust authentication mechanisms is vital to protect against unauthorized access.

Network Slice Selection Function (NSSF) The NSSF, a key component of the 5G network slicing feature, is responsible for the allocation of UEs to the appropriate slices. According to 3GPP TS 23.501, a significant security gap is the potential for inadequate isolation between different slices, which could enable attackers to exploit vulnerabilities across multiple slices, leading to unauthorized access and potential data breaches.

Policy Control Function (PCF) As per 3GPP TS 23.503, the PCF is tasked with the enforcement of network policies. Security lapses in policy enforcement can lead to unauthorized use of network resources, service disruptions, and unauthorized data access. Robust policy controls are essential to mitigate these risks.

Unified Data Management (UDM) The UDM, defined in 3GPP TS 23.502, centralizes the management of user data within the 5G core network. Potential vulnerabilities include data breaches due to weak encryption and insufficient access controls. These vulnerabilities could result in unauthorized access to sensitive user information, raising significant privacy concerns.

Network Repository Function (NRF) As described in 3GPP TS 23.501, the NRF maintains a registry of network function profiles and facilitates their discovery. Security gaps in the NRF include the risk of unauthorized manipulation of these profiles, which could disrupt network services and allow unauthorized access. Implementing stringent access controls is necessary to prevent such security breaches.

The transition to 5G presents both opportunities and challenges in network security. Addressing the identified security gaps in 5G core network functions, as outlined in the 3GPP specifications, is crucial for maintaining the network's robustness and reliability. Continuous enhancement of security measures, in alignment with 3GPP standards, is essential to mitigate potential vulnerabilities, ensuring a secure and resilient 5G network infrastructure.

5 Safeguarding 5G Core

5.1 Secure 5G Core

The following discussions highlight the significance of protecting the 5G core network using insights from 3GPP documents, emphasizing the need for an algorithmic security framework based on a thorough risk analysis.

According to the 3GPP TS 23.501 and TS 23.502, the service-based architecture (SBA) provides a greater degree of scalability and service provisioning while concurrently raising the risk level for a number of threats. Thus, an effective security framework for such architectural complexity and threats becomes mandatory.

The 3GPP has given detailed procedures for authentication and authorization in the 5G core in Technical Specification 33.501. The underlying procedure is called 5G-AKA (Authentication and Key Agreement), which allows secure identity verification and key management for user equipment (UE) and the network. This not only authenticates the UE but also associates this authentication with the serving network for an extra layer of security against unauthorized access. Nonetheless, the ever-evolving characteristics of 5G networks require solutions beyond fixed authentication techniques; it is essential to employ an algorithmic framework that can assess the risks linked to access requests in a dynamic manner to enhance these mechanisms.

Ensuring data integrity and confidentiality is paramount in the 5G core. 3GPP's security architecture mandates the use of encryption and integrity protection for sensitive data, as specified in 3GPP TS 33.501. These measures protect data from interception and tampering during transmission. The SBA of the 5G core leverages the use of secure transport protocols such as Transport Layer Security (TLS) to ensure secure communication between network functions. However, these measures must be part of a broader security strategy that includes continuous monitoring and anomaly detection algorithms to identify and mitigate potential security breaches proactively.

One of the most innovative features of the 5G core is network slicing, which allows operators to create multiple virtual networks on the same physical infrastructure. Each slice is tailored to specific service requirements and operates independently. The 3GPP specifications highlight the importance of isolating these slices to prevent cross-slice attacks. This isolation is achieved through stringent access controls and monitoring mechanisms that ensure slices remain secure and separate from one another. Implementing algorithmic solutions that dynamically adjust these controls based on real-time threat assessments is crucial for maintaining slice integrity and preventing unauthorized access. The security of network slices is covered in more detail in Sect. 5.2.

Risk analysis is a critical component of the security framework for the 5G core network. It involves a systematic process of identifying potential threats, assessing their impact, and determining the likelihood of their occurrence. The 3GPP has provided a foundational structure for conducting risk analysis, emphasizing the importance of a proactive and adaptive approach to security.

The first step in risk analysis is the identification of potential threats to the 5G core. These threats include unauthorized access, data breaches, denial-of-service (DoS) attacks, and insider threats. The impact of these threats on the 5G core can be significant, leading to service disruption, data loss, and damage to the network's reputation. The 3GPP recommends a detailed impact assessment to understand the severity of these threats and prioritize security measures accordingly.

Estimating the likelihood of potential threats materializing is the next step in the risk analysis process. This involves analyzing the vulnerabilities of the network and the capabilities of potential attackers. By combining impact and likelihood assessments, the security framework can focus on the most significant risks and implement appropriate countermeasures. The 3GPP's security specifications suggest employing machine learning algorithms to continuously assess the threat landscape and adjust security measures in real time.

Given the complex and dynamic nature of 5G networks, security needs an algorithmic approach. This calls for developing algorithms that can independently detect and mitigate security threats in real-time. The 3GPP emphasizes that algorithms should be able to adapt to changing conditions of the network and different threat landscapes to provide a flexible and adaptive security solution.

The algorithms should be capable of adaptive threat detection, utilizing machine learning and artificial intelligence to learn from network behavior and adapt to new threats as they emerge. Upon detecting a threat, the algorithms should initiate automated responses, such as isolating affected network segments or blocking malicious traffic, to minimize the impact of an attack. Additionally, continuous monitoring and analysis of network activity can help identify patterns indicative of potential security threats, enabling early detection and prevention of attacks.

By incorporating risk analysis and the algorithmic approach to security, a framework can be developed to effectively mitigate threats and ensure the integrity and reliability of the 5G core. As 5G networks continue to evolve, ongoing research and development in security technologies will be essential to address emerging threats and maintain the trust of users and stakeholders. The insights from 3GPP documents provide a solid foundation for developing these security measures and adapting them to the ever-changing telecommunications landscape.

Figure 3 shows a real-time framework that can monitor the message flow between UE, RAN, and AMF. It looks for any discrepancies in the structure or content of the initial registration request and the PDU session establishment request. The framework can notify the AMF if disparities are found, and then AMF can decide whether to reject the request or carry out more investigation. The figure provides an overview of the contents continually examined for irregularities. This framework allows the monitoring of all RRCs(Radio Resource Control), NAS (Non-Access Stratum), and AS (Access Stratum) messages.

5.2 Secure Network Slices

Given the complexities and multi-tenant nature of 5G networks, protection of the slices within 5G Core itself becomes paramount. The 3GPP standards, notably 3GPP TS 33.501, put in place a collective framework to ensure security at each network slice level. Network slice isolation, on a basic level, is one of the fundamental security approaches required for preventing unauthorized access and data leakage across slices. Above, it includes isolation in both logical and physical separation of slices. It shall be according to Section 5.15 of 3GPP TS 33.501, which states that S-NSSAI plays an important role in ensuring that the data and functionalities are handled in conformance with the varied security requirements of each slice; hence, stringent separation among the slices is necessary.

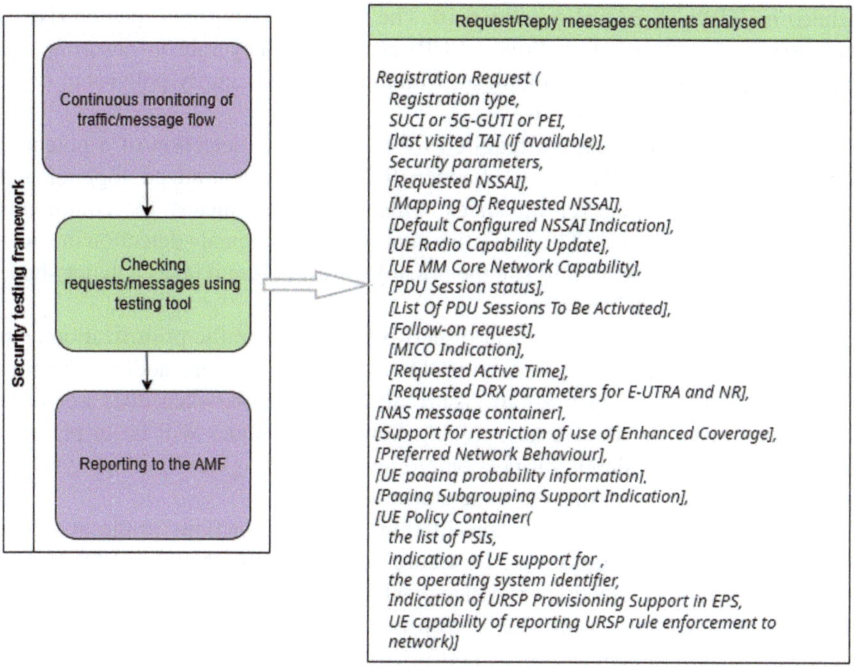

Fig. 3 Exploring message flow analysis within 5G infrastructure

Authentication and authorization processes customized for each slice introduce an additional dimension of security. As detailed in 3GPP TS 33.501 Sect. 6.1, the Authentication Server Function (AUSF) and Access and Mobility Management Function (AMF) collaborate to provide slice-specific authentication. This ensures that only authorized users can access resources within a specific slice. Here, the UDM system plays a major role in enforcing access control and managing slice-specific user subscriptions in such a way that the users will interact only with the slices they are allowed to.

Another important aspect is that each slice ensures data confidentiality and integrity. According to 3GPP TS 33.501 Sections 7.2 and 7.3, the control and user plane data shall be encrypted and integrity-protected, meaning each slice can implement different encryption keys controlled by the Key Management Function (KMF). This methodology includes the 128-NEAx and 128-NIAx algorithms that ensure that a breach of key integrity in one slice will not affect the security of other slices. Moreover, providing different key hierarchies for each slice, as described in 3GPP TS 33.501 Section 7.4, enhances it a lot by logically separating the cryptographic processes of each slice.

Security policies in the 5G Core are slice-specific, and the Policy Control Function enforces them. It may include traffic steering, firewall rules, and quality of service (QoS) requirements that cater specifically to the needs of each slice, as defined in 3GPP TS 33.501 Section 6.10. The Network Exposure Function (NEF) and Service Communication Proxy (SCP) also play a key role in ensuring any external applications that communicate with a slice fit its security policies in order to protect the integrity of the slice.

Monitoring and logging are required for the real-time detection of a potential security threat. 3GPP TS 33.501 Section 9.2 requires centralized logging and security event reporting for all slices. This provides a means for continuous monitoring of the network. This proactive approach with anomaly detection in slices gives a prompt response to mitigate the possible threat before it takes a major shape in terms of security incidents.

Mechanisms for the management of network load and traffic prioritization help protect the 5G Core against DoS and DDoS attacks. These are addressed under 3GPP TS 33.501 Section 6.5.4 to ensure an attack on one slice does not have a negative impact on the overall network. Several techniques will be in place to ensure that service availability is not compromised, including rate limiting, dynamic resource allocation, and other overload controls.

The interactions of APIs between different network functions in the 5G Core Service-Based Architecture should be secure. It states herein that 3GPP TS 33.501 Section 6.6 requires protection for API authentication, and OAuth 2.0 authentication should be used together with TLS, which is responsible for the transport of data securely. Mutual authentication of network functions is also performed to help each network function with isolation, thus protecting it from unauthorized access or tampering.

Those network slices operating across more than one PLMN require secure interconnects when roaming is involved. According to Section 8 of the 3GPP TS 33.501 specification, these types of connections should, by default, use encryption techniques at the IPsec level for data and signaling protection across different networks. User data would also be encrypted with respect to end-to-end encryption upon users roaming into other networks. It provides consistent security wherever they may be.

Therefore, ensuring conformance to 3GPP-mandated security requirements is of paramount importance for the secure operation of 5G network slices. Compliance testing, as called for by 3GPP TS 33.501, is extremely valuable in validating that all security controls, policies, and processes are effective and current. In fact, such assessment ensures the 5G Core provides the highest levels of security to protect all services delivered through network slices against emerging threats.

6 5G Enabled IoT and Related Security Challenges

The integration of 5G technology with the Internet of Things (IoT) represents a significant advancement in the realm of connected systems and smart applications.

6.1 5G Enabled IoT

According to the 3rd Generation Partnership Project (3GPP) standards, particularly 3GPP TS 23.501 and 3GPP TS 23.502, 5G provides a robust and scalable framework that enhances the capabilities of IoT beyond what was possible with previous generations of wireless technology. One of the most critical features of 5G is its capability for massive device connectivity. With support for up to 1 million devices per square kilometer, 5G networks can accommodate dense IoT ecosystems, such as those in smart cities, where numerous sensors and devices operate concurrently without compromising performance or reliability.

Another key advancement with 5G is its ultra-low latency, which can be as low as 1 millisecond. This is crucial for applications that require immediate feedback and rapid response, such as autonomous vehicles, remote surgical procedures, and industrial automation. In addition, 5G supports high data rates, with potential speeds reaching up to 10 Gbps. This high throughput is beneficial for applications that require large volumes of data transfer, such as high-definition video surveillance and real-time data analytics. The ability to handle such data-intensive applications without latency issues is a significant improvement over previous generations.

5G also introduces network slicing, which allows for the creation of multiple virtual networks within a single physical infrastructure. Each slice can be customized to meet the specific needs of different IoT applications, whether it be for enhanced security, low latency, or high data throughput.

Energy efficiency is another area where 5G makes a significant impact. The technology includes improvements in power management, such as advanced sleep modes and reduced power consumption during transmissions. These enhancements are particularly advantageous for battery-operated IoT devices, supporting longer operational lifetimes and reducing the need for frequent maintenance or battery replacement. This is especially important for remote or hard-to-reach sensors used in applications like environmental monitoring or agricultural sensing.

The impact of 5G on IoT is evident across various sectors. In smart cities, 5G enables real-time management of urban infrastructure, optimizing traffic flow, energy usage, and public safety. In industrial settings, 5G facilitates advanced manufacturing processes through real-time data exchange and automation, leading to increased efficiency and reduced downtime. Healthcare benefits from 5G-enabled IoT through improved telemedicine and remote monitoring capabilities, offering enhanced care and timely interventions. Additionally, the automotive industry leverages 5G for connected vehicles, which communicate with each other and with road infrastructure to enhance safety and traffic management.

However, the deployment of 5G for IoT is not without challenges. Security is a primary concern due to the increased number of connected devices and the critical nature of some IoT applications. Ensuring robust encryption, secure authentication, and privacy protections is essential to mitigate potential threats. Interoperability between diverse IoT devices and systems also presents a challenge, necessitating standardized protocols and frameworks to ensure seamless integration and operation. Infrastructure deployment is another significant consideration, as expanding 5G networks, especially in underserved areas, requires substantial investment and planning. Balancing the energy demands of network infrastructure with the efficiency of IoT devices is crucial for sustainable deployment.

In 5G networks, the identification and management of IoT devices are specially designed to accommodate their unique characteristics, particularly considering their often limited power and computational resources. The 5G core network is built to support Low-Power Wide Area (LPWA) IoT devices by reducing signaling overhead and optimizing resource usage, which is crucial for managing the vast number of devices typically involved in IoT deployments. For instance, in applications like smart metering, where multiple devices are deployed in a specific area, the network can employ group-based identifiers to manage these devices collectively. This group-based identification approach helps to significantly lower the signaling load and streamline the management processes, which is essential for efficiently handling large-scale IoT implementations.

6.2 *Large-scale IoT Networks*

In large-scale IoT networks, managing interoperability and security can be tricky. The 3GPP standards (TS 23.501 and TS 33.501) stress the need for consistent security practices across different devices to ensure they work well together. But this also means a bigger attack surface, where vulnerabilities in one device or protocol could potentially affect the whole network.

If an IoT device gets compromised, it can wreak havoc. It might intercept or alter data, launch DDoS attacks, or spread malware to other devices. This could disrupt services and impact network performance. To tackle these issues, 3GPP guidelines recommend secure device onboarding, segmenting the network, and keeping an eye on traffic for unusual activity. Techniques like network slicing and managing device identities help keep critical data separate and ensure that only authorized devices can connect.

By sticking to these standards and using strong security measures, the risks in large IoT networks can be better managed, keeping the system safe and running smoothly.

6.3 *Non-public 5G Networks and IoT Devices*

The private 5G networks, commonly referred to in 3GPP as nonpublic networks, become adopted to satisfy the security and performance requirements of industrial IoT applications since 5G networks are only isolated, customizable environments without the strict requirements for security that public 5G networks have. In technical specification 3GPP TS 23.501, 3GPP categorizes two main forms of

NPNs: standalone non-public networks (SNPNs) and public network-integrated non-public networks (PNI-NPNs). This kind of personalization and isolation makes NPNs a prime solution for the deployment of safe IoT systems. However, because of the diversities and scale of the devices involved in IoT, security proof has become robustly challenging, and it calls for an appropriate and flexible framework to address this challenge of security, and 3GPP takes care of it exhaustively. The security architecture for private 5G networks, as supported within the 3GPP, is founded on the underlying security mechanisms of the public 5G systems. However, it immediately raises new considerations, particularly because a whole variety of IoT devices with different capabilities and security profiles will be integrated. Key features in this architecture include mutual authentication between UE and the network, as specified in TS 33.501. This ensures that only authorized IoT devices can access the network. The AKA protocol is designed for resource-constrained light IoT devices, and with added extensions such as EAP-AKA, it supports authentication without significant overhead in computation. The security of slices could be a consideration in TS 33.210, where each slice enables independent security. This increases protection for several IoT use cases by providing an excellent layer of secure separation of services.

The heterogeneity of IoT devices is well-captured through the introduction of particular resource-constrained device-specific optimizations within the 3GPP framework. This includes smaller security contexts and scalable encryption protocols, thus helping to reduce the signaling overhead of low-power IoT communications (TS 33.501). Additionally, the use of NIDD mechanisms helps minimize complexity for devices that do not natively support IP-based communication, further enhancing security and efficiency in private 5G deployments over IoT environments. These optimizations support IoT with even mediocre capabilities to operate within the constrained security demands of the private 5G networks.

Private 5G networks, however, are also introducing new vectors of threats. Device compromise is the worst, mainly for the fact that the bulk of IoT devices may not possess mandatory security features to prevent such a breach. Compromised IoT devices may be used to release more widespread attacks, like DDoS attacks. Secondly, insider threats are also very difficult since internal teams usually operate the private network infrastructure in such environments. The threat of IoT devices and data manipulation by an insider calls for tight access controls and surveillance. Moreover, MitM attacks lead to PNI-NPN configurations where private networks connect to public networks. In such a case, the 3GPP security frameworks mitigate risks of attacks that allow safe network handovers as well as encrypted communications (TS 33.501).

To mitigate such threats, 3GPP has had to implement a range of mitigation mechanisms specifically designed for private 5G networks operating IoT. 3GPP TS 33.501 now uses end-to-end encryption across the control as well as user plane data to prevent sensitive IoT data from even being accessed if intercepted. Secure bootstrapping mechanisms defined in TS 33.220 ensure that IoT devices are securely initialized before they join the network, preventing unauthorized devices from being added. The zero-Trust security model, where each node in the network is constantly authenticated and validated, offsets the issues of insiders and unauthorized access. Continuous monitoring and anomaly detection enhance the posture of security by identifying anomalous traffic patterns or potential breaches ahead of the worst phases of the attack.

Private 5G networks do offer great opportunities for IoT applications but bring in special security challenges. The 3GPP standards totally adopt security architectures developed to address the challenges, including authentication, encryption, and security on the network slice. In more focused deployments specifically for IoT, advancements in protocol optimization ensure that light, resource-constrained devices may be securely integrated into the network. However, continuous evolving factors such as the possibility of compromise on the device, insider attacks, and interface vulnerabilities in the network call for enhancement in the security framework. A Zero-Trust model with continuous monitoring would serve as a good foundation for the long-term security of IoT systems within a private 5G environment.

6.4 IoT-Specific Identifiers

5G networks introduce specific identification mechanisms tailored to the needs of IoT devices. For example, the use of eSIM and Integrated SIM (iSIM) technologies allows IoT devices to be provisioned remotely, facilitating easier and more flexible deployment across various applications. These SIM technologies can include unique identifiers that are adapted to the specific requirements of IoT devices, such as their need for robust security and efficient management. By enabling dynamic and remote management, these identifiers ensure that IoT devices can seamlessly integrate into the 5G network while maintaining the necessary security protocols. This adaptability is particularly important in the context of IoT, where devices often need to operate reliably in diverse and evolving environments.

The integration of IoT devices into 5G networks necessitates a clear and systematic nomenclature, as defined by 3GPP standards. This structured classification is crucial for managing the diverse array of IoT devices within the 5G ecosystem, ensuring their effective operation and seamless integration.

Narrowband IoT (NB-IoT) devices are tailored for applications where low data rates, long battery life, and extensive coverage are critical. As outlined in *3GPP TS 38.300* and *3GPP TS 23.501*, NB-IoT devices operate within the 5G framework, supporting connectivity in challenging environments such as deep indoor spaces or remote areas. These devices are integral to 5G's strategy for massive IoT, facilitating applications like smart metering and environmental monitoring. The inclusion of NB-IoT in 5G demonstrates the network's capacity to support devices with specific power and coverage requirements while maintaining reliable connectivity.

Category M1 (Cat-M1) devices, also known as LTE-M, cater to IoT applications requiring moderate data rates and support for mobility and voice communication. According to *3GPP TS 38.306*, Cat-M1 devices are designed to provide more robust connectivity compared to NB-IoT, suitable for applications such as asset tracking and wearable technology. They leverage 5G features like extended Discontinuous Reception (eDRX) and Power Saving Mode (PSM) to enhance battery life, underscoring 5G's versatility in supporting diverse IoT use cases.

Massive Machine-Type Communications (mMTC) devices are pivotal to 5G's capability to handle a large number of devices simultaneously, especially in densely populated urban settings. As specified in *3GPP TS 22.261*, mMTC devices operate at low data rates but must coexist with other network services without causing interference. This category is fundamental to 5G's goal of supporting large-scale IoT applications, including smart cities and industrial automation. The classification of mMTC devices reflects 5G's emphasis on scalability and reliability, ensuring efficient performance even with millions of connected devices.

Ultra-reliable low-latency Communications (URLLC) devices are designed for high-performance IoT applications where ultra-reliability and minimal latency are essential. These devices are crucial for mission-critical uses such as autonomous vehicles and remote surgery. According to 3GPP TS 22.104 and 3GPP TS 23.501, URLLC devices must meet stringent requirements for low latency and high reliability, enabling near-instantaneous responses and exceptional dependability. This classification highlights 5G's commitment to supporting sophisticated IoT applications that require top-tier performance.

The nomenclature for User Equipment (UE) in 5G, as outlined in 3GPP TS 38.306, differs significantly from that of IoT devices. UE categories focus on defining the capabilities of smartphones, tablets, and laptops, emphasizing broad performance metrics, including maximum data rates, mobility, and support for high-bandwidth services. These categories are designed to address the general usage scenarios and performance expectations of consumer and business devices. In contrast, IoT device nomenclature is tailored to specific functional requirements and operational needs. For example, IoT device categories like Narrowband IoT (NB-IoT) and Category M1 (Cat-M1) prioritize aspects such as energy efficiency, extended coverage, and specialized data rates suited to applications like smart metering and environmental monitoring. The key differences lie in the purpose and scope of the nomenclature: UE classifications are oriented towards providing high-performance and versatile connectivity for a wide range of end-user applications, while IoT device classifications are more focused on optimizing network performance for particular use cases and ensuring efficient integration of a vast number of connected devices. This distinction reflects the different requirements and expectations for these devices within the 5G network.

In summary, the 3GPP-defined nomenclature for IoT devices in 5G is both detailed and precise, reflecting the varied needs of modern IoT applications. This classification enables 5G networks to optimize performance across a spectrum of IoT devices, from simple sensors to advanced industrial systems. In contrast, UE nomenclature addresses broader performance and usability aspects for consumer and business devices. This structured approach enhances the scalability, efficiency, and functionality of 5G networks, driving innovation and transforming interactions with the connected world.

6.5 Security Issues

For current and relevant security specifications related to Cellular IoT, it is essential to refer to the latest 3GPP technical reports and specifications. Notably, 3GPP TS 33.501 provides a detailed framework for the security architecture and procedures within the 5G system, including advanced security mechanisms tailored for IoT applications. Additionally, 3GPP TS 33.220 addresses security aspects for User Equipment (UE) in LTE networks, offering insights into security protocols and requirements that are also pertinent to IoT devices operating in LTE environments. These updated documents deliver comprehensive guidance on contemporary security frameworks and mechanisms, ensuring robust protection for modern IoT systems in line with the latest industry standards.

3GPP specifications, particularly in TS 23.501 and TS 33.501, address the unique security requirements of IoT devices within 5G networks, emphasizing ultra-low latency while ensuring robust attack detection. These standards propose lightweight cryptographic protocols that are well-suited for the resource-constrained nature of IoT devices, minimizing computational complexity and energy consumption. Additionally, 3GPP promotes the use of edge computing to perform localized security functions, such as attack detection and mitigation, thereby avoiding the delays associated with centralized processing. Network slicing, as detailed in 3GPP TS 23.501, allows IoT-specific slices to implement tailored security measures that align with both the low-latency and scalability demands of IoT deployments, ensuring security is maintained without introducing significant communication delays.

In the context of 5G IoT networks, addressing specific security threats while ensuring minimal latency and high performance is crucial. According to 3GPP standards (TS 33.501), several attack vectors are of particular concern:

6.5.1 Potential IoT Threats

DDoS Attacks Distributed Denial of Service (DDoS) attacks overwhelm IoT devices or networks with excessive traffic, causing service disruptions or outages. Attackers exploit the limited resources of IoT devices to generate traffic that can saturate network bandwidth or exhaust device processing capabilities. Network slicing and edge computing, as outlined in 3GPP TS 23.501, help mitigate these attacks by isolating IoT traffic and filtering malicious traffic locally before it impacts core network functions.

Spoofing Attacks Spoofing attacks involve malicious actors impersonating legitimate IoT devices to gain unauthorized network access. By mimicking valid devices, attackers can manipulate data, intercept communications, or inject malicious payloads. To counteract this, 3GPP TS 33.501 specifies the use of lightweight cryptographic protocols and mutual authentication mechanisms to ensure that only authorized devices can access the network and communicate securely.

Delay Attacks Delay attacks target time-sensitive IoT applications by introducing artificial latency, disrupting applications such as autonomous driving or industrial control systems that rely on timely data transmission. The 3GPP framework addresses this through network slicing and Quality of Service (QoS) management, which prioritize IoT traffic and ensure minimal delay. Edge computing also helps by processing data closer to its source, reducing potential latency impacts.

ProSe Communication Attacks Proximity Services (ProSe) allow direct device-to-device communication without routing through the core network, but this mode is vulnerable to eavesdropping, unauthorized access, and man-in-the-middle attacks. 3GPP TS 33.303 provides solutions such as device-level authentication and encryption to secure ProSe communications, ensuring that only authorized devices can participate in direct exchanges.

Mutable Attacks Mutable attacks involve intercepting and altering data transmitted between IoT devices, compromising data integrity. Attackers may modify data to disrupt operations, falsify information, or inject malicious commands. 3GPP TS 33.501 mandates robust integrity protection mechanisms, including cryptographic hashing and digital signatures, to detect and prevent data tampering, thus preserving the reliability of IoT communications.

Overall, while the 3GPP standards offer a robust foundation for securing IoT networks, ongoing advancements in edge computing, network slicing, and cryptographic protocols are essential to effectively address these evolving threats. These strategies ensure that security measures are scalable and minimally disruptive, maintaining the performance requirements of modern IoT applications.

6.6 Mitigation Techniques

One of the more significant security challenges from IoT is unauthorized access to those devices. As discussed in 3GPP TS 33.501 , strong authentication and access control capabilities will be an important feature in preventing any unauthorized parties from controlling those IoT devices. This would widely help to prevent attacks from spam, spoofing, and phishing, which compromise not only the functionality of the devices but the overall security on the network.

Several IoT devices crowded in the 5G network have opened the attack surface, which makes it more probable that the attack will be spread. 3GPP TS 23.501 states that IoT devices stand a chance of being threatened with DDoS attacks or might be exploited as entry points for further intrusions into the network. Accordingly, adequate security measures must be in place for the mitigatation of these risks and protect the network against disturbances that could lead to a breakdown of such critical services and applications. The overall reliability and stability of the 5G network is therefore guaranteed if the IoT devices are properly secured.

The next vital feature of IoT device security is compliance with regulatory and industry standards. 3GPP TS 33.501 and 3GPP TS 33.602 determine that IoT devices should adhere to some standard security procedures and guidelines. Thus, compliance is quite important legally and regulation-wise and to provide comfort for users and stakeholders. This compliance ensures that IoT devices will adhere to the prevalent security needs and may safeguard sensitive information based on the regulations implemented by the concerned industries.

With the increase in mission-critical applications that require deployment of 5G IoT devices, security and reliability have become more important. TS 22.261 of 3GPP states that applications like autonomous vehicles, remote surgery, and industrial automation require strong security measures because they might affect public safety and operational continuity. Thus, non-securing of these devices may lead to serious consequences such as accidents, equipment failure, or disruption of essential services. These critical applications thus necessitate strong security measurements for safe and reliable operation.

This means that the nature of threats to the system against cyberattacks evolves at a very rapid rate. Consequently, there is always a permanent need for security measures to be adapted and properly updated to ensure that all is well. Here, IoT devices are protected from emerging threats that could target vulnerabilities within the network through 3GPP TS 33.501. Continuous updates and developments in regard to security protocols are needed in dealing with such evolving threats as per the use of IoT devices, and for them to be resilient against forms of cyber attacks that are of sophisticated kinds.

Secure 5G IoT devices are imperative to ensure the security of sensitive data, maintain compliance with regulations, support critical applications, and ultimately safeguard against emerging threats. This structure of specifications from 3GPP underlines the role and further reasoning for having a holistic and proactive approach to IoT security within the context of the 5G ecosystem.

7 Open Source 5G Network Simulations and Tools

Several open-source projects for establishing, evaluating, and simulating 5G networks have been catalyzed by the emergence of 5G technology. The most salient open-source projects are free5GC, VeT5G, Open5GS, and UERANSIM. Each has different tools and functionalities to help build a 5G ecosystem. Scholars and developers utilize the projects written in various programming languages to emulate 5G network environments.

Free5GC [6] is an open-source project aimed at implementing the 5G core network per the standard defined by 3GPP. Free5GC provides a full-suite core network function including AMF, SMF, and UPF, which allows researchers and developers to explore and test the security of 5G core operations. Being implemented in Go, Free5GC is the best 5G core network simulation tool.

VeT5G[18] is another open-source virtualization and testing for 5G core networks. It is designed as an open-source project that offers an extensive system with flexibility for virtualizing and testing parts involved in 5G networks. Built using Python and C++, VeT5G makes it possible to realize virtualized network functions capable of methodically testing 5G networks under various scenarios. Its capacity to integrate into existing tools and platforms makes it a powerful enabler for researchers focused on the verification and optimization of 5G technologies within a cloud-centric, scalable framework.

Open5GS[15] represents a further advance in open-source projects, providing a complete, modular implementation of the 5G core network components. Written in C, Open5GS will provide flexibility and seamless integration with other elements of the network, therefore rendering it appropriate for both investigative studies and real-world applications. Its modular architecture provides users with the choice to customize and deploy partial core network functionalities as desired, which enables extensive testing and interoperability options with various diverse devices and simulators.

UERANSIM[16] is an open-source UE and RAN simulator intended to simulate the behavior of 5G devices in a network environment. The code for UERANSIM is in C++. Testing the interaction of 5G UEs and RANs with core networks is mostly done with the help of UERANSIM. It allows for detailed protocol testing, including registration, connection management, and data transfer procedures, making it an essential tool for validating the performance and reliability of 5G networks in a controlled, simulated environment.

8 Summary

The chapter explores the significant changes in the telecommunications sector, highlighting the 5G core, its security challenges, and its application in IoT. The introduction of SDN and NFV in the 5G core, along with the abstract concept of network slicing, is covered in detail. A comprehensive literature review identifies the possible 5G core security issues alongside mitigation techniques. Additionally, we aim to make 3GPP documents familiar to readers, which serve as the bible of specifications and requirements in 5G. The integration of IoT with 5G is explored, highlighting not only its transformative potential but also the critical security considerations required to safeguard connected ecosystems. This chapter provides an excellent starting point for beginners in the 5G core and may offer novel viewpoints to academics and professionals.

References

1. 3rd Generation Partnership Project (3GPP): Technical specification (ts) or technical report (tr), 3GPP (2023). Available at https://www.3gpp.org/
2. Abood, M.J., Abdul-Majeed, G.H.: Classification of network slicing threats based on slicing enablers: a survey. Int. J. Intell. Netw. **4**, 103–112 (2023). https://doi.org/10.1016/j.ijin.2023.04.002

3. Akon, M., Yang, T., Dong, Y., Hussain, S.R.: Formal analysis of access control mechanism of 5G core network. In: Proceedings of the 2023 ACM SIGSAC Conference on Computer and Communications Security (CCS), pp. 666–680. ACM (2023). https://doi.org/10.1145/3576915.3623113
4. Borsatti, D., Grasselli, C., Contoli, C., Micciullo, L., Spinacci, L., Settembre, M., Cerroni, W., Callegati, F.: Mission critical communications support with 5G and network slicing. IEEE Trans. Netw. Service Manag. **20**(1), 1–12 (2023). https://doi.org/10.1109/TNSM.2023.3239342
5. Chlosta, M., Rupprecht, D.: 5G SUCI-catchers: still catching them all? In: Proceedings of the 2021 ACM Conference on Security and Privacy in Wireless and Mobile Networks (WiSec), pp. 148–159. ACM (2021). https://doi.org/10.1145/3448300.3468272
6. Free5gc: An open source 5g core network. https://www.free5gc.org/ (2023). Accessed Oct 5, 2023
7. Abdul Ghaffar, A.A., Mahmoud, A., Sheltami, T., et al.: A survey on software-defined networking-based 5g mobile core architectures. Arab. J. Sci. Eng. 2313–2330 (2023). https://doi.org/10.1007/s13369-022-07183-9
8. Gomez, G.P., Batalla, J.M., Miche, Y., Holtmanns, S., Mavromoustakis, C.X., Mastorakis, G., Haider, N.: Security policies definition and enforcement utilizing policy control function framework in 5G. Comput. Commun. **177**, 1–13 (2021). https://doi.org/10.1016/j.comcom.2021.06.014
9. Hoq, M.N., Yao, J.W., Majumdar, S., Suarez, L., Wang, L., Boukhtouta, A., Pourzandi, M.: Evaluating the security posture of 5G networks by combining state auditing and event monitoring. In: Computer Security – ESORICS 2023, pp. 418–437. Springer (2023). https://doi.org/10.1007/978-3-031-51476-0_20
10. Kabir, H., Mohsin, M.H.B., Kantola, R.: Implementing a security policy management for 5G customer edge nodes. In: 2020 IEEE/IFIP Network Operations and Management Symposium, pp. 1–9. IEEE (2020). https://doi.org/10.1109/NOMS47738.2020.9110380
11. Kholidy, H.A., Karam, A., Sidoran, J.L., Rahman, M.A.: 5G core security in edge networks: a vulnerability assessment approach. In: 2021 IEEE Symposium on Computers and Communications (ISCC), pp. 259–266. IEEE (2021). https://doi.org/10.1109/ISCC53001.2021.9631531
12. Kuo, C.T., Chen, H.Y., Lin, T.N.: RAIN: risk assessment framework based on an interdependent-input propagation network for a 5G network. In: 2021 IEEE Symposium on Computers and Communications (ISCC), pp. 117–124. IEEE (2021). https://doi.org/10.1109/ISCC53001.2021.9631531
13. Mamushiane, L., Lysko, A.A., Makhosa, T., Mwangama, J.: Towards stress testing Open5GS core (UPF node) on a 5G standalone testbed. In: 2023 IEEE AFRICON, pp. 1–6. IEEE (2023). https://doi.org/10.1109/AFRICON55834.2023.10199397
14. Olimid, R.F., Nencioni, G.: 5G network slicing: a security overview. IEEE Access **8**, 153720–153733 (2020). https://doi.org/10.1109/ACCESS.2020.3018391
15. Open5gs: A free and open source 5g/4g mobile core network. https://open5gs.org/ (2023). Accessed Oct 5, 2023
16. Ueransim: Open source 5g ue and ran simulator. https://github.com/aligungr/UERANSIM (2023). Accessed Oct 5, 2023
17. Varadharajan, V., Tupakula, U., Karmakar, K.K.: Techniques for securing 5G network services from attacks. In: 2021 IEEE 20th International Conference on Trust, Security and Privacy in Computing and Communications (TrustCom), pp. 18–26. IEEE (2021). https://doi.org/10.1109/TrustCom53373.2021.00015
18. Vet5g: Virtualized and extensible testbed for 5g. https://vet5g.com/ (2023). Accessed Oct 5, 2023
19. Wehbe, N., Alameddine, H.A., Pourzandi, M., Bou-Harb, E., Assi, C.: A security assessment of HTTP/2 usage in 5G service-based architecture. IEEE Commun. Mag. **61**(1), 124–130 (2023). https://doi.org/10.1109/MCOM.001.2200751

20. Wijethilaka, S., Liyanage, M.: Survey on network slicing for internet of things realization in 5G networks. IEEE Commun. Surv. Tutor. **23**(2), 957–994 (2021). https://doi.org/10.1109/COMST.2021.3065740
21. Wijethilaka, S., Liyanage, M.: The role of security orchestrator in network slicing for future networks. J. Commun. Netw. **25**(3), 240–253 (2023). https://doi.org/10.1109/JCN.2023.0011

Part II
Advances in Internet of Drones (IoD) Security

Towards Resilient Internet of Drones: A Systematic Survey on Authentication and GPS Spoofing Countermeasures

Aiswarya S. Nair and Sabu M. Thampi

1 Introduction

Drones have transcended their traditional military uses and have become a common sight in our skies, propelled by technological advancements in hardware, software, and communications. These UAVs are now integral to numerous sectors, facilitating everything from package deliveries to breathtaking aerial photography, signaling a transformative shift in both industry and academia. UAVs serve multiple roles, including as network gateways, base stations, relay nodes, and in UAV-assisted ad-hoc networks [64, 111].

The functionality of drones has significantly expanded, leading to the innovative development known as the Internet of Drones (IoD). This network links multiple drones, creating a synergistic system capable of executing sophisticated tasks with enhanced efficiency and extensive reach. Initiated by Michael Müller and elaborated upon by Bekmezci [19], the IoD provides a considerable improvement over solitary drone operations by boosting operational efficiency, reliability, and cost-effectiveness, while also extending coverage and minimizing both individual drone workload and system failure rates. Common configurations in drone networks include star and mesh topologies. In a star topology, also known as a centralized

A. S. Nair (✉)
Indian Institute of Information Technology and Management- Kerala (IIITM-K), Trivandrum, Kerala, India

Connected Systems and Intelligence Lab, School of Computer Science & Engineering, Digital University Kerala, Trivandrum, Kerala, India
e-mail: aiswarya.res19@iiitmk.ac.in

S. M. Thampi
Connected Systems and Intelligence Lab, School of Computer Science & Engineering, Digital University Kerala, Trivandrum, Kerala, India
e-mail: sabu.thampi@duk.ac.in

S. M. Thampi et al. (eds.), *Securing the Connected World*,
https://doi.org/10.1007/978-3-031-82826-3_9

architecture, each drone communicates directly with a central ground station, ensuring direct line of sight connectivity. Meanwhile, the mesh topology or decentralized architecture involves drones communicating among themselves, with a master drone maintaining line of sight with the ground station and coordinating the network's broader communications.

A typical IoD architecture consists of drones that are deployed in clusters to monitor different road segments, reporting traffic conditions back to a central Ground Control Station (GCS). The GCS uses blockchain for secure data management and employs cloud services for efficient data processing and storage. The integration of 5G technology provides the drones with high-speed cellular connectivity [41], facilitating the real-time transmission of data. The architecture is designed to allow user interaction, enabling individuals or intelligent devices to access the data collected by drones for immediate insights into traffic conditions.

While the IoD offers remarkable capabilities, it also presents unique security challenges. Operating in the expansive, unbounded aerial environment, drones are susceptible to traditional cyber threats such as eavesdropping, man-in-the-middle, replay, tampering, Denial-of-Service (DoS) attacks, and GPS spoofing. These vulnerabilities are compounded by the inherent limitations of drones, including restricted battery life, limited processing power, and minimal storage capacity, making it challenging to implement comprehensive security measures.

To effectively secure the IoD and harness its full potential, it is crucial to develop security systems that are both robust and lightweight. This entails deploying a variety of security solutions designed to protect against specific threats. Advanced encryption methods, strong authentication and authorization protocols, and intrusion detection and prevention systems, vulnerability analysis techniques, localisation and privacy are essential.

Reliable verification of each drone's identity is essential, accomplished through advanced authentication protocols that prevent unauthorized access. These protocols use cryptographic methods to ensure that a drone's commands and data are accessible only to verified users or devices. Techniques such as Physical Unclonable Functions (PUF), Trusted Platform Modules (TPM), Radio Frequency Identification (RFID), hashing algorithms, Elliptic Curve Cryptography (ECC), and Public Key Infrastructure (PKI) enhance IoD security by using unique physical device characteristics, integrating cryptographic keys, and providing effective encryption methods, respectively.

Global Positioning System (GPS) signals play a pivotal role in the precise navigation of drones. GPS signals are unencrypted for civilian and commercial applications [52]. This lack of encryption and low signal power of GPS signals (around -130dBm) makes it vulnerable to GPS spoofing [71]. GPS spoofing involves an attacker altering the GPS coordinates and sending false navigation data with a signal of higher strength than the original signal to deceive the drone GPS receiver [8]. This manipulation is a highly threatening cyber attack within drone networks, and its consequences can be severe. It can result in drone hijacking, unauthorized access to sensitive areas, disruption in airspace leading to collisions between drones, fatalities, and ultimately mission failure. To counteract GPS spoofing, various defensive measures are employed. Multi-sensor fusion approaches are used, which combine GPS data with other sensor inputs to confirm location accuracy and identify any discrepancies that could indicate spoofing. Machine learning algorithms are applied to detect unusual patterns in navigation data, suggesting a possible GPS spoofing attack.

Both authentication and GPS spoofing are key challenges within the IoD that demand vigilant solutions to maintain the integrity and functionality of drone operations. Our survey focuses on these areas, evaluating the most effective strategies to mitigate risks associated with unauthorized access and navigational interference. This study aims to contribute to developing more secure and resilient IoD systems

2 The Landscape of IoD Security

Drones are now equipped with sophisticated navigation, communication, and payload systems, making them potent tools for a wide range of applications. IoD introduces unique security challenges due to the inherent characteristics of drones, including their compact size, limited resources, and wireless connectivity. These challenges are compounded by the dynamic nature of drone networks and the increasing deployment of drones in various sectors.

Their increasing accessibility and expanding capabilities have heightened the importance of securing these systems from unauthorized access and misuse. Privacy and data security are critical concerns, as drones equipped with cameras and sensors can gather extensive amounts of data. Physical security of drones also poses a challenge, as drones can be captured and reverse-engineered, providing adversaries with valuable technology or sensitive information.

2.1 Overview of IoD Vulnerabilities and Attacks

The increasing ubiquity of drones in our skies emphasises the critical need for robust and lightweight security measures. Drones are pivotal in supporting national defense, safeguarding privacy, and enhancing public safety, making the integrity, confidentiality, and availability of drone operations indispensable. This section highlights the importance of securing these aerial assets against diverse cyber threats, ensuring that sensitive information remains confidential and that control over these assets is shielded from adversarial interference.

IoD networks face various vulnerabilities that create attack surfaces, weakening the overall security framework. If exploited by attackers, these vulnerabilities can disrupt the security and integrity of IoD systems, leading to consequences like the loss of sensitive data, violations of privacy, interruptions to critical services, and even physical damage. Several key vulnerabilities include the susceptibility

Fig. 1 Vulnerabilities in IoD

of wireless communications to eavesdropping, jamming, and spoofing attacks, the physical accessibility of drones in the air making them prone to theft or tampering, and the dynamic nature of drone network topologies that complicates secure connections and access control. Several key vulnerabilities within IoD are detailed below and shown in Fig. 1:

1. Wireless Connectivity: Drone communication mostly relies on Wi-Fi or other wireless protocols susceptible to eavesdropping, jamming, and spoofing attacks if not adequately secured. Hence, implementing strong encryption and authentication protocols is crucial.
2. Physical Availability: Unlike ground-based networks, drones are physically accessible in the air, making them vulnerable to theft, tampering, or hijacking. Physical security measures need to be considered.
3. Dynamic Network Topology: The constant movement of drones creates a dynamic network topology. This dynamism presents challenges in maintaining secure connections and preventing unauthorized access. Secure routing protocols and dynamic authentication mechanisms are essential to address this issue.
4. Fleet Communication: Communication within a drone fleet can introduce vulnerabilities if not properly secured. Malicious actors could infiltrate the network and disrupt communication or inject false commands. Secure communication protocols and access control mechanisms are necessary to mitigate these risks.
5. Unencrypted GPS Data: Relying on unencrypted GPS data exposes drones to spoofing attacks that could lead to loss of control. Implementing robust GPS encryption protocols is essential to mitigate such problems.
6. Limited Resources: Drones have limited processing power, battery life, and memory. Security solutions need to be lightweight and efficient to minimize

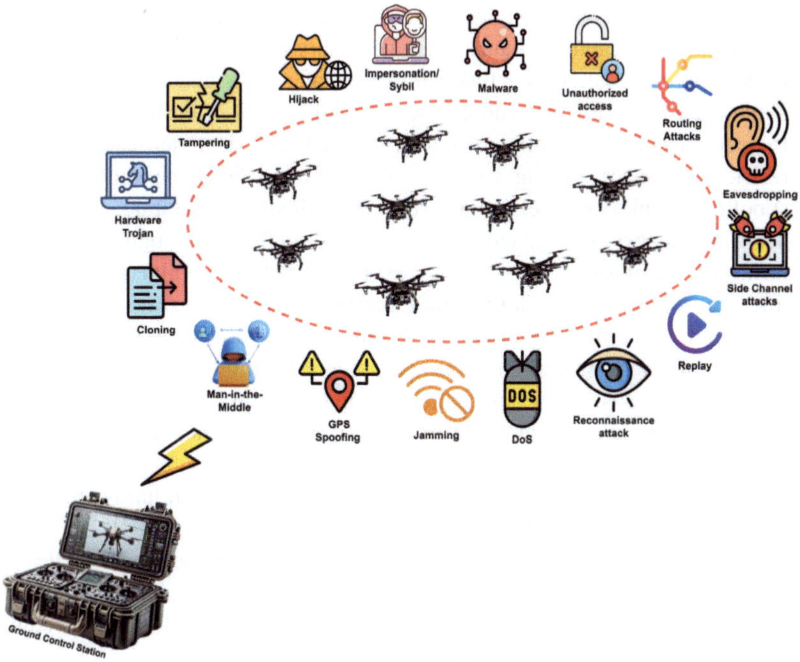

Fig. 2 Some of the attacks in IoD

resource consumption while offering strong protection. Lightweight encryption algorithms and efficient authentication mechanisms are crucial considerations.

7. Drone Hardware Vulnerabilities: Security vulnerabilities in the hardware components of drones themselves can be exploited by attackers.

The common attacks in IoD are detailed below and shown in Fig. 2:

1. Eavesdropping: Attackers can intercept sensitive data transmitted between drones or between drones and the ground control station. This stolen information could include flight paths, sensor data, video footage, or even confidential communication. Strong encryption protocols are essential to safeguard sensitive data in transit.
2. Denial-of-Service (DoS) Attacks: By flooding the network with fake traffic, attackers can overwhelm the system and disrupt legitimate communication. This can render drones inoperable at critical moments, causing accidents or hindering emergency response efforts. Robust network security measures and Intrusion Detection/Prevention Systems (IDS/IPS) are crucial to identify and mitigate DoS attacks.
3. Man-in-the-Middle (MitM) Attacks: In a MitM attack, attackers position themselves between the drone and the control station, intercepting and manipulating communication. This could allow them to steal data, issue false commands to

the drone, or even take complete control. Secure communication protocols with robust authentication mechanisms are necessary to prevent MitM attacks.

4. GPS Spoofing: Malicious actors can manipulate GPS signals to deceive drones about their location. This can be used to take control of drones, causing them to veer off course or even crash. The spoofed GPS data can lead drones into restricted airspace, posing a safety hazard. Robust GPS encryption and anti-spoofing techniques are essential to defend against GPS spoofing.
5. Malware Attacks: Drones can be infected with malware through various methods, such as physical access or by exploiting software vulnerabilities. Once infected, malware can disrupt drone operations, steal sensitive data, or even allow remote control by attackers. Secure coding practices, regular security updates, and anti-malware software are essential to mitigate malware threats.
6. Hardware Trojans: These are malicious modifications made during the manufacturing process of drone hardware components. Extremely difficult to detect, hardware trojans can provide attackers with a persistent foothold within the drone system. Rigorous supply chain security measures and hardware security audits are necessary to address this emerging threat.
7. Physical attack: This includes tampering the hardware of the drone and destroying the parts and rendering useless. Due to its physical availability in the air, drones can be hijacked or shot down. To make the system fail safe, it is required that no sensitive data is stored on drones.
8. Impersonation/Sybil attack: In this attack, an attacker impersonates or duplicates a drone and pretends to be legitimate drone.
9. Unauthorised access: Attacker may try to access the sensitive data that is securely stored.
10. Side channel attacks: It is a passive attack where the attacker monitors the side channels such as electromagnetic radiation, power, time and acoustic signals, to reveal the secret key or any other sensitive data.
11. Replay: In this attack, the attacker tries to replay the messages sent by the drone or GCS at a later time. This disrupts the communication process and is the authentication is not proper, the party receiving the message may respond to it thinking it is from a legitimate entity. Use of timestamps will help in preventing such attacks.
12. Reconnaissance attack: Through social engineering, and other automated tools, attacker gains information about the IoD such as IP address.
13. Jamming: The attacker tries to jam/flood the network with data. As the drones are resource constraint, this attack will lead to draining the drone battery, available memory and disrupts the overall operation.
14. Routing attack: In this type of attack, the data packets sent from the drone are captured by the attacker, leading to grey hole and black hole attacks. This disrupts the overall operation of the network.
15. Cloning attack: The attacker tries to clone the hardware of the drone and tries to duplicate it. The use of hardware fingerprints will eliminate this attack.

Drones are becoming more integral to our defense and civilian sectors, making the need for strong security measures crucial. The vulnerabilities present within IoD networks, if left unaddressed, have the potential to cause widespread damage, from compromising sensitive data to endangering human lives. It is imperative to develop new strategies to protect against these vulnerabilities to defend against immediate threats and future challenges, to ensure the safe and beneficial integration of drones into society's fabric.

2.2 Importance of IoD Security

Incidents like the SkyGrabber event, where unencrypted drone feeds were intercepted, and the hijacking of the RQ-170 drone due to GPS vulnerabilities, highlight the critical need for enhanced UAV security measures [129]. Over the past decade, the increase in drone incidents has highlighted the growing need for better safety protocols and regulatory frameworks. By 2015, the widespread use of drones in recreational and commercial sectors led to a notable increase in incidents, including privacy breaches, unauthorized flights near restricted areas, and minor collisions. From 2019 to 2021, India saw a markable rise in drone-related incidents due to the expanding drone market and the absence of stringent regulations. The most concerning trend appeared in 2023, with a 60% increase in drone-related incidents compared to the previous year. This sharp rise emphasized the urgent need for improved safety measures and robust regulatory frameworks. Incidents during this time ranged from minor collisions to severe cases involving critical infrastructure and public safety. This escalation underscores the importance of continuous efforts to develop and implement effective measures to mitigate the risks associated with drone operations.

The evolution of IoD security research has identified several core requirements essential for creating a resilient network, as shown in Fig. 3. Among these, confidentiality, integrity, and availability are fundamental. Confidentiality ensures that sensitive information transmitted between drones and control stations remains protected, using encryption and secure communication protocols to safeguard against eavesdropping and data breaches. Integrity preserves the accuracy and consistency of data during transmission, preventing operational failures due to corrupted information. Availability maintains the uninterrupted operation of drone networks, especially during critical missions, by implementing measures to prevent and mitigate DoS attacks.

Vulnerability analysis plays a pivotal role in identifying threats and assessing the robustness of IoD systems. Choi et al. [29] analyze IoD vulnerabilities in GPS jamming, ciphertext hacking, malware infection, and information theft. The vulnerability of the micro-air-vehicle communication (MAVLink) protocol, a common communication protocol for GCS-based UAVs, is analyzed by Kwon et al. [73]. Sharma et al. [110] proposed a Petri Net model based on security policies for

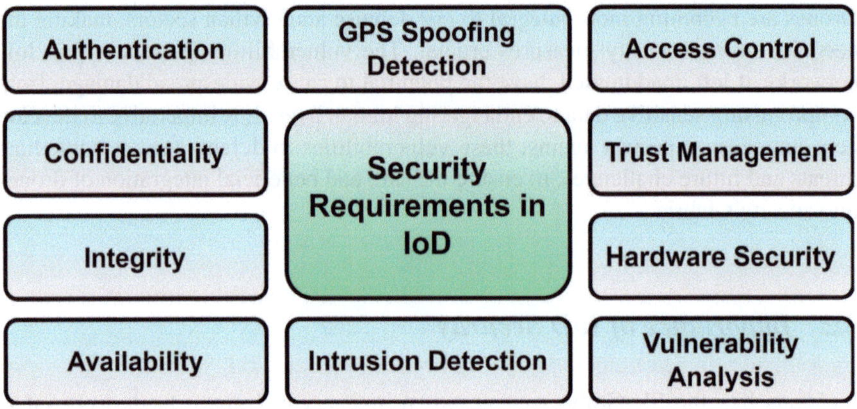

Fig. 3 Security requirements in IoD

behavior analysis and vulnerability analysis in a drone-enabled Industrial Internet of Things (IIoT) scenario.

Authentication is a cornerstone of IoD security, ensuring that only verified drones and operators can access the network, thereby preventing unauthorized entities from interfering with operations. This is crucial to maintain the integrity and safety of drone missions, especially in sensitive applications such as surveillance or delivery. Access to specific resources can be granted based on access control levels. A certificate-based access control was proposed by Chaudhry et al. [25], while Bera et al. [21] proposed a blockchain-based access control mechanism for IoD.

Evaluating the trustworthiness of drones is a vital aspect of managing their reliability within IoD, that relies on their historical communication behavior. The trustworthiness assessment hinges on a comprehensive analysis of a drone's historical communication and operational behavior, which is critical for predicting its future actions and determining whether it can be classified as reliable or adversarial. This trust assessment is not a static process but rather a dynamic evaluation that evolves as new data is collected and analyzed over time. Trust management systems within the IoD framework must address several technical challenges, including the heterogeneity of drone types, varying communication protocols, and the potential for malicious attacks that could compromise the network. Various methodologies have emerged for trust-based routing, employing techniques such as fuzzy logic, Bayesian networks, game theory and probability models. Petri nets and Markov chains are utilized to model and analyze the state transitions of drones within the network. Blockchain (BC) introduces a decentralized and tamper-resistant method for storing and verifying trust-related information, ensuring that trust data is immutable and verifiable across the IoD network. Researchers like Barka et al. [18], Singh et al. [113], and Barka et al. [17] have made significant contributions to developing drone trust models and management strategies.

The importance of intrusion detection and prevention cannot be overstated when it comes to safeguarding networks from attacks. These attacks may stem from external adversaries or insiders who have bypassed existing security protocols. IDS encompasses both host-based and network-based detection strategies. Host-based IDS focus on detecting irregularities within system logs and are effective in detecting insider threats or attacks that have already penetrated the network perimeter. Network-based IDS monitor traffic for any signs of unusual behavior to oversee the flow of traffic across the network, scanning for patterns or behaviors that deviate from the norm. This helps in identifying unauthorized access attempts. IDS can be categorized based on their detection techniques. Signature-based IDS rely on a pre-defined database of known threat signatures but they are limited in their ability to detect new, unknown threats. Anomaly-based IDS focus on identifying deviations from established behavioral patterns by using machine learning and statistical analysis and can detect previously unknown threats. In IoD, IDS plays a crucial role in analyzing data flows and can be implemented in either GCS or on the drone themselves. Current methodologies for IoD IDS include behavior rule-based approaches, deep learning based approaches [13], BC based [97], Q-learning [146], and federated learning [77].

Securing the routing of data in UAV networks is a complex task that involves selecting paths for data packets, which can be done through single-path or multi-path routing strategies. Single-path routing identifies a single optimal route, while multi-path routing finds multiple routes to ensure reliable data transmission. The dynamic and highly mobile nature of UAV networks adds significant complexity to this task. Various protocols have been developed for the IoD, including static, proactive, reactive, hybrid, geographic, and hierarchical routing. Malhotra et al. [80] and Arafat et al. [10] have provided extensive surveys on these protocols, detailing their advantages and limitations.

Ensuring hardware security is critical for protecting both drone and ground station equipment from malicious software and hardware attacks. Robust security measures help maintain system integrity even if a device is physically compromised. Key techniques involve the use of TPM, hardware security modules, and PUFs for secure key management and random number generation. Singh et al. [114] have explored the application of TPM in drones, highlighting its role in enhancing hardware security.

Drones depend heavily on GPS signals for localization, but due to their low power and unencrypted nature, these signals are susceptible to spoofing by attackers. Various levels of GPS spoofing, ranging from simple to severe, are countered by detection strategies employing on-board sensors [37, 49, 87], signal processing techniques [94, 132], and machine learning approaches [1, 81, 85, 148].

Among all security requirements, authentication and GPS spoofing detection and mitigation stand out as the most critical. Authentication serves as the foundation for IoD security, especially with the rising threat from attackers and unauthorized users attempting to access network secrets. Given the critical nature of these issues, this survey reviews existing techniques in authentication and GPS spoofing detection and mitigation within the IoD context. The goal is to enhance IoD security and ensure the safe integration of drones into various critical applications. This chapter systematically analyzes and compares current methodologies to identify gaps and propose improvements, ultimately aiming to strengthen IoD security. The survey provides a comprehensive overview, highlighting the strengths and weaknesses of existing approaches and exploring innovative solutions to ensure secure and reliable drone operations in critical applications. The findings will contribute to advancing the field by offering insights into effective strategies for robust drone security.

2.3 Impact of the Problem

Drones are frequently deployed in environments where security is essential, such as urban areas, critical infrastructure, and regulated airspaces. It is vital to implement robust authentication protocols to prevent unauthorized access and manipulation, which might lead to accidents, unauthorized data collection, and possible threats to both people and infrastructures. Effective authentication between drones, as well as between drones and GCS, is crucial for maintaining secure communication channels and operational integrity. Inadequate drone-to-drone authentication mechanisms increase the risk of unauthorized drones infiltrating a network, leading to data theft or malicious interference with operations. Similarly, weak drone-to-GCS authentication could allow unauthorized access to control systems, leading to manipulation of drone behavior. These security gaps disrupt operations and pose major risks to physical safety, in densely populated or sensitive areas.

Drones now operate across various domains and organizations, making strong cross-domain authentication crucial. Without secure mechanisms to verify the legitimacy of drones as they move between different operational zones, there is a heightened risk of security breaches, in collaborative or multi-agency operations. With advancements in quantum computing, existing cryptographic solutions will become obsolete. The absence of quantum secure authentication methods exposes drone networks to future threats, allowing adversaries to exploit emerging technologies to bypass traditional security measures. Transitioning to quantum-resistant algorithms is essential to safeguard sensitive data and secure communications against future quantum threats.

GPS spoofing presents one of the most immediate and disruptive threats to drone operations. This form of attack involves broadcasting false GPS signals to drones, misleading them about their actual location. The consequences of GPS spoofing range from minor disruptions in service delivery to severe threats such as collision, unauthorized entry into restricted airspace, or interference in critical operations like disaster response or environmental monitoring. Effective detection and mitigation techniques for GPS spoofing are essential to prevent these disastrous outcomes.

The failure to address these security challenges undermines the operational efficacy of drones and affects economic stability, national security, and public safety. Economically, security breaches can lead to operational downtime, increased costs due to loss of assets or information, and reduced trust among stakeholders. From a national security perspective, vulnerabilities in drone operations can be exploited to compromise sensitive information or disrupt critical infrastructure. Public safety is directly impacted in scenarios where drones are used in populated areas or for emergency responses, where failure to securely operate can lead to accidents or failures in critical missions. Thus, the development of advanced, quantum-resistant authentication systems and robust GPS spoofing countermeasures is essential for the sustainable growth of drone technologies in an increasingly connected and technologically sophisticated world.

2.4 *Key Developments and Discoveries*

Developments such as blockchain for secure, tamper-proof data logging and AI-driven attack detection systems have become crucial in protecting drone networks against a myriad of threats. The key technologies used in IoD security are shown in Fig. 4 and detailed below:

1. Blockchain: Blockchain technology has been proposed as a solution for securing UAV communication and data integrity. The decentralized and immutable nature of blockchain can enhance trust and security in UAV operations.
2. Software-Defined Networking (SDN): SDN is a technology that enhances network management and security by enabling programmability and providing visibility into the network. It allows centralized control through a controller and security policies, access control, and threat detection can be managed from a

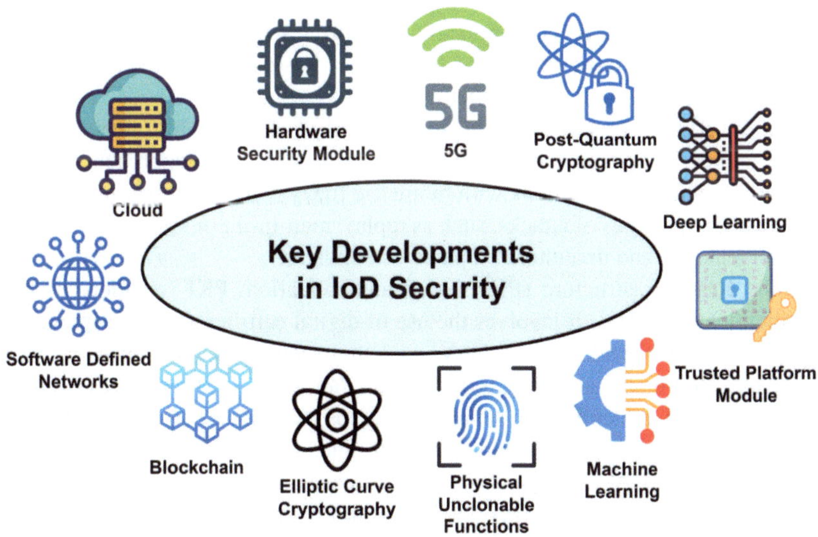

Fig. 4 Key developments and discoveries

single point. To address security challenges and cyber-attacks in SDN-enabled UAV networks, solutions were proposed in [82].

3. 5G Technology: The advent of 5G technology is expected to revolutionize UAV communications by providing high-speed, low-latency connections. This advancement is crucial for real-time data transmission and remote control of UAVs.
4. Physical Unclonable Functions (PUFs): PUFs are used to improve the security of UAV hardware by providing unique and tamper-evident identifiers. These functions help in ensuring the authenticity of UAV components and protecting against hardware-based attacks.
5. Post-Quantum Cryptography (PQC): With the emergence of quantum computing, traditional cryptographic methods may become vulnerable. PQC aims to develop cryptographic algorithms that are secure against quantum attacks.
6. Machine Learning/Deep Learning (ML/DL): ML/DL techniques are being utilized to enhance IoD security by enabling advanced threat detection and response mechanisms. AI models trained on large datasets can identify patterns and anomalies indicative of cyber threats.
7. Trusted Platform Module/Hardware Security Mechanism (TPM/HSM): TPM is a specialised chip whereas HSM is a specialised hardware device that can be mounted on drones. These methods can be utilized for storing private keys; however, they are more expensive, and the additional hardware requirements for mounting on drones need to be considered.

Authentication Authentication involves verifying the identity of entities within a network, whether it is a drone, ground control station, or a remote user interacting with the system.

- Biometric-Based User Authentication Protocols: In UAV networks, when a remote user intends to communicate with drones, it is crucial to verify their identity to maintain security. Only authenticated users are allowed access, which can be ensured through various methods like passwords, smart cards, or biometric data. To address this need in the IoD, Wazid et al. [139] introduced a robust user authentication protocol based on three factors. This approach integrates cryptographic hash functions with biometric fuzzy extractors, making it resilient against several types of attacks, such as replay, man-in-the-middle, drone capture, secret leakage, and unauthorized password updates.
- Public Key Infrastructure (PKI) based authentication: PKI is widely used for authenticating UAVs. It involves the use of digital certificates and cryptographic keys to verify the identity of UAVs and their controllers. Some of the works that use PKI-based authentication include Jan et al. [57], who developed an identity-based authentication scheme using PKI to enhance security and privacy in IoD communications. Cho et al. [28] introduced Sentinel, a PKI-based security framework for UAVs that provides end-to-end encryption and mutual authentication. Another notable work by Jan et al. [58] proposed a key management scheme using PKI to secure IoD against various cyber threats. De and Mittal

[33] presented UAVouch, a PKI-based authentication protocol designed to ensure secure and reliable communication in UAV networks.

- Hardware-Based Authentication: Hardware-based authentication identifies drones by using their unique hardware characteristics. Verifying the identity of each drone within the network is crucial for maintaining security. Various methods are employed for this purpose, including those based on PUFs [5, 6, 14, 90, 101, 103], as well as techniques that utilize acoustic signals, RFID, and MEMS gyroscopes. One approach detailed in [20] involves a scheme for drone authentication and tracking using RFID. In another study, Son et al. [116] focused on fingerprinting drones by exploiting the unique properties of the gyroscope sensor. Ramesh et al. [107] introduced a method for drone identification and authentication based on the distinct noise patterns from drone motors, which result from manufacturing variations.
- Blockchain based authentication: Blockchain provides a decentralized and immutable ledger for recording UAV identities and their authentication transactions. This technology ensures transparency and trust, making it difficult for malicious actors to spoof or hijack UAVs. Andola et al. [9] proposed SpyChain, a lightweight blockchain framework designed for authentication and anonymous authorization in the IoD. SpyChain ensures secure communication and prevents unauthorized access while maintaining user privacy through anonymous authorization. Javed et al. [63] introduced an efficient authentication scheme using blockchain as a certificate authority for IoD, using its decentralized nature to issue and verify digital certificates, enhancing security and scalability. Garcća et al. [43] presented a μTesla-based authentication method that integrates blockchain for reliable and secure broadcast communications in IoD, ensuring the integrity and authenticity of broadcast messages. Sripesh et al. [118] developed BAKP-IoDA, a blockchain-driven authentication and key agreement protocol for IoD applications, providing robust security by combining blockchain with traditional cryptographic techniques.

GPS spoofing is a persistant threat to UAV operations, as it can mislead UAVs by providing false location data. Detecting and mitigating GPS spoofing attacks are essential for maintaining the integrity and safety of UAV missions.

- Signal Anomaly Detection: Techniques like signal anomaly detection analyze the characteristics of GPS signals to identify discrepancies that may indicate spoofing. By comparing the received signals with expected patterns, UAVs can detect spoofing attempts. Some notable works in this area include Psiaki et al. [98], who developed a method to detect GPS spoofing by analyzing signal strength and timing anomalies. Jiang et al. [67] proposed a robust detection algorithm that uses machine learning to identify and classify GPS spoofing signals based on signal behavior.
- Cryptographic Approaches: Encrypting GPS signals and using cryptographic authentication can prevent unauthorized entities from injecting false signals. This method ensures that the UAV only accepts genuine signals from trusted sources. Wesson et al. [142] explored practical cryptographic civil GPS signal

authentication, providing a framework to secure GPS signals against spoofing attacks. Garratt et al. [44] estimated the true position of UAVs in INS/GPS integration systems during GPS spoofing conditions, it highlights the effectiveness of integrating cryptographic measures to enhance GPS signal security.

- Machine Learning Algorithms: Machine learning algorithms can be trained to recognize patterns associated with GPS spoofing. By analyzing historical data and real-time signals, these algorithms can detect anomalies and alert the UAV to spoofing. For example, Nayfeh et al. [88] developed a real-time machine learning-based GPS spoofing solution for location-dependent UAV applications.
- Inertial Navigation Systems (INS): INS can serve as a backup to GPS by providing continuous position data based on the UAV's motion sensors. Meng et al. [84] developed a resilient tightly coupled INS integration method for indoor UAV navigation under challenging scenarios. This method enhances navigation performance in environments where GPS signals are unreliable. Garratt et al. [44] presented an integrated GPS/INS/Vision navigation system for UAVs. This system uses a combination of GPS, INS, and vision sensors to provide robust and reliable navigation data even in GPS-compromised environments.

2.5 Challenges in IoD Security

In the current technological scenario, there are several challenges and limitations to implement solutions for the above problems. These include:

1. Resource Constraints: IoD devices, including drones, have limited computational power, memory, and energy. Any security mechanism must be lightweight and efficient.
2. Real-Time Requirements: Drones operate in dynamic environments, requiring real-time decision-making. Security mechanisms should not introduce notable latency and communication costs.
3. Resilience to Advanced Cyber Threats: With the emergence of quantum computing, there is a pressing need for security frameworks that are resistant to both current and anticipated cyber threats. Ensuring quantum resistance is crucial to safeguard against future vulnerabilities.
4. Physical Security: Drones can be physically tampered with, and storage devices can be accessed to extract data or insert malware. Ensuring physical security, especially when drones are deployed in remote or easily accessible areas, is critical.
5. Network Security and Data Integrity: Given the distributed nature of drone networks, securing communication channels is of utmost importance. Drones transmit sensitive data over insecure networks, where risks of interception and manipulation are significant. Ensuring data integrity and confidentiality during transmission and storage is a major challenge. Effective encryption and secure communication protocols are necessary but must be balanced with the drones' computational capabilities.

3 Authentication Mechanisms in IoD

Drones operating in dynamic environments require robust authentication systems to ensure secure network access, communication with ground stations, and data exchange. These networks face significant challenges, including susceptibility to impersonation, cloning, and location forgery attacks, primarily due to the aerial freedom of drone deployment and the unencrypted nature of location data. To counter these cyber threats and secure the network, an efficient and lightweight authentication mechanism is essential. This mechanism must be capable of identifying legitimate drones within a surveillance zone, resisting attacks such as eavesdropping, man-in-the-middle, impersonation, cloning, and replay. Moreover, it should enhance physical security and resilience by eliminating the need for key storage on drones.

With the advent of 5G technology, the operational capabilities of drones have expanded significantly. Drones can now travel greater distances and require authentication across various domains, zones, or organizations. For example, during emergencies such as hazardous chemical spills or wildfires, regions lacking advanced detection tools might seek drone support from neighboring domains equipped with the necessary technology. When drones transition between domains, they become vulnerable to cyber-attacks. The primary challenge in such scenarios is accurately distinguishing between legitimate drones and impostors as they enter new territories.

Authentication in IoD is a complex process that includes drone authentication, intra-domain authentication, and cross-domain authentication. Drone authentication ensures that each drone is verified and authorized to operate within the network. Intra-domain authentication secures communication within a single domain, requiring mutual authentication among users, drones, and GCS using various methods such as hash-based, PKI-based, ECC-based, and PUF-based mechanisms. Cross-domain authentication becomes crucial when drones operate across different domains or networks. Robust protocols are needed to maintain security continuity and trust across varying security infrastructures, often utilizing blockchain technology due to its decentralized and secure characteristics. The taxonomy of authentication and GPS spoofing detection and mitigation schemes in IoD are given in Fig. 5.

3.1 *Drone Authentication Mechanisms*

Consider a scenario where a military border is under surveillance by five drones. If a sixth drone attempts to join the network, it becomes crucial to determine whether it is authentic or a counterfeit. Hostile entities could deploy a duplicate drone that mimics the original drone, compromising the network by recording messages and replaying them to retrieve secret keys. In such situations, verifying the identity

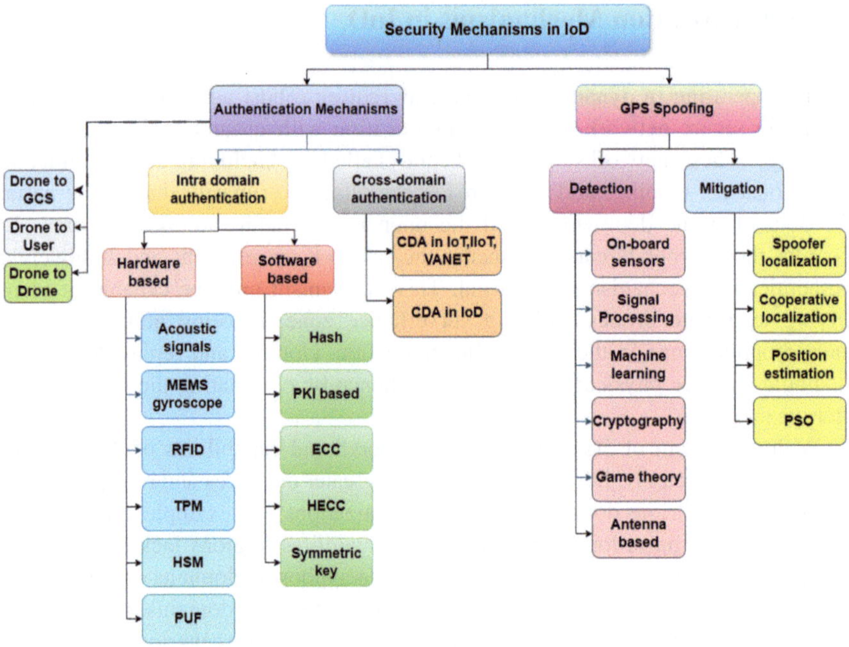

Fig. 5 Taxonomy of authentication and GPS spoofing detection and mitigation in IoD

Table 1 Drone authentication techniques

Author	Method	Limitations	Tools used
Benzarti et al. [20]	ID-based signcryption	Does not address mutual authentication or efficiency	RFID
Son et al. [116]	Using MEMS gyroscope offset as the device fingerprint	Best suited for small networks	MEMS gyroscope
Ramesh et al. [107]	Acoustic fingerprinting via differences in motor noise using machine learning (ML)	Limited scalability; does not account for manufacturing defects in propellers	Arduino Uno, Blue Yeti Pro microphone
Karimibiuki et al. [68]	Validation of flight path using K-NN, SVM, LR	High computational cost	ArduPilot

of drones within the network is essential to maintaining security. The existing techniques in drone authentication are listed in Table 1.

Benzarti et al. [20] investigated a novel approach for drone authentication combining the benefits of both RFID for efficient identification and signcryption for ensuring data security. The system involves six entities: base station (BS), BS controller, cloud and server. Each drone has an RFID tag for network registration. When a drone enters the BS range, its RFID is read and forwarded to the BS controller, which requests a temporary identity from the cloud. Drone identities are used to generate private keys for signature creation. The system facilitates drone-to-drone and drone-to-multi-drone interactions. However, it lacks crucial components such as security proofs, performance analysis, mutual authentication, and a thorough evaluation of communication efficiency.

Son et al. [116] developed a method using the unique characteristics of gyroscope sensors in drones for fingerprinting. MEMS gyroscopes measure the drone's orientation and rotation, with outputs varying due to manufacturing differences. These unique outputs can serve as identifiers for authentic drones. However, this method is more effective in small networks and may become less practical as the number of drones increases.

Ramesh et al. [107] utilized the distinct noise characteristics of drone motors, arising from manufacturing defects, for drone identification and authentication. This acoustic fingerprinting method employs digital signatures and motor sounds as factors for authentication. Electromagnetic and mechanical noise features from the motors are collected and analyzed using an SVM classifier. Motor sounds are captured via microphones, preprocessed to remove unwanted noise, normalized, and then used for authentication by predicting drone authenticity based on the analyzed motor sounds.

Karimibiuki et al. [68] applied K-Nearest Neighbor (KNN), SVM, and Logistic Regression (LR) to predict drone flight paths. The authentication process involves checking the flight path, where a failed authentication could indicate a hijack. These models are trained using both real and false data to predict new drone paths. The KNN model, which uses the Euclidean distance function, is effective at identifying incorrect data, although it is time-consuming. Simulations conducted using the ArduPilot simulator showed that KNN outperformed other classifiers in validating flight paths, while SVM and LR also contributed to detecting anomalies in the flight data.

Jiang et al. [67] introduced a system for real-time UAV identification that relies on analyzing the behavior of drones to detect any unauthorized attempts to alter flight paths. This system continuously gathers data such as location and sensor readings to evaluate the behavior of drones. It anticipates future flight routes and ensures that these routes are authentic for the purpose of verification by utilizing predictive modeling. Data parameters like longitude, latitude, speed, weight, and maximum speed are processed using a combination of a Kalman filter and Bayesian learning, which contributes to a Gaussian-Processes based Authentication (GPA) model. The central server manages this data processing and securely stores the information in a database. Each UAV is assigned a unique serial number and a QR code, while operators must provide verified credentials to receive the necessary operating license from the server. Nevertheless, this system is currently applicable only to single UAV scenarios, which limits its potential for broader applications.

3.2 Intra-Domain Authentication

Intra-domain authentication is a critical security process where entities within a single domain, such as users, drones, and GCS, mutually authenticate each other before exchanging sensitive information. This process ensures that the communication and data transfer are legitimate and secure. The authentication mechanisms employed can be categorized based on the underlying technology as hash based, PKI based, ECC based and PUF based authentication mechanisms.

Hash-Based Mutual Authentication Protocols TCALAS is a temporal credential based three factor authentication mechanism proposed by Srinivas et al. [117]. Three-factors are used for user authentication such as smart card, user password and biometrics. The protocol uses a combination of cryptographic hash function, bit-wise XOR operation, and fuzzy extractor. The drone-to-drone key management as in [139] is not considered here. Security analysis is performed using Real-or-Random model for validating the security of the session keys. Tanveer et al. in [121] discussed a mutual authentication mechanism between a user, management server and drone in a flying zone using hash function, bitwise XOR and an authenticated encryption scheme AEGIS. This scheme has secret key storage issues and does not consider physical security. Mutual authentication between mobile device and drone is done using a server. A similar work is done in [125], REAS-IoD, that uses authenticated encryption ACE, hash and XOR with a network of drones, ground station server, ground station, users and ground station registration centre. Sensitive parameters are accumulated in drone memory that makes the system vulnerable through physical attacks. Tanveer et al. [123] has also proposed a similar approach using another authenticated encryption, ASCON, for a network of users, GCS and UAVs.

Zhang et al. [155] proposed a lightweight hash and XOR-based mutual authentication mechanism between users and drones. Like other schemes, it neglected the drone physical security and stored sensitive data on them. Jan et al. [59] expanded the SENTINEL protocol by incorporating HMACSHA1 functions and randomized keys for authentication in IoD networks. This protocol includes dynamic drone addition and revocation phases and addresses stolen verifier and insider attacks, yet remains susceptible to physical attacks and clonability.

Cabuk et al. [24] discussed a group drone authentication protocol that uses contextual information without depending on a ground station. The protocol stores public-private key pairs in drone memory, which is a significant drawback, and does not address insider attacks or traceability issues. Deebak et al. [34] proposed a hash-based mutual authentication mechanism, employing bitwise XOR operations between drone and GCS. This approach focuses on the secure communication between the drones and the GCS but does not address drone-to-drone mutual authentication and drones hardware security.

Hu et al. [51] proposed a hash-based authentication scheme using SHA-256 and SPONGENT-128 for large groups of drones in military applications. The system includes relay drones, leader drones with higher computational capacities, and lightweight drones but does not address clonability or physical security. Wang et al. [151] analyzed Hussain's work [54] and proposed a user authentication protocol that uses only hash functions to reduce ECC computational costs. This network, consisting of users, servers, and drones, addresses mutual authentication between users and drones via the ground station but incurs high communication costs and does not consider the drone hardware security. The existing works in hash and PKI are summarized in Table 2.

Public Key Infrastructure (PKI) Based Protocols Cho et al. [28] developed the SENTINEL protocol to enhance security and prevent unauthorized drone activity within designated flight zones. This protocol assigns an encrypted flight session key to each approved drone, issued by the ground station, for authentication purposes. SENTINEL focuses on secure communication channels and authentication between drones and ground stations. However, it does not adequately address the risks associated with the hardware security of drones, such as tampering or physical capture. The protocol employs a lightweight Public Key Infrastructure (PKI) system that incorporates the Elliptic Curve Digital Signature Algorithm (ECDSA), Password-Based Key Derivation Function 2 (PBKDF2), and HMAC-SHA256. These cryptographic techniques establish mutual authentication between drones and ground stations and facilitate drone-to-drone authentication, which is centrally managed by the ground station. Although effective, the protocol faces challenges related to the scalability of certificate management and revocation in large IoD networks.

De et al. [33] introduced UAVouch, a PKI-based authentication method designed to verify the identity of drones before they are allowed to join a specific group or network. The method uses public key cryptography to mitigate common threats such as Sybil attacks, where a single entity claims multiple identities, and impersonation attacks. UAVouch includes mechanisms to verify the physical location and movement patterns of drones, adding an additional layer of security. The protocol does not fully address the issue of drone clonability, where identical copies of a drone could be created and used maliciously. While effective in preventing unauthorized drones from infiltrating a network, UAVouch lacks comprehensive solutions for mutual authentication between different network entities, which could leave gaps in overall network security.

Jan et al. [57] proposed an identity-based PKI protocol aimed at securing communication in sensitive environments, such as military zones. This protocol integrates pairing-based cryptography and aggregate signatures, allowing for efficient verification of multiple signatures at once, reducing the computational overhead associated with traditional PKI methods. The protocol ensures confidentiality and integrity of data transmitted within the IoD network while providing robust protection against insider threats and stolen verifier attacks. Identity-based cryptography simplifies key management by deriving public keys directly from the identities of the participating entities, eliminating the need for distributing and managing large numbers of public keys. Although strong in addressing certain security concerns, the protocol may still

Table 2 Existing hash and PKI-based authentication in IoD

Author	Network entities	Technique	Remarks
Srinivas et al. [117]	UAVs, Ground Station, Users	Hash, Fuzzy Extractor	User-to-UAV authentication utilizing smart cards, passwords, and biometrics
Tanveer et al. [121]	Drones, Server, Mobile Users	Hash, XOR, Authenticated Encryption (AEGIS)	Mutual authentication between drones and users; Not quantum secure
Tanveer et al. [125]	UAVs, GCS, Users	Authenticated Encryption (ACE), Hash, XOR	Lacks focus on drone-to-drone communication and location verification
Cabuk et al. [24]	Group of Drones	Context Information	Public-private keys stored in memory
Jan et al. [59]	External Users, Drones, Ground Station, Drone Service Provider	HMASHA1	Improves upon the work of Hussain et al. [54] by addressing issues like stolen verifier and insider attacks
Hu et al. [51]	Large Group of Drones	SHA-256, SPONGENT-128	Does not address clonability or physical security of drones
Deebak et al. [34]	Users, Mobile Sink, Gateway Node, Drones, Ground Server	Chebyshev Chaotic Maps, Hash, HMAC	High communication cost; lacks mutual authentication and physical security for drones
Zhang et al. [155]	Users, Drones	Hash, XOR	Ensures mutual authentication between users and drones
Wang et al. [151]	Users, Server, Drones	Hash	Mutual authentication through the ground station; approach has high communication cost
Cho et al. [28]	Drones, Operators, Certificate Authority, Ground Station	Certificates, ECDSA, PBKDF2, HMAC-SHA256	Developed a lightweight certificate; Drone-to-drone authentication facilitated by the ground station
De et al. [33]	UAVs	Public Key	Addresses Sybil, impersonation, considers drone location
Jan et al. [57]	UAVs	Pairing Cryptography, Aggregate Signature, Identity-Based Cryptography	Ensures confidentiality, integrity, and protection against insider and stolen verifier attacks

face challenges in terms of performance scalability when deployed in large-scale IoD networks.

Elliptic Curve Cryptography-Based Protocols Nyangaresi et al. [91] introduced a hybrid protocol that combines symmetric key techniques with ECC to enable mutual authentication among UAVs, operators, and registration authorities (RA). The protocol is designed to provide untraceability, anonymity, forward and backward key secrecy, and biometric privacy. However, the reliance on the RA for UAV-to-operator authentication results in increased communication costs and scalability challenges. This dependency on the RA could also introduce a single point of failure, making the system vulnerable if the RA is compromised. The existing works using ECC are listed in Table 3.

Nikooghadam et al. [89] developed an ECC-based user authentication protocol tailored for systems involving users, drones, and control servers. The protocol aims to reduce computational overhead while maintaining security, focusing on the interactions between users and control servers. However, it does not consider the hardware security of drones, leaving them vulnerable to capture or tampering, which could lead to unauthorized access or disruption of the network.

Ko et al. [72] designed an ECC-based authentication protocol specifically for military drone networks. This protocol involves certificate authorities, ground control stations (GCS), users, and drones, ensuring mutual authentication across all entities. The use of elliptic curve digital signatures, certificates, symmetric key encryption, hash functions, HMAC, and Diffie-Hellman key exchange strengthens the security of communications. However, the requirement for drones to store public/private key pairs increases computational costs and exposes the system to impersonation attacks, especially in hostile environments where drones may be physically compromised.

Chen et al. [26] proposed an ECC-based authentication mechanism that includes a trusted party, player devices, drone manufacturers, and ground stations. The protocol addresses mutual authentication and concerns related to integrity, availability, and privacy. However, it is vulnerable to key-escrow attacks, where a trusted third party could misuse stored keys. The mechanism also introduces significant computational and communication overheads due to the frequent key and signature exchanges required for secure operation.

Yahuza et al. [150] built upon Chen et al.'s approach by integrating a Mobile Edge Computing (MEC)-based architecture to enhance scalability. The architecture offloads processing tasks to the edge of the network, reducing latency and improving response times. However, the certificateless scheme does not fully address the hardware security of drones, as sensitive data on drones remain vulnerable to drone physical capture, allowing unauthorized access.

Tan et al. [120] discussed a BC-based mechanism for industrial IoD using elliptic curves. This approach uses the immutability and decentralized nature of blockchain combined with ECC's cryptographic efficiency to provide secure authentication and data integrity. The integration with blockchain introduces additional complexity and may increase latency, which could be problematic in time-sensitive applications.

Table 3 Existing ECC based authentication in IoD

Author	Network entities	Technique	Remarks
Nyangaresi et al. [91]	UAV, operator and registration authority	Symmetric key and elliptic curve	Untraceability, anonymity, forward key secrecy, backward key secrecy, biometric privacy
Nikooghadam et al. [89]	Users, drones, control serve	ECC	Physical security of drones was not considered
Ko et al. [72]	Certificate authority, GCS, users and drone	ECDS, certificates, symmetric key encryption, hash, HMAC, Diffie-Hellman key exchange	UAV to UAV authentication and UAV to ground mutual authentication
Chen et al. [26]	TA, player device, manufacturer, GCS	ECC	Higher communication and computation overheads
Yahuza et al. [150]	Trusted authority, MEC, drones, GCS	ECC, hash	They have improved the work in [26], considered authentication and communication between two entities, but has not addressed the physical security of drones
Rodrigues et al. [108]	Drones, ground station	ECC	
Tian et al. [130]	Network connected UAVs, MEC, drones, TA	Offline/online signature generation mechanism	Secret data are stored on the drones
Du et al. [35]	Trusted center, GCS, drone	Elliptic curve based operations	Trust-based, Only the trusted UAV communicates with GCS
Rajasekharan et al. [106]	Trusted server, drones, user	Bilinear pairing, hash	Mutual authentication between drone and user and group authentication with location privacy
Wu et al. [144]	Drones, user, server	Fuzzy extraction, hash	Cryptanalysis of [55], addressed drone capture attack, insider attack
Zhang et al. [156]	Users, drones, server	BPV pre-calculation with FourQ operations, HMAC, hash	Drone to user mutual authentication, smart card, biometric and password for user authentication
Teng et al. [128]	Drones, GCS, CA	ECC digital certificate, ECDSA signature algorithm and ECDH key exchange algorithm	Private key stored on drone, addresses drone to drone identity verification, lacks security analysis
Jan et al. [60]	TA, mobile device, drone and ground station	ECC	Suffers from key storage issues, mobile device to drone, drone to GCS, mobile device to GCS and device, drone and GCS authentication
Berini et al. [22]	User, drone, server	Hyperelliptic Curve Cryptography (HECC), blockchain and hash	User drone authentication, drone physical security not addressed

Rodrigues et al. [108] adapted an ECC-based mutual authentication protocol initially used in wireless sensor networks for application in drone-to-drone and drone-to-ground mutual authentication. This adaptation enables secure interactions between drones and ground stations. However, the lack of formal security verification leaves severe vulnerabilities unaddressed, which could be exploited in a real-world deployment.

Tian et al. [130] suggested a lightweight offline/online signature generation mechanism for network-connected UAVs involving MECs, drones, and a trusted authority (TA). The approach aims to reduce the computational burden on drones by allowing them to pre-compute signatures offline. However, the mechanism does not provide mutual authentication for all entities within the network and fails to address attack resiliency, as storing sensitive data on UAV increases storage requirements and the risk of data breaches.

Du et al. [35] introduced a mechanism where only trusted UAVs within a swarm communicate with the GCS. The system uses elliptic curve-based signatures for authentication. However, it remains vulnerable to bad-mouthing attacks, where malicious drones could undermine trust by providing false information. These attacks complicate the process of sending emergency alerts to the GCS, delaying critical communications.

Rajasekaran et al. [106] proposed a group authentication scheme for drones that incorporates location privacy features and public-private keys. The scheme enhances privacy by keeping the drone's location concealed during authentication but does not verify the actual location of the drone. Additionally, the storage of secret keys on drones makes them susceptible to hijacking and increases storage costs, which could be a limitation in resource-constrained environments.

Wu et al. [144] addressed issues identified in Hussain et al.'s protocol [54], which was vulnerable to drone capture, privileged insider, and session key disclosure attacks. Wu et al. improved the protocol by incorporating a location privacy scheme and proposing a batch authentication process that allows a group of drones to be authenticated simultaneously. This approach enhances efficiency but still leaves certain security concerns unresolved, regarding the hardware security of drones and the potential for large-scale attacks on the network.

Zhang et al. [156] discussed a user authentication protocol utilizing FourQ and Boyko-Peinado-Venkatesan (BPV) techniques, which aim to reduce the computational overhead of authentication processes. This method is designed for environments requiring high efficiency and low computational costs but does not address physical security, leaving the system vulnerable to drone capture and related attacks.

Teng et al. [128] suggested an identity authentication scheme based on ECC digital certificates, the ECDSA signature algorithm, and the ECDH key exchange algorithm. The scheme focuses on providing secure and efficient mutual authentication within IoD networks, yet does not address the risks associated with the hardware security of drones. Jan et al. [60] discussed an authentication scheme for networks involving a trusted authority, mobile devices, drones, and ground stations using ECC. The scheme offers strong security guarantees but suffers from key storage issues, when scaling to larger networks. The protocol does not fully address the physical security challenges faced by drones, such as tampering or unauthorized access to stored keys.

Berini et al. [22] introduced a user-drone authentication protocol using Hyperelliptic Curve Cryptography (HECC), blockchain, and hash functions. This protocol combines the advantages of HECC's smaller key sizes with the security provided by blockchain, offering a robust authentication mechanism. However, the increased complexity and computational requirements may limit its practical deployment in large-scale IoD networks.

Tanveer et al. [122] proposed a server-based authentication protocol utilizing ECC and Authenticated Encryption with Associated Data (AEAD) for user to drone communication. The protocol ensures secure communication but does not consider the hardware security of drones. Storing secret keys on the drone makes it vulnerable to physical attacks, compromising the integrity of the authentication process and exposing the network to breaches.

3.2.1 Symmetric Encryption Based

Tanveer et al. [124] introduced a mechanism ensuring that only authenticated users can access and control drones within a network. The protocol incorporates hash functions, ECC, and symmetric encryption to verify user identities, preventing unauthorized access and enhancing the overall security of user-to-drone communications. This combination of cryptographic techniques provides a robust and efficient solution for secure drone operations.

In another study, Tanveer et al. [126] proposed a mutual authentication mechanism based on chaotic maps and symmetric key encryption between drones and users. The use of chaotic maps in the encryption process adds an extra layer of security by making the encryption process more unpredictable, thus reinforcing the security of the communication between drones and users.

Tanveer et al. [127] also proposed a mutual authentication mechanism between users and drones that combines PUF, symmetric encryption, and hash functions. This method enhances the security of drone communications by utilizing the unique and inherent physical properties of hardware components, making it highly resistant to cloning and other types of attacks. The integration of PUFs with symmetric encryption and hash functions ensures that the authentication process is both secure and efficient, providing strong protection against unauthorized access.

PUF-Based Authentication Protocols Physically Unclonable Functions (PUFs) have emerged as a crucial method for secure authentication, in environments with limited resources, such as the IoD. PUFs rely on the unique physical characteristics inherent in hardware components to create distinct identifiers, offering a highly secure and tamper-proof method for authentication.

Yu et al. [152] introduced a user-to-drone authentication protocol based on PUFs, tailored for smart city scenarios within the IoD ecosystem. This protocol ensures secure communication between users and drones, making it highly suitable for scenarios where maintaining security and privacy is of utmost importance.

A two-stage drone authentication protocol was devised by Alladi et al. [5]. In this setup, a mini drone first communicates with the nearest leader drone, which then authenticates with the ground station. This hierarchical structure strengthens the security of the drone network by ensuring that only verified drones are permitted to communicate with each other and the ground station. Pu et al. [101] developed a drone authentication protocol integrating PUFs with chaotic systems, utilizing the Duffing map chaotic system. This approach enhances the security of drone communications by obfuscating messages, thus reducing the reliance on additional cryptographic methods while preserving a high level of security.

SecauthUAV, a protocol using PUF developed by Alladi et al. [6], secures drone communications by storing an initial challenge on the UAV. This design ensures that mutual authentication between drones is both secure and efficient, making it a dependable option for IoD networks. Aiming to secure RFID-enabled UAVs, Gope et al. [47] introduced a PUF-based mutual authentication scheme. This scheme emphasizes secure communication between the server and drone tag units, offering a robust solution in scenarios where RFID technology is employed alongside UAVs.

In a separate work, Gope et al. [48] presented a double PUF-based authentication protocol for UAV networks involving UAV service providers and Mobile Edge Computing (MEC) operators. This protocol facilitates the establishment of a secure session key between the UAV and the service provider, ensuring the confidentiality and security of data uploaded to the control center through MEC. Focusing on the integrity of drone systems, Vishal Pal [92] explored a protocol designed to verify both hardware and software by extracting PUF fingerprints from each unit inside the drone. This method enhances the overall security of the drone network by ensuring that each component within the drone is uniquely identified and authenticated.

Wu et al. [145] introduced an enhanced protocol that leverages lightweight operations to improve the efficiency of the authentication process. This protocol is crafted to ensure secure communication within IoD networks, focusing on minimizing communication costs while maintaining stringent security standards. Lei et al. [74] developed an identity authentication protocol optimized for IoD, which utilizes the Chinese Residual Theorem and PUF. This protocol ensures secure and efficient communication between sensors, drones, access points, and servers, making it a suitable choice for managing complex IoD networks.

In a network setup involving a leader drone and multiple mini drones, Alladi et al. [5] considered a protocol that uses lightweight functions. This protocol optimizes communication between drones and the GCS, ensuring that authentication processes are secure and scalable, thereby improving the overall network efficiency. A mutual authentication mechanism for IoD that combines PUFs with the Henon map chaotic system was discussed by Pu et al. [103]. This protocol provides a secure and efficient mutual authentication process between drones, enhancing the security of drone communications through the synergy of PUFs and chaotic systems.

Another significant contribution from Lei et al. [74] involves a robust authentication mechanism for IoD networks based on PUFs and the Chinese Residual

Theorem. This protocol is crafted to offer strong security features, ensuring that communication within the IoD network remains secure and resilient against various attacks. To enhance the security of IoD networks, Nyangaresi et al. [90] introduced a PUF-based mutual authentication technique. This approach ensures that all network communications are both secure and resistant to tampering. But they have not done the security analysis to validate their proposed technique.

Zhang et al. [157] developed a mutual authentication technique for drone networks using PUF, which guarantees secure inter-drone communications. This protocol offers a reliable method for authenticating drones within the network, thereby fortifying the security of the IoD. Alladi et al. [7] introduced a mutual authentication mechanism between drones and a 5G base station, utilizing PUFs. This protocol ensures that communications between drones and the base station are securely protected from unauthorized access, providing a strong security framework for IoD networks.

A multi-hop scalable authentication protocol for a swarm of drones using PUFs was proposed by Bansal et al. [14, 15]. The authors employed K-means clustering to form drone clusters based on location or proximity, while also implementing a spanning tree method to manage topology changes and message flow. These protocols enhance the scalability and security of drone networks, making them suitable for large-scale IoD deployments.

Alkatheiri et al. [4] proposed a lightweight authentication protocol for UAV networks utilizing PUF. This protocol offers strong defenses against physical capturing and cloning attacks, making it an effective solution for securing UAV communications in various scenarios. Byun et al. [23] introduced PUF-based drone identifiers (PUFDid) that feature secure authentication as a core component. This protocol is designed for drone-to-ground authentication, ensuring that communications between drones and ground stations remain secure and reliable. Pu et al. [102] proposed a lightweight authentication protocol for IoD networks that integrates bilinear pairing with PUFs. This protocol guarantees the confidentiality, integrity, and mutual authentication between drones and ground stations, making it a robust choice for securing IoD communications.

Park et al. [96] developed a mutual authentication mechanism that combines biometrics with PUF to enhance the security of user device-to-drone communications. This method ensures efficient mutual authentication by integrating PUFs, biometrics, and fuzzy extractors, resulting in a comprehensive security solution. Bansal et al. [16] proposed a distributed authentication mechanism for drone networks based on PUFs and Shamir's secret sharing scheme. This protocol addresses the challenges posed by noise in PUFs, ensuring that authentication remains secure and reliable under various conditions.

A mutual authentication technique for UAV-to-UAV communication utilizing PUFs and ECC was proposed by Zhang et al. [160]. This method combines the strengths of PUFs and ECC to provide a secure and efficient means for UAV-to-UAV interactions, ensuring all communications within the network are authenticated and secure. Karmakar et al. [69] discussed a mutual authentication mechanism for UAV-to-ground and UAV-to-UAV communications, based on PUFs and fuzzy extractors.

This protocol offers a secure and efficient method for mutual authentication, using the strengths of PUFs and fuzzy extractors to enhance UAV communication security. Irshad et al. [56] proposed a user-to-drone mutual authentication protocol that incorporates an intermediary controlling server. This mechanism utilizes PUFs and fuzzy extractors to ensure that the authentication process is both secure and efficient, providing strong protection against unauthorized access in IoD environments. The existing works are summarized in Table 4.

3.3 *Cross-Domain Authentication Mechanisms*

Blockchain technology has significantly transformed cross-domain authentication processes, bringing new solutions to the forefront. Jia et al. [65] presented a decentralized mechanism designed to enhance CDA within the IoT. This algorithm employs identity-based signatures and threshold cryptography (TC), offering robust security. However, its application to mobile objects remains challenging, and it does not sufficiently address the physical security concerns of the devices involved.

Alimoradi et al. [3] emphasized the importance of communication efficiency in wireless sensor networks, especially in intra-zone and inter-zone communications. While their research focused on enhancing communication, it left gaps in addressing the physical/hardware security of devices, which is a critical aspect of network security that must be considered.

To address privacy and scalability in IoT networks, Tong et al. [133] introduced a CDA scheme that integrates consortium blockchain, TC, and bilinear pairing. This mechanism incurs higher communication cost and higher number of interaction between the entities introduce cybersecurity risks and latency issues, affecting its real-world applicability.

In their exploration of consortium blockchain technology, Zhang et al. [159] developed a CDA mechanism for IoT that utilizes a digital token system linked to cryptocurrency. This innovative approach enhances security, yet it poses risks related to the physical safety of private keys stored on devices, which could jeopardize the integrity of the entire network.

Li et al. [75] approached CDA in IoT by integrating blockchain with edge computing and elliptic curve cryptography. Their dual-chain architecture, which includes a slave chain and a main chain, offers a structured security solution for managing identity information and domain data. Despite these improvements, the system remains vulnerable to cloning attacks, in environments where security measures are less stringent.

Privacy concerns within 5G heterogeneous networks (HetNets) have been addressed by Wang et al. [138], who proposed a CDA and handover scheme focused on preserving privacy. While the method enhances privacy protections, it is still susceptible to replay and physical attacks. The increased communication costs,

Table 4 Existing PUF based authentication in IoD

Author	Network entities	Technique	Remarks
Alkatheiri et al. [4]	UAVs, ground station, centralised	Multiple signature, elliptic curve based	Ground station based UAV to UAV authentication, response sent in raw form, susceptible to man-in-the-middle attacks, not quantum secure
Pu et al. [99]	Drone and ground station	ECC, PUF	Drone to GCS mutual authentication, Not quantum secure
Pu et al. [101]	UAVs, GCS	PUF, chaotic Duffing map system	Not addressed inter-drone communication and location validation
Gope et al. [48]	RFID enabled UAVs, server	Double PUF, fuzzy extractor	UAV to server mutual authentication, secret key is stored on drone
Yu et al. [152]	User, drone, server	PUF, fuzzy extractor	Drone to user mutual authentication via server
Lounis et al. [76]	UAVs	PUF, Extended challenge-response pairs, distributed value	Inter-drone authentication, Drone pairs are fixed, PUF reliability is not considered
Lei et al. [74]	Sensor node, UAV, Access point and server	PUF and Chinese residual theorem	Key storage issues, insider attacks and location validation
Karmakar et al. [69]	UAVs, Ground station	PUF, fuzzy extractor, Thompson Sampling	Ground station based UAV-UAV authentication and UAV ground station authentication, dynamic session adjustment
Zhang et al. [160]	UAVs, server	ECC, PUF	Drone to drone authentication, Not quantum secure
Alladi et al. [6]	UAVs, ground station	PUF	UAV to UAV authentication using ground station, initial challenge is stored on the UAV
Alladi et al. [5]	SDN UAVs, ground station	PUF	Software-Defined UAV networks leader drone to ground station authentication, mini drone to leader drone authentication via ground station
Pu et al. [102]	Drones, ground station	Bilinear pairing and PUF	Mutual authentication between drone and ground station, Incurs higher computation cost
Park et al. [96]	Users, Drones, Server	Biometrics, PUF, fuzzy extractor	Mutual authentication between user and drone, no forward secrecy, Susceptible to DoS attacks
Irshad et al. [56]	User, drone, server	PUF, fuzzy extractor	User to drone mutual authentication via server Higher Communication cost

due to additional network participants, may also present challenges in resource-constrained environments.

Yuan et al. [153] introduced a CDA scheme based on group signatures, aimed at securing communication within IoT networks. Although this method protects communication paths, it does not fully address the physical security of devices, leaving them exposed to certain risks. Jia et al. [66] suggested a IoT CDA solution that integrates identity-based cryptography (IBC) with edge computing. This approach strengthens network security, though the high communication costs associated with large-scale networks could limit its scalability. In traditional network environments, Zhang et al. [154] developed a technique based on a signature scheme that operates without the need for a trusted third party. While this method reduces reliance on external entities, it introduces security risks related to storing secret keys on devices, especially in environments where physical security is a concern.

Gong et al. [46] proposed a centralized CDA scheme for IoT that incorporates ECC and symmetric polynomial-based cryptographic methods. This approach is efficient, though it is prone to single points of failure, which could compromise the entire system if not properly addressed.

Ataei et al. [11] tackled secure data aggregation in wireless sensor networks by using a rail fence cipher algorithm for inter-cluster and intra-cluster communication. While this method improves communication security, it may not offer full protection against modern cryptographic attacks, leaving certain vulnerabilities in the system.

Mirsaraei et al. [86] explored a mutual authentication method that integrates user authorization via smart card registration and ECC. This method meets current security needs but could become less reliable as quantum computing advances, which might undermine the effectiveness of ECC-based systems.

In IIoT environments, Shen et al. [112] developed a framework called BASA that combines blockchain with identity-based cryptography (IBC). The reliance on a Key Generation Centre (KGC) for managing private keys introduces latency and vulnerabilities to cyberattacks during the authentication process.

Cui et al. [30] proposed a blockchain-based device authentication protocol for IIoT, utilizing tors (DACC) grounded in RSA assumptions. As quantum computing advances, the continued use of RSA might become problematic, necessitating a shift to more resilient cryptographic methods.

Singh et al. [115] devised a CDA scheme for IIoT that uses Identity-based Signature (IBS) and Ephemeral Elliptic Curve Diffie-Hellman (ECDHE). This scheme enhances security, but the practice of storing private keys on devices presents significant risks, making the network vulnerable to physical security breaches.

Zhang et al. [158] aimed to improve security in IIoT with a multi-factor CDA scheme that integrates DACC and PUFs. This method strengthens the security framework, it introduces delay in key generation and relies on ECC, which is not resistant to attacks from quantum computers, leading to future vulnerabilities. Gao et al. [42] suggested a certificate-less signature and BC based identity management CDA system for IIoT. Despite its innovative approach, the system's multiple communication paths make it vulnerable to physical and cloning attacks, which could compromise the system's integrity.

Wang et al. [135] introduced BlockCAM, a system designed to manage authorized certificates by storing their hashes on a blockchain ledger. The absence of encryption and decryption processes, coupled with the lack of a certificate revocation mechanism, creates vulnerabilities, especially in a system reliant on multiple communication pathways.

Zhong et al. [161] discussed a IIoT message authentication mechanism, which integrates blockchain with batch authentication, hash chains, and IBS. While the method secures communication, it does not adequately address the physical security of devices, leaving them exposed to cyber threats. Khalid et al. [70] explored mutual authentication for IIoT that combines AES and elliptic curve between edge and fog nodes. This system incurs high computational costs and relies on cryptographic methods that might not withstand future quantum-based threats.

Cross-Domain Authentication Protocols in IoD A Cross-Domain Authentication framework was developed for the IoD by Feng et al. [40]. This framework uses both private and consortium blockchains, incorporating multiple signatures and smart contracts to securely manage drone registrations. Despite enhancing security, the framework imposes considerable computational demands, impacting the performance of the drones. The existing CDA schemes are listed in Table 5.

In the pursuit of an alternative solution, Tian et al. [131] introduced a PUF-based multi-domain authentication protocol designed for drone networks, which operates without depending on blockchain. Emphasizing the security of 5G-enabled UAVs, a blockchain-based federated learning framework was proposed

Table 5 BC-based CDA schemes in various networks

Author	Network	Authentication technique	Issues
Feng et al. [40]	IoD	Multiple signatures, ECC	Physical security not considered, storage of secret keys on devices, privacy and scalability issues, not quantum secure
Qiao et al. [105]	IoD	Elliptic curve based	
Jia et al. [66]	IoT	ECC, IBC	
Zhong et al. [161]	IIoT	Batch authentication, TC	
Gao et al. [42]	IIoT	Non-Certificate based signature, ECC	
Shen et al. [112]	IoT	IBS, ECDHE	
Cui et al. [30]	IIoT	DACC, ECDHP	
Zhang et al. [154]	Basic network	Digital Signature, hash functions	
Wang et al. [137]	Self-operating	Multiple certificate authority	
Zhang et al. [158]	IIoT	PUF, DACC, ECC	Privacy and scalability issues not quantum resistant

by Feng et al. [40]. The framework focuses on ensuring data privacy through the use of multi-signature smart contracts for cross-domain authentication. However, physical security challenges for drones remain unresolved, highlighting a significant vulnerability.

For drone groups within the IoD, Qiao et al. [105] devised a cross-domain authentication protocol that integrates blockchain technology with ECC. Although robust in several aspects, the protocol overlooks critical considerations regarding the physical security of drones, which could expose the network to significant risks.

Shahidinejad et al. [109] presented a unique CDA scheme for the IoD utilizing Chebyshev's chaotic maps. This approach offers an innovative solution for authentication, yet it falls short in addressing the physical security of drones, leaving the system susceptible to physical threats.

To enhance security in the IoD, Pu et al. [100] combined Chebyshev polynomials with PUFs integrated into blockchain technology. This combination strengthens authentication but it does not consider the threats posed by quantum attacks, representing a critical gap in security. Li et al. [75] proposed a lightweight Unified Multi-domain Identity (UMI) mechanism. This mechanism simplifies identity management across various domains, but it does not provide adequate protection against quantum attacks, posing a serious security concern in IoD.

4 GPS Spoofing Detection Techniques

Current GPS spoofing detection techniques leverage on-board sensors, signal processing, machine learning (ML), game theory, and cryptographic methods. On-board sensors include cameras, accelerometers, gyroscopes, and magnetometers for position detection. The spoofing techniques are summarized in Table 6 and compared in Table 7.

4.1 On-Board Sensors

Qiao et al. [104] meticulously compared the drone's velocity derived from both the camera and Inertial Measurement Unit (IMU) with the velocity extracted from GPS data. Hacohen et al. [49] combined IMU with a LoRa sensor to detect spoofing within a drone swarm environment. These methods rely heavily on the accuracy of camera and IMU data, with their effectiveness limited in scenarios where LoRa connectivity is compromised or unavailable.

Feng et al. [38] utilized gyroscopes and accelerometers to deduce position, comparing it with GPS receiver data. Another technique involved integrating GPS data with optical flow sensors, as demonstrated by Meng et al. [83]. The primary limitation of sensor-based systems is that environmental conditions can cause

Table 6 Summary of GPS spoofing detection techniques

Main method used	Author	Technique used
On-board sensors	Qiao et al. [104]	Comparison of drone's velocity from camera and IMU with GPS data
	Hacohen et al. [49]	IMU combined with LoRa sensor
	Feng et al. [38]	Gyroscopes and accelerometers compared with GPS receiver data
	Meng et al. [83]	Integration of GPS data with optical flow sensors
	Mykytyn et al. [87]	Impulse radio ultra wideband ranging between drones
Signal processing	Pardhasaradhi et al. [94]	Radar analysis of signal parameters
	Javaid et al. [62]	Cross-referencing satellite signal packets with range information
	Titouna et al. [132]	Analysis of signal strength, pseudo-range, and frequency shift
Machine learning	Panice et al. [93]	SVM analysis of navigation system data
	Manesh et al. [81]	GPS spoofing detection model using pseudo-range, doppler shift, SNR
	Xiao et al. [148]	RNN for spoofing prediction
	Minhas et al. [85]	CNN-based technique for GPS spoofing detection
	Wang et al. [136]	LSTM for predicting flight paths
	Xue et al. [149]	DL techniques using satellite images
	Whelan et al. [143]	SVM and autoencoder neural networks using flight logs
	Feng et al. [39]	XGBoost and Genetic algorithm using GPS and IMU readings
	Dang et al. [31]	MLP trained on path loss between drone and ground station
	Agyapong et al. [1]	LSTM classifiers using flight logs and telemetry data
	Aissou et al. [2]	Tree-based ML models comparison, XGBoost performance
	Gasimova et al. [45]	Ensemble method for GPS spoofing detection
	Wei et al. [140]	ML models trained on flight data, XGBoost classifier
	Sun et al. [119]	PCA-CNN-LSTM model for GPS spoofing detection
Cryptographic	Humphreys et al. [53]	Model for replay type of spoofing attack
	Wesson et al. [142]	Navigation message authentication technique
Additional hardware	Pardhasaradhi et al. [94]	Extended Kalman filter framework and local tracker fusion
	Magiera et al. [78]	Antenna array processing for spoofing detection
	Hu et al. [50]	Array signal processing technique for anti-spoofing
	Wei et al. [141]	Analysis of signal envelope for spoofing detection
	Chen et al. [27]	Two antennas for GPS spoofing detection using carrier phase

Table 7 Comparison with state-of-the-art works based on the technique used

Author	Mitigation	Detection technique											Context aware	Dataset
		Ensemble	AE	MLP	DL	ANN	CNN	LSTM	SVM	Hybrid	GNN	MNN		
Panice et al. [93]									✓					Simulated
Manesh et al. [81]														–
Xiao et al. [148]						✓								Simulated
Minhas et al. [85]							✓							Real
Wang et al. [136]								✓						Simulated
Xue et al. [149]					✓									Real
Whelan et al. [143]			✓											Real
Dang et al. [31]				✓										Real
Agyapong et al. [1]								✓						Real
Aissou et al. [2]										✓				Real
Nayfeh et al. [88]										✓				Real
Gasimova et al. [45]		✓												[2]
Wei et al. [140]		✓												Real
Sun et al. [119]										✓				Real
Feng et al. [39]										✓				Real
SoCoMNNet	✓										✓	✓		[88]

deviations, leading to false positives or negatives in detection. Mykytyn et al. [87] discussed using impulse radio ultra-wideband ranging between two drones for detecting GPS spoofing, a system that fails if both drones are under attack.

4.2 Signal Processing Techniques

In signal processing for GPS spoofing detection, Pardhasaradhi et al. [94] employed radars to analyze signal parameters, including the carrier-to-noise ratio and signal correlation. Javaid et al. [62] scrutinized the authenticity of signal packets received from satellites by cross-referencing them with range information from different satellite sources. Titouna et al. [132] used factors like signal strength, pseudo-range, and frequency shift to discern GPS spoofing attempts. A notable drawback of these techniques is their reliance on predefined thresholds for signal values, and the need for specialized equipment for signal capture and analysis, which may not be practical for drones and incurs high communication overhead with ground stations.

4.3 Machine Learning-Based Techniques

Machine learning and on-board sensor systems are frequently employed for detecting GPS spoofing. ML-based methods identify deviations in GPS behavior compared to expected norms. However, these techniques are often too computationally intensive to be deployed on drones. Panice et al. [93] used data from diverse navigation systems analyzed through Support Vector Machines (SVM). Manesh et al. [81] employed pseudo-range, Doppler shift, and signal-to-noise ratio to create a GPS spoofing detection model. Xiao et al. [148] used recurrent neural networks (RNN) for spoofing prediction, while Minhas et al. [85] applied convolutional neural networks (CNN) for GPS spoofing detection. Wang et al. [136] utilized LSTM for predicting flight paths for fixed route applications. Xue et al. [149] employed satellite images from Google Earth for GPS spoofing detection using deep learning techniques. Whelan et al. [143] classified GPS attacks using SVM and autoencoder neural networks based on flight logs. Feng et al. [39] trained a model using GPS and IMU readings to detect abnormalities with XGBoost for offline analysis and genetic algorithms for model tuning. Dang et al. [31] studied path loss between drones and ground stations, training models using MLP. Agyapong et al. [1] used LSTM classifiers with flight logs and telemetry data. Aissou et al. [2] compared several tree-based ML models, finding XGBoost to perform best. Gasimova et al. [45] used ensemble methods for GPS spoofing detection. Wei et al. [140] demonstrated using flight data for training ML models to detect GPS spoofing, with XGBoost performing best. Sun et al. [119] used a PCA-CNN-LSTM model for GPS spoofing detection. These ML-based techniques, though effective, are computationally heavy for deployment on drones.

4.4 Cryptographic Techniques

Humphreys [53] developed a model for detecting replay-type spoofing attacks. Wesson et al. [142] proposed a navigation message authentication technique for civil GPS signals, combining cryptographic authentication of the GPS navigation message with statistical timing authentication, embedding a digital signature using the Elliptic Curve Digital Signature Algorithm (ECDSA).

4.5 Additional Hardware-Based Techniques

Radars have target detection capabilities independent of the environment. Pardhasaradhi et al. [94] utilized the extended Kalman filter framework for position estimation, fusing primary data from the drone and secondary data from a local ground tracker to detect and mitigate GPS spoofing attacks. If spoofing is detected, the fused track data is fed back to the drone to counteract the attack.

Magiera et al. [78] proposed a method for detecting and mitigating GPS spoofing using antenna array processing, utilizing phase delay for detection and spatial filtering for mitigation. Hu et al. [50] introduced an array signal processing technique to suppress GPS spoofing attacks, capturing spatial information from various directions using array sensors. This approach can be integrated into the software of array antennas without modifying GPS receiver hardware.

Wei et al. [141] proposed a method relying on signal envelope analysis, dynamically adjusting thresholds based on the dispersion value of the signal envelope's variance. Chen et al. [27] used two off-the-shelf antennas for GPS spoofing detection, employing carrier phase and known baseline length to detect single and multiple spoofing signals, estimating the baseline vector without relying on IMU data.

5 GPS Spoofing Mitigation Techniques

Majidi et al. [79] proposed an adapted particle swarm optimization filter for estimating the position of drones. This approach guides particles through search spaces, attracting them toward optimal solutions based on both their own experiences and the collective experiences of their neighbors.

Xiao et al. [147] introduced an anti-hijacking system for commodity drones called WiDrone. This system enhances security during drone operations by relying on WiFi fingerprint location cross-checks. When a drone receives a landing order, it verifies the destination by comparing the current WiFi fingerprint with the destination WiFi fingerprint, ensuring the drone is heading to the correct location.

Table 8 Summary of GPS spoofing mitigation techniques

Author	Main method used	Technique used
Majidi et al. [79]	Particle Swarm Optimization	Adapted filter for drone position estimation
Xiao et al. [147]	WiFi Fingerprinting	WiDrone anti-hijacking system
Javaid et al. [62]	Algorithmic Approach	Detection of attack source using satellite data
Jansen et al. [61]	Ground Infrastructure	Spoofer localization and detection
Wan et al. [134]	Attacker Location Tracking	ALT and ESC for guiding UAV away from spoofing range
Bada et al. [12]	Distributed Detection	Policy-based mechanism in FANETs
Pardhasaradhi et al. [95]	Advanced Positioning Algorithm	Combines robust positioning, Kalman filter, and M-best position algorithm
Eldosouky et al. [36]	Cooperative Localization	Mitigation using nearby UAVs' locations
Dang et al. [32]	3D Radio Map	Particle filters based on Wasserstein distance for precise UAV location

Javaid et al. [62] developed an algorithm designed to enhance the security of unmanned aerial vehicle (UAV) navigation against GPS spoofing. The algorithm detects the attack source, whether it is the host or a malicious satellite, by identifying anomalies in position calculations based on groups of five satellites divided into three. Once the specific PRN Code used in the attack is identified, the algorithm mitigates the attack by releasing the lock associated with that PRN Code. The mitigation techniques are summarized in Table 8.

In their research Jansen et al. [61] proposed a GPS spoofing detection and spoofer localization approach that involves continuous analysis of UAV position estimates using an independent ground infrastructure. By monitoring the contents and arrival times of these estimated positions, the system can detect spoofing attacks within seconds and accurately determine the spoofer's location after 15 minutes of monitoring, with a precision of up to 150 meters. Their novel localization method relies on analyzing position differences between pairs of spoofed aircraft, considering variations in signal arrival times at the GPS receivers of these aircraft. Wan et al. [134] proposed an Attacker Location Tracker (ALT) that monitors the attacker's location and estimates spoofing device output power. Using these estimates an Escape Controller (ESC) guides the UAV away from the spoofing device's effective range within the escape time, preventing sensor drift caused by spoofing.

In [12], Bada et al. introduced a policy-based distributed detection mechanism to combat colluding GPS spoofing attacks in Flying Ad Hoc Networks (FANETs). Based on the burglary scene and UAV locations during an attack, they distinguish between active and passive witnesses. Pardhasaradhi et al. [95] introduced an advanced positioning algorithm that combines robust positioning, a Kalman filter, and the M-best position algorithm. The algorithm considers all possible pseudo ranges. A gating technique within the Kalman filter estimates the vehicle's time-varying dynamics and removes unwanted position estimates. Eldosouky et al. [36] introduced a mathematical framework to analyze and mitigate the effects of GPS spoofing attacks on UAVs. It uses system dynamics to model UAV routes for reaching destinations. GPS spoofing is mitigated by using cooperative localization, using the location of nearby UAVs. Dang et al. [32] used a 3D radio map constructed using deterministic channel models and the Kriging method. They analyzed this data alongside real-time UAV Received Signal Strength (RSS) data using machine learning (ML) methods to detect signs of GPS spoofing. To mitigate spoofing, they employed particle filters based on the Wasserstein distance between radio map data and a set of RSS measurements, ultimately determining the precise location of the UAV.

6 Open Research Issues and Future Research Directions

In the rapidly evolving field of UAVs and the IoD, several open research issues need to be addressed. One of the critical challenges is the storage of sensitive data on drones. As UAVs are increasingly used for various applications, they carry sensitive information that needs robust protection against unauthorized access and tampering. Developing secure storage solutions that ensure data integrity and confidentiality is essential for the safe use of drones in sensitive operations.

Another important issue is the high communication and computation cost associated with existing IoD authentication schemes. These costs can be prohibitive and limit the scalability and efficiency of UAV operations. Research into more efficient authentication mechanisms that reduce these costs while maintaining high levels of security is crucial for the widespread adoption of IoD systems.

Physical security and location validation of drones also present major challenges. There is a pressing need for efficient mechanisms that can ensure the physical security of drones, preventing unauthorized access and tampering. Accurate location validation is also critical to ensure that drones operate within designated areas and follow predefined routes. Innovations in these areas are vital for maintaining the integrity and reliability of UAV operations.

The current server-based drone-to-drone authentication mechanisms require further refinement to enhance their security and efficiency. Developing decentralized authentication approaches could offer more scalable and resilient solutions. Cross-domain authentication in IoD is another area that needs attention, as drones increasingly operate across various jurisdictions and networks. Effective cross-domain authentication methods are necessary to ensure seamless and secure interactions between different IoD systems.

Existing mutual authentication mechanisms in IoD are vulnerable to future quantum attacks, which pose a markable threat to the future security of these systems. Developing quantum-resistant authentication protocols is essential to protect IoD systems from emerging quantum computing threats.

Moreover, attack resilience remains a critical concern, as UAVs are vulnerable to cloning, impersonation, man-in-the-middle (MitM) attacks, and eavesdropping. Enhancing the resilience of UAV systems against these attacks is crucial to ensure their safe and reliable operation.

There is also a need for lightweight GPS spoofing detection techniques on drones. Current methods are often resource-intensive, which can be challenging for UAVs with limited computational capabilities. Developing lightweight and efficient GPS spoofing detection methods is necessary to protect drones from navigation-based attacks. Many existing works do not adequately address spoofing mitigation, highlighting the need for efficient and secure techniques to counteract spoofing attempts.

7 Conclusion

The security challenges in IoD are complex, mainly concerning authentication mechanisms and GPS spoofing detection and mitigation. This chapter has provided a thorough literature survey, detailing the advancements and ongoing challenges in these areas. It has examined a range of strategies, from traditional cryptographic methods to innovative AI-based solutions, emphasizing the need for robust and adaptive security measures. Despite the progress, there remain critical gaps that require further research in developing seamless authentication protocols capable of handling the scale and complexity of IoD networks, and in creating effective, real-time GPS spoofing detection techniques that can function reliably in diverse environments.

References

1. Agyapong, R.A., Nabil, M., Nuhu, A.R., Rasul, M.I., Homaifar, A.: Efficient detection of GPS spoofing attacks on unmanned aerial vehicles using deep learning. In: 2021 IEEE Symposium Series on Computational Intelligence (SSCI), pp. 01–08. IEEE (2021)
2. Aissou, G., Slimane, H.O., Benouadah, S., Kaabouch, N.: Tree-based supervised machine learning models for detecting GPS spoofing attacks on UAS. In: 2021 IEEE 12th Annual Ubiquitous Computing, Electronics & Mobile Communication Conference (UEMCON), pp. 0649–0653. IEEE (2021)
3. Alimoradi, P., Barati, A., Barati, H.: A hierarchical key management and authentication method for wireless sensor networks. Int. J. Commun. Syst. **35**(6), e5076 (2022)
4. Alkatheiri, M.S., Saleem, S., Alqarni, M.A., Aseeri, A.O., Chauhdary, S.H., Zhuang, Y.: A lightweight authentication scheme for a network of unmanned aerial vehicles (UAVs) by using physical unclonable functions. Electronics **11**(18), 2921 (2022)
5. Alladi, T., Chamola, V., Kumar, N., et al.: Parth: A two-stage lightweight mutual authentication protocol for UAV surveillance networks. Comput. Commun. **160**, 81–90 (2020)

6. Alladi, T., Naren, N., Bansal, G., Chamola, V., Guizani, M.: SecAuthUAV: A novel authentication scheme for UAV-base station scenario. IEEE Trans. Veh. Technol. **69**, 15068 (2020)
7. Alladi, T., Venkatesh, V., Chamola, V., Chaturvedi, N.: Drone-MAP: A novel authentication scheme for drone-assisted 5G networks. In: IEEE INFOCOM 2021-IEEE Conference on Computer Communications Workshops (INFOCOM WKSHPS), pp. 1–6. IEEE (2021)
8. Altaweel, A., Mukkath, H., Kamel, I.: GPS spoofing attacks in FANETs: A systematic literature review. IEEE Access **11**, 55233 (2023)
9. Andola, N., Raghav, Yadav, V.K., Venkatesan, S., Verma, S.: Spychain: A lightweight blockchain for authentication and anonymous authorization in IoD. Wirel. Pers. Commun. **119**, 343–362 (2021)
10. Arafat, M.Y., Moh, S.: Routing protocols for unmanned aerial vehicle networks: A survey. IEEE Access **7**, 99694–99720 (2019)
11. Ataei Nezhad, M., Barati, H., Barati, A.: An authentication-based secure data aggregation method in internet of things. J. Grid Comput. **20**(3), 29 (2022)
12. Bada, M., Boubiche, D.E., Lagraa, N., Kerrache, C.A., Imran, M., Shoaib, M.: A policy-based solution for the detection of colluding GPS-spoofing attacks in FANETs. Transp. Res. A Pol. Pract. **149**, 300–318 (2021)
13. Badar, H.M.S., Kajla, N.I., Arshad, J., Saher, N., Ahmad, M., Jamil, M.A.: Lightweight intrusion detection for IoD infrastructure using deep learning. J. Comput. Biomed. Inf. (2024). Available at: https://jcbi.org/index.php/Main/article/view/433
14. Bansal, G., Sikdar, B.: Location aware clustering: Scalable authentication protocol for UAV swarms. IEEE Netw. Lett. **3**, 177 (2021)
15. Bansal, G., Sikdar, B.: S-MAPS: scalable mutual authentication protocol for dynamic UAV swarms. IEEE Trans. Veh. Technol. **70**(11), 12088–100 (2021)
16. Bansal, G., Sikdar, B.: Fault resilient authentication architecture for drone networks. In: 2022 IEEE International Conference on Communications Workshops (ICC Workshops), pp. 866–871. IEEE (2022)
17. Barka, E., Kerrache, C.A., Lagraa, N., Lakas, A., Calafate, C.T., Cano, J.C.: Union: A trust model distinguishing intentional and unintentional misbehavior in inter-UAV communication. J. Adv. Transp. **2018**, 7475357 (2018)
18. Barka, E., Kerrache, C.A., Benkraouda, H., Shuaib, K., Ahmad, F., Kurugollu, F.: Towards a trusted unmanned aerial system using blockchain for the protection of critical infrastructure. Trans. Emerg. Telecommun. Technol. **33**, e3706 (2019)
19. Bekmezci, I.F.: Flying ad-hoc networks (FANETs): A survey. In: Communications Surveys & Tutorials, IEEE, vol. 15, pp. 1699–1710. IEEE (2013)
20. Benzarti, S., Triki, B., Korbaa, O.: Privacy preservation and drone authentication using id-based signcryption. In: SoMeT, pp. 226–239 (2018)
21. Bera, B., Das, A.K., Sutrala, A.K.: Private blockchain-based access control mechanism for unauthorized UAV detection and mitigation in internet of drones environment. Comput. Commun. **166**, 91–109 (2021)
22. Berini, A.D.E., Ferrag, M.A., Farou, B., Seridi, H.: HCALA: Hyperelliptic curve-based anonymous lightweight authentication scheme for internet of drones. Pervas. Mob. Comput. **92**, 101798 (2023)
23. Byun, J.W.: Pufdid: Puf-based drone identifier and its application. In: 2023 International Conference on Artificial Intelligence in Information and Communication (ICAIIC), pp. 342–346. IEEE (2023)
24. Cabuk, U.C., Dalkilic, G., Dagdeviren, O.: CoMAD: Context-aware mutual authentication protocol for drone networks. IEEE Access **9**, 78400 (2021)
25. Chaudhry, S.A., Yahya, K., Karuppiah, M., Kharel, R., Bashir, A.K., Zikria, Y.B.: GCACS-IoD: A certificate based generic access control scheme for internet of drones. Comput. Netw. **191**, 107999 (2021)
26. Chen, C.L., Deng, Y.Y., Weng, W., Chen, C.H., Chiu, Y.J., Wu, C.M.: A traceable and privacy-preserving authentication for UAV communication control system. Electronics **9**(1), 62 (2020)

27. Chen, J., Xu, Y., Yuan, H., Yuan, Y.: A new GNSS spoofing detection method using two antennas. IEEE Access **8**, 110738–110747 (2020)
28. Cho, G., Cho, J., Hyun, S., Kim, H.: Sentinel: A secure and efficient authentication framework for unmanned aerial vehicles. Appl. Sci. **10**(9), 3149 (2020)
29. Choi, J.H., Lee, S.H., Jeong, I.R., Byun, J.W.: Analysis of security vulnerability in U2U authentication using MEC in IoD environment. J. Korea Inst. Inf. Secur. Cryptol. **31**(1), 11–17 (2021)
30. Cui, J., Liu, N., Zhang, Q., He, D., Gu, C., Zhong, H.: Efficient and anonymous cross-domain authentication for IIoT based on blockchain. IEEE Trans. Netw. Sci. Eng. **10**, 899 (2022)
31. Dang, Y., Benzaïd, C., Yang, B., Taleb, T.: Deep learning for GPS spoofing detection in cellular-enabled UAV systems. In: 2021 International Conference on Networking and Network Applications (NaNA), pp. 501–506. IEEE (2021)
32. Dang, Y., Karakoc, A., Norshahida, S., Jäntti, R.: 3D radio map-based GPS spoofing detection and mitigation for cellular-connected UAVs. IEEE Trans. Mach. Learn. Commun. Netw. **1**, 313–327 (2023)
33. De Melo, C.F.E., Silva, T.D.E., Boeira, F., Stocchero, J.M., Vinel, A., Asplund, M., De Freitas, E.P.: UAVouch: A secure identity and location validation scheme for UAV-networks. IEEE Access **9**, 82930 (2021)
34. Deebak, B.D., Al-Turjman, F.: A smart lightweight privacy preservation scheme for IoT-based UAV communication systems. Comput. Commun. **162**, 102–117 (2020)
35. Du, X., Li, Y., Zhou, S., Zhou, Y.: ATS-LIA: A lightweight mutual authentication based on adaptive trust strategy in flying ad-hoc networks. Peer-to-Peer Netw. Appl., **15**, 1–15 (2022)
36. Eldosouky, A., Ferdowsi, A., Saad, W.: Drones in distress: A game-theoretic countermeasure for protecting UAVs against GPS spoofing. IEEE Internet Things J. **7**(4), 2840–2854 (2019)
37. Feng, Q., He, D., Zeadally, S., Kumar, N., Liang, K.: Ideal lattice-based anonymous authentication protocol for mobile devices. IEEE Syst. J. **13**(3), 2775–2785 (2018)
38. Feng, Z., Guan, N., Lv, M., Liu, W., Deng, Q., Liu, X., Yi, W.: An efficient UAV hijacking detection method using onboard inertial measurement unit. ACM Trans. Embed. Comput. Syst. (TECS) **17**(6), 1–19 (2018)
39. Feng, Z., Guan, N., Lv, M., Liu, W., Deng, Q., Liu, X., Yi, W.: Efficient drone hijacking detection using two-step GA-XGBoost. J. Syst. Architect. **103**, 101694 (2020)
40. Feng, C., Liu, B., Guo, Z., Yu, K., Qin, Z., Choo, K.K.R.: Blockchain-based cross-domain authentication for intelligent 5G-enabled internet of drones. IEEE Internet Things J. **9**, 6224 (2021)
41. Ferrag, M.A., Maglaras, L., Argyriou, A., Kosmanos, D., Janicke, H.: Security for 4G and 5G cellular networks: A survey of existing authentication and privacy-preserving schemes. J. Netw. Comput. Appl. **101**, 55–82 (2018)
42. Gao, B., Yan, H., Tian, R.: A privacy-aware cross-domain device authentication scheme for IIoT based on blockchain. In: 2021 IEEE 23rd Int Conf on High Performance Computing & Communications; 7th Int Conf on Data Science & Systems; 19th Int Conf on Smart City; 7th Int Conf on Dependability in Sensor, Cloud & Big Data Systems & Application (HPCC/DSS/SmartCity/DependSys), pp. 561–570. IEEE (2021)
43. García, J.C.P., Benslimane, A., Braeken, A., Su, Z.: μtesla-based authentication for reliable and secure broadcast communications in IoD using blockchain. IEEE Internet Things J. **10**(20), 18400–18413 (2023)
44. Garratt, M., Lambert, A., Wang, J., Han, S., Wang, J., Sinclair, D.: Integration of GPS/ins/vision sensors to navigate unmanned aerial vehicles. Inf. Sci. **37**(B1), 963–970 (2008)
45. Gasimova, A., Khoei, T.T., Kaabouch, N.: A comparative analysis of the ensemble models for detecting GPS spoofing attacks on UAVs. In: 2022 IEEE 12th Annual Computing and Communication Workshop and Conference (CCWC), pp. 0310–0315. IEEE (2022)
46. Gong, B., Zheng, G., Waqas, M., Tu, S., Chen, S.: LCDMA: Lightweight cross-domain mutual identity authentication scheme for Internet of Things. IEEE Internet Things J. **10**, 12590 (2023)

47. Gope, P., Sikdar, B.: An efficient privacy-preserving authenticated key agreement scheme for edge-assisted internet of drones. IEEE Trans. Veh. Technol. **69**(11), 13621–13630 (2020)
48. Gope, P., Millwood, O., Saxena, N.: A provably secure authentication scheme for RFID-enabled UAV applications. Comput. Commun. **166**, 19–25 (2021)
49. Hacohen, S., Medina, O., Grinshpoun, T., Shvalb, N.: Improved GNSS localization and Byzantine detection in UAV swarms. Sensors **20**(24), 7239 (2020)
50. Hu, Y., Bian, S., Li, B., Zhou, L.: A novel array-based spoofing and jamming suppression method for GNSS receiver. IEEE Sensors J. **18**(7), 2952–2958 (2018)
51. Hu, F., Qian, H., Liu, L.: A random label and lightweight hash-based security authentication mechanism for a UAV swarm. Wirel. Commun. Mob. Comput. **2021**, 1–17 (2021)
52. Humphreys, T.: Statement on the vulnerability of civil unmanned aerial vehicles and other systems to civil GPS spoofing. University of Texas at Austin (July 18, 2012), pp. 1–16 (2012)
53. Humphreys, T.E.: Detection strategy for cryptographic GNSS anti-spoofing. IEEE Trans. Aerospace Electron. Syst. **49**(2), 1073–1090 (2013)
54. Hussain, S., Chaudhry, S.A., Alomari, O.A., Alsharif, M.H., Khan, M.K., Kumar, N.: Amassing the security: An ECC-based authentication scheme for Internet of Drones. IEEE Syst. J. **15**, 4431 (2021)
55. Hussain, S., Mahmood, K., Khan, M.K., Chen, C.M., Alzahrani, B.A., Chaudhry, S.A.: Designing secure and lightweight user access to drone for smart city surveillance. Comput. Stand. Interfaces **80**, 103566 (2022)
56. Irshad, A., Alzahrani, B.A., Albeshri, A., Alsubhi, K., Nayyar, A., Chaudhry, S.A.: SPAKE-DC: A secure PUF enabled authenticated key exchange for 5G-based drone communications. IEEE Trans. Veh. Technol. **73**, 5770–5780 (2023)
57. Jan, S.U., Khan, H.U.: Identity and aggregate signature-based authentication protocol for IoD deployment military drone. IEEE Access **9**, 130247–130263 (2021)
58. Jan, S.U., Abbasi, I.A., Algarni, F.: A key agreement scheme for IoD deployment civilian drone. IEEE Access **9**, 149311–149321 (2021)
59. Jan, S.U., Qayum, F., Khan, H.U.: Design and analysis of lightweight authentication protocol for securing IoD. IEEE Access **9**, 69287 (2021)
60. Jan, S.U., Abbasi, I.A., Algarni, F., Khan, A.S.: A verifiably secure ECC based authentication scheme for securing IoD using FANET. IEEE Access **10**, 95321–95343 (2022)
61. Jansen, K., Schäfer, M., Moser, D., Lenders, V., Pöpper, C., Schmitt, J.: Crowd-GPS-sec: Leveraging crowdsourcing to detect and localize GPS spoofing attacks. In: 2018 IEEE Symposium on Security and Privacy (SP), pp. 1018–1031. IEEE (2018)
62. Javaid, A.Y., Jahan, F., Sun, W.: Analysis of global positioning system-based attacks and a novel global positioning system spoofing detection/mitigation algorithm for unmanned aerial vehicle simulation. Simulation **93**(5), 427–441 (2017)
63. Javed, S., Khan, M.A., Abdullah, A.M., Alsirhani, A., Alomari, A., Noor, F., Ullah, I.: An efficient authentication scheme using blockchain as a certificate authority for the Internet of drones. Drones **6**(10), 264 (2022)
64. Jawhar, I., Mohamed, N., Al-Jaroodi, J., Agrawal, D.P., Zhang, S.: Communication and networking of UAV-based systems: Classification and associated architectures. J. Netw. Comput. Appl. **84**, 93–108 (2017)
65. Jia, X., Hu, N., Su, S., Yin, S., Zhao, Y., Cheng, X., Zhang, C.: IRBA: An identity-based cross-domain authentication scheme for the Internet of Things. Electronics **9**(4), 634 (2020)
66. Jia, X., Hu, N., Yin, S., Zhao, Y., Zhang, C., Cheng, X.: A2 chain: a blockchain-based decentralized authentication scheme for 5G-enabled IoT. Mob. Inf. Syst. **2020**, 1–19 (2020)
67. Jiang, C., Fang, Y., Zhao, P., Panneerselvam, J.: Intelligent UAV identity authentication and safety supervision based on behavior modeling and prediction. IEEE Trans. Ind. Inf. **16**(10), 6652–6662 (2020)
68. Karimibiuki, M., Aibin, M., Lai, Y., Khan, R., Norfield, R., Hunter, A.: Drones' face off: Authentication by machine learning in autonomous IoT systems. In: 2019 IEEE 10th Annual Ubiquitous Computing, Electronics & Mobile Communication Conference (UEMCON), vol. 10, p. 127 (2019)

69. Karmakar, R., Kaddoum, G., Akhrif, O.: A PUF and fuzzy extractor-based UAV-ground station and UAV-UAV authentication mechanism with intelligent adaptation of secure sessions. IEEE Trans. Mob. Comput. **23**, 3858 (2023)
70. Khalid, H., Hashim, S.J., Ahmad, S.M.S., Hashim, F., Chaudhary, M.A.: SELAMAT: a new secure and lightweight multi-factor authentication scheme for cross-platform industrial IoT systems. Sensors **21**(4), 1428 (2021)
71. Khan, S.Z., Mohsin, M., Iqbal, W.: On GPS spoofing of aerial platforms: a review of threats, challenges, methodologies, and future research directions. PeerJ Comput. Sci. **7**, e507 (2021)
72. Ko, Y., Kim, J., Duguma, D.G., Astillo, P.V., You, I., Pau, G.: Drone secure communication protocol for future sensitive applications in military zone. Sensors **21**(6), 2057 (2021)
73. Kwon, Y.M., Yu, J., Cho, B.M., Eun, Y., Park, K.J.: Empirical analysis of mavlink protocol vulnerability for attacking unmanned aerial vehicles. IEEE Access **6**, 43203–43212 (2018)
74. Lei, Y., Zeng, L., Li, Y.X., Wang, M.X., Qin, H.: A lightweight authentication protocol for UAV networks based on security and computational resource optimization. IEEE Access **9**, 53769–53785 (2021)
75. Li, W., Zhang, S., Chen, Z., Sen, L.: Cross-domain authentication scheme for IoT devices based on blockchain. In: 2022 IEEE 13th International Conference on Software Engineering and Service Science (ICSESS), pp. 67–73. IEEE (2022)
76. Lounis, K., Ding, S.H., Zulkernine, M.: D2d-map: A drone to drone authentication protocol using physical unclonable functions. IEEE Trans. Veh. Technol. **72**(4), 5079–5093 (2022)
77. Lu, Y., Yang, T., Zhao, C., Chen, W., Zeng, R.: A swarm anomaly detection model for IoT UAVs based on a multi-modal denoising autoencoder and federated learning. Comput. Ind. Eng. **196**, 110454 (2024)
78. Magiera, J., Katulski, R.: Detection and mitigation of GPS spoofing based on antenna array processing. J. Appl. Res. Technol. **13**(1), 45–57 (2015)
79. Majidi, M., Erfanian, A., Khaloozadeh, H.: A new approach to estimate true position of unmanned aerial vehicles in an INS/GPS integration system in GPS spoofing attack conditions. Int. J. Autom. Comput. **15**(6), 747–760 (2018)
80. Malhotra, A., Kaur, S.: A comprehensive review on recent advancements in routing protocols for flying ad hoc networks. Trans. Emerg. Telecommun. Technol. **33**, e3688 (2019)
81. Manesh, M.R., Kenney, J., Hu, W.C., Devabhaktuni, V.K., Kaabouch, N.: Detection of GPS spoofing attacks on unmanned aerial systems. In: 2019 16th IEEE Annual Consumer Communications & Networking Conference (CCNC), pp. 1–6. IEEE (2019)
82. McCoy, J., Rawat, D.B.: Software-defined networking for unmanned aerial vehicular networking and security: A survey. Electronics **8**(12), 1468 (2019)
83. Meng, L., Ren, S., Tang, G., Yang, C., Yang, W.: UAV sensor spoofing detection algorithm based on GPS and optical flow fusion. In: Proceedings of the 2020 4th International Conference on Cryptography, Security and Privacy, pp. 146–151 (2020)
84. Meng, Q., Song, Y., Li, S.y., Zhuang, Y.: Resilient tightly coupled INS/UWB integration method for indoor UAV navigation under challenging scenarios. Defence Technol. **22**, 185–196 (2023)
85. Minhas, D.: GPS spoofing attacks detection using defensive schemes in FANETs. In: 2023 International Conference on Data Science and Network Security (ICDSNS), pp. 1–8. IEEE (2023)
86. Mirsaraei, A.G., Barati, A., Barati, H.: A secure three-factor authentication scheme for IoT environments. J. Parallel Distrib. Comput. **169**, 87–105 (2022)
87. Mykytyn, P., Brzozowski, M., Dyka, Z., Langendoerfer, P.: GPS-spoofing attack detection mechanism for UAV swarms. In: 2023 12th Mediterranean Conference on Embedded Computing (MECO), pp. 1–8. IEEE (2023)
88. Nayfeh, M., Li, Y., Al Shamaileh, K., Devabhaktuni, V., Kaabouch, N.: Machine learning modeling of GPS features with applications to UAV location spoofing detection and classification. Comput. Secur. **126**, 103085 (2023)
89. Nikooghadam, M., Amintoosi, H., Islam, S.H., Moghadam, M.F.: A provably secure and lightweight authentication scheme for Internet of drones for smart city surveillance. J. Syst. Archit. **115**, 101955 (2021)

90. Nyangaresi, V.O., Petrovic, N.: Efficient PUF based authentication protocol for Internet of drones. In: 2021 International Telecommunications Conference (ITC-Egypt), pp. 1–4. IEEE (2021)
91. Nyangaresi, V.O., Jasim, H.M., Mutlaq, K.A.A., Abduljabbar, Z.A., Ma, J., Abduljaleel, I.Q., Honi, D.G.: A symmetric key and elliptic curve cryptography-based protocol for message encryption in unmanned aerial vehicles. Electronics **12**(17), 3688 (2023)
92. Pal, V., Acharya, B.S., Shrivastav, S., Saha, S., Joglekar, A., Amrutur, B.: PUF based secure framework for hardware and software security of drones. In: 2020 Asian Hardware Oriented Security and Trust Symposium (AsianHOST), pp. 01–06. IEEE (2020)
93. Panice, G., Luongo, S., Gigante, G., Pascarella, D., Di Benedetto, C., Vozella, A., Pescapè, A.: A SVM-based detection approach for GPS spoofing attacks to UAV. In: 2017 23rd International Conference on Automation and Computing (ICAC), pp. 1–11. IEEE (2017)
94. Pardhasaradhi, B., Cenkeramaddi, L.R.: GPS spoofing detection and mitigation for drones using distributed radar tracking and fusion. IEEE Sensors J. **22**(11), 11122–11134 (2022)
95. Pardhasaradhi, B., Srihari, P., Aparna, P.: Navigation in GPS spoofed environment using m-best positioning algorithm and data association. IEEE Access **9**, 51536–51549 (2021)
96. Park, Y., Ryu, D., Kwon, D., Park, Y.: Provably secure mutual authentication and key agreement scheme using PUF in Internet of drones deployments. Sensors **23**(4), 2034 (2023)
97. Perumalla, S., Chatterjee, S., Kumar, A.S.: Block chain-based access control and intrusion detection system in IoD. In: 2021 6th International Conference on Communication and Electronics Systems (ICCES), pp. 511–518. IEEE (2021)
98. Psiaki, M.L., OHanlon, B.W., Powell, S.P., Bhatti, J.A., Wesson, K.D., Schofield, T.E.: GNSS spoofing detection using two-antenna differential carrier phase. In: Proceedings of the 27th International Technical Meeting of the Satellite Division of the Institute of Navigation (ION GNSS+ 2014), pp. 2776–2800 (2014)
99. Pu, C.: A featherweight authentication and key agreement scheme for internet of drones applications. In: 2023 IEEE 34th Annual International Symposium on Personal, Indoor and Mobile Radio Communications (PIMRC), pp. 1–6. IEEE (2023)
100. Pu, C., Choo, K.K.R.: Chebyshev polynomial and private blockchain based cross-domain authentication protocol for IoD networks. In: 2024 IEEE 21st Consumer Communications & Networking Conference (CCNC), pp. 931–936. IEEE (2024)
101. Pu, C., Li, Y.: Lightweight authentication protocol for unmanned aerial vehicles using physical unclonable function and chaotic system. In: 2020 IEEE International Symposium on Local and Metropolitan Area Networks (LANMAN), pp. 1–6. IEEE (2020)
102. Pu, C., Wall, A., Choo, K.K.R.: Bilinear pairing and PUF based lightweight authentication protocol for IoD environment. In: 2022 IEEE 19th International Conference on Mobile Ad Hoc and Smart Systems (MASS), pp. 115–121. IEEE (2022)
103. Pu, C., Wall, A., Choo, K.K.R., Ahmed, I., Lim, S.: A lightweight and privacy-preserving mutual authentication and key agreement protocol for internet of drones environment. IEEE Internet Things J. **9**, 9918 (2022)
104. Qiao, Y., Zhang, Y., Du, X.: A vision-based GPS-spoofing detection method for small UAVs. In: 2017 13th International Conference on Computational Intelligence and Security (CIS), pp. 312–316. IEEE (2017)
105. Qiao, G., Zhuang, Y., Ye, T., Qiao, Y.: BCDAIoD: An efficient blockchain-based cross-domain authentication scheme for internet of drones. Drones **7**(5), 302 (2023)
106. Rajasekaran, A.S., Maria, A., Al-Turjman, F., Altrjman, C., Mostarda, L.: Anonymous mutual and batch authentication with location privacy of UAV in FANET. Drones **6**(1), 14 (2022)
107. Ramesh, S., Pathier, T., Han, J.: SoundUAV: Towards delivery drone authentication via acoustic noise fingerprinting. In: Proceedings of the 5th Workshop on Micro Aerial Vehicle Networks, Systems, and Applications, pp. 27–32 (2019)
108. Rodrigues, M., Amaro, J., Osório, F.S., RLJC, B.K.: Authentication methods for UAV communication. In: 2019 IEEE Symposium on Computers and Communications (ISCC), pp. 1210–1215. IEEE (2019)

109. Shahidinejad, A., Abawajy, J.: Anonymous blockchain-assisted authentication protocols for secure cross-domain IoD communications. IEEE Trans. Netw. Sci. Eng. **11**, 2661 (2023)
110. Sharma, V., Choudhary, G., Ko, Y., You, I.: Behavior and vulnerability assessment of drones-enabled industrial internet of things (IIoT). IEEE Access **6**, 43368–43383 (2018)
111. Sharma, A., Vanjani, P., Paliwal, N., Basnayaka, C.M.W., Jayakody, D.N.K., Wang, H.C., Muthuchidambaranathan, P.: Communication and networking technologies for UAVs: A survey. J. Netw. Comput. Appl. **168**, 102739 (2020)
112. Shen, M., Liu, H., Zhu, L., Xu, K., Yu, H., Du, X., Guizani, M.: Blockchain-assisted secure device authentication for cross-domain industrial IoT. IEEE J. Sel. Areas Commun. **38**(5), 942–954 (2020)
113. Singh, K., Verma, A.K.: A fuzzy-based trust model for flying ad hoc networks (FANETs). Int. J. Commun. Syst. **31**(6), e3517 (2018)
114. Singh, M., Aujla, G.S., Bali, R.S.: ODOB: One drone one block-based lightweight blockchain architecture for internet of drones. In: IEEE INFOCOM 2020-IEEE Conference on Computer Communications Workshops (INFOCOM WKSHPS), pp. 249–254. IEEE (2020)
115. Singh, P., Masud, M., Hossain, M.S., Kaur, A.: Cross-domain secure data sharing using blockchain for industrial IoT. J. Parallel Distrib. Comput. **156**, 176–184 (2021)
116. Son, Y., Noh, J., Choi, J., Kim, Y.: Gyrosfinger: Fingerprinting drones for location tracking based on the outputs of mems gyroscopes. ACM Trans. Priv. Secur. (TOPS) **21**(2), 1–25 (2018)
117. Srinivas, J., Das, A.K., Kumar, N., Rodrigues, J.J.: TCALAS: Temporal credential-based anonymous lightweight authentication scheme for Internet of drones environment. IEEE Trans. Veh. Technol. **68**(7), 6903–6916 (2019)
118. Sripesh, A., Wazid, M., Singh, D.P., Das, A.K., Verma, B.: BAKP-IoDA: Blockchain driven authentication and key agreement protocol for Internet of Drones based applications. In: Proceedings of the 5th International ACM Mobicom Workshop on Drone Assisted Wireless Communications for 5G and Beyond, pp. 25–30 (2022)
119. Sun, Y., Yu, M., Wang, L., Li, T., Dong, M.: A deep-learning-based GPS signal spoofing detection method for small UAVs. Drones **7**(6), 370 (2023)
120. Tan, Y., Wang, J., Liu, J., Kato, N.: Blockchain-assisted distributed and lightweight authentication service for industrial unmanned aerial vehicles. IEEE Internet Things J. **9**, 16928 (2022)
121. Tanveer, M., Zahid, A.H., Ahmad, M., Baz, A., Alhakami, H.: LAKE-IoD: Lightweight authenticated key exchange protocol for the Internet of Drone environment. IEEE Access **8**, 155645–155659 (2020)
122. Tanveer, M., Kumar, N., Hassan, M.M., et al.: RAMP-IoD: A robust authenticated key management protocol for the internet of drones. IEEE Internet Things J. **9**(2), 1339–1353 (2021)
123. Tanveer, M., Shah, H., Chaudhry, S.A., Naushad, A., et al.: PASKE-IoD: Privacy-protecting authenticated key establishment for internet of drones. IEEE Access **9**, 145683–145698 (2021)
124. Tanveer, M., Alkhayyat, A., Naushad, A., Kumar, N., Alharbi, A.G., et al.: RUAM-IoD: A robust user authentication mechanism for the Internet of Drones. IEEE Access **10**, 19836–19851 (2022)
125. Tanveer, M., Nguyen, T., Ahmad, M., Abdei-Latif, A., et al.: Towards a secure and computational framework for Internet of Drones enabled aerial computing. IEEE Trans. Netw. Sci. Eng. **10**, 3058 (2022)
126. Tanveer, M., Alasmary, H., Kumar, N., Nayak, A.: SAAF-IoD: Secure and anonymous authentication framework for the Internet of Drones. IEEE Trans. Veh. Technol. **72**, 11012–11024 (2023)
127. Tanveer, M., Aldosary, A., Kumar, N., Aldossari, S.A.: SEAF-IoD: Secure and efficient user authentication framework for the Internet of Drones. Comput. Netw. **247**, 110449 (2024)
128. Teng, L., Jianfeng, M., Pengbin, F., Yue, M., Xindi, M., Jiawei, Z., Gao, C., Di, L.: Lightweight security authentication mechanism towards UAV networks. In: 2019 Interna-

tional Conference on Networking and Network Applications (NaNA), pp. 379–384. IEEE (2019)
129. Thompson, C.: Drug traffickers are hacking US surveillance drones to get past border patrol. https://www.businessinsider.com/drug-traffickers-are-hacking-us-border-drones-2015-12?IR=T (2015) [Online]. Accessed 30 Dec 2015
130. Tian, Y., Yuan, J., Song, H.: Efficient privacy-preserving authentication framework for edge-assisted internet of drones. J. Inf. Secur. Appl. **48**, 102354 (2019)
131. Tian, C., Jiang, Q., Li, T., Zhang, J., Xi, N., Ma, J.: Reliable PUF-based mutual authentication protocol for UAVs towards multi-domain environment. Comput. Netw. **218**, 109421 (2022)
132. Titouna, C., Naït-Abdesselam, F.: A lightweight security technique for unmanned aerial vehicles against GPS spoofing attack. In: 2021 International Wireless Communications and Mobile Computing (IWCMC), pp. 819–824. IEEE (2021)
133. Tong, F., Chen, X., Wang, K., Zhang, Y.: CCAP: A complete cross-domain authentication based on blockchain for Internet of Things. IEEE Trans. Inf. Forens. Secur. **17**, 3789–3800 (2022)
134. Wan, W., Kim, H., Hovakimyan, N., Sha, L., Voulgaris, P.G.: A safety constrained control framework for UAVs in GPS denied environment. In: 2020 59th IEEE Conference on Decision and Control (CDC), pp. 214–219. IEEE (2020)
135. Wang, W., Hu, N., Liu, X.: BlockCAM: a blockchain-based cross-domain authentication model. In: 2018 IEEE Third International Conference on Data Science in Cyberspace (DSC), pp. 896–901. IEEE (2018)
136. Wang, S., Wang, J., Su, C., Ma, X.: Intelligent detection algorithm against UAVs' GPS spoofing attack. In: 2020 IEEE 26th International Conference on Parallel and Distributed Systems (ICPADS), pp. 382–389. IEEE (2020)
137. Wang, M., Rui, L., Yang, Y., Gao, Z., Chen, X.: A blockchain-based multi-CA cross-domain authentication scheme in decentralized autonomous network. IEEE Trans. Netw. Serv. Manag. **19**(3), 2664–2676 (2022)
138. Wang, M., Zhao, D., Yan, Z., Wang, H., Li, T.: XAuth: Secure and privacy-preserving cross-domain handover authentication for 5G HetNets. IEEE Internet Things J. **10**, 5962 (2022)
139. Wazid, M., Das, A.K., Kumar, N., Vasilakos, A.V., Rodrigues, J.J.: Design and analysis of secure lightweight remote user authentication and key agreement scheme in internet of drones deployment. IEEE Internet Things J. **6**(2), 3572–3584 (2018)
140. Wei, X., Sun, C., Lyu, M., Song, Q., Li, Y.: ConstDet: Control semantics-based detection for GPS spoofing attacks on UAVs. Remote Sens. **14**(21), 5587 (2022)
141. Wei, X., Aman, M.N., Sikdar, B.: A light-weight technique to detect GPS spoofing using attenuated signal envelopes. IEEE Open J. Comput. Soc. **4**, 158 (2023)
142. Wesson, K.D., Rothlisberger, M.P., Humphreys, T.E.: A proposed navigation message authentication implementation for civil GPS anti-spoofing. In: Proceedings of the 24th International Technical Meeting of the Satellite Division of the Institute of Navigation (ION GNSS 2011), pp. 3129–3140 (2011)
143. Whelan, J., Sangarapillai, T., Minawi, O., Almehmadi, A., El-Khatib, K.: Novelty-based intrusion detection of sensor attacks on unmanned aerial vehicles. In: Proceedings of the 16th ACM Symposium on QoS and Security for Wireless and Mobile Networks, pp. 23–28 (2020)
144. Wu, T., Guo, X., Chen, Y., Kumari, S., Chen, C.: Amassing the security: An enhanced authentication protocol for drone communications over 5G networks. Drones **6**(1), 10 (2021)
145. Wu, T., Guo, X., Chen, Y., Kumari, S., Chen, C.: Amassing the security: An enhanced authentication protocol for drone communications over 5G networks. Drones **6**(1) (2022). https://doi.org/10.3390/drones6010010, https://www.mdpi.com/2504-446X/6/1/10
146. Wu, M., Zhu, Z., Xia, Y., Yan, Z., Zhu, X., Ye, N.: A q-learning-based two-layer cooperative intrusion detection for internet of drones system. Drones **7**(8), 502 (2023)
147. Xiao, F., Zhou, M., Liye, Y., Yang, J., Wang, Q.: Poster: Enabling secure location authentication in drone. In: Proceedings of the 23rd Annual International Conference on Mobile Computing and Networking, pp. 600–602 (2017)

148. Xiao, K., Zhao, J., He, Y., Li, C., Cheng, W.: Abnormal behavior detection scheme of UAV using recurrent neural networks. IEEE Access **7**, 110293–110305 (2019)
149. Xue, N., Niu, L., Hong, X., Li, Z., Hoffaeller, L., Pöpper, C.: Deepsim: GPS spoofing detection on UAVs using satellite imagery matching. In: Annual Computer Security Applications Conference, pp. 304–319 (2020)
150. Yahuza, M., Idris, M.Y.I., Wahab, A.W.A., Nandy, T., Ahmedy, I.B., Ramli, R.: An edge assisted secure lightweight authentication technique for safe communication on the Internet of Drones network. IEEE Access **9**, 31420–31440 (2021)
151. Yimin, W., Shuhuan, W.: A new lightweight authentication for internet of drones (2023). Preprint, available at: https://www.authorea.com/users/599308/articles/631418-a-new-lightweight-authentication-for-internet-of-drones
152. Yu, S., Das, A.K., Park, Y., Lorenz, P.: Slap-IoD: Secure and lightweight authentication protocol using physical unclonable functions for internet of drones in smart city environments. IEEE Trans. Veh. Technol. **71**, 10374–10388 (2022)
153. Yuan, W., Li, X., Li, M., Zheng, L.: DCAGS-IoT: Dynamic cross-domain authentication scheme using group signature in IoT. Appl. Sci. **13**(10), 5847 (2023)
154. Zhang, H., Chen, X., Lan, X., Jin, H., Cao, Q.: BTCAS: A blockchain-based thoroughly cross-domain authentication scheme. J. Inf. Secur. Appl. **55**, 102538 (2020)
155. Zhang, Y., He, D., Li, L., Chen, B.: A lightweight authentication and key agreement scheme for Internet of Drones. Comput. Commun. **154**, 455–464 (2020)
156. Zhang, N., Jiang, Q., Li, L., Ma, X., Ma, J.: An efficient three-factor remote user authentication protocol based on BPV-FourQ for internet of drones. Peer-to-Peer Netw. Appl. **14**, 3319–3332 (2021)
157. Zhang, L., Xu, J., Obaidat, M.S., Li, X., Vijayakumar, P.: A PUF-based lightweight authentication and key agreement protocol for smart UAV networks. IET Commun. **16**, 1142 (2022)
158. Zhang, Y., Li, B., Wu, J., Liu, B., Chen, R., Chang, J.: Efficient and privacy-preserving blockchain-based multifactor device authentication protocol for cross-domain IIoT. IEEE Internet Things J. **9**(22), 22501–22515 (2022)
159. Zhang, Y., Luo, Y., Chen, X., Tong, F., Xu, Y., Tao, J., Cheng, G.: A lightweight authentication scheme based on consortium blockchain for cross-domain IoT. Secur. Commun. Netw. **2022**, 1–15 (2022)
160. Zhang, Y., Meng, L., Gan, J., Huang, Z., et al.: A novel and efficient authentication scheme based on UAV-UAV environment. Wirel. Commun. Mob. Comput. **2023**, 7107015 (2023)
161. Zhong, H., Gu, C., Zhang, Q., Cui, J., Gu, C., He, D.: Conditional privacy-preserving message authentication scheme for cross-domain industrial internet of things. Ad Hoc Netw. **144**, 103137 (2023)

Navigating the Skies: Exploring Dynamic Access Control in the Internet of Drones (IoD)

V. P. Jithu Vijay and Sabu M. Thampi

1 Fundamentals of Access Control

1.1 Introduction

Access control is a fundamental security measure designed to regulate and manage permissions within a system, determining which individuals or entities are authorized to access specific resources and perform certain actions. It is a major aspect of security architecture that ensures the confidentiality, integrity, and availability of services [38, 44].

Access control comprises three essential components: subjects, objects, and rules. Subjects are the entities seeking access, whether individual users, groups, or applications, often associated with specific roles or identities. Objects represent the resources or systems accessed, ranging from files and databases to physical spaces or airspace. The interaction between subjects and objects is governed by rules, which are policies dictating the conditions under which access is granted or denied. These rules, formulated based on security requirements, organizational policies, and regulatory considerations, specify who has access to what resources under various circumstances [11].

Access control mechanisms are broadly categorized into two classes: Traditional(Static) and Dynamic. Traditional access control mechanisms are characterized by static and predetermined permissions assigned to users or entities. In this model, the access rights are fixed and defined in advance, often based on roles and responsibilities. While traditional access control is straightforward to implement and manage, it is struggle to adapt with the dynamic nature of certain environments

V. P. Jithu Vijay (✉) · S. M. Thampi
Connected Systems and Intelligence Lab, School of Computer Science & Engineering, Digital University Kerala, Trivandrum, Kerala, India
e-mail: jithu.csres22@duk.ac.in; sabu.thampi@duk.ac.in

S. M. Thampi et al. (eds.), *Securing the Connected World*,
https://doi.org/10.1007/978-3-031-82826-3_10

[71]. Conversely, Dynamic access control mechanisms are designed to address the limitations of traditional models by introducing adaptability and responsiveness. Dynamic access control considers factors like the context of the access request, the current state of the system, or external conditions, allowing permissions to be adjusted dynamically. This approach is beneficial in environments with rapidly changing circumstances where the static nature of traditional access control is insufficient [20]. The different types of Traditional and Dynamic access control mechanisms are discussed in Sects. 4 and 5.

1.2 Need for Access Control in IoD

In the context of IoD systems, access control becomes more critical due to the unique challenges posed by UAVs operating in shared airspace. Unauthorized access to IoD systems can lead to safety hazards, privacy violations, and the misuse of drone capabilities. Effective access control also addresses privacy concerns by managing the collection, storage, and access to sensitive data and areas monitored by drones. Compliance to aviation regulations underscores the importance of strong access control in IoD systems. Also, it helps to optimize resources by preventing unauthorized use of airspace, bandwidth, and other valuable assets.

Without strong access controls, unauthorized individuals gain the control of IoD system, leading to coordinated attacks and operational disruptions. Effective access control systems are essential for limiting access to only authorized users, protecting the confidentiality of the data gathered by the drones, protecting mission goals, and preventing adversaries from exploiting compromised IoD systems.

2 Importance of Access Control in IoD Systems

Internet of Drones (IoD) is a collaborative network of drones that help in many fields, such as logistics, surveillance, military actions, and environmental monitoring. In IoD systems, one of the utmost security mechanism is access control that guarantees that only authorized entities have access to the IoD network. It safeguards information by limiting access to authorized users and preventing unauthorized access to data, apps, and devices. The access control mechanism enforces rules based on roles, identities, and attributes. It keep private information safe, maintain the system's integrity, and make sure it meets regulatory requirements [39, 44].

Implementing strong access control measures is important for ensuring the security, privacy, and integrity of data exchanged within the IoD ecosystem. Data breaches, malicious attacks, and the manipulation of drone operations are the possible consequences of intruders not following these precautions. Access control holds significant importance in IoD systems for various reasons. First and foremost, it prevents data leaks and secures sensitive information by limiting access to authorized drones only. Secondly, it prevents drones from being compromised and causing errors by preventing unwanted orders. Cyber threats like Distributed Denial of Service (DDoS) attacks can make IoD networks less safe by overloading them and stopping them from working. Strong access control systems can help lower these risks. The subsequent sections investigate the function of access control in IoD systems, with the focus on its enhancement of safety and security, prevention of unauthorized access, and establishment of trust and acceptance.

2.1 Safety and Security

Access control systems are very important for keeping IoD systems safe and secure. When someone gets illegal access to a drone in a sensitive area, it can cause major security breaches that put people's safety at risk and reveal private information [1]. It is important to make sure that only approved drones can get into sensitive areas. If someone gets in without permission, they might be able to change how the drone works and get important info from restricted areas, which could be used for bad things. Strong access control measures that confirm the names of drones and only let those enter who are authorized to do so protect against these threats. This method helps keep data safe and makes sure that drone actions follow safety rules [88].

2.2 Prevention of Unauthorized Use

The primary goal of regulating access in IoD systems should be to avoid illegal access. Several threats, which include the theft of sensitive information, unwanted monitoring, and the taking control of drones for malicious purposes, these can arise from unlawful access to the prohibited areas. These behaviors involve severe risks to privacy and might threaten the credibility of IoD operations [23]. Access control mechanisms helps in preventing illegal behaviors by ensuring that only authorized drones access and oversee coordinated tasks. Drones identities are validated before they are granted access through strict authorization processes. Certifying that only individuals with the required capabilities can carry out specific functions in the authorized region by restricting access to those locations [76].

2.3 Enhanced Trust and Acceptance

Access control procedures provide a basis for establishing trust and acceptability of IoD systems across partners including regulatory authorities, operators, as well as the public. The broad acceptance and deployment of drones in numerous industries rely on trust, which guarantees partners that operations involving drones are secure, dependable, and compliance with rules [40].

Strong access control measures show how to care about privacy and security, which is important for building trust among partners. One way to ensure that IoD systems are trustworthy is to follow all applicable regulations, conduct frequent security audits, and be transparent about how you handle data. This higher level of trust makes people more likely to accept drone technology. It makes easier to use in major regions like urban planning, emergency relief, healthcare delivery, and military operations [12].

3 Security and Privacy Considerations

IoD systems are vulnerable to various security and privacy threats due to their deployment in sensitive and high risk regions. These includes common cyber-attacks such as theft of encryption keys and unauthorised data access, as well as more complex attacks such as GPS spoofing and DDoS attacks. These attacks have the ability to disrupt the drone operations. The dynamic and unpredictable nature of the locations in which drones operate poses challenges in maintaining security and privacy protections. Addressing these challenges needs a comprehensive approach that includes context-aware authorization, effective risk management, continuous monitoring, and strict adherence to regulatory standards. The following sections will discuss the major security threats and vulnerabilities in IoD systems, then examine privacy concerns in IoD systems, and finally discuss the strategies needed to address the security and privacy of these systems.

3.1 Security Threats and Vulnerabilities in IoD Systems

The IoD is subjected to many security threats and flaws that could negatively impact the drone's availability, confidentiality, and integrity. Some of the important security threats and vulnerabilities in IoD systems are shown in Fig. 1. These threats pose an important issue as they take advantage of weaknesses by introducing undesired alterations [51]. As these systems handle extremely sensitive data, the threats they pose are similar to those in typical IoD systems. Drones collect sensitive information, which is then categorised based on its specific functions. Disclosure of this information can lead to violation of privacy and trust [3]. Below section discusses several threats and vulnerabilities associated with the IoD.

- **Compromise of Keys and Captured Communications:** A major threat to IoD systems is the risk of attackers compromising encryption keys and intercepting communications. The presence of this threat compromises the integrity and confidentiality of the system, resulting in privacy violations and the improper

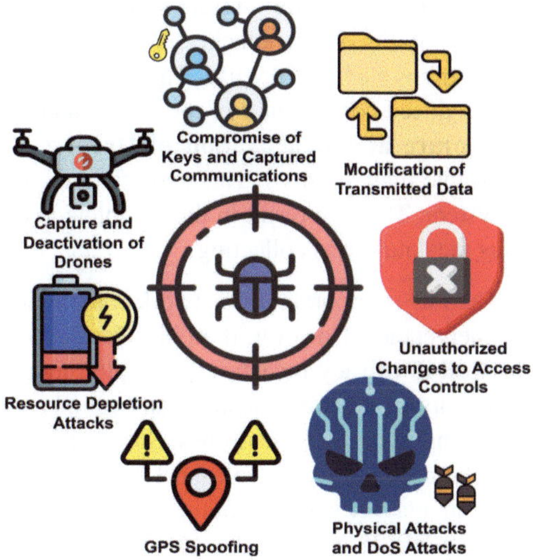

Fig. 1 Security threats and vulnerabilities in IoD systems

use of sensitive data. For example, A malicious operator with encryption keys can intercept the communications exchanged between drones and ground control station. The operator can disclose these confidential data to unauthorized parties by decrypting these communications.

- **Modification of Transmitted data:** Another critical vulnerability involves the alteration of transmitted data. This threat can change the integrity and confidentiality of information. As a result drones act on incorrect data. Such actions could lead to erroneous decisions and operational failures.
- **Unauthorized Changes to Access Controls:** Unauthorized changes to access controls and authorizations by illegitimate drones also pose a serious risk to the confidentiality and availability of IoD systems. This can enable attackers to modify permissions and execute unauthorized actions, leading to conflicts with legitimate operations and causing drone crashes.
- **Physical Attacks and Denial of Service (DoS) Attacks:** Physical attacks and excessive false requests target the availability of IoD systems. Attackers deploy out DoS attacks by flooding the system with an excessive number of requests, which prevents it from responding to valid commands. These disruptions severely affect drone operations. Especially the applications depend on prompt and accurate drone capabilities.
- **Coordination Disruption through GPS Spoofing:** The coordination of IoD can be compromised through GPS spoofing. This can impact the system's availability. The loss of drones navigation capabilities result in collision between other drones. GPS spoofing is the technique of altering the GPS signals that drones receive, as a result of which they navigate inaccurately and deviate from their intended path and fail to accomplish their tasks.

- **Resource Depletion Attacks:** Resource depletion attacks represent another vulnerability, where attackers affect the performance of IoD systems by draining resources such battery life. This threat targets the system's availability, leading to reduced performance of the drones and causing mission failures.
- **Capture and Deactivation of Drones:** An attacker can capture drones and disable their services. This can affect the confidentiality and availability of the system. This can result in the complete loss of the drone's functionality, as well as the data it was collecting.

The IoD is important for network communication during public safety operations or emergencies. However, if an intruder gains access to the communication keys, it can lead to privacy breaches. By exploiting vulnerabilities within the IoD and its application platforms, attackers can obtain keys. After that they modify the data and intentionally deceive the drones. So, access control is needed in IoD systems. It is must be done to guarantee robust security measures for access and authorization. Once an attacker gains unauthorised access to the access control system of a drone, they can readily modify the configuration of the IoD and cause disruptions.

In critical missions involving the IoD, Distributed Denial-of-Service (DDoS) attacks can severely impact the system [30, 70]. These attacks flood the ground control station with a high volume of requests. It affect the IoD availability of in major operations. Since drones have limited resources, So the attackers exploit this by overloading the system and leads to rapid depletion of resources.

Several other threats impact the availability of IoD. These include waypoint manipulation, and IoD freezing, which pose severe risks. Such attacks can alter coordination points, causing collisions within the IoD network. Better security measures and countermeasures are required to mitigate these threats. In order protect IoD systems against all these attacks, methods such as cryptography, dynamic security policies, and anomaly detection systems are used [57].

3.2 Privacy Concerns in IoD Systems

Today, drones are widely used in sensitive areas like restricted airspaces, military zones, and other critical infrastructure. The adaptive nature of these systems raises various privacy concerns and these should to be managed properly to stop illegal data leaks and access.

One of the primary privacy concerns with the IoD is the possibility of unauthorised collection and sharing. Drones operating in environments, they unintentionally record video footage and other data. This data is related to persons that is taken without their consent. Unintended recording can result in violation of privacy. For example, A drone is deployed to observe traffic patterns in an urban region and unintentionally capture footage of individuals in private regions. If the data is not effectively managed, it will be accessed by unauthorized operators and causing privacy violations [84].

Granting access to unauthorized drones in certain areas can result in privacy violations, including unauthorized monitoring, data breaches, and physical security risks. Strong policy enforcement mechanisms are important so those drones with permission can enter the areas. To detect and prevent these issues it is necessary to implement strong authorization mechanisms for drones and continuously monitor access attempts [74]. The complex nature of access control systems can lead to policy conflicts and misconfigurations. Their adaptable nature creates opportunities for cyber attackers to obtain unauthorized access. So, the access control policies are precisely defined and uniformly applied to minimize these risks. It is tough to maintain successful policy enforcement in adaptive contexts, frequent audits and updates to access control policies are required [13]. Such processes are needed for identifying and resolving issues that might threaten privacy and security in IoD systems.

Effective risk management is useful to guarantee that only authorised drones are allowed to enter critical areas. Dynamic risk-based access control methods continuously evaluate the risk of drones and adjust access permissions accordingly. It helps to maintain a precise and up-to-date model in order to avoid unauthorised access and keep sensitive data [83]. Systematic checks guarantee that drones undergo regular reassessment to reduce the likelihood of privacy violations. Incorporating dynamic access control mechanisms into the IoD also requires adherence to privacy laws and standards. Meeting these regulatory requirements is important for ensuring that drone operations remain lawful and ethical, especially in sensitive areas. In order to protect sensitive information, it must be done to conduct routine security assessments, maintain transparency regarding data handling practices, and implement strong access control measures [6]. By ensuring compliance with these regulations, trust among stakeholders is increased.

Thus, dynamic access control in IoD systems plays a major role for maintaining the secure and effective functioning of drones, especially when operating in sensitive areas. Important steps of managing privacy through limiting the data collection and sharing, preventing unauthorized access, resolving policy conflicts, handling risks, and adhering to regulatory standards. These steps are needed for protecting the sensitive data and secure drone operations. Effective dynamic access control methods allow IoD systems to balance operating flexibility with strong privacy protections. This allows for the safe use of drones in many areas.

3.3 Strategies for Addressing Security and Privacy Challenges

Deploying dynamic access control for drones in sensitive areas comes with its own set of security and privacy challenges that demand advanced solutions. Figure 2 shows different strategies for addressing security and privacy challenges and following sections describe each of these.

Fig. 2 Strategies for addressing security and privacy challenges

- **Context-Specific Authorization:** Dynamic access control in IoD systems needs to adjust in real-time to evolving contexts and operational needs. This means modifying access permissions based on the present environment and mission goals. The implementation of context-aware authorisation make sure that access is only provided when necessary, and thus minimising security vulnerabilities and preserving operational integrity. To achieve this, policies need to be flexible and automated. They should consistently evaluate recently collected information such as drone's location, battery level, and other environmental factors. These policies should be managed by properly, So that they can quickly adjust access permissions according to the current condition [4].
- **Preventing Unauthorized Drone Access:** Restricting unauthorized drones from entering sensitive areas is an important safety concern during IoD operations. Unauthorized drones present issues such as privacy breaches, unauthorized data collection, surveillance, and physical threats. Strong authorization techniques are essential to guarantee that only permitted drones access secured areas. The authorization mechanism consists of dynamic policies that will be updated in real-time based on the current operation condition, so that we can quickly mitigate these issues [16].
- **Addressing Threats Related to Policy Conflicts and Misconfigurations:** Dynamic access control systems offer flexibility, may sometimes encounter issues such as policy conflicts and misconfigurations. These vulnerabilities can be exploited by cyber attackers, So it is essential to ensure that access control policies are clearly defined and consistently enforced to address these threats. Regular audits and updates of these policies are necessary to identify and address

any vulnerabilities. Using automated tools for policy verification and conflict detection can help in maintaining the integrity of access control systems by guaranteeing that policies are accurate and consistent [22].

- **Risk Management and Continuous Monitoring:** Managing risks is needed for maintaining the security and privacy of IoD systems. In dynamic access control, it's important to keep evaluating the risks related to drones entering sensitive zones. This means recognizing and analyzing the effects of different risk elements on entering a specific area. Keeping a constant focus on drone operations is key to spotting any abnormal behaviors that might signal security issues [61].
- **Understanding and following privacy rules:** Complying with regulations means following set rules for safeguarding data and privacy, doing security checks often, and being open about how data is handled. To stay compliant, the IoD systems need strong access controls that follow rules and shield sensitive data. Regular checks make sure these controls work well and match the latest regulations [9].

4 Traditional Access Control in IoD

This section examines various traditional access control mechanisms and discusses the challenges and limitations of these traditional approaches in addressing the needs of modern IoD systems.

4.1 Traditional Access Control Mechanisms

Traditional access control mechanisms depend on predefined rules and policies set during system configuration to manage resource access. These rules are inflexible and do not adjust according to real-time context or situational changes [71]. Some of the well known traditional access control models are shown in Fig. 3 and listed below:

4.1.1 Mandatory Access Control

Mandatory access control (MAC) is a security framework designed to regulate access to resources based on predefined security policies, typically enforced by the operating system or security infrastructure [34]. In MAC, access decisions are not left to individual users or processes. Instead, a central authority establishes rules determining which subjects (e.g., users or processes) can access specific objects (e.g., files or devices). Both subjects and objects are assigned security labels or classifications, which indicate attributes like sensitivity levels or categories.

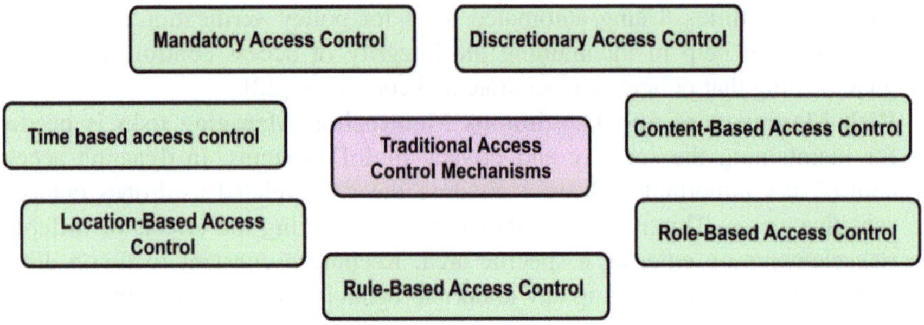

Fig. 3 Traditional access control mechanisms

Access is granted or denied by comparing these labels, ensuring that information is protected according to the predefined security policy.

4.1.2 Discretionary Access Control

Discretionary access control (DAC) functions as a security model that gives resource owners, such as those who possess files or directories, the power to manage access permissions. In DAC systems, resource owners have the authority to determine who can access their resources and what specific access levels are assigned to each user or group [69]. This decentralized approach allows individual users to independently manage access to their data and assets, enabling them to grant or revoke permissions according to their own criteria. Common permission levels in DAC include read, write, and execute, which can be assigned to the resource owner, particular users, or specified groups [56].

4.1.3 Content-Based Access Control

Content-based access control focuses on regulating access to resources based on the specific content or attributes of the data [98]. This approach involves creating rules that define conditions related to the content, with access being granted or denied based on whether the content meets certain predefined criteria. It is beneficial in scenarios where different data elements require different levels of security, allowing organizations to customize access controls based on the sensitivity of the content [62].

4.1.4 Role-Based Access Control

Role-based access control (RBAC) is a security framework that assigns access permissions based on the predefined roles within an organization. Instead of granting access directly to individual users, RBAC associates users with specific roles, each with designated access permissions. These roles represent certain job functions or responsibilities, and users assigned to a role automatically receive the corresponding permissions [28]. This approach simplifies access management, especially in large organizations, by making it easier to assign and revoke permissions through role assignments. RBAC enhances security and administrative efficiency by ensuring users access only the resources necessary for their roles, reducing the risk of unauthorized access and easing the burden of managing individual user permissions [21].

4.1.5 Rule-Based Access Control

Rule-based access control is a security framework that grants access permissions based on explicitly defined rules or policies. In this approach, access decisions depend on conditions specified in the rules, rather than on predefined roles or user attributes [60]. These rules can consider various factors such as time, location, and user behavior. This allows organizations to customize access policies to their specific requirements [85]. The rules are usually expressed through logical statements, form the basis for access decisions, determining whether access is granted or denied based on whether a user's request meets the specified conditions.

4.1.6 Location-Based Access Control

Location-based access control functions as a security measure that regulates access permissions based on the geographic location from which a user attempts to access a resource. When certain resources need to be accessed only from specific physical locations, this approach provides an extra layer of security [89]. This method involves creating rules that define acceptable locations for accessing particular resources. User authentication for accessing resources includes verifying both their identity and their physical location. Access is permitted only if the user is within an authorized geographic area, ensuring high security to particular physical boundaries. This system is useful for organizations that need to limit access to sensitive data or systems based on specific physical locations [2].

4.1.7 Time-Based Access Control

Time-based access control (TBAC) serves as a security measure that governs access permissions according to specific times or designated time ranges when a user attempts to access a resource. This type of access control is especially useful in situations where resources should be available only during certain predefined intervals [90]. Organizations utilize TBAC to enforce security policies, such as limiting access to sensitive data or critical systems outside of regular business hours.

This mechanism involves setting rules that specify permissible time frames for accessing particular resources [46]. Access is granted only when the current time matches the predefined criteria, and it is denied at all other times.

4.2 Challenges and Limitations of Traditional Approaches

Traditional access control approaches have long been the cornerstone of security frameworks in various organizations, primarily relying on static policies and predefined rules to manage user access to resources. However, these methods face several challenges and limitations in today's dynamic and complex environments. The challenges and limitations of traditional access control approaches are shown in Fig. 4 and listed below:

- **Lack of Granularity in Access Permissions:** Traditional access control methods lack the granularity required to define fine-tuned access permissions. These systems typically assign permissions based on predefined rules, which can lead to over-privileged access where users have more permissions than necessary for their tasks. This lack of granularity increases the possibility of data being compromised and accessed without authorization [63].
- **Inability to Enforce Dynamic Access Control Policies:** Here, the policies are typically static and lack the capability to adapt to changing contexts and environments. They do not support dynamic access control policies that can adjust permissions in real-time based on contextual factors. This inflexibility

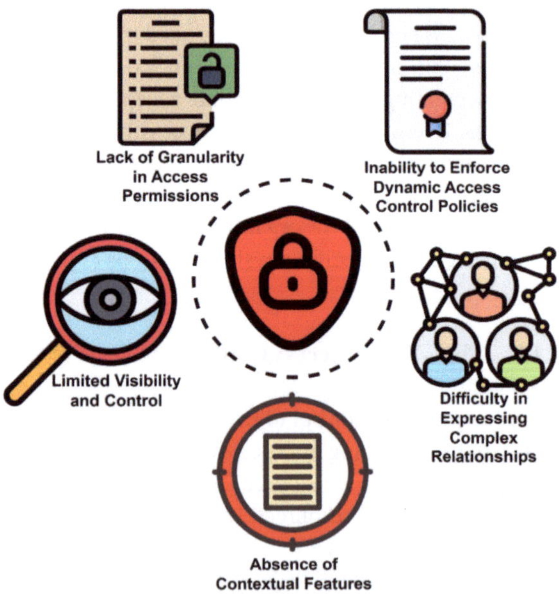

Fig. 4 Challenges and limitations of traditional approaches

makes traditional methods are not suitable for dynamic environments where access needs are continually evolving [67].
- **Difficulty in Expressing Complex Relationships:** They struggle to express complex relationships between users and resources. In modern environments, access requirements involve complex dependencies and conditional rules that are difficult to implement using traditional methods. This limitation restricts the ability to accurately model and enforce nuanced access control policies [77].
- **Absence of Contextual Features:** They do not typically incorporate contextual information to make access decisions. Contextual features such as behavior, environmental conditions, and real-time risk assessments to make more informed access control decisions. The absence of such contextual features in traditional methods limits their effectiveness in mitigating security threats [33].
- **Limited Visibility and Control:** These methods provide limited visibility into who is accessing what resources and when. This lack of visibility can restricts the ability to monitor and audit access activities effectively [77]. Without strong logging and real-time monitoring, organizations may find it challenging to quickly identify and address unwanted access attempts.

5 Dynamic Access Control in IoD

This section explores various dynamic access control mechanisms, examines their benefits, identifies the key components and principles of dynamic access control mechanisms for securing IoD operations.

5.1 Dynamic Access Control Mechanisms

Dynamic access control mechanisms evaluate access permissions based on real-time data about the user, resource, and environment [20]. This data includes factors such as user's identity, location, time of access, and the device being used. Unlike traditional methods, dynamic access control responds to current conditions, enabling more adaptive and context-aware resource management. some of the well-known dynamic access control models are shown in Fig. 5 and listed below:

5.1.1 Attribute-Based Access Control

Attribute-based access control (ABAC) operates as a security framework that determines access rights based on attributes related to users, resources, and contextual conditions. Unlike role-based access control, which relies on predefined roles for access decisions, ABAC offers a more flexible and adaptable approach [43]. This adaptability arises from the use of various attributes and their values

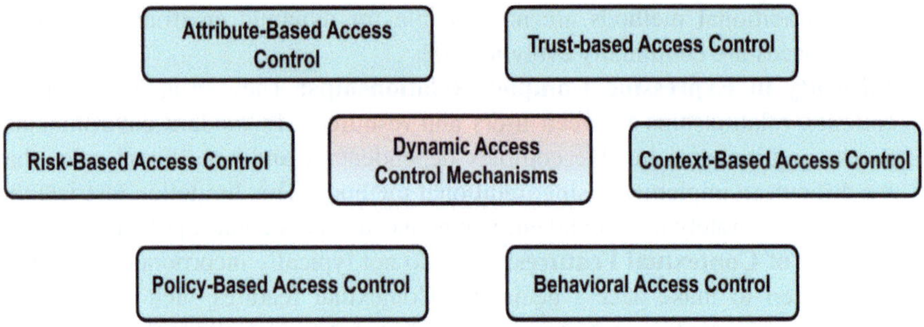

Fig. 5 Dynamic access control mechanisms

in defining access policies. In ABAC, policies are created using attributes such as user roles, time of day, geographical location, and specific user characteristics [29]. Access decisions are made by assessing these attributes against established policies, granting or denying permissions based on how well the attributes meet the specified criteria.

5.1.2 Trust-Based Access Control

Trust-based access control grants resource access based on the trust level established between entities within a system. It assesses the reliability of users, devices, or applications by considering factors such as their historical behavior, credentials, reputation, and endorsements from trusted sources [55]. Unlike traditional access control methods that depends on predefined permissions, trust-based access control incorporates dynamic and contextual elements when determining access rights. This method enables more flexible access control decisions, especially in complex and heterogeneous environments [73].

5.1.3 Context-Based Access Control

Context-based access control evaluates multiple contextual factors when making access control decisions. This approach adjusts access permissions based on the real-time context of the request [80]. It considers dynamic elements such as user identity, location, time of access, device characteristics, and environmental conditions. This method enhances security by customizing access control decisions to the specific circumstances of each access attempt, offering a more adaptive and responsive solution [80].

5.1.4 Behavioral Access Control

Behavioral access control focuses on analyzing and assessing user behavior to determine access permissions [96]. This approach examines users' past behavior patterns, closely analyzing irregularities that indicate security risks. By continuously monitoring and evaluating user behavior, behavioral access control identifies and responds to unusual activities that could indicate unauthorized access [75]. The system establishes a baseline of normal behavior for each user and triggers alerts when deviations are detected, thereby providing a proactive and adaptive security measure.

5.1.5 Policy-Based Access Control

Policy-based access control is a security model in which access permissions are determined dynamically through the real-time assessment of policies, considering various contextual factors. Unlike static access control methods, dynamic policy-based access control adapts to changing conditions, allowing organizations to apply access rules that align with the current status of users, resources, and the environment [19, 68].

5.1.6 Risk-Based Access Control

Risk-based access control assigns access permissions by assessing the risk associated with a user's current security context. This adaptive model considers factors such as the user's behavior, location, device characteristics, and the sensitivity of the resources being accessed to generate a risk score. Access decisions are then based on this score, allowing organizations to enforce strict controls in higher-risk situations and more permissive controls in lower-risk scenarios [78, 94]. This approach offers a flexible method for access control, ensuring that security measures are aligned with the assessed risk level at any given time.

5.2 Benefits of Dynamic Access Control in IoD Systems

Dynamic access control in IoD systems offers advantages by improving security and operational efficiency. Unlike static access methods, dynamic access control can adjust permissions in real-time based on factors such as drone location, time, mission status, etc. This method provides granular control, improves compliance with regulatory standards, and provides better auditing and accountability. Figure 6 shows these benefits and following sections describe it in detail.

Fig. 6 Benefits of dynamic access control in IoD systems

- **Real-Time Adaptability:** Dynamic access control systems offer high security by continuously adapting to changing conditions in real-time. Unlike traditional static access control mechanisms, dynamic access control can modify access permissions based on contextual factors such as the drone's location, time of access, and current operational status. This adaptability is important for maintaining security in IoD environments where access requirements are highly dynamic and context-dependent [27].
- **Granular Control:** It provides granular control over access permissions, providing more precise access management. This granularity allows IoD systems to define specific access rights for individual drones based on some criteria, reducing the possibility of unauthorized access and make sure each drone can only access the resources necessary for its mission [99].
- **Compliance with Regulatory Standards:** It helps to ensure compliance with regulatory requirements and industry standards. By continuously monitoring access activities and adjusting permissions in real-time, IoD systems can more effectively meet data protection laws and privacy regulations [72].
- **Increasing Operational Efficiency:** It makes operations more efficient by automated the tasks of allowing and denying access privileges. This automation reduces the administrative burden on security teams and ensures that access control policies are applied consistently and accurately. IoD systems can operate more efficiently with fewer disruptions and faster response times to changing operational needs [27].
- **Auditing and Accountability:** It provide detailed logging and auditing capabilities, enabling better tracking of access activities. This transparency increases

accountability by making it easier to trace access history back to specific drones. It helps to detect and investigate unauthorized access attempts [99].

5.3 Key Components and Principles of Dynamic Access Control

Dynamic access control in IoD systems is essential for managing access permissions in a highly dynamic and context-sensitive environment. By continuously adapting to changing conditions and make sure that only authorized drones can get to certain resources. The key components and principles of dynamic access control in IoD systems are shown in Figs. 7 and 8 and explained below:

5.3.1 Key Components of Dynamic Access Control

- **Access Control Lists (ACLs):** In dynamic access control systems, Access Control Lists are an essential component that must be present. It define which users are granted access to objects and the operations allowed on those objects [27]. In the IoD system, ACLs are dynamically updated to reflect real-time changes in access requirements.

Fig. 7 Key components of dynamic access control

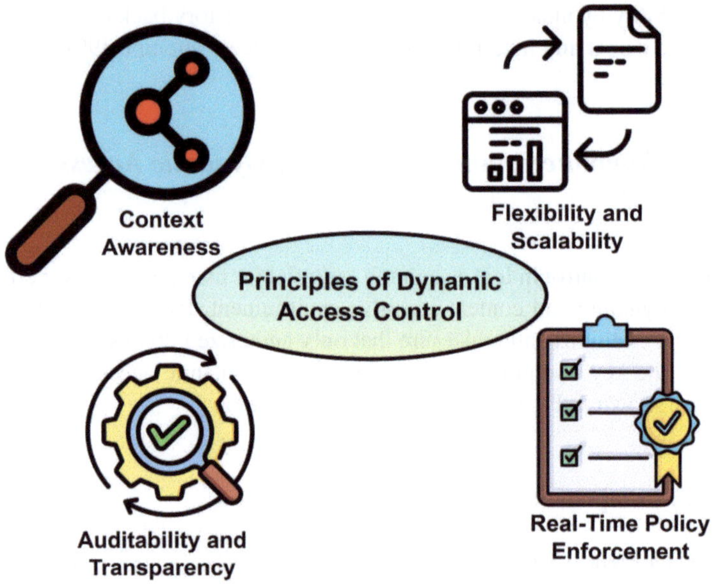

Fig. 8 Principles of dynamic access control

- **Security Groups:** Security groups aggregate user accounts, simplifying the management of access permissions [66]. In IoD systems, security groups help manage drone access efficiently by allowing policy changes to be applied to groups rather than individual drones.
- **Claim Types:** Claims are statements about a user or entity, such as their role, department, or clearance level [27]. In IoD systems, claims are used to make authorization decisions based on these attributes, providing more granular and context-aware access control.
- **Policy Enforcement Points (PEPs):** Policy Enforcement Points are responsible for enforcing access control policies within the system [36]. In an IoD system, PEPs ensure that drones comply with access policies by dynamically adjusting permissions based on current context and operational needs.

5.3.2 Principles of Dynamic Access Control

- **Context-Awareness:** Context-awareness is a core principle of dynamic access control, involving making access decisions based on the current context, such as the drone's location, operational status, and time of access. This ensures that permissions are relevant and appropriate for the situation [99].
- **Flexibility and Scalability:** It must be flexible and scalable to handle the diverse and evolving needs of IoD operations. Flexibility allows the system to adapt to

new access requirements and threats, while scalability ensures it can manage a large number of drones and access requests efficiently [66].

- **Real-Time Policy Enforcement:** It is important for maintaining security and operational integrity. This principle involves applying and updating access control policies instantly as conditions change, preventing unauthorized access and ensuring compliance with security policies at all times [36].
- **Auditability and Transparency:** It ensures that access control decisions are transparent and auditable. Auditability involves keeping detailed logs of access requests and decisions, which can be reviewed to ensure compliance and investigate security incidents. Transparency ensures that users and administrators understand how and why access decisions are made [99].

6 Technologies Enabling Dynamic Access Control

Dynamic access control is essential for managing access in environments where permissions need to adapt in real-time based on context and changing conditions. Figure 9 shows the technologies that enables dynamic access control systems and below sections explores each of these technologies.

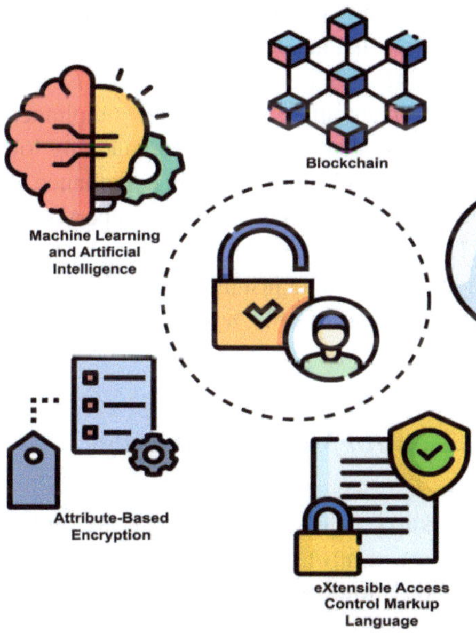

Fig. 9 Technologies enabling dynamic access control

6.1 Machine Learning and Artificial Intelligence

Machine Learning (ML) and Artificial Intelligence (AI) plays a important role in transforming modern access control systems. They bring advanced features that automate and improve security procedures. By processing large data sets, these technologies can detect patterns, predict security risks, and quickly modify access rights when needed.

ML models, such as supervised and unsupervised learning algorithms, can be trained on historical access data to recognize normal behavior and detect anomalies. For instance, a sudden deviation from established access patterns—like an employee trying to access sensitive data outside of normal working hours—can trigger an alert and prompt a reassessment of the user's access rights. This proactive approach helps mitigate risks before they escalate into security incidents [53, 86].

AI, especially through the use of neural networks and deep learning, allowing systems to handle complex and unstructured data. AI algorithms can process information from multiple sources, such as user behavior analytics, environmental sensors, and even social media feeds, to make strong access control decisions [50]. This capability is useful in environments such as IoT and IoD systems, where the context in which access requests are made can be highly dynamic and unpredictable. AI-driven dynamic access control systems can learn continuously. The more data fed into the system, the models resulting from the AI algorithms become increasingly refined; the accuracy and effectiveness thus improve over time. Such an improvement cycle ensures that the dynamic access control systems remain strong against evolving threats [24].

Eventually, ML and AI will help automate auditing and compliance-related tasks regarding dynamic access control systems. Their use for studying logs and finding abnormalities of access will let an organization maintain compliance with guidelines such as GDPR and HIPAA without much need for human supervision.

Integrating ML and AI further empowers decisions by providing the security analyst with actionable insights. Rather than just alerting to threats, for instance, AI systems can recommend remedial measures like temporary access suspension.

6.2 eXtensible Access Control Markup Language

eXtensible Access Control Markup Language is an agile, strong, and viable standard for defining and enforcing access control policies in dynamic environments. The XML-based format of XACML allows specifying complex rules, policies, and conditions governing access to resources. This level of granularity and flexibility is essential in dynamic access control systems, where the decisions about access are to be made based on several, often interrelated factors [18, 37].

XACML is based on a policy-based model for access control and is utilized when managing access within cloud computing, IoT, and IoD system environments. In such contexts, the concrete access control decisions are required to be dynamic and must adapt dynamically according to changes in context such as location, sensitivity of data, and current threat level. With XACML, access policies are defined at a granular level, so that access control decisions are consistent, transparent, and aligned with the organization's security objectives.

Fine-grained access control is one of the main benefits that XACML provides. This is a way to customize access permissions not just to drones, but also per actions, resources, and conditions. The XACML policy could specify that a drone can access secret data during a specific time window and from certain geolocations. This precision makes it more difficult to have unintended access and leads to permissions being as restricted as they need to be [64, 87].

XACML is intended to be extensible, enabling organizations to define their own data types, functions, and combining algorithms. This extensibility makes XACML very flexible with respect to different application domains and changes in the security requirements. For example, in a healthcare environment, XACML can be extended to include specific regulatory requirements for data access, such as those mandated by HIPAA.

XACML's architecture contains elements such as Policy Decision Point (PDP) and Policy Enforcement Point (PEP) that evaluate rules and ensure access decisions are enforced. PDP is the entity which makes decisions and defines exactly what kind of policies must be driven, while PEP allows or denies access based on those policies chosen by the former. This division of work also enables the scalability and versatility of the access control platform [35].

With XACML, it is possible to use access control systems in cross-domain. Drone networks involve multiple stakeholders operating in diverse environments, making the application of consistent and adaptable access control policies crucial. XACML provides a common language and framework to define and manage access control rules. These policies can be shared in a dynamic way among a variety of drones and ground control stations.

XACML is also used for auditing and compliance. With comprehensive policies, XACML enables every access control decisions to be traceable and are transparent. This is important for businesses required to prove regulatory compliance, like those involving data protection laws or industry standards [10].

6.3 Blockchain

Blockchain technology is revolutionizing the way we think of access control by providing full traceability, accountability, and privacy-centered immutability. Blockchains provide a decentralized and immutable ledger that tracks who accessed and any changes made to policies. This is very useful in environments where trust and consent are important [67, 91]. In dynamic access control contexts, blockchain can cryptographically store and validate access control transactions. For example, whenever an access permission is granted or revoked, the transaction is recorded on the blockchain. This ensures that all access changes are transparent and can be audited at any time [58]. This level of transparency makes it easier to discover policy violations and ensures that the access control system remains secure and compliant with regulations.

The biggest advantage of using blockchain in access control is that it eliminates tampering or fraud. Since data on the blockchain is immutable, once a transaction has been added, it will always be there and cannot be changed or removed. This provides a strong defense against insider threats and external attacks focusing on manipulating access control logs. Blockchain increases the scalability and flexibility of dynamic access control systems. In environments like IoD, where thousands of drones might be operating simultaneously, blockchain can efficiently handle the high volume of access transactions without compromising performance. Each drone's access permissions can be managed independently, with all transactions recorded on the blockchain for full accountability.

Blockchain supports smart contracts, which can automate and enforce access control policies without the need for manual intervention. Smart contracts are self-executing contracts with the terms of the agreement directly written into code. In a dynamic access control system, a smart contract could automatically revoke access rights when certain conditions are met, such as the expiration of a time-limited permission [45, 49].

The decentralized structure of blockchain enhances its durability. Without a single point of failure, distributed networks are more resistant to attacks. This decentralized structure ensures that even if a portion of the network is breached, the blockchain's integrity is preserved, maintaining the reliability of access control decisions [7]. Blockchain can facilitate greater collaboration and trust between different organizations. In situations where multiple entities need to manage and verify access to shared resources, blockchain provides a transparent and secure way to manage access control across organizational boundaries.

6.4 Attribute-Based Encryption

Attribute-Based Encryption (ABE) is a cryptographic method that support dynamic access control, by allowing for fine-grained access to encrypted data based on user attributes. ABE assures that only users with specific attributes, such as roles, departments, or clearance levels, can decrypt and access certain data.

ABE comprises two primary categories: Key-Policy Attribute-Based Encryption (KP-ABE) and Ciphertext-Policy Attribute-Based Encryption (CP-ABE). In KP-ABE, attributes are linked to the ciphertext, while the access policy is incorporated within the user's private key. By using this method, the system can regulate which users are able to decrypt data according to the characteristics they have. In an IoD system, a drone can encrypted flight data using specific attributes, allowing only operators possessing the corresponding attributes in their keys to decrypt and access the data [42, 100].

In CP-ABE, the access policy is linked to the ciphertext, while the attributes are incorporated within the user's key. This enables the formulation of more flexible and expressive access control policies, allowing the data owner to specify access permissions based on particular attributes. In a drone surveillance system, footage may be encrypted according to a policy that restricts access to operators assigned specific roles, such as individuals possessing a designated clearance level [47, 95].

The advantage of ABE lies in its capacity to implement access control independently of a centralized authority. The decentralized nature of ABE renders it appropriate for dynamic and distributed environments, where central management can be impractical.

ABE also supports multi-authority systems, where multiple independent authorities can issue attributes and keys. This enhances security by ensuring that no single entity has complete control over access permissions. In a multi-authority ABE system, different authorities could issue attributes based on their domain expertise, such as one authority issuing attributes related to drone roles and another issuing attributes related to geographic location. ABE provides fine-grained access control. By allowing access decisions to be made based on a combination of attributes, ABE enables highly specific and context-aware access policies [54, 59, 97].

ABE has some challenges, in terms of computational overhead and key management. Encrypting and decrypting data using ABE is more computationally intensive than traditional encryption methods, which can impact performance, especially in resource-constrained environments. Also, managing and distributing the large number of keys required in an ABE system can be complex [31].

6.5 Open Authorization

Open Authorization (OAuth) is an open standard for access delegation, widely used to grant third-party applications limited access to user data without exposing user credentials. OAuth operates by allowing users to grant tokens to third-party applications, which can then be used to access the user's data or resources for a specified period and with defined permissions. This token-based approach ensures that the user's credentials remain secure, while the third-party application only has access to the data it needs to perform its function [26, 65].

In a dynamic access control context, OAuth provides secure and flexible delegation of access rights. For example, in a multi-cloud environment, OAuth can be used to manage access to resources across different cloud providers, allowing users to securely share data between services without exposing their credentials. Similarly, in an IoD system, OAuth has been applied to allow temporary access to a certain area for authorized third-party drones.

It allows for granular control of who can access what. OAuth allow users to control access to data or resources by issuing tokens that have defined scopes and expiration times for third-party applications. This fine control is employed in dynamic contexts with context-dependent access control.

OAuth improves security by mitigating the risk of credential theft. The security of user credentials is minimised because third-party programs do not directly handle them. OAuth allows for the customisation of multiple flows and grant types to meet the needs of diverse use cases and security requirements. These include the authorisation code flow, the implicit flow, and the client credentials flow. OAuth is useful for a wide variety of applications due to its adaptability [82].

OAuth is compatible with various security frameworks and standards, including OpenID Connect (OIDC) and JSON Web Tokens (JWT). These integrations enable OAuth to offer both authorisation and authentication, as well as secure token exchange, thereby augmenting its effectiveness in dynamic access control systems [81].

It is important to carefully examine security best practices while adopting OAuth, including using secured token storage, putting in place token revocation procedures, and making sure that tokens are transferred securely. Incorrect configurations in OAuth deployments can result in security issues such as token stealing and unauthorized access.

7 Case Studies and Applications

The growing operations of the UAVs in various operation fields are indicative of adaptability and effectiveness in handling complex issues. Next case studies demonstrate how UAVs should be used, in realistic cases for different environments: observation of natural disasters, estimations of damage due to strong weather, and supporting military operations. These studies illustrate the capabilities of UAVs and indicate how dynamic access control is integral to enhancing the performance and efficiency of UAVs in various contexts. From landslide monitoring in Austria and support for disaster response in the United States to leading drone warfare during the Vietnam War, these case studies have provided insight into the evolution of UAV use in modern operations.

7.1 Case Study I: UAV-Based Monitoring of the Gallenzerkogel Landslide

In [32], it focuses on how UAVs were used in the Gallenzerkogel landslide, from Ybbs of Lower Austria. This area maintains steep slopes that are prone to landslides. Traditional methods in monitoring such areas are always difficult and dangerous to handle. However, with UAVs, they can collect detailed data from this challenging terrain.

They used a mini-octocopter UAV, MikroKopter OktoXL, with a Canon EOS 650D DSLR camera. They made three separate flights over the landslide area to capture high-resolution images of the UAV. The photos obtained from flights were then processed using SfM photogrammetry, which is a developing technique of creating three-dimensional models from a set of two-dimensional images. This Approach was followed here for the assessment of the landform over time.

DEM of Difference (DoD) method compares the elevation models of different times that quantify the landslide extension. They also used a multiscale model-to-model cloud comparison called M3C2 algorithm that allows one to delineate changes in terrain. The combination of these two allowed them to monitor the activity of the landslide closely and at the same time, evaluate the effectiveness of a stabilization effort.

A clear insight into the evolution of the Gallenzerkogel landslide with time has been achieved by UAV-based monitoring. DoD analysis showed that about 4380.1 cubic meters of slope material had been eroded, while 297.4 cubic meters amassed in the most active parts of the slope. About 688.3 cubic meters of the eroded material had destroyed a road in the area.

The M3C2 analysis helped them to visualize the changes between the first and second UAV flights. As there was dense vegetation around the landslide, the adopted method was helpful in order to reduce data noise. High-resolution orthophotos generated by the UAV helped to observe the impact of stabilization efforts between second and third flights.

Issue of data quality was initially affected by environmental factors such as wind, rain, and cloud conditions. Such factors normally make the operations of UAVs difficult across hilly regions such as Gallenzerkogel. Extensive heavy vegetation existed around the landslide area that initiated noise into the data, complicating the analysis. Another challenge lay in the limited flight time of the UAV because flight sessions are controlled by battery life. Each flight could only last for approximately 15 minutes, and therefore careful planning was required to gather sufficient data.

This could be very helpful in overcoming the various challenges by implementing dynamic access control and hence enabling the UAV to adapt its flight path with real-time changes of rain, cloud cover, and wind in order to improve both quality in data collected and smoothness in UAV operations.

It also optimizes the UAV's battery usage, allowing high battery capacity UAVs to access these areas and collect more data efficiently. In bigger operations, this will allow several UAVs to be used in a coordinated fashion, therefore offering higher coverage of the landslide area. By embedding dynamic access control, UAV-based monitoring can become even more effective than any other technique; it will help in better disaster management and environmental monitoring.

7.2 *Case Study II: UAV Use in Damage Assessment During the 2017 Hurricanes in Texas and Florida*

Following the widespread destruction caused by Hurricanes Harvey and Irma in 2017, UAVs or drones are used for assessing damage and assisting disaster response efforts in Texas and Florida. In [41] explores the use of drones during these crises, examining their effectiveness, the challenges encountered, and the important lessons learned for future applications.

These hurricanes were among the most severe storms to strike the United States, resulting in extensive damage and disruption. In response, various organizations including government agencies, NGOs, academic institutions, and private firms, deployed drones to quickly assess the situation and support relief efforts. These drones captured detailed visuals and created maps of the affected regions. This aerial data was important in determining the extent of the destruction, directing emergency operations, and planning the recovery.

In Texas, one of the most prominent civilian drone operations was coordinated by the Center for Robot-Assisted Search and Rescue (CRASAR) at Texas A & M University. Their team conducted 119 flights to map flood zones and assess damage, especially in areas that were difficult to access on the ground. These flights were used in identifying displaced hazardous materials, which posed serious public safety risks.

In Florida, post-Hurricane Irma drone operations were led by Florida State University's Center for Disaster Risk Policy, in collaboration with local emergency management agencies. The teams carried out 247 flights, covering 491 critical infrastructure sites. These operations provided FEMA with detailed property damage assessments, which were useful for prioritizing relief efforts and allocating resources efficiently. The data collected by the drones were also used to create 3D maps and orthomosaics, which offered a comprehensive view of the affected areas.

They highlighted several challenges that arose during these operations. Among the bigger issues was the lack of coordination across the different drone operators. In the absence of a central coordinating authority, redundant use of airspace and collection of data resulted in the wastage of efforts. The presence of drone operators not affiliated with any authentic body added to the problem; these were usually hobbyists who, while well-intentioned, contributed little more than to add to airspace congestion and sometimes without the proper authorization.

They also mentioned that while supportive, FAA regulations were not fully adapted to the specific requirements imposed by disaster response. Operators had to go through laborious and time-consuming procedures for flying permissions; sometimes this resulted in delays in significant operations. Flight restrictions were variably enforced, with unauthorized flights sometimes interfering with official disaster response activities.

Since the drone batteries had limited lives, all flights needed to be mapped out in advance; frequent recharging was often necessary to cover the ground that needed to be traveled. Besides, large-scale data volume management often poses challenges, especially in areas where communication infrastructure has been compromised. Delays in data transfer and its processing due to slow internet speeds and damaged networks could further restrain timely decision-making during disaster responses.

It is within this perspective that dynamic access mechanisms for drone operations can be implemented to address these challenges. These will be better coordination and communications among operators through the management of the flights of UAVs in real-time. The system would thus avoid airspace conflicts and redundancy and ensure that the missions are safely conducted. Dynamic access control could ease the process of retrieving flight permissions to ensure faster response situations during disasters.

It could also facilitate the optimization of UAV resource utilization, including battery power and data storage. By managing these resources in real time, drones could operate for longer periods, cover more area. This would enhance the efficiency of drone deployments and ensure that the data collected is immediately useful for disaster response teams. Implementing dynamic access control systems could address many of these challenges, making drones as an effective tool for managing natural disasters and supporting recovery efforts.

7.3 Case Study III: Use of UAV in the Vietnam War

In [79] provides a detailed exploration of the origins and development of drone warfare during the Vietnam War. This War is marked as a turning point in the development of drone technology, laying the foundation for the advanced UAVs used in military operations today. During this conflict, the United States developed and deployed the most advanced drone surveillance system of that era. These drones, called it as "Lightning Bug" UAVs, are essential in reconnaissance and intelligence gathering missions across hostile and dangerous territories. The Cold War, combined with the challenging environment of Vietnam, initiated the rapid development and deployment of these UAVs.

The "Lightning Bug" drones, formally known as Ryan Model 147, were initially developed by Ryan Aeronautical Company in response to the U-2 spy plane crisis in 1960, when a U.S. U-2 aircraft was shot down over Soviet territory. The Eisenhower administration, realizing the risks associated with manned reconnaissance missions, prioritized the development of UAVs to reduce human casualties and prevent the loss of sensitive intelligence. By 1962, the Lightning Bug program was fully operational, with these drones being launched from Lockheed DC-130 Hercules aircraft.

During the Vietnam War, the U.S. Air Force's Strategic Air Command utilized the Lightning Bugs in enormous amounts for reconnaissance over North Vietnam, Laos, and Cambodia. The drones were designated to fly pre-programmed routes; however, they could also be controlled by Airborne Remote Control Officers. After completion of the mission, the drone deployed a parachute and subsequently was retrieved by helicopters. These Lightning Bugs, flew more than 3500 combat sorties between 1964 and 1975, providing key intelligence that guided U.S. military operations during the war.

Major benefits were derived from the use of drones during the Vietnam War. First, drones could penetrate heavily defended areas without risking the lives of pilots, something very important given the advanced air defenses deployed by North Vietnam. Due to their small size and high speed, these drones were not easy marks for enemy forces, and thus they were able to accomplish many missions that could not be carried out by manned aircraft. These also operate in adverse weather conditions, including monsoon seasons.

The advanced sensors and cameras fitted in the Lightning Bug drones, enabled the capture of high-resolution images of enemy positions, the movement of troops and supplies, and real-time observation of enemy territory. This information is used in planning bombing missions, assessing damage, monitoring enemy activity, and giving a quick response to changing conditions on the battlefield.

Yet, despite the success of the drones in this operation, there are some limits to their viability and challenges which came out during that war. First and foremost, the cost of their survivability and maintenance was extremely high. In this respect, financial investment required to fund the Lightning Bug program was quite substantial considering the cost of the drone and its operation, which at the end of the war reached up to 250 million dollars annually. This costliness made the long-term sustainment of the program quite unfeasible.

Another challenge came from the limited operational flexibility of the drones themselves. Even though they might be remotely piloted, often the route of flight was pre-programmed, limiting their capability to make dynamic adaptations to battlefield conditions. This made them less effective in situations that called for real-time decision-making. While the drones were designed to avoid most enemy defenses, they were by no means immune to vulnerabilities. Advanced anti-aircraft systems installed by North Vietnam managed to shoot down a few such drones.

This dependence on remote control and pre-programmed routes created a narrow "soda straw" perspective for the drone operators, which significantly lessened their situational awareness and someone's ability to estimate the larger context of the battlefield. On the other hand, manned aircraft place pilots in a much more favorable position. Their visibility around them is much more complete, therefore helping make more informed decisions when on a mission. In this respect, since drones cannot integrate real-time intelligence, communication will become challenging and time-consuming to collect critical information, thus reducing the effectiveness of drones in dynamic combat situations.

The challenges identified during the Vietnam War encouraged furtherance and development of more advanced and flexible operational control systems for drones. Dynamic access mechanisms address most of the limitations identified above by managing UAV operations in real time. It provides for continued monitoring and adjustment in drone flight paths based on current conditions of the battlefield, environmental factors, and emerging threats. This allows the drones to be more responsive in dynamic conditions.

A mechanism like dynamic control of access would further enhance coordination among all flying drones in the same airspace. Dynamic management of access to this airspace would avoid conflict among them and ensure that each drone operates in a specific area, hence allowing better resource utilization. This will also enable more complex missions involving multiple drones with greater precision.

Situational awareness is further enhanced by integrating dynamic access mechanisms with advanced AI and machine learning systems. With the ability to scan real-time data from disparate sources, such a system would have a big picture view of the battlefield. This could potentially assist in better-informed decisions toward overcoming the "soda straw" limitation, thus enabling more effective mission planning and execution.

7.4 Applications of Dynamic Access Control in the Internet of Drones

The following sections examine the various applications of dynamic access control within the IoD systems, focusing on its importance in securing mission planning, managing air traffic, protecting privacy, and allowing safe and effective operations across various sectors.

- **Secure Mission Planning and Execution:** Mission planning and execution require high levels of security to restrict unauthorized access to confidential information including flight paths, drone configurations, and operational commands [92, 93]. Dynamic access control mechanism provide flexible and context-aware access control, ensuring that only authorized personnel can make modifications to mission plans and issue commands to drones. For instance, in a military operation, dynamic access regulation is established to limit access to mission-critical data according to the drone's role, location, and security clearance.

  Dynamic access control can be used to enforce event-driven access policies. For example, access to certain mission data might be granted only after particular conditions have been met, such as reaching a designated waypoint. This fine-grained control securing that access is tightly regulated and aligned with the operational requirements of the mission.
- **Real-Time Access Management for Air Traffic Control:** As the number of drones operating in shared airspace increases, managing their interactions with traditional air traffic control (ATC) systems becomes increasingly complex [8, 16]. Dynamic access control mechanisms are essential in managing these real-time interactions and make sure that only authorized drones can access ATC data and communication channels. For example, dynamic access control mechanism can dynamically adjust access permissions based on a drone's flight status, such as its proximity to no-fly zones, altitude, and speed.
- **Privacy Protection in Surveillance Operations:** Surveillance operations involving drones collect vast amounts of sensitive data, including video feeds,

images, and sensor readings [17, 92]. Protecting this data from unauthorized access is important, especially in law enforcement, border security, and private-sector applications [25]. Dynamic access control mechanism enables organizations to implement access control policies that restrict who can access, view, and modify the data collected by surveillance drones. As an example, only officers with the proper level of security clearance would be able to access encrypted video feeds obtained during a surveillance mission.

Dynamic access control enforces policies that restrict data retention and anonymise data in accordance with legal and regulatory requirements. For example, surveillance footage may be automatically deleted after a specific time and masked to protect the privacy of individuals who are not relevant to the investigation.

- **Emergency Response and Disaster Management:** Drones are increasingly deployed in emergency response and disaster management scenarios to provide real-time situational awareness, deliver supplies, and assist in search and rescue operations [15, 16]. In these environments, dynamic access control is important for ensuring that access to sensitive data and control systems is restricted to authorized personnel. For example, during a natural disaster, dynamic access control can dynamically adjust access permissions to allow emergency responders to access live video feeds, thermal imaging, and environmental data collected by drones, while restricting access to sensitive data to specific individuals.

  Dynamic access control can also manage temporary access for external entities such as government agencies, so that they can collaborate effectively without compromising security. Once the mission is completed, it can automatically revoke access.
- **Secure Data Sharing Between Drones and Ground Stations:** IoD systems involves distributed operations that require secure data sharing between drones and ground control stations [14]. Dynamic access control mechanism facilitates this secure data sharing by the process of encryption and data integrity policies, make sure that data is only accessible to authorized entities within the operational network and it is protected both in transit and at rest. For example, data collected by drones during an agricultural survey is shared with ground stations for analysis, but only authorized analysts within the network can access the raw data.
- **Autonomous Fleet Management:** Autonomous drones operating as part of a fleet require advanced dynamic access control mechanisms to manage access to control systems, navigation data, and communication channels [5, 48, 52]. In commercial applications, such as package delivery and smart city monitoring, it ensures that only authorized entities can issue commands to the drones and modify their operational parameters. For example, dynamic access control mechanism allow a logistics manager to reroute a drone in response to changing weather conditions while preventing unauthorized personnel from interfering with the drone's navigation.

8 Conclusion

As drones increasingly integrate into diverse fields, from surveillance to military operations, the need for secure, real-time management of dynamic access permissions becomes essential for drone networks or IoD. The chapter describes how dynamic access control mechanisms provide context-aware, real-time access management that adapts to the dynamic and complex nature of IoD environments. Maintaining safety, reducing risks, and building trust among stakeholders are all major outcomes of strong access control strategies. The integration of advanced technologies, such as machine learning and blockchain, further increases the effectiveness of these systems, ensuring that drones operate securely and efficiently across various scenarios. The concepts are illustrated through case studies, such as the use of UAVs for landslide monitoring in Austria, disaster assessment during the 2017 hurricanes in the United States, and drone warfare in the Vietnam War. Each case study shows how integrating dynamic access control can address challenges like unauthorized access, coordination in complex environments, and the need for real-time adaptability. The chapter further explores the application of dynamic access control in mission planning, air traffic management, privacy protection, disaster response, and autonomous fleet management, demonstrating its importance in modern drone operations.

References

1. Abdelmaboud, A.: The internet of drones: Requirements, taxonomy, recent advances, and challenges of research trends. Sensors **21**(17), 5718 (2021)
2. Abdulla, A.K., Bakiras, S., She, J.: ICMS: A flexible location-based access control system for mobile devices. IEEE Syst. J. **17**(1), 1536–1547 (2022)
3. Akram, R.N., Markantonakis, K., Mayes, K., Habachi, O., Sauveron, D., Steyven, A., Chaumette, S.: Security, privacy and safety evaluation of dynamic and static fleets of drones. In: 2017 IEEE/AIAA 36th Digital Avionics Systems Conference (DASC), pp. 1–12. IEEE (2017)
4. Al-Fuqaha, A., Guizani, M., Mohammadi, M., Aledhari, M., Ayyash, M.: Internet of things: A survey on enabling technologies, protocols, and applications. IEEE Commun. Surv. Tutorials **17**(4), 2347–2376 (2015)
5. Alami, R., Hacid, H., Bellone, L., Barcis, M., Natalizio, E.: Soreo: a system for safe and autonomous drones fleet navigation with reinforcement learning. In: Proceedings of the AAAI Conference on Artificial Intelligence, vol. 37, pp. 16398–16400 (2023)
6. Alharbe, N., Aljohani, A., Rakrouki, M.A., Khayyat, M.: An access control model based on system security risk for dynamic sensitive data storage in the cloud. Appl. Sci. **13**(5), 3187 (2023)
7. Alkhliwi, S.: An efficient dynamic access control and security sharing scheme using blockchain. Int. J. Adv. Appl. Sci. **9**(8), 28–40 (2022)
8. Allouch, A., Cheikhrouhou, O., Koubâa, A., Toumi, K., Khalgui, M., Nguyen Gia, T.: Utm-chain: blockchain-based secure unmanned traffic management for internet of drones. Sensors **21**(9), 3049 (2021)

9. Anedda, M., Floris, A., Girau, R., Fadda, M., Ruiu, P., Farina, M., Bonu, A., Giusto, D.D.: Privacy and security best practices for IoT solutions. IEEE Access **11**, 129156–129172 (2023)
10. Ashutosh, A., Gerl, A., Wagner, S., Brunie, L., Kosch, H.: XACML for mobility (xacml4m)—an access control framework for connected vehicles. Sensors **23**(4), 1763 (2023)
11. Atlam, H.F., Alassafi, M.O., Alenezi, A., Walters, R.J., Wills, G.B.: XACML for building access control policies in internet of things. In: IoTBDS, pp. 253–260 (2018)
12. Badshah, A., Abbas, G., Waqas, M., Tu, S., Abbas, Z.H., Muhammad, F., Chen, S.: USAF-IoD: Ultralightweight and secure authenticated key agreement framework for internet of drones environment. IEEE Trans. Veh. Technol. **73**(8), 10963–10977 (2024). https://doi.org/10.1109/TVT.2024.3375758
13. Banyal, R., Jain, V., Jain, P.: Dynamic trust based access control framework for securing multi-cloud environment. In: Proceedings of the 2014 International Conference on Information and Communication Technology for Competitive Strategies, pp. 1–8 (2014)
14. Bera, B., Chattaraj, D., Das, A.K.: Designing secure blockchain-based access control scheme in IoT-enabled internet of drones deployment. Comput. Commun. **153**, 229–249 (2020)
15. Bera, B., Saha, S., Das, A.K., Kumar, N., Lorenz, P., Alazab, M.: Blockchain-envisioned secure data delivery and collection scheme for 5g-based IoT-enabled internet of drones environment. IEEE Trans. Veh. Technol. **69**(8), 9097–9111 (2020)
16. Bera, B., Das, A.K., Garg, S., Piran, M.J., Hossain, M.S.: Access control protocol for battlefield surveillance in drone-assisted IoT environment. IEEE Internet Things J. **9**(4), 2708–2721 (2021)
17. Bera, B., Das, A.K., Sutrala, A.K.: Private blockchain-based access control mechanism for unauthorized UAV detection and mitigation in internet of drones environment. Comput. Commun. **166**, 91–109 (2021)
18. Bertolino, A., Daoudagh, S., Lonetti, F., Marchetti, E., Schilders, L.: Automated testing of extensible access control markup language-based access control systems. IET Softw. **7**(4), 203–212 (2013)
19. Bogaerts, J., Lagaisse, B., Joosen, W.: Sequoia: a middleware supporting policy-based access control for search and aggregation in data-driven applications. IEEE Trans. Depend. Sec. Comput. **18**(1), 325–339 (2018)
20. Boustia, N., Mokhtari, A.: A dynamic access control model. Appl. Intell. **36**, 190–207 (2012)
21. Butt, A.U.R., Mahmood, T., Saba, T., Bahaj, S.A.O., Alamri, F.S., Iqbal, M.W., Khan, A.R.: An optimized role-based access control using trust mechanism in e-health cloud environment. IEEE Access **11**, 138813–138826 (2023). https://doi.org/10.1109/ACCESS.2023.3335984
22. Chanal, P.M., Kakkasageri, M.S.: Security and privacy in IoT: a survey. Wirel. Pers. Commun. **115**(2), 1667–1693 (2020)
23. Chaudhry, S.A., Yahya, K., Karuppiah, M., Kharel, R., Bashir, A.K., Zikria, Y.B.: GCACS-IoD: A certificate based generic access control scheme for internet of drones. Comput. Netw. **191**, 107999 (2021)
24. Chauhan, A.: Leveraging machine learning to improve access control mechanisms in data warehousing. Afr. J. Biol. Sci. **6**, 2650–2658 (2024). https://doi.org/10.48047/AFJBS.6.12.2024.2650-2658
25. Chen, Y.J., Wang, L.C.: Privacy protection for internet of drones: A network coding approach. IEEE Internet Things J. **6**(2), 1719–1730 (2018)
26. Cirani, S., Picone, M., Gonizzi, P., Veltri, L., Ferrari, G.: IoT-oas: An oauth-based authorization service architecture for secure services in IoT scenarios. IEEE Sens. J. **15**(2), 1224–1234 (2014)
27. Covington, M.J., Long, W., Srinivasan, S., Dev, A.K., Ahamad, M., Abowd, G.D.: Securing context-aware applications using environment roles. In: Proceedings of the Sixth ACM Symposium on Access Control Models and Technologies, pp. 10–20 (2001)
28. Cruz, J.P., Kaji, Y., Yanai, N.: RBAC-SC: Role-based access control using smart contract. IEEE Access **6**, 12240–12251 (2018)
29. De Oliveira, M.T., Reis, L.H.A., Verginadis, Y., Mattos, D.M.F., Olabarriaga, S.D.: Smartaccess: Attribute-based access control system for medical records based on smart contracts. IEEE Access **10**, 117836–117854 (2022)

30. Douligeris, C., Mitrokotsa, A.: DDOS attacks and defense mechanisms: classification and state-of-the-art. Comput. Netw. **44**(5), 643–666 (2004)
31. Edemacu, K., Park, H.K., Jang, B., Kim, J.W.: Privacy provision in collaborative ehealth with attribute-based encryption: Survey, challenges and future directions. IEEE Access **7**, 89614–89636 (2019)
32. Eker, R., Aydın, A., Hübl, J.: Unmanned aerial vehicle (UAV)-based monitoring of a landslide: Gallenzerkogel landslide (Ybbs-Lower Austria) case study. Environ. Monit. Assess. **190**, 1–14 (2018)
33. Emami, S.S., Amini, M., Zokaei, S.: A context-aware access control model for pervasive computing environments. In: The 2007 International Conference on Intelligent Pervasive Computing (IPC 2007), pp. 51–56. IEEE (2007)
34. Fan, Y., Han, Z., Liu, J., Zhao, Y.: A mandatory access control model with enhanced flexibility. In: 2009 International Conference on Multimedia Information Networking and Security, vol. 1, pp. 120–124. IEEE (2009)
35. Farhadighalati, N., Barata, J., Nikghadam-Hojjati, S., Marchetti, E.: Behavioral and human-centric access control model in XACML reference architecture: Design and implementation of EHR case study. In: Doctoral Conference on Computing, Electrical and Industrial Systems, pp. 192–203. Springer (2024)
36. Ferraiolo, D.F., Kuhn, D.R.: Role-based access controls. CoRR abs/0903.2171 (2009). http://arxiv.org/abs/0903.2171
37. Ferraiolo, D., Chandramouli, R., Kuhn, R., Hu, V.: Extensible access control markup language (XACML) and next generation access control (NGAC). In: Proceedings of the 2016 ACM International Workshop on Attribute Based Access Control, pp. 13–24 (2016)
38. Ghaffari, F., Bertin, E., Crespi, N., Behrad, S., Hatin, J.: A novel access control method via smart contracts for internet-based service provisioning. IEEE Access **9**, 81253–81273 (2021)
39. Ghaffari, F., Bertin, E., Crespi, N., Behrad, S., Hatin, J.: A novel access control method via smart contracts for internet-based service provisioning. IEEE Access **9**, 81253–81273 (2021)
40. Gorrepati, R.R., Guntur, S.R.: Dronemap: an IoT network security in internet of drones. In: Development and Future of Internet of Drones (IoD): Insights, Trends and Road Ahead, pp. 251–268 (2021)
41. Greenwood, F., Nelson, E.L., Greenough, P.G.: Flying into the hurricane: A case study of UAV use in damage assessment during the 2017 hurricanes in Texas and Florida. PLoS One **15**(2), e0227808 (2020)
42. Guo, L., Yang, X., Yau, W.C.: TABE-DAC: Efficient traceable attribute-based encryption scheme with dynamic access control based on blockchain. IEEE Access **9**, 8479–8490 (2021)
43. Gupta, M., Awaysheh, F.M., Benson, J., Alazab, M., Patwa, F., Sandhu, R.: An attribute-based access control for cloud enabled industrial smart vehicles. IEEE Trans. Ind. Inf. **17**(6), 4288–4297 (2020)
44. Gupta, N., Prakash, A., Tripathi, R.: Medium access control protocols for safety applications in vehicular ad-hoc network: A classification and comprehensive survey. Veh. Commun. **2**(4), 223–237 (2015)
45. Gupta, R., Shukla, V.K., Rao, S.S., Anwar, S., Sharma, P., Bathla, R.: Enhancing privacy through "smart contract" using blockchain-based dynamic access control. In: 2020 International Conference on Computation, Automation and Knowledge Management (ICCAKM), pp. 338–343. IEEE (2020)
46. Hong, J., Xue, K., Xue, Y., Chen, W., Wei, D.S., Yu, N., Hong, P.: TAFC: Time and attribute factors combined access control for time-sensitive data in public cloud. IEEE Trans. Serv. Comput. **13**(1), 158–171 (2017)
47. Huang, W., Xie, X., Wang, Z., Feng, J.: A zero trust and attribute-based encryption scheme for dynamic access control in power IoT environments. In: The International Conference on Natural Computation, Fuzzy Systems and Knowledge Discovery, pp. 1338–1345. Springer (2022)
48. Hussein, M., Nouacer, R., Corradi, F., Ouhammou, Y., Villar, E., Tieri, C., Castiñeira, R.: Key technologies for safe and autonomous drones. Microprocess. Microsyst. **87**, 104348 (2021)

49. Hwang, D., Choi, J., Kim, K.H.: Dynamic access control scheme for IoT devices using blockchain. In: 2018 International Conference on Information and Communication Technology Convergence (ICTC), pp. 713–715. IEEE (2018)
50. Istiaque Ahmed, K., Tahir, M., Hadi Habaebi, M., Lun Lau, S., Ahad, A.: Machine learning for authentication and authorization in IoT: Taxonomy, challenges and future research direction. Sensors **21**(15), 5122 (2021)
51. Kanellos, L.: Safety, privacy and net neutrality aspects of civilian drones. In: Net Neutrality Compendium: Human Rights, Free Competition and the Future of the Internet, pp. 271–279 (2016)
52. Koubâa, A., Qureshi, B., Sriti, M.F., Allouch, A., Javed, Y., Alajlan, M., Cheikhrouhou, O., Khalgui, M., Tovar, E.: Dronemap planner: A service-oriented cloud-based management system for the internet-of-drones. Ad Hoc Netw. **86**, 46–62 (2019)
53. Kühl, N., Schemmer, M., Goutier, M., Satzger, G.: Artificial intelligence and machine learning. Electron. Mark. **32**(4), 2235–2244 (2022)
54. Li, J., Chen, X., Li, J., Jia, C., Ma, J., Lou, W.: Fine-grained access control system based on outsourced attribute-based encryption. In: Computer Security–ESORICS 2013: 18th European Symposium on Research in Computer Security, Egham, UK, September 9-13, 2013. Proceedings 18, pp. 592–609. Springer (2013)
55. Lin, G., Wang, D., Bie, Y., Lei, M.: MTBAC: A mutual trust based access control model in cloud computing. China Commun. **11**(4), 154–162 (2014)
56. Lin, T.Y.T., Vachon, P.: Secure information flow and file movements: A topological theory of discretionary access controls. In: 2017 IEEE International Conference on Big Data (Big Data), pp. 1821–1829. IEEE (2017)
57. Liu, C., Yang, J., Chen, R., Zhang, Y., Zeng, J.: Research on immunity-based intrusion detection technology for the internet of things. In: 2011 Seventh International Conference on Natural Computation, vol. 1, pp. 212–216. IEEE (2011)
58. Maesa, D.D.F., Mori, P., Ricci, L.: A blockchain based approach for the definition of auditable access control systems. Comput. Secur. **84**, 93–119 (2019)
59. MahdaviOliaee, M., Ahmadian, Z.: Fine-grained flexible access control: ciphertext policy attribute based encryption for arithmetic circuits. J. Comput. Virol. Hack. Techniq. **19**(4), 515–528 (2023)
60. Maheshkumar, M., Hemant, C.S., Zaddari, S.A., Jothimani, A.: Rule-based access control system in cloud-based environment. Int. J. Adv. Res. Ideas Innov. Technol. **5**(3) (2019). https://www.ijariit.com
61. Malik, V., Singh, S.: Security risk management in IoT environment. J. Discrete Math. Sci. Cryptogr. **22**(4), 697–709 (2019)
62. Mansoor, T., Ali, M.M.: Content-based access control in an online community. In: 2017 8th International Conference on Information Technology (ICIT), pp. 677–684. IEEE (2017)
63. Mohammad, Z.N., Farha, F., Abuassba, A.O.M., Yang, S., Zhou, F.: Access control and authorization in smart homes: A survey. Tsinghua Sci. Technol. **26**(6), 906–917 (2021). https://doi.org/10.26599/TST.2021.9010001
64. Nasim, R., Buchegger, S.: XACML-based access control for decentralized online social networks. In: 2014 IEEE/ACM 7th International Conference on Utility and Cloud Computing, pp. 671–676. IEEE (2014)
65. Oh, S.R., Kim, Y.G.: AFaaS: Authorization framework as a service for Internet of Things based on interoperable oauth. Int. J. Distrib. Sensor Netw. **16**(2), 1550147720906388 (2020)
66. Osborn, S.L.: Role-Based Access Control, pp. 55–70. Springer Berlin Heidelberg, Berlin, Heidelberg (2007). https://doi.org/10.1007/978-3-540-69861-6_5
67. Outchakoucht, A., Es-Samaali, H., Leroy, J.P.: Dynamic access control policy based on blockchain and machine learning for the Internet of Things. Int. J. Adv. Comput. Sci. Appl. **8**(7), 417–424 (2017)
68. Pal, S., Hitchens, M., Varadharajan, V., Rabehaja, T.: Policy-based access control for constrained healthcare resources in the context of the Internet of Things. J. Netw. Comput. Appl. **139**, 57–74 (2019)

69. Pan, X., Obahiaghon, A., Makar, B., Wilson, S., Beard, C.: Analysis of database security. Open Access Library J. **11**(4), 1–19 (2024)
70. Peng, T., Leckie, C., Ramamohanarao, K.: Survey of network-based defense mechanisms countering the DoS and DDoS problems. ACM Comput. Surv. (CSUR) **39**(1), 3–es (2007)
71. Pottier, F., Skalka, C., Smith, S.: A systematic approach to static access control. ACM Trans. Program. Lang. Syst. (TOPLAS) **27**(2), 344–382 (2005)
72. Prakash, S., Malaiyappan, J.N.A., Thirunavukkarasu, K., Devan, M.: Achieving regulatory compliance in cloud computing through ML. AIJMR-Adv. Int. J. Multidiscip. Res. **2**, 1038 (2024)
73. Putra, G.D., Dedeoglu, V., Kanhere, S.S., Jurdak, R., Ignjatovic, A.: Trust-based blockchain authorization for IoT. IEEE Trans. Netw. Serv. Manag. **18**(2), 1646–1658 (2021)
74. Rezaeibagha, F., Mu, Y.: Distributed clinical data sharing via dynamic access-control policy transformation. Int. J. Med. Inf. **89**, 25–31 (2016)
75. Rikhtechi, L., Rafeh, V., Rezakhani, A.: BBAC: Behavior-based access control to detect user suspicious behavior. J. Intell. Fuzzy Syst. **43**(6), 8207–8220 (2022)
76. Samanth, S., KV, P., Balachandra, M.: Security in internet of drones: A comprehensive review. Cogent Eng. **9**(1), 2029080 (2022)
77. Sandhu, R.S., Samarati, P.: Access control: principle and practice. IEEE Commun. Mag. **32**(9), 40–48 (1994)
78. Shaikh, R.A., Adi, K., Logrippo, L.: Dynamic risk-based decision methods for access control systems. Comput. Secur. **31**(4), 447–464 (2012)
79. Shaw, I.G.: Scorched atmospheres: The violent geographies of the Vietnam war and the rise of drone warfare. Ann. Am. Assoc. Geograph. **106**(3), 688–704 (2016)
80. Shebaro, B., Oluwatimi, O., Bertino, E.: Context-based access control systems for mobile devices. IEEE Trans. Depend. Sec. Comput. **12**(2), 150–163 (2014)
81. Shehab, M., Marouf, S.: Recommendation models for open authorization. IEEE Trans. Depend. Sec. Comput. **9**(4), 583–596 (2012)
82. Shehab, M., Marouf, S., Hudel, C.: Roauth: Recommendation based open authorization. In: Proceedings of the Seventh Symposium on Usable Privacy and Security, pp. 1–12 (2011)
83. Shrivastava, S., Srikanth, T.: A dynamic access control policy for healthcare service delivery in healthcare ecosystem using electronic health records. In: 2021 International Conference on COMmunication Systems & NETworkS (COMSNETS), pp. 662–667. IEEE (2021)
84. Son, J., Kim, J.D., Na, H.S., Baik, D.K.: Dynamic access control model for privacy preserving personalized healthcare in cloud environment. Technol. Health Care **24**(s1), S123–S129 (2016)
85. Srivastava, K., Shekokar, N.: Design of machine learning and rule based access control system with respect to adaptability and genuineness of the requester. EAI Endors. Trans. Pervas. Health Technol. **6**(24), e1 (2020)
86. Srivastava, K., Shekokar, N.: Machine learning based risk-adaptive access control system to identify genuineness of the requester. In: Modern Approaches in Machine Learning and Cognitive Science: A Walkthrough: Latest Trends in AI, pp. 129–143 (2020)
87. Standard, O.: extensible access control markup language (XACML) version 3.0. A: (22 January 2013). http://docs.oasis-open.org/xacml/3.0/xacml-3.0-core-spec-os-en.html (2013)
88. Tychola, K.A., Voulgaridis, K., Lagkas, T.: Beyond flight: Enhancing the Internet of Drones with blockchain technologies. Drones **8**(6), 219 (2024)
89. Vicente, C.R., Kirkpatrick, M., Ghinita, G., Bertino, E., Jensen, C.S.: Towards location-based access control in healthcare emergency response. In: Proceedings of the 2nd SIGSPATIAL ACM GIS 2009 International Workshop on Security and Privacy in GIS and LBS, pp. 22–26 (2009)
90. Wang, B., Li, W., Xiong, N.N.: Time-based access control for multi-attribute data in Internet of Things. Mob. Netw. Appl. **26**(2), 797–807 (2021)
91. Wang, P., Xu, N., Zhang, H., Sun, W., Benslimane, A.: Dynamic access control and trust management for blockchain-empowered IoT. IEEE Internet Things J. **9**(15), 12997–13009 (2021)

92. Wazid, M., Das, A.K., Kumar, N., Vasilakos, A.V., Rodrigues, J.J.: Design and analysis of secure lightweight remote user authentication and key agreement scheme in Internet of Drones deployment. IEEE Internet Things J. **6**(2), 3572–3584 (2018)
93. Wazid, M., Das, A. K., Lee, J.-H.: Authentication protocols for the Internet of Drones: Taxonomy analysis and future directions. J. Ambient Intell. Humanized Comput. **31**, 1–10 (2018)
94. Xie, P., Li, X., Feng, T., Zhang, M., Zhang, P., Li, P.: A trust and risk adaptive access control model for Internet of vehicles. Changes **20**, 22 (2024)
95. Yan, H., Li, J., Li, X., Zhao, G., Lee, S.Y., Shen, J.: Secure access control of e-health system with attribute-based encryption. Intell. Autom. Soft Comput. **22**(3), 345–352 (2016)
96. Yarmand, M.H., Sartipi, K., Down, D.G.: Behavior-based access control for distributed healthcare systems. J. Comput. Secur. **21**(1), 1–39 (2013)
97. Ying, Z., Li, H., Ma, J., Zhang, J., Cui, J.: Adaptively secure ciphertext-policy attribute-based encryption with dynamic policy updating. Science China. Inf. Sci. **59**(4), 042701 (2016)
98. Zeng, W., Yang, Y., Luo, B.: Content-based access control: Use data content to assist access control for large-scale content-centric databases. In: 2014 IEEE International Conference on Big Data (Big Data), pp. 701–710. IEEE (2014)
99. Zhang, G., Parashar, M.: Context-aware dynamic access control for pervasive applications. In: Proceedings of the Communication Networks and Distributed Systems Modeling and Simulation Conference, pp. 21–30. San Diego (2004)
100. Zhang, Y., Deng, R.H., Xu, S., Sun, J., Li, Q., Zheng, D.: Attribute-based encryption for cloud computing access control: A survey. ACM Comput. Surv. (CSUR) **53**(4), 1–41 (2020)

From Ground to Cloud: Integrated Multi-Attack Detection in IoT-Driven UAV Security Frameworks

Meenakshy S. Kumar and Sabu M. Thampi

1 Introduction to Internet of Drones

Imagine a world where drones coordinate seamlessly to manage crops, deliver packages, and monitor traffic, all without the need for human intervention. This is the promise of the Internet of Drones (IoD)—a revolutionary network that interconnects Unmanned Aerial Vehicles (UAVs), enabling them to communicate, collaborate, and operate autonomously across various industries [3]. The Internet of Drones (IoD) can be described as an infrastructure designed to provide control and access over the Internet between drones and users [1]. The Internet of Drones (IoD) derives its name from IoT by putting "Drones" in place of "Things." Thus, IoDs have similar properties to IoT [25]. In reality, drones are rapidly becoming readily available commodity items, allowing any user to fly different missions in controlled airspace using multiple drones [1]. The IoD has many other names. It is called an Unmanned Aerial Vehicle (UAV) when used on land, an Unmanned Aircraft System (UAS) when operated on air, and an Unmanned Under-Water Vehicle (UUV) when employed underwater [25]. The term drone originated from the military, while UAV and UAS were adopted by some regulators of the US Federal Aviation Administration (FAA) [15]. Although technology helps mass-produce the onboard components of Internet of Drones (IoD), including processors, sensors, storage, and battery life, the performance limitations of these components delay and reduce expectations. IoD offers drone coupling vehicles as well as cloud mobility functions to allow remote drone access and control, as well as seamlessly scalable offloading and capabilities of remote cloud storage [8, 20]. The IoD environment that includes base stations, signal links, and cloud environments has been illustrated in Fig. 1 [1].

M. S. Kumar (✉) · S. M. Thampi
Connected Systems and Intelligence Lab, School of Computer Science and Engineering, Digital University Kerala, Trivandrum, India
e-mail: meenakshy.cs22@duk.ac.in; sabu.thampi@duk.ac.in

S. M. Thampi et al. (eds.), *Securing the Connected World*,
https://doi.org/10.1007/978-3-031-82826-3_11

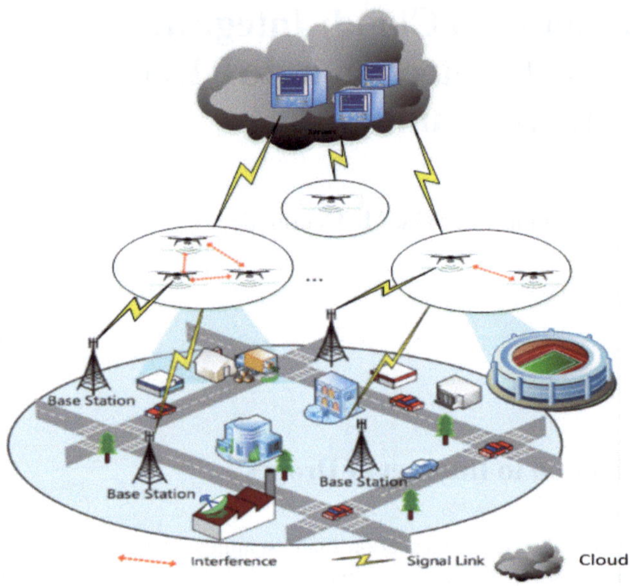

Fig. 1 IoD environment [1]

It is only by delving into the numerous ways in which IoD systems can be classified that one could have a complete understanding of the complexities and potential of the Internet of Drones. A clear classification can have the power to be a huge enabler for the successful deployment of drones in different scenarios, but it also plays a very critical role in identifying unique cybersecurity challenges inherent in each category.

1.1 Classification of Internet of Drones

The Internet of Drones is an advanced infrastructure in terms of networking that connects multiple drones and helps them transmit information, coordinate efforts, and work effectively within various environments. Conversely, isolated standalone drones have less to do in contrast, since integrated and scalable solutions offered by IoD systems are crucial for implementation in several sectors-from agriculture to security. With such cross-connected networks, the drones interrelate with live data optimize their routes and work on complicated tasks with even greater efficiency.

To entirely exploit the potential of IoD technology, it becomes crucial to categorize the classes of IoD systems based on their application-specific and operational environments. This approach will allow us to highlight the specific challenges and requirements for different domains where drones can be deployed. Focusing on their applications, benefits, and particular cybersecurity threats, IoD

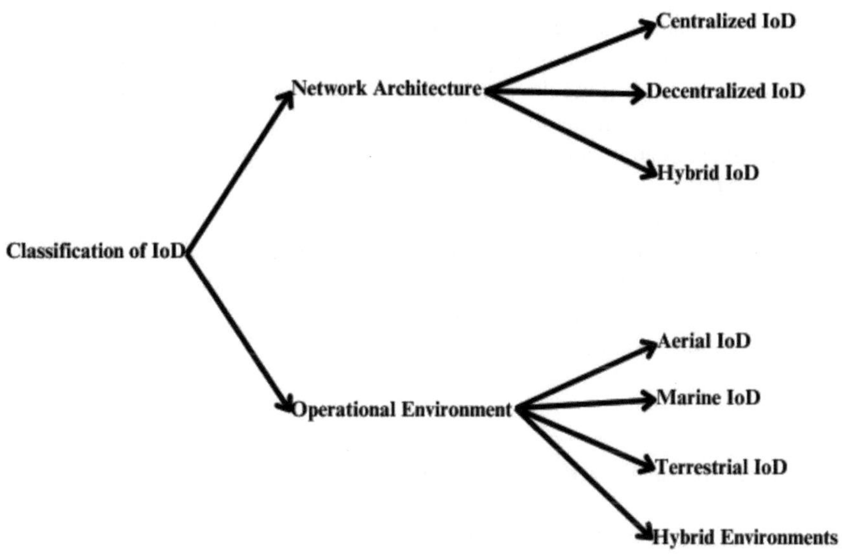

Fig. 2 Classification of IoD

systems are categorized into two types: Network architecture-based and Operational environment-based as shown in Fig. 2.

1.1.1 Network Architecture Based IoD

The Network Architecture classification describes how drones within an IoD system are organized, managed, and interact with each other. This classification can be broadly classified into three types:

- ***Centralized IoD:***
  In a centralized IoD system, all the drones are connected and controlled by a central server or control unit. These central hubs process data, coordinate drone activities, and issue commands. Centralized systems make it easier to manage large fleets but may suffer from scalability issues and vulnerabilities as the entire network relies on the central server.
  Applications: Urban air mobility, agricultural monitoring, centralized surveillance
- ***Decentralized IoD:***
  Decentralized IoD systems allow for peer-to-peer communication of drones, without the need for a centralized control point. Every drone is allowed to make autonomous decisions. That makes it possible for more flexible and robust network behaviour. This kind of configuration does exist in dynamic environments with fast, real-time communication requirements. In simple terms, group work implies working as a unit; one person submits his work directly to

fellow teammates and does not have everything pass through one group leader. In this way, if one person is busy or drops out, the others can continue working without delay. Such is the direct coordination between the decentralized systems of IoD; drones coordinate directly to accomplish tasks.
Applications: Search and rescue, disaster response, cooperative mapping

- ***Hybrid IoD:***
  Hybrid IoD systems comprise an integration of central and decentralized architectures. Perhaps with an overarching coordination central hub, the same drones are also capable of peer-to-peer operation for local tasks, thereby balancing management and adaptive, autonomous operation.
  Applications: Smart city operations, multi-domain logistics, military operations.

1.1.2 Operational Environment Based IoD

The classification of the Operational Environment is based on the physical environments through which drones operate and are deployed. Drones are made appropriate for various terrains and conditions according to the use case, which brings out the following subcategories:

- ***Aerial IoD:*** Aerial IoD is comprised of drone networking that works in the air. It is the most common type of drone and has applications in almost all industries such as surveillance, delivery, and agricultural control. In order for Aerial IoD systems to operate efficiently, they should encompass precise navigation, safe communication, and protection measures.
  Applications: Delivery service, crop monitoring, aerial photography, emergency response.
- ***Marine IoD:*** Marine IoD systems comprise Unmanned Underwater Vehicles - UUVs that operate underwater, underneath water bodies. These drones have been developed to be deployed in applications ranging from environmental monitoring and underwater explorations to offshore inspections. Operating in underwater environments poses special difficulties, such as communication and navigation challenges.
  Applications: Environmental research, oil rig inspections, marine life studies.
- ***Terrestrial IoD:*** Land-based or Terrestrial IoD networks contain land-vehicle drones, also referred to as Unmanned Ground Vehicles (UGVs). The earth-oriented drones can carry out missions on challenging or changing terrains, including logistics, infrastructure surveying, and agriculture. Hybrid vehicles offer automatic delivery and ground surveillance functionality.
  Applications: Last-mile delivery, autonomous farming, infrastructure maintenance.
- ***Hybrid Environments:*** Hybrid IoD systems are designed to integrate drones that operate in air, land, and water environments. Such systems will be coordinative in multi-domain operations, thus extending the scope of tasks they can accomplish-

such as those that involve an individual's combination of capabilities. Such versatility is important when considering items that cut across different terrains-for example, search and rescue missions or environmental monitoring.
Applications: Disaster relief coordination, comprehensive environmental monitoring, integrated logistics networks.

In fact, with a complex understanding of the various configurations of IoD systems, the identification of each of the distinctions—whether by network architecture or the operating environment becomes easier and is peculiar to a set of its own cybersecurity challenges or not.

1.2 Multi-Attack Detection in Internet of Drones

Drones are soaring higher, expounding new industries and opportunities through the concept of the Internet of Drones (IoD), in which UAVs are as interconnected as the IoT. IoD brings changes into airspace as what was once unthinkable becomes real: drones that are not only connected but also cooperating as they enhance the new fields [5]. Multi-Attack Detection (MAD) is the process of identifying and countering different cyber attacks that aim at a system or network either concurrently or consecutively. To analyze, detect, and respond to a wide range of cyber-attacks, Multi-Attack Detection (MAD) in the IoD and other networked systems make use of sophisticated algorithms, security precautions, and monitoring tools. Going beyond the detection of individual attacks like DDoS attacks or GPS Spoofing attacks, this method aims to provide a comprehensive defence plan against sophisticated and coordinated attacks that may exploit many vulnerabilities at once. Its proactive nature allows it to monitor coordinated attacks early enough that escalation can be prevented.

Moreover, Multi-Attack Detection (MAD) is equipped with a multi-layered security architecture. These comprise firewalls, IDS, and encryption protocols. They make sure that if one layer is compromised, then the other layers will keep protecting the critical components. Real-time monitoring and automated responses are very important features of Multi-Attack Detection (MAD). It helps the system quickly detect new threats and begin implementing predefined actions to reduce further damage. Adaptive learning capabilities further make Multi-Attack Detection (MAD) much more effective, improving algorithms in terms of detection from past incidents that occurred and could expect and prepare to encounter new ones.

Data correlation of several sources is also important in multi-attack scenarios, and Multi-Attack Detection (MAD) systems aggregate logs that enable comprehensive forensic analysis, support direct responses, and insights into future defences. In return, while key stakeholders like manufacturers and cyber security experts collaborate and share threat intelligence and best practices, it will make it easier to enhance the overall effectiveness of Multi-Attack Detection (MAD). Implementing Multi-Attack Detection (MAD) also ensures an organization would

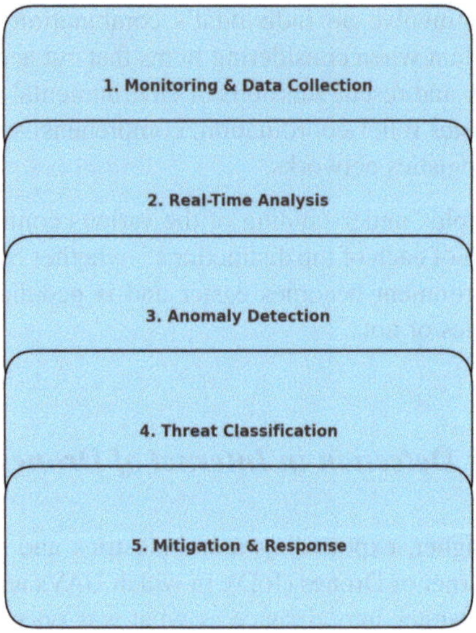

Fig. 3 Multi-attack detection system operation

demonstrate proper regulatory compliance-even a steadfast commitment to cyber security through standardized protocols and effective incident response. In this context, Multi-Attack Detection (MAD) itself has the highest significance for the IoD-just as much as it can safeguard the organization from threats even of the present times but still ensure that the organization is much better prepared for future arising challenges-for example, down the line.

An outline of how the Multi-Attack Detection system operation takes place is shown in Fig. 3.

- ***Monitoring & Data Collection:***
  It constantly monitors the IoD network itself, on telemetry data, communications logs, and performance metrics generated by all drones from the data traffic perspective.
- ***Real-time Analysis:***
  It looks at real-time data. It can spot any unusual pattern or anomaly that may give off a hint of the existence of a threat through algorithms. This could be anything from skewed traffic spikes to unauthorized access attempts or even anomalous behaviour from drones.
- ***Anomaly Detection:***
  It detects alterations in the data against predefined baselines that represent normal operating conditions. It uses machine learning models for detecting subtle attacks including patterns of evolving threats.

- ***Mitigation & Responses:***
  The instant it feels a MAD, the MAD system identifies the type of attack, say GPS spoofing, DoS attack, or jamming. Such identification helps decide the response to be taken. Therefore, the classification prompts specific protection protocols for the system against the threat. Such denial access, isolation of some compromised drones, or even a switch to redundant communication channels are common.

And, the Multi-Attack Detection (MAD) system improves its past errors/mistakes by remembering its past incidents, just like how humans learn from their previous mistakes.

1.3 Significance and Scope of Multi-Attack Detection in Internet of Drones

The importance and scope of multi-attack detection (Multi-Attack Detection (MAD)) in any environment of security of IoT-driven UAVs are paramount. Multi-Attack Detection (MAD) provides a comprehensive defence strategy since it combats advanced and organized cyber attacks, as it creates room to defend the integrity of UAVs and operational performance besides the IoT infrastructures. Thus, it supports the detection of several attacks at once, thus preventing a potential cascading effect that may cause the blocking of some critical operations and information. In Multi-Attack Detection (MAD), the very nature of reliance upon connected devices, wireless communication channels, and autonomous decision processes makes it fundamentally important in IoT-enabled UAVs. This means Multi-Attack Detection (MAD) can identify threats proactively because it can respond in time to emerging attack vectors and protect against vulnerabilities otherwise not detected [24]. Furthermore, to this end, with the consciousness of shifting threat landscapes, Multi-Attack Detection (MAD) facilitates the setting of an overall security posture for the IoT system and informs mechanisms for achieving robust security measures.

Safeguarding data integrity is only one aspect of Internet of Drones (IoD) security; confidentiality, authentication, and non-repudiation are all part of an all-encompassing strategy. Strengthening the security of the IoD and its supporting infrastructure is the main objective. The necessity of this is highlighted by the difficulties presented by conventional security measures, which are distinguished by their slow speed, large size, high power consumption, and possible inability to provide the necessary data protection inside the network. Because of the wide variety of applications across many circumstances and the diversity of communication protocols, IoD security is intrinsically complicated.

There are several vulnerabilities that exist in the IoD that could compromise the security of the system like impersonation attacks, wormhole attacks, sinkhole attacks, Sybil attacks, GPS spoofing attacks, DDoS attacks, channel jamming, and routing attacks. Therefore, a strong security solution is essential for bolstering IoD security. Cryptographic methods, authentication procedures, and intrusion detection systems are all integrated into this solution. IoD nodes are susceptible to a variety of attacks, including impersonation, wormhole, sinkhole, sybil, and coagulation attacks. As a result, prompt methods, countermeasures, and readily modifiable solutions are required. Drones have a significant influence on security and privacy because of their range of sizes. Compact drones present particular difficulties since it is typically more difficult to add security and privacy features than it is for bigger drones with more powerful computing power.

It is crucial and something that has received little attention—to address the privacy and security issues related to various drone models. A strong security solution is essential for sustaining IoD security. Cryptographic methods, authentication procedures, and intrusion detection systems are all integrated into this solution. IoDs are susceptible to multiple attacks such as GPS Spoofing attacks, DDoS attacks, and Man-In-The-Middle attacks, etc. As a result, prompt methods, countermeasures, and readily modifiable solutions are required. Drones have a significant influence on security and privacy because of their range of sizes. Compact drones present particular difficulties since it is typically more difficult to add security and privacy features than it is for bigger drones with more powerful computing power.

To validate security in an IoD network that has been developed, techniques that use security logic or models must be used. Specialized tools must also be used for the validation process. In this context, the severity of privacy and security concerns is especially noticeable in mission-critical operations (MCO), where multi-attack detection in real-time is crucial. Here are some more arguments emphasizing the significance of real-time multi-attack detection in the Internet of Things devices:

(a) ***Data Integrity Preservation:*** The integrity of data transported inside the Internet of Things network is guaranteed by multi-attack detection. During drone operations, any compromise to the validity of data might result in erroneous decision-making and potentially dangerous outcomes.
(b) ***Protection Against Malicious Actors:*** The Internet of Things is vulnerable to attacks by malevolent actors who want to take advantage of weaknesses for different objectives, such as stealing data, spying, or stopping vital services. As a preventative measure, real-time detection systems spot and neutralize such threats before they have a chance to do any damage.
(c) ***Mitigation of Complex Threat Landscapes:*** Emerging cyber dangers are constantly changing in the dynamic environment in which the Internet of Things functions. Multi-attack detection systems offer a complete defence plan against a constantly shifting threat landscape by being flexible enough to handle a wide range of dynamic threats.

(d) ***Maintaining Continuity of Operations:*** Drones are frequently used for urgent and vital missions including delivery, emergency response, and surveillance. By quickly mitigating any disturbances brought on by cyber-attacks, real-time multi-attack detection is essential to ensuring the continuation of these activities.
(e) ***Enhanced Trust and Reliability:*** In applications where sensitive data or human lives are at stake, the reliability of IoD systems is critical. Because it shows a dedication to the security and dependability of drone networks, real-time multi-attack detection promotes confidence.
(f) ***Adaptability to Diverse Attack Vectors:*** Systems for detecting multiple attacks are Multi-Attack Detection (MAD)e to identify complex attack vectors in addition to DDoS and GPS spoofing. Maintaining this flexibility is essential to fending off cyber attacks that might use a variety of methods to undermine IoD security.
(g) ***Regulatory Standards Compliance:*** Following security guidelines and procedures is crucial as drone use becomes increasingly regulated. IoD operators may ensure responsible and safe drone deployments by adhering to industry and regulatory security regulations with the use of real-time multi-attack detection.

2 Attacks in the Internet of Drones

Real-time multi-attack detection is essential in the Internet of Drones (IoD) domain to tackle the intricate security issues brought about by diverse attacks.

Drone navigation systems can lose accuracy due to GPS spoofing attempts, which alter location data [2]. DDoS attacks, on the other side, might overload the communication infrastructure, causing service outages and potentially compromising drone operations. There are various types of attacks on the Internet of Drones such as GPS Spoofing attacks, DoS attacks, DDoS attacks, jamming attacks, hijacking attacks, collision attacks, and wormhole attacks as shown in Fig. 4.

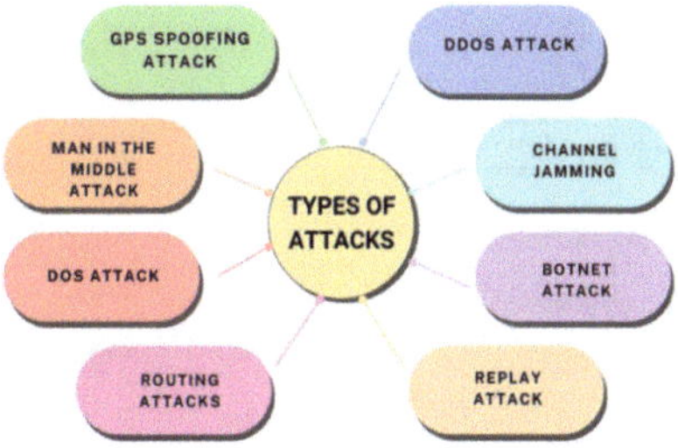

Fig. 4 Types of attack in IoD

2.1 *Types of Attacks*

The different types of attacks illustrated in Fig. 4 are explained in this section in detail.

2.1.1 GPS Spoofing Attacks

Suppose you are travelling to a friend's place using GPS navigation, but someone hacks it to provide you with the wrong locations, causing you to end up in an entirely different location. That's similar to what happens during a GPS Spoofing attack. GPS Spoofing attacks also known as Global Positioning System spoofing entail an effort to send false or interfered GPS signals to a drone's GPS receiver. i.e., the original trajectory of the internet of drones is spoofed by the attacker and false trajectory is set for their traversal. The major impacts or risks posed by GPS spoofing attacks include misdirection of drones, collisions, safety threats, unauthorized control, and data integrity. The GPS Spoofing attack is illustrated in Fig. 5 [4].

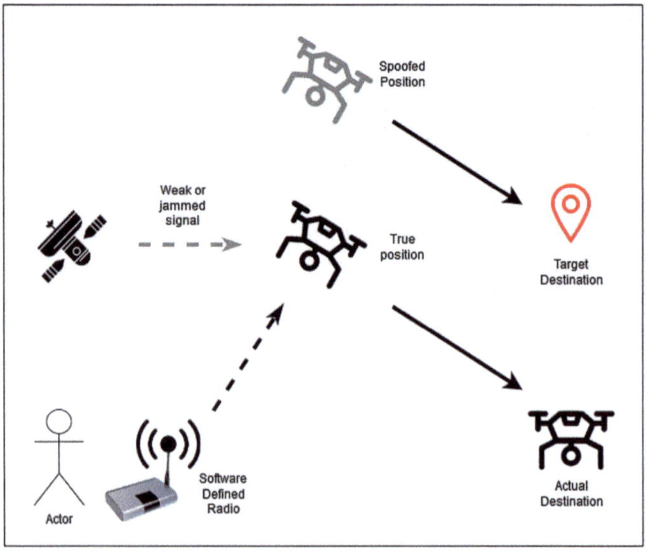

Fig. 5 GPS spoofing attacks [4]

2.1.2 Denial of Service (DoS) Attacks

Think of DoS attacks as if someone, repeatedly dialed your phone so it never rings out-but, meanwhile, you don't get any other calls. This drone gets so many unwanted requests it cannot respond to the real, necessary tasks and falls apart. Denial of Services (DoS) attack can also be the point of easiest access to the drone network and sometimes it makes it useless, or sometimes it becomes dangerous. A high number of unnecessary requests limit the resources available to be shared by other legitimate users thus congesting the system and risking some, if not all, legitimate requests.

This process may eventually deny the authentication of the network connection between the drone and the ground controller because the adversary sends large amounts of data to the drone, thus causing the failure in the computational power of the drone. Therefore, these data packets are easily produced by any packet generator application and sent directly into the network of the drone. Then, at an extremely high rate, the ICMP packets are sent so that overflows happen within the network of the drone and it loses its control by both the drone and its ground controller. Such attacks should be performed with malicious malware in one of the packets of data sent hence further weakening the Drone. In such attacks, hackers would be able to crash the drone and cause damage not only to civilians but to government agencies themselves. Figure 6 [10] illustrates a DoS attack on UAV.

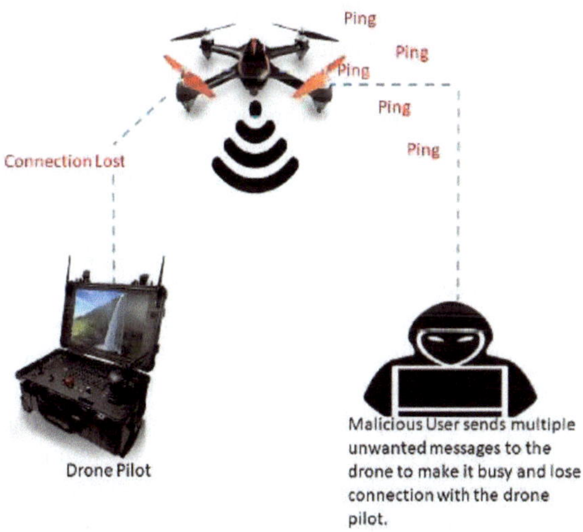

Fig. 6 Denial of Service (DoS) attacks on drones [10]

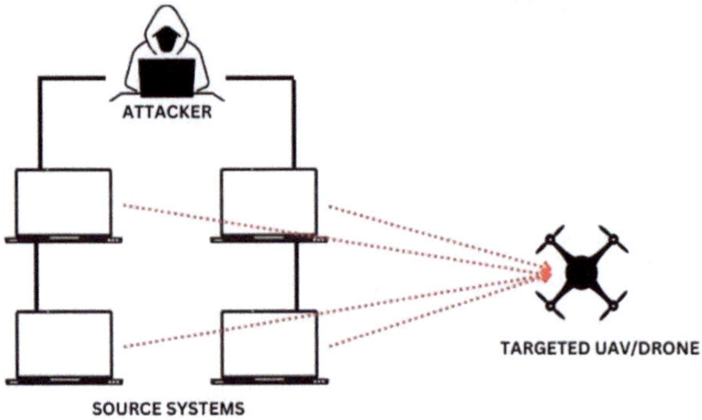

Fig. 7 Distributed Denial of Service (DDoS) attacks on drones

2.1.3 Distributed Denial of Service (DDoS) Attacks

A Distributed Denial of Service (DDoS) attack in the framework of drones involves an attacker attempting to overwhelm a drone by sending large amounts of requests or data. The objective of a DDoS attack is to render the drone unavailable to perform its intended tasks, thus denying access to legitimate users or operators. The DDoS attack is illustrated in Fig. 7.

2.1.4 Jamming Attacks

Imagine you're trying to listen to your favorite radio station, but someone nearby turns on a device that blasts static noise, making it impossible to hear anything. Jamming attacks do the same thing to drones—they create "noise" that blocks important signals from getting through. A jamming attack in the Internet of Drones (IoD) involves an attacker transmitting powerful radio frequency signals on the same frequency band as the drones, disrupting communication between the UAV and the ground control station. This interference overwhelms the UAV systems, causing it to lose control, disconnect from the network, or operate unpredictably, potentially leading to crashes or mission failures. Prolonged jamming can drain the drone's battery and may be part of a broader attack strategy that includes injecting malicious code, further compromising the drone's operations. Such attacks are particularly dangerous in critical applications like surveillance or emergency response, posing serious risks to public safety. This attack is illustrated in Fig. 8 [10].

2.1.5 Collision Attacks

A collision attack in the Internet of Drones (IoD) involves deliberately causing two or more drones to crash into each other or into other objects by manipulating their

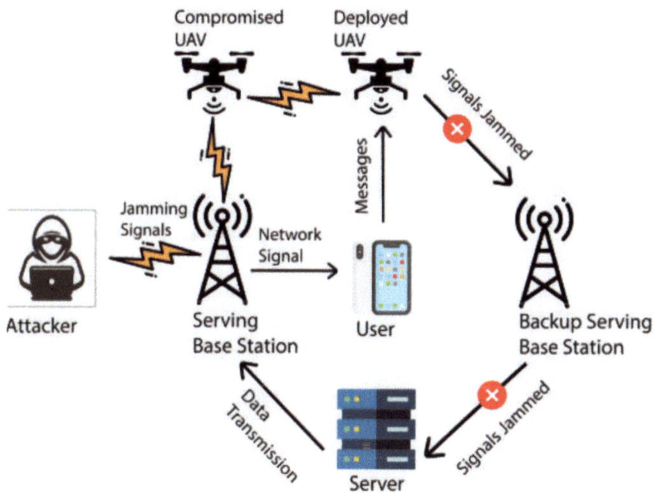

Fig. 8 Jamming attacks in IoD [10]

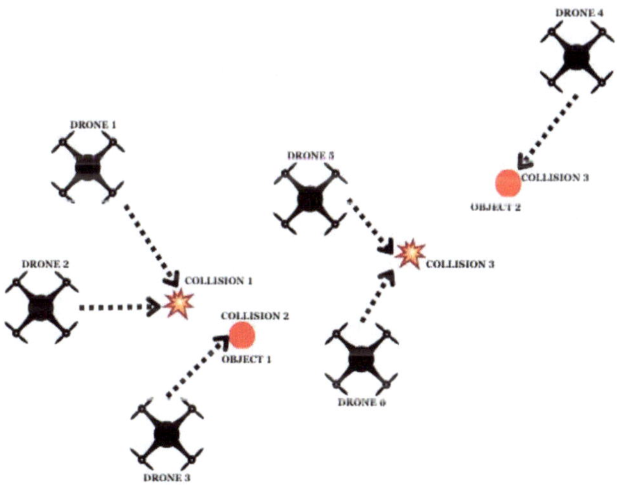

Fig. 9 Collision attacks in IoD

flight paths or communication protocols. This is achieved by an attacker intercepting and altering the drones' navigation data, injecting false location information, or disrupting their coordination systems. As a result, the drones may be directed onto a collision course, leading to physical damage, mission failure, and potential harm to people or property. Such attacks are particularly concerning in densely populated areas or during coordinated drone operations, as they can create hazardous situations and disrupt critical services. This attack is illustrated in Fig. 9.

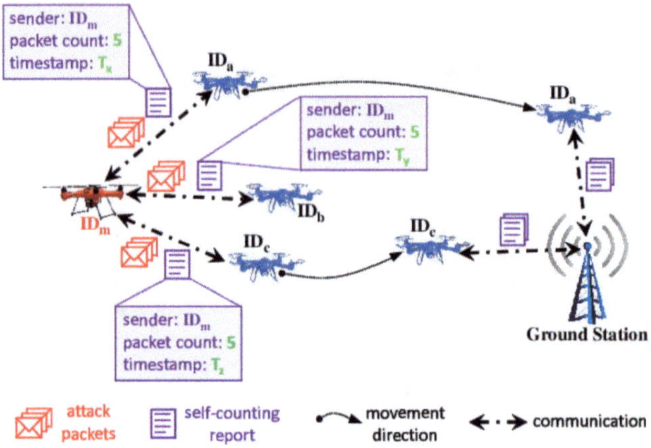

Fig. 10 Flooding attacks on drones [18]

2.1.6 Flooding Attacks

A flooding attack on the Internet of Drones (IoD) involves overwhelming a drone network with an excessive amount of traffic or data requests, causing it to become overloaded and unresponsive. In this type of attack, the adversary floods the network with superfluous requests, consuming all available resources and preventing legitimate communications between drones and their control stations. This can lead to delays, loss of control, or complete system failure. The attack can also exhaust the drones' battery power as they attempt to process the excessive data, ultimately disrupting their operations and posing significant risks to the success of missions, especially in critical applications like search and rescue or surveillance. The Flooding attack is illustrated in Fig. 10 [18].

2.1.7 Hijacking Attacks

A hijacking attack on the Internet of Drones (IoD) occurs when an attacker takes unauthorized control of a drone, redirecting it from its intended mission. This can be achieved by intercepting and manipulating the communication signals between the drone and its ground controller or by exploiting vulnerabilities in the drone's software. Once hijacked, the drone can be used for malicious purposes, such as espionage, delivering harmful payloads, or crashing into targets. Hijacking attacks are particularly dangerous because they allow the attacker to fully control the drone, potentially turning it into a weapon or using it to disrupt critical operations, posing serious threats to security and public safety. The hijacking attack on the internet of drones is illustrated in Fig. 11 [11].

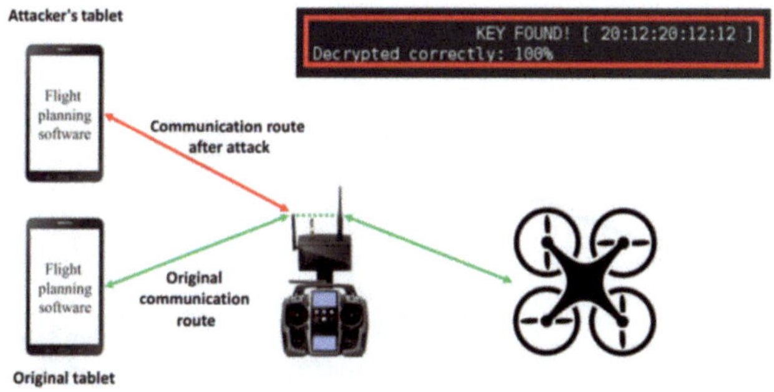

Fig. 11 Hijacking attacks on drones [11]

2.1.8 Man-In-The-Middle (MITM) Attacks

Man-in-the-middle attack puts an adversary between the client and the drone. The adversary uses a device called Wi-Fi Pineapple [24]. With this attack, flight planning software will be broadcasting the plan to the drone controller that will forward it to the drone. Upon successful receipt of commands from the controller, the drone will send the acknowledgement, and the acknowledgement will then be received by the attacker between the drone and the controller. The attacker, with Wi-fi Pineapple, will forward the forced commands to the controller. After configuring the pineapple, it will initiate recon mode tracing out all probable access points the client software might be using. Once traced to the access point or drone, it gets added to the Pine-AP SSID pool. This order is forwarded to the drone and the planned activities of the adversary remain unnoticed as carried out by the drone. One example of a man-in-the-middle attack is active eavesdropping [24] in which the adversary connects himself with the drone controller. After acquiring the SSID of the drone, the hacker proceeds to the spoofing of commands to the controller and makes them believe that they are communicating with the drone. The several vulnerabilities identified in UAVs include the following: it uses a weak encryption scheme then its password is easily broken, and the man-in-middle attack is performed using the Wi-Fi link. Such attacks can be caused by insecure encryption schemes at the different stages of the chain of communication. Researchers found that to be able to conduct such an attack, they would need hardware worth only 40 dollars. This is pretty obvious as an attack in which the middle layer hacker is never known by the controller. The Man-In-The-Middle attack on the IoD is illustrated in Fig. 12 [10].

2.1.9 De-authentication Attacks

It is one form of Denial Of Service attack particularly where the communication between the client and the Wi-Fi access point is fragmented. In this case, the attacker de-authenticates the ground pilot leaving the pilot to look for control of the drone.

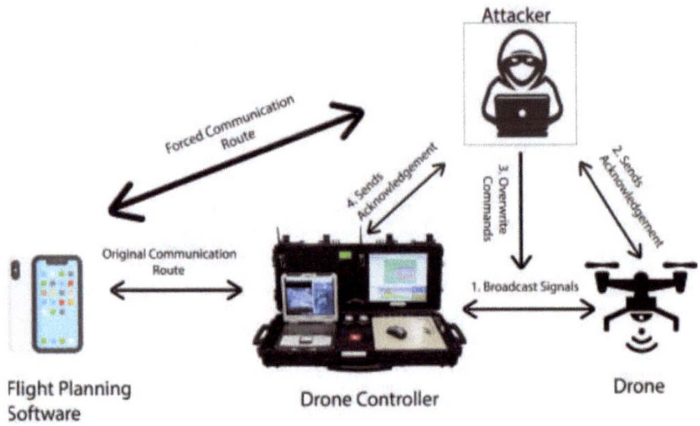

Fig. 12 Man-in-the-middle attacks [10]

Fig. 13 De-authentication Attacks on drones [19]

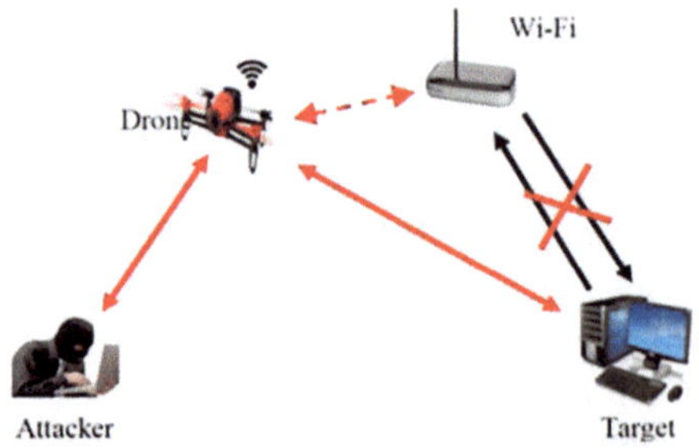

Since encryption is not a must in sending the frame, at any point in time, the attacker can easily send a de-authentication frame to a wireless access point irrespective of the technique of privacy used. Also, the attacker only needs the Mac address of the drone which is available through any of the tools like 'Aircrack-ng'. In the case of a de-authentication attack, this tool hijacks the drone by specifying the mac address of the drone. The moment when the Aircrack-ng tool has been set it de-authenticates the connection between the drone and the ground controller. This tool can be used to communicate with the drone and maliciously send the drone out of control. This particular attack causes huge losses. De-authentication attacks are slowly turning into one of the newest concerns in the industry nowadays as e-commerce giants like Amazon look towards making mechanisms for delivering products through drones. Among the most famous methods to execute this attack is SkyJack [14] which uses an AR. Drone 2.0 along with a Raspberry Pi and wireless Adapters in order to hack and control drones. It would send a de-authentication request to Aircrack-ng that would disconnect the target drone from its user. Then it would communicate with the target drone using a node-ar-drone library. Figure 13 [19] portrays the de-authentication attack on IoD.

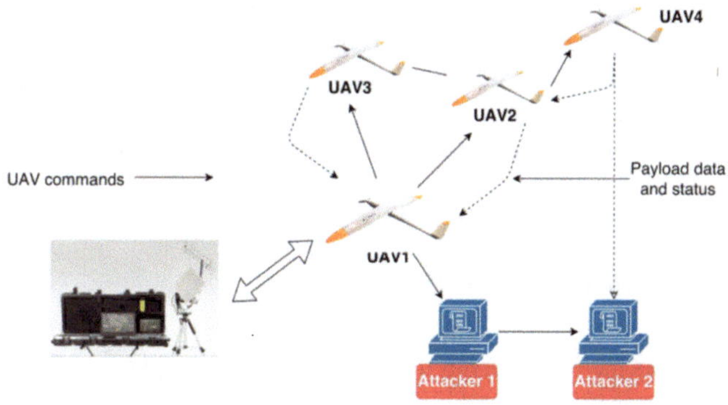

Fig. 14 Wormhole attacks on drones [12]

2.1.10 Wormhole Attacks

UAV networks that utilize FANET or MANET are susceptible to routing-based attacks like wormholes. The communication between UAVs relies not only on the information exchange between the UAV and the ground control station but also among the UAVs [9]. FANET uses a system of auto-configuration and self-healing to improve its reliability, but it makes it vulnerable to wormhole attacks. A wormhole attack is one of the most severe and grave attacks in MANETs. In a wormhole attack, two attackers place themselves strategically in the network to listen in on the communication between the drone network. The attacker records the communication at one point in the drone network and tunnels the information to the second attacker, where the recorded information is replayed [3]. As the routing protocol algorithm looks for the nearest node to transfer the information, wormholes are placed to make the distant nodes believe that they are their closest neighbours. This kind of re-routing compromises the confidentiality of sensitive information and also enables the attacker to launch an attack from any point in the network because it practically controls all the routes discovered after the wormhole.

Figure 14 [12] illustrates the wormhole attack in the IoD. Moreover, wormhole attacks in a UAV Ad Hoc Network (UAANET), Multi-Attack Detection (MAD) of a swarm of UAVs, and a ground control station, are high-level risks, and special attention needs to be paid to this multi-node attack. Even without the knowledge of any of the cryptographic keys or hash functions, the attacker can affect the integrity of the network by transferring control packets, and further, capturing the data traffic.

3 Impacts of Attacks

Disruptions in the drone networks affect them first directly at mission-critical operations and pose serious threats to industries, public safety, privacy, and even national security. Understanding these potential impacts of cyberattacks on IoD systems would be critical in developing robust defence mechanisms and mitigating vulnerabilities inherent to such technologies. There are mainly two impacts caused by these cyber attacks on the Internet of Drones: Operational Disruptions and Economic Consequences. They also pose safety risks to the infrastructure.

3.1 Operational Disruptions

IoD system attacks have the potential to completely interrupt operational processes, stopping vital services and risking the successful completion of missions. Multi-vector attacks, including DDoS combined with GPS spoofing, may severely impact drone fleet operations by flooding control systems and sending unmanned aerial vehicles in the wrong path. Among the repercussions are:

- Loss of control over UAVs: Operators may be unable to communicate with drones in real-time, which makes it difficult to give corrective orders or efficiently monitor the system.
- Service disruptions: Important services that put lives and property in danger, such as the delivery of medical supplies, surveillance, or search and rescue missions, may be postponed or completely stopped.
- Longer recovery durations are usually necessary for coordinated attack disruptions since several system components, such as drone firmware, control systems, and communication networks, need to be recovered.

3.2 Economic Consequences

Cyberattacks on IoD systems can have significant negative economic effects, including the following direct and indirect costs:

- Financial losses: Due to service interruptions, maintenance expenses, and jeopardized assets, businesses that depend on UAVs for delivery, logistics, or surveillance may suffer direct financial losses.
- Reputational harm: A company's reputation may be harmed by persistent or serious cyberattacks, which may result in a decline in clientele and market share. Businesses and consumers can decide not to use drone-based services if security flaws are not fixed.
- Costs associated with liability and insurance: Businesses that use UAVs must have extensive insurance coverage to protect themselves from any liability resulting from compromised drone operations. Lawsuits or penalties may also follow an attack if private information is compromised or if a service is rendered unavailable.

3.3 Safety Risks

Cyberattacks on IoD systems pose serious safety issues, especially in areas where drones are used to interact with humans and vital infrastructure. Among the possible safety hazards are:

- Physical damage: Drone crashes caused by cyberattacks such as GPS spoofing, hijacking, or collision attacks can result in serious property damage or even human casualties in crowded regions.
- Emergency services compromised: Mission failures resulting in casualties and impeding rescue attempts can be caused by attacks against unmanned aerial vehicles (UAVs) used for emergency response, including disaster management and medical delivery. Misuse of hijacked drones: A hijacked UAV poses a serious risk to public safety and national security as it may be used for hostile purposes like espionage, weaponized attacks, or information collection.

4 Case Study

There have been various UAV-related attacks that have been reported since the emergence of technology. In recent years, the rate of UAV-related cyber attacks has been at the peak at about 89%. This section discusses a few case studies of Multi-attack incidents in the Internet of Drones which signifies the importance and need for more efficient Multi-attack Detection Systems.

4.1 Real World Incidents of Attacks in the Internet of Drones

- ***Case Study 1:GPS Jamming and Malware Attack on Drones during Kumbh Mela***
  The police deployed drones during the Kumbh Mela in Prayagraj (India) in 2019 when billions of people gathered there. But most of them fell prey to GPS jamming attacks that disrupted the flight patterns, and ground control systems had malware with malicious tampering effects on the possibility of real-time transmission of video footage. Such simultaneous attacks would have altogether disabled the surveillance utilities of UAVs that even risked the lives of participants in such huge congregations. Very soon though cyber security team interference cooled down the intensity but eventually arose serious questions as far as protected deployment of drones in mass congregations was concerned. It rather raised some critical questions relating to UAV systems safety in mass networking whose failure can lead to disastrous consequences.
- ***Case Study 2: Multi-Vector Attack on Surveillance Drones in Jammu and Kashmir***
  During the Indian security forces' counter-terrorism operations in Jammu and Kashmir in 2020, they used drones for surveillance activities. The latter was

attacked by multiple agents: firstly, jamming devices were used to break communication links that had already been set between the UAVs and their ground control stations. Moreover, the attackers used GPS spoofing techniques to manipulate the flight paths of the drones and seize control at critical moments during security operations. Apart from that, one of the seized drones had malware which would have compromised its data collection and would have transmitted wrong imagery to the command centers. As the drones were recovered without much security breach, this attack again emphasized the sophistication of cyber attacks, especially in sensitive regions like Jammu and Kashmir. This incident occurred at such a time that it demanded the protection of UAVs deployed in counter-terror operations on a war footing, particularly within conflict-prone areas.

4.2 Simulated Attacks In the Internet of Drones

- ***Case Study 3: Simulated UAV Cyberattack during DEFEXPO India***
  Indian defence agencies conducted mock cyber attacks against UAV systems on the battalion level scenario within an international defence exhibition, DEFEXPO India 2020 in Lucknow, Uttar Pradesh, on strength against cyber attacks, where testing ranged from signal jamming, GPS spoofing to malware insertion as it affected the flight patterns and communication systems of the UAV. These simulated cyberattacks specifically concentrated on how the UAV could provide real-time reconnaissance and intelligence to the ground forces. The exercise was aimed at testing the military's readiness to identify multi-tiered cyberattacks and take necessary steps to ensure that future UAVs are properly defended against such attacks in the real world. Simulations indicated that the UAV's communication encryption and navigation systems had serious deficiencies.

Considering these attacks and incidents, it is crucial to understand how the Internet of Drones (IoD) systems can defend against such multi-vector attacks. Effective defence mechanisms must be robust, adaptive, and capable of identifying and mitigating diverse forms of multiple cyber attacks.

5 Emerging Trends and Technologies in Multi-Attack Detection

Attacks against the Internet of Drones (IoD) are becoming significantly sophisticated and demand a much more robust multi-vector attack detection system. Various emerging technologies such as Machine Learning (ML), Blockchain, Digital Twin, Federated Learning, and Post Quantum Cryptography, have significantly improved over the years in terms of detection and mitigation capabilities of multi-vector attacks of IoD systems.

5.1 Machine Learning and AI-Based Detection

Machine learning and Artificial intelligence have been playing a strong role in changing the structure of Multi-Attack Detection (MAD) systems for IoD. Initially, signature-based systems cannot cope up with increased complexity and variability in multi-vector attacks, DDoS, GPS spoofing, and sensor tampering. With the advancement of ML and AI, IoD systems can perform learning from historical data to adapt towards new attack patterns thus responding in real-time hence enhancing their ability in the detection and mitigation of advanced threats.

In a work of T P Voung et al. [22], they analyzed the limitations of traditional IDS on IoD networks and proposed new solutions based on ML by using critical metrics like network load rates, velocity, and energy consumption so as to detect emerging patterns related to attacks. The study indeed shows that ML overcomes the dynamic nature of the IoD environments. The work showed real-time monitoring with adaptive mechanisms for detection in the IoD environment. The merit in the contribution of Dapeng Wu et al. [24] was bringing BP neural networks and the use of RBF neural networks to enhance anomaly detection within an IoD system, which outperformed the detection of certain types of attacks—namely DDoS and GPS spoofing attacks, with gigantic amounts of training and fine-tuning within UAV activity datasets, allowing complex threats to be detected in a more efficient way. Shenqing Wang et al. [23] furthered the domain by applying LSTM models in the detection of real-time GPS spoofing attacks. Their research assumed deep learning models can hold great capabilities that can, in turn, detect many restrictions of conventional sensing mechanisms in high-speed IoD operations, especially in mission-critical operations. The LSTM models can track and evaluate real-time telemetry from drones so as to enable the system to detect attacks and initiate immediate countermeasures at the very moment when the attacks are underway.

Supervised and unsupervised models of ML have revolutionized the real-time anomaly detection ability and predictive capability of threat analysis for a Multi-Attack Detection (MAD) system integrated into the IoD network. It is certainly possible for IoD systems to detect actual attacks and predict future threats based on historic patterns observed and current telemetry.

- ***Supervised Learning Models:***
  Supervised algorithms of learning are deep neural networks that can detect and classify various types of attacks, which may range from GPS spoofing to jamming or any type of DDoS attack. In light of massive training on large datasets related to UAV activities, supervised learning strengthens the detection capabilities of multi-vector complex attacks. It identifies the signature of items so that a quick response is provided, thus offering security in the IoD system.
- ***Unsupervised Learning Models:***
  The techniques that consist of unsupervised learning for anomaly detection are clustering and autoencoders. Such techniques are useful to determine recent or new threats by identifying anomalies from normal UAV behaviour. In such an environment, it will have disparate attack vectors that the system may not have

been preprogrammed to follow; hence, a Multi-Attack Detection (MAD) system would flag suspicious activity that does not fit within the previously existing norms. This can determine real-time unknown attack strategies.

Machine learning techniques such as Naive Bayes, SVM, LSTM, etc have been in wide use for attack detection purposes in the IoT domain. They possess several advantages and challenges.

5.1.1 Advantages of AI/ML in Attack Detection in IoD

- *Predictive capabilities:*
  An ML algorithm might use deep learning and unsupervised models that can detect changed patterns over time. Data learned historically may also allow it to evolve and adapt dynamically in response to new, unforeseen attack vectors. This may be impossible for traditional signature-based systems because they are not able to handle multi-vector attacks.
- *Adaptability to new threats:*
  A smarter system, as against a manual static detection system, is better adept at dealing with large and varying attack patterns in the amounts of data. For example, the BP neural networks utilized by Dapeng Wu et al. provided some improvement in detection concerning particular kinds of attacks, especially DDoS and GPS spoofing, fine-tuned and learned from UAV activity datasets.

5.1.2 Disadvantages of AI/ML in Attack Detection in IoD

- *Computational Overhead:*
  Indeed, the use of ML-based Multi-Attack Detection (MAD) systems may have high computational requirements and even infrastructural support for real-time computation, especially in those environments where the drones are generating telemetry. That may imply an elevated power consumption as well as network load, which is not at all practicable in every IoD environment.
- *False positives and False negatives:*
  While anomaly detection is very strong concerning AI and ML models, they are nowhere near perfect. They sometimes flag good behaviour as bad or vice versa-miss the actual attacks. Precision of detection has much to do with the choice and configuration model, and it's tough to get those models right so that you don't make errors in this way.

5.2 Blockchain Technology for Advanced Detection

Blockchain technology, which is a decentralized and distributed technology, provides tamper-proof and robust mechanisms for securing communications within the

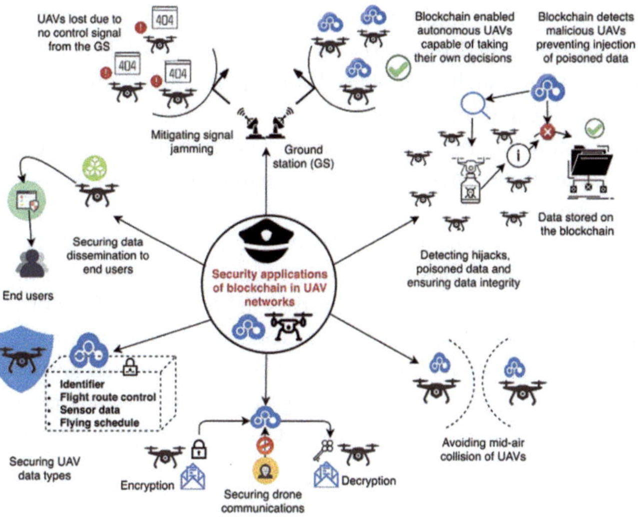

Fig. 15 Security applications of blockchain technology in UAV networks [2]

Internet of Drones (IoD), defending against attacks such as Man-In-The-Middle (MITM) attacks, command injection, and unauthorized access. The blockchain ensures that all the transactions and communications are immutable; hence, the data exchange between drones and their corresponding control systems is ensured decentralized for integrity and security. Figure 15 [2] shown here portrays the security applications of blockchain technology in UAV networks. The figure explains the security mechanisms and also the identified malicious UAVs, prevents poisoned data injected, and ensures that all the data within the network remains confidential and its integrity is maintained. Other notable data of UAVs, such as identifiers, flight routes, sensors, and flight schedules have been encrypted and decrypted to make UAV communications tamper-resistant. Decentralization in blockchain mechanism also enables UAV real-time coordination without many chances of mid-air collisions from the safe availability of sharing flight information. Apart from this, the system ensures that data is secure and trustworthy once it reaches the user end, thereby ensuring operational integrity under extreme conditions of hijacks or jamming.

In the work of G. Panice et al. [17], he emphasized the use of blockchain technology in protecting RPAS against the man-in-middle attack on unauthorized control signal manipulation. The series of experiments that the researchers demonstrate reveal that communications of this high stakes cannot be intercepted and, therefore, only authenticate command is received by the drone. Li et al. [22] in their work further advance smart contracts automatically validating the validity of drone commands in furtherance of work by Christian Petersson Nielsen et al. [16]. The contracts make sure that only authenticated messages are processed at the drones' end, thus reducing malicious interference. In this regard, smart contracts permit automated authentication, ensuring that commands and data received by drones get validated to prohibit false injection or alteration of the drone's activities. Yagmur Yigit et al. [26] performed the study on the scalability of Blockchain applied to complex environments, such as 5G-based smart ports, where drones play an integral role in data gathering and management. Their work established how Blockchain can indeed offer real-time tamper-resistant communication between thousands of nodes so that large-scale drone operations can be maintained securely and efficiently in dynamic environments.

There is a need to protect the system from multistage attacks, like coordinated DDoS and GPS spoofing. This relates to its capability of ensuring intact data and communicating in transparent manners across the board. As if the drone command stream has been targeted on both the network side and signal side, Blockchain ensures all the instructions received by the drone are validated and protected from tampering. Since the decentralized technology does not allow any point of failure to happen within the IoD network, this makes it highly resistant to cyber-attacks.

5.2.1 Key Features of Blockchain in the IoD Multi-Attack Detection System

The key features of blockchain technology in the IoD Multi-Attack Detection System are:

- *Immutability and Data Integrity:*
  Since blockchain technology permanently records each transaction, command, or exchange of data between drones and their controllers in an immutable ledger, it ensures legitimacy in all activities performed through drones and completely avoids a possibility wherein a piece of data becomes tampered with or even manufactured.
- *Automatic authentication:*
  Automatic authentication among communications of ground control stations and drones using smart contracts would prevent any unauthorized party from hijacking a drone or gaining access to the data related to the device, thus minimizing the possibilities of MITM attacks or any form of intercept. Through decentralization, one of the most significant aspects in which Blockchain can be scaled up adequately and support complex IoD environments such as large fleets of drones operating within smart cities or industrial zones, is. The decentralized architecture ensures that there is no single point of failure from attacks on a cyber level, which makes the system generally more resilient against cyberattacks.

5.2.2 Advantages of Blockchain Technology in Attack Detection in IoD

- *Scalability for Complex Environments:*
  A blockchain technology can be utilized in large-scale operations, like a smart city or an industrial zone, where drones play a major role in gathering and

managing data; thousands of drones can be added in a decentralized manner without dropping their level of security.

- *Real-Time Coordination and Collision Avoidance:*
  The free exchange of flight information is possible among UAVs through real-time communication and coordination, enabling efficient flight management with possible prevention of in-flight collisions by real-time determination of each other's paths.

5.2.3 Disadvantages of Blockchain Technology in Attack Detection in IoD

- *Computational Overhead:*
  Indeed, the use of ML-based Multi-Attack Detection (MAD) systems may have high computational requirements and even infrastructural support for real-time computation, especially in those environments where the drones are generating telemetry. That may imply an elevated power consumption as well as network load, which is not at all practicable in every IoD environment.
- *Energy Consumption:*
  While anomaly detection is very strong for AI and ML models, they are nowhere near perfect. They sometimes flag good behaviour as bad or vice versa-miss the actual attacks. Precision of detection has much to do with the choice and configuration model, and it's tough to get those models right so that you don't make errors in this way.

5.3 Digital Twin for IoD Simulation and Threat Analysis

A Digital Twin (DT) is referred to as a virtual representation of a real-world entity, device, machine, process, or other abstraction. Physical sensors, computer programs, machine learning algorithms, and software models are used to simulate real-time digital models of the physical entity.

The general structure of Digital Twin technology in the IoD is illustrated in Fig. 16.

A DT, which is simply a virtual replica of the physical system has various definitions: "A Digital Twin (DT) [7] is a computerized model of a physical device or a system that represents all functional features and links with the working elements".

"The digital twin is a living model [7] of the physical asset or system, which continually adapts to operational changes based on the collected online data and information, and can forecast the future of the corresponding physical counterpart".

"A Digital Twin is a virtual instance [7] of a physical system (twin) that is continually updated with the latter's performance, maintenance, and health status data throughout the physical system's life cycle".

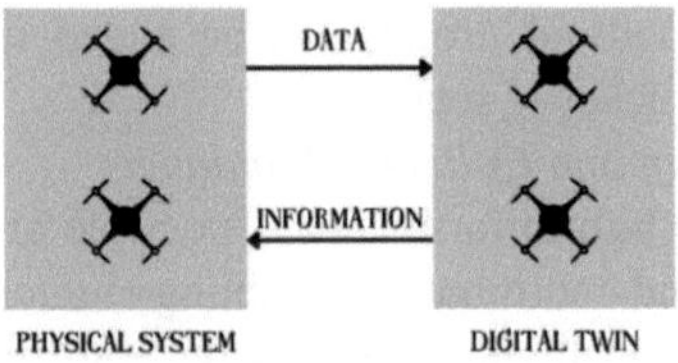

Fig. 16 General structure of digital twin data transfer in IoD

Digital Twin (DT) can be used for multi-attack detection in the internet of drones because of its ability to provide a real-time virtual representation of physical drones with real-time monitoring by enabling continuous monitoring of the physical drones and analyzing the performance and environment. DT can also predict potential issues and schedule maintenance before any failure occurs and enhance the reliability and lifespan of the drones. It also facilitates the optimization of IoD operations and working by analyzing performance data and simulating different scenarios, enabling more efficient and effective use of resources.

Christian Petersson Nielsen et al. [16] pushed the Digital Twin to a new level by incorporating it with Blockchain technology. That integration will allow for secure communication and real-time synchronization between drones and their virtual replicas. The blockchain-securing channels would enable their work to further demonstrate how, through the IoD system, one could predict and mitigate attacks against UAV systems by simulating the latter. Integration assures the authenticity and integrity of data being transmitted between the real-world drones and the Digital Twin. Fadhila Tlili et al. [21] used adaptive deep learning frameworks within the Digital Twin ecosystem that gives fault tolerance with attack detection in UAVs. They focused on developing dual entry schemes for fault identification and repelling attacks in large decentralized IoD networks. The proposed system was expected to enhance the robustness of UAV networking so it could function effectively even during cyberattacks and malfunctioning hardware.

5.3.1 Advantages of Digital Twin Technology in Multi-Attack Detection (MAD) Systems

- *Simulating Multi-Attack Scenarios:*
  The digital twin allows the operators to model and simulate complex, coordinated attacks in a risk-free virtual environment. These include DDoS types of attacks, GPS spoofing, and jamming types of attacks that aid in simulating attacks without having at-risk physical UAVs. IoD systems can, therefore, test and evaluate the resilience of UAV networks toward numerous coordinated attacks and adapt their defense strategy.

- *Predictive analytics and real-time threat monitoring:*
  With the use of Digital Twin technology, it can ensure continuous synch of its real-world drones with their virtual counterparts using predictive analytics and real-time monitoring. Such synching would help detect vulnerabilities and threats even before they materialize in the physical system, while Multi-Attack Detection (MAD) systems prevent them by analyzing real-time telemetry data that provide early indicators of cyber-attacks and take corrective actions proactively and stop them from escalating into a threat that could compromise critical UAV operations.
- *Fault Tolerance and Attack Resilience:*
  This also allows the UAV to detect system failure as well as cyber-attacks because of deep learning models integrated into the framework of Digital Twin. Digital Twins track drone health in operations and simulate faults to strengthen the fault-tolerant aspects of the IoD systems, highly indispensable during mission-critical operations where each fault or attack brings about a significant disruption in operations.

5.3.2 Disadvantages of Digital Twin Technology in Multi-Attack Detection (MAD) Systems

- *Scalability Concerns in Large-Scale Networks:*
  With the number of drones and operations increasing, it becomes challenging to maintain real-time synchronism, simulation, and analysis of the DT system on all these drones. Thousands of drone twins may stretch resources to the breaking point of bottlenecking in a smart city or large industrial zone.
- *Security Risks from Digital Representation:*
  Although the DT technology improves the security of the physical system, the virtual replica itself is insecure. If unauthorized access into the DT system is obtained, the attackers may modify the digital replica, and this leads to improper simulations or vulnerabilities in the physical UAVs. Therefore, new protection mechanisms should be developed to secure the virtual twin from unauthorized access.

5.4 Federated Learning for Decentralized Threat Detection

Federated Learning (FL) is a method that allows multiple parties to train collaboratively without sharing data. The general framework of Federated Learning is illustrated in Fig. 17 [5]. The core concept of federated learning is to create machine learning models that are built on distributed datasets across different devices while avoiding the leakage of data [6]. Federated learning, in particular, is a novel approach in which local IoT data is used to calculate an updated model on IoT devices after downloading the current model. After the IoT devices send these

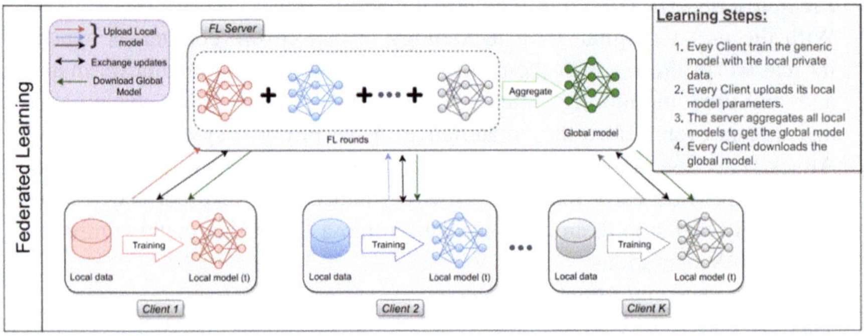

Fig. 17 Federated learning [5]

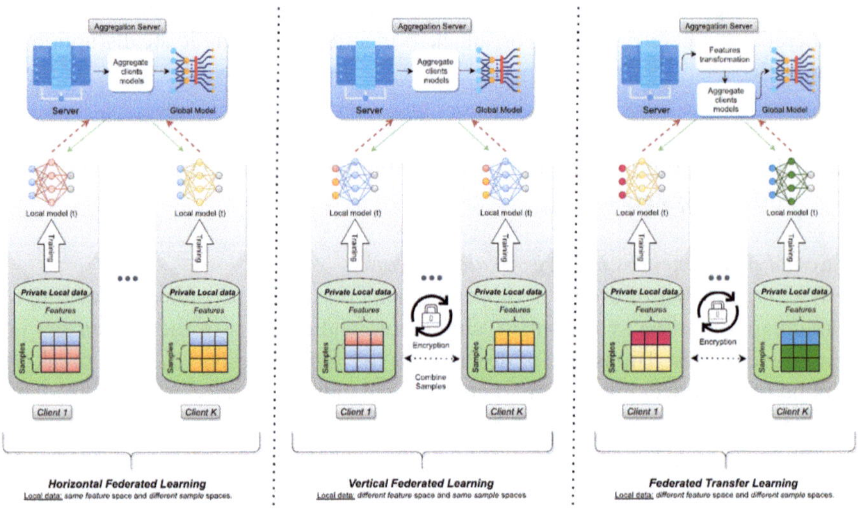

Fig. 18 Types of federated learning [5]

locally trained models to the central server for aggregation (weights, for example), a merged and improved single global model is reverted to the IoT devices.

5.4.1 Types of Federated Learning

Regarding the deployment of federated learning and the related technical and practical difficulties, data dissemination is crucial. Currently, there are three forms of federated learning available: The types of Federated Learning are illustrated in Fig. 18 [5].

- ***Horizontal federated learning:*** This type is implemented in situations in which the data sets share the same feature space but differ in the sampling space.

- ***Vertical federated learning:*** This type is implemented in situations in which the data sets differ in the feature space but share the same sampling space.
- ***Federated transfer learning:*** This type is implemented in situations where the data sets have different feature spaces as well as different sampling spaces.

5.4.2 Advantages of Federated Learning

- *Collaborative Learning Across Unmanned Aerial Vehicle Networks:*
  Federated learning involves drones sharing their locally learned models with a central server, which then combines these models to detect threats worldwide. This method uses the collective learning of many UAV networks to identify a variety of attack patterns while protecting the privacy of your data.
- *Privacy-Preserving Threat Detection:*
  Federated learning is a great option for Internet of Things (IoD) systems where data security is crucial since it removes the requirement for raw data transfer, which lowers the possibility that sensitive information may be captured by attackers.

5.4.3 Disadvantages of Federated Learning

- *Heterogeneity of Devices:*
  Devices within an IoT or a UAV network can be heterogeneous in terms of connectivity and processing abilities. Such heterogeneity in the devices can lead to unpredictable training results and a delay in ensuring model updates get synchronized in all devices participating in the process disadvantage for the model.
- *Limited Applicability for Small-Scale Datasets:*
  However, it may not be too effective in the context of federated learning when data is not spread out or when datasets in local nodes are too small to give meaningful updates. In this case, less populated local devices lack meaningful updates contributing to the improvement of the global model.

5.5 Post Quantum Cryptography for Enhanced Security

After the emergence of quantum computing technology, it is the turn of Post Quantum Cryptography (PQC) now. These are traditional techniques of encryption—RSA and ECC, which stand vulnerable to attacks by a quantum computer. As a result, the time has now come to design cryptographic frameworks that can provide safety against emerging threats. In IoD, Post Quantum Cryptography becomes an essential requirement for making sure communications and integrity of sensitive data exchanged by drones and ground control stations are secured.

Post Quantum Cryptography refers to algorithms designed so that they remain secure against both classical and quantum computational attacks. Rising powerful quantum computers will most likely break commonly used encryption methods, which makes IoD systems extremely vulnerable. Transitioning to PQC means all security measures are future-proof as well as keeping vital communication flows in applications that may well be military or otherwise with infrastructure management.

5.5.1 Advantages of Post Quantum Cryptography in IoD Security

- *Enhanced Security Against Quantum Attacks:*
  PQC algorithms are specifically designed to withstand the unique threats posed by quantum computers, making them significantly more secure than traditional methods like RSA or ECC. This enhanced security ensures that sensitive data, such as communications between drones and ground control stations, remains protected from interception or decryption by potential quantum adversaries.
- *Future Proofing:*
  Implementing PQC now allows organizations to prepare for a future where quantum computing capabilities could compromise existing encryption standards. This proactive approach minimizes the risk of vulnerabilities emerging as quantum technology advances, ensuring that critical communications remain secure over time.

5.5.2 Disadvantages of Post Quantum Cryptography in IoD Security

- *Standardization Issues:*
  The field of PQC is still in its infancy. Not all the algorithms are vetted and standardized by authorities. Hence, one is usually in two minds regarding which algorithms to employ or use because selecting a less secure or untested method may occur.
- *Resource Limitations:*
  Drones will typically use power processing, memory, and battery life and may quite often badly limit the range of resource-intensive PQC algorithms considerably. Organizations therefore need to decide and implement those PQC methods that could be run without imposing a severe performance cost on IoD systems.

5.6 Future Trends in MAD Technologies in IoD

There are many limitations for the above-mentioned technologies when they are used alone to tackle multi-vector attacks as stated. In recent works, researchers have been integrating these technologies using various algorithms to get more efficiency in the detection of attacks in the IoT ecosystem. Some of the integrated technologies mainly being worked upon are mentioned below.

5.6.1 Digital Twin and Blockchain for Secure Communication and Attack Validation

This integration creates avenues toward a strong framework for secure UAV communications and the validation of attacks. More so, blockchain will record all commands and communications between a drone and its ground control system to create an immutable and tamper-proof record of every interaction. This decentralized ledger prevents unauthorized access, manipulation, or data tampering and, most importantly, improves the safety of UAV operations through protection from MITM and command injection attacks. Through logging all transactions, Blockchain also allows operators to trace every command back to its source, thereby ensuring the transparency and accountability that is maintained across the process of communication.

Meanwhile, the Digital Twin technology provides for real-time virtual modelling of the UAV system that can be continually monitored and validated in real-time. For example, the Digital Twin can simulate in a virtual environment the effects of a command well before that command is executed in the physical environment, thereby setting the legitimacy of the command with no strings attached. Pre-testing commands feature is greatly helpful against a command-injection attack wherein an attacker can hijack or mislead a drone using evil commands. Digital Twin checks the behavior of the UAVs validates the correctness of the received commands and makes sure that only valid actions are performed.

Another area of protection that the combined Blockchain and Digital Twin affords against the various forms of attacks, including signal jamming or GPS spoofing is the Blockchain log that ensures accepted commands are legitimate even when all channels of communication are infiltrated. The Digital Twin is the main actor here simulates and validates the commands in real-time intending to eliminate unauthorized actions before their execution. This two-layer defense system is useful for security against data tampering, eavesdropping, and drone operation manipulation; which helps the integrity and security of UAV networks.

Nielsen et al. [16] highlighted an integration of Digital Twin and Blockchain technologies showcasing a proof concept in secure communication between UAVs, thus demonstrating how the decentralized nature of Blockchain, when combined with the real-time simulation capability of DT, might indeed prevent Multi-Vector Cyberattacks such as MITM without having any negative impacts on operational efficiency in complex environments. Together the two technologies form a system that is extremely resilient and tamper-proof for UAV operations steadily bringing performance as well as security to the IoD.

5.6.2 Blockchain and Federated Learning for Decentralized Multi-Attack Detection Models

Blockchain and Federated Learning together provide the decentralized and secure mode of network attack detection to the IoD by multi-vector attacks. It becomes possible to share and aggregate the models of attack detection safely across the decentralized UAV networks due to the application of FL frameworks with enforced data privacy. Such IoD systems can further empower drones to acquire particular localized threat information like anomalous GPS signals or network interference and then apply that information to update models of machine learning locally on these drones. as mentioned by Zhu et al. [13]. Such models, with knowledge about real-time threats, can further be securely transferred between drones using blockchain in a fashion that ensures models remain resilient against tampering, even to manipulation or poisoning attacks in sporadic communications environments.

This ensures that blockchain maintains the integrity and traceability of these models, thus making a process of Federated Learning exist without aggregating data in one place. In other words, it is decentralized, which means there is no single point of failure with which an attacker may end all communication with this system or even complete stopping of model sharing. This decentralized approach would be particularly critical for UAV systems because they are very often deployed in situations wherein communication networks have been compromised or may altogether be unreliable. For instance, those drones deployed in combat zones or disaster areas require robust multi-attack detection systems to handle complex attacks which may even involve network disruption coupled with sensor manipulation.

In such scenarios, Federated Learning enables the drones to learn all the various threats identified on the IoD network. Contributions from locally trained models from drones are going to make the system better with time in recognizing emerging patterns of sophisticated attacks. The use of Blockchain provides security in the process of model-sharing since there is no unauthorized access or tampering with the models in transmission. Khan et al. [13], Federated Learning in Digital Twin-based vehicular networks apply Blockchain to improve security and robustness of multi-attack detection, thus suited for UAV networks operating in dynamic hostile environments. The IoD system can maintain robust, real-time threat detection capabilities combining the advantages of Blockchain and Federated Learning while keeping data private, secure, and operationally efficient.

5.6.3 Federated Learning and Digital Twin for Predictive Multi-Attack Scenario Planning

Drones outfitted with Federated Learning models in large-scale IoD networks may recognize and thwart threats by drawing on prior experience. By offering a virtual environment where different multi-attack scenarios (such as coordinated GPS spoofing, network jamming, and malware insertion) can be tested and assessed without disrupting the real drone operations, digital twins improve this process [9]. This would be realized through massive IoD networks where the drones, equipped with Federated Learning models, can identify and prevent attacks possibly based on experience earlier incurred. Digital twins promote this process by allowing multiple scenarios, such as coordinated GPS spoofing, network jamming, or even malware insertion, to be tested and assessed without interfering with the activities of actual drones. DT-FL systems of drones do not share any highly confidential data with their replicas; instead, they share model parameters. This greatly lowers the possibility of privacy violations because the data collected by drones are concealed. Furthermore, DT-FL decreases network load because of the limited transfer of data, and this is useful for areas with limited access to bandwidth, for example, rural zones, where drones are increasingly significant. However, the benefits do not stop at the enhancement of efficiency and confidentiality. For local and collaborative learning, the Digital Twin acts as a training field for drones. Compared to the regular central processing method, this procedure may fasten training and optimize the use of the available resources. This is especially the retention of large quantities of information and a sharp increase in the overall level of intelligence of the network when individual drones are involved in the learning process.

Moreover, DT-FL improves security. In most cases, cyber attackers focus on the central servers or unique drones. However, the influence reach is only towards the Digital Twin with DT-FL. The overall function of the network is less prone to data theft and model tampering since this central objective is easier to protect. DT-FL is incredibly versatile. As has been inferred, the Digital Twin can be updated thoroughly based on alterations in the environment or the network topology. It would integrate real-time simulation of multi-vector attacks on UAVs through the digital twin, and federated learning increases the adaptability of the system towards new and unforeseen attacks as they evolve across the network, hence allowing for the continuous building of proactive safety mechanisms and detection algorithms against dynamic coordinated attacks. For instance, that would expose an autonomous fleet of drones in a smart city to DDoS or GPS spoofing, endangering the public.

For evaluating the performance metrics of these systems, accuracy, F1 score, and recall are usually calculated. Generally, the accuracy, F1 score, and Recall can be calculated using these measures.

$$\text{Accuracy} = \frac{TP + TN}{TP + TN + FP + FN} \tag{1}$$

$$\text{F1 Score} = 2 \times \frac{\text{Precision} \times \text{Recall}}{\text{Precision} + \text{Recall}} \tag{2}$$

$$\text{Recall} = \frac{TP}{TP + FN} \tag{3}$$

The integration of these modern technologies like blockchain, digital twins, machine learning, federated learning, and Post Quantum Cryptography have many benefits for multi-attack detection (Multi-Attack Detection (MAD) in the Internet of Drones (IoD)) as they have proved they enhance the efficiency of attack detection, and reduce false positives and false negatives as compared to other attack detection frameworks. There are several obstacles to overcome in putting them into practice. Numerous prospects for improved capabilities in sectors including emergency services, agriculture, logistics, and surveillance are presented by the Internet of Drones (IoD). Nevertheless, it also has some built-in difficulties that need to be resolved to guarantee safe, dependable, and effective operation. If not handled properly, these problems, which cross operational, technological, and regulatory boundaries, might prevent IoD systems from being widely used. The integration of these technologies such as Digital Twin with Blockchain and also Digital Twin with Federated Learning has given significant results based on these values, especially accuracy which calculates to about 96%.

5.7 *Technical Challenges, Concerns and Ethical Considerations*

To fully achieve the promise of an all-inclusive Multi-Attack Detection (MAD) system in IoD contexts, several obstacles need to be overcome as mentioned below.

5.7.1 Technical Challenges

The technical challenges in the IoD system can be defined on the basis of the following:

- ***Interoperability Issues:***
  The hardware and software platforms from many manufacturers make up the IoD ecosystem. It can be challenging to ensure compatibility across different drone models, GCSs, and communication networks, particularly when including diverse security technologies like Blockchain, Federated Learning, or Post Quantum Cryptography. Interoperability and standardization issues can cause security lapses or communication failures, which increases the susceptibility of IoD systems to coordinated attacks. For instance, a drone's onboard systems and ground station security protocols may not be integrated, which leaves room for vulnerabilities in either system to be exploited by an attacker. Furthermore, multi-vendor settings could find it difficult to put unified threat detection frameworks into practice, which would lessen the potency of multi-attack detection (Multi-Attack Detection (MAD)) systems.

- ***Insider Threats:***
  IoD systems are vulnerable to insider attacks because anyone with access to communication networks or drone control systems might purposefully jeopardize security. Insider attacks may include data manipulation, interfering with drone software, or disclosing private information to outside enemies. It can be challenging to identify insider threats, particularly in settings where a variety of stakeholders have access to drone systems, such as operators, maintenance staff, and service providers. There are serious hazards to security and safety from these attacks since they may lead to espionage, sabotage, or purposeful redirection of UAV operations.
- ***Computational and Resource Constraints:***
  Drones have very tight resource constraints in terms of processing power, battery, and storage. Even prudent use of security measures such as Post Quantum Cryptography or machine learning-based attack detectors consumes a large amount of computer resources. Energy consumption algorithms for assault detection may cut down the time allowed for a drone operation. The computations that are performed in drones, like blockchain verification or digital twin simulations, thus need to have hardware that is more efficient or lightweight to be adopted as effective or lightweight alternatives.
- ***Resource Overhead:***
  Concerning that, blockchain and digital twin technologies bring an increase in security as well as predictability but incur some extra costs associated with computing power, bandwidth usage, and data storage. Its decentralized and irreversible nature because of consensus processes may slow down transactions, making it difficult to make decisions in real-time in an IoD setting where speed is associated with a lot of movement. It would necessitate a rather large bandwidth to keep updating constantly in synchronization with the real-time data of drones and perhaps might not be achievable at times, like that from remote locations.

5.7.2 Regulatory and Legal Concerns

Drone usage is increasing faster than adequate regulatory frameworks have been developed. The majority of nations lack clear laws governing the administration of expansive IoD networks, particularly those about privacy, airspace management, and the moral use of drones. Additionally, the lack of uniform security guidelines for drone operations results in uneven safety precautions in various areas. Insufficient rules may lead to privacy infringements, such as unapproved monitoring or the improper use of drones for illicit purposes. The employment of drones in delicate contexts, including border security, law enforcement, or military operations, raises ethical questions as well since improper usage or malfunctioning drones may result in abuses of human rights or worsened conflicts.

5.7.3 Ethical Considerations

As the technologies are increasingly embedded in people's daily lives, issues that arise in the context of responsible deployment need to be addressed. While the protection of these systems from cyber attacks is paramount, wider implications of UAV utilization should be recognized: privacy, data security, and ethical exploitation of autonomous systems. The most serious ethical concerns involved are the following:

- ***Privacy and Surveillance:*** One of the significant ethical conflicts is the potential for invasive surveillance and unapproved data collection using drones. It may be the case that there is no comprehensive legislation to handle the mishandling of drones and the infringement of people's private information rights. This raises an important question ethically, particularly in regions that have an unregulated environment for drones. It is going to require ethical frameworks to explain what data is being collected, by whom and under what circumstances so that people understand what is going on and can hold someone accountable.
- ***Prevention of Misuse and Arms Risings:*** A very versatile UAV could be used for task alterations, including such tasks as unauthorized surveillance data theft, or worse, a weapon. IoD will ensure the system can't be altered easily for nefarious purposes, which will combine technical security measures with the law's constraints. Much ethical reasoning will inform development so serious security protocols are in place to prevent misuse while allowing beneficial, legitimate uses.
- ***Responsibility and Transparency:*** The deployment of drones in sensitive environments makes accountability more significant in IoD networks. Effective reporting mechanisms are to be developed with required checks to report any incidence or data breach related to the activities of drones. Blockchain technology can play a very crucial role in enhancing accountability, with tamper-proof records of all interactions within the IoD network, thereby building trust and clarity.
- ***Balancing Innovation with Regulation:*** Innovation in IoD technology happens so fast that the regulatory frameworks get left behind and ethical dilemmas start arising in deployment and usage. Technological development needs to be furthered, as well as regulations that ensure the rights and safety of individuals. Responsible innovation should be called for in safety and privacy among other advancements in technologies.

6 Conclusion

Significant operational capability improvements are being brought about by the Internet of Drones (IoD) as it develops in fields including military applications, disaster management, logistics, and surveillance. IoD networks, however, also face a rising number of cyber risks as they develop and become more integrated into vital infrastructures. Securing these systems now requires the capacity to identify and counter multi-vector attacks including GPS spoofing attacks, DDoS attacks, jamming attacks, and hijacking attacks. The many attack vectors against IoD systems have been examined in this chapter, highlighting the necessity of Multi-Attack Detection (Multi-Attack Detection (MAD)) frameworks. Through the utilization of cutting-edge technologies like Post Quantum Cryptography, Digital Twins, Federated Learning, Blockchain, and Machine Learning, Internet of Things networks can implement multi-layered security architectures that can react in real-time to planned and clever attacks. However, there are some difficulties in putting these technologies into practice, such as resource limitations, latency, scalability, and interoperability issues. Despite all these limitations, drone proliferation has also outpaced legal frameworks, raising privacy, security, and ethical issues that need to be resolved with extensive legal and technological solutions. Improved industry stakeholder engagement, worldwide standards and laws, and ongoing research and development in Multi-Attack Detection (MAD) technologies are all needed to exploit the potential of IoD while maintaining its security properly. IoD systems may develop into strong, secure networks that not only increase efficiency but also preserve resistance against more complex attacks by addressing the difficulties and successfully integrating developing technology. To guarantee safe, dependable, and scalable drone operations in a connected environment, the future of IoD security hinges on using a proactive, adaptive, and layered strategy like Multi-attack Detection.

Enhancing security within the Internet of Drones has tremendous broad implications that are totally transformative, crossing sectors that are industrial and societal. Such is the case for industries whose operations entail the use of Unmanned Aerial Vehicles (UAVs), such as emergency services, agriculture, and military logistics; an effective framework for Multi-Attack Detection is critical. These frameworks ensure that there is an unbroken continuity of vital services, which could mitigate operational disruption resulting from the cyber attack. Examples include, in emergency response scenarios, a great deal would depend on drones' critical roles in medical supply delivery, surveying disaster zones, and rescue efforts coordination. Such service disruptions due to a cyber attack could have very grave, even life-threatening, impacts. Similarly, in agricultural applications where UASs monitor crop health and optimize resource distribution, it can prevent manipulated data from causing the wrong actions, damaging crops, or resulting in financial loss.

Furthermore, security enhancement in IoD networks entails trust, which remains a salient feature in the wide application of drone technology. As industries and consumers become more confident in the safety and reliability of UAV systems, it encourages their further integration into a whole range of applications bringing tangible benefits for society. For example, drones can be helpful in environmental monitoring in more efficient ways to track wildlife, deforestation, and water resources in real-time. The UAVs can help assist in the smart cities' management of traffic flow, infrastructure inspection, and pollution control at lower costs of operation. This means that autonomous delivery systems would be able to benefit as well, along with easier transportation, lesser chances of human errors, and less delay in logistics by secured IoD networks. Securing IoD systems is no longer just about preventing cyber-attacks; it unlocks the entire potential of UAVs for their application towards unlocking life better on a sector-to-sector level.

Acknowledgments Deepest gratitude is extended to C3iHub for their unwavering support, guidance, and resources throughout the research and development of the cybersecurity frameworks discussed in this chapter. Their contribution has been invaluable, and heartfelt thanks are expressed for their essential role in this work.

References

1. Abdelmaboud, A.: The internet of drones: Requirements, taxonomy, recent advances, and challenges of research trends. Sensors **21**(17) (2021). https://doi.org/10.3390/s21175718, https://www.mdpi.com/1424-8220/21/17/5718
2. Abualigah, L., Diabat, A., Sumari, P., Gandomi, A.H.: Applications, deployments, and integration of Internet of Drones (IoD): A review. IEEE Sensors J. **21**(22), 25532–25546 (2021). https://doi.org/10.1109/JSEN.2021.3114266
3. Basan, E.S., Sushkin, N.A., Babenko, L.K.: Methodology for detecting attacks in the context of destructive influences. In: 2023 IEEE XVI International Scientific and Technical Conference Actual Problems of Electronic Instrument Engineering (APEIE), pp. 1120–1124 (2023). https://doi.org/10.1109/APEIE59731.2023.10347616
4. Brewington, J., Kar, D.: Uav GPS spoofing detection via neural generative one-class classification. In: Proceedings of the Twenty-Fourth International Symposium on Theory, Algorithmic Foundations, and Protocol Design for Mobile Networks and Mobile Computing, pp. 492–497. MobiHoc '23, Association for Computing Machinery, New York, NY, USA (2023). https://doi.org/10.1145/3565287.3617628
5. Derhab, A., Cheikhrouhou, O., Allouch, A., Koubaa, A., Qureshi, B., Ferrag, M.A., Maglaras, L., Khan, F.A.: Internet of drones security: Taxonomies, open issues, and future directions. Veh. Commun. **39**, 100552 (2023). https://doi.org/10.1016/j.vehcom.2022.100552, https://www.sciencedirect.com/science/article/pii/S2214209622000997
6. Ferrag, M.A., Friha, O., Maglaras, L., Janicke, H., Shu, L.: Federated deep learning for cyber security in the internet of things: Concepts, applications, and experimental analysis. IEEE Access **9**, 138509–138542 (2021). https://doi.org/10.1109/ACCESS.2021.3118642
7. He, X., Chen, Q., Tang, L., Wang, W., Liu, T., Li, L, Liu, Q., Luo, J.: Federated continuous learning based on stacked broad learning system assisted by digital twin networks: an incremental learning approach for intrusion detection in UAV networks. IEEE Internet Things J. **10**(12), 19825–19838 (2023). https://doi.org/10.1109/JIOT.2023.3282648
8. Gharibi, M., Boutaba, R., Waslander, S.L.: Internet of drones. IEEE Access **4**, 1148–1162 (2016). https://doi.org/10.1109/ACCESS.2016.2537208
9. Gupta, D., Moni, S.S., Tosun, A.S.: Integration of digital twin and federated learning for securing vehicular internet of things. In: Proceedings of the 2023 International Conference on Research in Adaptive and Convergent Systems. RACS '23, Association for Computing Machinery, New York, NY, USA (2023). https://doi.org/10.1145/3599957.3606250
10. Hassija, V., Chamola, V., Agrawal, A., Goyal, A., Nguyen, C., Niyato, D., Yu, F., Guizani, M.: Fast, reliable, and secure drone communication: A comprehensive survey. IEEE Commun. Surv. Tutorials (2021). https://doi.org/10.1109/COMST.2021.3097916
11. https://www.facebook.com/thehackernews: Iranian engineer hijack U.S. drone by GPS hack [video explanation]. thehackernews.com, https://thehackernews.com/2011/12/iranian-engineer-hijack-us-drone-by-gps.html. Accessed 16 Jan 2024

12. Jean aime, M., Ben Mahmoud, M.S., Larrieu, N.: Secure routing protocol design for UAV ad hoc networks. Research Gate (2015). https://doi.org/10.1109/DASC.2015.7311581
13. Khan, L.U., Mustafa, E., Shuja, J., Rehman, F., Bilal, K., Han, Z., Hong, C.S.: Federated learning for digital twin-based vehicular networks: Architecture and challenges. IEEE Wirel. Commun. **31**(2), 156–162 (2024). https://doi.org/10.1109/MWC.012.2200373
14. Krasnyánszki, B., Brassai, S.T., Németh, A.: UAV weaknesses against deauthentication based hijacking attacks. In: 2024 IEEE 22nd World Symposium on Applied Machine Intelligence and Informatics (SAMI), pp. 000493–000498 (2024)
15. Mitka, E., Mouroutsos, S.G.: Classification of drones. Am. J. Eng. Res. **6**, 36–41 (2017)
16. Nielsen, C.P., da Silva, E.R., Yu, F.: Digital twins and blockchain – proof of concept. Procedia CIRP **93**, 251–255 (2020). https://doi.org/https://doi.org/10.1016/j.procir.2020.04.104, https://www.sciencedirect.com/science/article/pii/S2212827120307381, 53rd CIRP Conference on Manufacturing Systems 2020
17. Panice, G., Luongo, S., Gigante, G., Pascarella, D., Di Benedetto, C., Vozella, A., Pescapè, A.: A SVM-based detection approach for GPS spoofing attacks to UAV. In: 2017 23rd International Conference on Automation and Computing (ICAC), pp. 1–11 (2017). https://doi.org/10.23919/IConAC.2017.8081999
18. Pu, C., Zhu, P.: Defending against flooding attacks in the internet of drones environment. In: 2021 IEEE Global Communications Conference (GLOBECOM), pp. 1–6 (2021). https://api.semanticscholar.org/CorpusID:245139760
19. Sethuraman, S.C., Vijayakumar, V., Walczak, S.: Cyber attacks on healthcare devices using unmanned aerial vehicles. J. Med. Syst. **44**(1), 29 (2019). https://doi.org/10.1007/s10916-019-1489-9
20. Tian, Y., Yuan, J., Song, H.: Efficient privacy-preserving authentication framework for edge-assisted internet of drones. J. Inf. Secur. Appl. **48**, 102354 (2019). https://doi.org/10.1016/j.jisa.2019.06.010, https://www.sciencedirect.com/science/article/pii/S2214212618307038
21. Tlili, F., Ayed, S., Fourati, L.C.: A new hybrid adaptive deep learning-based framework for UAVs faults and attacks detection. IEEE Trans. Serv. Comput. **16**(6), 4128–4139 (2023). https://doi.org/10.1109/TSC.2023.3311045
22. Vuong, T.P., Loukas, G., Gan, D., Bezemskij, A.: Decision tree-based detection of denial of service and command injection attacks on robotic vehicles. In: 2015 IEEE International Workshop on Information Forensics and Security (WIFS), pp. 1–6 (2015). https://doi.org/10.1109/WIFS.2015.7368559
23. Wang, S., Wang, J., Su, C., Ma, X.: Intelligent detection algorithm against UAVs' GPS spoofing attack. In: 2020 IEEE 26th International Conference on Parallel and Distributed Systems (ICPADS), pp. 382–389 (2020). https://doi.org/10.1109/ICPADS51040.2020.00058
24. Wu, D., Yan, J., Wang, H., Wang, R.: Multiattack intrusion detection algorithm for edge-assisted Internet of Things. In: 2019 IEEE International Conference on Industrial Internet (ICII), pp. 210–218 (2019). https://doi.org/10.1109/ICII.2019.00046
25. Yahuza, M., Idris, M.Y.I., Ahmedy, I.B., Wahab, A.W.A., Nandy, T., Noor, N.M., Bala, A.: Internet of drones security and privacy issues: Taxonomy and open challenges. IEEE Access **9**, 57243–57270 (2021). https://doi.org/10.1109/ACCESS.2021.3072030
26. Yigit, Y., Nguyen, L.D., Ozdem, M., Kinaci, O.K., Hoang, T., Canberk, B., Duong, T.Q.: Twinport: 5G drone-assisted data collection with digital twin for smart seaports. Sci. Rep. **13**(1), 12310 (2023)

Tactical Trust: A Comprehensive Exploration of Trust Management in the Internet of Drones

B. S. Smitha Rani and Sabu M. Thampi

1 Introduction

Drones, or Unmanned Aerial Vehicles (UAVs), are cyber-physical systems (CPS), integrating computation, networking, and physical processes. They are crucial for civilian and military applications such as remote sensing, border patrolling, surveillance, package delivery, and medical services, disaster monitoring, and communication coverage extension. The Drones converse with a reference ground structure in tandem, gathering and extending data to facilitate services or provide up-to-date information to users who are connected to dedicated application servers from a distance. Drones fly in the sky with full network capabilities and this interconnected system of drones forms the Internet of Drones (IoD), akin to the Internet of Things (IoT) [1]. Figure 1 illustrates the general architecture of IoD environment that includes swarms of drones, ground control station, zone service provider and signal link connecting the nodes.

IoD is a "layered network control architecture," according to Gharibi et al. [2] that aids in the coordination of UAVs. In an IoD environment, a large number of drones come together to transmit and receive data from one another, forming a network. IoD technology is anticipated to drive significant innovations in areas such as logistics, surveillance, agriculture, and emergency response, thereby unlocking new potential and applications for drones. Like any other network, IoD faces various security issues that can compromise its functionality and safety.

B. S. Smitha Rani (✉) · S. M. Thampi
Connected Systems and Intelligence Lab, School of Computer Science and Engineering, Digital University Kerala, Trivandrum, India
e-mail: smitha.csres24@duk.ac.in; sabu.thampi@duk.ac.in
https://duk.ac.in

S. M. Thampi et al. (eds.), *Securing the Connected World*,
https://doi.org/10.1007/978-3-031-82826-3_12

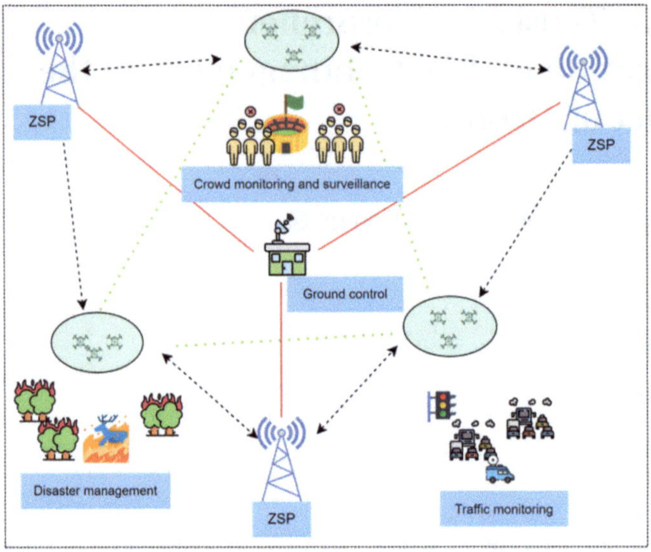

Fig. 1 General architecture of Internet of Drones

Thus, regardless of the progress and the various methods to enhance drone communication, security remains a primary concern in IoD because transmissions encompass delicate as well as critical information. Therefore, the security of IoD is perhaps one of the most critical necessities in the proper applicability of multiple UAVs.

1.1 Common Features of Internet of Drones

The prominent features of Internet of Drone network is discussed below (see Fig. 2). They collectively enhance the operational capabilities of drones, making the IoD a powerful tool in sectors like logistics, surveillance, agriculture, and environmental monitoring.

Hierarchical Network Structure An IoD typically employs a multi-layered hierarchical structure. A central controller that manages the entire network usually makes up the top layer. Drones themselves make up the bottom layer, while groups of drones are managed by local controllers or edge nodes in the middle layers. Since strategic instructions are provided by upper layers and carried out by lower layers, the hierarchical structure facilitates effective command and control.

3D Mobility and Coverage Drones in the Internet of Drones (IoD) move in three dimensions, which makes routing, communication, and collision avoidance

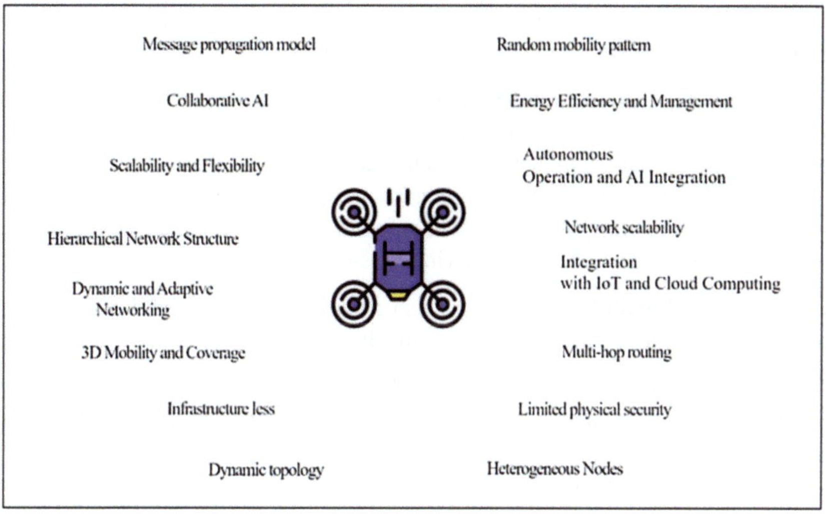

Fig. 2 Features of Internet of Drones

more challenging than in conventional networks. Wide-area coverage provided by Internet of Drones supports applications such as environmental monitoring, security surveillance and delivery services since they can reach places that are difficult or impossible to reach otherwise.

Dynamic and Adaptive Networking Drones operating in the Internet of Drones (IoD) can react in real-time to mission objectives, environmental changes, and drone status (such as battery level) to ensure seamless operations. To enhance efficiency and ensure mission success, dynamic resource allocation in the IoD optimizes bandwidth, power, and computing resources based on the real-time demands of both the mission and the network [3].

Heterogeneous Nodes Drones of multiple types with varying capacities are included in the Internet of Drones (IoD) (e.g., size, sensors, endurance, processing power). For the network to run effectively, these resources must be managed and optimized.

Energy Efficiency and Management Drones in the IoD have limited battery life, making energy efficiency a critical concern. Energy-efficient communication protocols, flight path optimization, and power management strategies are integral features of the IoD.

Integration with IoT and Cloud Computing The IoD often integrates with other Internet of Things (IoT) devices, allowing drones to interact with ground sensors, cameras, and other connected devices to collect and process data. The Internet of Drones (IoD) utilizes cloud and edge computing to handle data processing, storage, and analysis, allowing drones to make real-time decisions while shifting heavy computational tasks away from the drones themselves.

Autonomous Operation and AI Integration The majority of Internet of Drone (IoD) systems are equipped with artificial intelligence (AI) algorithms that enable drones to operate autonomously, evaluate data, and make basic decisions based on mission objectives, environmental conditions, and gathered data. Drones within the IoD can collaborate using AI techniques to perform complex tasks, such as coordinated surveillance, formation flying, or swarm behavior.

Scalability and Flexibility The IoD is also scalable, with the capability to add new drones or sensors to the network without much compromise of connection speeds.

Multi-Hop Routing In the Internet of Drones (IoD), multi-hop routing is a communication technique where data is transmitted through multiple intermediate drones or nodes rather than relying on a direct, long-distance connection between the source and destination.

Infrastructure Less Internet of Drones are infrastructure-less networks because they do not rely on any pre-established infrastructure, such as fixed routers or base stations, for communication. Instead, these networks are self-organizing and dynamically create the network on demand, allowing devices or drones to communicate directly with each other.

Dynamic Topology Due to the frequent departure and arrival of drones, the network topology remains constantly dynamic.

Random Mobility Pattern The mobility patterns of nodes are unpredictable, allowing them to move in any direction at random.

Limited Physical Security In these networks, physical security is minimal because the drones are constantly moving in different directions. This makes it challenging to provide them with proper physical protection.

Network Scalability IoD is easily scalable. New drones can join or exit the network at any time as needed [3].

1.2 Motivation

In the rapidly evolving Internet of Drones (IoD) domain, the frequent joining and leaving of highly mobile nodes leads to significant challenges such as link breakage and packet loss. These issues necessitate robust mechanisms for monitoring and assessing node behavior within the network. The decentralized nature of IoD further complicates matters, as each drone autonomously determines its communication partners based on perceived reputation. This underscores the critical need for a system that provides accurate and reliable reputation feedback across the network. Information forwarding and sharing are also vital in the real-time, dynamic environments typical of ad-hoc networks like IoD. However, these networks are increasingly vulnerable to various attacks, including the dissemination of false information, packet forgery, and malicious alterations to routing data. In such contexts, trust management systems become indispensable. They are crucial in identifying untrustworthy nodes, tracking their activities, and calculating trust values to maintain network integrity.

This book chapter, "Tactical Trust: A Comprehensive Exploration of Trust Management in the Internet of Drones," delves into these challenges. It provides an in-depth analysis of trust computation techniques and their application within the IoD, offering solutions to enhance the reliability and security of drone networks. By examining recent advancements and ongoing research, this chapter aims to contribute to the development of resilient and trustworthy IoD systems, essential for the safe and efficient operation of drones in a wide range of applications.

1.3 Our Contribution

In this book chapter, we conduct a comprehensive analysis of state-of-the-art trust management techniques in the Internet of Drones (IoD). This review contributes to the research community focused on enhancing the security of IoD networks. We identify various threats targeting drone networks and explore the complete process of trust management, including trust composition, formation, computation, propagation, and updating. We evaluate trust management techniques based on their effectiveness in addressing complexity, dynamicity, scalability, and security challenges in IoD. Finally, we recommend best practices for building trust among drones and provide future research directions to strengthen trust management in IoD.

2 Security Requirements

Researchers have developed various security and privacy techniques to protect the Internet of Drones (IoD) network, which is essential for safeguarding the location and operations of drones (unmanned aerial vehicles, or UAVs) and addressing the security and privacy issues that arise with IoD use. In the past, inaccuracies in drone positioning caused significant issues for the entire network, posing serious risks. One of the main goals of the IoD network is to ensure security and privacy at levels that cannot be easily compromised.

To achieve this, the IoD network must meet several critical security requirements: availability, confidentiality, integrity, authenticity, and non-repudiation [4].

Availability in the context of the Internet of Drones refers to ensuring that all legitimate or authorized entities within the IoD ecosystem have uninterrupted access to the services, resources, and data they need, whenever required. This means that drones, ground control systems, operators, and other connected infrastructure can seamlessly communicate and operate without delay or downtime. **Confidentiality** in the Internet of Drones refers to ensuring that only authorized and legitimate entities within the IoD ecosystem have access to the data and communications being exchanged. This means that sensitive information, such as telemetry data, control commands, and mission-critical communications, must be protected from unauthorized access or interception by malicious actors.

Integrity in the Internet of Drones refers to ensuring that the data and messages transmitted between drones, ground stations, and other components remain unaltered and are delivered without manipulation or tampering by unauthorized parties. This concept is critical in maintaining trust in IoD communications, as compromised data can lead to incorrect decisions, failed missions, or even catastrophic events. **Authentication** in the Internet of Drones ensures that every entity participating in the network, such as drones, ground control systems, and communication nodes, is legitimate and can be trusted. Authenticity is fundamental to the security of IoD systems, as it prevents unauthorized or malicious actors from infiltrating the network, ensures that communications originate from valid sources, and establishes trust among IoD entities. **Non-repudiation** refers to ensuring that a drone cannot deny sending a message or performing a specific action within the network. This requirement is crucial for maintaining accountability and trust between drones and other entities in the IoD network.

2.1 Security Threats and Vulnerability Issues with IoD

Potential threats to IoD security encompass key compromise, communication interception, and access control manipulation, which can lead to privacy breaches. Vulnerabilities in IoD and its application platforms are exploitable by attackers seeking to gain unauthorized access. Emphasis should be placed on robust access and authorization security measures. Tampering with access control information can lead to configuration changes, resulting in conflicts. Services-oriented IoD, employed in critical tasks like real-time surveillance and air traffic control, are susceptible to node capture and service shutdown, leading to mission failures.

Critical mission-oriented IoD may suffer from Denial-of-Service (DoS) or Distributed Denial-of-Service (DDoS) attacks, impacting availability due to limited resources. Attackers may exploit excessive resource utilization by enabling numerous services, causing rapid depletion. Additional threats affecting IoD availability include waypoint alteration, GPS spoofing, and IoD Freezing, potentially resulting in collisions. Effective security measures, including Intrusion Detection Systems (IDS), cryptographic tools, and stringent security policies, are imperative to safeguard IoD.

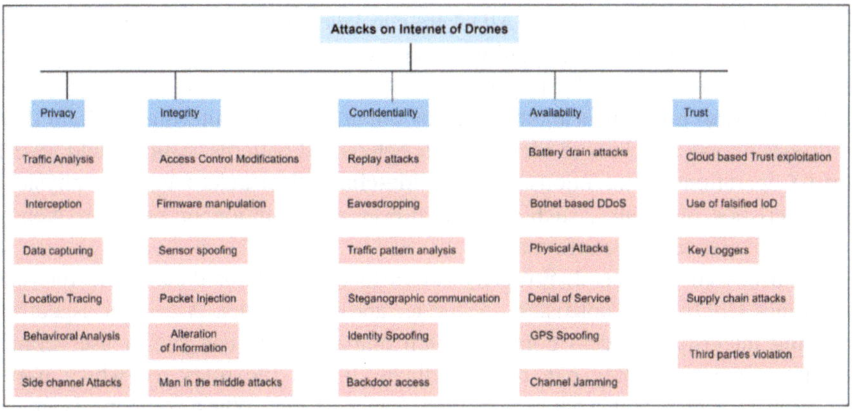

Fig. 3 Types of known attacks in Internet of Drones

2.2 *Attacks in Internet of Drones*

These attacks can be classified into three main classes: device-based attacks, network-based attacks, and software-based attacks [5] (see Fig. 3).

1. Device-based attacks: Getting physical access to drone parts, like memory, in order to take control of the drone or steal information.
2. Network-based attacks:Attacks targeting the network such as Man-in-the-middle, replay, eavesdropping, and modification attacks that intercept and modify data.
3. Software-based attacks:Attacks such as DoS/DDoS attacks are caused by exploiting vulnerabilities in the software, operating system or other applications.

Privacy is a significant concern for data-driven security in the Internet of Drones (IoD). An attacker can obtain sensitive information through a range of attacks.

One such attack is **traffic analysis** where attackers examine network traffic as it flows to and from the targeted systems. Attackers employ statistical techniques to understand and interpret the communication patterns exchanged across the network. By analyzing this data, they can glean insights about the interactions and potentially uncover sensitive information. Another attack vector is **interception** attacks which grant unauthorized users access to drone data, applications, or environments, posing a significant risk to confidentiality.

Closely related to interception is **data capturing** where a malicious actor can capture network packets to intercept or steal unencrypted data traffic. Sniffers analyze the streams of data packets exchanged between computers on a network and with the Internet. By using a packet sniffer in "promiscuous mode," an intruder can examine any packet, regardless of its intended destination.

Additionally, **location tracing** is a growing concern due to the use of GPS receivers on unmanned aerial vehicles (UAVs), making them susceptible to intentional disruptions like spoofing. Attackers can leverage this information to create location profiles, tracking the positions and movement patterns of these nodes. Such data can then be exploited for targeted attacks.

Behavioural analysis is another privacy threat, where monitoring the flight data of drones allows attackers to identify their behavioral patterns, which could reveal private operations or intentions. Lastly, **Side-channel attacks** target the physical characteristics of drones, such as their power consumption or radio frequency signals, to infer sensitive information.

As discussed in Sect. 2, **integrity** refers to the need for data in the Internet of Drones (IoD) to be consistent, accurate, and trustworthy. A critical aspect of ensuring integrity is access control, which manages who can see or use certain resources and what they can do with them. It sets the rules for which users are allowed access and what actions they can perform. When someone is given permission to access a resource, that process is called authorization. This system helps keep information safe by ensuring that only authorized users can access it. However in **access control modification** attacks, an attacker could modify permission and privileges leading to loss of data integrity. **Firmware manipulation attack** poses a serious risk to the integrity of drones. Unauthorized modifications or tampering with the embedded software (firmware) that controls the hardware of drones. It poses significant risks can compromise both the functionality and security of drones, undermining trust within the network. One particularly serious form of attack is the **Man in the Middle attack,** where an adversary position themselves in between the client and the drone to capture the data communicated between IoD and other devices in the IoD network.

Furthermore, **sensor spoofing** involves manipulating GPS signals, spoofing data from sensors like temperature, wind speed, or obstacle detection, manipulating visual or distance-measuring sensors, causing the drone to misinterpret its environment or make incorrect decisions. **Alteration of Information** attack involves tampering with our assets. Although these attacks primarily target data integrity, they can also threaten availability. For instance, data injection attacks change sensitive information and may upload infected data, creating a backdoor into the ground control system. Lastly, **packet injection** is another form of attack where malicious actors inject fabricated or manipulated data packets into the communication network between drones or between drones and ground control stations.

In Sect. 2, we discussed the importance of **confidentiality** within the Internet of Drones environment. A breach in confidentiality can have serious consequences, as it can lead to unauthorized parties obtaining information that could be used to exploit or compromise the IoD or the systems it interacts with. Therefore, maintaining robust confidentiality measures is crucial for safeguarding the integrity and security of IoD operations. **Identity Spoofing** occurs when an attacker deceives a system by assuming the identity of a legitimate user. In the context of IoD networks, this means the attacker effectively poses as a genuine user with the same identification credentials and gains unauthorized access to the IoD network and its communication links. Similarly **unauthorized access** is the act of gaining entry to the IoD server and its associated services without proper authorization. This security breach carries a notable risk of disclosing confidential and critical information from the IoD without proper authorization.

Replay Attack is another significant threat to drones operating within the Internet of Drones ecosystem. These attacks typically occur in two main stages. First, an attacker intercepts and records the authentic data transmitted by drones, such as navigation signals or telemetry information. Later, the attacker can use this captured data to replace the genuine signals being sent, leading to various issues. This manipulation can cause a drone to experience degraded performance or instability, and it may even allow for stealthy physical attacks on the drone or its operations, all without detection. **Eavesdropping** attack refers to the unauthorized real-time interception of communications within the IoD network. This type of attack is particularly perilous because it grants an attacker the ability to surreptitiously collect confidential information being exchanged between IoD devices.

Moreover, **traffic pattern analysis** enables attackers to infer sensitive information by analyzing patterns of encrypted traffic without decrypting it. A more covert method of attack is **steganographic communication,** where confidential data is embedded in seemingly innocent drone communication packets to exfiltrate information without detection. **Identity spoofing** occurs when an attacker deceives a system by assuming the identity of a legitimate user. In the context of IoD networks, this means the attacker effectively poses as a genuine user with the same identification credentials and gains unauthorized access to the IoD network and its communication links. In **backdoor access attacks**, backdoors are installed into drone software, allowing unauthorized users to gain access to confidential information at will.

Availability in the context of IoD, refers to the capability of services to be promptly initiated whenever they are required to maintain proper functionality. Given that IoD is deployed in mission-critical sectors and environments, ensuring its uninterrupted availability is a paramount concern in terms of security. In these mission-oriented fields, any disruption or downtime in IoD services can have severe consequences. Various types of attacks specifically target the availability of IoD systems. **Physical attacks** are one such threat, as ensuring the physical security of IoD devices is crucial due to their high value and the potential ramifications of a successful physical attack. Implementing robust protective measures is essential to mitigate the risks associated with these types of threats.

DoS and DDoS attack in the context of drones involves a deliberate attempt to overwhelm a drone's capabilities, typically by flooding it with a high volume of requests or data. The goal of a DoS attack is to render the drone incapable of performing its intended functions, effectively denying its service to legitimate users or operators. In more severe cases, **botnet based DDoS** attacks involve compromising multiple IoD nodes (drones) and using them to launch large-scale distributed denial-of-service attacks against central drone controllers or networks. **GPS Spoofing** involves a deliberate attempt to deceive a drone's Global Positioning System (GPS) receiver by transmitting false or manipulated GPS signals. The misdirection of drones, collisions and safety risks, unauthorized control and data integrity are major concerns of GPS spoofing attacks.

In **channel jamming** attacker floods the designated frequency band with high levels of noise or signals, disrupting or preventing the normal exchange of data between the drone and its control station. **Battery Drain attack** involves forcing drones into energy-intensive operations to drain their battery and render them inoperable.

Trust in IoD refers to the confidence and reliance placed in the security, reliability, and integrity of the communication and operations of drone networks. It encompasses the assurance that drones and their associated systems will perform as expected and not pose risks to safety, privacy, or data integrity. However, several attacks specifically target the trust in IoD systems. One such threat arises during the deployment phase, known as the **use of falsified IoD**. This occurs When a fabricated IoD device is maliciously substituted for a legitimate one. This fraudulent IoD can then transmit data to an eavesdropper who has gained unauthorized access to the IoD network.

Key Loggers attacks in drones involve the deployment of malicious software or hardware designed to capture and record keystrokes made on the drone's control systems. In the Internet of Drones (IoD), many applications rely on trusted third parties for communication, such as certification bodies and central management authorities. However, if these trusted entities sell or leak the data they collect from their applications or deployments, it can result in significant financial losses or theft of intellectual property. This breach of trust due to **third parties violations** not only jeopardizes sensitive information but can also have far-reaching consequences for businesses and users alike.

Firmware replacement attack present another vulnerability. When an IoD device is sent for repair or maintenance, it typically undergoes a process where its firmware or software is updated. This is done to implement improvements, fix bugs, and introduce new features. However, if this process is not adequately secured, it can become a potential vulnerability [4].

2.3 Importance of Security in Internet of Drones

The security of the internet of Drones is critical due to the complex and interconnected nature of drone networks, which operate across various communication standards and contexts [2]. Ensuring confidentiality, integrity, authentication, and non-repudiation of transmitted data in IoD networks is essential to prevent unauthorized access, data breaches, and potential exploitation by malicious actors. Without adequate security mechanisms, such as intrusion detection systems, cryptographic algorithms, and authentication techniques, drones can become vulnerable to a range of cyber-attacks, including Sybil, Wormhole, Sinkhole, and Impersonation attacks. These attacks can severely disrupt the functionality of IoD systems, leading to compromised mission-critical operations, such as flight control, obstacle avoidance, and airspace regulation conformance [2].

Additionally, the variation in drone sizes poses significant challenges in maintaining security. Smaller drones, with limited computational capabilities, struggle to incorporate robust security and privacy mechanisms, making them particularly susceptible to attacks. In contrast, larger drones, with greater processing power, are better equipped to implement and maintain advanced security protocols. The importance of securing IoD networks extends beyond just preventing immediate cyber threats; it ensures trust among devices in the network, especially during sensitive missions. Trust validation and assurance among drones are crucial for their safe operation, particularly in environments where the stakes are high, such as military or disaster recovery missions. Therefore, a comprehensive security framework for IoD must be adaptive, resilient, and capable of addressing both known and emerging threats [6].

2.4 Use Case Scenario

Two hypothetical use cases involving trust critical applications of Drones are discussed below:

Scenario 1 A military operation involves deploying multiple drones for autonomous surveillance and reconnaissance over hostile territory. These drones must collaborate in real-time, sharing information about enemy positions, terrain, and potential threats. However, some drones are captured or compromised by the enemy, attempting to transmit false information to mislead the military forces.

Importance of Trust Management In this scenario, trust management is crucial for ensuring that only reliable and authentic drones are allowed to share and propagate information within the network. The system needs to assess the trustworthiness of each drone based on past behavior, origin, and consistency of the information provided. By implementing a robust trust management system, the military can filter out compromised drones and prevent misinformation from affecting critical decisions. This ensures that only trusted drones contribute to the intelligence gathered, maintaining the integrity and effectiveness of the operation.

In a military operation using autonomous surveillance and reconnaissance drones, if an attacker successfully hacks or attacks the drone network, the consequences can be severe and multifaceted. Here's a breakdown of what could go wrong:

1. *Misinformation and False Intelligence* If an attacker hacks into the drone network, they could inject false information into the system. This might include:

- Fake enemy positions: The attacker could make it seem like enemy forces are concentrated in an area where they are not, leading the military to allocate resources inefficiently or miss the real threat.
- Manipulated terrain data: Altering geographical information could cause troops to navigate into dangerous zones, such as ambush points, traps, or hazardous environments.
- Inaccurate threat detection: The attacker could suppress the detection of actual enemy forces or create phantom threats, leading to operational paralysis or faulty decision-making.

2. *Loss of Control and Hijacking* A compromised drone network might lead to loss of control over drones. The attacker could:

   - Take control of individual drones or the entire fleet, rerouting them away from mission objectives or using them against friendly forces.
   - Crash drones into friendly troops or military assets, causing physical damage or exposing vulnerabilities.
   - Use drones for espionage, gathering intelligence on military operations and transmitting sensitive information to the enemy.

3. *Compromised Communication Network* Military drone networks are often integrated into broader command-and-control (C2) systems. A hack could allow attackers to:

   - Disrupt communication between drones and ground forces, causing real-time intelligence to be delayed or manipulated.
   - Intercept sensitive communications, giving the enemy access to critical military data.
   - Break the coordination between drones, causing them to malfunction, collide, or become ineffective in executing their mission.

4. *Friendly Fire or Operational Errors* If the attacker manipulates drone data or drone commands, it could result in operational errors, such as:

   - Targeting friendly units: The altered data could cause drones to mistakenly classify friendly forces as hostile, leading to friendly fire incidents.
   - Inaccurate airstrikes: Misleading information might result in wrong coordinates for airstrikes, potentially hitting civilian areas, allies, or even own troops.

5. *Exposure of Military Positions and Tactics* The attacker could:

   - Reveal the position of friendly forces: Hacked drones might relay the exact locations of military units, supply lines, or command posts to the enemy, putting the entire operation at risk.
   - Understand military tactics and strategies: By observing drone behavior and data exchanges, attackers could gain insight into military tactics, leading to more effective counter-strategies by the enemy.

6. *Physical Damage to Military Assets* The attacker might sabotage drones to:

- Self-destruct in proximity to critical military assets, causing damage to military equipment, infrastructure, or personnel.
- Deploy payloads or create diversions, causing confusion, panic, or unnecessary resource allocation.

7. *Security Breach of Broader Military Infrastructure* Since military drones often form part of a broader network of interconnected systems, a breach in the drone network could serve as a gateway for attackers to infiltrate other sensitive military systems, such as satellite communications or intelligence networks. This would widen the scope of damage far beyond the drone fleet itself.
8. *Consequences for Human Life and National Security*

    - Loss of Personnel: Manipulated or hijacked drones could directly harm soldiers on the battlefield through misdirected attacks, or indirectly by misinforming troop movements into ambushes or enemy territory.
    - Civilian Casualties: Inaccurate drone strikes or reconnaissance might lead to collateral damage, with devastating effects on civilian populations.
    - Compromised National Security: If critical military information is exposed or the operation fails, it can have strategic consequences, such as emboldening enemy forces, undermining public trust in the military, and weakening national security.

Scenario 2 During a large public event, such as a protest or a sporting event, a fleet of drones is deployed for crowd control and surveillance. These drones monitor the crowd, detect potential threats, and provide real-time data to law enforcement agencies to ensure public safety. The drones operate in a coordinated manner, sharing information on crowd movement, identifying suspicious behavior, and providing live video feeds to control centers.

Potential Attack An attacker, aiming to disrupt the event or cause chaos, targets the drone network. They could attempt to hack into one or more drones to gain control, inject false information, or even disable the drones entirely. Alternatively, the attacker might use jamming technology or physical means to destroy or incapacitate multiple drones in the network.

Impact on the Internet of Drones
Compromised Data Integrity: If an attacker successfully hacks into a drone, they could manipulate the data being sent back to the control center. This could result in false reports of threats or alter the perception of crowd behavior, leading to inappropriate or delayed responses by law enforcement.

- For example, directing resources away from a real threat to a fabricated one could result in unprotected areas, increasing the risk of harm.
- Network Disruption: By hacking or destroying one or more drones, the attacker could create a ripple effect throughout the entire drone network.

Loss of Control If the attacker gains control of even a single drone, they could potentially command it to perform unauthorized actions, such as flying into restricted areas, dropping hazardous materials, or crashing into the crowd. Such actions could cause panic, leading to injuries or property damage, and escalate the situation from a controlled environment to a chaotic one.

3 Trust Management

Trust refers to the level of confidence or reliability associated with an individual, be it a human or an intelligent machine. It is typically determined by assessing feedback ratings and aggregating them to establish a measure of trustworthiness. According to Mui et al. [7], "Trust is a subjective expectation an agent has about another's future behavior based on the history of their encounters." Another definition from Grandison and Sloman [8] refers to the "competence" to act, "Trust is the firm belief in the competence of an entity to act dependably, securely, and reliably within a specified context." In computer science, trust is often established through feedback based on prior interactions, as highlighted by Mui et al. [7]. Trust can be categorized into two types: direct and indirect. Direct trust refers to the confidence a user develops from their own interactions with a system, while indirect trust, also known as recommendation trust, is based on feedback or experiences shared by other users (see Fig. 4).

Trust management encompasses the processes involved in defining and handling trust within a computing system. This includes identifying the factors that contribute to trust, developing mechanisms for computing, propagating, and aggregating trust, as well as storing trust-related data. Additionally, trust management covers the ways trust is utilized in service provisioning. Blaze et al. [9], introduced "Trust Management" as a framework that addresses various security components within network systems. It begins with establishing trust, updating trust values based on ongoing interactions, and revoking trust when it falls below an acceptable threshold.

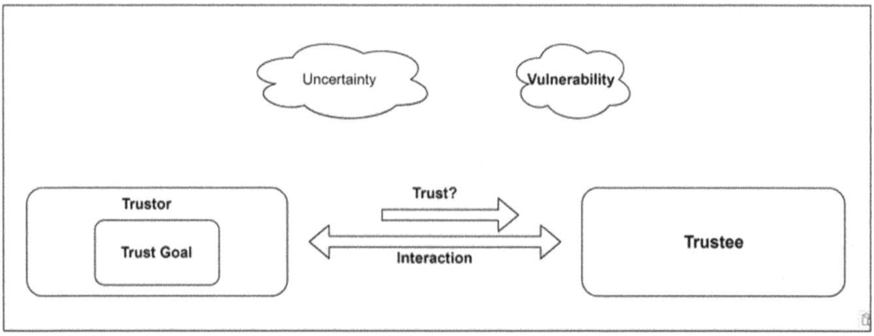

Fig. 4 Trust definition

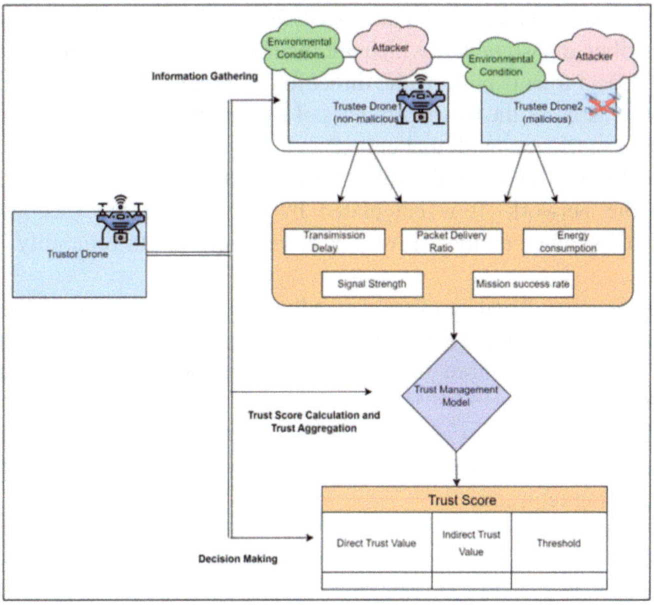

Fig. 5 A Trust Management model depicting interaction between trustor and trustee drones

Managing trust in ad-hoc networks, such as those with mobile nodes, presents greater challenges compared to traditional centralized systems (see Fig. 5).

The Internet of Drones (IoD) is an example of a Mobile Ad Hoc Network (MANET), where Unmanned Aerial Vehicles (UAVs) operate collaboratively without relying on fixed infrastructure. IoDs dynamic nature can lead to nodes exhibiting malicious behavior or unintentional misbehavior. Thus, securing IoDs with limited resources is crucial. Trust management, known for fortifying ad-hoc networks, emerges as a viable approach.

3.1 Characteristics of Trust

Trust can be evaluated in numerous ways by considering the following characteristics [10]:

(1) Subjective: This type of trust is shaped by personal perception, often from a social standpoint. It involves evaluating trust based on an individual's direct experiences (known as direct trust) and also the opinions or feedback from others (referred to as indirect trust).

(2) Objective: Unlike subjective trust, objective trust is more impartial, drawing from feedback provided by all the participants in a network. This collective

trust information is transparent and accessible to everyone through mechanisms like distributed hash tables, which are maintained by trusted entities.

(3) *Local:* Local trust is built on the direct interaction between two entities, where one entity assesses the trustworthiness of another based on its own observations and past experiences with that entity.

(4) *Global:* On the other hand, global trust reflects an entity's overall reputation within the network. It is calculated by aggregating the trust assessments provided by other entities, giving a broad view of its reliability across the network.

(5) *Context-Specific:* Trust can vary depending on the situation or context. Factors such as time, location, or the energy status of the entities involved can influence how much trust is placed in one entity by another, making trust a dynamic relationship.

(6) *Asymmetric:* Trust is not always reciprocal. If one entity trusts another, it does not automatically mean the feeling is mutual—trust can exist in one direction without being returned.

3.2 *Trust Management Components*

The essential components that are to be considered for trust management process are:

Trust Composition Trust metrics refer to the specific characteristics used to evaluate and establish trust. These metrics can be based on two main aspects: social trust metrics and quality of service (QoS) trust metrics.

Social Metrics Social trust metrics focus on the behavior of nodes in a network, particularly in terms of their relationships with other IoT device owners. These metrics assess factors like integrity, benevolence, honesty, friendships, shared interests, and selflessness [11–13].

QoS Metrics Quality of Service metrics assess a node's ability to deliver reliable and efficient performance. This includes factors such as reliability, competence, data delivery rate, throughput, and the ability to complete assigned tasks [14–16].

Trust Formation Trust formation can be established in two ways: it can either be based on a single factor, such as positive or negative QoS performance, or it can involve multiple factors. In the latter case, trust models incorporate both QoS metrics and social trust metrics to provide a more comprehensive assessment.

Based on Property

- Single Trust: Single trust refers to the use of just one trust metric, such as a quality of service (QoS) measure, to determine the overall trust level of an entity [17–19].

- Multi Trust: Multi trust treats trust as a multidimensional concept, where various factors, like both social and QoS metrics, are combined to create a comprehensive trust score [11–13].

Based on Observation

- Direct Observation: In direct observation, a node (the trustor) assesses the behavior of another node through firsthand interaction with it.
- Indirect Observation: Indirect observation occurs when the trustor evaluates a node's behavior by observing its interactions with other nodes in the network, rather than through direct engagement.
- Recommendation: In the recommendation approach, the trustor gathers trust-related information about a node from other nodes in the network, relying on their experiences to form its trust judgment.

Trust Computation Trust computation involves determining the overall trustworthiness of a network node. This is accomplished through the application of two methods: trust prediction and trust aggregation, both of which are utilized to assess the trust value of a node within an ad-hoc network. Some of the common parameters used for trust computation are depicted in Fig. 6.

- Trust Prediction: Trust prediction is a method that anticipates the level of trust between nodes by examining their past and present behaviors within the network. This technique also incorporates recommendations from fellow nodes to forecast trustworthiness.

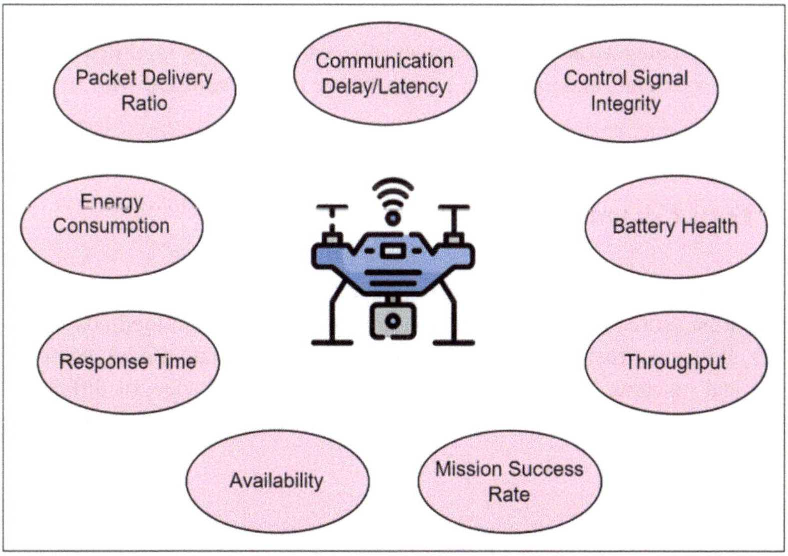

Fig. 6 Common parameters used for trust computation in IoD

- Trust Aggregation: Trust aggregation techniques are employed to compute the trustworthiness of a network node when trust is disseminated through multiple routes. This method involves combining these various values to arrive at a singular trust score for a node within the network.

Trust Propagation Trust propagation is a method by which the trust levels of nodes in a network are disseminated. This approach serves to avoid the repetitive recalculation of trust for a node, thereby conserving resources. Within this framework, there exist two schemes for propagating node trust in the network: distributed and centralized.

- Distributed Trust: In the distributed scheme, a node's trustworthiness can be conveyed either through trust chaining or recommendation. Trust chaining involves the sequential passing of trust from one trusted node to another. In the recommendation approach, a node's trust value is relayed by another node that possesses information about the recommended node, either directly or indirectly.
- Centralized Trust: In the centralized trust propagation scheme, a designated node in the network assumes the role of a central authority responsible for managing trust propagation for every node in the network.

Trust Updation Trust Updation involves determining when and how the trustworthiness of a network node is adjusted. This can be achieved through two schemes: time-based and event-based.

- Time Based: Trust is updated either periodically, at specified intervals, or continuously, without fixed time intervals, based on observations or properties.
- Event Based: Trust is updated in response to specific occurrences. This can be further categorized into certain events, where trust is modified only upon predefined events, and uncertain events, where trust is adjusted with any event.

3.3 Trust Computation

Trust Aggregation consists of techniques that aggregate trust observation to obtain a single trust score. Trust and reputation are evaluated through methods like fuzzy models, Bayesian trust models, weighted sum, Markov Chain model, game theory models and machine learning etc. Table 1 provides an overview of different trust computation techniques and details their underlying principles and notable features.

Table 1 Trust computation methods

Methods	Key characteristics	Key principle
Fuzzy Logic models	Trust values range between 0 and 1, representing degrees of trust. Unlike Boolean logic, fuzzy logic deals with partial truths and approximations	Fuzzy controllers convert real inputs into fuzzy sets, while fuzzy logic rules use operators like union and intersection to combine values. Membership functions transform inputs into outputs, and defuzzification converts fuzzy outputs back to real-world value back to real-world values
Bayesian Trust model	Leverages probability theory to compute trust based on a node's behavior over time	Bayes' Theorem updates trust based on past (prior) and present (posterior) behavior: $p(A\|B) = \frac{p(B\|A) \cdot p(A)}{p(B)}$ Here $p(A\|B)$ is the posterior probability of A given B is true, $p(B\|A)$ is the likelihood of B given A is true, p(B) is the probability of A happening, and p(A) is the prior probability of A
Weighted sum model	Aggregating multiple trust metrics into a single trust score. Each metric is assigned a weight, and the weighted sum provides an overall trust value	1. Simple to implement and interpret. 2. Weights can either be static or dynamic, allowing flexibility in different contexts. M = m1, m2, m3, m4.....,mn represents the n trust metrics and W = w1, w2, w3 ....wn the weights of each n trust metrics, the weighted sum aggregation (WSA) is computed as: $\text{WSA} = \sum_{i=1}^{n} W_i \cdot M_i$
Markov chain model	A stochastic method that calculates trust based on a node's current state without considering previous history beyond the current state	1. A node's future behavior depends only on its present state. 2. Transitions between states are based on probabilistic rules, making the model suitable for short-term trust predictions
Game theory Model	Mathematical models that analyse the decisions of two parties who can either collaborate or compete. Effective in identifying selfish behavior in network nodes and devising optimal strategies, often using Nash equilibrium, to maximize gains	1. Models interactions as strategic games where outcomes depend on the decisions of both parties. 2. Nash equilibrium is often used to determine the optimal strategy, where no node has an incentive to change its behavior unilaterally
Machine Learning model	Machine learning techniques provide a sophisticated approach to trust computation, especially when dealing with large, complex datasets	1. Unsupervised Learning (Clustering): Groups interactions or nodes without prior labels. 2. Supervised Learning (Classification): Classifies interactions as trustworthy or untrustworthy based on labelled training data

4 Recent Advancements in Trust Management in Internet of Drones

Recent advancements in drone technology include the integration of AI and machine learning for enhanced navigation, automated inspections, and efficiency. Increased autonomy enables tasks like automated take-off, landing, and swarm technology for coordinated operations. Drones now feature high-quality sensors and cameras, including thermal imaging and multispectral sensors, while improvements in battery life support longer flight times. Additionally, AI-powered image analysis and cloud integration streamline data processing and transfer, and eco-friendly drones are being developed using electric power and solar energy.

Let us now discuss few of the latest works on trust management in Internet of Drones (IoD). The work [20] introduces the "TMIoDT" (Trust Management in IoDT) framework, which integrates Digital Twin technology with blockchain to enhance communication security in the Internet of Drone Things (IoDT) within Open Radio Access Networks (Open RAN). The novelty of this framework lies in the seamless integration of Digital Twin technology with blockchain. Digital Twins provide real-time virtual models of physical entities while blockchain ensures transparent and secure trust management. The framework employs an advanced Intrusion Detection System (IDS) using Stacked Variational Autoencoder (SVA) and Attention-based Bidirectional LSTM (ABL) for detecting anomalies. This deep learning-based IDS strengthens the security of IoDT by accurately identifying multi-vector cyber-attacks.

The work [21] introduces GALTrust, a novel Generative Adversarial Learning-based trust management framework for Internet of Drone Things (IoDT) in spatial crowdsourcing. The framework combines Generative Adversarial Networks (GANs) with Type-2 Fuzzy Logic to handle trust management challenges and distinguish between trustworthy and malicious drones. The framework uses a GAN-based codec structure, trained with trust vectors to accurately classify drones as malicious or trustworthy. A key innovation is the GAN-based trust redemption model, which reduces false positives. It rehabilitates benign drones that might have been mistakenly labelled as malicious, thereby maintaining overall network integrity.

The work [22] introduces FUBA (Fuzzy-based UAV Behavior Analytics), a trust management system for Flying Ad-Hoc Networks (FANETs). It uses fuzzy logic to analyse the behavior of unmanned aerial vehicles (UAVs) to detect malicious nodes while considering environmental conditions like humidity and signal strength. FUBA uses several critical parameters for trust evaluation, including Received Signal Strength Indicator (RSSI), battery level (energy), Packet Delivery Ratio (PDR), Transmission Delay (TD), and weather conditions (humidity). These factors are integrated into the fuzzy logic system to assess drone behavior under dynamic conditions. The most innovative aspect of this work is the consideration of weather conditions, specifically humidity, as a parameter for trust management in FANETs.

The impact of these conditions on RSSI and overall drone behavior is addressed, making FUBA adaptable to real-world outdoor environments.

The work [23] "DDRM: Distributed Drone Reputation Management for Trust and Reliability in Crowdsourced Drone Services" uses Ethereum smart contract capabilities to ensure transparency and security. The use of a dual-token system strengthens the verification of drone service reviews, improving reliability and mitigating fraud. Service Review Authorization Token (SRAT) token is required for posting reviews, ensuring only legitimate users provide feedback. Drone Reputation Enhancement Token (DRET) rewards drones that consistently perform well, incentivizing reliability and quality of service. DDRM has mechanisms to counteract reputation frauds like ballot-stuffing and bad-mouthing, enhancing the authenticity of drone reviews. DDRM leverages Ethereum's create a transparent and immutable review system, addressing the major challenge of verifying the authenticity of drone service reviews.

The work [24] titled "A Hierarchical Blockchain-Based Trust Measurement Method for Drone Cluster Nodes" introduces a novel approach to trust evaluation in drone clusters, addressing several key issues in dynamic environments where drones enter and exit the network frequently. The paper proposes a method for accurate trust evaluation of drone nodes in highly dynamic UAV (Unmanned Aerial Vehicle) clusters. One of the key innovations of this works the layered blockchain architecture, which ensures that trust evaluation is both secure and efficient, despite the limited resources available in drone networks. The proposed method introduces an information entropy-based optimization for calculating trust, making it adaptive to the evolving behavior of nodes. It also incorporates a dynamic trust decay factor, which ensures that trust values remain current and relevant by accounting for the timeliness of past interactions. The integration of Practical Byzantine Fault Tolerance (PBFT) and Proof of Work (PoW) consensus mechanisms across different blockchain layers allows for better security and efficiency in trust management.

The paper titled "Bio-Inspired Dynamic Trust and Congestion-Aware Zone-Based Secured Internet of Drone Things (SIoDT)" [25] focuses on integrating the Internet of Drone Things (IoDT) into the Internet of Vehicles (IoV) to mitigate traditional IoV challenges, including congestion, security issues, and energy consumption. One of the major innovations is the development of a triple-layer dynamic trust estimation model, which improves security at three levels of communication: vehicle-to-cluster head (CH), CH-to-drone, and drone-to-base station (BS). This trust system is designed to protect against various attacks, including flooding, insider, wormhole, and position falsification attacks. The research employs a hybrid optimization technique combining Ant Colony Optimization (ACO) and Grey Wolf Optimization (GWO) to enhance the routing process which is a significant novelty.

5 Trust Management Obstacles in IoD: Challenges and Solutions

Decentralization of Trust Management IoD systems often face challenges in decentralized environments where trust management between drones can be complex, especially when the network grows.

Data Security and Privacy Concerns Trust management systems must secure data from unauthorized access and tampering, especially in sensitive operations like emergency services.

Connectivity and Network Reliability Ensuring trust when the network experiences disruptions or connectivity losses is crucial, especially for real-time applications.

Authentication and Misbehavior Detection Ensuring that drones behave as expected and have the right authentication processes in place.

Scalability of Trust Models The challenge of developing trust models that scale efficiently as the number of drones in the network grows.

Handling Malicious Drones Detecting and mitigating the impact of compromised or malicious drones in the network.

Integration with Existing IoT Infrastructure Ensuring that trust models for IoD integrate well with existing IoT security and trust management frameworks.

Adversarial Attacks on Trust Models Trust models are vulnerable to adversarial attacks, where drones may attempt to manipulate trust values for malicious purposes.

Regulatory and Compliance Issues Meeting regulatory standards and ensuring compliance with local and international drone operation laws while maintaining trust across diverse jurisdictions.

5.1 Attacks on Trust Management in IoD: Network Vulnerabilities and Their Impact

The following section outlines key trust management attacks that pose significant risks to IoD networks, illustrating how attackers can undermine trust to deceive or disrupt services (see Fig. 7).

Good-mouthing Attack/Self-Promoting Attack To Increase the likelihood of being selected as a service provider, a malicious node promotes itself by falsely enhancing its own reputation within the network. This makes it appear as a

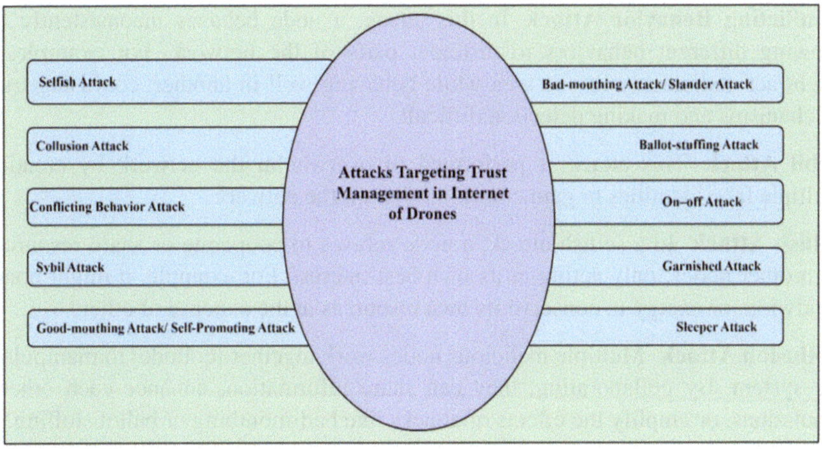

Fig. 7 Attacks on trust management models

trustworthy and efficient service provider. The attack exploits trust mechanisms, which rely on reputation scores to determine reliability.

Bad-mouthing Attack/Slander Attack To decrease the likelihood of well-behaved nodes being chosen as service providers, malicious nodes seek to damage the reputation of well-behaved or honest nodes by spreading false negative feedback. As a result, the well-behaved nodes are sidelined, while attackers or compromised nodes may gain prominence.

Ballot-Stuffing Attack To increase the selection chances, conspire to artificially boost the reputations of other malicious nodes. By inflating their trust scores, these compromised nodes increase their chances of being selected as service providers, allowing them to exploit or disrupt services once chosen.

On–Off Attack The Objective here is to exploit trust-redeeming mechanisms by alternating between honest and malicious behavior. A malicious drone alternates between good and bad behavior in this attack. During the "on" phase, the node behaves well and gains reputation, but during the "off" phase, it behaves maliciously, often just before another attack occurs. This cyclical behavior allows the malicious drone to continuously re-establish trust, making it harder to detect and mitigate.

Garnished Attack A garnished attack occurs when malicious nodes manipulate or tamper with data or transactions to subtly alter outcomes while avoiding detection. This is typically a low-key manipulation of data for malicious gains.

Sleeper Attack The objective here is to launch an attack after gaining trust by being inactive or behaving benignly for an extended period.

Conflicting Behavior Attack In this attack, a node behaves inconsistently by showing different behaviors to different parts of the network. For example, it might act maliciously in one area while behaving well in another, confusing trust mechanisms and making detection difficult.

Sybil Attack This attack is performed to overwhelm the network by creating multiple fake identities to gain control or disrupt the network.

Selfish Attack In a selfish attack, a node refuses to cooperate or share resources with other nodes, only acting in its own best interest. For example, it might hoard bandwidth or energy to conserve its own resources at the expense of others.

Collusion Attack Multiple malicious nodes work together (collude) to manipulate the system. By collaborating, they can share information, enhance each other's reputations, or amplify the effects of attacks like bad-mouthing or ballot stuffing.

5.2 Mitigation Strategies

In the Internet of Drones (IoD) network, several strategies can be applied to mitigate trust-related attacks between drones. *Reputation aging* helps by gradually reducing a drone's trust score over time, ensuring malicious drones can't rely on brief periods of good behavior, as seen in on-off attacks. Similarly, *weighted feedback* ensures that feedback from more reliable drones carries more weight, reducing the effectiveness of self-promoting and ballot-stuffing attacks. New drones entering the network should follow a trust bootstrap mechanism, starting with limited trust to prevent malicious drones from resetting their reputation after misbehavior. *Context-aware trust evaluation* assesses a drone's trustworthiness based on specific missions or tasks, preventing drones from acting maliciously in one context while behaving well in others. Additionally, *feedback credibility validation* ensures that positive or negative feedback is tied directly to actual mission outcomes, protecting against false reports like bad-mouthing attacks.

Other defenses in the IoD include *collaborative trust management*, where multiple drones assess each other's trust collectively, making it harder for Sybil and colluding drones to manipulate the network. *Anomaly detection methods* can identify suspicious behavior, such as drones switching between good and bad performance (as in on-off or conflicting behavior attacks). *Threshold-based trust mechanisms* ensure drones can't quickly build or lose reputation without consistent behavior across missions. Penalizing drones for inconsistent or suspicious behavior through monitoring can prevent erratic activity. Finally, *identity verification* methods, such as using unique physical attributes or cryptographic proofs, help mitigate Sybil attacks by ensuring each drone in the network is legitimate and not part of a malicious multi-identity scheme. These strategies strengthen the trust system within drone networks, protecting against various forms of attack.

6 Conclusion

In conclusion, this chapter provides a comprehensive exploration of trust management within the Internet of Drones (IoD), emphasizing its critical role in ensuring secure and reliable aerial operations. Integrating advanced technologies such as Digital Twin, Blockchain, Federated Learning, Quantum cryptography, Bio inspired dynamic trust calculation and 5G will revolutionize trust management and security in IoD, creating a robust, scalable, and adaptive system capable of meeting the evolving demands of drone networks. The convergence of these technologies will not only improve security and resilience but also foster innovation in drone operations, paving the way for the seamless integration of drones into modern intelligent infrastructures. Furthermore, the discussion of potential threats and mitigation strategies underscores the importance of strengthening trust systems to safeguard IoD networks from malicious attacks. The chapter reaffirms the significance of ongoing research efforts in enhancing the security and resilience of trust management, highlighting its vital contribution to the future development of trustworthy drone ecosystems and secure drone operations.

Acknowledgments We extend our gratitude to the C3i Hub, the Technology Innovation Hub for Cyber Security of CyberPhysical Systems, and the Department of Science and Technology (DST), under the Government of India, for providing the financial resources and infrastructure that made this work possible.

References

1. Choudhary, G., Sharma, V., Gupta, T., Kim, J., You, I.: Internet of Drones (IOD): Threats, vulnerability, and security perspectives. arXiv.org (2018, August 1). https://arxiv.org/abs/1808.00203
2. Choudhary, G., Sharma, V., Gupta, T., Kim, J., You, I.: Internet of Drones (IOD): Threats, vulnerability, and security perspectives. arXiv (Cornell University) (2018)
3. Agrawal, D.P., Wang, H.: Computer and Cyber Security. Auerbach Publications eBooks (2018). https://doi.org/10.1201/9780429424878. Integration. Technical report, Global Grid Forum (2002)
4. Heidari, A., Navimipour, N.J., Unal, M., Zhang, G.: Machine learning applications in Internet-of-Drones: Systematic review, recent deployments, and open Issues. ACM Comput. Surv. **55**(12), 1–45 (2022). https://doi.org/10.1145/3571728
5. Rawat, S.S., Alotaibi, Y., Malsa, N., Gupta, V.: Enhancement of UAV data security and privacy via Ethereum blockchain technology. Comput. Mater. Continua/Comput. Mater. Continua (Print) **76**(2), 1797–1815 (2023). https://doi.org/10.32604/cmc.2023.039381
6. Akram, R.N., et al.: Security, privacy and safety evaluation of dynamic and static fleets of drones. In: 2017 IEEE/AIAA 36th Digital Avionics Systems Conference (DASC), St. Petersburg, FL, USA, 2017, pp. 1–12. https://doi.org/10.1109/DASC.2017.8101984
7. Mui, L., Mohtashemi, M., Halberstadt, A.: A computational model of trust and reputation. In: Proceedings of the 35th Annual Hawaii International Conference on System Sciences, Big Island, HI, USA, pp. 2431–2439 (2002). https://doi.org/10.1109/HICSS.2002.994181
8. Grandison, T., Sloman, M.: A survey of trust in internet applications. IEEE Commun. Surv. Tutorials **3**(4), 2–16, Fourth Quarter (2000). https://doi.org/10.1109/COMST.2000.5340804

9. Blaze, M., Feigenbaum, J., Lacy, J.: Decentralized trust management. In: Proceedings 1996 IEEE Symposium on Security and Privacy, Oakland, CA, USA, 1996, pp. 164–173 (1996). https://doi.org/10.1109/SECPRI.1996.502679
10. Ghafari, S.M., Beheshti, A., Joshi, A., Paris, C., Mahmood, A., Yakhchi, S., Orgun, M.A.: A survey on trust prediction in online social networks. IEEE Access **8**, 144 292–144 309 (2020)
11. Xia, H., Xiao, F., Zhang, S., Hu, C., Cheng, X.: Trustworthiness inference framework in the social Internet of Things: A ContextAware approach. In: Proceeding of IEEE Conference on Computer Communications (INFOCOM), pp. 838–846 (2019)
12. Chen, I., Bao, F., Guo, J.: Trust-based service management for social Internet of Things systems. IEEE Trans. Depend. Sec. Comput. **13**(6), 684–696 (2016)
13. Nitti, M., Girau, R., Atzori, L., Member, S.: Trustworthiness management in the social Internet of Things. IEEE Trans. Knowl. Data Eng. **26**(5), 1253–1266 (2014)
14. Xiao, H., Sidhu, N., Christianson, B.: Guarantor and reputation based trust model for Social Internet of Things. In: 2015 International Wireless Communications and Mobile Computing Conference (IWCMC), Dubrovnik, Croatia, pp. 600–605 (2015). https://doi.org/10.1109/IWCMC.2015.7289151
15. Sun, X., Ansari, N.: Dynamic resource caching in the IoT application layer for smart cities. IEEE Internet Things J. **5**(2), 606–613 (2018)
16. Li, X., Zhu, G., Gong, Y., Huang, K.: Wirelessly powered data aggregation for IoT via over-the-air function computation: beamforming and power control. IEEE Trans. Wirel. Commun. **18**(7), 3437–3452 (2019)
17. Saied, Y.B., Olivereau, A., Zeghlache, D., Laurent, M.: Trust management system design for the Internet of Things: A context-aware and multi-service approach. Comput. Secur. **39**, 351–365 (2013). https://doi.org/10.1016/j.cose.2013.09.001
18. Mendoza, C.V.L., Kleinschmidt, J.H.: Mitigating on-off attacks in the Internet of Things using a distributed trust management scheme. Int. J. Distrib. Sensor Netw. **11**(11), 1–8 (2015)
19. Chen, R., Guo, J., Bao, F.: Trust management for SOA-Based IoT and its application to service composition. IEEE Trans. Serv. Comput. **9**(3), 482–495 (2016). https://doi.org/10.1109/TSC.2014.2365797
20. Akram, J., Anaissi, A., Rathore, R.S., Jhaveri, R.H., Akram, A.: Digital twin-driven trust management in open RAN-based spatial crowdsourcing drone services. IEEE Trans. Green Commun. Netw. **8**(3), 1061–1075 (2024). https://doi.org/10.1109/TGCN.2024.3403901
21. Akram, J., Anaissi, A., Rathore, R.S., Jhaveri, R.H., Akram, A.: GALTrust: Generative adverserial learning-based framework for trust management in spatial crowdsourcing drone services. IEEE Trans. Consumer Electron. (2024). https://doi.org/10.1109/TCE.2024.3384978
22. Benfriha, S., Labraoui, N., Bensaid, R., Salameh, H.B., Saidi, H.: FUBA: A fuzzy-based unmanned aerial vehicle behaviour analytics for trust management in flying ad-hoc networks. IET Netw. **13**(3), 208–220 (2023). https://doi.org/10.1049/ntw2.12108
23. Akram, J., Anaissi, A.: DDRM: Distributed drone reputation management for trust and reliability in crowdsourced drone services. Preprint. arXiv:2407.00591 (2024)
24. Zuo, J., Cao, R., Qi, J., Gao, P., Wang, Z., Li, J., Zhang, L., Lu, Y.: A hierarchical Blockchain-Based trust measurement method for drone cluster nodes. Drones **7**(10), 627 (2023). https://doi.org/10.3390/drones7100627
25. Jghef, Y.S., Jasim, M.J.M., Ghanimi, H.M.A., Algarni, A.D., Soliman, N.F., El-Shafai, W., Zeebaree, S.R.M., Alkhayyat, A., Abosinnee, A.S., Abdulsattar, N.F., Abbas, A.H., Hariz, H.M., Abbas, F.H.: Bio-inspired dynamic trust and congestion-aware zone-based secured Internet of Drone things (SIODT). Drones **6**(11), 337 (2022). https://doi.org/10.3390/drones6110337

Smart Surveillance in Physical Security Systems and Ethical Frameworks in IoD

M. V. Neha and Sabu M. Thampi

1 Introduction

Surveillance and monitoring behaviors and activities have been integral to human society for thousands of years. From the formation of early human civilizations up to this modern day of digital times, methods and tools for Surveillance have continually changed and have been shaped by technology and social needs.

Historically, the practice of Surveillance was significantly done manually and rudimentarily. For example, the Roman, Greek, and Egyptian Civilizations relied on human observation to monitor activities and detect potential threats. Watchtowers, sentinels, and patrols were common, where the functions comprised the eyes and ears of the kingdoms and empires [55]. These rudimentary methods set the foundation for more organized and systematic types of Surveillance.

The conceptualization of security tied to Surveillance can be traced back to medieval Europe. Watchtowers and sentry posts were a feature of castles and fortified towns, while guards would remain ever watchful for invaders. It was also a time that saw secret police and networks of paid informants used as a means whereby rulers exerted their control and suppressed dissent [26].

For this purpose, the nineteenth century, with its Industrial Revolution, turned out to be a critical point in the history of Surveillance. In the wake of rapid development, factories, and urban centers were unable without new monitoring forms, allowing workers' productivity and maintaining discipline. Factory managers employed overseers who kept workers at labor and optimized the efficiency of this labor [21]. The middle of the nineteenth century invented photography, which became a great surveillance tool. Photography began to be employed by the police

M. V. Neha (✉) · S. M. Thampi
Connected Systems and Intelligence Lab, School of Computer Science & Engineering, Digital University Kerala, Trivandrum, India
e-mail: neha.csres22@duk.ac.in,; sabu.thampi@duk.ac.in,https://duk.ac.in

S. M. Thampi et al. (eds.), *Securing the Connected World*,
https://doi.org/10.1007/978-3-031-82826-3_13

for criminal records, thus making the identity and follow-up of particular individuals possible as never before.

It was not until the mid-twentieth century that wartime and the Cold War spawned electronic Surveillance. Wiretapping was also one of the joint operations to spy on and gather information from adversaries. In this context, radio and television development expanded this reach more and allowed monitoring broadcasts and communications [29]. CCTVs were invented in 1942. While initially, CCTVs had military and industrial applications, and they spread rapidly to commercial and public premises too [36].

The seismic shift in surveillance technologies came with the digital revolution of the 1980s and 1990s. Computers and the Internet completely changed how information was collected, stored, and analyzed. Analog CCTV systems gave way to high-resolution digital cameras and more accessible storage options [51]. It was also during this era that databases and digital record-keeping emerged, increasing the efficiency and effectiveness of Surveillance considerably. In this way, the growth of the Internet opened up new dimensions of Surveillance whereby both governments and private agencies started to monitor persons' activities, which were initiated online: the log-ins into email accounts, and even web browsing histories [6].

The early twenty-first century was characterized by the proliferation of mass surveillance programs, particularly in response to security threats worldwide. In response to the terrorist attacks of September 11, 2001, for instance, there were far-reaching surveillance programs such as the USA PATRIOT Act. Next came the proliferation of smartphones and social media, enabling Surveillance through constant location tracking, communication, and social interaction [14].

Nowadays, using developed technologies, Surveillance has reached a whole new level. Artificial Intelligence makes it truly intelligent, with machine learning at its core for advanced analytics. Big Data analytics changed the game by comprehensively processing and making sense of vast chunks of information. Surveillance systems can detect data patterns and real-time anomalies for proactive reactions against potential threats [43]. Drones and robotic systems for monitoring are increasingly used in various contexts, ranging from military operations to monitoring public events and traffic management [39]. Biometric technologies, such as fingerprint, iris, and voice recognition, increased the level of identification and authentication processes and allowed for more complete and reliable surveillance [50].

As surveillance technologies continue to evolve, ubiquitous surveillance is becoming a reality. Figure 1 shows the importance of surveillance in diverse sectors. Intelligent cities, equipped with interconnected sensors and surveillance systems, aim to enhance security and efficiency [14]. However, expanding surveillance also brings challenges related to privacy and ethical use. Balancing security needs with individual privacy rights remains critical, requiring careful consideration and regulation. Intelligent surveillance has revolutionized the way we ensure security and monitor environments. This chapter delves into the evolution, significance, and technological advancements shaping modern surveillance systems.

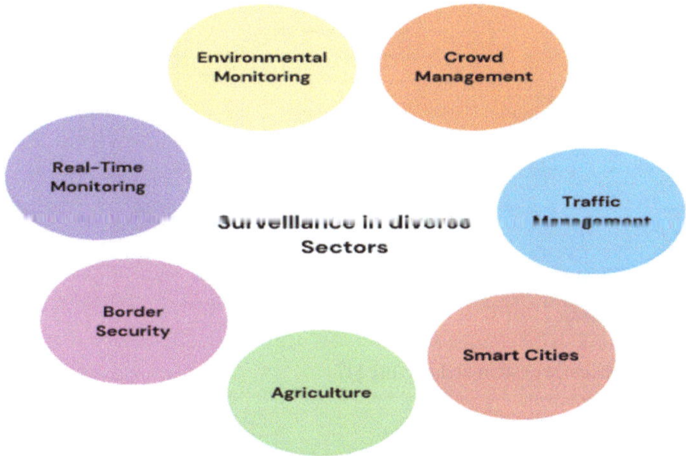

Fig. 1 Surveillance in diverse sectors

1.1 Evolution and Importance in Security Systems

Over the past twenty years, there has been significant growth in audio-video information across various settings. The increase in population and the rise in terrorist attacks at the start of the twenty-first century, along with the surge in criminal activities, have led to the widespread deployment of surveillance cameras in cities [40]. As a result, there has been a notable interest in scientific and artificial vision research. Today, video surveillance systems cover entire cities, utilizing millions of cameras. Various surveillance techniques are now used to enhance security and manage society [10, 49]. The advent of the internet has facilitated the collection, recording, and analysis of vast amounts of data, raising concerns about the privacy of individuals under surveillance.

The importance of video surveillance for security systems can not be exaggerated. Video surveillance deters criminal activities, evidence gathering, and public safety. Intelligent surveillance today offers all benefits regarding real-time monitoring, better image quality, and automatic threat detection; it is irreplaceable in the modern concept of security. These days, intelligent surveillance systems are essential in many respects in different fields of urban areas, businesses, and critical infrastructure. Among many of these attack methods, they implement advanced technologies such as AI, machine learning, and deep learning to make them more effective. The algorithms of AI and machine learning permit systems to identify patterns and detect anomalies, greatly enhancing the speed and precision of threat detection [4].

Recently, the demand for video surveillance security has increased, driven by technological advancements that improve the architecture and analysis of these systems. Figure 2 illustrates the components of a video surveillance architecture,

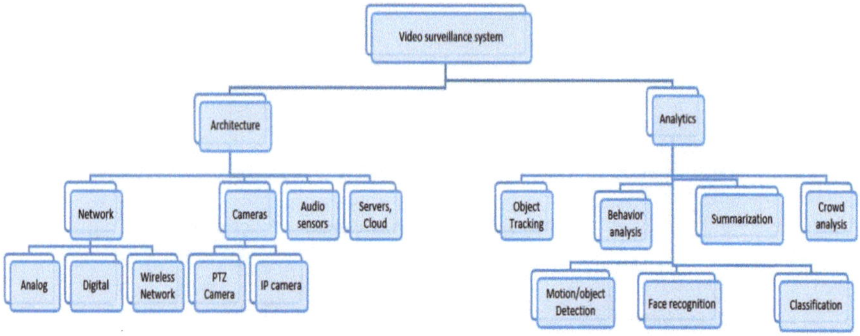

Fig. 2 Video surveillance system architecture [12]

including sensors, servers, and network types. The analysis component comprises processing algorithms essential for effective surveillance. In this context, the devices within the architecture function as the system's eyes, while the analytics serve as its brain.

Modern systems are hallmarked by real-time monitoring of video surveillance. These systems continually capture data and analyze information to allow immediate responses to security threats. For example, intelligent surveillance systems will automatically alert security personnel whenever unusual activities are occurring. This way, dependence upon human monitoring will decrease, while the response times will be minimized [36].

Integration of high-definition cameras with image-processing technologies significantly enhances captured surveillance footage. Enhanced clarity of captured images reinforces identifying and tracking people and objects, which will be helpful for preventive and investigative reasons [27]. Also, automated threat detection systems utilize such clear images to detect potential threats without human interference with significant accuracy, further upgrading the security measures [5].

Advancing technology in surveillance has grown these systems into an essential component in modern security infrastructure. By nature, surveillance systems enable real-time monitoring, improved image quality, and automated threat detection-thereby aiding in deterring criminal activities and gathering crucial evidence to ensure safety.

1.2 Role of Technological Advancements

Various researchers have contributed to developing automatic video surveillance systems over the last couple of decades. They took up most of the burning problems related to architecture and functionality. Works have been done on video surveillance tasks such as object recognition, object classification, and detection and

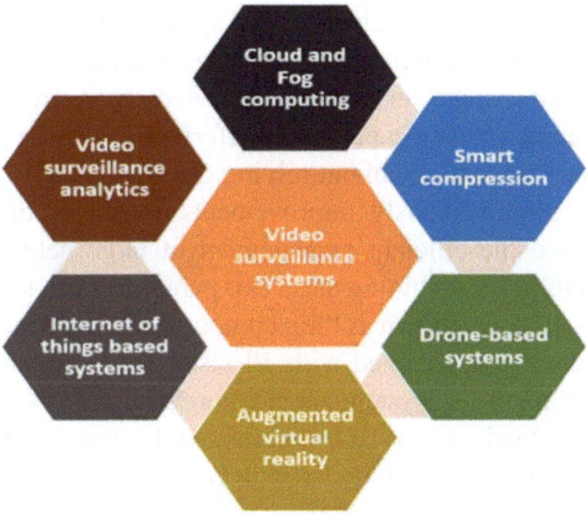

Fig. 3 Technological advancements in video surveillance [12]

tracking of moving objects that are crucial for security. Many proposed methods and algorithms have solved problems and yielded effective and satisfactory results. However, further work is required to enhance these systems. Two issues common in every video surveillance system are false alarms and ecological changes. The false alarm can be annoying, especially in sensitive sectors; automatic alarms are generally disabled. On the other hand, ecological alteration and wildly unexpected weather changes can also cause system failures. The limitations among these are the robustness and precision that need to be improved in some video surveillance algorithms.

Technological advancements have significantly impacted surveillance systems. Integrating digital technologies, high-definition cameras, and networked systems has enhanced surveillance capabilities. Innovations such as video analytics, facial recognition, and motion detection have further improved the efficiency and effectiveness of surveillance. Researchers are now exploring new topics to align with emerging technologies such as IoT, augmented virtual reality, Fog computing, and intelligent compression. Figure 3 illustrates these technologies, which can potentially drive developments in video surveillance systems.

Moreover, the rise of the Internet of Things (IoT) and artificial intelligence (AI) has introduced new dimensions to smart surveillance. These technologies enable collecting and analyzing vast amounts of data, facilitating predictive analytics and proactive security measures.

2 IoT in Surveillance

In the past decade, significant efforts have been made by the research community in surveillance and safety. These demands have driven the study and development of new solutions to more rapidly detect and respond to warning situations and threats.

Surveillance in public spaces such as airports, bus stations, and train stations has notably increased, particularly in countries with high terrorism risks. Technological advancements in embedded devices have created more powerful, compact computing devices capable of performing fundamental analysis and recognition tasks independently, without relying on cloud architecture.

Simultaneously, improvements in Internet of Things (IoT) protocols have facilitated the efficient management of large networks with minimal delay and high stability. Combining these two paradigms has led to the development of an intermediate layer known as "fog computing." This approach prevents the cloud layer from being overwhelmed with all tasks. The computational capabilities of the devices within the ecosystem handle more straightforward tasks, while communication with the cloud is reserved for more complex tasks or data that require further analysis. By empowering edge nodes with computational capabilities, quicker responses can be achieved when cloud analysis is unnecessary. Even when cloud analysis is needed, the process is expedited by initiating basic computations at the edge nodes, thus saving time and resources. The Internet of Things (IoT) has transformed various industries, including surveillance. This section explores the concept of IoT and its application in modern surveillance systems.

2.1 *Definition and Concept of IoT*

The term "Internet of Things," commonly abbreviated as IoT, is derived from two components: "Internet" and "Things." The Internet refers to a worldwide network of interconnected computer systems that utilize the standard Internet protocol suite (TCP/IP) to cater to billions of users around the globe. This vast network comprises millions of private, public, academic, business, and government networks, ranging from local to global scales, all interconnected through various electronic, wireless, and optical networking technologies.

The Internet of Things (IoT) can be viewed as a global network facilitating communication between humans, between humans and devices, and between devices by assigning a unique identity to every object [37]. IoT envisions a world where virtually anything can be interconnected and communicate more intelligently. Typically, "being connected" brings to mind electronic devices like servers, computers, tablets, telephones, and smartphones. However, in IoT, sensors and actuators embedded in physical objects from roadways to pacemakers are interconnected through wired and wireless networks, often utilizing the same Internet IP that connects the broader Internet. These networks generate vast amounts of data, which are then processed by computers for analysis. When objects can sense their environment and communicate, they become valuable tools for swiftly understanding and responding to complexity. IoT's revolutionary aspect lies in deploying these physical information systems, many of which operate largely without human intervention. Figure 4 depicts the relationship of IoT between humans, things, and the internet.

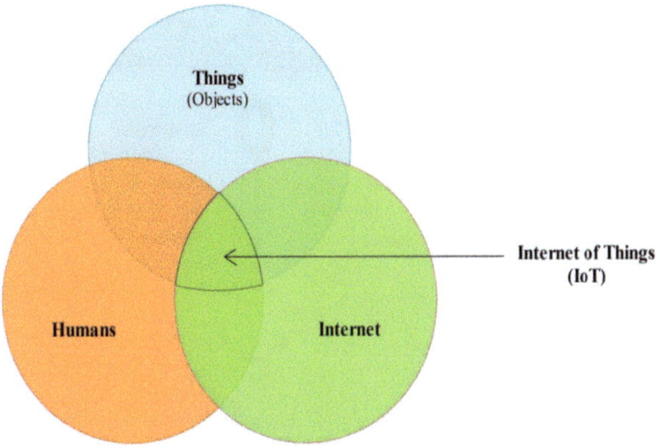

Fig. 4 Relationship among three different aspects of IoT [25]

The evolution of the term Internet to Internet of Things (IoT) has undergone several phases. The initial Pre-Internet phase involved communication through fixed telephone lines and Short Message Service (SMS). This was followed by introducing mobile telephony devices, enhancing communication capabilities. The second phase, the Internet of Content, enabled the transmission of large messages, such as emails with attachments, and facilitated information sharing and entertainment. The third phase, the Internet of Services, focused on electronic applications like e-productivity and e-commerce. The fourth phase, the Internet of People, connected individuals through social media platforms and other mediums like Facebook, Orkut, Skype, and YouTube.

This emerging phase is known as the Internet of Things powered by Artificial Intelligence (IoTAI), and the transformation phases of IoT are illustrated in Fig. 5. As IoTAI continues to be adopted across various sectors, it holds significant potential for social, environmental, and economic impact. Key IoTAI-based concepts include Mobility, Smart Grid, Smart Homes/Buildings, Public Safety and Environment Monitoring, Medical and Healthcare, Industrial Processing, Agriculture and Breeding, and Independent Living. These applications are deeply integrated into our daily lives, offering numerous benefits and creating a substantial dependency on their functionality. In recent years, the presence and usability of IoTAI applications have grown to a visionary scale, becoming critically important.

It is not an exaggeration to state that the future of the Internet is fundamentally tied to the concept and vision of IoT, which is propelling us into a more connected and intelligent future. Various application areas of IoT, illustrated in Fig. 6, demonstrate its wide-ranging impact. As IoT devices are integrated to enhance various applications, surveillance emerges as a crucial area where different sensors and cameras come together to form IoT-based surveillance systems. The next section discusses utilizing various IoT devices in these surveillance systems.

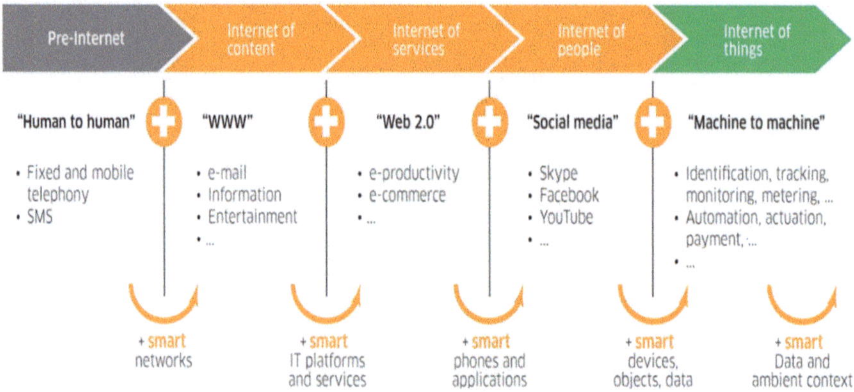

Fig. 5 Transformation phases of IoT [25]

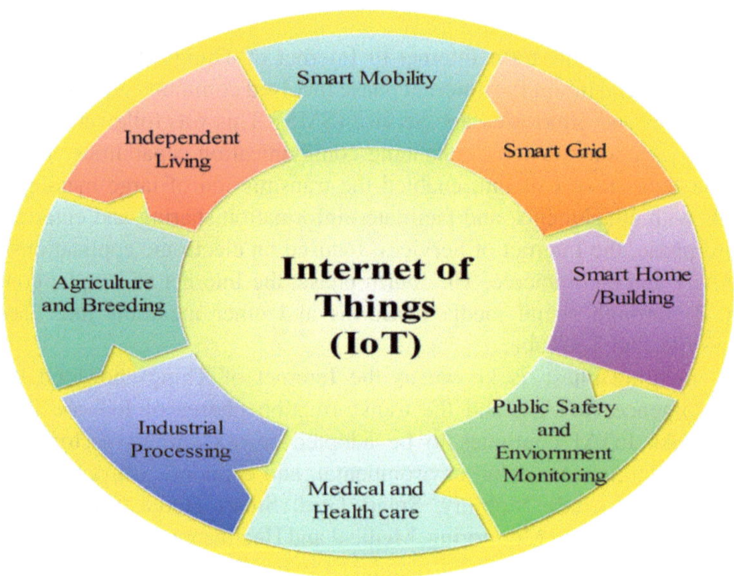

Fig. 6 IoT based applications [25]

2.2 Leveraging IoT Devices in Surveillance Systems

With advancements in the Internet of Things (IoT), artificial intelligence, and communication technologies, edge computing provides a novel solution by processing all or part of the data locally at the edge of a surveillance system.

In surveillance, IoT devices are crucial in enhancing monitoring and security. These devices include cameras, sensors, and alarms connected to a central system. They provide real-time data, enabling continuous monitoring and prompt response to security threats. IoT devices can be deployed in various environments, from homes and offices to public spaces and critical infrastructure. They offer remote access, allowing users to monitor and control surveillance systems from anywhere, enhancing convenience and security.

The Internet of Things (IoT) has recently been integrated into surveillance systems to enhance security and ensure personal protection. This technology connects numerous physical devices globally to the internet, allowing them to collect and exchange data autonomously without human intervention. IoT's benefits include faster operations, automation and control, easy information access, and cost savings. In security and monitoring, IoT devices are critical in improving surveillance robots' capabilities and developing systems for rapid response.

Several studies have focused on developing mobile surveillance robots using various processors and features [31]. For example, in [42], the authors implemented an intelligent surveillance robot equipped with a Raspberry Pi 3 Model B. This robot can be operated remotely via the internet and streams live video to a website using Wi-Fi technology. It includes an obstacle avoidance module and a metal detector that helps the robot navigate and identify metal objects.

Similarly, a spy robot built using a Raspberry Pi 3 is presented in [1]. Designed for military applications, this robot monitors war zones and detects suspicious individuals. It is equipped with various sensors, including PIR, LDR, and IR, alongside a Pi camera. When the PIR sensor detects movement, the Pi camera captures and displays the object on a web page. The robot can avoid obstacles using infrared sensors and is controlled manually via a web interface, with the LDR sensor enabling night time functionality by flashing the camera.

Another IoT-based surveillance robot aimed at household security is described in [22]. Built around a Raspberry Pi 3 Model B, this robot uses a webcam to stream live video and send email notifications to the user upon detecting motion. The system employs a motion detection algorithm developed with SimpleCV and is controlled via keyboard commands.

In [48], a domestic surveillance robot is introduced, featuring a Raspberry Pi board, camera, PIR sensor, buzzer, and GSM module. Upon detecting an intruder with the PIR sensor, the buzzer sounds, and the GSM module alerts the user. The camera records the video and sends it to the user's device via the internet. This system can be operated from a PC or Android phone through a website interface.

Finally, in [3], a spy robot car is developed using IoT technology and an Arduino UNO, designed for continuous surveillance in hazardous environments. It features cameras, PIR, ultrasonic, and gas sensors. The robot's movements are controlled through an Android application built on Blynk software, allowing long-distance navigation via Wi-Fi. Although the system offers live video streaming to connected Android devices, it cannot send alert notifications to users.

While these surveillance robots [1, 3, 22, 42, 48] excel at detecting human movements and objects, they do not incorporate facial recognition to distinguish between authorized and unauthorized individuals.

2.3 Examples of IoT Devices in Surveillance

Examples of IoT devices in surveillance include smart cameras, motion detectors, and environmental sensors. Smart cameras with AI capabilities can recognize faces, detect unusual activities, and send alerts to security personnel. Motion detectors trigger alarms when unauthorized movements are detected, while environmental sensors monitor conditions such as temperature and air quality, ensuring a comprehensive security solution.

Smart doorbells [19] with cameras and intercom also enable homeowners to see and communicate with visitors, boosting residential security remotely. Wearable devices with GPS and communication features facilitate real-time tracking and monitoring of security personnel, ensuring their safety and coordination during operations. Drones with high-resolution cameras and sensors provide aerial surveillance, offering extensive coverage of large areas such as industrial sites, agricultural fields, and public events.

Networked video recorders (NVRs) [24] and cloud-based storage solutions are vital components of IoT-based surveillance systems. These devices allow for the efficient storage and retrieval of substantial video data, ensuring easy access and analysis. Advanced analytics software processes this data to detect patterns, anticipate potential security breaches, and optimize resource allocation. Moreover, smart lighting systems can be integrated with surveillance networks to enhance visibility in low-light conditions and deter criminal activities. These systems can automatically activate when motion is detected or during specific times, adding an extra layer of security. Access control systems utilizing IoT technologies, such as biometric scanners and RFID readers, bolster the security of sensitive areas by ensuring only authorized personnel gain entry.

IoT devices are also crucial for remote surveillance and monitoring. Security systems can be accessed and controlled from anywhere using mobile applications, allowing users to receive real-time updates and take immediate action if needed. This remote capability is particularly advantageous for managing multiple sites or for security personnel who are constantly mobile. Integrating IoT devices into surveillance systems like mobile robots and different systems has transformed security management, making it more efficient, reliable, and scalable. These technologies improve the ability to detect and respond to security threats and support the proactive management of safety and security across various environments.

As discussed in the previous section, Mobile robots [1, 22, 42, 48] offer an appealing solution for numerous applications. In video surveillance systems, they monitor crowds, supervise moving objects, and track them. Robots have the potential to become a future trend in video surveillance systems. Drones, for instance, are robots used to monitor areas. In the next section, we will discuss integrating surveillance in drone-based systems.

3 Integration of Surveillance in Drone Technology

As society rapidly advances towards smart homes and smart cities, deploying Internet of Things (IoT) devices is increasingly necessary. Continuous surveillance is essential to achieve smart urbanization. While video surveillance using Closed-Circuit Television (CCTV) cameras has been extensively researched over the decades, it faces several challenges, such as limited area coverage, lack of location sharing, and insufficient tracking capabilities. In contrast, vision sensors mounted on drones offer greater scalability and flexibility, providing more extensive surveillance coverage. Data captured by drones is transmitted to central stations, where nodes analyze it to trigger responses to potential events [35]. For traffic monitoring, drones can cover specific areas, such as highways and streets, that are not equipped with cameras, providing real-time tracking of vehicles. Additionally, drones help track fugitives and oversee borders. This section discusses the concept of the Internet of Drones (IoD), applications of drones in surveillance, and their advantages and challenges.

In recent years, various fields have explored the use of surveillance drones in smart cities, with applications spanning areas such as transportation, environmental monitoring, infrastructure management, object or people detection, disaster response, and data collection, as discussed by [18]. Although some studies on drone surveillance are relevant to multiple categories, each study was assigned to the single most suitable category. For instance, research on monitoring road pavement conditions was classified under infrastructure instead of transportation. Figure 7 provides a detailed breakdown of the articles according to their application areas. The results indicate that most articles fall under the transportation and environment categories (each constituting 20.9%), followed by infrastructure (16.2%). Overall, the articles covered thirty application areas for using drones in smart city surveillance. Among these, air pollution monitoring emerged as the most frequently addressed topic (7 articles), followed by traffic monitoring (6 articles) and power line inspection and traffic safety (2 articles each). All other application areas were covered by only one article each.

Among the 43 reviewed articles, nine (20.9%) focused on the application of drones for surveillance in the transportation sector. Of these, six (66.6%) specifically discussed using drones for traffic monitoring in smart cities. One article explored the concept of cooperative intelligent transportation systems (C-ITS). De Frias et al. [11] proposed a system that leverages drones and a lightweight semantic neural network for urban traffic monitoring. Their system processes RGB images to produce segmented photos of vehicles, determines the 2D real-world positions of detected vehicles, and disseminates information about nearby traffic. The system was evaluated and found suitable for traffic monitoring due to its low mean error in vehicle position estimation.

Two articles explored the use of multiple drones for traffic monitoring. In the SwarmCity project, Roldan et al. [44] examined the efficiency of using aerial swarms as an alternative to fixed sensors or sensors on public transport, which

Category	Application area	Number of articles	Total number of articles	Percentage
Transportation	1. Traffic monitoring	6	9	20.9%
	2. Traffic safety	2		
	3. Parking management	1		
Environment	4. Air pollution monitoring	7	9	20.9%
	5. Waste incineration management	1		
	6. Weather monitoring	1		
Infrastructure	7. Bridge inspection	1	7	16.2%
	8. Bridge and pavement inspection	1		
	9. Bridge deck condition monitoring	1		
	10. Power line inspection	2		
	11. Road pavement condition monitoring	1		
	12. Building inspection	1		
Object or people detection and tracking	13. Tracking people and objects	1	6	13.9%
	14. Urban tree detection	1		
	15. Runways trees detection	1		
	16. Night-time pedestrian detection	1		
	17. Foreign object debris detection	1		
	18. Criminal tracking	1		
Disaster management	19. Humans body detection	1	5	11.6%
	20. Evacuation map building	1		
	21. Fire detection	1		
	22. Firefighting management	1		
	23. Search and rescue	1		
Data collection	24. General	1	3	6.9%
	25. Data collection and fusion-city monitoring	1		
	26. Multimedia streaming	1		
Others	27. 3D spectrum mapping	1	4	9.3%
	28. 3D city modeling	1		
	29. Farming	1		
	30. City and extensive ocean monitoring	1		
	Total	43	43	100%

Fig. 7 Drone surveillance articles based on application areas

are often hindered by blind spots and uncontrolled sensor movement. The study concluded that aerial swarms are adequate for data collection and traffic modeling in simulated intelligent cities. Similarly, Garcia-Aunon et al. [15] proposed a method for traffic surveillance using a behavior-based algorithm to control multiple drones. The algorithm showed promising results, with low variability in performance, scalability, and adaptability to different traffic volumes.

Additionally, nine (20.9%) articles detailed the use of drones for environmental monitoring in smart cities. Five focused on measuring airborne particulate matter (PM), consisting of solid particles and liquid droplets in the air. Chen et al. [9] developed a LoRa-based air quality monitoring system mounted on a drone to measure PM2.5, a harmful and unpredictable air pollutant. They also introduced a web interface to configure the drone's route and view real-time data. Field tests showed the system's ability to collect and transmit PM2.5 data in real-time with minimal human involvement. Similarly, Mayuga et al. [30] tested a drone with PM, temperature, and humidity sensors to measure PM at different altitudes under various traffic conditions. Hu et al. [23] implemented an IoT-based 3D air quality monitoring system using aerial and ground sensors. Their multi-layered system (sensing, transmission, processing, and presentation) provided real-time, detailed, and energy-efficient air quality data, using UAVs to address the variability in air quality across urban environments.

Several studies also focused on using drones for infrastructure monitoring in smart cities. Two studies specifically addressed bridge inspections. Seo et al. [46] evaluated the effectiveness of drones for inspecting bridges by assessing image quality and damage detection on a particular type of bridge (a three-span glued-laminated timber girder with a composite concrete deck). Their approach involved reviewing the bridge's structure, assessing environmental risks, establishing pre-flight protocols, conducting drone-based inspections, and identifying damages. The results demonstrated that drones with digital cameras and photogrammetry software are highly effective for detailed bridge inspections.

Similarly, Shang et al. [47] developed a data fusion platform to monitor bridge deck conditions and detect defects. The platform is composed of three main components: data collection (via unmanned aerial vehicles and ground inspections), image processing (including techniques like perspective projection and image stitching), and a user-friendly web interface (with map integration and a defect layer). By combining images from both aerial and ground sources, the system can identify, describe, and pinpoint surface cracks and subsurface delamination across different scales.

Another study took a broader approach, focusing on bridge and pavement inspections. Wu et al. [53] developed a framework that integrates drones with deep learning techniques to detect and classify cracks and other forms of structural damage. Their system employed high-resolution photos and infrared thermal images captured by drones, which were used to train deep convolutional neural networks (CNNs) to improve damage detection accuracy.

As discussed in the section, drones are widely used in various surveillance applications. The key focus areas include transportation, environmental monitoring, and infrastructure inspection, with traffic and air pollution monitoring among the most significant use cases. Whether used alone or in combination with modern technologies such as IoT, wireless sensor networks (WSNs), computer vision (CV), cloud computing, and artificial intelligence (AI), drones provide real-time data and effectively carry out complex surveillance tasks in smart cities. This method overcomes the limitations of traditional techniques, offering cost-effective, time-efficient, labor-saving, and highly accurate solutions.

The concept of the Internet of Drones (IoD) [16] plays a critical role in enhancing the capabilities of drone surveillance systems. The IoD allows for seamless communication and coordination among multiple drones, enabling them to share data, optimize flight paths, and collaborate to cover larger areas more efficiently. This interconnected network of drones uses advanced communication protocols and cloud computing to process and analyze large amounts of data in real-time, delivering a comprehensive and integrated surveillance solution. The IoD ensures drones can operate autonomously with high accuracy and reliability, ultimately improving smart cities' overall security and monitoring infrastructure. The following section will explore the potential applications of IoD technology in surveillance and other domains.

3.1 Definition and Scope of IoD Technology

IoD is designed for coherent and coordinated access to controlled airspace by unmanned aerial vehicles, also known as drones. During this period, while sensors and processors continue to miniaturize and wireless connectivity becomes ubiquitous, drones find applications in several innovative means to improve our daily life, ranging from on-demand package delivery, traffic and wildlife monitoring, infrastructure inspections, search and rescue operations, agriculture, cinematography, among others. It is easy to note that common underpinning factors shared across all these applications are effective navigation and airspace management. IoD finds application in many fields of life, like in smart cities, where many associated components transfer data, thereby making life in the city easy to live (Fig. 8).

Above is the architecture of the IoD-based surveillance system of a smart city, representing the most advanced approach for monitoring and managing urban environments within a smart city. Every drone within a swarm in such an architecture comes with high-resolution cameras and sensors. Operating conjointly, they would capture diverse data through images, videos, and environmental readings. These drones communicate over a wireless network, enabling transparent data exchange and agreed operations. Real-time communication is highly needed in the integrity

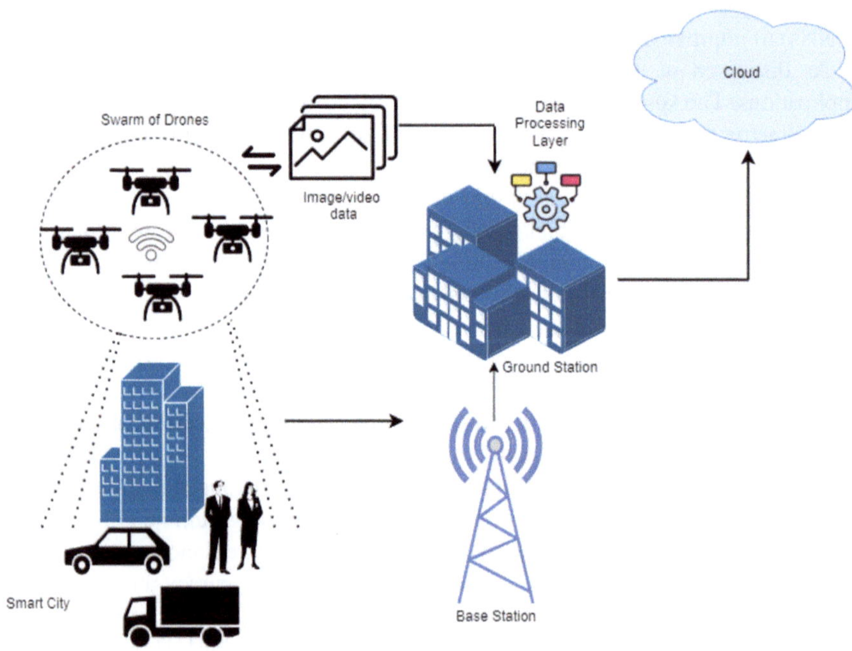

Fig. 8 IoD-based surveillance system

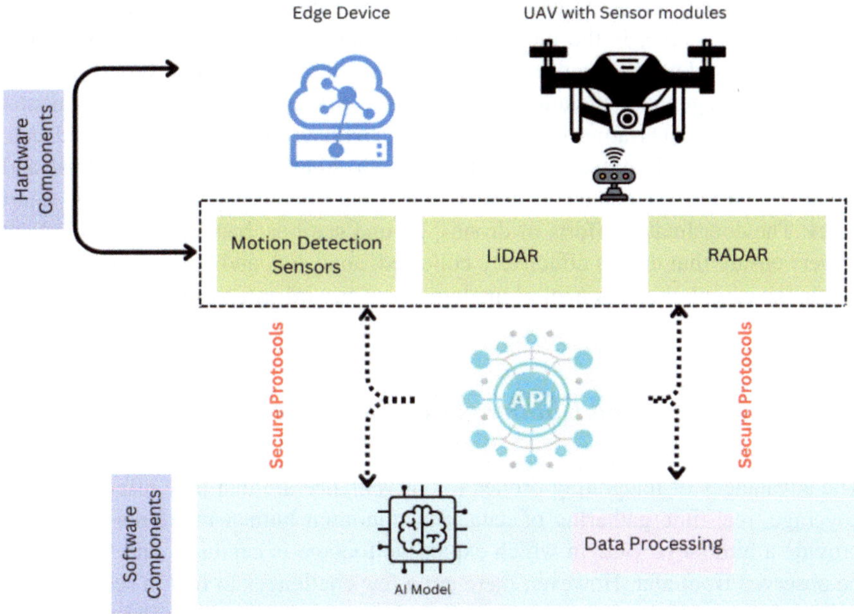

Fig. 9 Architecture with UAV sensor modules using AI model

and coverage of the surveillance network, as drones in the network relay information when some fall out of direct range from the central control station.

The data collected by the drones is transmitted to a ground station, which acts as the central hub for initial data processing. Using robust communication protocols such as 5G [20], Wi-Fi, or specialized radio frequencies, the drones ensure that the transmission is efficient and reliable. The ground station houses the data processing layer, where initial data analysis and aggregation occur. This layer employs algorithms and machine learning models to perform object detection, anomaly identification, and pattern recognition tasks. The processed data is then visualized on dashboards or maps, providing operators with an easily interpretable real-time overview of the monitored area.

A base station facilitates further communication between the ground station and cloud servers. This base station ensures the data is transmitted to the cloud for more extensive processing and long-term storage. Advanced analytics, big data processing, and machine learning algorithms are applied in the cloud to derive deeper insights and actionable intelligence. The following section will discuss the architecture (Fig. 9), showing how a single drone in a swarm of drones is equipped with an AI-based model and multi-fusion drone sensors for data processing. The cloud infrastructure provides scalable storage solutions, enabling historical data retention for future analysis. The results of the cloud-based analysis are sent back to the ground station, where they inform real-time decision-making and updates.

The smart city environment, which includes various elements like buildings, vehicles, and people, is the monitored area where the drones are deployed. The comprehensive data collected from this environment helps improve various aspects of urban management, including safety, traffic management, and environmental monitoring. By integrating drone technology with ground and cloud-based data processing, this IoD-based surveillance system architecture offers a robust and scalable solution for enhancing urban safety and operational efficiency in smart cities. The coordinated efforts of drones, ground stations, base stations, and cloud servers ensure that data is effectively collected, analyzed, and utilized, making this system an essential component of modern smart city infrastructure.

3.2 Advantages and Challenges of IoD in Security

The advantages of integrating drones for surveillance are that they offer increased coverage, real-time gathering of data, and minimum human interference. Drones provide a bird's-eye view in which expansive footage is captured, and threats can be observed from afar. However, there are a few challenges to IoD in security. IoD suffers from regulatory, privacy, and technical limitations. Such safe and responsible usage of drones demands considerable regulations and policies. Protecting confidentiality and addressing cybersecurity risks are crucial for winning public confidence in drone surveillance. The Internet of Drones will revolutionize fields with enhanced precision and intelligence, integrating next-generation smart technologies. As a new technology, IoDT faces several challenges and shortcomings that must be overcome.

IoD's main challenges are security and dealing efficiently with big data. IoD integrates several drones for cooperative data collection; hence, large chunks of data are produced that get transmitted to cloud servers in an unstructured manner. The processing needs to be done in real-time using significant data clustering and mining techniques, which require abundant computational resources and technologies; hence, this makes implementing IoD very expensive.

Real-time applications will require a fleet of drones, depending on the scenario. Addressing and managing devices, along with QoS, is an issue with an increasing number of devices. This can be mitigated by ad-hoc deployment, allowing drones to join and leave the network. Hence, all the applications should be customized from scratch, allowing extensible services and operations.

Another huge challenge is connectivity. For IoD's seamless performance, at least 4G/5G connectivity is required. If there is no connectivity, the IoD loses enormous performance operational range. Thus, with sensitive tasks and data security, vulnerabilities are opened. Therefore, reliability in ensuring continuous connectivity has become crucial for the successful implementation and operation of IoD systems.

4 Integration of AI and Machine Learning

AI and machine learning have completely changed the thought processes of the smart surveillance system by allowing it to conduct a lot of data analysis and predict various things. Without human intervention, this will increase efficiencies, versatility, and complexity in drone tasks. The convergence of these technologies can enable a drone to fly through an environment, recognize objects, and make decisions all on its own, thus opening up a wide vista of applications across various industry verticals.

The hinterland of this autonomous drone technology is artificial intelligence. AI allows drones to process vast amounts of data, learn patterns from their experiences, and adapt to new situations. Most important among all, one subset of AI pertains to machine learning, which enables improvement in the performance of drones by identifying patterns and thus making predictions. Deep learning, an improved version of machine learning, uses neural networks to take inspiration from the human brain's decision-making process. Using such methods, drones can achieve very high levels of autonomy and thus become appropriate for applications requiring real-time decision-making and adaptability.

Another critical complement to AI in developing autonomous drones is computer vision [52]. This technology relies on capturing and interpreting visual data from the drone using cameras and sensors. Algorithms and techniques such as image recognition, object detection, and optical flow enable drones to perceive their environment like human vision. This important navigation capacity allows a drone to detect obstacles and recognize landmarks along predefined paths. Moreover, with computer vision, they can conduct specific drone activities, such as infrastructure inspection, crop monitoring, and search and rescue operations, by processing real-time visual data.

The interaction of AI with computer vision increases the functionality and efficiency of autonomous drones manifold. In applications such as navigation, for instance, AI algorithms process data from computer vision systems to develop a detailed environmental map and plan routes dynamically to avoid obstacles. This feature is handy in complicated or GPS-denied environments where traditional navigation means fail. Besides that, integrating AI with drones enables them to identify and track objects or people using computer vision for easier surveillance, delivery, and environmental monitoring applications.

AI-driven and computer vision-based autonomous drones keep track of crop health in agriculture [2] by analysis of aerial images of the crop regarding signs of disease, yield estimation, etc. The informatics-driven strategy helps farmers make informed decisions regarding irrigation, fertilization, and control against pests, which improves productivity and enhances sustainability. Also, in infrastructure inspection, drones can independently survey constructions such as bridges, electric wires, and pipelines to detect defects or any abnormalities requiring maintenance. This makes the inspection process more efficient and much safer because human inspectors are no longer exposed to hazardous conditions. Besides, integrating AI and computer vision in drones is essential in disaster response and search and rescue missions. Drones will independently analyze the whole catastrophe region quickly and send real-time images and information to rescue teams. By finding survivors, mapping areas of the catastrophe, and delivering goods, they help to raise the productivity of rescue operations and save people's lives.

4.1 Role of AI in Smart Surveillance Systems

Artificial intelligence enhances intelligent surveillance by automating video analysis, threat detection, and decision-making activities. AI-driven systems can analyze significant data in real-time and identify patterns and anomalies that may suggest security threats. In addition, the multi-fusion of sensors for drone surveillance with AI capability is an efficient means of detecting patterns in data. Figure 9 illustrates an architecture that shows the integration of the critical components: UAVs with multiple sensor modules, edge computing, and secure communication protocols.

The architecture consists of UAVs, which are designed to be equipped with essential sensors like motion detection sensors, LiDAR, and RADAR. All these sensors will work together to collect important data, detect movement, map high-resolution environmental information, and the object's distance, speed, and direction.

It thus acts as a local processing unit for the swarm: receiving and processing data from the UAV sensors, it is close to the source. Secure communication protocols grant integrity and privacy to the data exchanged between the UAVs and the edge device. The processed information is further sent to the data processing layer, which includes value-added software components, such as AI models incorporating new algorithms and data processing tools. AI models further analyze the data for object detection, anomaly identification, decision-making, etc.

The API allows for smooth communication between architecture segments, ensuring data is transferred and integrated efficiently. This is what the API does using secure protocols that ensure the confidentiality and integrity of data in transit. The hardware parts of the architecture include UAVs, sensors, and edge devices, while the software parts include algorithms, AI models, and tools for data processing. Such a holistic architecture will provide all the facilities for real-time data collection, processing, and analysis.

The proposed enhanced AI-based architecture finds an excellent fit for implementing efficient and intelligent surveillance and monitoring by swarms of drones, given a broad range of applications in smart cities. Advanced sensor technology, edge computing, and AI-driven data processing provide the platform where such a system can deliver real-time actionable insight to enhance operational efficiency and decision-making in complex environments. Employing a swarm of drones improves coverage and reliability, offering more decadent data collection and faster response times to any anomalies or threats detected.

By leveraging the collective capabilities of multiple drones, this architecture offers scalable and resilient surveillance solutions capable of adapting to dynamic and challenging environments, thus significantly improving the operational effectiveness of smart city infrastructures.

4.2 Machine Learning Algorithms for Anomaly Detection

Machine learning algorithms play a vital role in anomaly detection, a critical component of smart surveillance threats, and predict future incidents by analyzing data and detecting deviations that may indicate security incidents. Anomaly detection is "the problem of identifying patterns in data that deviate from the expected behavior" [7, 34]. This technique is extensively utilized across various applications, including surveillance. Anomalies are categorized into three types,

1. Point Anomalies: In the context of surveillance, a point anomaly occurs when a single event or instance is detected as unusual compared to the typical behavior observed in the surveillance data.
2. Contextual Anomalies: A contextual anomaly occurs when a data instance is anomalous within a specific context but not in another. Regarding surveillance, contextual anomalies happen when an event is considered abnormal in a specific context but may appear normal in another. These anomalies are identified based on contextual attributes (like time and location) and behavioral attributes (like actions or movements).
3. Collective Anomalies: In surveillance, collective anomalies occur when a group of events or instances is collectively unusual compared to the overall dataset. For example, if multiple individuals gather in a typically unoccupied area, this group behavior might be flagged as a collective anomaly. These anomalies are more complex and involve detecting patterns among related data points, such as a sudden crowd forming in a typically deserted area or multiple vehicles stopping simultaneously on a normally quiet road.

Abnormal event detection [41] is crucial in video surveillance and smart camera systems. Existing methods in the literature are often not good at object awareness, meaning they do not distinguish between different objects during processing. These methods typically rely on trajectory feature extraction or semantic analysis based on initial categories derived from detection or tracking results to detect anomalies. For instance, track-matching issues and dynamic event detection are handled across frames.

Processing surveillance data, especially in crowded events, presents significant challenges. Advanced machine learning techniques, such as deep learning, are considered one of the most effective ways to handle this data and achieve goal-oriented pattern recognition. However, the problem of anomaly detection remains largely open to interpretation. Research efforts are scattered regarding how the problem is defined, the assumptions made, and the goals pursued. This study aims to provide a focused review of recent publications on automated surveillance, allowing for a deeper exploration of the specific challenges associated with this field. Instead of reviewing specific pattern classification methods, this review will emphasize the broader problem formulations and assumptions used in anomaly detection studies within the context of automated surveillance.

A work by Sahu et al. [45] developed a K-means algorithm specifically designed for effective crowd anomaly detection. This approach demonstrated superior accuracy to deep learning (DL)-based and handcrafted feature-based methods. A notable aspect of this work was the implementation of a low-power FPGA, which extracted features over non-overlapping pixels, allowing for the gating of inputs to multiple modules, thereby achieving high power efficiency. The energy consumption per pixel was minimal, at 2.43 nJ, with the ability to process 126.65 million pixels per second. However, the approach did not address noisy data or outliers.

Similarly, Claudio Piciarelli et al. [38] introduced a single-class Support Vector Machine (SVM) for trajectory-based anomalous event detection. This method focused on trajectory analysis, particularly relevant in video surveillance and traffic monitoring applications. The SVM clustering approach was employed to recognize anomalous trajectories, with detection capabilities leveraged for identifying these anomalies. Specific attention was given to trajectory classification without prior information about outlier distributions. While the validity of the approach was demonstrated, it did not conclusively prove good generalization performance when classifying unseen patterns.

Xinfeng Zhang et al. [54] explored a K-Nearest Neighbor (KNN) technique for video anomaly detection and localization. This method detected anomalies over time and space by assessing whether the similarities between test samples and the retrieved K-NN samples conformed to homogeneous intra-class similarities distribution patterns. The approach was an unsupervised one-class learning method that did not require clustering or prior assumptions. Using probability as a judgment criterion, the system was advantageous over existing solutions as it was not affected by motion distortions caused by perspective changes. However, the need for specialized training for different scenes significantly slowed the training speed, limiting its practical deployment.

In another study, Sondos Fadl et al. [13] proposed a Gaussian RBF multi-class SVM (RBF-MSVM) for detecting video forgery in surveillance footage. Their system, designed for inter-frame forgery detection, utilized a 2D-CNN to process spatiotemporal information and fusion for feature extraction. The system detected inter-frame forgeries, such as frame deletion, insertion, and duplication. Despite its efficiency, the lack of motion modeling made it unsuitable for direct application to videos.

Using machine learning, Shaoci Xie et al. [54] focused on video crowd detection and abnormal behavior modeling. They aimed to enhance detection accuracy by learning from disparate data mining techniques. They proposed an intrusion detection system and anomaly detection model tailored for the absence of user behavior anomaly detection. The model improved the representation of user behavior patterns and profiles, incorporating a similarity task. Experiments based on UNIX user shell command data demonstrated high detection performance. However, determining the optimal sequence length for specific users proved challenging.

4.3 Real-Time Data Analysis and Predictive Analytics

Real-time data analysis and predictive analytics are essential for proactive security measures. Surveillance systems can identify threats and predict future incidents by analyzing data from sensors and cameras. Effective monitoring solutions involve integrating advanced sensor technology, data analytics, and IoT devices. This allows real-time data collection, analysis, and predictive capabilities to optimize surveillance for safety. Real-time object detection for predicting location and performing localization is a critical capability of UAVs in surveillance. Figure 10 illustrates the components and methodologies of real-time data analysis for detection used in surveillance for UAVs (Unmanned Aerial Vehicles).

The sensors employed in UAVs can be broadly categorized into vision-based and non-vision-based types. Vision-based sensors, such as RGB cameras, stereo cameras, and infrared cameras, rely on capturing and processing visual data. RGB cameras provide standard color images, essential for general object detection tasks. With their dual-lens configuration, stereo cameras enable depth perception by mimicking human binocular vision, allowing the UAV to estimate distances to objects. Infrared cameras extend the UAV's capabilities to low-light conditions by detecting infrared radiation, making them particularly useful for night-time surveillance or thermal imaging applications.

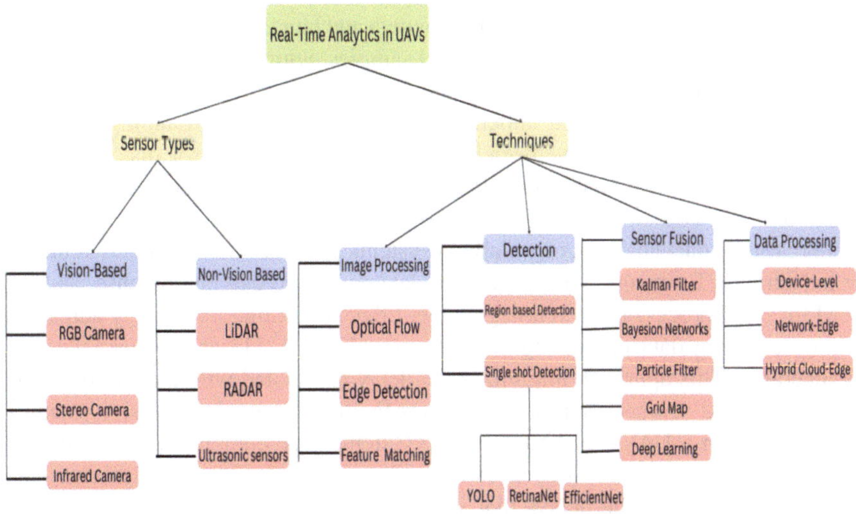

Fig. 10 Components and techniques for real-time analytics using UAVs

In contrast, non-vision-based sensors do not depend on visual data but use alternative methods to detect objects. LiDAR (Light Detection and Ranging) is a prominent example that utilizes laser pulses to measure distances, creating precise three-dimensional maps of the environment. RADAR (Radio Detection and Ranging) employs radio waves to detect objects and determine their distance and speed, offering robust performance in various weather conditions. Ultrasonic sensors, which use sound waves for short-range detection, are often employed in scenarios where precision nearby is required.

Various image processing techniques are applied to process the data collected by these sensors. Optical flow methods analyze the movement of objects between consecutive frames in a video, providing insights into object dynamics. Edge detection techniques are used to identify the boundaries of objects within images, which is a crucial step in isolating the object from the background. Feature matching compares distinctive features across images to detect and track objects over time.

Two primary methodologies are employed for object detection: Region-based and Single-shot. Region-based detection [17] techniques identify potential regions of interest within an image where objects might be located before applying more detailed analysis to confirm their presence. Single-shot detection methods [28], such as YOLO (You Only Look Once), RetinaNet, and EfficientNet, streamline the detection process [56] by identifying objects in a single forward pass through the network. YOLO is renowned for its speed, making it suitable for real-time applications, while RetinaNet and EfficientNet focus on balancing accuracy and efficiency.

Sensor fusion techniques play a pivotal role in enhancing the reliability and accuracy of object detection by integrating data from multiple sensors. The Kalman filter is commonly used to predict the future location of objects based on past observations, improving tracking consistency. Bayesian networks provide a probabilistic framework for effectively combining sensor data and handling uncertainties. Particle filters track objects using a set of weighted samples, which is particularly useful in dynamic environments. Grid mapping techniques represent the environment in a grid format, aiding the spatial understanding of the UAV's surroundings. Finally, deep learning approaches have been increasingly applied to sensor fusion utilizing neural networks to combine sensor data for more sophisticated and accurate object detection.

In real-time data analysis, especially in systems like UAVs, autonomous vehicles, or industrial IoT networks, the volume of data generated can be immense, and the need for rapid processing is non-negotiable. Edge computing technology addresses this by enabling data processing at the network's edge, closer to where the data is generated. This approach minimizes the delay associated with transmitting data to distant cloud servers for processing, thus facilitating quicker decision-making. For instance, in a UAV-based surveillance system, edge computing allows for the immediate processing of video streams to detect objects, track movements, and trigger alerts without the delays that would occur if the data had to be sent to a centralized server.

Enabling cognitive computing [32], powered by artificial intelligence (AI) and machine learning (ML) into edge computing, enables edge devices to process data and learn from it, make intelligent predictions, and adapt to new situations in real-time. Cognitive computing enhances edge computing by enabling more sophisticated data analysis at the edge. Instead of merely processing data, edge devices with cognitive capabilities can understand context, recognize patterns, and make decisions akin to human reasoning.

Combining edge computing and cognitive abilities thus provides a powerful framework for real-time data analysis. This synergy allows systems to process and analyze data with minimal latency, adapt to changing conditions, and make intelligent decisions in real-time. This is particularly valuable in applications where time is of the essence, such as in healthcare, autonomous driving, and security, where the ability to process data quickly and make informed decisions can significantly impact outcomes.

5 Case Studies and Examples

This section presents real-world case studies of smart surveillance systems by highlighting the importance of practical insights in the application.

5.1 Case Study 1: Smart Drone-Based Crowd Surveillance in Sabarimala

Sabarimala is a revered Hindu temple in Kerala's hills, attracting millions annually. Given the hilly terrain, the Makaravillakku festival transforms it into a massive religious gathering, presenting challenges for safety and movement. Traditional surveillance faces difficulties in this context, making drone-based crowd surveillance a promising solution. Deploying smart drones equipped with high-resolution cameras and advanced sensors can significantly enhance crowd monitoring and safety in Sabarimala. They are as follows:

- Real-time crowd monitoring: Drones provide a bird's-eye view of the entire pilgrimage area, enabling real-time tracking of crowd density and movement patterns. The cognitive ability of the drone automatically recognizes the patterns in the crowd, can predict congestion points, identify bottlenecks without human aid, and divert crowds to ensure smooth flow.
- Interpretable crowd surveillance: Traditional crowd surveillance system uses either deep learning or machine learning algorithms for analysis. Explainable AI is provides data processing along with explanation in a precise and "white box" nature.

- Real-time crowd management employs a cognitive-based smart drone displaying context-specific information. This system mimics human commonsense, highlighting high-density areas during peak seasons and blurring sensitive spots like bathing ghats during rituals.

5.2 *Case Study 2: Smart City Surveillance in Barcelona*

Barcelona, a vibrant city in Spain, has emerged as a global pioneer in "smart city" initiatives. At the heart of this transformation lies a sophisticated network of surveillance technologies to enhance safety, security, and urban efficiency. This case study explores the critical components of Barcelona's innovative city surveillance system and how drone surveillance with intelligence can be brought to the scene for real-time surveillance.
System Components are as follows:

- Extensive Camera Network: Barcelona's fixed camera network captures real-time footage of streets and critical areas. Though fixed cameras have limitations covering the entire city, drones offer comprehensive data on city streets, providing insights beyond fixed cameras.
- Advanced Sensor Technology: Sensors embedded in the city's infrastructure monitor diverse parameters like air and noise pollution, traffic flow, and environmental conditions.
- AI-powered Analytics: Powerful artificial intelligence algorithms analyze the data collected by cameras and sensors, extracting valuable insights and generating actionable intelligence. i.e., Cognitive intelligence makes the system more efficient in making predictions.

The system must be designed with privacy and ethical considerations. Also, drones should be robust in various environmental conditions and have fail-safe mechanisms to prevent accidents.

6 Ethical and Privacy Considerations

Ethical and privacy concerns arise in the deployment of intelligent surveillance systems. This section raises considerations regarding balancing security with confidentiality, ensuring responsible usage of surveillance technologies, and increasing public concerns.

6.1 *Informed Consent*

An important ethics-based principle involved in surveillance is that of informed consent. Individuals have a right to know and either approve or reject when data concerning them is being collected and monitored. When it comes to drones, this can become somewhat tricky. Drones can collect data over broad ranges and sometimes in unrecognizable ways. Any drone monitoring would have to be done entirely with awareness of the individuals being watched, with their consent given. This would protect their autonomy and control over their information.

6.2 *Data Security*

There are several issues regarding data security in general, but it is much more susceptible in the case of drones since the latter can gather plenty of confidential information. All entities using drones must be adequately prepared with security measures that will prevent unauthorized access or data breaches and misuse. Without robust security, there is a risk of significant privacy violations and loss of trust in managing surveillance systems.

6.3 *Transparency and Accountability*

Transparency regarding the practice of surveillance is of prime importance. In this light, it means stating what drones do, how they capture data, and for what reason. "Accountability requires not only that organizations be responsible for their actions but also that they be liable to review and scrutiny by others." Lack of transparency, because drones can operate surreptitiously, leads to data abuse and destroys trust among the masses. Being open about conducting surveillance instills confidence in people and ensures ethical use is maintained.

6.4 *Legal and Regulatory Compliance*

The surveillance law must be followed, even with the employment of drones. Regions have different regulations concerning drone surveillance; therefore, an organization should consider such rules to ensure it does not violate any of these laws. This will ensure that the measures put in place to prevent crimes are within the law and do not violate the privacy rights of all individuals. This will avoid legal implications and violations of individual rights.

6.5 Purpose Limitation

Data from surveillance is to be used strictly for the purpose for which it is collected. This, especially in drone surveillance, makes the ethical practice a requirement that forbids the use of data in unrelated or secondary purposes without consent. This ensures the curbing of misuse and builds trust in managing the surveillance systems.

7 Future Trends and Challenges

Recently, drones have participated increasingly in real-time surveillance [33] over the areas where it would be impossible to install many fixed cameras. The video data is streamed to nearby servers for real-time video processing to track people or animals if they go out of the range of the camera. Besides that, drones also participate in environmental monitoring; however, their contribution has many caps regarding weather conditions like extreme winds and heavy rain.

However, this all changes in the case of drones: they involve significant risks from a security point of view. With drones, sensitive personal information such as house addresses and facial images is within reach. More robust privacy measures and data protection will be essential. Besides, compliance with data protection legislation and transparency of data use are required to safeguard individual privacy.

Drones serve not only in search and rescue operations and disasters, all the way to estimating flood levels or delivering medical supplies, but they also can inadvertently or even inadvertently stray into areas where entry is denied, compromising national security by engaging in unauthorized surveillance or interfering with air traffic. That's why counter-drone technologies have been devised to mitigate those risks for ensuring control in drone access to secure zones, thereby averting misuse.

Despite their advantages, drones have restricted battery life, lack computing power, and have several security vulnerabilities. Solar-powered solutions with power lines from ground stations will be possible; each has constraints and limitations concerning weather and movement.

7.1 Surveillance System Based on Unsupervised Learning

Classification often uses supervised learning methods in video surveillance, which rely on labeled data. Unsupervised learning, however, processes unlabeled data to discover patterns and anomalies independently. This approach is beneficial when encountering new or unlabeled objects.

Unsupervised learning frameworks, such as ISTL [8], adapt to new data and detect anomalies dynamically. This method benefits scenarios with limited labeled data, such as marine surveillance. However, from a security standpoint, challenges include the risk of inaccurate anomaly detection and the need for continuous human oversight to validate and adjust the system.

These systems must address scalability and interpretability to prevent errors and ensure effective monitoring.

7.2 Reduction of False Alarm

Real-time analytics that detect imminent danger are handled through video surveillance systems, but false alarms erode the system's reliability and waste resources. Advanced analytics with deep learning algorithms can generate false alarms when not set right.

The work can be extended by introducing blockchain Smart Contracts and multifactor authentication to reduce false alarms, thus increasing security. Blockchain presents a tamper-proof, decentralized alarm management system, while multilevel verification procedures ensure that only genuine threats trigger alarms. Regular updates and research are required to fine-tune these systems to reduce the number of false positives and maintain security integrity.

7.3 Multi-Modal Fusion

This can be limiting when relying totally on cameras. Integrating other sensors, such as sound, temperature, and movement, into a multi-modal system amplifies the capability of surveillance in giving a fuller insight into the environment.

From a security point of view, multimodal systems ensure better accuracy and are more reliable. Different sensors' complementary information on the data aids in detecting and verifying threats. However, with the approach also come challenges in managing diverse formats and ensuring real-time processing speed. Responding to the challenges will be of great essence to the system's effectiveness and security.

7.4 Resource Management

Surveillance systems generate vast amounts of data, requiring efficient resource management to ensure security and operational effectiveness. Key considerations include:

- Networking: This would ensure data is transmitted securely and efficiently. This includes several techniques like content filtering, compression, and edge computing to optimize bandwidth, hence reducing latency on data. Software-defined networking could have better traffic management to avoid congestion and improve general network security.

– Storage: The safety of video data is paramount, and storing it locally on the cloud and using blockchain is possible. In this respect, blockchain is a decentralized way of video data storage, thus safer and more resistant to tampering and other attack types than a centralized system.

Effective management of these resources ensures that surveillance systems operate smoothly and securely, providing reliable monitoring and data protection.

8 Conclusion

Intelligent surveillance systems revolutionize the idea of security by empowering both monitoring capabilities and proactive threat detection. IoT, AI, and drone technologies combined in surveillance practices have brought comprehensive and effective solutions to security. Smart surveillance systems ensure that wider and more crucial roles will be played in guaranteeing public safety and security with further technology developments. All these technological developments must be weighed properly against consideration for ethics and privacy in their proper and productive deployment. The chapter, therefore, discusses the advances made in developing and deploying smart surveillance systems, considering the technological development and bringing together IoT, drones, and AI. It deals with major applications, advantages, challenges, and emerging trends and thus provides useful insight to security and surveillance researchers, practitioners, and policymakers.

References

1. Abdalla, G.O.E., Veeramanikandasamy, T.: Implementation of spy robot for a surveillance system using internet protocol of raspberry Pi. In: 2017 2nd IEEE International Conference on Recent Trends in Electronics, Information & Communication Technology (RTEICT), pp. 86–89. IEEE (2017)
2. Ahirwar, S., Swarnkar, R., Bhukya, S., Namwade, G.: Application of drone in agriculture. Int. J. Curr. Microbiol. Appl. Sci. **8**(01), 2500–2505 (2019)
3. Akilan, T., Chaudhary, S., Kumari, P., Pandey, U.: Surveillance robot in hazardous place using IoT technology. In: 2020 2nd International conference on Advances in Computing, Communication Control and Networking (ICACCCN), pp. 775–780. IEEE (2020)
4. Avinashiappan, A., Thiagarajan, H., Mahesh, H.C., Suresh, R.: Smart surveillance using deep learning. Int. J. Reconfig. Embedded Syst. (IJRES), 423–432 (2023). https://doi.org/10.11591/ijres.v12.i3.pp423-432
5. Calba, C., Goutard, F., Hoinville, L., Hendrikx, P., Lindberg, A., Saegerman, C., Peyre, M.: Surveillance systems evaluation: a systematic review of the existing approaches. BMC Public Health **15** (2015). https://doi.org/10.1186/s12889-015-1791-5
6. Chan, S., Camp, L.J.: Law enforcement surveillance in the network society. IEEE Technol. Soc. Mag. **21**, 22–30 (2002)

7. Chandola, V., Banerjee, A., Kumar, V.: Anomaly detection: A survey. ACM Comput. Surv. (CSUR) **41**(3), 1–58 (2009)
8. Chen, B.H., Shi, L.F., Ke, X.: A robust moving object detection in multi-scenario big data for video surveillance. IEEE Trans. Circuits Syst. Video Technol. **29**(4), 982–995 (2018)
9. Chen, L.Y., Huang, H.S., Wu, C.J., Tsai, Y.T., Chang, Y.S.: A LoRa-based air quality monitor on unmanned aerial vehicle for smart city. In: 2018 International Conference on System Science and Engineering (ICSSE), pp. 1–5 (2018). https://doi.org/10.1109/ICSSE.2018.8519967
10. Cumming, D., Johan, S.: Cameras tracking shoppers: the economics of retail video surveillance. Eurasian Bus. Rev. **5**, 235–257 (2015)
11. de Frías, C.J., Al-Kaff, A., Moreno, F.M., Madridano, Á, Armingol, J.M.: Intelligent cooperative system for traffic monitoring in smart cities. In: 2020 IEEE Intelligent Vehicles Symposium (IV), pp. 33–38 (2020). https://doi.org/10.1109/IV47402.2020.9304649
12. Elharrouss, O., Almaadeed, N., Al-Maadeed, S.: A review of video surveillance systems. J. Vis. Commun. Image Represent. **77**, 103116 (2021). https://doi.org/10.1016/j.jvcir.2021.103116, https://www.sciencedirect.com/science/article/pii/S1047320321000729
13. Fadl, S., Han, Q., Li, Q.: CNN spatiotemporal features and fusion for surveillance video forgery detection. Signal Process. Image Commun. **90**, 116066 (2021)
14. Foresti, G., Micheloni, C., Piciarelli, C., Snidaro, L.: Visual sensor technology for advanced surveillance systems: Historical view, technological aspects and research activities in Italy. Sensors **9**, 2252–2270 (2009)
15. Garcia-Aunon, P., Roldán, J.J., Barrientos, A.: Monitoring traffic in future cities with aerial swarms: Developing and optimizing a behavior-based surveillance algorithm. Cogn. Syst. Res. **54**, 273–286 (2019). https://doi.org/10.1016/j.cogsys.2018.10.031, https://www.sciencedirect.com/science/article/pii/S1389041718303279
16. Gharibi, M., Boutaba, R., Waslander, S.L.: Internet of drones. IEEE Access **4**, 1148–1162 (2016)
17. Girshick, R., Donahue, J., Darrell, T., Malik, J.: Region-based convolutional networks for accurate object detection and segmentation. IEEE Trans. Pattern Anal. Mach. Intell. **38**(1), 142–158 (2015)
18. Gohari, A., Ahmad, A.B., Rahim, R.B.A., Supa'at, A.S.M., Abd Razak, S., Gismalla, M.S.M.: Involvement of surveillance drones in smart cities: A systematic review. IEEE Access **10**, 56611–56628 (2022)
19. Gomathy, C.K., Satyaa, D.: Study on IOT smart doorbells. Int. Res. J. Eng. Technol. (IRJET). E-ISSN: 2395 **56** (2021)
20. Gupta, A., Jha, R.K.: A survey of 5g network: Architecture and emerging technologies. IEEE Access **3**, 1206–1232 (2015)
21. Haering, N., Venetianer, P.L., Lipton, A.: The evolution of video surveillance: an overview. Mach. Vis. Appl. **19**(5–6), 279–290 (2008)
22. Harshitha, R., Hussain, M.H.S.: Surveillance robot using raspberry Pi and IoT. In: 2018 International Conference on Design Innovations for 3Cs Compute Communicate Control (ICDI3C), pp. 46–51. IEEE (2018)
23. Hu, Z., Bai, Z., Yang, Y., Zheng, Z., Bian, K., Song, L.: UAV aided aerial-ground IoT for air quality sensing in smart city: Architecture, technologies, and implementation. IEEE Netw. **33**(2), 14–22 (2019). https://doi.org/10.1109/MNET.2019.1800214
24. Karlsson, K.: A hands-on guide to use network video recorders, internet protocol cameras, and deep learning models for dynamic monitoring of trout and salmon in small streams. Ecol. Evol. **14**(5), e11246 (2024)
25. Khanna, A., Kaur, S.: Internet of things (IoT), applications and challenges: a comprehensive review. Wirel. Pers. Commun. **114**, 1687–1762 (2020)
26. Lauer, J.: Surveillance history and the history of new media: An evidential paradigm. New Media Soc. **14**(4), 566–582 (2012)
27. Lin, T., Pham, H.: Modeling security surveillance systems with state dependent inspection-maintenance strategy. IEEE Trans. Comput. Soc. Syst. **10**, 2467–2478 (2023). https://doi.org/10.1109/TCSS.2022.3183238

28. Liu, W., Anguelov, D., Erhan, D., Szegedy, C., Reed, S., Fu, C.Y., Berg, A.C.: Ssd: Single shot multibox detector. In: Computer Vision–ECCV 2016: 14th European Conference, Amsterdam, The Netherlands, October 11–14, 2016, Proceedings, Part I 14, pp. 21–37. Springer (2016)
29. MacWillie, J.: From keyhole to big brother: The legacies of early cold war surveillance. Surveill. Soc. **16**(2), 1–16 (2018)
30. Mayuga, G.P., Favila, C., Oppus, C., Macatulad, E., Lim, L.H.: Airborne particulate matter monitoring using uavs for smart cities and urban areas. In: TENCON 2018 - 2018 IEEE Region 10 Conference, pp. 1398–1402 (2018). https://doi.org/10.1109/TENCON.2018.8650293
31. Meddeb, H., Abdellaoui, Z., Houaidi, F.: Development of surveillance robot based on face recognition using raspberry-pi and IoT. Microprocess. Microsyst. **96**, 104728 (2023). https://doi.org/10.1016/j.micpro.2022.104728, https://www.sciencedirect.com/science/article/pii/S0141933122002575
32. Modha, D.S., Ananthanarayanan, R., Esser, S.K., Ndirango, A., Sherbondy, A.J., Singh, R.: Cognitive computing. Commun. ACM **54**(8), 62–71 (2011)
33. Myagmar-Ochir, Y., Kim, W.: A survey of video surveillance systems in smart city. Electronics **12**(17), 3567 (2023)
34. Nassif, A.B., Talib, M.A., Nasir, Q., Dakalbab, F.M.: Machine learning for anomaly detection: A systematic review. IEEE Access **9**, 78658–78700 (2021). https://doi.org/10.1109/ACCESS.2021.3083060
35. Patil, N., Ambatkar, S., Kakde, S.: IoT based smart surveillance security system using raspberry Pi. In: 2017 International Conference on Communication and Signal Processing (ICCSP), pp. 0344–0348. IEEE (2017)
36. Pavlidis, I., Morellas, V., Tsiamyrtzis, P., Harp, S.: Urban surveillance systems: from the laboratory to the commercial world. Proc. IEEE **89**, 1478–1497 (2001)
37. Perera, C., Zaslavsky, A., Christen, P., Georgakopoulos, D.: Context aware computing for the internet of things: A survey. IEEE Commun. Surv. Tutorials **16**(1), 414–454 (2013)
38. Piciarelli, C., Micheloni, C., Foresti, G.L.: Trajectory-based anomalous event detection. IEEE Trans. Circuits Syst. Video Technol. **18**(11), 1544–1554 (2008)
39. Pîrjol, P.: Aerial surveillance – evolutions and enduring trends. Roman. Mil. Think. **3**, 144 (2022)
40. Porikli, F., Bremond, F., Dockstader, S.L., Ferryman, J., Hoogs, A., Lovell, B.C., Pankanti, S., Rinner, B., Tu, P., Venetianer, P.L.: Video surveillance: past, present, and now the future [dsp forum]. IEEE Signal Process. Mag. **30**(3), 190–198 (2013)
41. Raja, R., Sharma, P.C., Mahmood, M.R., Saini, D.K.: Analysis of anomaly detection in surveillance video: recent trends and future vision. Multimedia Tools Appl. **82**(8), 12635–12651 (2023)
42. Raut, A., Raj, A., Patil, S., Katkar, A.: Internet controlled techrobot using raspberry Pi. Int. J. Eng. Res. **9** (2020)
43. Remagnino, P., Velastín, S., Foresti, G., Trivedi, M.: Novel concepts and challenges for the next generation of video surveillance systems. Mach. Vis. Appl. **18**, 135–137 (2007)
44. Roldán, J.J., Garcia-Aunon, P., Peña-Tapia, E., Barrientos, A.: Swarmcity project: Can an aerial swarm monitor traffic in a smart city? In: 2019 IEEE International Conference on Pervasive Computing and Communications Workshops (PerCom Workshops), pp. 862–867 (2019). https://doi.org/10.1109/PERCOMW.2019.8730677
45. Sahu, A.K., Sharma, S., Tanveer, M., Raja, R.: Internet of things attack detection using hybrid deep learning model. Comput. Commun. **176**, 146–154 (2021)
46. Seo, J., Duque, L., Wacker, J.: Drone-enabled bridge inspection methodology and application. Autom. Constr. **94**, 112–126 (2018). https://doi.org/10.1016/j.autcon.2018.06.006, https://www.sciencedirect.com/science/article/pii/S0926580517309755
47. Shang, Z., Cheng, C., Shen, Z.: A data fusion platform for supporting bridge deck condition monitoring by merging aerial and ground inspection imagery, pp. 299–305. https://doi.org/10.1061/9780784482445.038, https://ascelibrary.org/doi/abs/10.1061/9780784482445.038
48. Sunitha, M., Vinay, P.D., Lokesh, V., Kumar, B.D.: Ip based surveillance robot using IoT. In: 2020 Fourth International Conference on I-SMAC (IoT in Social, Mobile, Analytics and Cloud) (I-SMAC), pp. 337–342. IEEE (2020)

49. Tang, Y., Ma, B., Yan, H.: Intelligent video surveillance system for elderly people living alone based on ODVS. Scientific Research Publishing (2013)
50. Teixeira, E.H., Mafra, S., Rodrigues, J., da Silveira, W.A.A.N., Diallo, O.: A review and construction of a real-time facial recognition system. In: SBCUP (2020)
51. Tsakanikas, V., Dagiuklas, T.: Video surveillance systems-current status and future trends. Comput. Electr. Eng. **70**, 736–753 (2018)
52. Voulodimos, A., Doulamis, N., Doulamis, A., Protopapadakis, E.: Deep learning for computer vision: A brief review. Comput. Intell. Neurosci. **2018**(1), 7068349 (2018)
53. Wu, W., Qurishee, M.A., Owino, J., Fomunung, I., Onyango, M., Atolagbe, B.: Coupling deep learning and UAV for infrastructure condition assessment automation. In: 2018 IEEE International Smart Cities Conference (ISC2), pp. 1–7 (2018). https://doi.org/10.1109/ISC2.2018.8656971
54. Xie, S., Zhang, X., Cai, J.: Video crowd detection and abnormal behavior model detection based on machine learning method. Neural Comput. Appl. **31**, 175–184 (2019)
55. Yekutieli, Y.: Is somebody watching you? Ancient surveillance systems in the southern Judean desert. J. Mediterr. Archaeol. **19**(1), 65–89 (2006)
56. Zaidi, S.S.A., Ansari, M.S., Aslam, A., Kanwal, N., Asghar, M., Lee, B.: A survey of modern deep learning based object detection models. Digit. Signal Process. **126**, 103514 (2022)

Index

S. M. Thampi et al. (eds.), *Securing the Connected World*,
https://doi.org/10.1007/978-3-031-82826-3

MIX
Papier aus verantwortungsvollen Quellen
Paper from responsible sources
FSC® C105338

If you have any concerns about our products,
you can contact us on
ProductSafety@springernature.com

In case Publisher is established outside the EU,
the EU authorized representative is:
Springer Nature Customer Service Center GmbH
Europaplatz 3, 69115 Heidelberg, Germany

Printed by Libri Plureos GmbH
in Hamburg, Germany

MIX
Papier aus verantwortungsvollen Quellen
Paper from responsible sources
FSC® C105338
www.fsc.org

If you have any concerns about our products,
you can contact us on
ProductSafety@springernature.com

In case Publisher is established outside the EU,
the EU authorized representative is:
Springer Nature Customer Service Center GmbH
Europaplatz 3, 69115 Heidelberg, Germany

Printed by Libri Plureos GmbH
in Hamburg, Germany